WORLD BANK WORKING PAPER NO. 182

The Education System in Malawi

THE WORLD BANK
Washington, D.C.

BREDA

Pôle de Dakar
EDUCATION SECTOR ANALYSIS

Education For All
Fast Track Initiative

gtz

Copyright © 2010
The International Bank for Reconstruction and Development / The World Bank
1818 H Street, N.W.
Washington, D.C. 20433, U.S.A.
All rights reserved
Manufactured in the United States of America
First Printing: January 2010

 Printed on recycled paper

1 2 3 4 5   13 12 11 10

World Bank Working Papers are published to communicate the results of the Bank's work to the development community with the least possible delay. The manuscript of this paper therefore has not been prepared in accordance with the procedures appropriate to formally-edited texts. Some sources cited in this paper may be informal documents that are not readily available.

The findings, interpretations, and conclusions expressed herein are those of the author(s) and do not necessarily reflect the views of the International Bank for Reconstruction and Development/The World Bank and its affiliated organizations, or those of the Executive Directors of The World Bank or the governments they represent.

The World Bank does not guarantee the accuracy of the data included in this work. The boundaries, colors, denominations, and other information shown on any map in this work do not imply any judgment on the part of The World Bank of the legal status of any territory or the endorsement or acceptance of such boundaries.

The material in this publication is copyrighted. Copying and/or transmitting portions or all of this work without permission may be a violation of applicable law. The International Bank for Reconstruction and Development/The World Bank encourages dissemination of its work and will normally grant permission promptly to reproduce portions of the work.

For permission to photocopy or reprint any part of this work, please send a request with complete information to the Copyright Clearance Center, Inc., 222 Rosewood Drive, Danvers, MA 01923, USA, Tel: 978-750-8400, Fax: 978-750-4470, www.copyright.com.

All other queries on rights and licenses, including subsidiary rights, should be addressed to the Office of the Publisher, The World Bank, 1818 H Street NW, Washington, DC 20433, USA, Fax: 202-522-2422, email: pubrights@worldbank.org.

ISBN-13: 978-0-8213-8198-4
eISBN: 978-0-8213-8199-1
ISSN: 1726-5878   DOI: 10.1596/978-0-8213-8198-4

Library of Congress Cataloging-in-Publication Data

The education system in Malawi : country status report.
  p. cm.
  ISBN 978-0-8213-8198-4
  1. Education--Malawi. I. World Bank.
  LA1551.E385 2010
  370.96897--dc22

2009045470

Contents

Foreword from the Minister of Education, Government of Malawi xviii
Foreword from the World Bank xx
Acknowledgments xxiv
Acronyms and Abbreviations xxvi
Executive Summary xxviii
    Policy Recommendations Matrix by Sub-Sector lii
    Technical, Entrepreneurial, and Vocational Education and Training (TEVET) lviii
    Higher Education lxiii

1. Demographics, Social Development, and Macroeconomic Conditions 1
    Summary of the Chapter 1
    Demographics 2
    Social Development 4
    Macroeconomic Conditions 5

2. Enrollment Patterns 12
    Summary of the Chapter 12
    The Education System in Malawi 13
    Coverage in Primary and Secondary Education: Schooling and Survival
        Profiles 18
    Understanding Dropouts at the Primary Level 26

3. Education Expenditure and Financing 32
    Summary of the Chapter 32
    Total Public Recurrent Expenditure for Education 34
    Public Recurrent Expenditure by Level of Schooling 38
    Public Recurrent Unit Costs by Level of Schooling 42
    Household Financing 46
    Donor Financing for the Education Sector (2005–2008) 51
    Comparisons of School Construction Costs 52

4. Internal Efficiency, Learning Outcomes, and Management Issues 54
    Summary of the Chapter 54
    Internal Efficiency of the Education System 57
    Quality and Learning Outcomes 64
    Administration Management 76
    Pedagogical Management: Transforming Inputs into Learning Outcomes 96

5. Equity and Disparities 101
Summary of the Chapter 101
Disparities among Social Groups 102
Equity in Distribution of Public Resources for Education 114

6. Technical, Entrepreneurial, and Vocational Education and Training 118
Summary of the Chapter 118
Introduction 119
Enrollment 121
Equity 124
Costs and Financing 127
Internal Efficiency and Quality 135
Governance Issues and Institutional Set-up 141

7. Higher Education 147
Summary of the Chapter 147
The Genesis and Growth of Higher Education in Malawi 148
Higher Education Enrollments and Fields of Study 149
Financing 158
Internal Efficiency 169
Equity in Higher Education 175
Governance and Management 177

8. External Efficiency 182
Summary of the Chapter 182
Education and Human Development in Malawi 183
Relevance of Education for the Labor Market 187

Appendixes 206
Appendix 1.1: Demographic and Social Development Indicators 207
Appendix 1.2: Context Index, Methodology of Calculation 211
Appendix 2.1: Education System Structure 212
Appendix 2.2: Enrollment Trends 213
Appendix 2.3: Population Estimates for the Malawi CSR 215
Appendix 2.4: Cross-Sectional Schooling Profiles According to EMIS and UN Population Data 224
Appendix 2.5: How to Read Educational Pyramids? 226
Appendix 2.6: Factors Explaining Why Some Children Never Go to Primary Education 228
Appendix 2.7: Model Result for Retention Explanation, Based on EMIS Data 231
Appendix 2.8: Quantitative Efficiency of Education Expenditure 232
Appendix 3.1: Expenditure by Type and Source of Funding 235

Appendix 3.2: Ministries with Some Education Activities and Education Institutions Outside of the Ministry of Education 237
Appendix 3.3: Recurrent and Capital Allocations to ECD and Adult Literacy 238
Appendix 3.4: Adjustment Methodology for Comparing Distribution of Recurrent Expenditure by Level of Education 239
Appendix 3.5: Comparative Data on Expenditure Breakdown in Higher Education 240
Appendix 3.6: Teachers' Salaries in Primary and Secondary Education by Category of Teachers 241
Appendix 4.1: Internal Efficiency and Resources Management 242
Appendix 4.2: SACMEQ Levels Definitions 247
Appendix 4.3: Examination Pass Rates Analysis 248
Appendix 4.4: Consistency in Resource Allocations 251
Appendix 4.5: Teacher Training 253
Appendix 5.1: Internal Efficiency Tables by Gender 256
Appendix 5.2: Disparities 257
Appendix 6.1: TEVET Recurrent Unit Cost and Financial Management Issues 264
Appendix 6.2: Other TEVET Indicators 265
Appendix 7: Higher Education 272
Appendix 8.1: Duration of Job Search 283
Appendix 8.2: Results of the Impact of Education on Social Behavior Calculations 284
Appendix 8.3: Rates of Return of Education Investments: Calculation Method 288
Appendix 8.4: Employment and Income Data 293

Appendix 9: Tracer Study of TEVET and Higher Education Completers 295

Part I: General Background 297
    1. Introduction 297
    2. Objectives of the Study 298
    3. Methodology 299

Part II: Higher Education Tracer Study 301
    Introduction: The Context of the University System in Malawi 301
    1. Methodology 302
    2. Results of Graduate Study 304
    3. Results of Dropout Study 313
    4. Summary and Conclusions 315
    5. Conclusions and Recommendations 316

Part III: TEVET Tracer Study 318
    Introduction: The Context of the TEVET System in Malawi 318
    1. Methodology 319

2. Results of TEVET Study 320
4. Summary and Conclusions 331
Part IV: Final Remarks **334**
References **335**

Tables

Table 1: STR in Public Schools by Level of Education (2007) xl
Table 2: Higher Education Teachers' Average Salary, as Units of GDP Per Capita for Countries with GDP per Capita Lower than US$500 (2007 or last year available) xlvii
Table 3: Annual Average Income and Expected Annual Income According to Level of Education xlix
Table 1.1: Evolution in Real GDP Growth, Inflation, and Exchange Rate (MK/US$) 6
Table 1.2: Evolution in Total Government Revenue and Expenditure and Deficit 7
Table 1.3: GDP Per Capita and Domestic Resources as a Percentage of GDP for SADC Countries (ca. 2006) 8
Table 1.4: Annual External Aid for Education as Percentage of GDP (2004–2006 Average) 9
Table 2.1: Enrollment Trends per Education Level (1998–2007) 15
Table 2.2: Schooling Coverage by Level of Education (2000–2007) 17
Table 2.3: International Comparison on GER (SADC countries) 18
Table 2.4: Percent of Repeaters in Primary Education According to Different Data Sources (in %) 19
Table 2.5: Construction of Survival Profile 23
Table 2.6: Share of Schools and Pupils According to the Number of Standards Supplied 26
Table 2.7: Percentage of Pupils Who Cannot Continue on to the Next Standard in the Same School, 2006–07 (in %) 27
Table 2.8: Main Reasons for Dropping Out of School Declared by School Heads (in %) 29
Table 2.9: Main Reasons for Dropping Out of School, Declared by Pupils (in %) 29
Table 3.1 Education Public Recurrent Expenditure 35
Table 3.2: Percentages for Education in Public Recurrent Expenditure, SADC countries 35
Table 3.3: Breakdown of Total Public Recurrent Expenditure by Nature of Spending and by Level of Education (in %) 37
Table 3.4: Breakdown of Public Recurrent Expenditure (revised 07/08 budget) by level of Schooling 39
Table 3.5: Distribution of Recurrent Expenditure by Level of Schooling, SADC Countries, (2008 or last year available) 40
Table 3.6: Public Recurrent Unit Costs by Level of Schooling 43
Table 3.7: Primary and Secondary Public Recurrent Unit Costs, SADC Countries (2007 or last year available) 44

Table 3.8: Higher Education Teachers' Average Salary, as Units of GDP Per Capita for Countries with GDP per Capita Lower than US$500 (2007 or last year available) 45
Table 3.9: Student-Teacher Ratios in Public Schools, 2007 46
Table 3.10: Estimated Breakdown of the Household Expenditure by Level of Education and Household Unit Costs, 2007 47
Table 3.11: Decomposition of Household Education Expenditure (in %) 49
Table 3.12: Cross-country Comparison of Distribution of Household Education Expenditure 50
Table 3.13: Share of Education in Household Expenditure by Quintile of Household Income 50
Table 3.14: Donor Financing and Extra Budgetary Grants to Education (MK Millions) 51
Table 3.15: Unit Construction Costs in Primary School Construction (US$) 52
Table 4.1: Trend in Repetition Rates by Standard in Primary Schools of All Types (1999 and 2006) (in %) 60
Table 4.2: Repetition Rates by Form in Secondary Schools of All Types (2006) (in %) 60
Table 4.3: Dropout Rates at the Primary Level in All Types of Schools (1999 and 2006) (in %) 62
Table 4.4: Dropout Rates at the Secondary level in All Types of Schools (2006) (in %) 62
Table 4.5: Internal Efficiency Coefficient in Primary and Secondary Schooling (1999/00–2006/07) 63
Table 4.6: Reading (English) and Mathematics Scores and Percentage of Students Reaching Minimum and Desirable Levels of Reading Mastery (SACMEQ I and II) 65
Table 4.7: Leaving School Examination Results at the Primary Level by School Type in % (2006) 67
Table 4.8: JCE and MSCE Examination Results (2006) 68
Table 4.9: JCE and MSCE Examinations Pass Rates by School Types in % (2006) 68
Table 4.10: Determinants of PSLE Results at the National Level (2006)— Marginal Effect 71
Table 4.11: Determinants of MSCE Results at the National Level (2006)— Marginal Effect 75
Table 4.12: Teacher Status by Location (in %), Government-Funded Primary Schools (2007) 78
Table 4.13: Teacher Distribution by Gender and Location (in %), Government-Funded Primary Schools (2007) 78
Table 4.14: Teacher Qualifications and Training Status by Location and Gender (in %), Government-Funded Primary Schools (2007) 79
Table 4.15: Types of Training among Trained Teachers (in %), Government-Funded Primary Schools (2007) 79
Table 4.16: Reasons for Attrition among Government-Funded Primary Schools 80
Table 4.17: STR by Location in All Government-Funded Schools (1999 and 2007) 80

Table 4.18: STRs and Class Size, Standards 1–8, in Government-Funded Public Schools (2000 and 2007) 82
Table 4.19: Degree of Randomness at Division Level, Government-Funded Schools (2007) 85
Table 4.20: Book Allocation by Standards in Government-Aided Schools (2007) 87
Table 4.21: Book Allocation Coherence by Standards in Government-Aided Schools (2007) (in %) 88
Table 4.22: Teacher Characteristics in Government-Funded Secondary Schools by Type of School (2007) (in %) 90
Table 4.23: Teacher Attrition by Reason at the Secondary Level (2007) 91
Table 4.24: STR by Types of Schools and Location, Government-Funded Secondary Schools (2007) 92
Table 4.25: Recap of the Funds Allocated to Secondary Schools 93
Table 4.26: Relationship between the Wage Unit Cost and the Number of Students at the Primary Level 94
Table 4.27: Relationship between the Wage Unit Cost (Teachers Only) and the Number of Students at the Secondary Level 95
Table 5.1: Social Structure by Highest Level of Education and Comparison Group, 5–24 Years Old (in %) 102
Table 5.2: Gender Parity Indexes at Different Education Levels, 2000–2007 103
Table 5.3: Percentage of Pupils Reaching Minimum and Desirable Levels of Reading Mastery (SACMEQ II) 105
Table 5.4: Leaving School Examination Results at the Primary Level by Gender (2006) 106
Table 5.5: JCE and MSCE Examination Results at the Secondary Level by Gender (2006) 106
Table 5.6: Differences of Access and Completion Rates in Primary and Secondary Education 107
Table 5.7: Survival Rates and Transition Across Levels (in %) 110
Table 5.8: Percentage of Pupils Reaching Minimum and Desirable Levels of Reading Mastery (SACMEQ II) 113
Table 5.9: Distribution of Public Education Spending According to the Highest Level Attended (Pseudo-Cohort of 100 Children) 114
Table 5.18: Benefit Incidence 117
Table 6.1: Synopsis of Different TEVET Provider Types in Malawi 119
Table 6.2 Number of Regular and Parallel Students in Technical Colleges (2007) 122
Table 6.3: Sources of TEVET Funding by Training Provider System 128
Table 6.4: Total Public Spending for TEVET 2007/08 (MK) 129
Table 6.5: Summary per Trainee of Public Allocations to TCs, 2007/08 130
Table 6.6: Expenditure in TC 2007/08 (Revised Budget) by Subprograms (in %) 131
Table 6.7: TEVETA Income from 2003–2007 (MK) 132
Table 6.8: TEVETA Expenditure Structure 2002/03 to 2006/07 (in %) 133
Table 6.9: Qualifications of Teachers in TCs (2007) 140
Table 7.1: Enrollment, Actual Number, and Number per 100,000 Inhabitants 149
Table 7.2: Fields of Study (2008) 152
Table 7.3: Postgraduate Students by Fields of Study and College (2008) 156

Table 7.4: Comparison of Fees in Public and Private Universities (in MK) 160
Table 7.5: Surplus and Deficit in Expenditures 164
Table 7.6a: Unit Cost Per Expenditure Category: UNIMA (in MK) 166
Table 7.6b: Unit Cost per Expenditure Category: MZUNI (in MK) 166
Table 7.7: Staff Profile in Public and Private Universities 169
Table 7.8: Qualifications of Staff in Public Institutions 170
Table 7.9: Student/Staff Ratios for 2008 171
Table 7.10: Cumulative University Graduate Output (2003–2007) 172
Table 7.11: Enrollment of Women by Fields of Study (2008) 176
Table 8.1: Simulated Net Impact of Education on Social Behaviors in Malawi 184
Table 8.2: Impact of a Mother's Education on Various Adult Behaviors (Share
   for the Different Cycles) (in %) 187
Table 8.3: Distribution of Workforce by Level of Education and Type of
   Employment in Percentages for 15-years-old and Over (2004) 188
Table 8.4: Annual Average Income and Expected Annual Income According to
   Level of Schooling 189
Table 8.5: Months Needed by HE Graduates to Properly Carry out Professional
   Tasks 193
Table 8.7: Employment Status of TEVET Completers 194
Table 8.8: Employment (of All Kinds) Rate of TEVET Graduates or Leavers,
   Aged 25–34 and 35–59 in Different African Countries (in %) 195
Table 8.9: Position of TEVET Completers at First Employment and Time of Study
   (in %) 198
Table 8.10: Private and Social Rates of Return to Education 200
Table 8.11: ROR in Malawi Compared to Selected Other African Countries 200
Table 8.12: Percentage of Firms that Report Labor Regulations and Skill Levels
   of Workers as a Major or Severe Constraint in Malawi 202
Table 1A.1: 5-16-Year-Old Population as % of Total, SADC Countries (2008) 208
Table 1A.2: Population Living Below Poverty Lines and Gini Index (2005 or
   Closest Year) (in %) 208
Table 1A.3: Orphans (0–17 Years) Due to AIDS, SADC Countries (2007) 209
Table 1A.4: African Context Indexes 209
Table 1A.5: Other Social Development Indicators 210
Table 2A.1: Outreach Population by Literacy Programs 214
Table 2A.2: Expected School-Age Population for 2006 and 2007, NSO Projections 217
Table 2A.3: Differences of Estimates (2006) 222
Table 2A.4: Comparison of Some Schooling Indicators According to the Sources
   of Data Used for the Population Estimates (2006) 223
Table 2A.5: Evolution of Gross Intake Rate (Access Rate to Standard 1) since
   2000 225
Table 2A.6: Model for Access Rate to Standard 1 Using Household Survey Data 228
Table 2A.7: Main Reason Declared for Having Never Attended School (in %) 229
Table 2A.8: Results of Econometric Model Explaining Retention Rate at the
   School Level 231
Table 2A.9: ASR and School-Life Expectancy Calculation for Malawi (2007) 232

Table 2A.10: School Life Expectancy, Recurrent Expenditure for Education as a Share of GDP and Index, Low-Income African Countries (2007 or closest Year) 233
Table 3A.1: Methodology of Recalibration to a 6–7 Year Duration Structure 239
Table 3A.2: Recalibration of Malawian 2008 Recurrent Expenditure Data 239
Table 3A.3: Breakdown of Public Recurrent Expenditure in Higher Education, African Countries (2007 or last year available) 240
Table 3A.4: Primary Education Salaries 241
Table 3A.5: Secondary Education Salaries 241
Table 4A.1: Degree of Randomness (1 − R^2) in Public Teacher Allocations in Various African Countries (2002–2007) 243
Table 4A.2: Reading and Mathematics Skill Levels 247
Table 4A.3: Correlates of PSLE Results at National Level (2006)—Basic Statistics 248
Table 4A.4: Correlates of MSCE Results at National Level (2006)—Basic Statistics 249
Table 4A.5: Some Characteristics of CSSs and CDSSs 250
Table 4A.6: Consistency of Teacher Allocation across Government-Funded Primary Schools at District Level (2007) 251
Table 4A.7: Consistency in Book Allocation across Government-Funded Primary Schools, by Divisions: R^2 Analysis 252
Table 5A.1: Repetition Rate Trends by Standard in Primary, 1999 and 2006 (All Types of Schools) 256
Table 5A.2: Repetition Rates by Form in Secondary, 2007 (All Types of Schools) 256
Table 5A.3 Dropout Rates in Primary By Gender, 1999 and 2006 (All Types of Schools) 256
Table 5A.4 Dropout Rates in Secondary by Gender, 2006 (All Types of Schools) 256
Table 5A.5: GER and PCR for the 28 Administrative Districts (2007) 258
Table 5A.6: Leaving School Examination Results at the Primary Level by School Types, Location, Division and Gender (2006) 259
Table 5A.7: JCE and MSCE Examination Pass Rates by School Types, Location, Division, and Gender (2006) 259
Table 5A.8: Access Rates to Standard 8 and GER, According to Education Division and Gender 260
Table 5A.9: Access Rates to Different Forms and GER on Secondary Education, According to Region, Education Division, and Gender 261
Table 5A.10: Probability of Enrollment in Standards 1–8 of Primary School, by District 262
Table 5A.11: Probability of Enrollment in Forms 1–4 of Secondary School, by District 263
Table 6A.1: Number of Regular and Parallel Students in Technical Colleges (2007) 265
Table 6A.2: Records of the TEVET Provider Directory 1999 265
Table 6A.3: Enrollment in Regular Apprenticeship Programs (2003–2007) 265
Table 6A.4: Female Participation in TEVETA-Sponsored Courses by Applications, Short Listing, and Enrollment from 2001 to 2008 266

Table 6A.5: Girls' Participation in Malawi Craft and Malawi Advanced Craft Examinations (in %) 266
Table 6A.6: Expenditure in Public Technical Colleges 2007/08 (Revised Budgeted) by Subprograms (in %) 266
Table 6A.7: Budget Execution Rates for Technical Colleges (2005/06) 267
Table 6A.8: TEVETA Expenditure 2002/03–2006/7, in '000 MK 267
Table 6A.9: Examination Fees for Malawian Qualification 268
Table 6A.10: Calculation of Private Cost (Tuition Fees, Boarding, Testing Fees) for Formal TEVET in Technical Colleges (Prices as of 2008) 268
Table 6A.11: Synopsis of Programs Offered and Qualifications Achieved in the Malawian TEVET Environment 269
Table 6A.12: STR in Technical Colleges (2007) 269
Table 6A.13: Trade Test Participation by Grade 270
Table 6A.14: Trade Testing Candidates by Trade and Gender (2003–2008) 270
Table 6A.15: Trade Testing Pass Rate by Type of Institution 271
Table 7A.1: Categories of Expenditure as Percentage of Total Expenditure: UNIMA 274
Table 7A.2: Categories of Expenditure as Percentage of Total Expenditure: MZUNI 274
Table 7A.3: Categories of Expenditure as Percentage of Total Expenditure: Livingstonia 275
Table 7A.4: Categories of Expenditure as Percentage of Total Expenditure: Catholic 275
Table 7A.5: Enrollments in Higher Education by Gender 277
Table 7A.6: Sources of Income for UNIMA 278
Table 7A.7: Percentages of Sources of Income for UNIMA 279
Table 7A.8: Sources of Income for MZUNI 279
Table 7A.9: Percentages of Sources of Income for MZUNI 279
Table 7A.10: UNIMA Actual Expenditure: 2003/04 to 2006/07 280
Table 7A.11: MZUNI Actual Expenditure: 2003/04 to 2006/07 280
Table 7A.12: Unit Cost by Institution 280
Table 7A.13: Percentage of Females in Postgraduate Studies 282
Table 8A.1: Mincerian Earning Function of Malawi (2004) 288
Table 8A.2: Job Sector of Employed People According to Their Education Level, 15+ Years Old 289
Table 8A.3: Means of Variables Other Than the Highest Grade Completed 289
Table 8A.4: Logarithm of Annual Income According to Education Level 290
Table 8A.5: Expected Income According to Education Level, 15+ Years Old 290
Table 8A.6: Schooling Duration, Unit Cost, and Rates of the Different Education Levels 291
Table 8A.7: Mean Income by Education Level as Units of GDP per Capita in Selected African Countries 293
Table 8A.8: Expected Annual Income by Job Sector Taking into Account Unemployment Risk (MK) 293
Sampling Frame 303
Table A9.1: Rating of Study Condition and Provision 304

Table A9.2: General Satisfaction with Studies 305
Table A9.3: Rating Usefulness of Studies 305
Table A9.4: Occupational Situation after Graduation and Present (in %) 308
Table A9.5: Extent of Use of Qualification 310
Table A9.6: Degree of Abilities and Knowledge of the Graduates 311
Table A9.7: Extent of Appropriateness of Professional Situation 312
Sampling Frame 320
Table A9.8: Type and Grade of Qualification 321
Table A9.9: Duration of Training Courses 321
Table A9.10: Changes as Result of Program/Course 323
Table A9.11: Weaknesses of Program/Course 323
Table A9.12: Current Employment Status 324
Table A9.13: Duration of Employment Seeking 324
Table A9.13: Level of Position 325
Table A9.14: Number of Employees 325
Table A9.15: Relative Risk of Unemployment for High Risk Groups 325
Table A9.16: Mean Income by Positional Level 327
Table A9.17: Mean Income by Occupational Status 327
Table A9.18: Mean Income by Way of Getting Skills 327
Table A9.19: Mean Income by Field of Occupation 328
Table A9.20: Mean Income by Type and Level of Certificates 329
Table A9.21: Degree of Abilities and Knowledge of TEVET Completers by Type
  and Level 330

Figures

Figure 1: Educational Pyramids for Malawi and Sub-Saharan Africa xxx
Figure 2: Access Rate to Each Grade (2007) xxxi
Figure 3: SACMEQ Scores in English and Mathematics (SACMEQ II) xxxii
Figure 4: Teacher Allocation in Government-Funded Schools (2007) xxxiii
Map 1a: STR at the District Level xxxiv
Map 1b: SqTR at the District Level xxxiv
Figure 5: Access Rates to the Different Grades According to Wealth Index xxxv
Figure 6: Share of Public Education Expenditure for the 10 Percent Most
  Educated, Africa Region xxxvi
Map 2a: Primary Completion Rates by District xxxvii
Map 2b: Secondary Completion Rates by District xxxvii
Figure 7: Evolution of the Distribution of Recurrent Expenditure by Level of
  Schooling xxxviii
Figure 8: Contribution of Public Financing by Level of Education (2007) xl
Figure 9: Flows of Funds to TEVET xlii
Figure 10: Number of Higher Education Students per 100,000 Inhabitants in
  Sub-Saharan Africa xliv
Figure 11: Higher Education Public Recurrent Unit Costs (2007 or last year
  available) xlvi
Figure 12: Job Insertion Rate (Modern Sector Only) of Higher Education Leavers .. xlviii

Figure 13: Mean Income by Education Level in Relation to GDP Per Capita l
Figure 14: Unmet Labor Demand as a Percentage of Employed in Selected
    TEVET Occupations.. li
Figure 1.1: Trends and Projections of School-Age Populations (1998–2018) 3
Figure 1.2: Evolution in Real GDP Per Capita (1987–2008)... 7
Figure 2.1: Cross-Sectional Schooling Profile with Revised Repetition Structure
    from IHS-2 20
Figure 2.2: International Comparison for Gross Intake Rate and Primary
    Completion Rate (Access Rate to Grade 6 to Be Comparable Across
    Countries) 21
Figure 2.3: Percentage of People Who Have Ever Attended Primary School
    (by Age).. 22
Figure 2.4: Probalistic Schooling Profile 22
Figure 2.5: Evolution of Survival Profile in Primary and Secondary Education,
    2003–2007 24
Figure 2.6: Educational Pyramid for Malawi (2007) 25
Figure 2.7: Educational Pyramid for Sub-Saharan Africa (2005/06) 25
Figure 3.1: Domestic Resources as a Percentage of GDP and Budget Allocation
    Towards Education, SSA Countries 36
Figure 3.2: Evolution of the Distribution of Recurrent Expenditure by Level of
    Schooling 39
Figure 3.3: Distribution of Recurrent Expenditure by Level of Schooling, SADC
    Countries, (2008 or Last Available Year) 41
Figure 3.4: Higher Education Public Recurrent Unit Costs, Sub-Saharan
    Countries (2007 or last year available) 44
Figure 3.5: Contribution of Public Financing by Level of Education (2007)..................... 48
Figure 4.1: Repetition Rate at Primary and Secondary Levels in SADC Countries
    (2006 or Closest Year) (in %)... 61
Figure 4.2: Percentage of Students Reaching Literacy and Mathematics
    Competency Levels in Malawi (SACMEQ II) 65
Figure 4.3: Mean for the Reading and Mathematics Test Scores of Learners in All
    SACMEQ Countries (SACMEQ II) 66
Figure 4.4: STR at the Primary Level, SADC Countries (2006 or Closest Year) 81
Figure 4.5: Teacher Allocation in Government-Funded Schools (2007)............................ 83
Figure 4.6: STRs by Location (1999 and 2007)... 84
Figure 4.7: STR in Government-Funded Primary Schools, by Division (2000 and
    2007).. 84
Map 4.1a: STR at the District Level 86
Map 4.1b: SqTR at the District Level.. 86
Figure 4.8: Relationship between the Wage Unit Cost and the Number of
    Students (School Level) at the Primary Level 95
Figure 4.9: Relationship between the Unit Cost (for Teachers and All School
    Staff) and the Number of Students at the Secondary Level 96
Figure 4.10: Relation between PSLE Results and Spending on Cost per Student
    at the Primary Level (Government-Funded Schools) 97
Figure 5.1: Access to and Completion of the Different Levels by Gender 104

Figure 5.2: Access to and Completion of the Different Levels by Wealth Quintile 107
Figure 5.3: Access Probability to the Different Grades According to Living Area 108
Figure 5.4: PCR Urban /PCR Rural in Some African Countries 108
Figure 5.5: Regional Disparities 109
Map 5.1a: Access Rate to S1 by District 111
Map 5.1b: Primary Completion Rate by District 111
Maps 5.2a: Access Rate to Form 1 by District 112
Map 5.2b: Secondary Completion Rate by District 112
Figure 5.6: Education Lorenz Curve 115
Figure 5.7: Share of Public Resources for the 10 percent Most Educated, African Countries 116
Figure 6.1: Number of Formal Apprentices Recruited 122
Figure 6.2: TEVET Students per 100,000 Inhabitants in Selected SADC Countries 123
Figure 6.3: Female Participation in Malawi (Advanced) Craft Examinations (2003–2007) 125
Figure 6.4: Malawi Craft Pass Rates by Gender and Year 125
Figure 6.5: Poverty and TEVET Admission by District (2005 Compared to 2008) 127
Figure 6.6: Pass Rates for MC and MAC Examinations by Trades (2003–2007) 136
Figure 6.7: STRs in TCs for Regular Programs and Total Enrollment (2007) 139
Figure 7.1: Enrollments in Higher Education in Malawi (2003–2008) 150
Figure 7.2: Percentage of Non-Residential Students (2003–2008) 151
Figure 7.3: Postgraduate Students in the Total Enrollment (% of) 155
Figure 7.4: Sources of Income for UNIMA Colleges and Central Office (2004/05–2007/08) 159
Figure 7.5: Sources of Income for MZUNI: 2002/03–2004/05 159
Figure 7.6: Unit Cost (in relation to GDP Per Capita 165
Figure 7.7: Trends in Graduate Output by Institution by Year 173
Figure 7.8: Trends in Graduate Output by Field of Study 173
Figure 7.9: Masters Graduates by Gender and by Institution (2003–2008) 174
Figure 8.1: Relations between Education, Income, and Behavior 183
Figure 8.2: Mean Income by Level of Education in Relation to GDP per Capita (in %) 189
Figure 8.3: Occupational Situation of HE graduates by Field of Study 190
Figure 8.4: Employment Rate (Modern Sector Only) of Higher-Education Leavers in Different Age Groups in Different African Countries 191
Figure 8.5: Mean Monthly Income of HE Graduates by Field of Study, Degree, and Work Situation 192
Figure 8.6: Duration of Job Search of TEVET Completers: Findings from Two Tracer Studies (2008) (in %) 196
Figure 8.7: Net Income per Month of TEVET Graduates (MK) 196
Figure 8.8: Level of Position of TEVET Graduates in Employment (in %) 197
Figure 8.9: Mean Monthly Net Income of TEVET Completers 199
Figure 8.10: Distribution of Employed by Economic Sector 202
Figure 8.11: Unmet Labor Demand as a Percentage of Employed in Selected TEVET Occupations (in %) 204
Map 1A.1: Population Density by District (2008) 207

Figure 2A.1: Structure of the Education System in Malawi 212
Figure 2A.2: Enrollment Trends in Primary Education (in Thousands) 213
Figure 2A.3: Enrollment Trends in Secondary Education Since 2000, by Provider (in Thousands) 213
Figure 2A.4: Projections of the Malawian Population, Based on the 1998 National Census (1999–2023) 215
Figure 2A.5: Projections of Single-Age Population 216
Figure 2A.6: Population Projections for the Rural Blantyre District 218
Figure 2A.7: Single-Age Population for Malawi in 2006 According to MICS Data 218
Figure 2A.8: Projections of Malawian Population, Compared to the UN and NSO 220
Figure 2A.9: Malawian Population per Age for 1998, Comparison between NSO and UN 220
Figure 2A.10: Malawian Population Projections per Single Ages, According to the UN 221
Figure 2A.11: Difference between the Two Estimates (2007) 222
Figure 2A.12: Cross-Sectional Schooling Profile, School Year 2006 and 2007 224
Figure 2A.13: Educational Pyramid 227
Figure 2A.14: International Comparison on School-Life Expectancy (2007 or Closest Year) 232
Figure 2A.15: School Life Expectancy and Current Expenditure for Education as a Share of GDP for Some Low Income African Countries (2007 or Closest Year) 234
Figure 3A.1: Teachers' Average Salary (Primary and Secondary) as Units of GDP Per Capita for Countries with GDP Per Capita Lower than US$500 (2007 or last year available) 235
Figure 3A.2: Public Recurrent Expenditure Excluding Teachers' Salaries As a Percentage of Total Recurrent Expenditure (Primary Education) (2007 or last year available) 235
Figure 3A.3: Household Education Expenditure As a Percentage of GDP 236
Figure 3A.4: Education Household Expenditure as a Percentage of Total Household Expenditure 236
Figure 3A.5: Evolution of Budget Allocation to ECD and Adult Literacy (in MK Millions) 238
Figure 4A.1: Trend of Repetition Rates by Cycle (2000–2006) 242
Figure 4A.2: Student Flow Efficiency Index in Various SADC Countries, (2006 or Closest Year) 242
Figure 4A.3: Internal Efficiency Coefficient (IEC) in SADC Countries (2006 or Closest Year) 243
Figure 4A.4: Consistency of Allocation of ORT at the Primary Level According to Enrollment at the District Level (2007/08) 244
Figure 4A.5: Teacher Allocation in All Secondary Publicly Funded Schools (2007) 244
Figure 4A.6: Coherence on Allocation of ORT Funds at the Secondary School Level (For Cost Center Schools and Grant-Aided Secondary Schools) 245

Figure 4A.7: Relation between JCE Results and Spending on Cost of Salaries per Student at the Secondary Level (Government-Funded Schools) 245
Figure 4A.8: Relation between MSCE Results and Spending on Cost of Salaries per Student at the Secondary Level (Government-Funded Schools) 246
Figure 5A.1: Urban Completion Rate/Rural Completion Rate for Lower Secondary in Some African Countries (ca. 2007) 257
Figure 6A.1: TEVET Public Recurrent Unit Cost as a Percentage of GDP per Capita in Selected African Countries 264
Figure 6A.2: Trade-Testing Candidates by Training Background and Year 269
Figure 6A.3: Trade Test Candidates by Gender and Year (2003–2008) 270
Figure 6A.4: Trade Testing Pass Rates by Gender (2003–2008) 271
Figure 7A.1: Comparison of Enrollments per 100,000 Inhabitants in SSA 272
Figure 7A.2: Percent of Sources of Income for UNIMA Colleges and Central Office (2004/05–2007/0) 272
Figure 7A.3: Percent of Sources of Income for UNIMA Colleges and Central Office (2004/05–2007/08) 273
Figure 7A.4: Percentage of Female Enrollment by Type of Institution 273
Figure 7A.5: Comparison of Average Annual Change in Enrollments per 100,000 Inhabitants 276
Figure 7A.6: Enrollment by Institution: 2003–2008 276
Figure 7A.7: Postgraduate Enrollments by Field of Study (2003–2008) 277
Figure 7A.8: Education Expenditure in Tertiary as a Percentage of Total Education Expenditure 278
Figure 7A.9: Student/Lecturer Ratios for Selected SSA Countries (2006) 281
Figure 7A.10: Percentage of Females Enrolled in Fields of Study 281
Figure 8A.1: Duration of Job Search after Leaving University, HE Grads/Dropouts 283
Figure 8A.2: Probability of Antenatal Care According to Education Level (in %) 284
Figure 8A.3: Probability of Using Iron Tablets During Pregnancy, According to Education Level (in %) 284
Figure 8A.4: Probability for Women to Be Assisted at Delivery, According to Education Level (in %) 285
Figure 8A.5: Probability of Using Anti-Malaria Treatments for Children Under the Age of Five (in %) 285
Figure 8A.6: Average Woman's Age at Her First Birth 286
Figure 8A.7: Birth Interval (in Years) 286
Figure 8A.8: Knowledge about HIV/AIDS (on [0–11] Scale) 287
Figure 8A.9: Probability for Women to Be Literate According to Education Level (in %) 287
Figure A9.1: Predominant Job Situation since Graduation by Year of Completing 306
Figure A9.2: General Satisfaction with Professional Situation (in %) 307
Figure A9.3: Gross Income per Month in Malawi Kwacha 308
Figure A9.4: Average Income in the First and the Actual Occupation by Cohort 309
Figure A9.5: Differences between Graduates from Different Institutions 312
Figure A9.6: Reasons for Dropping Out (in %) 314
Figure A9.7: Rating of Professional Opportunities in the Next Years (in %) 315

Figure A9.8: Rating of Usefulness of Training (in %) 322
Figure A9.9: Net Income per Month in Malawi Kwacha (in %) 326
Figure A9.10: Differences between Completers from Different Institutions (in %) 331

Boxes

Box 3.1: Why Use the Reference to GDP Per Capita? 42
Box 4.1: The Impact of Repetition on Schooling Efficiency 57
Box 6.1: More about the TEVET Levy Fund 132
Box 6.2: The Malawian TEVET Landscape—A Jungle of Qualifications and
   Programs 137
Box 2A.1: Data Used by the UN Population Unit to Estimate and Project the
   Population for Malawi 219
Box 6A.1: Financial Management Issues in Technical Colleges 264

Foreword from the Minister of Education, Government of Malawi

The Country Status Report is an important tool in diagnosing the problems that the education sector is facing in the county. It intends to provide an accurate snapshot of the current status of the education in Malawi and thus offer policy makers and their development partners a solid basis for policy dialogue and decision making.

This study on the education sector in Malawi adds to the growing list of country status reports that the World Bank has been sponsoring in the Africa region. As with similar reports, its preparation involved the collaboration of a national team and the donor community. The team included members of government education ministries; staff from the World Bank; and staff from development partners, particularly the Pôle de Dakar team from UNESCO BREDA (the UNESCO regional office in Dakar, Senegal).

This Country Status Report not only updates the original report completed in 2004, but also includes deeper analysis of areas such as early childhood development; literacy; external efficiency; and, particularly, technical, entrepreneurial, and vocational education and training (TEVET) and higher education. This report comes at a time when the government is finalizing the National Education Sector Plan and preparing for a funding request to the Education for All-Fast Track Initiative catalytic fund. The findings of this report are therefore very useful for providing analytical inputs for future reforms.

This report has a number of important features, two of which deserve special mention. First, it was prepared through a combined effort by a dedicated government team and its counterparts in the donor community. The report is therefore not an external evaluation of the system but a collaborative attempt to deepen understanding of the sector and the challenges it faces and to create a common ground of joint action. In this sense, the report is a tangible arrangement for implanting the aspirations of the Paris declarations on aid effectiveness. In addition, this collaboration also built capacity for sector analysis within Malawi's Ministry of Education, Science and Technology and other involved ministries. Second, the report's methodology and information sources go beyond the ordinary. The team has taken advantage of existing data sources, mostly from ministry administrative sources, as well as household surveys to develop more in-depth indicators than the basic indicators of enrollment that typify education system monitoring. For example, a trace study of TEVET and higher education graduation was prepared to rigorously examine skills needs and the links between education and the labor market.

The report highlights some recent achievements and challenges in the education sector. More broadly, it offers a valuable and comprehensive resource for anyone interested in education in Malawi. It is the hope of the ministry that this document will be of use to all stakeholders in the education sector.

Dr. George T. Chaponda MP
Minister of Education, Science and Technology

Foreword from the World Bank

This study on the education sector in Malawi adds to the growing list of Country Status Reports (CSRs), which the World Bank has been sponsoring in the Africa Region. As with other similar reports, it involved the collaboration of a national team consisting of members from the government ministries—including the ministries in charge of education—and staff from the World Bank and development partners, particularly the Pôle de Dakar team from the UNESCO regional office in Dakar, Senegal (UNESCO-BREDA). The report is intended to provide an accurate snapshot of the current status of education in Malawi, and thus to offer policy makers and their development partners a solid basis for policy dialogue and decision-making.

In recent years, the development context for education has evolved in ways that increase the relevance and demand for this type of analytic work. Governments are striving toward poverty reduction and the Millennium Development Goals, and the international development community has pledged to complement their efforts by providing financial assistance to implement credible plans for sector development. The launch of the Education for All-Fast Track Initiative (EFA-FTI) in 2002 has put the necessary aid architecture in place and as of September 2009, 21 African countries have already received grants (a total of $1,233 million) to implement sector development plans that have been endorsed by the EFA-FTI partners.

This is the second CSR for Malawi. It not only updates the original CSR completed in 2004, but also includes a more in-depth analysis of some areas, such as early childhood development, literacy, external efficiency, and particularly technical, entrepreneurial, and vocational education and training (TEVET) and higher education. The report comes at a time when the government is finalizing the national education sector plan. The findings of this report are therefore very useful for providing analytical inputs in this process.

This report has a number of noteworthy features—two of which are worth special mention here. First, it was prepared through a combined effort by a dedicated government team and its counterparts in the donor community. The report is therefore not an external evaluation of the system, but a collaborative attempt to deepen understanding of the sector and the challenges it faces and to create common ground for joint action. In this sense, the report is a tangible arrangement for implementing the aspirations of the Paris Declaration on Aid Effectiveness. In addition, this collaboration also had the benefit of building capacity for sector analysis within the Malawian Ministry of Education and other involved ministries. Second, the report's methodology and information sources go beyond the ordinary. The team has taken advantage of existing data sources, mostly from ministry administrative sources as well as household surveys, to develop more in-depth indicators than the basic indicators of enrollment that typify monitoring education systems. For this report, a TEVET and higher education graduates tracer study was also prepared to provide a more in-depth examination of the issue of skill needs and the links between education and the labor market.

This CSR highlights some recent achievements, among them the following:

- Between 2004 and 2007, enrollments increased considerably in early childhood development programs (+44 percent per year), in adult literacy programs (+19 percent), in secondary education (+ 5 percent), and in higher education (+4 percent).
- Education in Malawi has an important impact on social development. Education in general, particularly for girls, has a strong impact on behavior in terms of reproductive health, maternal and child health, and knowledge of HIV/AIDS. The primary cycle contributes to almost half of the total effect of education on social development.
- External efficiency in relation to employability and income is high, in particular for TEVET and higher education graduates. The job insertion rates of higher education graduates are among the highest in Africa and the wage premium for higher education is extremely high in relation to comparable countries. TEVET completers also show a high acceptance in the labor market when recording the job insertion rates of all African countries.

The CSR also points to the key challenges in the coming years for educational development in Malawi, among them:

- **Increasing the amount of public resources to primary education.** The share of recurrent education expenditure allocated to primary education (when calibrated to a six-year duration for comparative purposes) is only 32 percent—far from the African average of 44 percent. This lack of budget priority leads to a student-teacher ratio (STR) of 80:1 for primary education, twice the Southern African Development Community's average value, while the higher education student-teacher ratio of 11:1 is better than the Organisation for Economic Co-operation and Development's average of 16:1.
- **Reducing the high dropout rates in primary education.** Currently only 35 children out of every 100 complete primary school. Promising reforms for reducing dropout rates include: (i) building new classrooms to complete incomplete schools (13 percent of pupils attend a school that does not provide a continuous educational supply up to Standard 8); (ii) decreasing the repetition rate with both pedagogical and administrative measures; and (iii) reducing the number of overloaded classes by improving consistency in the deployment of teachers in schools.
- **Raising the level of student achievement.** Evaluations show that Malawian children perform far below expectations. Malawi has the weakest performance in English reading and the second weakest in mathematics among countries whose pupils have been tested using the same Southern African Consortium for Monitoring Educational Quality standardized tests. A possible option for raising learning achievement may be to improve the management of official instructional time. An estimated 20 percent of teaching time is lost due to

teacher absenteeism and 16 percent of schools use overlapping shifts. Moreover, pupil absenteeism, holidays, and other events that cause schools to close also contribute to a decrease in teaching time.
- **Reducing the repetition rate.** In primary education, repetition rates have increased to 20 percent from 1999–2006; this level is the highest in the region. Evidence, at the national and international level, shows that high repetition rates do not favor a better mastery of school subjects, have adverse effects on STR, and increase dropouts and costs. An estimated MK1.97 billion is used annually to deliver primary education services to repeaters. A promising option is to reorganize the primary cycle into subcycles, within which repetition would not be allowed, in addition to implementing measures on quality improvement.
- **Improving consistency in the deployment of teaching staff to schools.** Large disparities exist among education divisions and schools in Malawi. While some schools have only two teachers for 200 pupils, others have twelve teachers for the same number of pupils. The Shire Highlands and South Eastern divisions have the lowest allocated number of government-funded teachers compared to the number of students.
- **Improving the coordination and flexibility of TEVET.** Three parallel qualification systems currently co-exist—trade testing, Malawi (Advanced) Craft, and the TEVET Authority/Competency-Based Education and Training (TEVETA/CBET)—which all maintain their own assessment and certification structures. This is unnecessarily costly for students and the government and hampers quality improvements at the school level. TEVETA, the Ministry of Education, Science, and Technology, and the Ministry of Labour need to agree on an approach to integrate all formal TEVET and the trade testing system under the TEVETA/CBET system so that it becomes the one and only national benchmark of recognized TEVET provision in Malawi.
- **Increasing cost-sharing in higher education.** Higher education is highly subsidized by public resources and is delivered at an extremely high public unit cost when compared to countries with similar incomes. Higher education is the level of education to which households contribute the least, while it is also the level with the lowest share of students from the poorest families. Giving universities the latitude to charge higher fees and improving the mechanism to recover student loans once graduates get a job could be a promising reform avenue to implement.

These and other findings in the CSR have already stimulated discussions within the government and between the government and its development partners regarding the challenges for the country in the education sector. They have informed the finalization of the education sector plan and the preparation of the EFA-FTI endorsement process.

More broadly, this CSR offers a valuable and comprehensive resource for anyone interested in education in Malawi. It is, however, a snapshot of the system at a particular time. Thus, as the country makes progress in implementing its sector plan, this report's findings are likely to become dated. I therefore look forward to a third

CSR in the years ahead. Hopefully, the effort would be led by a national team, with minimal support from external technical assistance. This approach has started to take hold in other countries, highlighting strong ownership for this type of product and has enhanced ownership for the product. I hope the third CSR will reveal tangible evidence of continued educational progress in Malawi, both in the number of children who gain access to better quality schooling and in the number of youth who exit the system with the skills and competencies to support the country's democratic, social, and economic development.

Yaw Ansu
Director
Human Development Department
Africa Region
The World Bank

Acknowledgments

This country status report was prepared in close collaboration with the government of Malawi, the World Bank, UNESCO/Pôle de Dakar, and the GtZ.

The government team consisted of staff from the different ministries in charge of education, as well as other relevant ministries and departments: the Ministry of Education, Science and Technology (MOEST), the Ministry of Finance (MOF), the Ministry of Labour (MOL), the Ministry of Women and Child Welfare (MOWCW), the National Statistical Office (NSO), the Technical, Entrepreneurial, and Vocational Education and Training Authority (TEVETA), and public and private universities.

The government team was led by Mathews Makalande, Deputy Director of Research and Planning (MOEST), under the overall leadership of Bernard Sande, Principal Secretary I (MOEST) and Moffat Chitimbe, Principal Secretary II (MOEST). It consisted of Lamulo Nsanja (Chapter Head/MOEST), Stanley Nkhata (MOF), and Dunstan Matekenya (NSO) for Chapter 1; Martin Masanche (Chapter Head/MOEST), Charles Mkunga (MOWCW), and B. V. Kayala (MOWCW) for Chapter 2; Grace Banda (Chapter Head/MOEST) and Lamulo Nsanja (MOEST) for Chapter 3; Job Mwamlima (Chapter Head/MOEST) and McNight Kalanda (MOEST) for Chapter 4; Grace Milner (Chapter Head/MOEST), C.P. Inani (MOEST), and Chikondi Maleta (MOEST) for Chapter 5; Ackim Phiri (Chapter Head, TEVETA), Aubrey Mathemba (MOEST), Wesley Muwalo (MOL), Modesto Gomani (TEVETA), and Brain Ng'oma (MOL) for Chapters 6 and 8; and Amlata Persaud (Chapter Head/MOEST) and John Bisika (University of Malawi) for Chapter 7.

The World Bank team consisted of Mathieu Brossard (Task Team Leader, Senior Education Economist), Michael Mambo (Co-Task Team Leader, then Consultant), Jutta Franz, Koffi Segniagbeto, and Gerald Chiunda (Consultants), under the overall guidance of Christopher Thomas (Sector Manager), Luis Benveniste (Lead Education Specialist), and Jee-Peng Tan (Adviser). The UNESCO/Pôle de Dakar team consisted of Nicolas Reuge and Diane Coury (Education Policy Analysts) under the overall guidance of Jean-Pierre Jarousse (Head of Pôle de Dakar). The GtZ team consisted of Dietmar Pfeiffer (Consultant in charge of the tracer survey) under the supervision of Wilfried Goertler and Friis Jorgen. Borel Foko and Jean-Marc Bernard (Pôle de Dakar) also contributed to the preparation of this report. The team also gives thanks to Amina Sharma and Kara Suter for their editing work. Administrative support was received from Maggie Mwaisufanana Mshanga and Pauline Kayuni (World Bank Lilongwe office) and Brigida Arriaza de Figueroa (World Bank Headquarter).

The team received very precious comments from the peer reviewers Carlos Rojas, Robert Prouty, Muna Meky, Riham Shendy, Kirsten Maajgard, and Michael Drabble.

The Development Partners group (first led by Sandra Burton, DFID and then by Simon Mphisa, UNICEF) provided valuable inputs at the concept note stage, strong support throughout the process, and facilitated the policy dialogue during the presentation of the findings of the report.

The report was mainly funded by the Education Program Development Fund, a trust fund of the Education for All/Fast Track Initiative managed by the World Bank. The Tracer Study (Appendix 9 of the report) was jointly funded by GTZ and the World Bank.

Acronyms and Abbreviations

AIR	Apparent Intake Rate
ASR	average schooling ratio
CDSS	Community Day Secondary Schools
CIDA	Canadian International Development Agency
CPD	Continued Professional Development
CSS	Conventional Secondary Schools
DFID	Department For International Development
DTED	Department of Teacher Education and Development
ECD	early childhood care and development
EFA-FTI	Education for All-Fast Track Initiative
EGRA	Early Grade Reading Assessment
EFA	Education for All
EMIS	Education Management Information System
FPE	Free Primary Education
GER	gross enrollment ratio
GTZ	German Society for Technical Cooperation
HE	higher education
IEC	internal efficiency coefficient
IPTE	Initial Primary Teachers Education Programme
JICA	Japan International Cooperation Agency
JCE	Junior Certificate Examination
KFW	Kreditanstalt Für Wiederaufbau (German Development Bank)
LMI	labor market information
MANEB	Malawi National Examinations Board
MASTEP	Malawi Special Teacher Education Programme
MGDS	Malawi Growth and Development Strategy
MDG	Millennium Development Goal
MICS	Multi Indicators Cluster Survey
MIITEP	Malawi Integrated In-service Teacher Education Programme
MIT	Malawi Institute of Tourism
MOEST	Ministry of Education, Science and Technology
MOL	Ministry of Labour
MSCE	Malawi School Certificate of Examination
NCHE	National Council for Higher Education
NESP	National Education Sector Plan
NSO	National Statistical Office
NUSLT	National University Student Loan Trust
OECD	Organisation for Economic Co-operation and Development
ODL	Open and Distance Learning
ODSS	Open-Day Secondary Schools

ORT	other recurrent transactions
PCAR	Primary Curriculum and Assessment Reform
PETS	Public Expenditure Tracking Survey
PSLE	Primary School Leaving Examination
PSLCE	Primary School Leaving Certificate of Education
PTA	Parent-Teacher Association
PTR	pupil-teacher ratio
SACMEQ	Southern African Consortium for Monitoring Educational Quality
SADC	Southern African Development Community
SIDA	Swedish International Development Cooperation Agency
SLE	school life expectancy
SMASSE	Strengthening Mathematics and Science in Secondary Education
SMC	School Management Committee
SqTR	student-to-qualified-teacher ratio
STR	student-teacher ratio
TEVET	technical, entrepreneurial, and vocational education and training
TTC	teacher training college
UNIMA	University of Malawi
UPE	Universal Primary Education
USAID	United States Agency for International Development

Executive Summary

The context of the education system in Malawi is strongly marked by demographic pressure, a high prevalence of HIV/AIDS, striking poverty, and very low human and social development.

The Malawian education system has to develop within a heavier demographic context than that of its neighboring countries. Malawi's population, estimated at 13 million inhabitants in 2008, is increasing at the rate of 2.4 percent per year. The 5–16-year-old age group represents 37 percent of the total population. This is the highest proportion of that age group in the entire Southern African Development Community (SADC) region. It is estimated that the population growth rate will slowly decrease, but that the primary school age group (6–13 years old) will increase by 20 percent between now and 2018. If universal primary education is reached before 2018, primary school places for 4.8 million children[1] will be needed in 2018. This represents 45 percent more primary school places compared to 2008.

The large majority of the population (82 percent) still lives in rural areas where school supply and demand are weaker. Sixty-three percent of Malawians live on less than US$2 a day. Malawi has the highest malnutrition prevalence in the SADC region and an overwhelming 44 percent of preschoolers have stunted growth. There are an estimated 122 children per 1,000 who die before the age of five, which is similar to the SADC average. The adult (15 years and older) literacy rate is estimated to be 69 percent in Malawi, which is lower than the SADC average (75 percent). Illiteracy of parents impedes the achievement of education for all because these parents are less likely to enroll their children in school than literate parents.

The HIV/AIDS pandemic also dramatically affects the development of the education sector, because of the deaths of both teachers and parents. The pandemic also increases teachers' absenteeism and the number of orphans, who are less likely to go to school than children with families. The adult (15–49 years old) prevalence rate is 12 percent, whereas children orphaned by AIDS represent 7 percent of the children under 17 years old (in addition to the 5 percent of children orphaned by other reasons). HIV/AIDS occurrences are highest in the Southern region and are concentrated in urban areas.

The Malawian economy is getting better but still remains one of the poorest in the world.

Malawi's economy has been growing steadily since 2005, mainly due to recent sound economic policies and favorable weather conditions for agriculture. The continual increase in economic growth has allowed Malawi to reach a GDP per capita of around US$300 in 2008. In comparison to the entire SADC region, Malawi still has the third lowest GDP per capita and one of the five lowest in all of Africa. However, with the government's increased emphasis on value addition on domestic products, coupled with the discovery and mining of uranium, there is the prospect of improved GDP levels.

Compared to countries with a comparable level of economic development, Malawi's performance is very satisfactory for mobilization of public revenue. The rate of domestic revenue as a proportion of GDP is higher in Malawi than the average observed in low-income non-oil producing African countries (19 compared to 17 percent). Thus, while reducing the budget deficit at around 1 percent of GDP, the government has increased the volume of its expenditures up to more than 33 percent of GDP. This creates a good opportunity to increase spending for the education sector.

The ratio of enrollment increased very differently for the different levels of education. Compared to other African countries, education coverage remains very low, for post-primary levels in particular.

Since 2000, the gross enrollment ratio (GER) has decreased in primary education. In 2007, it was 101 percent. In the same period, early childhood care and development showed a very high increase in the enrollment ratio (from 2 to 23 percent), while coverage in secondary education stayed stable (16 percent). Enrollment in adult literacy programs is 1,074 learners per 100,000 inhabitants.

Compared to other Sub-Saharan African (SSA) countries, Malawi performs worse in post-primary levels and technical, entrepreneurial, vocational education and training (TEVET) (see the educational pyramids in figure 1).

Malawi still stands far from the Education Millennium Development Goal of universal primary completion because of the high number of dropouts within the primary cycle.

Access to Standard 1 in primary education is almost universal but the dropout rate is still very high, leading to only a 35 percent primary completion rate. The retention rate within the primary cycle improved from 23 percent in 2004 to 32 percent in 2007, but remains largely insufficient. The retention rate in secondary education is much better, with very few dropouts within the cycle (see figure 2).

The poor retention rate in primary education comes from a lack of school demand, in particular among the poorest. Economic difficulties and behavior such as early marriage, pregnancy, and family responsibilities explain the fragility of school demand. The lack of supply (crowded classrooms, open-air or temporary classrooms, and incomplete schools) also has a negative effect on retention. Sixteen percent of pupils are enrolled in a school that does not provide the eight grades of the primary cycle and these students are likely to drop out before completion.

Figure 1: Educational Pyramids for Malawi and Sub-Saharan Africa

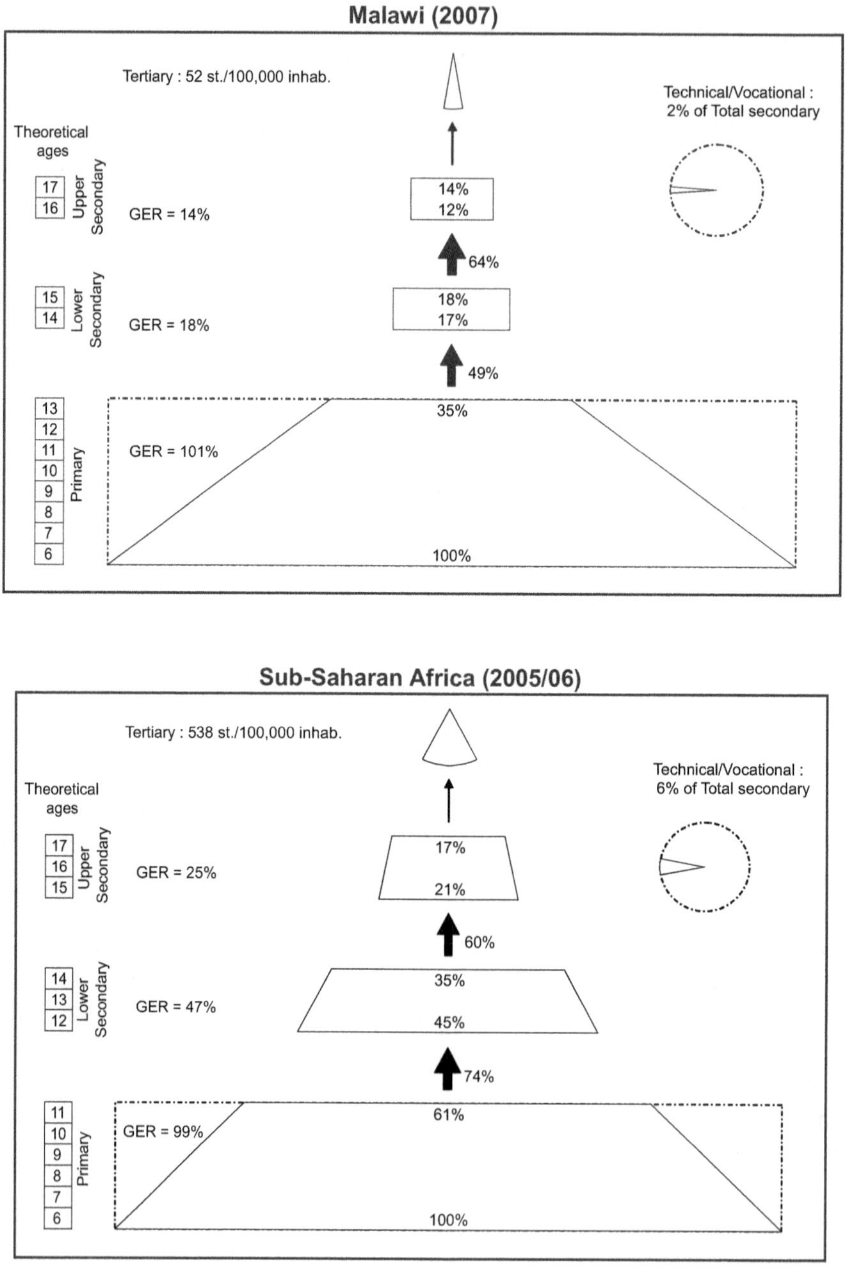

Malawi (2007)

Tertiary : 52 st./100,000 inhab.

Technical/Vocational : 2% of Total secondary

Theoretical ages

- Upper Secondary (ages 16–17): GER = 14% — 14% / 12%
- ↑ 64%
- Lower Secondary (ages 14–15): GER = 18% — 18% / 17%
- ↑ 49%
- Primary (ages 6–13): GER = 101% — 35% / 100%

Sub-Saharan Africa (2005/06)

Tertiary : 538 st./100,000 inhab.

Technical/Vocational : 6% of Total secondary

Theoretical ages

- Upper Secondary (ages 15–17): GER = 25% — 17% / 21%
- ↑ 60%
- Lower Secondary (ages 12–14): GER = 47% — 35% / 45%
- ↑ 74%
- Primary (ages 6–11): GER = 99% — 61% / 100%

Sources: Calculation from EMIS, UN population data, and World Bank database.

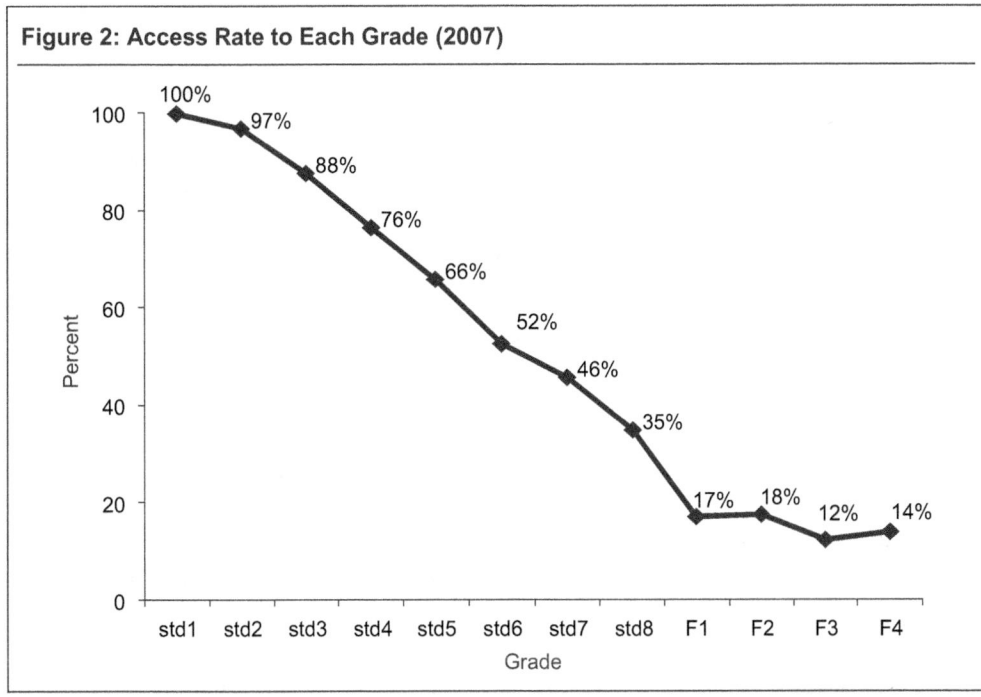

Figure 2: Access Rate to Each Grade (2007)

Sources: Calculation with EMIS 2007 database, IHS 2004 repetition structure, and UN population data.

The internal efficiency of the system is weak, in particular due to very high repetition rates.

The internal efficiency coefficient (IEC) at the primary level is particularly low (35 percent), which implies that 65 percent of public resources are wasted in paying for repeated grades or schooling for students who dropout before cycle completion. Currently, the system requires 23 student years to produce one Standard 8 graduate, instead of 8 years with an ideal internal efficiency. The situation has slightly worsened since 1999, when the IEC was 39 percent. A higher level of repetition is mainly responsible for this degradation.

Repetition rates have increased over the 1999–2006 period to reach 20 percent in primary education—a level that is the highest in the region. At the national and international level, evidence shows that too high repetition rates do not favor a better mastery of learning, increase the risk of dropping out, and have adverse effects on the STR (student-teacher ratio) and costs. An estimated MK1.97 billion is used annually to deliver primary education services to repeaters.

The Ministry of Education, Science and Technology is well aware of the issue, especially as it affects standards 1 to 4 of the primary cycle, where the highest repetition rates are to be found. The Ministry, inspired by success stories in other countries, is thinking of a policy to favor direct promotion between certain standards and for the others, (such as 4, 6, and 8) allowing a student to repeat only after failing to achieve a 50 percent pass in two subjects (standards 4 and 6), and after failing Standard 8.

Education in Malawi suffers from a flagrant problem of poor quality.

Malawi is offering poor and deteriorating quality education in primary schools, as documented by the Southern African Consortium for Monitoring Educational Quality (SACMEQ) scores and national examination pass rates. The number of children who reach a minimum level of mastery in English reading was cut in half in the period from 1998–2004, and in 2004 was barely nine percent. The decline may be partly explained by the 1994 Fee Free primary policy, which led to an increase of lower-performing students in the system. Nevertheless, examples of other countries who improved both quantity and quality in primary education at the same time shows that the free policy is not the only factor affecting the decrease of quality in Malawi.

At the primary level, high STRs are associated with lower Primary School Leaving Examination (PSLE) pass rates, as well as overlapping shifts, whereas school facilities tend to have a positive impact. At the secondary level, teacher characteristics have a major impact on Malawi School Certificate of Examination (MSCE) pass rates: While female teachers tend to perform better (all other things being equal), PT4 to PT1 teachers (teachers normally trained to work only at the primary level) do not teach as well as better qualified teachers, such as MSCE holders.

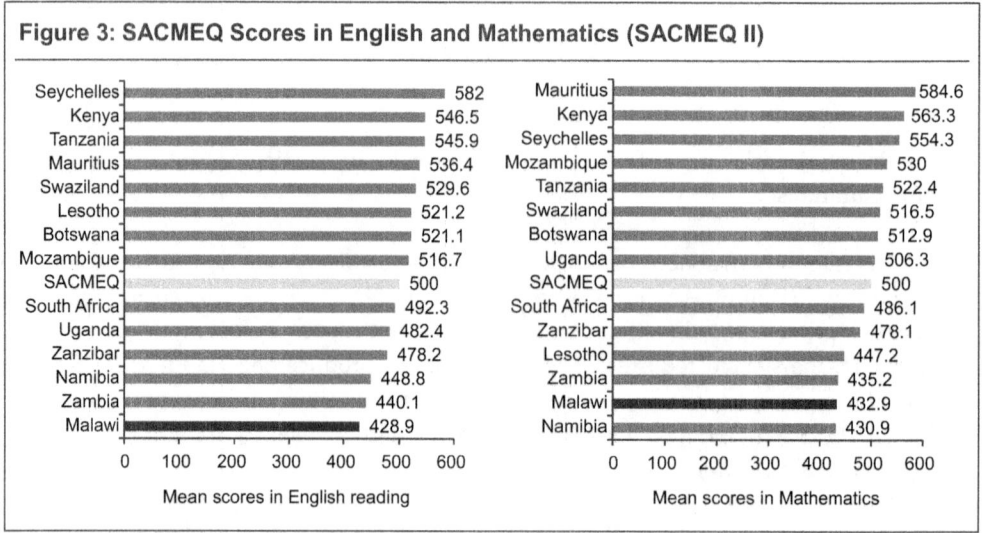

Figure 3: SACMEQ Scores in English and Mathematics (SACMEQ II)

Source: SACMEQ II report, 2005.
Note: SACMEQ scores are scaled so that the average of all students is 500 and the Standard deviation is 100.

The lack of qualified teaching staff in primary education is combined with a fairly incoherent distribution, reflecting the lack of efficient administrative management.

Malawi is characterized by a severe lack of teachers at the primary level, as shown by its high STR, which was 80:1 in 2007. In 2000, the STR was 63:1; it rose through a combined increase in student enrollment and pupil retention and a reduction in the number of teachers. However, the recruitment of volunteers teachers has somewhat eased the pressure (bringing the STR down from 86:1 to 80:1).

Teacher qualification still remains a major challenge. Although the situation has improved in primary schools, the student-to-qualified-teacher ratio (SqTR) is still high, at 88:1 (down from 118:1 in 1999). The Ministry's training efforts over the last few years need to be pursued if the situation is to be significantly improved.

The number of teachers assigned to different schools at the primary school level is erratic. There is little connection between the number of teachers allocated by the government and the number of students. For instance in a 1,000-student school, the number of teachers varies from less than 10 to more than 50 (see figure 4), making the class size range from 20 to 100.

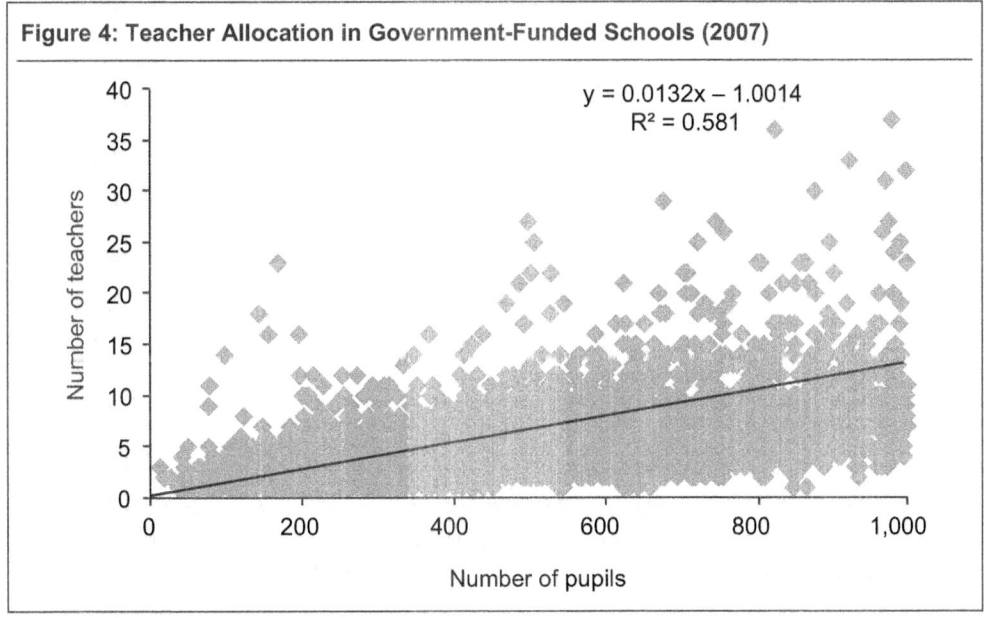

Figure 4: Teacher Allocation in Government-Funded Schools (2007)

$y = 0.0132x - 1.0014$
$R^2 = 0.581$

Source: Calculation based on EMIS 2007 data
Note: Volunteer teachers are not included.

The degree of randomness in teacher allocation is estimated at 42 percent (against 35 percent in 2000), which is well above the average of African countries (31 percent). This means that 42 percent of teacher allocation can be explained by factors other than the number of students enrolled in the school.

Teacher allocation across location and divisions/districts is uneven, with the deployment of teachers highly skewed toward urban areas (46:1) instead of rural area (86:1). At the division level, the STR ranges from 66:1 in the Northern division to 104:1 in the Shire Highlands. Some districts benefit from a SqTR lower than 60:1 while other districts have to handle a SqTR above 100:1 (see maps 1a and 1b).

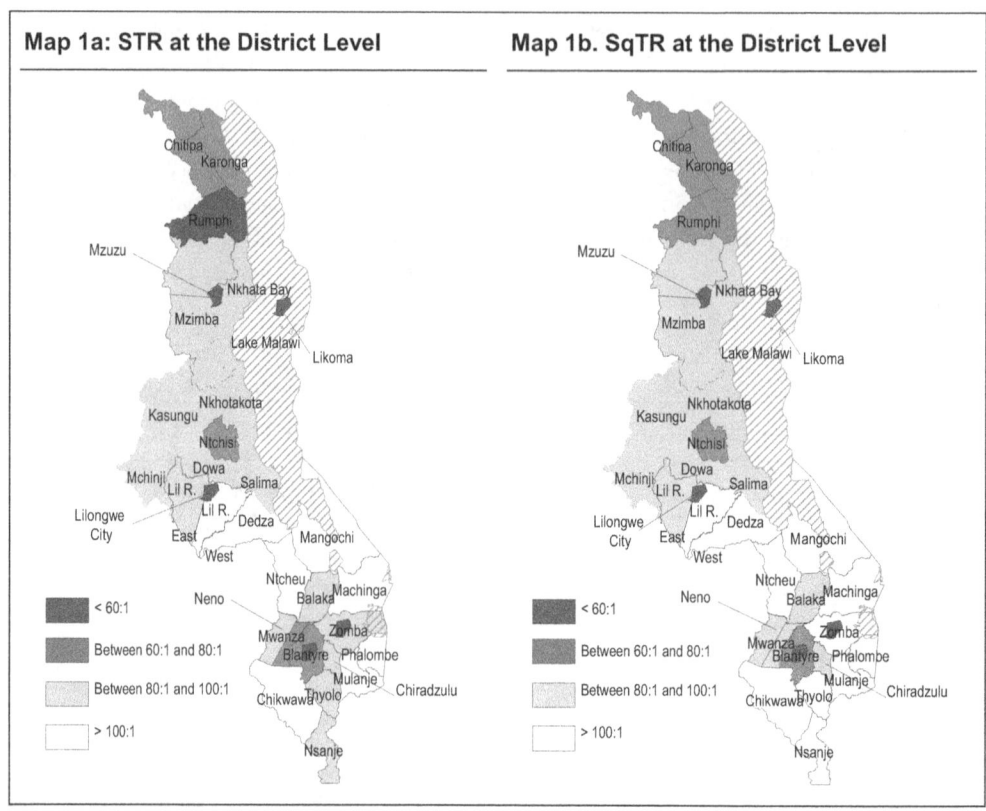

Source: EMIS, 2007

At the secondary level, coherence in teacher deployment is better but there are still discrepancies between Conventional Secondary Schools (CSSs) and Community Day Secondary Schools (CDSSs), to the detriment of the latter.

At the secondary level, in spite of a relatively good average STR, more than 60 percent of teachers are underqualified, with a SqTR ratio of 51:1. Most of the underqualified teachers work in CDSSs; 81 percent of the CDSS teaching force is unqualified and 27 percent of the teachers in CSSs are unqualified. Globally, CDSSs have fewer resources than other schools, although they enroll nearly half of the secondary student population. They are generally underfunded, have underqualified teachers, a poorer learning environment, and lack appropriate teaching and learning materials and equipment.

Teacher deployment across secondary schools is fairly consistent, as indicated by the value of the statistical coefficient of determination (R^2) of 72 percent. This is a sharp improvement from 2000, when only 41 percent of the variation in teacher deployment was explained by school size. Yet, there remains room for improvement throughout the system, since 28 percent of teacher allocation still depends on factors other than the number of students enrolled in each school.

The lack of connection between available resources and results in the different schools shows that there is a serious pedagogical management problem.

In primary education, schools with the same expenditure per student (MK4,000 for example) show PSLE results that vary from less than 10 to 100 percent. Similarly, in junior secondary education, schools with a unit expenditure of around MK10,000 have Junior Certificate Examination (JCE) pass rates ranging from 15 to 100 percent. The education system is suffering from serious problems of pedagogical management insofar as some schools with higher than average expenditures show poorer results.

These observations raise questions about the process underlying the way resources are transformed into learning achievement at the school level. Beyond their allocation, the way resources are used seems to be a major factor influencing the level of learning outcome. Improving supervision, transparency, and accountability mechanisms at the local level are known to be effective interventions.

Considerable disparities in access exist and they increase along with the level of education. A family's standard of living is the greatest factor in discrimination.

Schooling patterns suffer from disparities according to gender. Gender parity indexes decrease from 1.04 (that is, a better enrollment for girls than for boys) in the first four standards to 0.50 in higher education and 0.38 in TEVET.

Access to each level of education suffers even more from location and income disparities. The difference in the primary completion rate is 14 percent between boys and girls, yet 34 percent between urban and rural students. And the disparity is still greater—44 percent—between the richest 20 percent of the population and the poorest 20 percent (see figure 5). Furthermore, university students from the poorest quintile make up only 0.7 percent of students, while the richest quintile accounts for 91 percent.

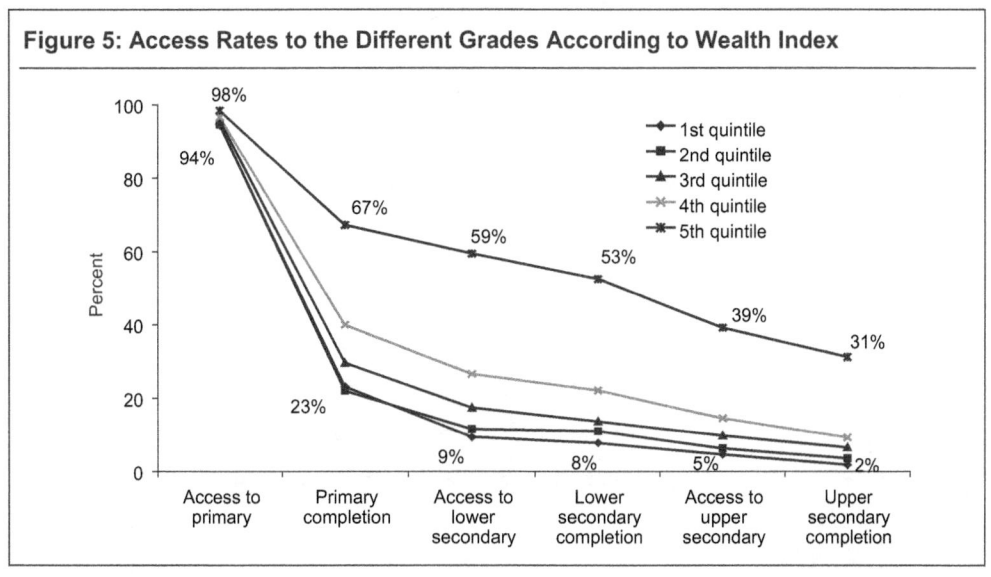

Figure 5: Access Rates to the Different Grades According to Wealth Index

Sources: Calculation from MICS 2006.

The majority of public resources for education benefit the most privileged students.

Each child benefits from part of the public education expenditure through his or her schooling. The longer a child stays in the education system, the greater the share of public resources used, which corresponds to what the government pays for the child's education. In Malawi, the 10 percent most educated (those who study longest) benefit from 73 percent of the public resources allocated to the education sector. This makes the Malawian education system the most elitist system in Africa. Malawi appears to be the country that provides the most inequitable distribution of public resources for education (see figure 6). The SSA average value for this indicator is 43 percent.

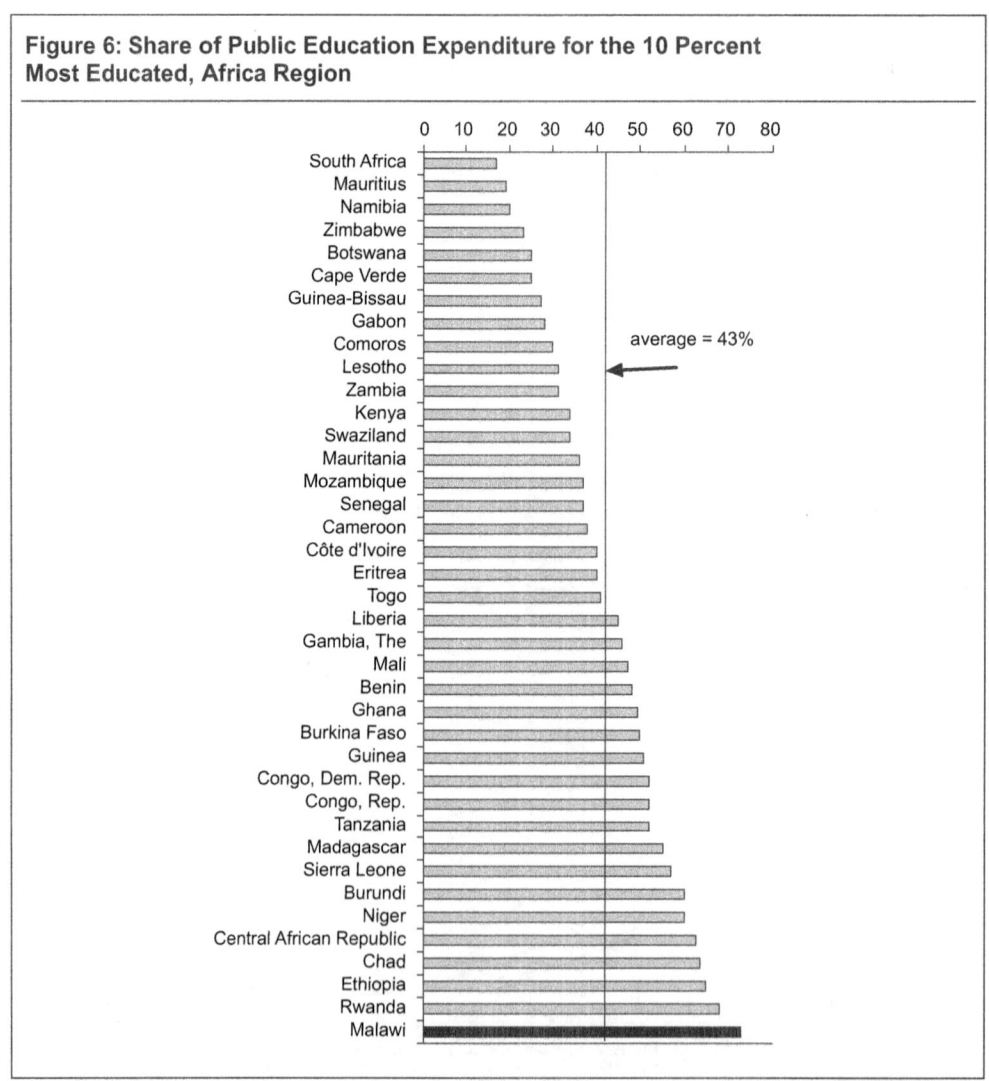

Figure 6: Share of Public Education Expenditure for the 10 Percent Most Educated, Africa Region

Source: World Bank database.

Schooling inequalities according to socioeconomic characteristics are thus reflected in an unequal appropriation of public resources for education. For example, girls only benefit from 48 percent of the public expenditure on education, compared to 52 percent for boys. Due to longer schooling for children from the wealthiest households, 68 percent of the public education expenditure goes towards education for the 20 percent most privileged children. Conversely, the poorest 20 percent of children only benefit from 6 percent of these resources (that is, 11.5 times less).

Schooling inequalities are also geographical.

The Northern region has better educational coverage than the two others. The GER in primary (134 percent) and secondary education (28 percent) are much higher than at the national level (101 and 16 percent, respectively). The primary completion rate is more than 50 percent in a few districts (Mzimba, Rumphi, and Nkhatabay) while it is below 30 percent in six others (Dedza, Mangochi, Ntcheu, Machinga, Phalombe, and Thyolo). The secondary completion rate (proxied by the access rate to Form 4) is very low. The Northern region is at the same level as the Southern (12 percent), and Central is lower (9 percent). At the district level, Blantyre has the maximum value (30 percent), while 19 districts have less than 10 percent; three of them (Chitipa, Balaka, and Machinga) being under 5 percent (see maps 2a and 2b).

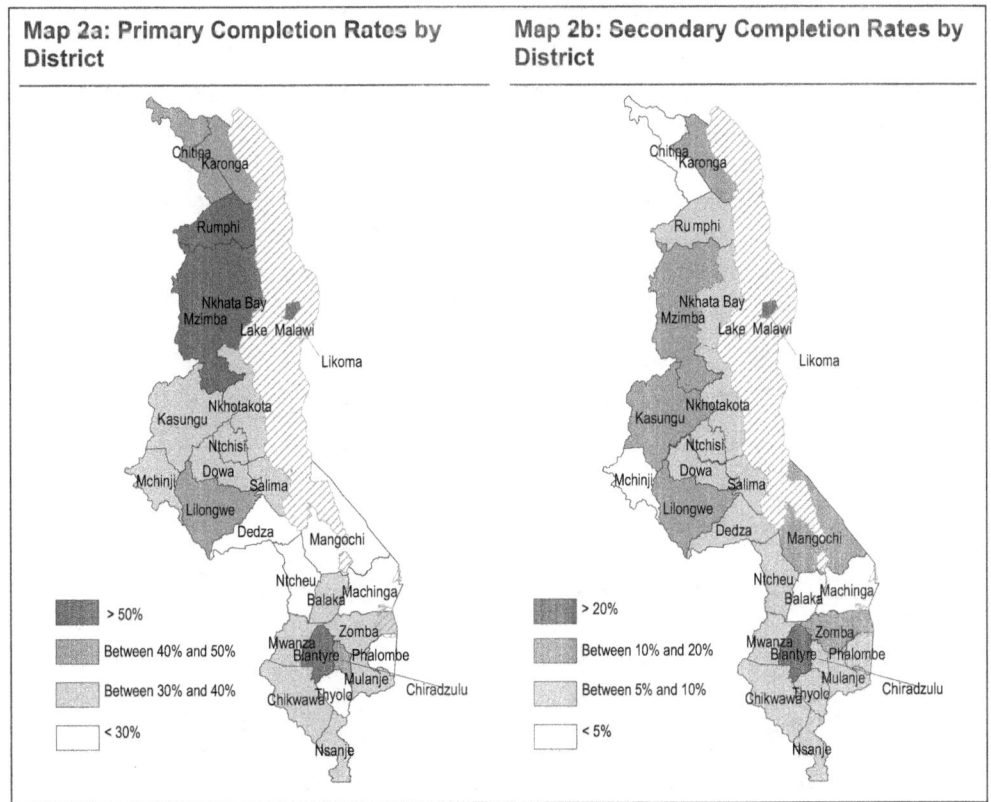

Map 2a: Primary Completion Rates by District

Map 2b: Secondary Completion Rates by District

Source: Calculations from MICS 2006.
Note: Related figures are reported in Appendix 5.3.

The budget priority for education is still in the bottom half when compared to other African countries.

Total education public recurrent expenditures amounted to MK22.3 billion in the 2007/08 fiscal year.[2] This represents 19.4 percent of total government recurrent expenditures and it is an increase compared to 2001/02 (16 percent). However, the budget share for education can certainly be increased further. In the 10 low-income African countries that most highly prioritize their education system, the share for education equals an average of 28.8 percent. Unfortunately, preliminary data for 2008/09 indicates a decreasing trend that would prevent Malawi from catching up with both the SADC average (20.8 percent) and the EFA-FTI reference benchmark (20 percent).

Development partners provided US$53.8 million to support the education sector in 2007/08. On average between 2004 and 2006, education in Malawi benefited from aid equivalent to 1.9 percent of GDP (compared to 1.1 percent of GDP on average in SSA). Direct support to education accounted for 1.2 percent of GDP and 0.7 percent of GDP was the estimated education share from the global budget support.[3]

Within the education budget, there is a lack of priority for the primary level and it keeps decreasing.

Primary education gets the largest share of the recurrent education expenditures with 44 percent of the total. The share for higher education (27 percent) is higher than that for secondary education (22 percent). The amounts allocated to preschool, literacy, TEVET, and teacher training does not exceed 7 percent when added together. In particular, very low priority is placed on ECD and literacy when allocating public resources (less than 1 percent for each). The 2000–2008 trends show a decrease in the priority of primary education to the benefit of higher education (see figure 7).

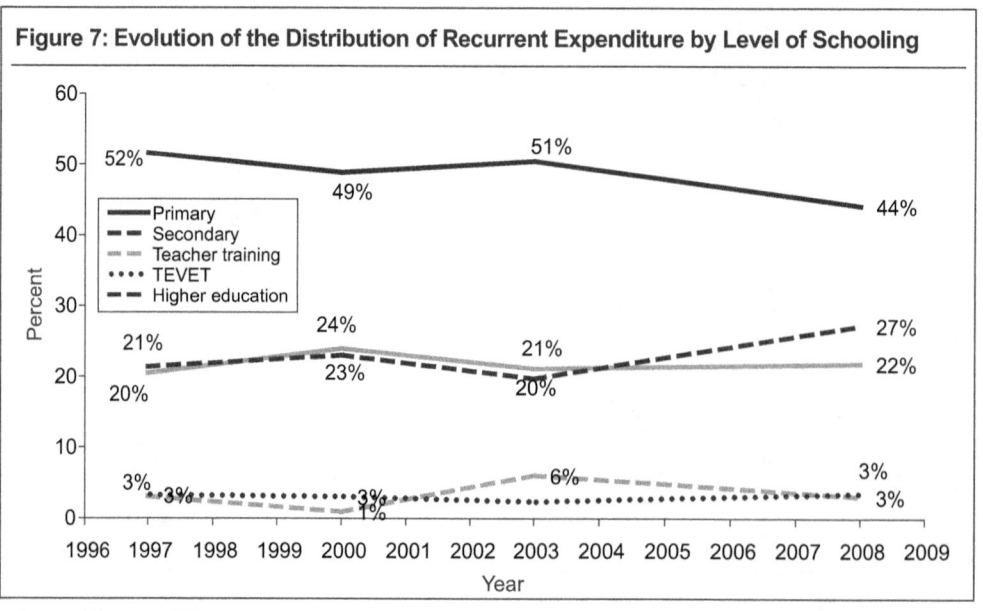

Figure 7: Evolution of the Distribution of Recurrent Expenditure by Level of Schooling

Source: Ministry of Finance.

In 2008, Malawi's allocation to primary education, when calibrated to a 6-year cycle (as is common in most African countries), was one of the lowest (32.5 percent) in a continent where the average is 44.4 percent. Compared to other countries, Malawi prioritizes higher and secondary education above primary education. Malawi's recurrent allocations to secondary (40.4 percent when adjusted to a 7-year cycle duration for a comparative perspective) and higher education (27 percent) are above average—the SSA average is 34.4 percent for secondary and 21 percent for higher education.

As a result of making comparatively poor budget allocations to primary education, the public recurrent unit cost for primary is very low and the unit costs for secondary and higher education are very high.

In 2007/08, the recurrent expenditure per student in primary education was around MK3,000, which is equivalent to only 8.3 percent of GDP per capita (compared to an average of 12 percent in the SADC region and 11 percent in SSA).

At the secondary level, the public unit cost is estimated to be MK30,300 (83 percent GDP per capita versus 30 percent for the SSA average) and it is four times higher (in terms of GDP per capita) than it was in 2000. However, this average unit cost for secondary hides the disparities that exist between the CSSs and the CDSSs, to the detriment of the latter. TEVET, when parallel students are included, costs the government MK136,500 per year per student (equivalent to 45 times the primary unit cost).

Larger secondary schools would help to reduce the unit cost. While potential economies of scale are modest in primary schools, they are quite important at the secondary level. This has to do with student-teacher ratio levels and school size: While the average number of students in secondary schools is relatively low at 212, it reaches an average of 642 pupils in primary schools. Scale economies are possible at the secondary level, by favoring larger schools of more than 150 students and increasing the STR level.

The public recurrent unit cost of university education is the highest in the world in terms of GDP per capita (2,147 percent of GDP per capita, or seven times more than the SSA average). One year of study for one university student costs the same amount to the government as 259 school years of primary pupils.

Consequently, schooling conditions are comparatively very bad in primary education and better than average in secondary and higher education.

Unit cost in primary education is low mainly because of the very high student-teacher ratio—80:1 vs. 48:1 for the SSA average (see table 1) and the low rate of other recurrent transactions (ORT) allocated to primary education. Inversely, the secondary education unit cost is high because the student-teacher ratio is low (20:1 compared to 28:1 for the SSA average) while the ORT rate is relatively higher than in primary education.

The extremely high unit cost in higher education is mainly due to a very low student-lecturer ratio and comparatively high teacher salaries. The student-lecturer ratio is 11:1, which is below the Organization for Economic Co-operation and Development (OECD) average of 16:1 and half the SSA average. The teacher salaries account for 64 units of GDP per capita, compared to an average of 19 units of GDP per capita in the five economically similar countries with available data. The very small number of university students in Malawi does not help reduce unit cost by economies of scale.

Table 1: STR in Public Schools by Level of Education (2007)

	Primary education	Secondary education	Higher education
Malawi	80	20	11
SADC average	41	22	17
SSA average	45	28	20

Sources: Chapter 4, Chapter 7, and World Bank data.

Higher education is, along with primary education, the level to which households contribute the least. It is also the level with the lowest number of students from the poorest families.

Primary education is mostly funded by public resources (92 percent of the total cost), which is in line with the implementation of Free Primary Education and the MDG. The cost-sharing structure between public and private funding is the same in higher education as in primary education with 92 percent of the financing coming from public resources (see figure 8).

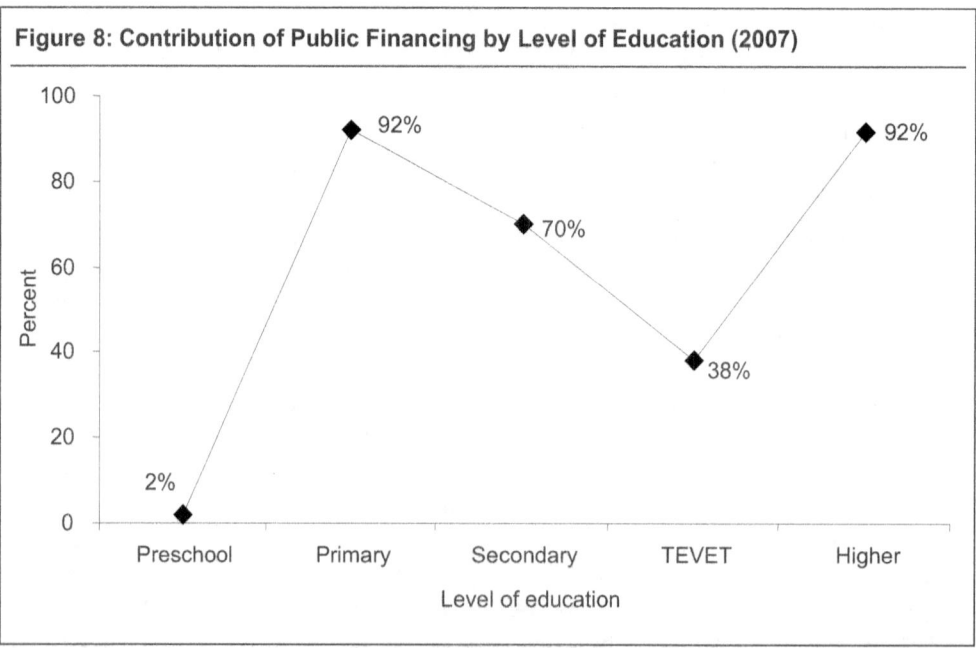

Sources: Tables 3.4 and 3.7 in Chapter 3.

This raises an equity issue in the way public resources are allocated to education because 90 percent of the students in higher education are from the wealthiest 20 percent of households (see Chapter 5) and these students get a very high level of private return (salaries) when working after graduation (see Chapter 8). It would be relevant to discuss ways to create a more equitable cost-sharing of the higher education service delivery.

The TEVET system is very fragmented and formal general TEVET programs enroll very few learners.

The TEVET system in Malawi is highly diverse, fragmented, and uncoordinated, with multiple private and public provider systems. Reasonable, robust data are available only for the formal general TEVET provided in public technical colleges (TCs) under the auspices of the Ministry of Science, Education and Technology (MOEST). Access to the regular TEVET programs is very low; these are regulated and administered by the TEVET Authority (TEVETA) and provided mainly as four-year apprenticeship training.

With an annual intake of around 700, only 3.9 percent of MSCE graduates have access. Including so-called "parallel" students, who are directly recruited by the TEVET institutions, annual enrollment in the public TEVET system under MOEST was 4,807 in 2007. This represents 35 TEVET students per 100,000 inhabitants, by far the lowest access rate in the group of SADC countries for which data are available. TEVET enrollment in Malawi represents only two percent of the secondary education enrollment, three times less than the African average of six percent; see the educational pyramids in figure 1.

The training supply in the formal system is limited to mainly traditional technical trades. Additional skill development opportunities are provided by other ministries, NGOs, and church-run schools in the private training market and, not least, by companies. Of particular importance for the informal sector, and for low income groups, is the system of traditional apprenticeship (mastercraftsman training).

As far as the formal TEVET system is concerned, access is biased against girls, school leavers from poorer districts, and those with lower educational attainment.

The female participation rates in the country's main TEVET examination systems—trade testing and Malawi (Advanced) Craft—are 10 percent and 23 percent, respectively. This indicates the low access girls have to TEVET. However, at least in the public TCs, the female share is slowly increasing to 30 percent, which is the result of an antidiscrimination policy employed by TEVETA.

School leavers from the Northern region are overrepresented in regular TEVET. Access to regular TEVET programs has recently been limited to MSCE holders, effectively excluding the majority of the country's youth from the publicly subsidized general TEVET system.

TEVET is funded by multiple sources, including household contributions and investment from the business sector.

TEVET in Malawi, including the public TEVET system, is funded by multiple sources. Although again, a comprehensive picture of all contributions is not readily available, it can be assumed that public expenditure is one, but most likely not *the* most important funding source. Figure 9 depicts the major flow of funds and summarizes the different sources by the type of training they are funding.

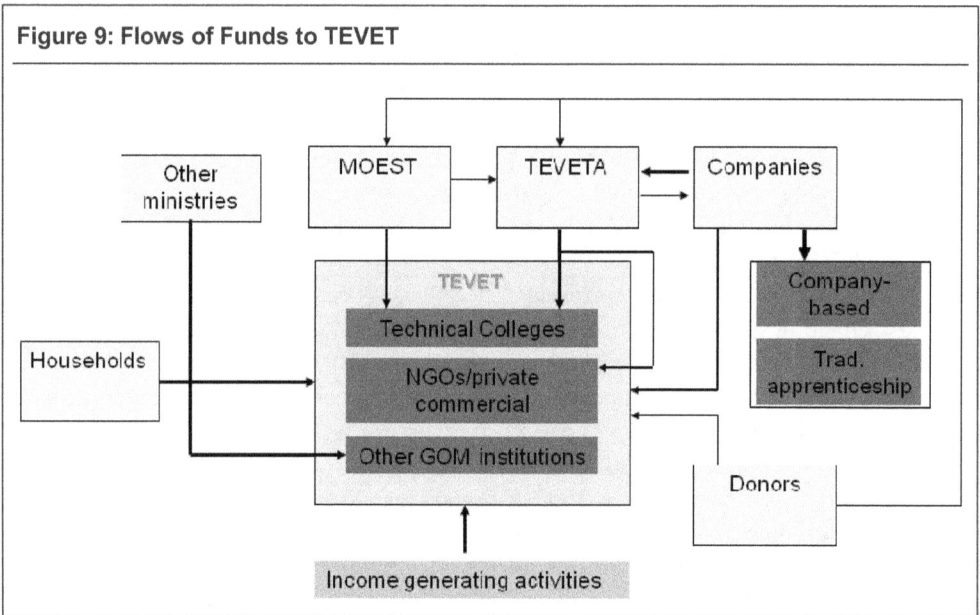

Figure 9: Flows of Funds to TEVET

Overall public expenditure for TEVET, including examination systems, amounted to MK760 million in 2007/08, of which MK250 million were allocated through MOEST in support of general TEVET. This represents a recurrent public expenditure per student of 141 percent of GDP per capita, a relatively high value compared to other African countries. The average public allocation per TC student is MK35,100, but this varies a lot across the different TCs and is not related to enrollment or other performance indicators.

The TEVET Fund administered by TEVETA has been successful in increasingly mobilizing private sector resources for TEVET. Levy income from private companies in 2007 contributed 84 percent of the entire TEVET Fund.

Direct TEVETA subsidies for training programs, including training for companies and the informal sector, has grown to 36 percent of the annual fund expenditure. Administration cost as a share of TEVETA's budget has fallen substantially in recent years; however, it still represents a relatively high 38 percent.

Household contribution is highly differentiated according to the status of the students.

Private households contribute significantly to the cost of TEVET in Malawi, mainly through fees (tuition and examination), boarding fees, the cost of living of trainees (if boarding is not an option), as well as opportunity costs if a trainee would have otherwise been employed and earned an income.

In the formal TEVET programs provided in the TCs, private contributions are highly differentiated according to the status of the students—whether they are regular (TEVETA-sponsored) apprentices or parallel students recruited directly by the colleges. The former are subsidized by TEVETA and the public budget (through MOEST base-funding of the institutions). Over the entire four-year training period, parallel students pay 5 to 6.6 times the amount of regular students. It should be recalled that admission to TEVETA-sponsored apprenticeships is limited to around 700 students annually, which represent only 38 percent of all students in enrolled TCs.

The quality of the TEVET provision is negatively affected by multiple factors, including lack of clarity about the roles of main stakeholders.

The main factors affecting quality are inadequate equipment and facilities; a shortage of training materials due to financial constraints; and, in particular, deficient practical competences of TEVET teachers coupled with an absence of a systematic TEVET teachers training system. A low quality of training leads to low pass rates in national examinations of between 50 and 67 percent.

The most important impediment to sustainable quality improvement is the coexistence of the three local qualification systems—trade testing, Malawi (Advanced) Craft, and CBET (implemented by TEVETA), which prevents the development of a unified employer-involved quality assurance system, and forces teachers to train on the basis of parallel curricula.

The lack of clarity about the division of roles and responsibilities among the main actors—TEVETA, MOEST, and the Ministry of Labour (MOL)—and major stakeholders such as the private sector, has been a major reason why implementation of the agreed TEVET sector reform has been slow. It also affects the status of the public TCs, whose current scope of responsibility is not appropriate to the diverse funding and program structures they have to manage.

Higher education enrollment is one of the smallest in the world but it is growing at a quick pace.

Malawi, with 51 students per 100,000 inhabitants, has the lowest university enrollment when compared to other African countries whose average is 337 (see figure 10). Nevertheless, university enrollments almost doubled from 2003–2008, in partly because of the enrollment of non-residential students and the establishment of private universities, which contributed 12.4 percent of the total enrollment in 2008.

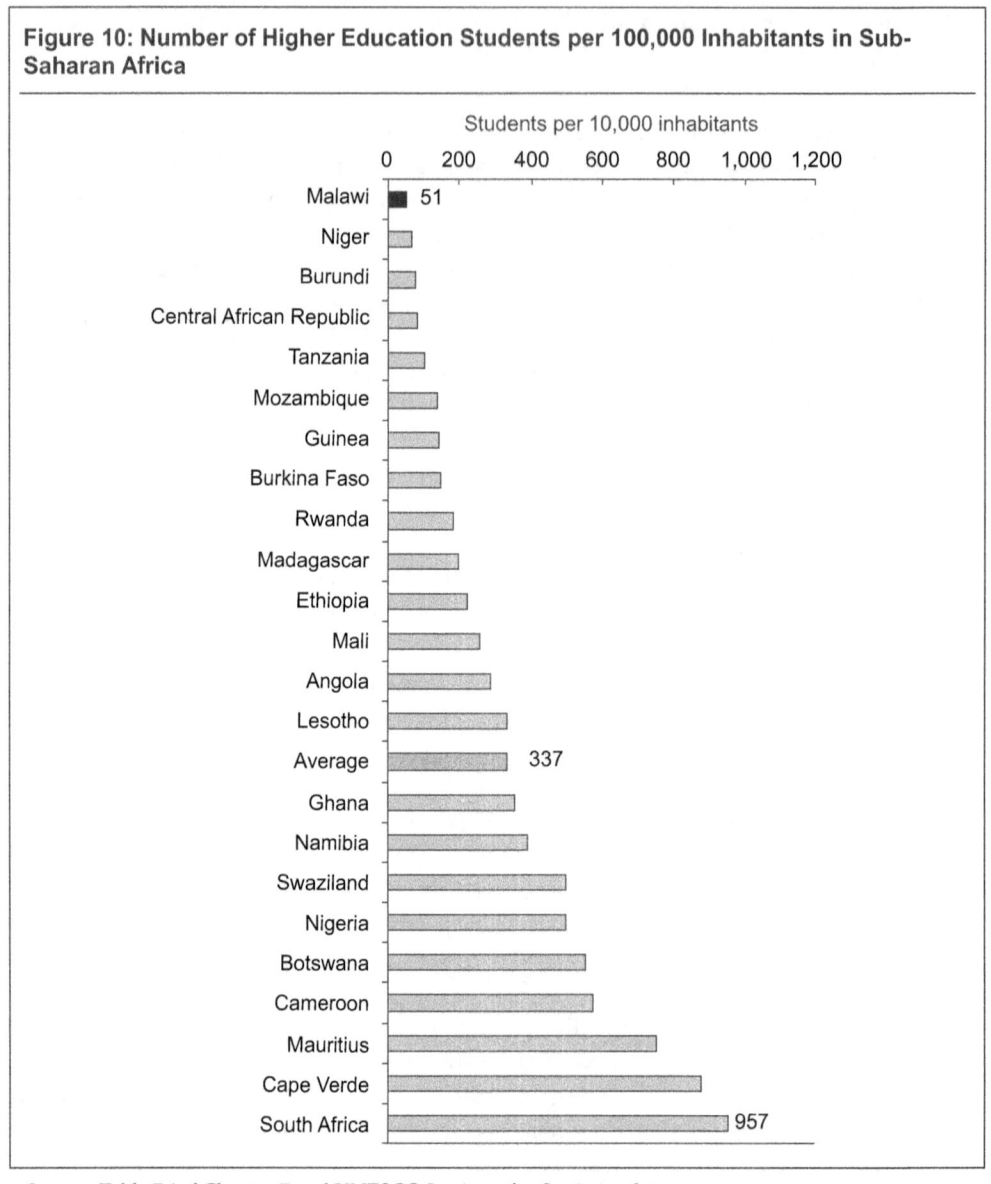

Figure 10: Number of Higher Education Students per 100,000 Inhabitants in Sub-Saharan Africa

Sources: Table 7.1of Chapter 7 and UNESCO Institute for Statistics data.

Postgraduate enrollments account for less than 10 percent of total enrollment. Private colleges are not offering postgraduate programs yet. The highest enrollments are in the social sciences and sciences. Areas critical to the implementation of the Malawi Growth and Development Strategy are not adequately covered.

There are still huge gender disparities in the access to higher education.

Female enrollment has remained around 30 percent in public institutions and around 45 percent in private institutions. There are a number of reasons why female enrollments are low in higher education. The first has to do with the dropout rates for females throughout the education cycle in primary and secondary levels (see Chapter 2). This reduces the percentage of females who enter for the MSCE examination to below that of males. In addition, the percentage pass for female-to-female[4] is lower than that for male-to-male. As a result, there is a double screening in the numbers of females that eventually qualify for university entry.

Bed space is also an important constraint in enrolling more females as the institutions have more bed space allocated for males than females. In 2008, the total bed space for all the University of Malawi (UNIMA) colleges was 2,761 for males and 1,383 for females.

The introduction of non-residential programs has increased enrollments for both genders but the enrollment statistics show that the percentage of non-residential female students is consistently lower than that for males and also lower than that for residential female students. This may be attributed to problems of financing, having to live alone in rented accommodations, and commuting to college daily.

Higher education is highly subsidized by public resources and is delivered at an extremely high unit cost when compared to other countries.

The percentage of the education public budget allocated to higher education (27 percent) is higher than the average (21 percent) for SSA countries. The subventions account for over 80 percent of the income of public universities, while student fees and other income contribute less than 10 percent each. Student fees are the main source of income for private universities.

The higher education recurrent unit cost of 21.5 times the GDP per capita is the highest among all the SSA countries, whose average is 3.14 times the GDP per capita (see figure 11). It varies widely from one institution to another.

The way public universities use expenditures is not efficient.

Emoluments and benefits consume more than 50 percent of expenditures in public institutions. Very little is spent on teaching materials and equipment, books and periodicals, and research. Emolument comprises less than 40 percent of the total expenditure in private universities, which also spend more on teaching materials than public institutions.

The average student/lecturer ratio at 11:1 is very low, compared to other countries in SSA of similar GDP whose average is 20.4:1. Lecturer salaries expressed at 65.8 times GDP per capita are also higher compared to other SSA countries with similar GDP whose average is 24.3 times GDP per capita (see table 2). This also contributes to a very high unit cost.

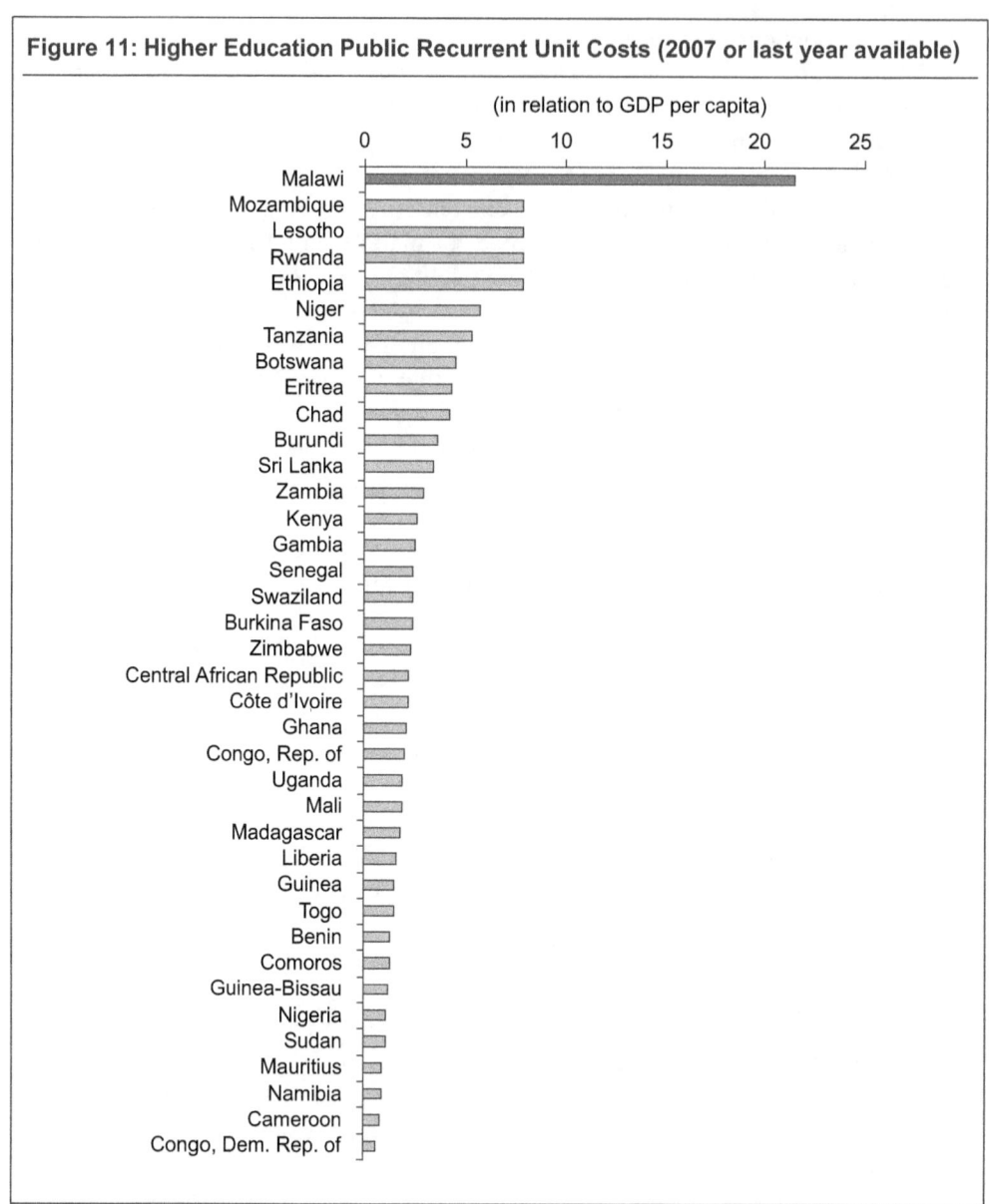

Sources: Revised 07/08 budget (Ministry of Finance and our own calculations) and World Bank data.

Table 2: Higher Education Teachers' Average Salary, as Units of GDP Per Capita for Countries with GDP per Capita Lower than US$500 (2007 or last year available)

	Higher Education Average Lecturers' Salaries as Units of GDP Per Capita
Congo, Dem. Rep. of	4.1
Guinea	10.3
Mali	12.1
Madagascar	12.8
Malawi	**65.8**
Ethiopia	27.1
Burundi	37.2
Average 7 countries	**24.2**

Sources: Malawian higher education institutions and World Bank data.

The student loan scheme is inefficient and not targeted to the neediest.

Initially, students were provided with a straight grant. Around 1994, the policy shifted to a loan system in which students were expected to repay their loans after graduation. However, recovery mechanisms were not established and the loans effectively became grants. In 2005, there was another policy shift that led to the National University Student Loan Trust, which would lend and recover the loans from the graduates. The Malawi model is the mortgage-type loan with a fixed rate of payment over a period of time. Other countries use the income contingency system, which is based on a percentage of the salary of the borrowers when they are in employment until the loan is repaid.

As currently constituted, recovery relies on the cooperation of the employers as there is no legal framework in place that obligates employers to report on graduates in their employment and deduct repayments and remit these to the Trust. A serious backlog of loans is building up.

Countries like Zimbabwe and South Africa have such legal frameworks, which have proved effective in improving loan repayments. A legal framework that spells out the responsibilities and obligations of all parties and the sanctions applicable is therefore a critical prerequisite to the success of this scheme.

The Loan Trust meant for the needy does not apply a "Means Test," and as result almost all applicants access it. The system is not equitable because those who access loans are mainly among the wealthiest in the country.

Education has an important impact on social development. Primary education is the level of education that has the greatest impact.

Education in general (particularly for girls) has a strong impact on literacy, on behavior in terms of reproduction and maternal and child health, and on knowledge of HIV/AIDS. For example, with all else being equal, women who have never attended school benefit from medical help at childbirth in only 43 percent of all cases, while those who have completed primary education do so in 67 percent of all cases, and those who have completed secondary education do so in 79 percent of all cases.

The primary cycle contributes to almost half (48 percent) of the total impact of education on social development. It reinforces the rationale that efforts need to be implemented for all Malawian children to achieve at least the primary cycle. Finally, it is important to indicate that all costs being equal, the efficiency of the primary cycle in enhancing human development is 18 and 243 times higher than that of the secondary cycle and of tertiary education, respectively.

External efficiency in relation to employability is high, in particular for TEVET and higher education graduates.

Tracer studies show a generally high satisfaction with higher education outcomes among graduates and employers. The average duration between graduation and job entrance is relatively low. Job insertion rates of academically trained people are among the highest in Africa (see figure 12).

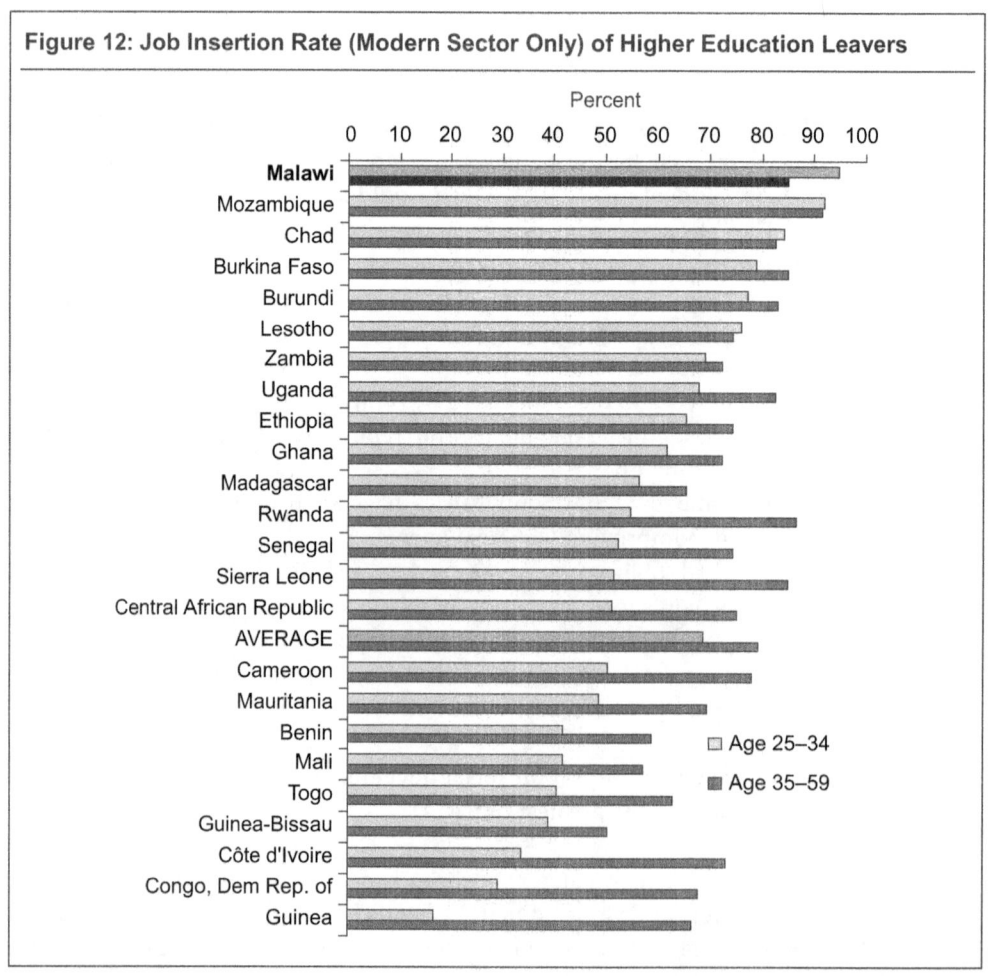

Figure 12: Job Insertion Rate (Modern Sector Only) of Higher Education Leavers

Source: World Bank database.

TEVET completers also show a high acceptance in the labor market when recording the job insertion rates of all African countries for which comparative data are available. The time it takes to find a job after graduation is lower for former apprentices than for completers of other programs.

For higher education in particular, the wage premium is extremely high compared to other countries. The private rate of return for higher education graduates is particularly high.

The relevance of education to the labor market is indicated by increasing average annual incomes gains for each additional level of education. The additional average income of people working in 2004 compared to the lower educational level was 14 percent for lower primary, 60 percent for upper primary, 92 percent for lower secondary, 155 percent for upper secondary, and 177 percent for TEVET. The income gain for higher education as compared to TEVET is 440 percent (see table 3).

Table 3: Annual Average Income and Expected Annual Income According to Level of Education

	Annual average income for people working (MK)	Expected annual income taking into account unemployment risk (MK)	Income increase compared to previous level of education (%)
No school	7,095	7,015	
Lower primary	8,112	8,005	14.1
Upper primary	12,983	12,715	58.8
Lower secondary	24,969	24,038	89.1
Upper secondary	63,566	57,121	137.6
Technical college	176,582	169,221	196.3
Higher education	952,027	929,233	449.1

Source: IHS 2004.

The average income of TEVET completers remains relatively low compared to higher education graduates. The income prospects for graduates who ventured into self-employment appear to be higher than for the wage-employed. Income variations among occupational areas are more pronounced in TEVET than in higher education.

No significant correlation exists between the duration of TEVET training and income, which raises concern about the appropriateness of the long duration of the public regular TEVET program.

The average incomes of higher education graduates are highest for lawyers, engineers, and pure scientists, indicating labor market shortages.

Comparable data of mean income by educational level as a percentage of GDP per capita are available for five African countries in addition to Malawi. Up to the lower secondary level, the mean income as a percentage of GDP stays low in comparison with the other countries. It approaches the higher end of the group with three times the GDP per capita in upper secondary, and rises above all other countries for people with a technical training background, who can expect to earn 8.25 times the country's per capital income. The ratio of expected incomes to GDP per capita rises to an enormous

44.5 for people with a higher education background, way beyond what was found in other countries (see figure 13).

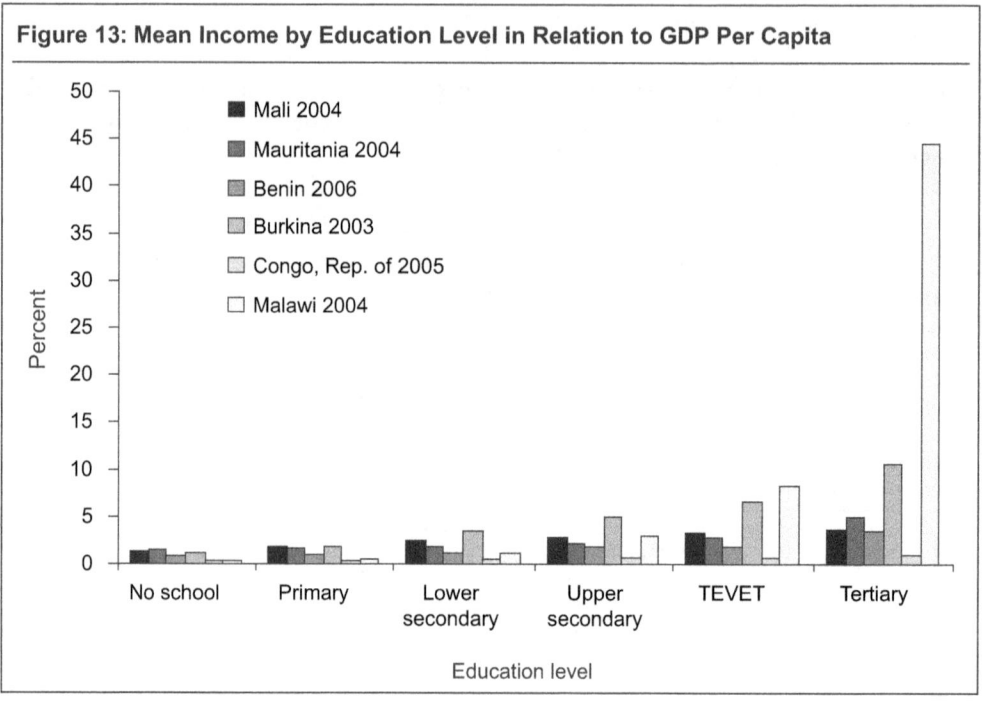

Figure 13: Mean Income by Education Level in Relation to GDP Per Capita

Source: World Bank database.

The rates of return (ROR) to education in Malawi are very high, in particular at higher education levels, which reflect Malawi's low overall access to education. Private ROR of 54 percent for TEVET and 171 percent for higher education also indicate severe shortages of skilled and highly educated human resources, demonstrating the country's urgent need to ensure greater access rates to stimulate growth.

A comparison between social and private ROR at different education levels again reflects the high public subsidization for higher education, although the benefits are mainly private.

Some indications exist regarding skill demands but there is a need for additional surveys.

Recently, only the TEVETA Labour Market Survey (JIMAT, 2008) tried to identify skill demands in more concrete terms. According to JIMAT, which focused on occupational areas for which formal TEVET programs exist, unmet training needs are significant in advanced mechanics, welding and fabrication, general fitting, electronics, administration, building, calibration equipment, computer knowledge, machine maintenance, plant operators, steel fixing, advanced molding, and fire drill evacuation.

A lack of practical skills was recorded as a key weakness by the majority of companies. JIMAT also found that on average across occupational fields, the demand for further skilled labor as a percentage of all employed in the specific occupational field was 47.6 percent, with occupations such as water plant operators, instrumentation mechanics, mechatronics, plumbers, refrigeration technicians, painters and decorators, roofers, drivers, electricians, plant operators and welders showing an above-average shortage (unmet demand) of the skilled workforce (see figure 14).

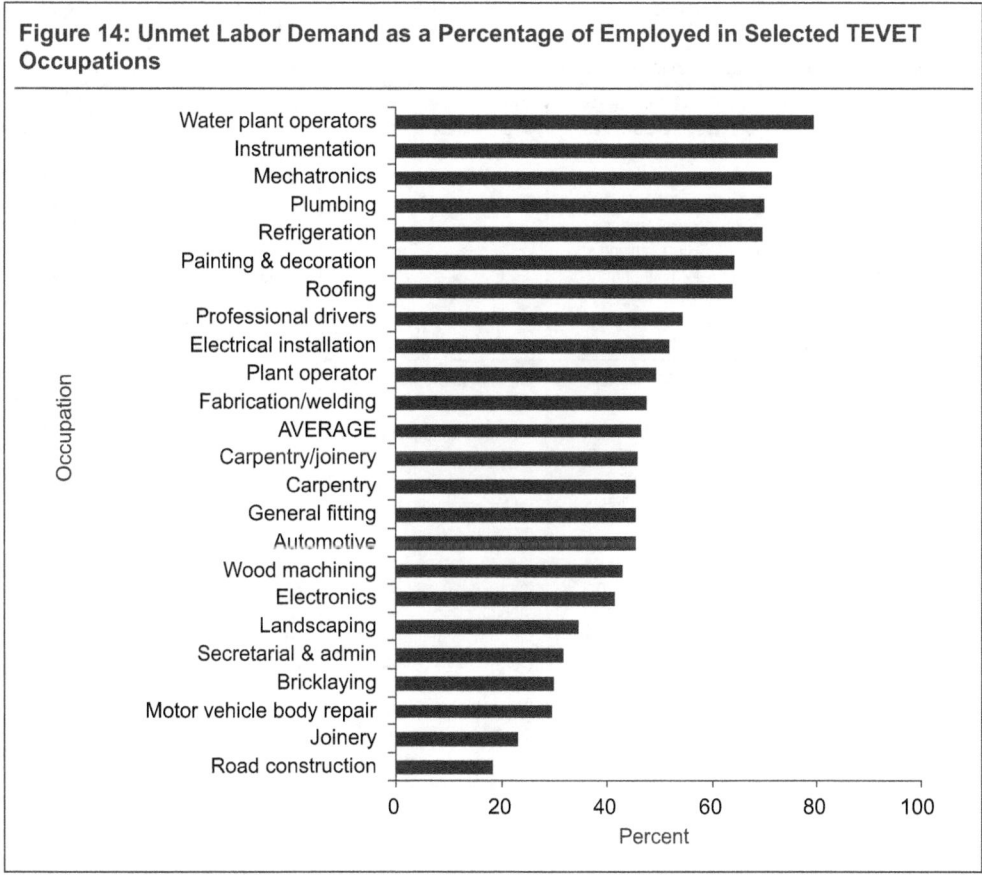

Figure 14: Unmet Labor Demand as a Percentage of Employed in Selected TEVET Occupations

Source: JIMAT 2008.

In view of the occupational limitations, methodological problems as well as resources needed for studies such as the one JIMAT undertook, considerable doubts remain as to whether comprehensive quantitative attempts to assess skill shortages and forecast future needs is the right approach to training needs assessment in a country like Malawi, where research capacities and resources are scarce. More qualitative assessment methods, such as sector-specific consultative meetings with employers and experts, complemented by targeted surveys of selected economic sectors, may be more promising.

Policy Recommendations Matrix by Sub-Sector

SECTOR-WIDE

Main challenges: i) Share knowledge transparently to enhance smooth implementation of reforms, ii) Strengthen capacity to better plan policies and monitor performance.

Rationale	Situation in Malawi	Policy Proposals	Financial Cost ($) Political Cost (*)	Expected Results
Enhance knowledge sharing about the education system's strengths and weaknesses.				
Sharing knowledge about the education system is key to maximizing the chances of smooth implementation of necessary reforms at the local level.	The 2008/09 Country Status Report (CSR) has been done with much greater government participation than the first CSR. Some major findings of the CSR are striking and call for reforms that may be politically sensitive.	Implement the dissemination strategy of the CSR in order to reach all stakeholders up to the local level.	$/** Good communication skills will be needed to explain the needs of some reforms (based on the CSR results), which may be unpopular for some groups of people.	Better knowledge of the education system and of the need for reforms to achieve goals.
Strengthen capacity to ensure better data production for planning policies, monitoring, and performance.				
National population data are important in order to adequately monitor progresses in schooling attendance.	Birth registration suffers from large under-declaration. As a result, the school-age population is not adequately known, making the calculation of schooling indicators inaccurate.	Improve demographic data production. Advocate and take action in favor of birth registration generalization (at birth and retroactive procedures).	$$/*	Better estimates of the school-age population and more reliable indicators to inform planning and support relevant monitoring of the sub-sectors.
Planning and the efficient monitoring of a system depends on reliable and recent statistical data.	Some statistical data in Malawi are incomplete or not reliable enough. Access rates to first standards based on Education Management Information System (EMIS) data are over-estimated due to the double count of some new entrants. Data on non-state education and training are weak, in particular for Technical, Entrepreneurial, and Vocational Education and Training (TEVET) and Early Childhood Development (ECD).	Improve the way EMIS monitors dropout/reintegration (some children dropout and come back to school the next year without being counted as repeaters) to adequately assess intake rates. Strengthen the capacity to improve the statistical information system, in particular for TEVET and ECD.	$/* Measures costs that are more technical than political	

Notes:
$ No or low cost, $$: moderate cost, $$$: high cost
* Low political cost, **: moderate political cost, ***: high political cost

PRIMARY EDUCATION

Main challenges: i) increase the budget priority for primary education, ii) reduce repetition and dropouts, iii) improve the quality, and iv) improve teacher and other resources management

Rationale	Situation in Malawi	Policy Proposals	Financial Cost ($) Political Cost (*)	Expected Results
Increase the budget priority for primary education.				
Budget priority for primary education is a necessity if the education system is expected to reach universal primary completion (UPE).	In the last decade, the budget priority for primary education declined. Schooling conditions, such as class size, have deteriorated due to an expansion of enrollments, which was not matched by corresponding increases in teachers for the sub-sector. The student-teacher ratio (STR) is 80:1 in Malawi is around twice the Southern African Development Community (SADC) average (41:1). When calibrated to a six-year duration (for comparative purposes), the share allocated to primary is only 32.5 percent—far from the African average of 44.4 percent. The recurrent expenditure per student in primary education is around MK3,000, which is equivalent to only 8.3 percent of GDP per capita (compared to an average of 12 percent in the SADC region and 11 percent in Africa).	Increase the amount of public resources for primary education by making it a priority to allocate new resources to this sub-sector, in particular for training and recruiting additional teachers.	$$$/** Possible opposition from other sub-sectors for the allocation of new resources.	Improved schooling conditions will make for an improved quality of education.
Enroll the last unreached children who never went to school.				
Universal access to Standard 1 is necessary to reach UPE.	Four percent of children never attend primary education, which affects the achievement of UPE and limits enrollment in post-primary cycles.	Identify the unreached children and assess their specific needs to ensure they go to school.	$$/** Targeting the most vulnerable may be difficult as it raises questions about the criteria to be used and the type of actions to take to have them in school.	There will be universal access to Standard 1.

Rationale	Situation in Malawi	Policy Proposals	Financial Cost ($) Political Cost (*)	Expected Results
Reduce dropouts within the cycle.				
UPE requires that all children access and complete the full primary cycle.	Due to very frequent dropouts within the primary cycle, the primary completion rate is only 35 percent. Poor student retention comes from both the supply and demand side. Incomplete schools are still an issue because 13 percent of pupils attend a school that does not provide a continuous educational supply up to Standard 8, making them more likely to dropout if another school does not exist close to their home. Crowded classrooms, open-air, and temporary classrooms also significantly affect retention rates. Economic difficulties and behavior such as early marriage, pregnancy, or family responsibilities are reported as major reasons for dropping out.	Build new classrooms and hire and train new teachers to complete incomplete schools. Enhance school demand among the poorest population (via cash transfers, school meals, and advocacy for the school). Advocate in favor of postponing pregnancies and early marriages	$$$/** Building classrooms is expensive. Targeting the most vulnerable may be difficult as it raises questions about i) the criteria to be used, ii) the type of actions to take to have them in school (e.g., grants/in kind advantages), and iii) the type of monitoring mechanism to be put in place. Some resistance may arise concerning issues related to early marriages and pregnancies.	The completion rate will be improved.
Reduce repetition rate.				
A rate of repetition that is too high negatively affects educational outcomes and costs.	Repetition rates have increased over the 1999–2006 period to reach 20 percent in primary education—a level that is the highest in the region. Evidence, at national and international level, shows that high repetition rates do not favor a better mastery of school subjects, have adverse effects on STR, and increase dropouts and costs. An estimated MK1.97 billion is used annually to deliver primary education services to repeaters.	Reorganize the primary cycle into sub-cycles (Std1-Std2, Std3-Std4, Std5-Std6), within which repetition would not be allowed. Sensitize/train school participants (e.g., head teachers, teachers, parents, inspectors) on the real impact and cost of repetition.	$/** Possible resistance from some parents and teachers who may believe that repetition has a positive effect on learning outcomes.	Repetition will decrease, the completion rate will improve, and the use of public expenditures will be more efficient.

Rationale	Situation in Malawi	Policy Proposals	Financial Cost ($) Political Cost (*)	Expected Results
Improve quality.				
Teaching time, when effectively respected, has an important positive impact on student learning achievement.	The learning outcomes for primary students have worsened over the years. Malawi's scores on student learning tests are among the worst in the SACMEQ countries. The official schooling time is not always respected in Malawi. It is estimated that 20 percent of teaching time is lost due to teacher absenteeism and 16 percent of schools use overlapping shifts. Moreover, pupil absenteeism, holidays, and other events when the schools are closed also contribute to a decrease in teaching time.	Implement measures to better respect official schooling time, such as increasing the responsibility of the community in school management; supervision; and evaluating results (look at the example of multi-partite school management committees in Niger).	$$/** Difficult to measure because it involves communities and should therefore be organized with a large sensitization campaign. However, impact can be important. Communitarian management school was successfully implemented in Niger and contributed to the increased efficiency of schools and an improved quality of teaching.	Accountability at the school level will increase and this will improve the quality of education.
Efficiently trained teachers are key to ensuring a good quality of learning.	There is still a lack of qualified teachers. Trends show an improvement in the situation as indicated by the decrease in the Student per Qualified Teacher Ratio (SqTR) from 118:1 in 1999 to 91:1 in 2007 but further improvements are needed to reach the 40:1 Education for All-Fast Track Initiative (EFA-FTI) reference benchmark.	Pursue efforts in teacher training development (e.g., pre- and in-services, continuing professional development). Evaluate the different training courses provided to scale up the most cost-effective ones.	$$/*	More qualified teachers will make for an improved quality of education
Female teachers show better results than their male counterparts in learning outcomes.	The proportion of teachers who are female in Malawi is very small (26 percent of all primary teachers) compared to other countries.	Recruit more female teachers, if necessary through a positive affirmative action process.	$/* Measure relatively easy to organize.	A higher proportion of female teachers will increase student learning and school retention.

Rationale	Situation in Malawi	Policy Proposals	Financial Cost ($) Political Cost (*)	Expected Results
Better manage the allocation of teaching staff and other resources in schools.				
The government is responsible for providing equal learning conditions for all children. This means ensuring that the allocation of teaching staff is well-balanced throughout the territory and matches the needs of the schools (contingent on the number of pupils/students).	Large disparities exist among education divisions and schools in Malawi. While some schools have two teachers for 200 pupils, others have six teachers for 100 pupils. The Shire Highlands and South Eastern divisions have the lowest allocated number of government-funded teachers compared to the number of students. The average SqTR is 99:1 in rural schools and 47:1 in urban schools. The STR is one of the highest in the world in primary education (80:1 in Malawi vs. 48:1 for the African average) while the STR in secondary education is much better than the African average (20:1 compared to 28:1). Fifty-five percent of teachers teaching in secondary schools were trained to only teach in primary schools. Books at the primary level are not allocated consistently and they are not always adequately used by teachers and school staff.	Implement— without exception—the school-based, post-recruitment system. In consultation with teachers' unions, design and implement a stable, incentive-based system for rural and remote areas. Favor the reallocation to primary schools of primary school teachers currently based in secondary schools. Improve the consistency of book allocation and use at the school level.	$$/** Some resistance may arise as it may be difficult to force people to move to remote areas, meaning that required incentives could be costly. Transferring teachers from secondary schools to primary schools may also be politically sensitive.	Inequalities in learning conditions among students will be reduced once there is a more consistent allocation of teaching staff and textbooks.
Regular evaluations and transparency in the results of student learning will strengthen the accountability of stakeholders and improve the overall efficiency of schools.	The evaluation of pupils in Malawi is neither systematic (in time) nor uniform (throughout the territory).	Regularly evaluate learning achievements in a standardized manner and organize performance evaluations at the school level.	$$/** Measure is more technical than political; it is included in the 10-year plan and Fast Track implementation. The study on efficient schools goes in the same direction.	The existence of an educational system in which quality is scientifically measured and transparent will give lower-performing schools an incentive to improve.

Notes:
$ No or low cost, $$: moderate cost, $$$: high cost
* Low political cost, **: moderate political cost, ***: high political cost

SECONDARY EDUCATION

Main challenges: i) Improve the equity in learning conditions, ii) improve quality, and iii) increase efficiency.

Rationale	Situation in Malawi	Policy Proposals	Financial Cost ($) Political Cost (*)	Expected Results
Development of a better quality, more equitable and efficient secondary education.				
Providing equal learning conditions for all secondary students is very important in increasing equity.	The allocation of other recurrent transactions (ORT) to secondary schools is very weakly related to the number of students. Community Day Secondary Schools (CDSSs) are systematically less well endowed (in teachers and in ORT per student) than are Conventional Secondary Schools (CSSs).	Ensure more equitable teachers and resource allocation among secondary schools and in particular between CSSs and CDSSs (revise the allocation formula of ORT to include school environment and hardship).	$/** Some resistance may arise because it may be difficult to force teachers to move from CSSs to CDSSs.	Inequalities in learning conditions among students will be reduced.
Economies of scale are possible in secondary education to improve efficiency	The average school size in secondary schools is very low (212 students in secondary vs. 642 students in primary education). Economies of scale savings are possible by favoring bigger secondary schools (of more than 150 students).	Build new classrooms and deploy new teachers with priority given to the smallest secondary schools (in areas with a population density large enough to attract a sufficient amount of students).	$$$/* In the short-term, building new classrooms will be very costly, but mid-term it saves resources because a more efficient service delivery comes from economies of scale.	Secondary education service delivery will be more efficient.
Textbooks are vital to ensuring a good quality education. Labs in secondary school are very important to enhance effective learning in science.	All other things being equal, textbooks and labs are associated with better exam pass rates. The average number of textbooks per student is 3.7, but some schools have no textbooks at all. Only 23 percent of secondary schools have a lab.	Increase the number of textbooks and labs in secondary schools.	$$/* Textbooks are not expensive. Labs are more costly.	The quality of learning will be increased.
The knowledge economy requires better human capital skills, particularly in scientific and technological fields.	There is a dramatic lack of secondary teachers in the sciences.	Pursue the program called Strengthening Mathematics and Science in Secondary Education (SMASSE).	$$/* Measure already implemented. This was tested from 2004–2007 in the South Eastern education division. This is now being rolled out to the remaining divisions.	A higher quality general secondary education will emerge, more in line with the needs of the modern economy

Notes:
$ No or low cost, $$: moderate cost, $$$: high cost
* Low political cost, **: moderate political cost, ***: high political cost

Technical, Entrepreneurial, and Vocational Education and Training (TEVET)

Main challenges: i) Improve flexibility, coordination and clarify roles, ii) increase access, in particular for training focused on the informal job sector, iii) increase efficiency by revising the duration of the longest programs.

Rationale	Situation in Malawi	Policy Proposals	Financial Cost ($) Political Cost (*)	Expected Results
Development of a more coordinated and flexible TEVET.				
A stringent and transparent TEVET qualification system provides the base for the testing and quality assurance of the TEVET programs, and quality benchmarks for TEVET providers. In order to ensure labor market responsiveness, qualification systems are usually built as outcome-based systems, founded on occupational standards that are set by experts from the world of work.	In Malawi, three parallel qualification systems currently co-exist—trade testing, Malawi (Advanced) Craft, and the TEVET Authority /Competency-Based Education and Training (TEVETA/CBET)—which all maintain their own assessment and certification structures. This is unnecessarily costly for students and government and hampers quality improvements at the school level. Two of the qualification systems can be considered outcome-based, however only the TEVETA/CBET approach is based on the updated demands of today's market. The CBET approach developed and administered by TEVETA was initiated in the late 1990s to overcome the parallel qualification structure of Malawi (Advanced) Craft and trade testing. Instead, a third parallel qualification system has now been introduced in practice.	TEVETA, the Ministry of Education, Science, and Technology, and the Ministry of Labour agree on an approach to integrate all formal TEVET and the trade testing system under the TEVETA/ CBET system to become the one and only national benchmark of recognized TEVET provision in Malawi.	$/ * Integration might affect vested interests in different ministries to maintain existing structures. Substantial financial gains can be expected from integration, as no parallel structures would need to be maintained. However, a universal orientation towards CBET qualifications will increase quality assurance costs by TEVETA for standard setting, certification, and accreditation.	There will be one recognized outcome-based TEVET qualification system based on occupational standards developed by experts from the world of work, applicable to all TEVET provisions, and in line with SADC standards. An indirect result will be an improved quality of training and a more well-trained Malawian workforce.

Rationale	Situation in Malawi	Policy Proposals	Financial Cost ($) Political Cost (*)	Expected Results
Due to its provider and program diversity and multi-stakeholder nature, TEVET systems require an integrative and conducive governance structure. Such a structure would ensure effective stakeholder involvement, the articulation of different provider systems, and broad-based coverage of accepted quality assurance mechanisms. In many countries, this is reflected by the emergence of more or less independent, stakeholder-governed TEVET regulatory bodies in charge of regulation, facilitation, and quality assurance, while training provision and delivery remains with a variety of different actors in accordance with the needs of specific target groups.	The TEVET Policy of 1998 and the TEVET Act of 1999 assigned the regulatory and policy-making authority for the broad TEVET system to the newly created TEVET Authority (TEVETA). Stakeholder involvement is inter alia facilitated through the TEVET Board. However, TEVETA's role does not appear to be unanimously accepted by all major ministerial stakeholders, as is shown in the parallel initiatives of standard and curriculum development and examination regulations. This lack of clarity about roles and responsibilities in the national TEVET system reinforces existing obstacles to the development of an integrated and labor-market driven TEVET system. It particularly affects training quality in a negative way as scarce resources available at the TEVET institution level are used to accommodate the different requirements, procedures, and standards of various authorities with regulatory functions.	Facilitate a clarification of roles and responsibilities in the national TEVET system, confirm or adjust existing policies and legal documents as needed, and ensure subsequent implementation.	$ ** Financial savings expected through avoidance of parallel development activities, such as standard and curriculum development. Considerable opposition can be expected against an institutional reform that may reduce the scope of responsibility of existing institutions.	There will be a functioning TEVET authority with broad responsibilities for the regulation, standard development, and quality assurance of the entire public and private TEVET provision.

Executive Summary

Rationale	Situation in Malawi	Policy Proposals	Financial Cost ($) Political Cost (*)	Expected Results
Against the very diverse educational and social backgrounds of TEVET target groups in Malawi, public TEVET resources should be used to support the development of flexible TEVET offers. These should accommodate a broad range of target groups and ensure access to disadvantaged groups in line with labor market demands. The new outcome-based TEVET paradigm (CBET approach) facilitates the flexibility of training approaches by integrating different learning environments under one outcome-based qualification system.	Regular (formal) TEVET programs, which are supported (very low tuition and boarding fees, privileged access to resources and quality assurance) through public budget allocations to Technical Colleges and subsidies from TEVETA, are de facto limited to rigid formal long-term training programs. These programs are mainly delivered as apprenticeship training and accessible only to senior secondary school leavers upon merit. Low educational achievers, including socially disadvantaged groups, have to find training opportunities in the open training market, which includes the parallel programs in technical colleges. With few exceptions, high fees are charged in this market. Only regular programs are properly facilitated and supervised. As a consequence, public resources and modern (CBET-oriented) TEVET management is serving a very limited group of relatively high-educational achievers—without deliberate social targeting—and leaving behind the large group of youth who left school before Form 4 and lack the financial means to continue (TEVET) education on their own.	Revise public (including TEVETA) subsidization principles to include a larger array of TEVET delivery modes (based on accreditation) that address a broader range of TEVET target groups. Introduce outcome-based subsidization principles. Systematically apply the CBET approach to parallel students and participants of other TEVET programs.	$$/ * Significant opposition among TEVET providers and other stakeholders against a broad based application of CBET is not expected. It will be necessary to make substantial efforts to upgrade the competencies of technical teachers in order to adapt the new approach on a broad base. The regular apprenticeship system will lose its privileged status if public support is broadened for programs and target groups. The potential loss of privileges needs to be analyzed in the context of other educational opportunities. It may act to further reduce the attractiveness of TEVET among the better-educated.	The public TEVET subsidization system will be based on training outcomes, open to a large range of accredited TEVET programs, and geared to defined social, economic and/or labor market targets. Target groups with different training and learning backgrounds will have a broad access to CBET qualifications.

Rationale	Situation in Malawi	Policy Proposals	Financial Cost ($) Political Cost (*)	Expected Results
The informal sector is an important employment destination mainly for TEVET graduates in Malawi. Labor-market responsive TEVET offers and delivery modes have to take the sector's special requirements into account. An integration of trade testing with the CBET qualification system would provide an important avenue for skills improvement and modernization in the informal sector.	Recent research (tracer studies) have demonstrated that the informal sector is not only an important target labor market for TEVET graduates in terms of numbers absorbed, but also a rather attractive destination as incomes tend to be relatively high. The formal TEVET system, however, is still largely oriented on formal sector needs. For example, informal entrepreneurs are not targeted as cooperation partners in the formal apprenticeship training. The trade testing system is accessible and presents the most important avenue to formal skills certification for informal sector operators and traditional apprentices. However, the system's standards are outdated.	Systematically incorporate the informal sector into TEVET as a target employment destination (with special modules oriented towards work in the informal sector); as apprenticeship providers (including in the formal apprenticeship system); and as a partner in TEVET planning (including labor market assessments). Revive previous activities to strengthen traditional apprenticeship training in order to increase quality and enrollment. Integrate trade testing with the CBET qualification system.	$/ * There is a substantial history of TEVETA working with and for informal sector operators on which to build. Current informal sector activities by TEVETA need to be extended and approaches mainstreamed in the TEVET system. Some resistance expected among TEVET stakeholders to systematically integrating informal sector operators into formal training.	TEVET programs will be more responsive to the needs and conditions of the informal sector labor market. The quality and relevance of the TEVET provided in the informal sector will be increased.
A flexible TEVET system of delivery modes and program duration ensures better targeting to specific competence and qualification requirements. in the labor market. A flexibilization, which may lead to shortened average training durations, increased cost effectiveness of the TEVET system.	The TEVET tracer study showed that no correlations exist between the duration of training and expected incomes. This means that graduates of four-year apprenticeship programs are not significantly better remunerated than graduates from shorter TEVET programs, suggesting that the market is not honoring the long-training duration that is common in the formal TEVET system.	Reconsider the predominance of four-year programs in the formal TEVET system in accordance with labor market needs for specific occupational areas. Provide incentives for flexible TEVET provision.	$/** The four-year apprenticeship system has a long tradition in Malawi as the heart of formal TEVET. The system is getting more flexible with the introduction of the modular CBET programs.	Will provide flexible TEVET programs that are in line with labor market needs. Will engender the increased cost-effectiveness of TEVET and a larger enrollment (through lower unit cost via shortened duration).

Rationale	Situation in Malawi	Policy Proposals	Financial Cost ($) Political Cost (*)	Expected Results
Improve external efficiency with an updated labor market information system.				
In view of high public and private cost, TEVET (and higher education) offers need to be continuously fine-tuned to respond to changing labor market needs. To facilitate this, up-dated labor market information (LMI) is necessary.	TEVET and higher education (HE) planning in Malawi suffer from serious data and information gaps about labor market needs and trends. TEVETA has recently initiated a labor market database; however, the analytical approach appears limited to occupational fields that target current TEVET programs. Tools to rapidly and cost-effectively identify new and emerging occupational fields and their training and qualifications are not yet in place.	Initiate development of a network between TEVETA, higher education institutions, investment planners, the Ministry of Labour, the National Statistics Office, and other potential partners with a concerted strategy to systematically and continuously assess labor market trends and related skill requirements.	$$/* Any LMI approach in Malawi should focus on cost-effective methods to collect and analyze labor market data for TEVET (and HE) that relies on the appropriate analysis of available data and institutionalized discussions with industry representatives (industry panels), rather than focusing on comprehensive surveys and large database creation. Participation of TEVET institutions in acts (e.g., tracer studies) to improve the relationship between TEVET and the labor market at a grassroots level.	A cost-effective approach to observe labor market trends in operation will be implemented. There will be up-to-date labor market information to support TEVET (and HE) planning at the national level, as well as the program decisions of TEVET institutions and universities.

Notes:
$ No or low cost, $$: moderate cost, $$$: high cost
* Low political cost, **: moderate political cost, ***: high political cost

Higher Education

Main challenges: i) Increase access and equity, ii) increase cost-sharing with households and the private sector, iii) revise the structure of public universities' expenditure, and iv) increase accountability

Rationale	Situation in Malawi	Policy Proposals	Financial Cost ($) Political Cost (*)	Expected Results
Enrollments in higher education: Increase space and opportunities for all eligible Malawians.				
Higher education is an important component of the entire education system because of its role in creating and advancing new knowledge through teaching and research. It also produces people who have the high level skills that are critical to Malawi's socioeconomic development and the implementation of the Malawi Growth and Development Strategy. Through research, higher education is able to provide solutions to the country's many technological, social, and economic challenges.	Access to higher education is the lowest in the world, with only 64 higher education students per 100,000 inhabitants. Lack of investment in increased infrastructure and habilitation of the old infrastructure has constrained enrollments and the introduction of new programs in public institutions. Private institutions are still relatively new and small, although their contribution to enrollments and new programs is increasing. But they are set to play an increasingly important role in this sub sector.	Invest in infrastructure and in rehabilitation in order to increase enrolments and expand relevant programs and introduce new programs needed in the country. Establishing an open university (distance learning) as a more economic option to increasing access. Reviewing the current policy of offering loans to students in public institutions (which are already heavily subsidized) to include non-residential students and Malawi students in accredited private universities. Encouraging the private sector to invest in student accommodation near university centers as a way of increasing the amount of non-residential students. Introducing flexibility in the curriculum by adopting the credit-hour system. Exploring the use of the SADC Protocol on Education and Training in order to increase access, especially in specialist areas for which Malawi does not currently have capacity.	$$$/* University education was provided by only public institutions until quite recently. UNIMA in particular, is now particularly constrained by increasing enrollments because of space and an old, dilapidated infrastructure. Addressing this requires a lot of financing at a time when the allocation share to higher education is already among the highest in the region. There is a need to develop a five-year phased rehabilitation and construction program based on the availability of resources. The establishment of private universities will definitely have an impact on enrollments, but this will be gradual because their source of financing is mainly through student fees.	Greater access to higher education will result in increased enrollment per 100,000 inhabitants. More programs will be implemented that address Malawi's human resource needs and research will be conducted on Malawi's socioeconomic and technological development.

Executive Summary

Rationale	Situation in Malawi	Policy Proposals	Financial Cost ($) Political Cost (*)	Expected Results
Reduce disparities at both the gender and the socioeconomic level and take people with disabilities into account.				
Issues of equity are important for social, political, and economic stability. The Millennium Development Goals place great emphasis on equity issues, particularly in relation to gender. Malawi is signatory to many international and regional conventions that require equity issues to be addressed so that all citizens have opportunities to develop themselves and actively participate in national development.	Gender disparities are huge in spite of affirmative action at UNIMA. The situation is particularly bad in science, engineering, and ICT. Over 90 percent of the students enrolled in higher education come from the wealthiest quintile. Regular students are heavily subsidized while non-residential students are not aided. Few institutions have facilities for students with physical handicaps.	Provide bridging courses to upgrade females to the required entry levels, especially for the targeted fields of science and engineering. Provide grants to girls in these targeted areas and explore the possibility of private-sector involvement in such a scheme. Increase bed-space for female students and prioritize accommodations for females in non-residential programs. Increase the enrollment of low-income students by addressing the shortcomings of the Student Loan Trust to ensure that it benefits the needy from low-income families, and by implementing a means-test on loan applications. Provide facilities for physically disabled students in the institutions.	$$/ * Providing grants and expanding access to the Student Loan Trust will require moderate additional funding, but with good management and efficient recovery methods, the long-term cost will be small compared to the benefits to be derived. Introducing equity measures can only have positive political advantages.	An equitable higher education system will be in place, allowing all Malawians to have an equal opportunity to develop to their fullest potential. This would benefit the socioeconomic development of the country and aid in the alleviation of poverty.

Rationale	Situation in Malawi	Policy Proposals	Financial Cost ($) Political Cost (*)	Expected Results
Increase cost-sharing, improve student loan recovery, and restructure expenditure priorities.				
While higher education is critical to development, it is expensive and should be adequately funded if it is to achieve its stated objectives. Diverse and sustainable sources of financing therefore need to be explored. Public resources at this level should be used to fund the core functions of teaching.	Financing is highly dependent on subventions from government. This is clearly unsustainable, especially if enrollments are expected to increase and new programs are introduced. Student loans are almost never recovered although graduates can easily find well-paid jobs soon after graduation (there are very high individual rates of return). The expenditure in universities is concentrated on emoluments, administration, and student provisions at the expense of the core areas of teaching and learning materials.	Give universities latitude to charge higher fees and agree to regular reviews of fees. Improve the mechanism of recovery of student loans once graduates get a job. Diversify sources of income through more coordinated and accountable schemes of sale of products and services. Set minimum enrollment figures for courses to be offered in order to reduce unit costs. Have universities restructure their expenditure priorities so that they are aligned to their core functions of teaching. Set a limit of approximately 3 percent of total recurrent expenditure on management functions.	$$/** Very little cost will be required by the universities in generating additional income. What they need is a mechanism that properly coordinates and manages the sale of products and services. Implementing cost-sharing and student loan recovery has a political cost as the public may complain about the increase in fees. These can be offset by having a properly targeted loan and bursary scheme.	Will create adequately funded and sustainable institutions where resources are efficiently used. More resources will be available to finance core functions once those able to pay are made to do so.

Rationale	Situation in Malawi	Policy Proposals	Financial Cost ($) Political Cost (*)	Expected Results
Make management of public institutions more accountable and more focused on reducing inefficiencies.				
Good management is critical to the efficiency of any organization. The autonomy of higher education institutions is also critical to their success. Autonomy, however, also comes with accountability—especially in institutions that are heavily dependent on public resources.

Good management and good decision making should be backed by current and reliable data and information about the institution. | Public universities are quite autonomous and the decentralization of management functions from the University Office of UNIMA to the UNIMA constituent colleges is underway. However, guidelines for implementing the decentralization were not developed and this has created problems in a number of areas.

Staff management and the allocation of staff have led to inefficiencies that resulted in very low student-lecturer ratios and extremely high unit costs.

Institutions have not established robust management information systems, and as a result data and information on many aspects of the universities are not readily available.

Institutions also lack performance indicators against which they can measure their performance and make themselves accountable for the resources entrusted to them. | Review university structure and governing bodies to determine whether there are financial and administrative advantages that can accrue from converting the UNIMA colleges into fully-fledged independent universities, in view of the decentralization that is already taking place.

Expedite the passage of the Higher Education Act and the establishment of the National Council for Higher Education (NCHE). This is critical for maintaining standards and quality in higher education institutions.

University councils should create guidelines for the roles and responsibilities of all stakeholders in the higher education sector and for the ongoing decentralization process at UNIMA colleges.

Set up a monitoring and evaluation mechanism to assess the achievement of outsourcing objectives.

Ensure that universities have accountability mechanisms based on good Management Information Systems and key outcome indicators to periodically assess their performance and support policy-decision making. | $/*
The policy options proposed are not costly as they require some reorganization of resources that are already available.

Converting UNIMA colleges into free-standing universities may have some political cost due to resistance but this can be overcome if there are benefits to be accrued, given that the decentralization process is already underway.

Some resources may be needed for setting up Management Information Systems and training personnel in their use, but cost is low. | Will provide for a well-managed, effective, and efficient higher education system, accountable for its mandate to the public and consumers of the system.

Information on operations and functions of the universities will be easily available and used for policy-decision making. |

Notes:
$ No or low cost, $$: moderate cost, $$$: high cost
* Low political cost, **: moderate political cost, ***: high political cost

Notes

[1] The assumption used is that repetition rate will stay constant between 2008 and 2018; 20 percent of the students would be repeaters.

[2] This figure includes all education expenditures from the Ministry of Education (MOE) and all other ministries outside of MOE.

[3] For cross-country comparisons, the usual assumption is to estimate that 20 percent of global budget support goes to the education sector (that is, the average share for education in recurrent budgets in SSA countries).

[4] This refers to the percentage of females passing against the number of females who entered the examination.

CHAPTER 1

Demographics, Social Development, and Macroeconomic Conditions

Summary of the Chapter

The Malawian education system has to develop within a heavier demographic context than those of its neighboring countries. The country's population, estimated at 13 million people in 2008, is increasing at the rate of 2.4 percent per year. The 5-to-16-year-old age group represents 37 percent of the total population, which is the highest proportion of this age group in the entire Southern African Development Community (SADC) region. The population growth rate is estimated to decrease slowly, but the primary school age group (6-to-13-year-olds) will increase by 20 percent between now and 2018. If universal primary completion is reached before 2018, primary school places for 4.8 million children[1] will be needed in 2018. This represents a 45 percent increase from 2008.

The large majority of the population (82 percent) still lives in rural areas where school supply and demand are weaker. Sixty-three percent of Malawians live on less than US$2 a day. Malawi has the highest rate of malnutrition in the SADC region and an overwhelming 44 percent of preschoolers have stunted growth. There are an estimated 122 children per 1,000 who die before the age of five, which is similar to the SADC average. The adult (15 years and older) literacy rate is estimated to be 69 percent in Malawi, which is lower than the SADC average (75 percent). Illiteracy of parents impedes the achievement of education for all because these parents are less likely to enroll their children in school than literate parents.

The HIV/AIDS pandemic dramatically affects the development of the education sector because of the deaths of both teachers and parents. The pandemic also increases teachers' absenteeism and the number of orphans, who are less likely to go to school than children with families. The adult (15–49 years old) prevalence rate is 12 percent, whereas children orphaned by AIDS represent 7 percent of the children under 17 years of age (in addition to the 5 percent of children orphaned by other reasons). HIV/AIDS occurrences are highest in the Southern region and are concentrated in urban areas.

Malawi's economy has been growing steadily since 2005, mainly due to recent sound economic policies and favorable weather conditions for agriculture. The continual increase in economic growth has allowed Malawi to reach a GDP per capita of around US$300 million in 2008. In comparison to the entire SADC region, Malawi still has the third lowest GDP per capita and one of the five lowest in all of Africa. However, with the government's increased emphasis on value addition on domestic products, coupled with the discovery and mining of uranium, there is the prospect of improved GDP levels.

Compared to countries with a comparable level of economic development, Malawi's performance is very satisfactory for mobilization of public revenue. The rate of domestic revenue as a proportion of GDP is higher in Malawi than the average observed in low-income, non-oil producing African countries (19 compared to 17 percent). Thus, while reducing the budget deficit at around 1 percent of GDP, the government has increased the volume of its expenditures up to more than 33 percent of GDP. This creates a good opportunity to increase spending for the education sector.

Development partners provided US$53.8 million in support of the education sector in 2007/08. On average, between 2004 and 2006, education in Malawi benefited from aid equivalent to 1.9 percent of GDP (compared to 1.1 percent of the average GDP in Sub-Saharan Africa). Direct support to education accounted for 1.2 percent of GDP, and 0.7 percent of GDP was the estimated education share from global budget support.[2]

* * *

An education system develops within a national context, which is largely determined by the socio-demographic characteristics of the population, the strength and size of the economy (the macroeconomic conditions), and by decisions about expenditure on education versus other sectors. Chapter 1 is a discussion of the demographic makeup, social context, and macroeconomic environment affecting the education sector in Malawi. This chapter is divided in three parts: i) the demographic trends (with a particular focus on the school-age population), ii) the social development context (including the prevalence of HIV/AIDS), and iii) the macroeconomic conditions.

Demographics

General Information

Located in southeast Africa, Malawi is a land-locked country of 118,484 square kilometers—20 percent of which is water. Eighty-two percent of the population lives in rural areas where the main means of subsistence is smallholder, rain-fed agriculture.

From 1987 to 2008, the population of Malawi grew at an average annual rate of 2.4 percent. The 2008 Population and Housing Census conducted by the Malawi National Statistics Office estimated the country's population to be slightly greater than 13 million—a 39 percent increase from 1987's estimate of 8 million inhabitants. In 2008, 49 percent of the population was male and 51 percent was female.

Population Density across Regions and Districts

The Southern region of Malawi is the most densely populated, with 5.9 million people (45 percent of the total population). The Central region has 5.5 million people (42 percent). The Northern region is the least urbanized and has the lowest share of the population with only 1.7 million people (13 percent).

The country averages a population density of 139 people per square kilometer. Density by district ranges from less than 53 up to more than 3,000 (see map 1A.1 in Appendix 1.1 for more details).

School-Age Population

To assess the potential demand for education, it's important to look at population trends and projections by school-age groups. Figure 1.1 shows Malawi's population of 3–5-year-olds, 6–13-year-olds, and 14–17-year-olds from 1998 to 2018 (projected). These three age groups correspond with the official Ministry of Education ages for attending early childhood development programs (ECD), primary school, and secondary school, respectively.

Thanks to the ongoing demographic transition[3], the average annual growth rates for the three school-age groups are expected to be lower between 2008 and 2018 than those observed between 1998 and 2008. As figure 1.1 shows, the ECD school-age population grew at an average annual rate of 2.6 percent between 1998 and 2008 and is projected to increase by only 1.6 percent a year for the next ten years. The same patterns are projected for the two other school-age groups (3.7 percent and 1.9 percent for the primary school-age group and 3.1 percent and 2.9 percent for the secondary school-age group). From 1998 to 2018, the primary school age group had (and is projected to have) the highest share of the population relative to the other two age groups. The share of the population in the ECD age group will be overtaken by the secondary education category after 2008.

If a universal primary completion of 100 percent is reached, school seats will be needed for 4.8 million children in 2018,[4] which implies a 45 percent increase from the 3.3 million primary school pupils in 2008.

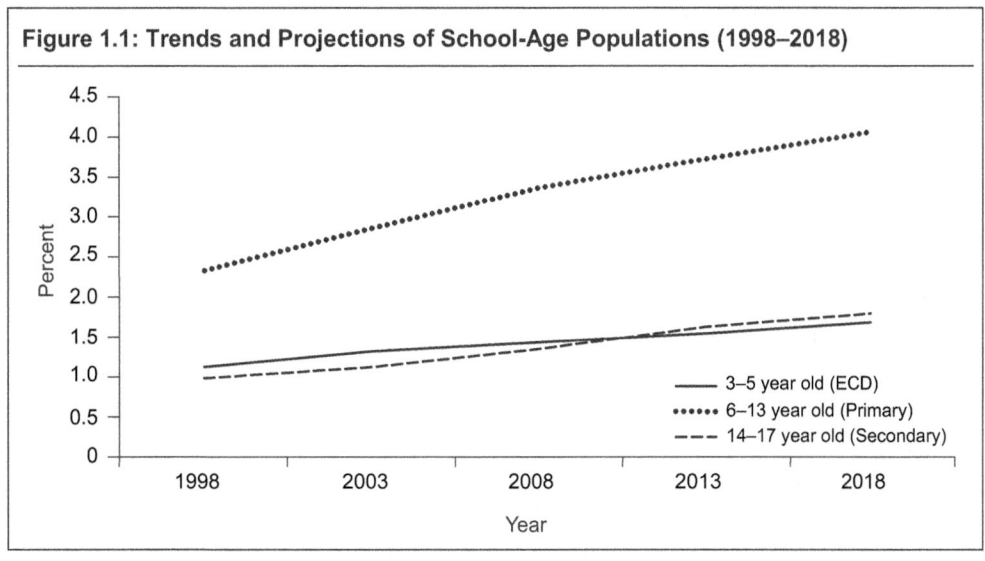

Figure 1.1: Trends and Projections of School-Age Populations (1998–2018)

Source: UN Population Statistics.

To assess the demographic burden in Malawi compared to the other South African Development Communities (SADC) countries, it is useful to compare the share of 5–16-year-olds to the total population. This age group comprises the bulk of the children expected to attend primary and secondary school in most countries. In 2008, Malawi's proportion of children ages 5–16 was 37 percent. This is the highest in the SADC region and much higher than in the country with the next largest share—Zambia with 33 percent (see table 1A.1 in Appendix 1.1). This implies that the demographic burden for the education sector in Malawi is heavier than that of its neighboring countries.

Social Development[5]

Poverty and Inequality

According to the last United Nations Development Programme (UNDP) development report (2007/08), 63 percent of the Malawian population is living below the US$2 a day income poverty line and 21 percent below the US$1 a day poverty line.[6] Nevertheless, those percentages are lower than the SADC average (41 percent and 69 percent, respectively).

The Gini index[7] (39 in Malawi) indicates significant inequalities in access to resources, services, and opportunities among Malawians. There is a large discrepancy between the average per capita income of the richest and poorest sections of the population. The richest 10 percent of Malawi's population have an average per capita income that is 11 times higher than the average per capita income of the poorest 10 percent. Nevertheless, when compared to other SADC countries, Malawi appears as one of the least unequal countries. The SADC average of the Gini index stands at 52.

Malnutrition and the Child Mortality Rate

Malnutrition in Malawi is extensive and a major social development challenge. The prevalence of malnutrition[8] is estimated to be 49 percent. Dietary diversity and the average amount of calories consumed daily are low across the country (for instance, rural people eat mainly maize). Nationwide in 2008, an overwhelming 44 percent of preschoolers were stunted (with 18 percent being severely stunted). These figures have remained more or less constant over the past 15 years.

Malawi has the highest malnutrition in the SADC region (the SADC average is 33 percent). Malawi's mortality rate for children below the age of five is 122 children per every 1,000, which is similar to the SADC average of 131.

HIV/AIDS

The HIV/AIDS pandemic has affected all levels of social development in Malawi, including mortality, life expectancy, and infant mortality. In the education sector, HIV/AIDS is killing both teachers and parents. It also contributes to teachers' absenteeism, since the affected teachers are often sick. The pandemic has significantly increased the number of orphans in the country and these children are less likely to go to school than children with families (World Bank, 2008).

Malawi's HIV/AIDS prevalence rate is 11.9 percent—this is the sixth lowest rate in the region, out of the 14 countries. Nevertheless, the prevalence rate in Malawi is much higher than the African average of 6.7 percent.

HIV/AIDS occurrences are higher in urban areas than in rural one and higher in the more populous south of the country compared to other regions. The incidence of HIV/AIDS is reportedly higher among women (13 percent) than men (10 percent). Overall, 97 percent of women and almost all men report having heard of HIV/AIDS. However, the number of adults who report knowing all the main ways of preventing HIV transmission is low (52 percent).

Other Social Development Indicators

Adult Literacy Rates

When parents are more literate, they are more likely to enroll their children in school. The adult literacy rate is clearly a context factor for school demand and it is noteworthy to compare Malawi to other countries in that regard. The adult (meaning 15 years and older) literacy rate in Malawi is estimated to be 69 percent,[9] which is better than the African average (62.9 percent) but lower than the SADC countries average (75.3 percent).

Urbanization Rate

The percentage of people living in an urban setting is also an important context indicator because the demand for education is higher in urban areas than in rural ones and it's easier to deliver education services in urban areas (probably because it's easier to allocate teachers in urban areas). Malawi however, has one of the lowest urbanization rates with only 17.7 percent of the population living in cities. This proportion is much lower than both the African average (37.9 percent) and the SADC countries average (35.9 percent).

Composite Index of Social Context

The World Bank recently computed an aggregate social context index that takes into account demographic dependency, malnutrition rate, the child mortality rate, the HIV/AIDS prevalence rate, the adult literacy rate, and the urbanization rate. On that scale, Malawi with an index of 39, is the SADC country with the lowest value— meaning that it is the SADC country with the most difficult social context. Among all Sub-Saharan African (SSA) countries, Malawi is the country with the fourth most difficult social context. Only Niger, Burundi, and Ethiopia have a lower composite social context index.

Macroeconomic Conditions

Economic Growth and Policy

Since 2005, Malawi's economy has been growing rapidly due to sound economic government policies and favorable weather conditions for agriculture. This follows a prolonged period of weak policy implementation, which resulted in the rapid build-up of domestic debt, accelerating inflation, dwindling external reserves, and low economic growth rates. Due to these fiscal policy slippages, the International Monetary Fund (IMF) suspended its balance of payments to support the Malawi government in April 2004 under the Poverty Reduction and Growth Facility (PRGF).

After the third multiparty general elections in May 2004, the new government began implementing the IMF Staff Monitored Programme (SMP), which was aimed at dealing with impediments to sound fiscal and economic management. The government successfully implemented the SMP, leading to the approval of a PRGF arrangement by the IMF in August 2005. After further progress in economic management, the international community approved a significant debt relief package for Malawi under the Heavily Indebted Poor Countries (HIPC) program and the Multilateral Debt Relief Initiative (MDRI). Consequently, the external debt stock was reduced significantly from US$3 billion to US$0.5 billion in 2006. This has lead to the availability of significant debt service savings for poverty reducing expenditures in education, healthcare, and other sectors.

This strengthening of the country's fiscal position has led to macroeconomic stability, lowered domestic debt, and lowered interest rates. The exchange rate has stabilized at MK140 per U.S. dollar over the past two years. A stable exchange rate and sound agricultural policies have helped reduce inflation from 13.3 percent in the 2005/06 financial year. Inflation stayed at single digit levels in 2008 despite the recent surge in international food and petroleum prices. Economic growth has been strong, averaging 7.3 percent for 2005–08, compared to 4.0 percent in 2002–04 (see table 1.1). Continued favorable conditions and policies in 2008 will allow Malawi's output growth to remain above 7 percent in real terms.

Table 1.1: Evolution in Real GDP Growth, Inflation, and Exchange Rate (MK/US$)

Variable	2003/04	2004/05	2005/06	2006/07	2007/08
Real GDP growth rates	5	2.6	5.2	8.1	8.7
Inflation	12.3	10.5	13.3	8.8	7
Exchange rate (MK/US$, average)	103.1	113.6	127.2	138	140.3

Source: *Ministry of Finance.*

The recent increase in economic growth allowed Malawi to reach a GDP per capita slightly over MK42,000 in 2008, a value similar to what was observed at the end of the 1990s before weather conditions (lack of rain that led to famine in 2002) and macroeconomic instability reduced GDP per capita (see figure 1.2).

Government Revenues and Expenditures

Government revenues, including grants, have increased significantly from 19.4 percent of the GDP in the 2003/04 financial year to 32.3 percent in 2007/08, largely due to improved domestic tax administration and increases in donor support in the form of both grants and loans. As indicated in table 1.2, domestic revenues increased from 16.4 percent of the GDP to 19.2 percent during the 2004–2008 period, while grants increased from 8.8 percent of the GDP to 13.2 percent.

Figure 1.2: Evolution in Real GDP Per Capita (1987–2008)

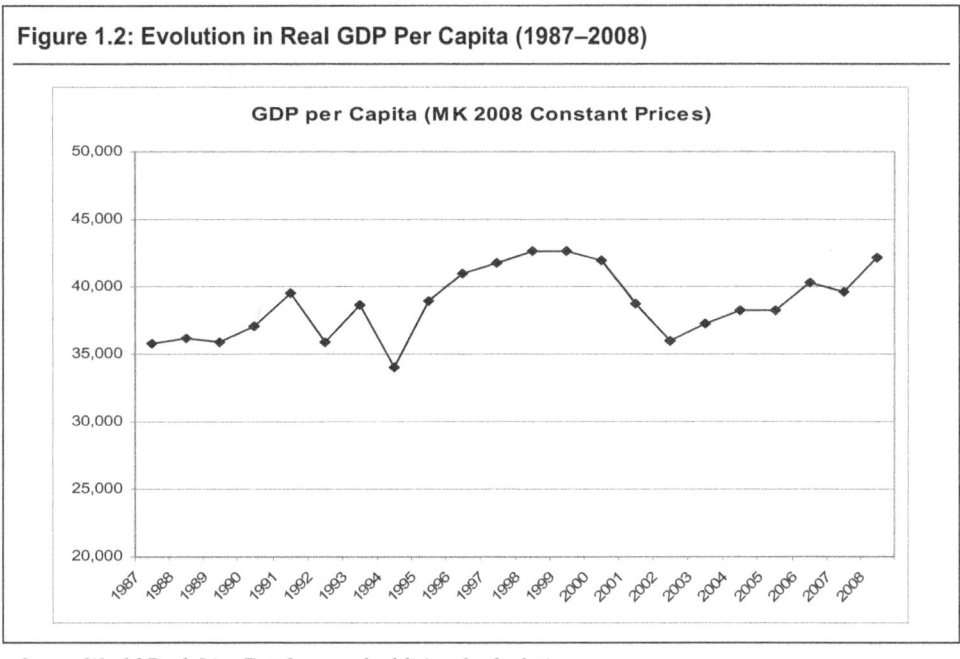

Source: World Bank Live Database and additional calculations.

On the other hand, expenditures have increased only marginally during the same period because of strengthened control over the wage bill and utility payments. (These were the main sources of over-expenditure in the period leading up to 2003/04. As a proportion to GDP, expenditures increased from 30.9 percent in 2003/04 to 33.4 percent in 2007/08. Most of this expenditure is on recurrent activities. However, the proportion of development expenditure to GDP has risen significantly during the 2004–2008 period, from 8 percent to 12 percent, reflecting the government's policy of investing in and improving infrastructural development.

Consequently, the fiscal deficit has been reduced from 8.5 percent of GDP in 2002/03 to 1.1 percent in 2007/08.[10]

Table 1.2: Evolution in Total Government Revenue and Expenditure and Deficit

Variable	2003/04	2004/05	2005/06	2006/07	2007/08
Total govt. rev. (including grants) as % of GDP	25.2	27.2	30.5	31.8	32.3
- Revenue (excluding grants) as % of GDP	16.4	18.2	17.5	18.1	19.2
- Grants as % of GDP	8.8	9	12.9	13.6	13.2
Total govt. expenditures as % of GDP	30.9	31.2	31.2	31.7	33.4
- Recurrent expenditure as % of GDP	22.8	23	24.4	20	21.4
- Development expenditure as % of GDP	8	8	6.8	11.6	12
Deficit including grants as % of GDP	−5.6	−3.9	−0.8	0.1	−1.1
Deficit excluding grants as % of GDP	−14.5	−13	−13.6	−13.5	−14.2

Source: Ministry of Finance.

Comparisons to Other African Countries

GDP Per Capita and Domestic Resources as a Percentage of GDP

In comparison to the SADC region and SSA, and in spite of the recent good macroeconomics performance, Malawi's GDP per capita and domestic resources (excluding grants) as a percentage of GDP remain relatively low. With the exception of the Democratic Republic of Congo, Malawi has the lowest GDP per capita in the SADC region at US$263 million (see table 1.3). This is far below the SADC average of US$2.413 million and the SSA average of US$1.7 million. This is partly because Malawi has comparatively fewer precious minerals available and low levels of manufactured exports. However, with the government's increased emphasis on value addition on domestic products coupled with the discovery and mining of uranium, the prospect of having improved GDP levels is brighter.

The Malawian value of 19.2 percent of GDP for domestic resources is also lower than both the SADC average (29 percent) and the SSA average (23.5 percent). Nevertheless, when compared with similar GDP per capita countries, this indicator is relatively high in Malawi.

Table 1.3: GDP Per Capita and Domestic Resources as a Percentage of GDP for SADC Countries (ca. 2006)

SADC country	GDP per capita (US$)	Domestic resources (excluding grants) as % GDP
Angola	2,728	46.4
Botswana	5,704	41.4
Congo, Dem. Rep. of	141	18.0
Lesotho	749	50.8
Madagascar	287	11.2
Malawi	**263**	**19.2**
Mauritius	5,071	19.6
Mozambique	326	15.6
Namibia	3,208	28.1
Swaziland	2,336	29.7
South Africa	5,285	26.7
Tanzania	324	12.9
Seychelles	8,600	52.5
Zambia	918	17.2
Zimbabwe	260	45.0
Average for SADC countries	**2,413**	**30.0**
Average for SSA countries	**1,700**	**23.5**

Source: World Bank.

External Aid for Education

According to the Debt and Aid Management Report (2008), donors provided US$53.8 million in support of education activities in 2007/08 compared to US$42.8 million in the previous financial year.[11] Over one third of donor resources in 2007/08 were provided by the Department for International Development (DFID) in the United Kingdom. The other donors are the Japanese International Cooperation Agency (JICA), the United States Agency for International Development (USAID), UNICEF, the Canadian International Development Agency (CIDA), the German Society for Technical Cooperation (GTZ), the African Development Fund, the World Bank, and the government of Ireland.

On average, from 2004 to 2006, Malawi benefited annually from external aid for education equivalent to 1.9 percent of its GDP (using data from the donors' headquarters, compiled by the OECD Development Assistance Committee).Direct support for education accounted for 1.2 percent of the GDP and 0.7 percent of the GDP was the estimated education share from global budget support.[12] As presented in the table 1.4, the total support as a percentage of Malawi's GDP is higher than both the SADC average (0.9 percent of GDP) and the SSA average (1.1 percent of GDP).

Table 1.4: Annual External Aid for Education as Percentage of GDP (2004–2006 Average)

SADC country	Annual external aid for education as % of GDP (2004–2006 average)
Angola	0.1
Botswana	0.1
Congo, Dem. Rep. of	0.5
Lesotho	0.5
Madagascar	1.6
Malawi	**1.9**
Mozambique	2.6
Namibia	0.2
Swaziland	0.0
South Africa	0.0
Tanzania	2.1
Zambia	1.3
Zimbabwe	0.3
Average for SADC countries	**0.9**
Average for SSA	**1.1**

Source: OECD Development Assistance Committee data, including 20 percent of the global budget support received.

Composite Index of Economic Context and Composite Index of Context

The World Bank recently computed an aggregate economic context index that takes into account GDP per capita, domestic resources as a percentage of GDP, external aid for education, and the percentage of students enrolled in private education.[13] On that scale, Malawi with an index of 41.5 is the SADC country with the second lowest value (right after the Democratic Republic of Congo), meaning that it is the second SADC country with the most difficult economic context for the education sector. Among all SSA countries, Malawi is ranked as the country with the seventh most difficult economic context, right after DRC, Ethiopia, Sierra Leone, Niger, Central African Republic, and Burundi.

A composite index of global context has also been computed by the World Bank, by combining the composite index of social context (see part II.4.3 above) and the composite index of economic context. On this global context index, Malawi is, with a value of 39, ranked as the SADC country with the most difficult global context and the fourth among all SSA countries (right after Niger, Burundi, and Ethiopia). See Appendix 1.1.

Notes

[1] The assumption used is that repetition rate will stay constant between 2008 and 2018; 20 percent of the students would be repeaters.

[2] For cross-country comparisons, the usual assumption is to estimate that 20 percent of global budget support goes to the education sector (i.e., the average share for education in recurrent budgets in Sub-Saharan countries).

[3] Demographic transition happens when the population growth starts to decrease, even if the population itself is increasing.

[4] This figure is estimated using the assumption than the repetition rate for 2018 will be the same as in 2008.

[5] See Appendix 1.1 for data for all African countries.

[6] Income poverty lines are calculated at 1985 international prices and adjusted for purchasing power parity.

[7] The Gini index measures the extent to which the distribution of income (or consumption) among individuals or households within a country deviates from a perfectly equal distribution. A Lorenz curve plots the cumulative percentages of total income received against the cumulative number of recipients, starting with the poorest individual or household. The Gini index measures the area between the Lorenz curve and a hypothetical line of absolute equality, expressed as a percentage of the maximum area under the line. A value of 0 represents absolute equality, a value of 100 absolute inequality (one individual concentrating 100 percent of the national income). An education Gini index is also presented in Chapter 5 of this report.

[8] The prevalence of child malnutrition (height for age) is the percentage of children under five whose height for age is more than two standard deviations below the median for the international reference population ages 0–59 months. For children up to two years of age, height is measured by recumbent length. For older children, height is measured by stature while standing. The reference population adopted by the WHO in 1983 is based on children from the United States, who are assumed to be well nourished (source: World Health Organization, Global Database on Child Growth and Malnutrition).

[9] Source: United Nations Educational, Scientific and Cultural Organization (UNESCO) Institute for Statistics.

[10] The domestic debt has been reduced from 25 percent in 2003/04 to 16 percent in 2007/08.

[11] These amounts are based on the information that development partners reported to the Ministry of Finance for inclusion in the budget. However, donor support that is not reported at the time of budget preparation is treated as off-budget, together with resources that are directly managed by donors even though they may be in support of government activities.

[12] For cross-country comparisons, the usual assumption is to estimate that 20 percent of global budget support goes to the education sector (i.e., the average share for education in recurrent budgets in Sub-Saharan countries).

[13] The percentage of students enrolled in private education is included in the index of economic context because when more children go to private schools, the government has to pay less to enroll students in public schools.

CHAPTER 2

Enrollment Patterns

Summary of the Chapter

Since 2000, enrollment has increased at all educational levels. There has been a high average annual growth rate since 2004 in preschool education (44 percent) and a much lower growth rate in primary (1.5 percent) and secondary (5.3 percent) education. Private enrollment increased the most but general education is still mainly provided by public institutions, which enroll 99 percent of pupils in primary and 77 percent in secondary. In addition, enrollment in public universities has doubled since 1998 and enrollment in adult literacy programs multiplied by 2.5 since 2000.

Because of the school-age population increase, the gross enrollment ratio (GER) has decreased in primary education since 2000. Ranking 101 percent in 2007, it is more than twice as important for the first four standards (136.6 percent) as for the last four (61.4 percent). During the same period, the GER in secondary education stayed stable (16 percent). Enrollment in adult literacy programs is 1,074 per 100,000 inhabitants while global coverage in technical, entrepreneurial, and vocational education and training (TEVET) and higher education remains low: 35 and 52 students per 100,000 inhabitants, respectively.

Access rates in the first four standards, particularly in Standard 1, show a high multi-cohort phenomenon due to a large proportion of over-age new entrants. This can be attributed to unknown ages and double counts of new entrants, with some pupils dropping and attending the same standards for at least two consecutive years. Household surveys (IHS-2, 2004–2005) show that among pupils attending Standard 1 in 2004, 47 percent had attended the same grade the year before, while official repetition is 25 percent. This has affects access rates to Standard 1, which according to the Education Management Information System (EMIS), were 142 percent in 2007.

EMIS enrollment data and alternate repetition structure (from household surveys) show that access to Standard 1 is almost universal but survival until the end of the primary cycle remains poor (that is, there is a high dropout rate), leading to only a 35 percent completion rate. These figures show that Malawi still stands far from universal primary completion. Survival improved within primary education, from 23 percent in 2004 to 32 percent in 2007, but remains insufficient. Completion is not expected to improve according to the most recent data on promotion between standards.

Poor retention comes from both supply and demand. Incomplete schools are still an issue—13 percent of pupils are in a school that does not provide educational supply continuity up to Standard 8, making them more likely to drop out if another school doesn't exist close to their home. Crowded classrooms, open-air, and temporary classrooms are also significantly affecting retention rates. Economic difficulties and early marriage, pregnancy, and family responsibilities are also reported as major reasons for dropping out. The schools with higher repetition rates show a significantly higher dropout rate as well.

* * *

This chapter describes the enrollment patterns of all education levels in Malawi. It focuses primarily on general education (preschool, primary, and secondary) as well as non-formal education. Technical, entrepreneurial, and vocational education and training (TEVET) and higher education will be analyzed in more detail in subsequent chapters. Chapter 2 provides a global description of the education system in Malawi, with an overview of enrollment trends from 1998[1] for each level and type of schooling. Education is then addressed for: i) global coverage, which compares enrollments by level and the age group that can attend; ii) actual coverage, which uses the schooling profile on primary and secondary education; and iii) the main reasons dropping out, which are identified by different analytical methodologies and data sources.

The Education System in Malawi

The Structure

In general, basic education has three main components: ECD; adult literacy, including out-of-school youth literacy; and primary education. In Malawi however, basic education is synonymous only with primary education. Indeed, while ECD is part of infant care and support, adult and out-of-school youth literacy are considered non-formal education.

The formal education system in Malawi follows an 8–4–4 structure: eight years of primary education (Standard 1–Standard 8), four years of secondary (Form 1–Form 4), and four years of university-level education[1] (see figure 2A.1 in Appendix 2.1).

At the end of their primary education, students take the Primary School Leaving Certificate Examination (PSLE), which determines their eligibility for entry into secondary school.

Public school secondary students attend either Community Day Secondary Schools (CDSSs, previously MCDE) or Conventional Secondary Schools (CSSs). At the end of two years of secondary education, pupils take the national Junior Certificate of Secondary Education (JCE), which is followed by the Malawi School Certificate Examination (MSCE) two years later.

Tertiary education is provided by an array of educational institutions, including primary and secondary teacher training colleges, technical and vocational training schools, and university colleges. For university entrance and for the secondary teacher training college, an MSCE certificate is required. For primary teacher training, the policy is to take MSCE graduates, but those who passed the JCE may also be accepted. Technical and vocational training can start after either JCE or MSCE.

Primary, secondary, teacher, and higher education levels fall under the authority of the Ministry of Education Science and Technology.

Early Childhood Development in Malawi falls under the authority of the Ministry of Women and Child Development and contains programs for children from birth to age five. Its main purpose is to protect children's rights and foster full cognitive, emotional, social, and physical development. Examples of ECD activities include opening preschool centers, recruiting caregivers, and providing instructional materials and some nutrition. ECD services are categorized into two levels. The first—baby care centers for children aged 0–2 years—is usually offered by the private sector. The second level—for children aged 2–5 years—is either provided by the private sector (preschools/nurseries) or the public sector (community-based childcare centers), and the government contributes by training caregivers and sometimes providing instructional materials.

Adult literacy tries to give adults (aged 15 years and older) a second chance at learning opportunities that may have been missed when they were young. The programs teach the specialized knowledge, skills, and attitudes that are needed to independently engage in active citizenship. Improving adult literacy in Malawi involves opening adult literacy classes, recruiting instructors, and providing teaching and learning materials. It also involves giving adults opportunities for post-literacy activities that may include easy-reading booklets, skill training, and information about small-business management. These programs are free but provided by both governmental and non-state entities, including NGOs and private-sector and faith-based organizations.

Enrollment Trends

ECD

As table 2.1 shows, enrollment grew steadily from 38,166 children in 1998 to 683,826 in 2007. Growth can be mainly explained by an increased advocacy for ECD in early 2000, which allowed private and public institutions to join in the government's efforts to provide ECD education.

Primary education

Growth was constant from 1998 to 2001 (figure 2A.2 in Appendix 2.2). High enrollment in primary education is a direct result of the introduction of free primary education in 1994. The sudden decline in 2002 and 2003 was a result of a famine brought on by lack of rain and resulted in most pupils, especially the youngest, dropping out of school. There was a noticeable increase in enrollment from 2004 to 2007, reaching 1.5 percent annually. Enrollment in private institutions (table 2.1) grew more quickly (17.1 percent per year) than in public institutions (1.3 percent), likely a result of a national policy to authorize education provisioned by private institutions that was set up in the early 2000s. Nevertheless, primary education in Malawi is mainly provided by public institutions (religious agencies and the government), which still enrolled nearly 99 percent of the total pupils attending that level of education in 2007. Annual growth is higher in the last four grades of primary schooling (3.4 percent) than in the first (0.7 percent): This could be the consequence of the previous increase in Standard 1's enrollment consecutive to the introduction of free primary education in 1994.

Table 2.1: Enrollment Trends per Education Level (1998–2007)

	1998	2001	2004	2006	2007	Average Annual Growth Rate 2001–2004	Average Annual Growth Rate 2004–2007
ECD	38,166	72,760	229,823	615,478	683,826	47%	44%
Primary Education	2,805,785	3,187,835	3,166,786	3,280,714	3,306,926	0%	1%
public	n.a.	n.a.	3,140,440	3,242,483	3,264,594	n.a.	1%
private	n.a.	n.a.	26,346	38,231	42,332	n.a.	17%
Including:							
Std1–Std4	2,090,728	2,296,039	2,315,171	2,379,302	2,365,307	0%	1%
public	n.a.	n.a.	2,298,971	2,356,063	n.a.	n.a.	1%*
private	n.a.	n.a.	16,200	23,239	n.a.	n.a.	20%*
Std5–Std8	715,057	891,796	851,615	901,412	941,619	–2%	3%
public	n.a.	n.a.	841,469	886,420	n.a.	n.a.	3%*
private	n.a.	n.a.	10,146	14,992	n.a.	n.a.	22%*
Secondary Education							
Form1–Form4	59,636	176,252	180,157	218,310	210,325	1%	5%
Public	n.a.	153,119	137,822	166,307	161,575	–3%	5%
CDSS	n.a.	114,751	83,492	104,161	99,172	–10%	6%
conventional	n.a.	25,738	36,051	47,996	42,734	12%	6%
grant-aided	n.a.	8,764	16,322	9,717	12,730	23%	–8%
open school	n.a.	3,866	1,957	4,433	6,939	–20%	52%
Private	n.a.	23,133	42,335	52,003	48,750	22%	5%
Adult Literacy	63,035	88,240	103,965	146,301	n.a.	6%	19%*
state	63,035	85,807	95,515	128,967	n.a.	4%	16%*
non-state	n.a.	2,433	8,450	17,334	n.a.	51%	43%*
University	3,385	4,304	6,478	6,346	7,263	15%	4%
Public	3,385	4,304	6,478	6,346	6,458	15%	0%
Bunda	490	592	666	780	886	4%	10%
Chancellor	1,292	1,555	2,017	2,252	1,108	9%	–18%
Kamuzu Nursing	263	180	331	251	454	23%	11%
Polytechnic	1,031	1,239	2,345	1,980	2,147	24%	–3%
Medicine	93	88	179	n.a.	419	27%	33%
Mzuzu	n.a.	264	475	1,083	1,444	22%	45%
Board of Governors	216	386	465	n.a.	n.a.	6%	n.a.
Private	n.a.	n.a.	n.a.	n.a.	805	n.a.	n.a.
TEVET	n.a.	n.a.	n.a.	n.a.	4,807	n.a.	n.a.

Source: Education Management Information System (EMIS) data from the Ministry of Education Science and Technology and from the Ministry of Women and Child Development.
n.a.: not available.
*Due to the absence of 2007 data, the average annual growth rate is calculated for those levels from 2004 to 2006.

The increased enrollment in open schools was the highest overall for the recent period: 52.5 percent on average annually since 2004. This trend can be explained by open schools absorbing most of the increase in the demand for secondary school. Thus in 2007, records show that 77 percent pupils were enrolled in public institutions, most of them attending either CDSS (47 percent) or conventional schools (20 percent). The share of open school and grant-aided schools remains low among the global enrollment in secondary education: 3 percent and 6 percent.

Adult literacy

Enrollment increased substantially, from 63,035 students in 1998 to 146,301 in 2006. The average annual growth in enrollment since 2001 was a high 10.6 percent. Data for non-state providers became available in 2001 and since then, their share has increased. They showed a 48 percent average annual growth rate from 2001–2006, while the rate for state providers was about 8 percent. However, the state continues to be the primary provider of the adult literacy program; it enrolled 88 percent of students in 2006.

TEVET

Data regarding TEVET are scarce in Malawi; the only figures available are for 2007 and concern only the number of students enrolled in formal public technical colleges. Chapter 6 of this CSR discusses TEVET in more detail.

Higher education

Enrollment showed an 8.9 percent average annual growth rate between 1998 and 2007. This figure is based primarily on public institutions, as data on private structures were not available. In 2007, enrollment in higher education was mainly public (89 percent); Polytechnic, Chancellor College, and Mzuzu University enroll about 65 percent of the total number of students. Higher education is examined in greater depth in Chapter 7.

I.3 Enrollment Ratio Evolution

It is important to analyze enrollment trends in the context of overall changes in population demographics. In other words, enrollment patterns can be better understood when compared to the theoretical population that would be expected to attend certain levels of school over time. Table 2.2 displays the evolution of coverage indicators from 2000–2007 for all educational levels in Malawi.

ECD

- Enrollment has picked up since 2002, reaching 23 percent in 2007.
- The gradual increase, in particular since 2005, suggests that the support of non-state institutions (UNICEF and NGOs) greatly helped increase coverage.
- However, the majority of children still enter primary education without being exposed to ECD services.

Primary Education

- The GER decreased from 120 percent in 2000 to 101 percent in 2007.[2] This value still means that the system is potentially able to accommodate all the pupils within the school-age group, according to the present schooling conditions (which are very bad, with a student to teacher ratio (STR) of 80:1. See Chapter 4 for more information.)
- Nevertheless, this GER does not ensure universal primary completion because of the high level of repetition and over-age enrollment,[3] which artificially inflate the GER, and the high number of dropouts throughout the primary cycle (in particular between the two sub-cycles).

Table 2.2: Schooling Coverage by Level of Education (2000–2007)

Age group	Gross Enrollment Ratio (GER) ECD (0–5)	Gross Enrollment Ratio (GER) Primary (%)			Gross Enrollment Ratio (GER) Secondary (%)			# of learners per 100,000 inhabitants TEVET	# of students per 100,000 inhabitants Higher Education	# of learners per 100,000 inhabitants Adult Literacy
		Std1–Std4 (6–9)	Std5–Std8 (10–13)	Std1–Std8 (6–13)	Form 1–2 (14–15)	Form 3–4 (16–17)	Form 1–4 (14–17)			
2000	2	158.6	73.3	119.8	18.7	13.3	16.0	n.a.	34	759
2001	3	160.3	74.9	121.5	18.9	14.6	16.8	n.a.	36	739
2002	5	153.4	70.5	115.7	12.1	9.3	10.8	n.a.	38	792
2003	5	146.6	64.5	109.1	13.7	9.9	11.9	n.a.	37	811
2004	8	144.7	62.5	106.9	18.0	13.3	15.8	n.a.	44	806
2005	21	141.3	61.2	104.2	17.4	13.3	15.5	n.a.	48	983
2006	21	140.5	60.9	103.4	19.7	15.5	17.7	n.a.	55	1,078
2007	23	136.6	61.4	101.2	18.3	14.1	16.3	35	61	

Sources: Calculation based on EMIS, Data from the Ministry of Women and Child Development and UN population statistics. (Reasons for use of the UN population database are mentioned in Appendix 2.3.)
Note: GER for pre-primary, primary, and secondary education are computed by dividing the total enrollment by the reference age-group population. GER is not computed for TEVET, higher education, and adult literacy because there is not a unique reference age group for those levels of education and they are not delivered with a unique curriculum and for a unique duration.

Secondary Education

- The GER did not change significantly from 2000, staying at around 18 percent for forms 1–2 (lower secondary) and 14 percent for forms 3–4 (upper secondary).

Adult Literacy

- Enrollment slowly grew between 2000 and 2006— from 759 learners per 100,000 inhabitants to 1,078.
- However, the percentage of the targeted population enrolling in adult literacy education (those aged 15 to 49) remains low (5.7 percent). See table 2A.1 in Appendix 2.2.

TEVET

- Results show very low educational coverage—in 2007, the number of learners per 100,000 inhabitants was only 35.

Higher Education

- Coverage was only 61 students per 100,000 inhabitants.
- Nevertheless, higher education coverage has increased a lot since 2000, when it was only 34 students per 100,000 inhabitants.

Using data summarized in Table 2.3, it is possible to compare the educational coverage in Malawi to that of the other SADC countries. For both preschool and primary education, Malawi is close to the average; however, it remains far from the average in secondary and higher education.[4]

Table 2.3: International Comparison on GER (SADC countries)

	ECD	Primary	Lower Secondary	Upper Secondary	Higher Education
Malawi	23	101	18	14	52
Angola	n.a.	64	22	11	299
Botswana	15	107	89	58	596
Congo, Dem Rep of.	1	61	30	18	411
Lesotho	18	114	45	24	426
Madagascar	8	139	32	11	259
Mozambique	n.a.	105	22	5	138
Mauritius	101	102	100	80	1,340
Namibia	22	107	74	30	644
Seychelles	109	125	116	106	n.a.
Swaziland	17	106	56	33	502
South Africa	38	106	98	92	1,536
Tanzania	28	110	8	3	133
Zambia		117	53	18	235
Zimbabwe	43	101	58	31	416
SADC average	35	104	55	36	518
Africa average	22	98	47	25	416
Malawi/SADC	0.71	0.97	0.33	0.39	0.10

Sources: EMIS data for Malawi, World Bank database for the other countries.

Note: Data are from 2007 or thereabouts.

Coverage in Primary and Secondary Education: Schooling and Survival Profiles

While the GER gives an indication for a given cycle of the system's capacity to enroll students of the corresponding age groups, its value can be inflated by repetition rates. These can result in an average measure of coverage without reflecting the schooling history of a cohort at each grade. It is preferable to compute schooling profiles that describe access at each grade, thereby measuring the proportion of children that have access to Standard 1 and the proportion of pupils that stay in school.

There are several methods and data sources available for computing schooling and survival profiles.[5] Two different schooling profiles exist: the cross-sectional schooling profile and the probalistic schooling profile. The cross-sectional computes access rate to each grade by dividing the new repeaters (repeaters are not counted for avoiding double count) by the population of the theoretical single age for that grade. Some access rates of the cross-sectional profile may be higher than 100 percent due to multi-cohort phenomena (over-age enrollment). The probalistic schooling profile is made by computing for each cohort (a single-age population group) the share of children who attend or have attended each grade. Access rates of a probalistic schooling profile are always below or equal to 100 percent.

A survival profile differs from a schooling profile because it does not reference the total population of children but only those who entered Standard 1. It is computed using the available enrollment data from the last two consecutive years and gives the most recent status of the retention throughout the cycle (pseudo-cohort method).

An expected schooling profile can also be computed by applying the survival profile to the access rate to grade 1. The profile then provides the expected access rates to different grades (including the access rate to the last standard, proxy of the completion rate) in the coming years if promotion rates between standards stay the same.

Cross-Sectional Schooling Profile

The usual practice is to compute a cross-sectional schooling profile using the administrative enrollment data (EMIS) and the population data. Nevertheless, in Malawi, data on repetition (which greatly affects the profile) are subject to discussion. The EMIS data use the official definition of repeaters and regard as repeaters only the children for whom a decision of repetition was taken by the school. (All other students are regarded as non-repeaters.) In Malawi a lot of children drop out during the school year and come back to the same standard the next year (or years later). Those children are not regarded in EMIS as repeaters although they should be for accurate calculation of access rates. Then the cross-sectional schooling profile computed without changing the repetition rate (see Appendix 2.4) should be adjusted.

Household surveys (DHS, 2000 and IHS-2, 2004–2005) provide some alternate information about the actual repetition structure in the education system in Malawi (see table 2.4[6]). This survey contains information about the standard attended in school during the current year as well as the year before. It then becomes possible to compute the proportion of pupils that attended the same grade the year before for each standard. Of course, this is not an official repetition rate, as it includes both the children for whom a decision of repetition was taken by the school, and the children that had drop out during a school year and decided to attend the same grade the year after (no administrative decision of repetition).

Table 2.4: Percent of Repeaters in Primary Education According to Different Data Sources (in %)

	Std1	Std2	Std3	Std4	Std5	Std6	Std7	Std8
EMIS 2007	25	21	23	17	16	13	11	16
IHS-2 2004	47	27	30	21	19	17	13	24
DHS 2000	45	24	27	17	15	13	11	38

Sources: Calculation from EMIS 2007 and IHS-2 2004; DHS 2000 repetition structure as reported in Malawi in first CSR

The global repetition structure provided by IHS-2 is consistent with the information provided by DHS 2000. Applying the IHS-2 repetition structure to the EMIS 2007 enrollment allows the user to compute a cross-sectional profile that is not overestimated by the repetition definition problem (see figure 2.1).

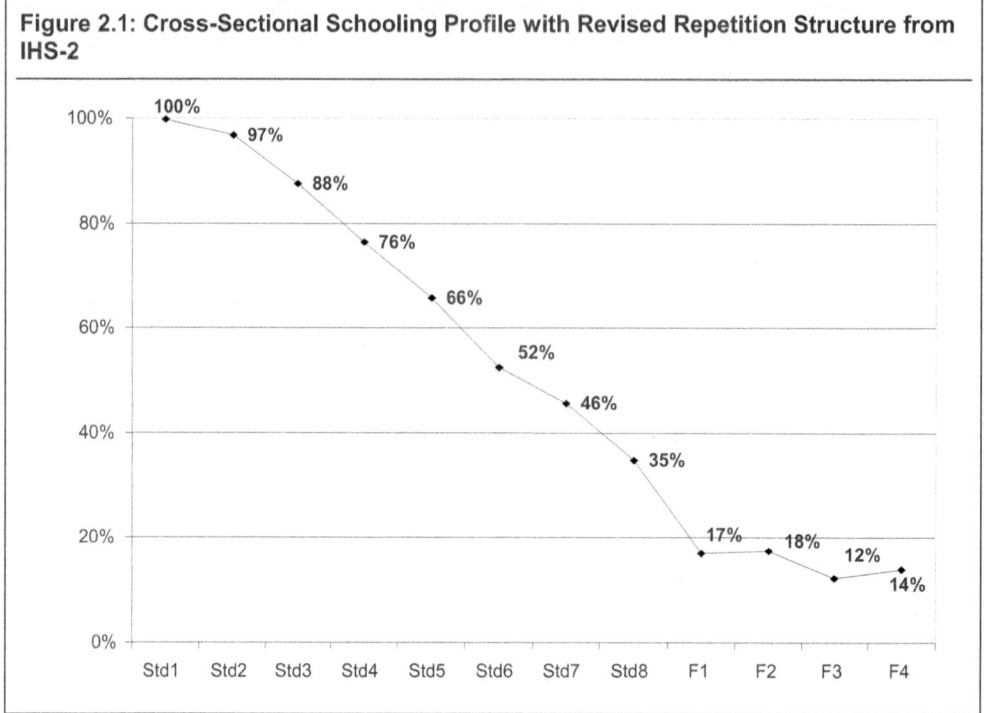

Figure 2.1: Cross-Sectional Schooling Profile with Revised Repetition Structure from IHS-2

Sources: Calculation with EMIS 2007 database; IHS-2 2004 repetition structure; and UN population data

The gross intake rate (access rate to Standard 1) is 99.9 percent, which would situate Malawi close to universal access in Standard 1.[7] The primary completion rate (access rate to Standard 8) is 35 percent, which indicates that there is still 65 percent of a cohort that does not reach the end of the primary cycle.

These results lead to two main observations:

- Due to the low level of completion, Malawi remains far from the goal of universal primary education, which supposes each child to enter school and complete the whole cycle.
- As access to Standard 1 seems to be nearly universal, this 35 percent completion rate is mainly the consequence of poor retention (a very high level of dropping out) between Standard 1 and Standard 8. This is analyzed in section III of this chapter.

The figures for secondary education give a 17 percent access rate to Form 1 and a 14 percent completion rate.

In comparison to other countries, Malawi stands above the African average (92 percent) but falls under the SADC average (116 percent).[8] See figure 2.2. For comparability purpose, this figure displays access rates to the sixth grade of primary education[9], instead of comparing primary completion rates, which would rely on a different duration of primary education.

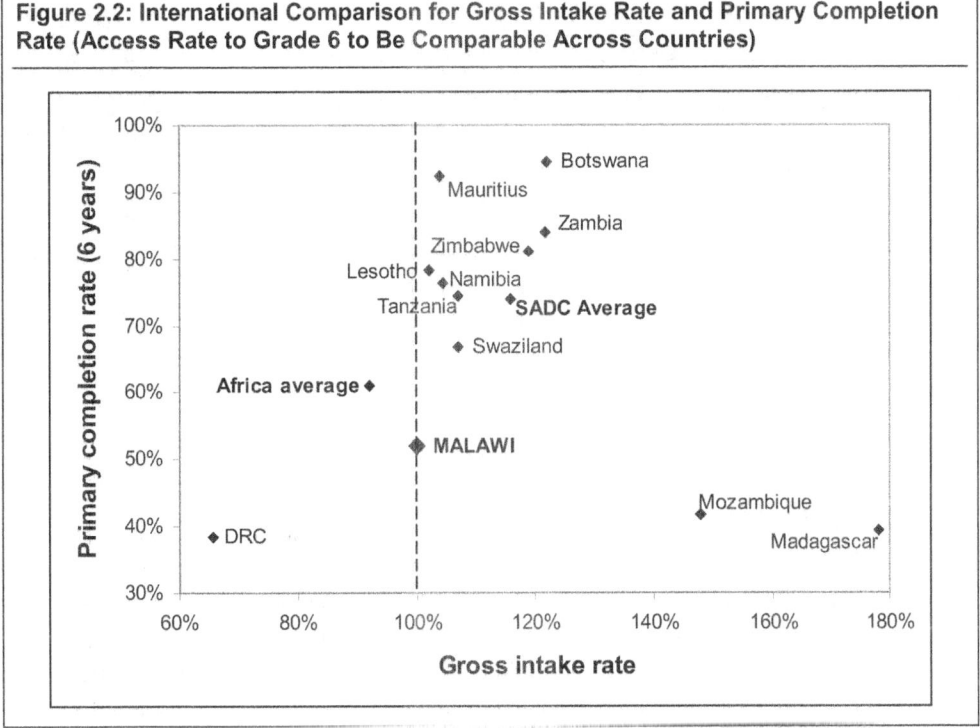

Figure 2.2: International Comparison for Gross Intake Rate and Primary Completion Rate (Access Rate to Grade 6 to Be Comparable Across Countries)

Sources: Figure 2.4 for Malawi and World Bank database for the other countries.

The access rate to the sixth grade of primary education, however, is quite a different story. With a 52 percent access rate to Standard 6, Malawi remains far behind the SADC average (74 percent), yet stays above countries like DRC (38 percent), Madagascar (39 percent), or Mozambique (42 percent). Moreover, Malawi is still under the average value of Africa (61 percent), which places the country among those who will have the longest way to go in achieving universal primary completion.

Probalistic Schooling Profile

A probalistic schooling profile allows to the user to access rates without the effect of multi-cohort phenomena. Data from household surveys can again be of interest, as they provide some information on education attendance. The data could also validate the results obtained with administrative data (adjusted on the repetition structure). Both MICS and IHS-2 information can be used to calculate the proportion of people who have ever attended school, whether they are currently enrolled or not, which includes individuals who may have accessed school but do not attend anymore (figure 2.3).

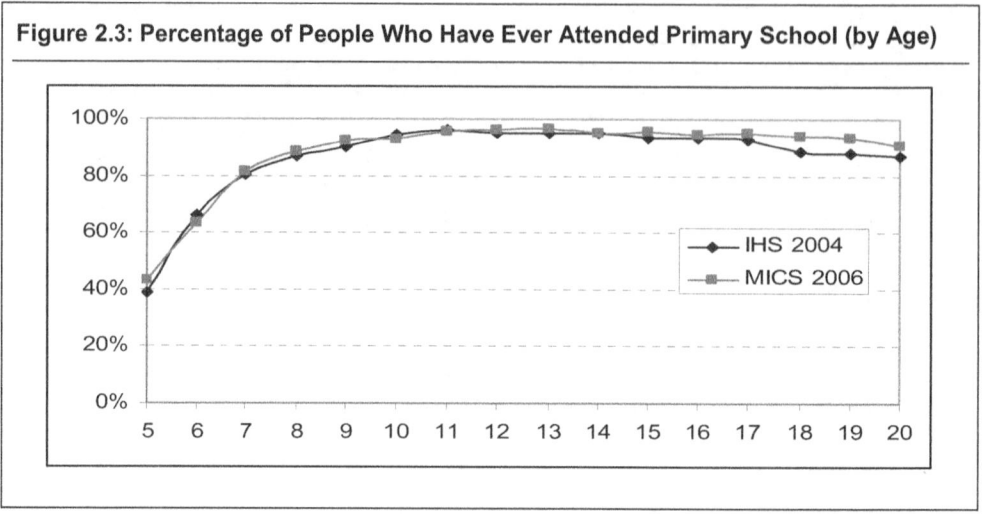

Figure 2.3: Percentage of People Who Have Ever Attended Primary School (by Age)

Sources: Calculation from MICS 2006 and IHS-2 2004 databases.
Note: In the MICS questionnaire, this item concerns only people above age five.

The two curves are almost identical, which suggests consistency in the results. The proportion of individuals who have accessed Standard 1 is only 60 percent for six-year-olds, while this age-specific group is the official one that should access school each year. This figure is 40 percent for five-year-olds, and becomes higher for children ages seven and above. The maximum value is reached for age 11 (96 percent), meaning that there should be a lot of late enrollments, and little probability of entering Standard 1 after 11.[10] The probability for a cohort to access Standard 1 can be estimated at 96 percent. The full probalistic schooling profile computed from MICS 2006 is presented in figure 2.4.[11]

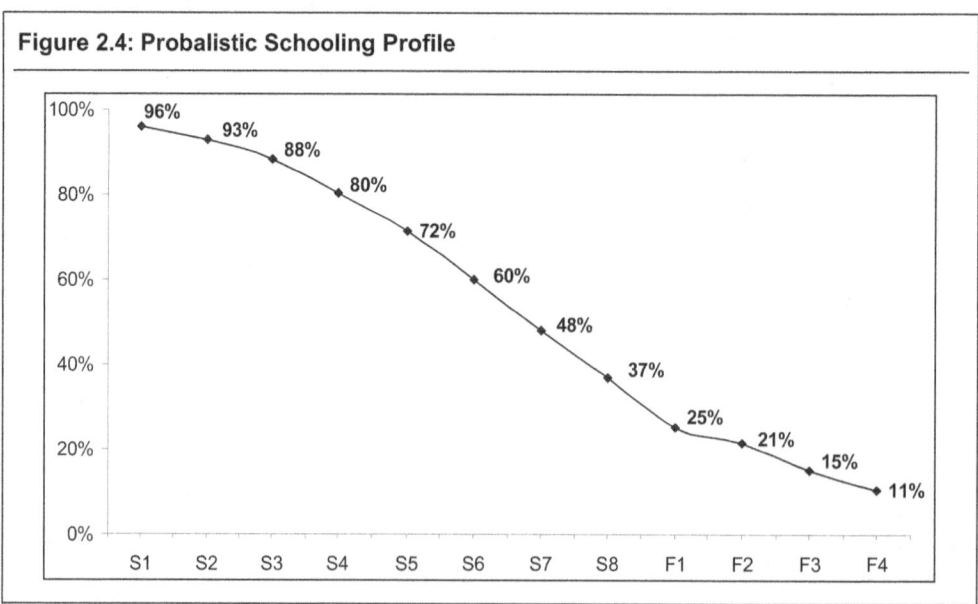

Figure 2.4: Probalistic Schooling Profile

Source: Calculation from MICS 2006 data.

These figures are consistent with those based on administrative data: There is a high access to Standard 1 of primary education, with an estimated probability of 96 percent, which would confirm a near universal access to first grade (there would still be 4 percent of a cohort with no access at all to school). Access to Standard 8 is 37 percent, which is nearly the same as the access rate computed with EMIS data. The enrollment for secondary education is different (with an access rate to Form 1 of 25 percent), but MICS does not differentiate between general secondary education and technical and vocational secondary education, so this figure includes part of TEVET.

Survival Profile and Expected Schooling Profile (Pseudo-Cohort Analysis)

Focusing now on the children that entered school, it is possible to compute a survival profile (using a pseudo-cohort method). This computes the share of pupils attending Standard 1 who will access the other standards: Each point of this profile is the retention or survival rate to the corresponding standard, calculated from the actual promotion rates of one standard to the next (see table 2.5).

Table 2.5: Construction of Survival Profile

	Estimated Non-Repeaters Using EMIS enrollment and IHS-2 Repetition Rates*		Promotion Rate from One Standard to the Next One	Survival Profile
	2006	2007		
Standard 1	470,738	449,722	100%	100%
Standard 2	416,945	424,851	424,851 / 470,738 = 90%	90 x 100 = 90%
Standard 3	371,760	374,219	374,219 / 416,945 = 90%	90 x 90 x 100 = 81%
Standard 4	307,873	316,741	316,741 / 307,873 = 85%	69%
Standard 5	254,181	265,329	86%	59%
Standard 6	197,270	205,288	81%	48%
Standard 7	164,978	172,563	87%	42%
Standard 8	119,641	125,674	76%	32%
Form 1	60,179	58,729	49%	16%
Form 2	60,167	58,010	96%	15%
Form 3	44,038	38,644	64%	10%
Form 4	40,301	41,521	94%	9%

Source: Calculations from EMIS data and HIS-2 data.
*These non-repeaters are not reported by EMIS but estimated with EMIS 2006 and 2007 enrollment per grade, on which was applied the repetition structure reported by IHS-2 2004.

If the promotion rates between each standard remain unchanged, the probability for a child attending Standard 1 to reach Standard 6 is 48 percent and to reach Standard 8 is only 32 percent:[12] This clearly remains insufficient to reach the target of universal primary completion. Figure 2.5 shows a graphical representation of the survival profile from 2003–2007 using the same method.

Figure 2.5: Evolution of Survival Profile in Primary and Secondary Education, 2003–2007

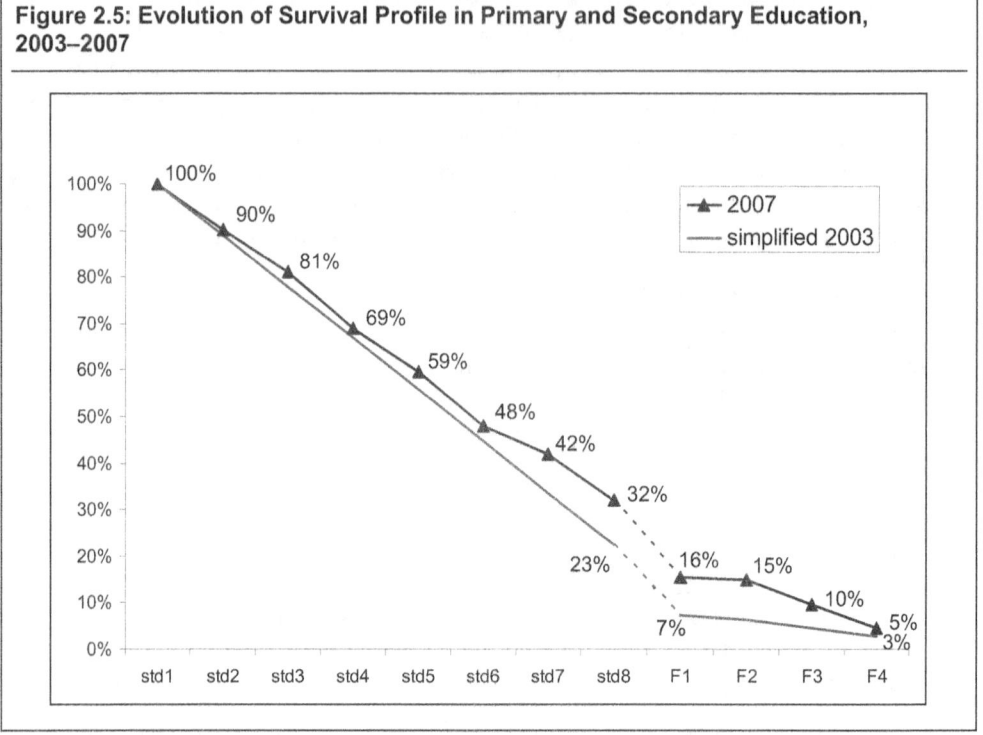

Sources: Calculation from EMIS database and IHS-2 repetition structure for primary education.

A positive evolution of retention within the primary level can be seen, even if it is still lacking. It grew from 23 percent in 2003 to 32 percent in 2007. In secondary education, retention declined after 2003.

Finally, combining a gross intake rate (access rate to Standard 1) and the survival profile[13] can lead to the expected schooling profile if the access to Standard 1 and retention rates remain the same as they are now. For Malawi, since the gross intake rate is estimated at 100 percent, the expected schooling profile and survival profile are the same. If the present condition of intake and promotion between grades remains unchanged, it is expected to face a 32 percent primary completion rate within the eight years, which would denote a decline, considering the present value of 35 percent in 2007.

Summary of Schooling Coverage: the Educational Pyramid Compared to Africa

The educational pyramid (see figure 2.6 and Appendix 2.5 for the detailed methodology) summarizes the different results obtained in the section regarding access, retention, and completion of the different levels of primary and secondary education, as well as coverage in higher education and TEVET. These results can be compared to the SSA-average pyramid (see figure 2.7).

The Education System in Malawi 25

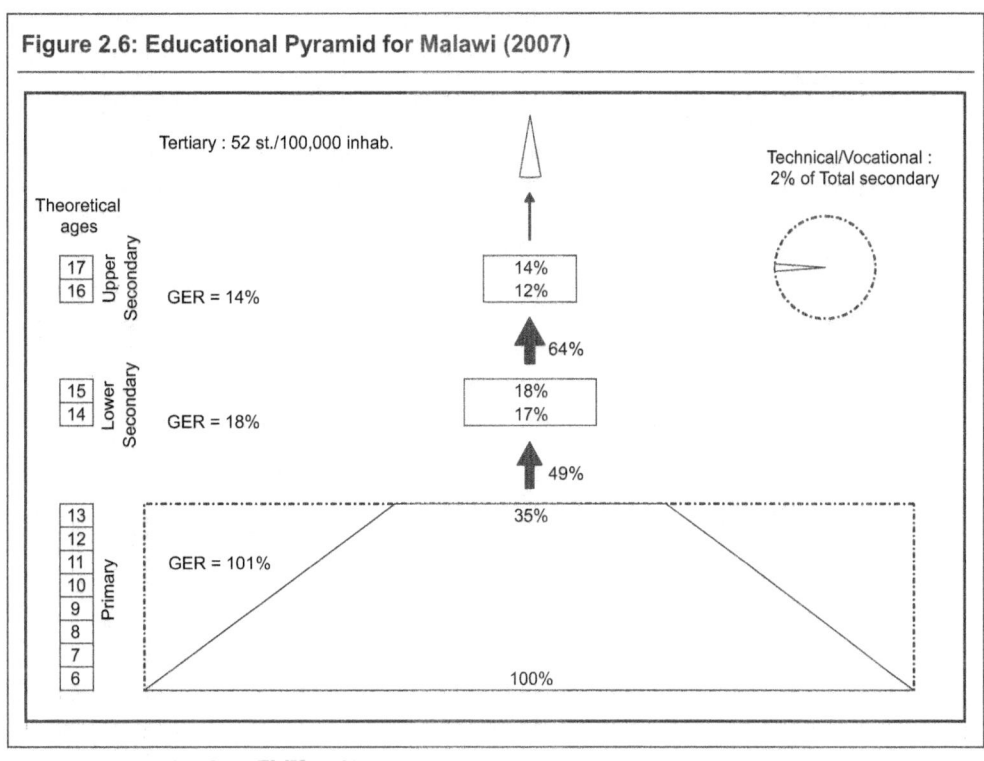

Sources: Calculation from EMIS and UN population data.

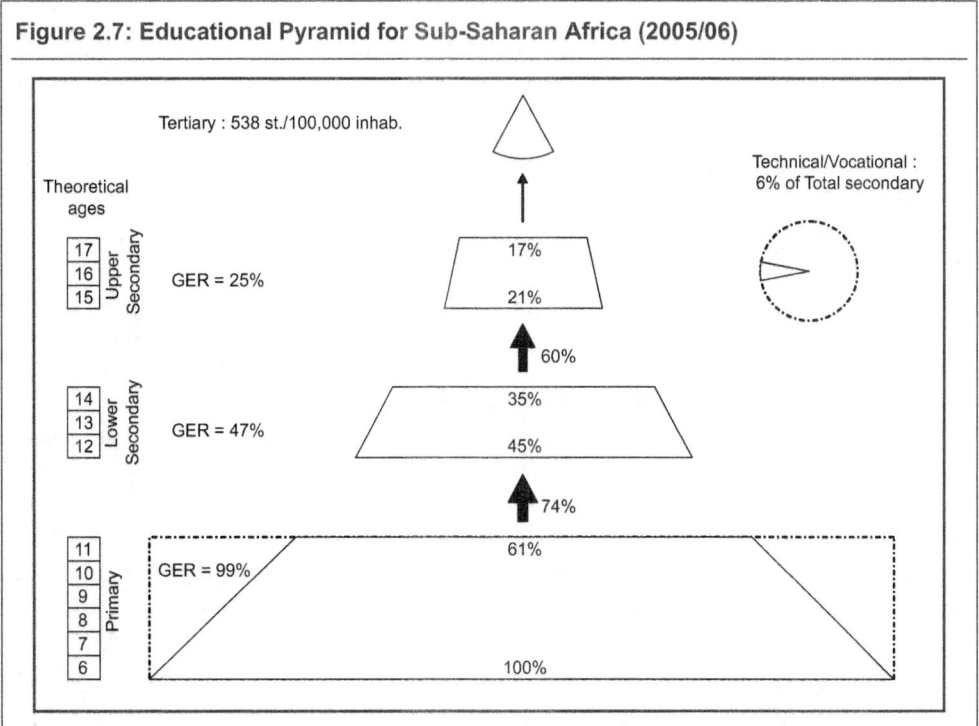

Source: World Bank database.

Understanding Dropouts at the Primary Level

Educational Supply Continuity

The low primary completion rate is mainly due to high level of dropouts rather than to a lack of first access to children in Standard 1.[14] One main reason that students drop out is that some schools are incomplete. A school that does not provide all standards forces children to find another school if they want to continue primary education. This introduces the problem of distance and some pupils drop out if they cannot continue attending school in the same place. Table 2.6 shows the distribution of schools according to the number of standards supplied and the corresponding share of pupils enrolled in these schools in 2006 and 2007.

Table 2.6: Share of Schools and Pupils According to the Number of Standards Supplied

Number of Standards Supplied	2006		2007	
	% of Schools	% of Pupils	% of Schools	% of Pupils
1 standard only	0.2	0.0	0.1	0.0
2 standards	1.8	0.4	1.5	0.4
3 standards	2.3	0.7	2.5	0.7
4 standards	7.1	2.9	7.2	2.9
5 standards	7.9	3.8	8.3	4.1
6 standards	6.8	3.9	6.4	3.8
7 standards	5.8	3.8	6.3	4.0
Total Incomplete Schools	31.9	15.5	32.3	16.0
8 standards	68.1	84.5	67.7	84.0
Total	100.0	100.0	100.0	100.0

Source: Calculation from EMIS databases.

The proportion of incomplete primary schools is around 32 percent and the corresponding schools enroll 16 percent of the pupils. Among them, some will probably be exposed to a high dropout risk.

This result is based on a static analysis and probably overestimates the number of cases where pupils face discontinuity in the educational supply. Indeed, among those incomplete schools, some are likely to provide educational continuity from one year to another by setting up new classes as the students progress through the primary cycle. (This can be the case with new schools.) With data from two consecutive school years the number of pupils who couldn't attend the next standard in the following year can be measured. Table 2.7 shows the results for Malawi, based on 2006–2007 school data.

At the national level, there are few situations of supply discontinuity between Standard 1 and Standard 4. For instance, only 0.11 percent of pupils attending Standard 1 in 2006 were in a school that didn't provide Standard 2 in 2007. This discontinuity is 0.69 percent between standards 2 and 3, and 0.83 percent between standards 3 and 4. In 2006, only 1.6 percent[15] of pupils attending Standard 1 were enrolled in a school that did not provide supply continuity until Standard 4. This small proportion should not have strong consequences on retention within the first four standards.

Table 2.7: Percentage of Pupils Who Cannot Continue on to the Next Standard in the Same School, 2006–07 (in %)

	Std1–Std2	Std2–Std3	Sdt3–Std4	Std4–Std5	Std5–Std6	Std6–Std7	Std7–Std8	Std1–Std8
Region								
Central	0.04	0.60	0.90	3.19	2.58	3.68	3.50	14
North	0.07	0.89	0.69	1.52	1.62	2.20	2.16	9
South	0.20	0.71	0.80	3.39	2.67	3.57	3.44	14
Education Division								
Central Eastern	0.01	0.09	0.60	2.84	2.38	4.38	3.77	13
Central Western	0.06	0.92	1.08	3.43	2.72	3.21	3.31	14
Northern	0.07	0.89	0.69	1.52	1.62	2.20	2.16	9
Shire Highlands	0.34	0.82	0.78	3.59	2.54	2.48	2.69	13
Southern Eastern	0.22	0.71	0.57	3.02	3.10	4.51	4.81	16
Southern Western	0.00	0.59	1.10	3.63	2.37	3.54	2.77	13
Malawi	**0.11**	**0.69**	**0.83**	**3.00**	**2.44**	**3.34**	**3.19**	**13**

Sources: Calculation from EMIS 2006 and EMIS 2007 databases.

However, the lack of supply continuity becomes more important between standards 4 and 8. The proportion of pupils attending a given standard, enrolled in schools that do not provide the next standard, fluctuates between 2.44 percent (std5–std6) to 3.34 percent (std6–std7). Globally, the share of pupils attending Standard 4 in a school that does not provide continuity until the end of the cycle is 11.4 percent,[16] nearly ten times the share observed in the first four standards.

Finally the share of pupils attending Standard 1, and enrolled in a school that does not provide continuity on the whole cycle is 13 percent.[17] This is slightly below the proportion of pupils enrolled in an incomplete school (16 percent).

The data are nearly homogenous across the country, except for the northern region where this proportion is only 9 percent, and in the South Eastern education division where 16 percent can be observed. Educational supply continuity is an issue countrywide, and among those 13 percent of pupils enrolled in discontinuous schools, the dropout risk increases if there is no alternative school nearby that students can attend.

This affects the global survival rate of the system. On the sub-sample of schools providing full continuity (from standards 1 to 8), the survival rate to Standard 8 is 42 percent. It is 10 percentage points higher than the global (including all schools) survival rate of 32 percent. A policy targeting the completion of incomplete schools might help to improve survival rate within the primary cycle. Nevertheless, it may not be enough for achieving universal completion and other levers should also be found.

Other Factors Affecting Dropout Rate

An Econometric Model Using EMIS Data at the School Level

An econometric model has been computed using the EMIS data at school level in order to assess the potential effects on retention rate of school characteristics. It should be noted that the determination level of the model is quite low (6 percent) meaning that the main factors affecting retention are other characteristics than those present in the model. However, it is useful to underline the effects of the factors found as statistically significant for explaining differences on retention rate across schools (see the model in Appendix 2.5).

Repetition and the student-teacher ratio have negative significant effects on retention.[18] Repetition is the factor that has the highest quantitative negative effect. This must be related to parents' perception of school. A high repetition rate in primary education may be considered by parents as a reason why their children shouldn't continue to attend school, increasing the dropout risk. International studies (Mingat and Sosale, 2001) done in 50 countries have confirmed this, showing that one percentage point less of repetition is associated with an increase of survival rate by 0.8 percentage point (for more details see Chapter 4).

Temporary and open-air classrooms also have a negative effect on child retention within the whole primary cycle. "However, there is no empirical evidence proving that school equipment (e.g., electricity, water, library, and latrine) has a negative effect on retention."

A policy targeting i) the completion of incomplete schools and ii) a reduction in repetition (from 20 percent to 10 percent) might help to increase the global retention in primary education from 32 to 50 percent. Ten percent more would be due to the supply of educational continuity and 8 percent more (0.8 x (20% − 10%)) would come from repetition reduction.

Reasons for Dropping Out As Declared by School Heads and Students

It is useful to complement the previous quantitative analysis with more qualitative information that could be gathered from declarations of school heads (EMIS 2007) and from students themselves (IHS-2 2004).

In EMIS 2007 (table 2.8), the main reason given by school heads for explaining dropout is the **family responsibilities** of the students (44 percent for boys and 41 percent for girls). Hidden within this reason could be children who drop out of school because they become heads-of-household as a result of the death of their parents.

Marriage appears to be a major issue, particularly for girls. Marriage is responsible for 9 percent of dropouts as declared by school heads. It increases after Standard 5 and reaches 41 percent at the end of the cycle.

Pregnancy is also the reason that 4 percent of all girls drop out, starting with 2 percent in Standard 4 and reaching 21 percent in Standard 8. These figures seem to be consistent with information from EMIS 2007, stating that 69 percent of girls attending Standard 8 are over-age (more than 13 years old), with 22 percent being over 16. Another report (MICS, 2006) mentions that 15 percent of women have their first birth between 16 and 18 years of age.

Employment is stated as the main reason in 12 percent of the cases for boys; **sickness and death** account for a total 4 percent.

IHS-2 2004 provides similar information, but this time as declared by students themselves (see table 2.9).

Three main reasons (75 percent of the explanations) are given by students to explain dropouts:

Table 2.8: Main Reasons for Dropping Out of School Declared by School Heads (in %)

	Std1	Std2	Std3	Std4	Std5	Std6	Std7	Std8	Total
Boys									
Family responsibilities	44	46	45	45	42	42	39	36	44
Marriage	0	0	0	1	3	6	11	20	2
Fees	0	1	1	1	1	1	2	2	1
Employment	2	5	9	11	12	12	12	10	7
Sickness	4	4	3	3	3	2	2	2	3
Death	1	1	1	1	1	1	1	1	1
Dismissed / disobedience	0	0	1	1	1	1	2	3	1
Other reasons	47	43	40	38	37	33	32	27	41
Girls									
Family responsibilities	45	48	47	44	37	30	23	19	41
Pregnancy	0	0	0	2	6	12	17	21	4
Marriage	0	0	1	6	18	27	36	41	9
Fees	0	1	1	1	1	1	2	1	1
Employment	2	4	8	10	7	4	3	2	5
Sickness	4	4	3	3	2	2	1	1	3
Death	1	1	1	1	1	1	1	1	1
Dismissed / disobedience	0	0	0	0	1	0	1	1	0
Other reasons	47	41	37	33	28	22	16	13	36

Source: Calculation from EMIS 2007.

Table 2.9: Main Reasons for Dropping Out of School, Declared by Pupils (in %)

Reasons Expressed	Std1	Std2	Std3	Std4	Std5	Std6	Std7	Total
Acquired all education wanted				2.0			2.9	0.6
No money for fees/ uniform	17.3	14.2	18.0	19.2	11.7	11.3	20.3	16.1
Too old to continue		5.3	1.8	5.8	1.7	4.5	3.1	2.9
Married/became pregnant	1.3		2.7	15.3	17.7	21.2	26.2	10.9
Illness or disability	9.9	5.5	5.7	2.8	5.6	3.9	6.1	6.0
Found work	0.9	2.0	3.7	4.0	2.0			1.7
Not interested, lazy	54.7	63.5	57.4	46.9	50.4	36.4	22.6	48.4
Parents told me to stop	2.4	1.6	2.2			1.5	1.7	1.4
Had to work or help at home	1.3	0.0	1.8	3.9	5.1	9.4	4.8	3.5
Poor/crowded school							2.3	0.3
Poor quality instruction	1.6						2.7	0.7
School too far from home	0.9	2.2			2.1	1.5		1.0
Failed promotion exam			4.6		3.6			1.1
Dismissed/expelled	1.1					3.9	2.9	1.1
Other	8.7	5.8	2.0			6.3	2.3	4.0
Teachers' abuse/ill treatment							2.1	0.3
Total number of individuals (weighted)	22 472	13 386	13 344	12 959	14 178	12 890	12 419	101 649
Number of individuals in the sample	93	55	54	51	56	51	50	410

Source: Calculation from IHS-2 2004 data.
Note: Reasons given by individuals who were attending primary education in 2003 for not continuing primary education the following year.

- The first reason, given in over 48 percent of cases, is that children might not be interested in school or may be lazy. This comes up more frequently in the first standards and decreases significantly at the end of the cycle. It probably results from the feedback schools give to parents on their children's success, and should be correlated to repetition practice. Indeed, the high repetition rates observed in Malawi (20 percent) can be perceived as a signal of student failure. This may result in parents preferring to keep their children at home, making them work in the fields or take care of younger children, instead of continuing to send them to school.
- The second reason involves poverty—16 percent of students drop out because of a lack of money.
- The third main reason is marriage and pregnancy, which is given as the explanation for dropping out in about 11 percent of the cases. This argument becomes particularly significant from Standard 4 onward and accounts for 26 percent of Standard 7's dropouts.

Notes

[1] When appropriate information is available.

[2] The results obtained for primary education with administrative data demonstrate a high level of consistency with available household survey data: IHS-2 data led to a 107 percent GER for 2004 (148 percent for Std1–Sd4 and 60 percent for Std5–Std8) and MICS data led to a 110 percent GER for 2006.

[3] The late entry in primary education leads to multi-cohort phenomena. It has been favored in the past by the introduction of free primary education in 1994.

[4] SADC averages are pushed up by countries like Mauritius or Seychelles, for which coverage indicators for preschool and primary are around 100 percent.

[5] For more details, see N. Reuge, *Schooling Profiles, Methodological Note n°2*, UNESCO-BREDA, Note du Pôle de Dakar (www.poledakar.org).

[6] The repetition structure of secondary education can't be derived from IHS-2 due to the sample size of pupils enrolled in secondary education that is too small. It is also assumed that the phenomenon of "drop out and come back" is mainly a problem for primary education.

[7] A 100 percent gross intake rate (GIR), computed by dividing non repeaters in the first grades by the total population of official age to attend the grade, must not be considered strictly as an indication of universal access due to multi-cohort phenomenon.

[8] However, SADC average is certainly over estimated due to the presence of countries like Madagascar or Mozambique, which may overestimate intake and probably face the same bias and data problems as described for Malawi in the previous section.

[9] The reported access rate is related to the sixth grade of primary education if the duration of the cycle is six years or more. For countries with five years, like Madagascar, the reported figure is the access rate to grade five.

[10] Information concerning age is weak due to the lack of birth registration certificates.

[11] The results of IHS-2 2004 are nearly the same but the MICS information is presented because it is more recent.

[12] These figures are computed, using the IHS-2 repetition structure but one should consider that using EMIS official repeaters should lead to 14 percent and 25 percent, respectively.

[13] Technically, the pseudo-cohort schooling profile is estimated by multiplying all point of the survival profile but the gross intake rate.

[14] Analysis of the factors explaining the lack of access some children have to Standard 1 (four percent according to the probalistic schooling profile) has also been done. The results of this analysis are presented in Appendix 2.4.

[15] 1.6% = 1-(1-0.11%) x (1-0.69%) x (1-0.83%)

[16] 11.4% = 1-(1-3%) x (1-2.44%) x (1-3.34%) x (1-3.19%)

[17] 13%= 1-(1-0.11%) x (1-0.69%) x (1-0.83%) x (1-3%) x (1-2.44%) x (1-3.34%) x (1-3.19%)

[18] Even if there is a link between repetition and the student-teacher ratio, non-collinearity is observed between those two variables.

CHAPTER 3

Education Expenditure and Financing

Summary of the Chapter

The total public recurrent expenditure for education amounted to MK22.3 billion in the 2007/08 fiscal year. This represents 19.4 percent of total government recurrent expenditures and is an increase compared to 2001/02 (16 percent). However, the budget share for education can certainly be increased further. In the ten low-income African countries that most highly prioritize their education system, the share for education averages 28.8 percent. Unfortunately, preliminary data for 2008/09 indicates a decreasing trend that would prevent Malawi from catching up with both the SADC average (20.8 percent) and the Education for All-Fast Track Initiative (EFA-FTI) reference benchmark (20 percent).

The 2000–2008 trends show a decrease in the priority of primary education to the benefit of higher education. In 2008, Malawi's allocation to primary education is one of the lowest (at 32.5 percent) in the continent where the average is 44.4 percent. Compared to other countries, Malawi prioritizes higher and secondary education above primary education. Malawi's recurrent allocations to both secondary and higher education are above average—40.4 percent against an SSA average of 34.4 percent for secondary education and 27 percent against an average of 21 percent in higher education.

Malawi has made comparatively poor budget allocations to the largest education sub-sector—primary education—so the public recurrent unit cost for primary is very low. In 2007/08, the recurrent expenditure per student in primary education stood at around MK3,000 which is equivalent to only 8.3 percent of GDP per capita (compared to 12 percent on average in the SADC region and 11 percent in SSA). At the secondary level, the public unit cost is estimated to be MK30,300 (83 percent of GDP per capita versus 30 percent for the SSA average) and it is four times higher (in terms of GDP per capita) than it was in 2000. However, this average unit cost for secondary hides the disparities that exist between the conventional and the Community Day Secondary Schools, at the detriment of the latter. TEVET, when parallel students are included, costs the government MK136,500 per year per student (equivalent to 45 times the primary unit cost). Finally, the public recurrent unit cost of university education is the highest in the world in terms of GDP per capita (2,147 percent of GDP per capita, which is seven times more than the SSA average). In fact, one year of study for one university student costs the same amount to the government as one year of study of 259 primary school pupils.

Unit cost in primary education is low, mainly because of the very high student-teacher ratio (80:1 vs. 48:1 for the SSA average) and the small amount of other recurrent transactions (ORT) allocated to primary education. Inversely, the secondary education unit cost is high because the student-teacher ratio is low (20:1 compared to 28:1 for the SSA average) while their ORT is relatively higher than in primary education. The extremely high unit cost in higher education is mainly due to a very low student-lecturer ratio (11:1 which is below the Organisation for Economic Co-operation and Development [OECD] average of 16:1 and equivalent to half the SSA average) and comparatively high teacher salaries (64 units of GDP per capita, compared to an average of 19 units of GDP per capita in the five economically similar countries with available data). Malawi has a very small university student population, which does not help reduce unit cost by economies of scale.

The total household spending on education is estimated to be 1.43 percent of the GDP (MK4.4 billion in 2004), a relatively low value when compared to the 2 percent of GDP average in SSA. Primary education is mostly funded by public resources (92 percent of the total cost), which is in line with the implementation of free primary education and the Millennium Development Goal (MDG). The cost-sharing structure between public and private funding is the same in higher education as in primary education with 92 percent of the financing coming from public resources. It raises an equity issue in the way education public resources are allocated because i) 90 percent of the students at higher education are from the wealthiest 20 percent of households (see Chapter 5), and ii) the students get very high level of private returns (salaries) when working after graduation (see Chapter 8). It would be relevant to discuss ways to progress towards a more equitable cost-sharing of the higher education service delivery.

* * *

This chapter analyzes and reviews recurrent and development expenditures in the education sector and is divided into six sections:

- Section I analyzes the 2007/08 total public recurrent expenditure for education activities, compares the budget priority for education with other countries, and presents the breakdown of recurrent expenditure by the nature of spending.
- Section II presents the breakdown of total public recurrent expenditure by level of schooling, its evolution from 1995/96 to 2007/08 and compares the 2007/08 situation with comparable countries.
- Section III analyzes recurrent unit costs by level of education and includes a comparative analysis of teachers' salaries.
- Section IV discusses household education financing by type of spending and by family level of income.
- Section V presents development partners for education expenditures.
- Section VI addresses school building costs.

Total Public Recurrent Expenditure for Education

Malawi's Budgetary System (with Adjustments Made for Analytical Purposes)

Education sector public expenditures fall into two categories: recurrent and development (or capital). The recurrent expenditures are financed by domestic revenues from taxes and non-tax sources and from budget support grants.

The development expenditures are financed by multilateral and/or bilateral loans or grants and from governments' own resource counterparts. In the Malawian budget typology, the recurrent expenditures are divided in two main categories: personal emolument (PE) and other recurrent transactions (ORT).

For analytical purposes, several adjustments have been made for analyzing expenditures in a more detailed way and for capturing all expenditures for education and training activities. The first type of adjustment was made to the different categories of recurrent expenditures. In order to get more details and to be more accurate, a thorough review was done of all budget lines by cost center for reallocating the different recurrent expenditures into four categories:

- personal expenditures;
- student welfare expenditures;
- subventions to institutions; and
- ORT.

It is important to note that leave grant/disturbance allowances have been subtracted from ORT and included in personal expenditures and that student welfare expenditure includes boarding expenses and student grants.

The second type of budget data adjustments captures all public expenditures for the education sector by including expenditures for education/training activities that are charged to ministries other than the Ministry of Education. Such is the case with:

- decentralized expenditures reported in the budget under city and district assemblies;
- early childhood development and literacy program expenditures that are charged under the Ministry of Women and Child Development;
- the subventions to public universities and to some other education or education-related institutions (other subvented organizations), as well as the student grants that are reported in the Ministry of Finance budget; and
- the public expenditures devoted to some vocational training institutions that are charged under different ministries, such as the Ministry of Agriculture or Ministry of Energy and Mines (the full list is presented in Appendix 3.2).

Share for Education in the Total Public Recurrent Expenditure and Comparison with Other Countries (2007/08)

The data presented are based on the 2007/08 revised estimates, which are more accurate than the 2007/08 approved budget and more recent than available data on actual expenditures.[1] When including all the expenses on education activities outside the Ministry of Education budget, the 2007/08 recurrent expenditures add up to MK22.3 billion, compared to MK14.5 billion when only counting the expenditure reported under the Ministry of Education (see table 3.1). This is a significant raise compared to 2001/02 (16 percent of total public recurrent expenditure and 3.7 percent of GDP), which shows an increase in the priority given to education in budget allocation. Nevertheless, it will be important to follow up in the coming years because the first data available for the 2008/09 budget seems to show a decrease from 2007/08.

Table 3.1 Education Public Recurrent Expenditure

	Ministry of Education Only	All Ministries with Education Activities
Education Recurrent Expenditure (MK millions)	14,520	22,311
as a % of total recurrent expenditure	12.6	19.4
as a % of GDP	3.1	4.8

Source: Calculations from the revised 07/08 Ministry of Finance budget

When compared to other SADC countries, Malawi positions itself as a median country in terms of budget priority for the education sector (see table 3.2). Out of the 12 countries with recent available data, Malawi ranks 6th for its share of recurrent expenditures devoted to education. Malawi is slightly below the SADC countries average (19.4 percent versus 20.8 percent) and the SSA average (20.3 percent). The budget priority for education in Malawi is still much smaller than what is observed in countries like Madagascar, Tanzania, Lesotho, or Kenya where the share for education is around 30 percent or above.

Table 3.2: Percentages for Education in Public Recurrent Expenditure, SADC countries

	Percentages for Education in Public Recurrent Expenditures
Lesotho	31.5
Tanzania	29.7
Madagascar	28.7
Botswana	27.6
Mozambique	25.6
Malawi	**19.4**
South Africa	18.6
Swaziland	17.7
Zambia	16.8
Seychelles	13.5
Mauritius	13.0
Congo, Dem. Rep.	7.1
Average SADC countries	**20.8**
Average SSA countries	**20.3**

Sources: Calculations from the revised 07/08 Ministry of Finance budget for Malawi and the World Bank for the other countries.
Note: Data are from 2008 or thereabouts.

Figure 3.1: Domestic Resources as a Percentage of GDP and Budget Allocation Towards Education, SSA Countries

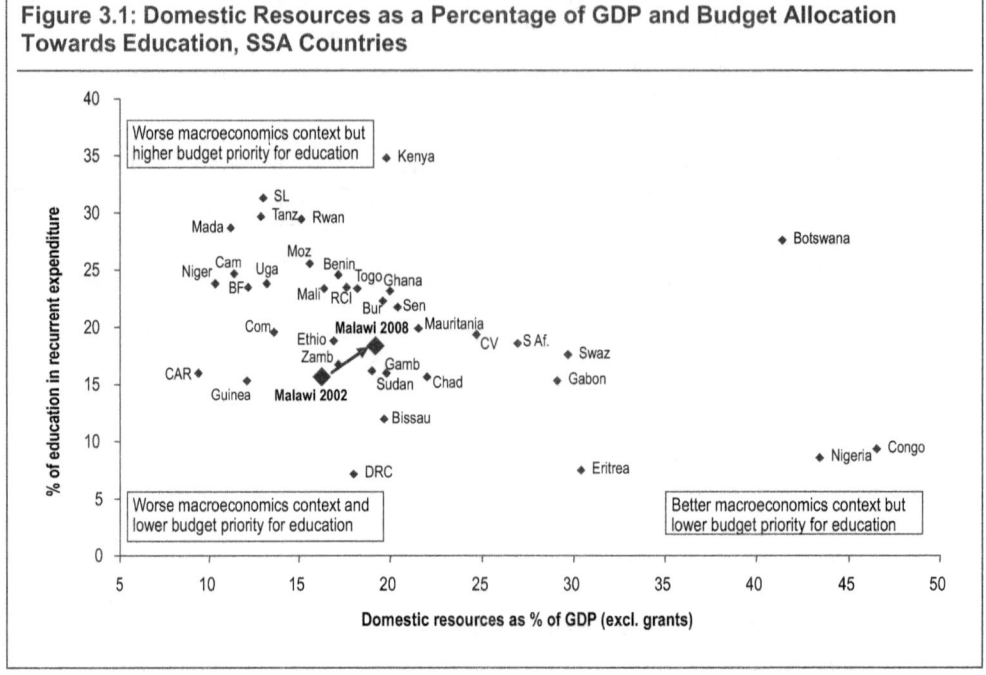

Sources: Calculations from the revised 07/08 Ministry of Finance budget and World Bank data.
Note: Data are from 2008 or thereabouts.

Figure 3.1 combines the data on domestic resources (as a percentage of GDP—described in Chapter 1 of this report) and on the share for education in recurrent expenditures for 37 African countries. If the two indicators are high, a country will have a good amount of resources for education activities. This is the ideal situation for all SSA countries.

Countries in the top-right quadrant of figure 3.1 have a good macroeconomic scenario and a high allocation of the total national budget towards education. The countries in the bottom-right quadrant have a better than average macroeconomic context but a lower than average allocation towards education. Countries situated in the top-left quadrant have a below-average macroeconomic context but a high allocation of the total national budget towards education. Countries in the bottom-left quadrant have both a below-average macroeconomic scenario and a below-average budget allocation towards education.

Although Malawi is progressing towards the average mark, which happens to be the point of intersection of the four quadrants, the country still falls into the bottom-left quadrant. This indicates that Malawi still needs to improve its macroeconomic condition and also allocate more of its total national budget towards education.

Decomposition of Total Public Recurrent Expenditure by Type of Spending

In addition to the information in section I.1 regarding data adjustments, it is important to note two additional methodological points on the following estimations. First, it appeared after cross-checking the budget data with the EMIS data that the salary of some secondary school teachers (those who have the certificate for normally teaching only in primary schools) was reported in the budget data under the primary education component instead of being included in the secondary education component.[2] Therefore, an adjustment has been made to reallocate those teachers' salaries under the secondary education component. The second methodological point relates to the administrative costs that cannot be primarily allocated to one single specific level of schooling (for example the expenditure of central level administration units). For analytic and comparative purposes, calculations have been done to make pro-rata distributions of this kind of expenditure across the different levels of schooling.[3]

With this done, the education public recurrent expenditures for financial year 2007/08 can be broken down into the four major functional groups (as described in section I.1) and by level of education. Table 3.3 shows the result of this breakdown.

In the education sector as a whole, the highest share of recurrent expenditures (70 percent) was allocated to personal expenditure while 24 percent of all recurrent expenditures went towards operating costs (for example, transport, travels, funerals allowance) or ORT. Student welfare and subventions to institutions together account for 6 percent of total recurrent expenditures.

A large share (58 percent) of the division's budget for ORT was passed on to teachers in the form of allowances and other subsidies such as coffins, while departments spent nearly their entire budget on transport costs, of which funeral use reportedly accounted for more than half of vehicle usage (Bellew, 2008). Coffins alone consumed an estimated 11 percent of the divisions' ORT budgets. Expenditures that directly benefit students, schools, and the community were a miniscule share of total expenditure and came mainly through donor-financed projects, such as the School Grant-Whole School Development pilot.

Table 3.3: Breakdown of Total Public Recurrent Expenditure by Nature of Spending and by Level of Education (in %)

	Teachers' Emolument	Non-Teachers' Emolument	ORT	Student Welfare (boarding, feeding, student loans)	Subventions to Institutions	Total
ECD	15		85	0	0	100
Literacy	74		26	0	0	100
Primary	82	1	16	0	0	100
Secondary	57	8	29	5	0	100
Teacher training	39		44	17	0	100
TEVET	43		43	5	9	100
Higher education	38	21	26	13	2	100%
Total (in %)	70		24	5	1	100
Total (Millions MK)	15,634		5,268	1,186	222	22,311

Source: Calculations from the revised 07/08 Ministry of Finance budget.

When analyzing the expenditure breakdown by level of education, the main findings are as follows:

- The public recurrent expenditures on ECD are mainly ORT (85 percent). This is consistent with the fact that this level receives a very low public allocation (see table 3.4).
- In the literacy and primary education sub-sectors, the largest share goes to PEs (74 percent and 83 percent, respectively) and only a minor share goes to ORT (26 percent and 16 percent, respectively).
- In secondary education, the breakdown is more balanced, with 65 percent for PE, 29 percent for ORT, and 5 percent for student welfare. The share for ORT being higher in secondary than in primary is consistent with reports on other countries. Secondary education needs more learning material per student than primary education does.
- In teacher training and TEVET, the share of expenditure for ORT is higher than in the other levels of education (44 percent and 43 Percent, respectively). In teacher education, 17 percent of recurrent expenditure goes to student welfare (5 percent in TEVET). More details on the financing and expenditure of TEVET can be found in Chapter 6.
- In higher education, 59 percent goes to PE, 26 percent to ORT, and 13 percent to student welfare. Comparative data are provided in Appendix 3.5 and a more detailed analysis of cost and financing of the higher education subsector is provided in Chapter 7.

Public Recurrent Expenditure by Level of Schooling

After analyzing the level of the education recurrent expenditure and its breakdown by type of spending, it is important to look at the distribution by level of schooling and compare it to other countries over time.

Distribution by Level of Schooling in 2007/08

Table 3.4 shows the situation in 2007/08 and points out the main findings:

- Primary education gets the largest share (44.2 percent) of public recurrent expenditures.
- The share for higher education (27 percent) is higher than that of secondary education (22 percent).
- The share of public recurrent resources allocated to teacher education, TEVET together with ECD and adult literacy does not exceed 7 percent when added together. In particular, ECD accounts for only 0.1 percent and Literacy for only 0.3 percent.

Table 3.4: Breakdown of Public Recurrent Expenditure (revised 07/08 budget) by level of Schooling

	Millions MK	Percentage
ECD	20	0.1
Literacy	61	0.3
Primary	9,857	44.2
Secondary	4,894	21.9
Teacher training	669	3.0
TEVET	760	3.4
Higher Education	6,050	27.1
Total	22,311	100.0

Source: Calculations from the revised 07/08 Ministry of Finance budget.

The Evolution of the Distribution by Level of Schooling

The comparison over time of the distribution by level of schooling is not easy due to the absence of data for the fiscal years previous to 2007/08. Nevertheless, estimates of the distribution of recurrent expenditure for the five main levels of schooling (primary, secondary, teacher training, TEVET, and higher education) have been done for 1996/97, 1999/2000, and 2002/03.[4] Trends of recurrent and development expenditure for ECD and literacy are provided in Appendix 3.3.

The main findings for the evolution of the breakdown of expenditure by level of schooling (see figure 3.2) are as follows:

- The budget priority for primary education has been decreasing during the 1996–2008 period, going from 52 percent of the total education recurrent spending in 1996 to 44 percent in 2008.

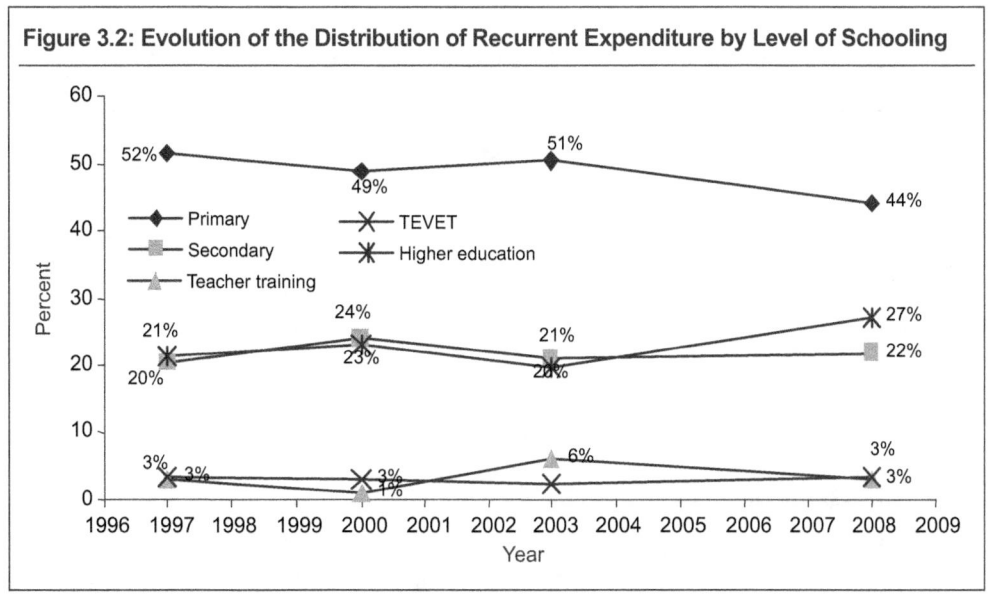

Figure 3.2: Evolution of the Distribution of Recurrent Expenditure by Level of Schooling

Source: Calculations from the Ministry of Finance.

- The decrease of the primary education share benefited higher education, whose share increased from 21 percent in 1996 to 27 percent in 2008.
- The share allocated for the three other main levels of schooling (secondary, TEVET, and teacher training) remained more or less constant during the considered period.

Comparison with Other African Countries

Calibration of Expenditure Data by Level of Education

For comparative purposes, some data adjustments are again needed. Primary education in Malawi (eight grades) is longer than the most common primary duration in other African countries (six grades). And inversely, the duration of secondary education in Malawi (four grades) is shorter than the most common duration for secondary in other African countries (seven grades). Therefore, for comparative purposes, calculations have calibrated what would be the share of expenditures for both primary and secondary education if the duration were six and seven grades, respectively. Details of the calibration methodology are provided in Appendix 3.4.

Cross-Country Comparison

With those adjustments it is possible to compare the breakdown by level of schooling. The three main levels of schooling are primary (including teacher training expenditure to train primary teachers), secondary (including TEVET), and higher education. Table 3.5 shows the comparative data.

The following two main observations emerge: Malawi's allocation of recurrent expenditure to primary education is one of the lowest compared to other SSA countries and the SADC average. And compared to other countries, Malawi prioritizes secondary and higher education above primary education when making recurrent allocations.

Table 3.5: Distribution of Recurrent Expenditure by Level of Schooling, SADC Countries, (2008 or last year available)

	% Primary (calibrated to 6 grades)	% Secondary (calibrated to 7 grades)	% Higher Education
Madagascar	59.2	24.4	16.5
Namibia	55.4	35.9	8.7
Ethiopia	54.9	26.1	18.9
Mozambique	48.0	30.0	21.9
Zambia	45.6	35	19.4
Botswana	43.7	37.7	18.6
Malawi	**32.5**	**40.4**	**27.1**
Congo, Dem Rep. of	32.2	34.9	32.8
Swaziland	22.6	51.9	25.5
Average SADC countries	**43.8**	**35.1**	**21.0**
Average SSA	**44.4**	**34.4**	**21.2**

Sources: Calculations from the revised 07/08 Ministry of Finance budget and World Bank data.

Comparisons of the Priority to Primary Education When Taking into Account the Level of Development towards the MDG

To enhance sound policy dialogue, it is important to contextualize the comparison with other countries by taking into account the differences across countries in achieving universal primary completion.

Countries that are closer towards achieving universal primary completion should allocate a bigger proportion of their education expenditure to post-primary education. The demand for secondary and higher education in those countries is greater than it is in countries that are further from universal primary completion.

Inversely, it is logical that countries that struggle with universal primary education should prioritize finances for the primary level; achieving the MDG is the first priority and the demand for post-primary education is smaller (and so less demanding financially) than in countries with a more advanced education system.

Figure 3.3 shows the relationship between the primary completion rate (calibrated to six grades for comparative purposes) and the share of primary education in education expenditure (calibrated to six grades, as well). Globally, countries less advanced in terms of primary education put on average a higher share of their spending into primary education. Nevertheless, there are a lot of disparities around this correlation and Malawi's is particularly interesting.

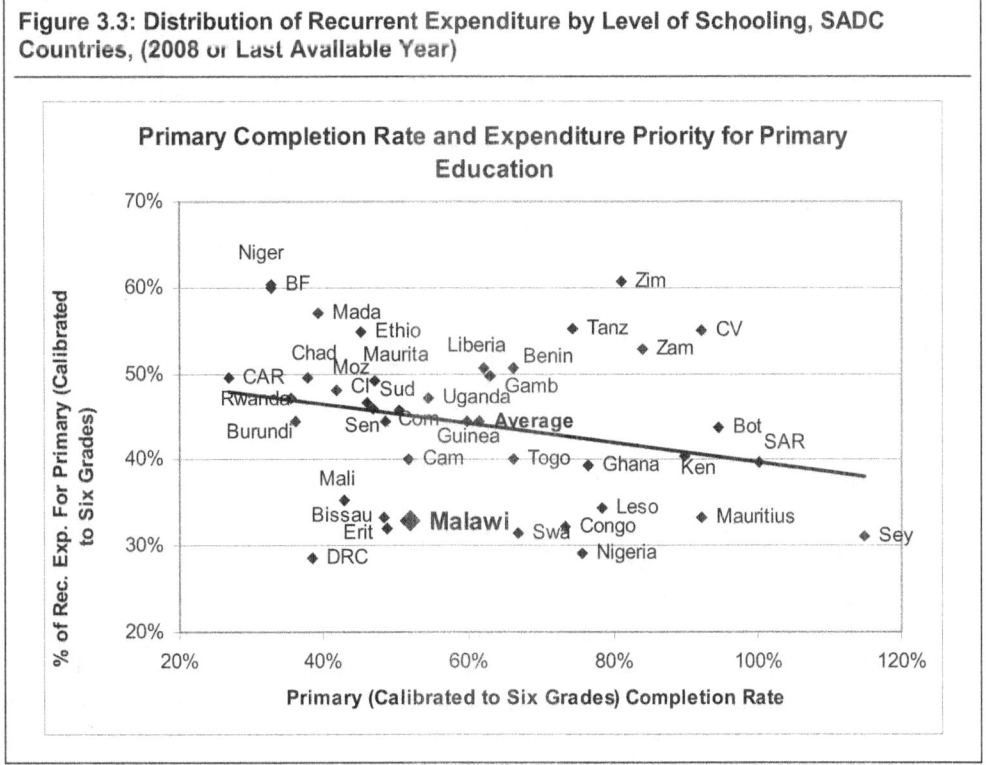

Figure 3.3: Distribution of Recurrent Expenditure by Level of Schooling, SADC Countries, (2008 or Last Available Year)

Sources: Calculations from the revised 07/08 Ministry of Finance budget and World Bank data.

Compared to countries with a similar primary completion rate (52 percent when calibrated to six grades), the share of expenditure devoted to primary education is particularly low in Malawi. The data suggest that finding ways to increase future resources for primary education (even more than the resources for the other levels) would be useful.

Public Recurrent Unit Costs by Level of Schooling

Public Recurrent Unit Costs and Comparisons over Time

Public recurrent unit costs are calculated by dividing the public recurrent expenditure devoted to each level by the number of students in public schools and institutions enrolled in the same level. They are interpreted as the average cost per student for one year of schooling.

Table 3.6 shows the recurrent unit costs, including administrative costs, for the seven levels of education using 2007/08 revised recurrent budget figures and the 2007 EMIS enrollment in public schools. The costs are expressed in MK and in terms of the percentage of GDP per capita. For comparing trends over time, the values in 2000 (from the first CSR done in Malawi) are also reported.

Box 3.1: Why Use the Reference to GDP Per Capita?

The reference to GDP (Gross Domestic Product) per capita is very important because it leads to thinking about cost in terms of sustainability. The GDP per capita is an estimate of the average wealth produced by a Malawian. As an example, if a year of study for one person costs 50 percent of GDP per capita, it means that the cost of one year of study is equivalent to half the average Malawian annual production (value of his work). Also, if a teacher's salary is five units of GDP per capita, then the production of five average Malawians is needed to pay this teacher's salary. The reference to GDP per capita gives costs of education service delivery (and in particular recurrent costs, meaning repeated annual costs) related to the domestic annual resources available in the country. Because the bulk of recurrent expenditure is paid by domestic resources, the reference to GDP per capita is key for thinking about education expansion in a sustainable way.

Another advantage of using finance indicators in reference to GDP per capita is for making comparisons. The use of the GDP per capita reference allows comparisons between countries that do not use the same currency. Nevertheless, the countries compared should have similar GDP per capita.

The main findings from table 3.6 are as follows:

1. In primary education, per-student public recurrent expenditure is MK3,019. In GDP per capita, this unit cost has doubled since 2000.
2. The public recurrent unit cost at the secondary level is ten times higher than at the primary level. In terms of GDP per capita, it has grown four times larger since 2000. It is worth noting that there are huge disparities between CDSS and CSS unit costs. Full unit costs has not been separately calculated for those two types of secondary schools but the information from EMIS indicates that the government grant received by CSS is much higher on average than the one received by CDSS (see Chapter 4 for details).

Table 3.6: Public Recurrent Unit Costs by Level of Schooling

	2007					2000
	Students (in public institutions)	Public Recurrent Expenditure (MK million)	Public Recurrent Unit cost (MK)	As % of GDP Per Capita	As a Multiple of Primary Education	As % of GDP Per Capita
ECD (level 2)	287,206	20	69	0.20	0.02	n.a.
Literacy	128,967	61	476	1.3	0.16	n.a.
Primary	3,264,594	9,857	3,019	8.3	1	4
Secondary	161,575	4,894	30,292	83	10	21
TEVET (technical colleges)	4,807	247	51,408	141	17	n.a.
TEVET (technical colleges with only residential students)	1,810	247	136,529	376	45	355
Teacher training	6,029	669	110,905	305	37	n.a.
Higher education	7,700	6,010	780,479	2,147	259	1,489

Sources: Calculations from the revised 07/08 Ministry of Finance budget; EMIS data.

3. One year of study in TEVET costs 17 times the primary level unit cost (and 45 times the primary level unit if "parallel" students are not taken into account). It has stayed more or less stable since 2000 in GDP per capita.
4. The per student recurrent costs for teacher training is 305 percent of GDP per capita and 37 times the primary level unit cost.
5. The higher education recurrent unit cost is very high (21.5 times the GDP per capita) and has increased a lot since 2000. The public annual cost of one student in a public university is equivalent to the public annual cost of 259 primary level students. The small number of students in Malawi (see chapters 2 and 7) does not help for having economies of scale and constitutes one of the main reasons why the unit cost is so high. Other reasons that explain the high public unit cost of higher education are explained in this section of the chapter and in Chapter 7.
6. Public unit costs for ECD and adult literacy are negligible when compared with the other levels of education.

Comparison of Public Recurrent Unit Costs with Other African Countries

Table 3.7 compares public primary and secondary unit costs in Malawi with other SADC countries. In primary education, Malawi and Zambia are the SADC countries with the lowest unit cost in GDP per capita. With 8 percent of GDP per capita, Malawi is much lower than both the SADC average (12 percent) and the SSA average (11 percent).

In secondary education, the reverse is true: Malawi shows the highest unit cost among all SADC countries with available data. The Malawian secondary public unit cost is more than two times higher than SADC and SSA averages.

In higher education, the comparison with other African countries is similar to what can be observed in secondary education. The Malawian unit cost is highest among all African countries (see figure 3.4), with a unit cost 6.8 times higher than the SSA average (314 percent of GDP per capita). The very high unit cost at this level of education is partly due to the fact that the number of higher education students is very small in Malawi compared to the other countries.

Table 3.7: Primary and Secondary Public Recurrent Unit Costs, SADC Countries (2007 or last year available)

	Public Recurrent Unit Cost in Primary Education (in % of GDP per capita)	Public Recurrent Unit Cost in Secondary Education (in % of GDP per capita)
Botswana	n.a.	41
Congo, Dem. Rep. of	15	n.a
Lesotho	18	50
Madagascar	9	13
Malawi	8	83
Mauritius	9	17
Mozambique	9	75
Namibia	21	22
Seychelles	n.a	17
South Africa	14	17
Swaziland	11	44
Tanzania	12	n.a
Zambia	7	8
Zimbabwe	13	21
SADC average	12	34
SSA average	11	30

Sources: Calculations from the revised 07/08 Ministry of Finance budget and World Bank data.

Figure 3.4: Higher Education Public Recurrent Unit Costs, Sub-Saharan Countries (2007 or last year available)

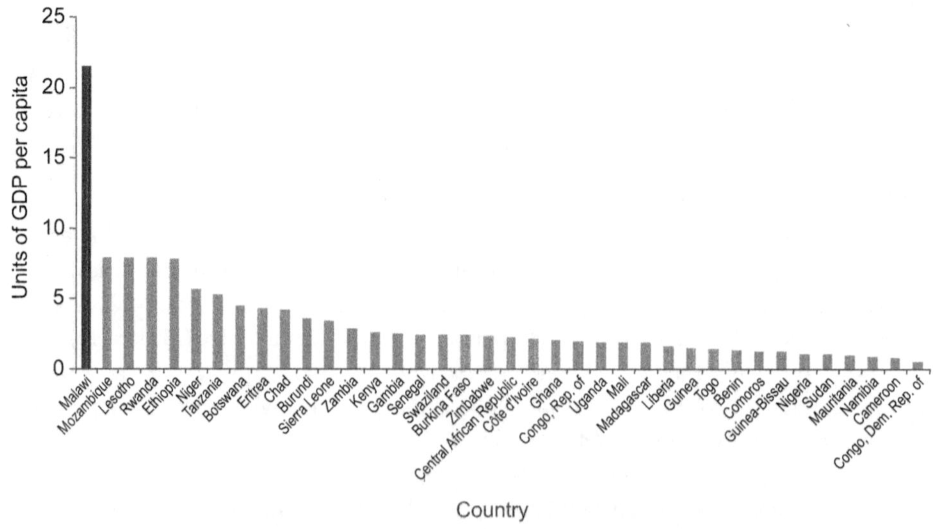

Source: Calculations from the revised 07/08 Ministry of Finance budget and World Bank data.

Factors Affecting the Public Unit Costs and Comparisons

Three main factors affect the level of unit costs:

- teachers' salaries,
- the student-teacher ratio (the lower the student-teacher ratio the higher the unit cost), and
- recurrent expenditures other than teachers' salaries (for example, personal, ORT, and salaries of non-teachers).

Teachers' Salaries

The annual average salary of a primary school teacher in 2007 was MK195,000; this is 5.8 times Malawi's GDP per capita. The annual average salary of a secondary school teacher was MK350,000, which is 9.8 times the GDP per capita. In 2008, after the salary increase and the implementation of the new salary scale, the average annual salaries were estimated at 6.3 and 11.6 units of GDP per capita, respectively. The salaries vary widely across categories of teachers within the same level of teaching (see Appendix 3.6 for detailed data).

When the annual average primary and secondary school teachers' salaries are compared with other SSA countries with similar GDP per capita (see figure 3A.1 in Appendix 3.1), the data show that Malawi's teachers are paid above the average for both primary (an average of 4 units of GDP per capita) and secondary (an average of 8.5 units of GDP per capita) levels. As a reference point for primary education, the EFA-FTI benchmark for teacher salaries (calculated as the average observed in the countries closest to achieving universal primary completion) is 3.5 times GDP per capita.

In higher education, Malawi looks like an outlier: The average annual teachers' salary is 66 units of GDP per capita, which is 2.7 times higher than the average in economically similar countries with the same information (see table 3.8).

Table 3.8: Higher Education Teachers' Average Salary, as Units of GDP Per Capita for Countries with GDP per Capita Lower than US$500 (2007 or last year available)

	Average Teachers' Salaries in Higher Education as Units of GDP Per Capita
Congo, Dem. Rep. of	4.1
Guinea	10.3
Mali	12.1
Madagascar	12.8
Malawi	**65.8**
Ethiopia	27.1
Burundi	37.2
Average 7 countries	**24.2**

Sources: Chapter 7 and World Bank data.

Student-Teacher Ratios

The second factor that affects the level of unit cost is the student-teacher ratio. The very low unit cost for primary education in Malawi is mainly explained by this factor. With a student-teacher ratio in government-funded schools of 80:1, Malawi has one of the highest values in Africa, equal to twice the SADC average (41:1). In contrast, the student-teacher ratio of 20:1 in secondary is very low compared to other countries (the SSA average is 28:1) and contributes significantly to the high unit costs. Higher education is similar with a ratio of 11:1 for Malawi and an average of 20:1 for the SSA (see table 3.9 and Chapter 7 for more details).

Table 3.9: Student-Teacher Ratios in Public Schools, 2007

	Primary Education	Secondary Education	Higher Education
Malawi	80	20	11
SADC average	41	22	17
SSA average	45	28	20

Sources: Chapter 4, Chapter 7, and World Bank data.

Recurrent Expenditure Excluding Teachers' Salaries (Primary Education)

The third main factor affecting the unit cost is the remaining recurrent expenditure excluding teachers' salaries. For this indicator, only primary-level data is available for comparison with other countries. As previously noted, expenditures for spending outside of salaries are very small in Malawi. Out of all African countries with available data, Malawi has the fourth lowest share for this type of spending (see figure 3A.2 in Appendix 3.1). In addition to the high pupil-teacher ratio, this factor contributes to the low unit cost observed in primary education in Malawi.

Household Financing

Total Household Education Expenditure and Comparisons

The household education expenditure includes both the monetary (for example, fees and other financial contributions by parents) and non-monetary support that communities are encouraged to contribute for rehabilitating schools and other building projects. According to the 2004 Integrated Household Survey, Malawi's total household spending on education is estimated at MK4.4 billion, which is 1.43 percent of GDP.

Compared to other African countries with available data, Malawi is the in the middle in terms of household contribution to education (in 9 countries the contribution as a percentage of GDP is lower than in Malawi and in eight other countries it is higher). Malawi's contribution is slightly lower than the average calculated on the 18 African countries with available data (1.4 percent of GDP vs. 2 percent, see figure 3A.3 in Appendix 3.1).

Compared to other African countries, the share of education to total household expenditures in Malawi is in the bottom half (see figure 3A.4 in Appendix 3.1). The share of education expenditures accounts for only 1.7 percent of total household expenditures, compared to an SSA average of 3.6 percent. This is likely related to the fact that for many poor households there is very little money left after subsistence spending (in particular, for food). It is noteworthy that countries such as Benin, Cameroon, or Côte d'Ivoire are richer and have a larger number of households that find it easier to save money for spending beyond subsistence.

Household Expenditure by Level of Education and Comparison with the Public Expenditure

Household Unit Costs by Level of Education

As table 3.10 shows, almost half of total household education expenditure goes to secondary education and 20 percent goes to preschool. The share of household education expenditure that goes to primary education—the level that enrolls a majority of the students—is only 17 percent. (In Malawi, primary education has been free since 1994 and this partly explains the lower share for that level.)

Table 3.10: Estimated Breakdown of the Household Expenditure by Level of Education and Household Unit Costs, 2007

	Share of the Total Education Household Expenditure (%)	Household Unit Cost (Per Student) in MK	Household Unit Cost (Per Student) as % of GDP Per Capita
Preschool	20	1,980	5.4
Primary	17	252	0.7
Secondary	44	9,925	27.3
TEVET*	8	34,444	94.8
Higher education*	11	63,725	175.3

Source: Estimates for 2007 based on IHS-2 2004.
*Estimates for TEVET and higher education should be taken with caution because they are based on a small number of individuals in the household survey.

Consequently the household expenditure per student is very low in the primary level. Nevertheless, students still state that lack of money is one of the main reasons for dropping out of primary school (see Chapter 2, table 2.9) and it is worth noting that for the poorest families the indirect costs of education (such as uniforms and contributions) are likely to still be too high.

Higher education accounts for the highest household expenditure per student, as shown in table 3.10. This is mainly due to fees (see Chapter 7, table 7.4 for details). There are also school fees in secondary education. The average household spending per junior secondary school student (forms 1–2) is half that allocated to a senior secondary school student (form 3–4).

For all levels of schooling, the average annual spending per student is higher in the urban regions than in the rural regions.

Comparisons of Public and Private Financing by Level of Education

To enhance sound policy dialogue on the allocation of additional public resources for the education sector, it is beneficial to analyze the structure of cost-sharing between public and private resources by education level. This analysis (see figure 3.5) suggests very interesting findings:

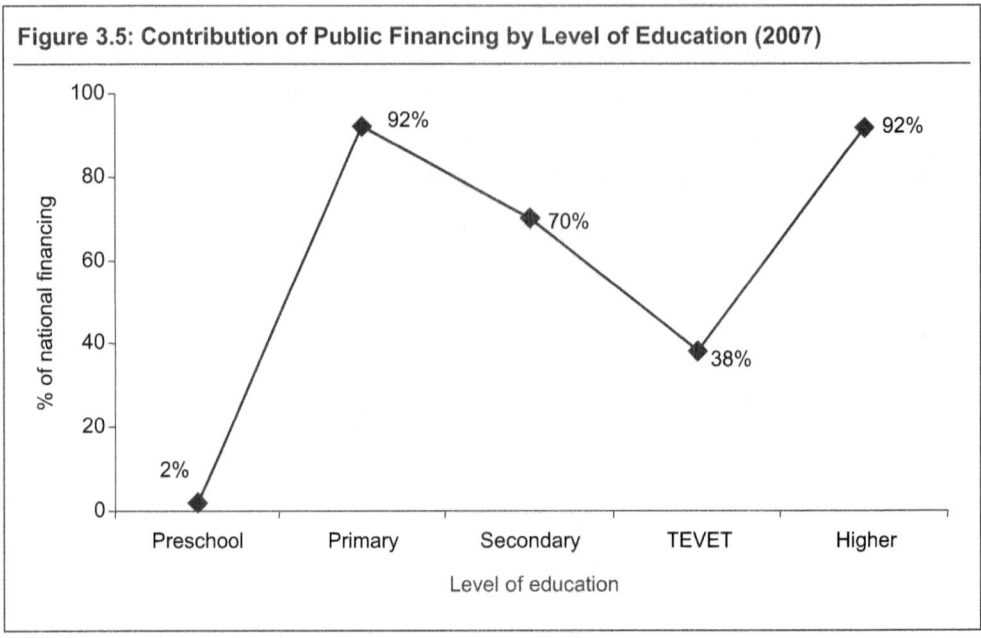

Figure 3.5: Contribution of Public Financing by Level of Education (2007)

Sources: Tables 3.4 and 3.7.

1. The share of public funding for preschool is negligible (2 percent), which is consistent with the observation that the share of ECD in the public recurrent education expenditure is only 0.1 percent (see section II.1).
2. Primary education is mostly funded by public resources (92 percent of the total recurrent cost), which is in line with the free policy at this level and the government's goal to achieve the education MDG.
3. Household contributions for the delivery of secondary education account for 30 percent of the total recurrent cost. This is lower than what can be observed on average in Africa (44 percent) and probably due to the higher public contribution to secondary education in Malawi than in most African countries and that the relative poverty of Malawian households.
4. In higher education, the cost-sharing structure between public and private funding is the same as in primary education, with 92 percent of the financing coming from public resources. This raises an equity issue in the way education public resources are allocated. Students in higher education are almost all from the wealthiest income quintiles of the country (see Chapter 5) and investment returns in higher education are mainly private, which results in much better salaries for university graduates than for individuals who drop out (see Chapter 8). It would be relevant to address this issue and discuss ways to reach a more equitable cost-sharing of the higher education service delivery. As stated in the Malawi Growth and Development Strategy MGDS, higher education is an important pillar for contributing to economic growth, in particular in the context of competition with neighboring SADC countries that have more developed higher education systems. Then, public financing of higher education makes sense to a certain extent.

5. Nevertheless, international research shows that for the poorest countries primary education is the level of education that contributes most to economic growth.[5] Consequently, primary education has a greater legitimacy to be seen as a "public good" for which government involvement is crucial.
6. Ultimately, it is a question of going towards the right balance of public-private cost sharing. In terms of scarcity of resources, a high level of public financing for higher education should not exist at the detriment of primary education, where unit costs are so low that they impede student retention and learning achievements, which are important drivers of economic growth.

Decomposition of Household Education Expenditure by Type of Spending

Out of the total MK4.4 billion that households spend annually for education in Malawi, the largest share goes to tuition (58 percent). School uniforms account for 10 percent of the spending, boarding school fees for 9.6 percent and school books (and other learning materials) for 8.3 percent. Table 3.11 shows the percentages allocated to each of the different categories.

Table 3.11: Decomposition of Household Education Expenditure (in %)

Type of Spending	% of total
Tuition (including any extra tuition fees)	58.1
School books and other materials	8.3
School uniform clothing	10.0
Boarding school fees	9.6
Contribution for school building or maintenance	2.6
Parent association & other school related fees	0.9
Other expenses	10.6
Total	100.0

Source: IHS-2 2004.

For comparative purposes, it is necessary to reclassify household education expenditures into three broad categories: "Tuition," "School Books and Other Materials," and "Other Education Expenses." Using these three categories, it is possible to better understand how Malawian households prioritize their expenditures compared to households in other countries. Table 3.12 shows a cross-country comparison among 12 African countries. Malawi's household allocations to tuition and other education expenses are slightly above the cross-country average while inversely, the allocations to school books and other materials are below average.

These findings are consistent with the high allocation in Malawi. The number of pupils taking tutoring increased from 22 percent in 1998 to 80 percent in 2005 (Bellew, 2008). It illustrates the increasing loss of trust families have in the quality of education and emphasizes the need for improving this quality (see Chapter 4 for analytical inputs that should lead to policy reforms meant to improve the quality of learning).

Table 3.12: Cross-country Comparison of Distribution of Household Education Expenditure

Country	Tuition	School Books/Other Materials	Other Education Expenses
Benin	48.4	37.2	14.4
Burkina Faso	63.7	29.4	6.9
Cameroon	45.7	37.4	16.9
Côte d'Ivoire	36.3	40.1	23.6
Madagascar	33.6	30.9	35.5
Malawi	**59.0**	**18.2**	**22.8**
Mauritania	37.8	37.2	25.0
Niger	48.9	38.2	12.9
Uganda	73.0	13.3	13.7
Sierra Leone	20.9	48.5	30.6
Tanzania	62.4	26.4	11.2
Togo	53.4	37.8	8.8
Average	**48.6**	**32.9**	**18.5**

Sources: IHS-2 2004 and F. Ndem, Education Household Expenditure, Senegal: Pôle de Dakar, 2008.

Household Education Expenditure According to Family Income

The information on family income in the IHS 2004 survey enables comparisons of the priority given to education expenditure according to family income quintiles. As presented in table 3.13, in Malawi the share of spending that a household allocates to education increases according to the economic status of the household. On average, the 20 percent richest households allocate 2.8 percent of their total spending to education. This is nine times higher than the proportion that the poorest 20 percent allocate to education (0.3 percent of their total expenditure).

Table 3.13: Share of Education in Household Expenditure by Quintile of Household Income

Household Income Quintile	Share of Education in Total Household Spending (in %)
Q1 (20% poorest)	0.31
Q2	0.53
Q3	0.64
Q4	0.90
Q5 (20% richest)	2.84

Source: IHS-2 2004.

As noted before when comparing countries, the poorest households cannot afford education spending that is proportionate to the wealthiest households because they need to first pay for subsistence (in particular, for food). This is consistent with the fact that non-schooling and dropping out are mainly an issue of lack of demand (see Chapter 2) and that lack of demand is exacerbated by poverty. In the coming years, it will be interesting to follow up with the findings of the Zomba Cash Conditional transfers pilot project for girls in school (or who dropped out school during the last three years). The preliminary results of this pilot project show that stimulating the demand for schooling by subsidizing young women could lead to a dramatic increase in retention rates and cause girls who have dropped out of school to return.

Donor Financing for the Education Sector (2005–2008)

In the government budget typology, development (or capital) expenditures are classified in two parts: Development Part 1 and Part 2. Part 1 is expenditures from multilateral and bilateral donors' grants and loans. Part 2 is the government's own development expenditures. Few donors use the government's "Integrated Financial Management System" (IFMIS) to process their expenditures. Of the ten major education donors (DFID, USAID, KFW & GTZ, World Bank, CIDA, SIDA, JICA, PLAN INTERNATIONAL, Action Aid, and UNICEF), only the expenditures from UNICEF and the counterpart contribution of Malawi's government to multilateral loans pass through IFMIS. Government literature is not consistent in the way that it documents donor contributions to education. In some years, the expenditures of donors who do not use the IFMIS are included (for instance in 2007/08), while in other years (for instance 2008/09) they are. Therefore, the variations in Development Part I are not accurate and could miss the true picture of the actual changes in capital expenditures. In order to get a better idea of donor activities in the education sector, our analysis used data from a survey conducted by the DFID.

Donor contributions play a critical role in the development budget of the government. On average, their contribution amounts to 86 percent of the total development budget. Over 60 percent of donor support to education goes towards construction in primary education. In both 2005/06 and 2006/07 about 63 percent was committed to the construction of primary schools (66 percent in 2007/08). The commitment towards secondary education is very low, even if it has increased from 1 percent of total donors financing in 2005/06 to 3 percent in 2007/08. This increase is due to the current African Development Bank project, which has focused on improvements in secondary education. Universities have received very little official development assistance in the recent past (1 percent in 2005/06) and none in 2006/07 and 2007/08.

Table 3.14: Donor Financing and Extra Budgetary Grants to Education (MK Millions)

Level of Education	Objective of Assistance	Committed 05/06	Disbursed 05/06	Committed 06/07	Disbursed 06/07	Committed 07/08
General	General	3,973	1,650	2,619	2,224	2,113
	TA and Other	396	243	387	270	460
Primary	Construction	608	599	916	739	1,618
	Curriculum and books	1,343	931	2,346	1,557	1,346
	PRESET	1,092	409	616	510	792
	School feeding	1,335	1,261	1,428	1,406	1,685
Secondary	PRESET	40	40	33	30	290
Higher	Universities	30	30,45	—	—	—
Total		8,818	5,163	8,346	6,737	8,303

Source: DFID.

Comparisons of School Construction Costs

Unit classroom construction costs for primary school do not vary greatly. For the purposes of comparison of the unit construction costs in Malawi, table 3.12 provides various donors' unit costs (net). Most donors build a single classroom for about US$7–8,000 (excluding the contingencies and supervision fees customarily added to the construction budget). When furnishing is added, the cost of a classroom increases to around US$8,500–10,000 million. The difference in cost from one donor to the next is fairly moderate; this may be an indication of a good level of coordination of construction standards for primary schools in Malawi. It should be noted that the construction of an entire school often includes various site works, such as the construction of an administration block, a borehole, and latrines (this may vary from donor to donor). The greatest variation in unit construction cost is in the cost of a teacher's house.

Only MASAF (Malawi Social Action Fund) has provided a unit classroom cost lower than this range: The MASAF classroom unit cost is US$5,000 for an unfurnished classroom and US$7,000 for a furnished one. The difference between MASAF and other donors' costs is likely due to a greater community input in the MASAF school construction, but it would be useful to further explore the cost differential and undergo a deeper analysis that takes into account the life expectancy of the different constructions. Unfortunately, data gathered within the CSR process did not permit this analysis.

Table 3.15: Unit Construction Costs in Primary School Construction (US$)

Donor/Program	Per Classroom (rural)	3-Bedroom Teacher's House	Furnishing of 1 Classroom	Furnished classroom
DFID	7,115	10,000	1,625	8,740
EU/Micro-projects	7,600	16,800	1,600	9,200
PLAN INTERNATIONAL	8,600	14,400	1,850	10,450
UNICEF	7,749			
WB/MASAF	5,035	9,143	1,921	6,956

Source: Ministry of Education, Science and Technology.

Notes

[1] There are differences between approved, revised budgets and actual expenditures that span 2–3 years for the same fiscal year. While revised estimates tend to be higher than the approved amounts, actual expenditures usually lie (but not always) in between the approved budget and the revised estimate.

[2] In the central western division, the misreporting of secondary teachers with a primary teaching certificate is great. The personal emolument reported in budget data under secondary education is only MK6.1 million, while the estimate done with EMIS data is MK688 million.

[3] The pro-rata distribution key is calculated on all the spending devoted to one single level of schooling, which is a common technique in education economics.

[4] Caution should be used when discussing the data for those years as the estimates are not as solid as they are for the 2007/08 year.

[5] For the middle-income countries, the best contributor to economic growth is secondary education and for the high income countries, the best one is higher education. See for instance,

UNESCO BREDA, *Education for All in Africa: Top Priority for Integrated Sector-Wide Policies*, Dakar+7: UNESCO, Dakar 2007 and also B. Foko and M. Brossard, Couverture scolaire des années 1970 et impacts sur la croissance entre 1970 et 2003, UNESCO-BREDA, Document de travail du Pôle de Dakar (www.poledakar.org), 2007.

CHAPTER 4

Internal Efficiency, Learning Outcomes, and Management Issues

Summary of the Chapter

Internal efficiency coefficient (IEC) at the primary level remained particularly low in 2007 (35 percent), which implies that 65 percent of public resources are lost due to repetition and dropouts before cycle completion. Currently, the system requires 23 student-years to produce one graduate, instead of 8 years with perfect internal efficiency. The situation has worsened slightly since 1999, when the IEC was 39 percent. An increase in repetition is mainly responsible for this degradation. However, high dropout rates have the greatest adverse effect on the internal efficiency of the system. At the secondary level, internal efficiency is slightly better, with an index of 55.4 in 2007. Yet, the situation has significantly deteriorated over the period from 1999–2006. Inefficiencies resulting from repetition remained low over the period (5–6 percent). Major problems came from dropouts, which alone led to a 29 percent waste of public resources in 2007. Much gain in internal efficiency could be realized from a reduction in dropouts and repetitions.

Repetition rates have increased over the 1999–2006 period and are now 20 percent in primary education—a level that is the highest in the region. Yet, evidence at the national and international level, shows that such high repetition rates do not favor a better mastery of learning and have adverse effects on student-teacher ratios, retention, and costs.

Malawi is offering poor and deteriorating quality education in primary schools, as can be concluded by the Southern African Consortium for Monitoring Educational Quality (SACMEQ) scores and national examination pass rates. The percentage of children who reached a minimum level of mastery in reading in English has been reduced by half over the 1998–2004 period, and was barely 9 percent in 2004. In mathematics, 98 percent of the students did not possess skills beyond basic numeracy and none of them had skills beyond competent numeracy. Compared to other countries, Malawi fares poorly, being at the bottom of all the SACMEQ countries in English reading and next to last in mathematics. There is a strong need to further investigate those results and better understand why competency levels are so poor and have fallen over the last past years.

Failure rates in national examinations vary from 74 percent for the PSLE, 62 percent for the JCE, and 44 percent for the MSCE. The low achievement in the MSCE is striking and raises serious issues about the skill level acquired throughout the schooling system. At the secondary level, poorer outcomes are associated mainly with CDSSs.

At the primary level, high STRs are associated with lower PSLE pass rates, as well as overlapping shifts, whereas school facilities tend to have a positive impact. At the secondary level, teacher characteristics have a major impact on MSCE pass rates: While female teachers tend to perform better (all other things being equal), PT4 to PT1 teachers fare less well than their better-qualified peers, as MSCE holders fare less well than higher education graduates.

Malawi is characterized by a severe lack of teachers at the primary level, as illustrated by its high STR of 80:1 in 2007. The concomitant increase in student enrollment and pupil retention and the reduction in teachers have led to a deterioration of the STR; this was 63:1 in 2000. However, the recruitment of volunteer teachers has been somewhat able to ease the pressure (reducing the STR from 86:1 to 80:1). This is in sharp contrast to what can be found at the secondary level, where STRs stood at 20:1 in 2007—one of the lowest levels in Africa.

Teacher qualification still remains a major challenge, both at primary and secondary levels. Although the situation has improved in primary schools, the student-to-qualified-teacher Ratio (SqTR) is still high—currently reduced to 88:1 from a level of 118:1 in 1999. The ministry's training efforts over the last years need to be pursued to significantly improve the situation. At the secondary level, more than 60 percent of teachers are underqualified, with a SqTR ratio of 51:1. Most of the underqualified teachers work in CDSSs— 81 percent of their teaching force is unqualified compared to 27 percent in CSSs.

Improvement in the administrative management of human resources at the primary level will be crucial. The degree of randomness for primary teacher allocation is somewhat high, 42 percent in 2007 (against 35 percent in 2000), well above the average observed in a sample of African countries (31 percent). This means that 42 percent of the allocation of teachers is explained by factors other than the number of students enrolled in the school. The situation is different from that of secondary schools; teacher deployment across public schools is fairly consistent as indicated by the value of R^2 of 72 percent. This is a sharp improvement on the situation in 2000, where 41 percent of teacher deployment variation was explained by school size. Yet, there remains room for improvement throughout the system, 28 percent of teacher allocation still depends on factors other than the number of students enrolled in each school.

Teacher allocation across location and divisions/districts is quite uneven, with their deployment highly skewed toward urban zones (46:1 against 86:1 in rural areas). At the division level, the STR ranges from 66:1 in the Northern division to 104:1 in the Shire Highlands division. Teacher deployment shows even more disparities when qualified teachers are taken into account. Their allocation has benefited urban settings (47:1), leaving rural areas seriously deprived of qualified teachers (95:1). This highlights the challenges of having teachers work and remain in rural settings.

Globally, CDSSs are less well resourced than other schools, although they enroll nearly half of the secondary student population. They generally are underfunded, staffed by underqualified teachers, have a poorer learning environment, and lack appropriate teaching and learning materials and equipment.

While economies of scale are modest in primary schools, they are quite important at the secondary level. This is very much related to student-teacher ratios and school size. The average number of students in secondary schools is relatively low at 212, but it reaches 642 pupils in primary schools. Scale economies are possible at the secondary level by favoring *bigger* schools of more than 150 students and increasing the PTR level.

Finally, there is a particularly weak relationship at the school level between national examination pass rate results and spending per pupil (at primary and secondary levels). This raises questions about the underlying process that transforms resources into learning achievement. Beyond the issue of resource allocation, the way they are used seems to be a major influence on the level of learning outcome. Improving supervision and accountability mechanisms at the local level are known to be effective interventions.

* * *

It is important that all children have access to and remain in school, but it is equally crucial that those enrolled acquire the relevant human capital and cognitive skills. This raises the issue of the quality of the education services being offered, which needs to be considered along with the efficient use of education resources. A given education system needs to have a maximum number of students reach the end of the cycle (rather than dropping out) in a minimum amount of time (by repeating as little as possible).

There are many ways to organize the education process for a given level of resources per student. For classroom organization, a school can have 40 or 60 students per classroom and offer or not offer multi-grade classes or double-shifting courses. A school may recruit teachers after 9 or 12 years of schooling followed by a specific training of 1 or 3 years. School buildings can be modern buildings of international quality or more traditional ones built by the community. The system may or may not allow for a high level of repetition. These are all normative, often contradictory, decisions on education policies and school management, so it is crucial to get objective empirical evidence to support the decision-making process.

In Chapter 4, these aspects of internal efficiency, quality, and education system management are examined and addressed in four sections:

- Section I deals with the internal efficiency of the education system. It provides a close look at the capacity of the education system to bring the maximum number of students that enter the cycle to the end in a minimum number of years. Student flows, repetition, dropout trends, and the loss in internal efficiency due to dropouts and repetition are examined.
- Section II addresses the issue of quality through analyses of the SACMEQ standardized test scores of Standard 6 primary school students and national examination pass rates at primary and secondary levels.

- Section III reviews administrative management issues concerning the allocation of resources (for example, human, books, and financial) from the central level to the decentralized level and the school level.
- Section IV focuses on the pedagogical management that deals with the transformation, at school level, of the allocated resources into student learning achievement.

Internal Efficiency of the Education System

This section looks at the progression of students within and between the different cycles of education by analyzing repetition, dropouts, and retention. We compare the internal efficiency of the education system in Malawi with that of other comparable countries by calculating a synthetic measure of internal efficiency.

Repetition

Each standard, from one to eight, corresponds to a qualitative standard to be achieved by the learner. The primary education curriculum in Malawi is designed to encourage cumulative learning. It requires a learner to have a good mastery of the knowledge and skills taught in each standard to understand the subject matter in the following grade. This is the rationale for repetition. In this respect, repetition is perceived as a tool to improve learning since students who achieve below the expected masterly levels are made to repeat a standard. There are also some fears that subsequent reductions in repetition would result in a sacrifice of education quality. However, more and more empirical evidence challenges these opinions (see box 4.1). There is a growing recognition that high levels of repetition have adverse effects on schooling efficiency, as:

- the decision to have a student repeat is not always fair;
- the impact on learning achievement is not empirically proven;
- repetition tends to increase the risk of dropout; and
- repetition is a costly pedagogical measure.

Box 4.1: The Impact of Repetition on Schooling Efficiency

The debate on repetition is not new. Supporters of repetition point out the sequential nature of learning, the need for classes to be homogenous, a failing student's loss of interest in the class, and the motivating effect of sanctions. Opponents say that the student's disinterest in repeating a class is the first step to dropping out and decry the subjective ways this repetition is decided, along with the cost of an extra school year. Knowledge based on solid empirical studies has progressed, particularly in the context of African countries, and the main results show the negative effects of too high a level of repetition, which can be summed up as follows:

a) The decision to oblige a student to repeat a year is not always fair.

A student's knowledge and skills are not the only explanation for repetition. Decisions often depend on subjective factors, such as the student's relative position in the class, the environment, the schooling conditions, and the teacher's qualifications (PASEC, 1999). In the Côte d'Ivoire, for example, more than 30 percent of repeaters are not in the lower third of students at the national level, as measured by the standard PASEC assessment test.

(Box continues on next page)

Box 4.1 (continued)

The debate on repetition is not new. Supporters of repetition point out the sequential nature of learning, the need for classes to be homogenous, a failing student's loss of interest in the class, and the motivating effect of sanctions. Opponents say that the student's disinterest in repeating a class is the first step to dropping out and decry the subjective ways this repetition is decided, along with the cost of an extra school year. Knowledge based on solid empirical studies has progressed, particularly in the context of African countries, and the main results show the negative effects of too high a level of repetition, which can be summed up as follows:

a) The decision to oblige a student to repeat a year is not always fair.

A student's knowledge and skills are not the only explanation for repetition. Decisions often depend on subjective factors, such as the student's relative position in the class, the environment, the schooling conditions, and the teacher's qualifications (PASEC, 1999). In the Côte d'Ivoire, for example, more than 30 percent of repeaters are not in the lower third of students at the national level, as measured by the standard PASEC assessment test.

b) The impact of repetition on learning achievement is not empirically proven.

Macroanalyses show that the argument aimed at justifying students' repetition for reasons linked to the quality of the education cannot be verified empirically (Mingat and Sosale, 2000). Good education systems (that is, a high level of student learning) can have a high or low repetition rate; there is no significant relationship between the students' learning achievement and the frequency of repetitions. The same is shown in the studies at the school level (for instance in Benin, Chad, and Cameroon) which conclude that with equal resources and environment, schools where the students have repeated the most grades do not have better results at the end of the cycle (Brossard, 2003; World Bank 2004, 2005). Finally, analyses at an individual level show that the students (excepting the especially weak) who are made to repeat a year do not improve more by repeating than by moving on to the next grade (PASEC, 1999; PASEC 2004b).

c) There is a significant negative effect on students who drop out.

Studies at country, school, and individual levels reinforce this point. At the macro level, Mingat and Sosale (2000) and Pôle de Dakar (2002) studies show that repetition increases the dropout rates during the cycle, and this remains the main disincentive for reaching Universal Primary Enrollment (UPE);. The families of students who repeat a year feel that is the students are unsuccessful and do not benefit from being at school. As the opportunity costs always create an argument against school attendance, repetition encourages parents to take their children out of school. Mingat and Sosale estimate that one more percentage point of repeaters results in a 0.8 percentage point increase in the dropout rate. They also show that these negative effects are even more distinct among the population groups where the demand for schooling is already low (for example, girls, children from underprivileged economic environments). For girls, the effect of one more percentage point is estimated to be a 1.1 point increase in the dropout rate.

The results of analyses at the school level take the same direction. In Chad, with all other factors being equal, one more percentage point of repetition is related to a 0.53 percent less survival rate (World Bank, 2005). At the individual level, studies also confirm this trend. In Senegal, at a given student level, the decision to make a grade 2 student repeat a year increases the risk of the student dropping out at the end of the year by 11 percent (PASEC, 2004).

(Box continues on next page)

> **Box 4.1 (continued)**
>
> **d) Costs are affected.**
>
> Repetition costs the system two years of study while only one year is validated. In other words, for a given budget constraint, repeating students occupy places that overload the classes and may prevent other children from going to school. The link between repetition rate and the STR is shown empirically (Mingat and Sosale, 2000 and Pôle de Dakar, 2002).
>
> Bruns, Mingat and Rakotomalala (2003) observed that among the highest performing African countries in 1990–2000 (in terms of universal primary education), the average proportion of repeaters was 10 percent, which is lower than the current African average (16 percent). This benchmark of 10 percent has been established as a reference value within the indicative framework of the Fast Track Initiative. The practices—because it is really a case of practices and habits rather than an objective system of remedial action designed to improve student learning—relating to repetition vary greatly. The percentage of repeaters ranges from under 3 to 40 percent. Thirty-one of the 43 countries for which data was available had over 10 percent of repeaters. In all, the analysis does not suggest a generalized automatic promotion to the next grade (which poses other problems), but leads us to conclude that a figure of 10 percent for repeaters is both desirable and possible.
>
> Being aware of a need to reduce repetition rates, a number of African countries have chosen to:
>
> - put in the primary cycle three sub-cycles of two years each that correspond to well-defined units of skills;
> - no longer allow repetitions within these two-year sub-cycles; and
> - limit the frequency of repetitions between consecutive sub-cycles.
>
> This strategy has proven its efficiency: Niger has reduced repetition in primary education from 18 percent in 1992/93 to 7 percent in 2002/03; in Guinea repetition has decreased even more rapidly, from 21 percent in 2001/02 to 11 percent in 2003/04.
>
> In conclusion, an efficient in-cycle flow management necessitates:
>
> ***An improvement in the survival rate during the cycle.*** It is necessary to eliminate dropouts in the primary cycle to attain UPE. In the other cycles, in view of the fact that the learning programs are put together according to the homogenous units per education cycle, the dropouts during a cycle represent a waste of resources; the system invests in years of studies that do not yield the expected results (completion of a cycle).
>
> ***The reduction of repetitions in countries where these are high.*** Although the requirements of teachers who make students repeat a year when they have not acquired all the knowledge expected in the syllabus is understandable, education systems can not realistically allow repetition rates over 10 percent to be accepted. This represents an additional cost for which the pedagogical efficiency is not proven. It seriously reduces the chances of achieving full UPE.
>
> *Source*: EFA in Africa: Paving the Way for Action, 2005 UNESCO BREDA.

In Malawi, repetition rates are high in primary education. More concerning is the fact that they are strongly tending upward, increasing from 15 percent in 2000 to 20 percent in 2006.[1]

Repetition rates generally decline as students progress through the grades, with Standard 8 being the exception where repetition increases (table 4.1).[2]

Table 4.1: Trend in Repetition Rates by Standard in Primary Schools of All Types (1999 and 2006) (in %)

	Std 1	Std2	Std3	Std4	Std5	Std6	Std7	Std8
2006	24.5	21.4	22.8	17.2	16.1	12.8	11.1	15.6
1999*	18.8	16.6	16.6	13.9	11.7	11.3	10.1	13.9

Sources: *CSR, 2004; EMIS 2006, 2007.
Note: Repetition is calculated here as the number of repeaters in standard X in year t divided by the total enrollment in standard X in year t – 1. Thus repetition refers to the year t – 1.

At the secondary level, the repetition rate remains low at 6 percent (for the whole cycle);[3] it has been stable since 2004 (with a 1 percentage point increase since then) (table 4.2).[4] Repetition rates are highest in Form 2 (10 percent in 2006) and Form 4 (12 percent in 2006). This may be linked to exam failure or to the willingness of candidates to obtain the required number of subjects or grades for the award of a certificate (especially to qualify for entry into universities and other colleges). The examination system tends to encourage repetition in that it allows for the accumulation of subjects passed for the award of a certificate and an improvement in grades. Repetition rates for forms 1 and 3 are comparatively low because moving on to form 1 and 4 is almost automatic, unless school management and parents agree that a student should repeat. Such an approach could be applied in the primary level by reorganizing the cycle into two sub-cycles within which repetition would not be allowed.

Table 4.2: Repetition Rates by Form in Secondary Schools of All Types (2006) (in %)

Form 1	Form 2	Form 3	Form 4
1.0	9.8	2.2	12.1

Sources: EMIS 2006, 2007.
Note: Repetition is calculated here as the number of repeaters in standard X in year 2007 divided by the total enrollment in standard X in year 2006. Thus, repetition refers to the year 2006.

How does Malawi fare compared to other countries? As shown in figure 4.1, Malawi has the highest repetition rate at the primary level in the region, twice as high as that of the SADC. In the secondary level, Malawi is in line with the average of the SADC countries.

The Ministry of Education, Science and Technology is well aware of the issue, especially regarding the situation in standards 1 to 4 of the primary cycle, where the highest repetition rates are to be found. The Ministry is thinking of a policy to favor direct promotion between certain standards and for the others (for example, standards 4, 6, and 8) a student would repeat only after failing to achieve a 50 percent pass in two subjects (standards 4 and 6) and after failing Standard 8.

Figure 4.1: Repetition Rate at Primary and Secondary Levels in SADC Countries (2006 or Closest Year) (in %)

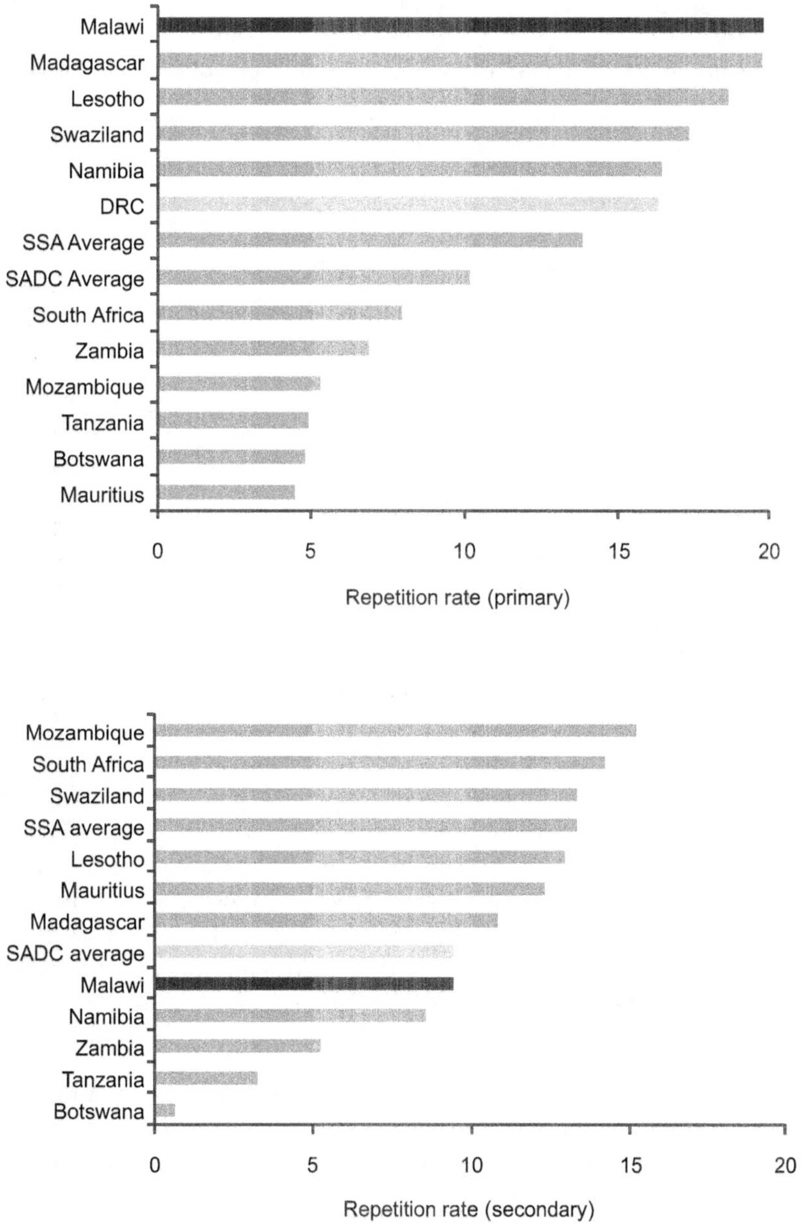

Source: World Bank data 2009.

Dropout

2006 EMIS data[5] show an average dropout rate at the primary level of around five percent—a sharp decrease compared to 1999 (table 4.3).

Table 4.3: Dropout Rates at the Primary Level in All Types of Schools (1999 and 2006) (in %)

	Std 1	Std2	Std3	Std4	Std5	Std6	Std7	Std8
2006	6.1	5.2	4.6	4.7	4.5	4.9	5.1	5.5
1999*	13.9	11.1	9.3	8.9	7.7	8.3	8.3	8.2

Sources: *CSR, 2004; EMIS 2006, 2007.

Dropout rates are much higher at the secondary level, averaging 8.3 percent, as shown in table 4.4.

Table 4.4: Dropout Rates at the Secondary level in All Types of Schools (2006) (in %)

	Form 1	Form 2	Form 3	Form 4
Total	9.9	7.6	8.0	7.1

Sources: EMIS 2006, 2007.

The student flow efficiency index, based on survival rates within and between cycles (primary and secondary), helps to assess the effect of dropping out within cycles and between cycles. While dropouts within cycles tend to be endured by the system (which is not ideal as each cycle corresponds to a set of competencies that are meant to be fully acquired by completing the given cycle), dropouts between cycles are usually influenced by education policy decisions (such as the number of places available at the next education level). A well-managed education system—in terms of student flow—would have the majority of dropouts occur between cycles instead of within cycles.

Computations for 2007 provide an index of 0.21.[6] This means that 21 percent of student dropouts occur between cycles while 79 percent occur within cycles. Problems of dropout are thus particularly striking within cycles. This pattern is generally less skewed in other SADC countries (which have an index averaging 0.54) as figure 4A.2 in Appendix 4.1 shows.

Internal Efficiency Index

What does the preceding analysis of student flow patterns (for example, repetition, dropout, retention) say about the internal efficiency of the education system? It may help to compare the resources the system consumes to produce its annual output of primary and secondary school completers with the resources that it would have used if there were no grade repetitions and dropouts.

Table 4.5 provides an estimation of the global internal efficiency of the primary and secondary systems, summarized by the internal efficiency coefficient and its related partial indicators. These give us some insights into the proportion of inefficiency and wastage due to perturbation in the student flows following dropouts or repetitions. Sending a child to school is costly for the system, whether or not that child completes the cycle. And, those children who do not complete primary school have very little chance of getting literate. The consumption of student-years by students dropping out before the end of the cycle entails a waste of public resources. Similarly, repetition creates extra charges for the system, as it costs two or more schooling years to validate only one year. The consumption of unproductive years of schooling following dropouts or repetition can lead to an inefficient use of already scare public resources.

The IEC is defined as the ratio between the cumulative student-years invested in a system with no student flow problems and the actual cumulative student-years invested given the current pattern of dropout and grade repetition (for example, those additional years due to repetition and those useless years due to dropouts). An education system with no dropouts and no repetitions would have a coefficient of 100.[7,8]

Table 4.5: Internal Efficiency Coefficient in Primary and Secondary Schooling (1999/00–2006/07)

	1999/00*	2006/07
Primary		
Internal efficiency coefficient	39%	35%
Dropout related (w/o repetitions)	50%	49%
Repetition related (w/o dropouts)	80%	71%
Student-years required to produce one graduate	20.1	23
Secondary (lower and upper)		
Internal efficiency coefficient	76%	66%
Dropout related (w/o repetitions)	81%	71%
Repetition related (w/o dropouts)	95%	94%
Student-years required to produce one graduate	5.2	6

Sources: *CSR 2004, EMIS 2006, 2007; HIS 2004 for repetition structure.

The internal efficiency coefficient at the primary level remains particularly low (35 percent in 2007). This implies that 65 percent of public resources are used for repeated years or for school years of students who are dropping out before completing the cycle. Indeed, the system requires 23 student-years to produce one graduate instead of 8 years with a perfect efficiency. The situation has slightly worsened since 1999, when the IEC was 39 percent. An increase in repetition is mainly responsible for this degradation and the related rise in wasted resources. In 1999, repetition induced a 20 percent waste of resources (partial IEC of 80 percent); in 2007, the waste of resources was 29 percent (partial index of efficiency of 71 percent). Dropout also remains a major issue, inducing a 50 percent waste of resources. Indeed, in a system with no repetitions, the partial efficiency index (dropout-related only) would be 49 percent. High dropout rates have the greatest adverse affect on the efficiency of the system.

Internal efficiency at the secondary level is slightly better, with a coefficient of 66 percent in 2007, although the situation has significantly deteriorated over the period (the IEC was 76 percent in 1999). Thirty-four percent of resources are currently used for repeated years or for school years of students who drop out before cycle completion. It takes six student-years to produce a graduate instead of the four years theoretically needed. This is higher than in 1999/00, when 5.2 years were required to produce a graduate. Inefficiencies resulting from repetitions remained low over the period (5–6 percent); major problems stemming from dropouts, which alone led to a 29 percent wastage of public resources in 2007. Additional efforts are necessary, despite constraints on resources, to reduce student dropout rates.

Allowing for international comparisons sheds some light on the magnitude of inefficiencies in the Malawian education system. As shown below, Malawi fares poorly on that issue compared to other countries in the region. Indeed, the internal efficiency coefficient (computed over a primary cycle of six years)[9] stands at 0.45 (or 45 percent): the lowest level among the SADC countries.

Quality and Learning Outcomes

The quality of education is becoming a major issue for most education sector planners in Africa and constitutes a specific EFA goal. Yet, what does this notion cover? Defining quality is actually tricky and measuring it is even trickier. In many instances, the measure of quality refers to the level and type of resources poured into the system, such as the STR, the level of teacher training, or the type of school buildings. This measure is often favored when there is a lack of adequate data on student learning outcomes. Yet, as many studies have shown, the relationship between education inputs and learning outcomes is somewhat weak. Indeed, if resources do matter, the way they are being used tends to matter even more.

Referring to the EFA goal on quality,[10] quality can be defined as what students actually learn. In that context, the level of learning achievement becomes a major issue as it provides interesting insights into the level of human capital build, which are crucial for the development of the nation. To assess quality and learning outcomes, two major sources of data are mobilized: i) standardized tests performed at the primary level—Southern African Consortium for Monitoring Educational Quality (SACMEQ) data—and ii) national examinations at the primary and secondary levels.

Level of Learning Outcomes

SACMEQ Scores

Malawi, along with other 13 countries in the region, is participating in the SACMEQ which is measuring student performances in grade 6 in English reading and mathematics. Malawi is currently undergoing its third round; yet data will not be available for this report. We will therefore rely on the results of the last SACMEQ surveys conducted in 2004 and 1999.

Evidence from SACMEQ data gathered in table 4.6 would suggest a decline in quality of learning,[11] as expressed by the score in English reading, which dropped from 463 (SACMEQ I) to 429 (SACMEQ II). The percentage of children who attained a minimum level of mastery in English reading fell by 50 percent from 1999 to 2004, to reach barely 9 percent in 2004. This poor result is a major concern in itself, and since English is the language used in instruction, this overall poor performance could have very adverse effects on the entire student learning process.

Table 4.6: Reading (English) and Mathematics Scores and Percentage of Students Reaching Minimum and Desirable Levels of Reading Mastery (SACMEQ I and II)

	SACMEQ I	SACMEQ II	
	Reading	Reading	Mathematics
Means score	462.6	428.9	432.9
Students reaching minimum level of mastery	19.4%	8.6%	
Students reaching desirable level of mastery	1.3%	0.3%	

Source: SACMEQ 2005 report.

An interesting feature of SACMEQ data is that student skills level can be assessed. There are eight skill levels for each subject area. Levels are hierarchical and enable an assessment of the skills that students have or have not reached (see table 4A.1 in Appendix 4.1 for a detailed presentation). If level 4 is taken as the point where children can read independently, then data show that 78 percent of students have not mastered that level.

Two major conclusions can be drawn from those observations: More and more students have drifted into lower literacy levels and a sizeable number of students have proceeded to higher levels without a good mastery of relevant skills. In mathematics, 98 percent of students did not possess skills beyond basic numeracy and none of them had skills beyond competent numeracy (level 5). The results are clearly unsatisfactory and show that Malawi offers a poor quality of education in primary schools.

Figure 4.2: Percentage of Students Reaching Literacy and Mathematics Competency Levels in Malawi (SACMEQ II)

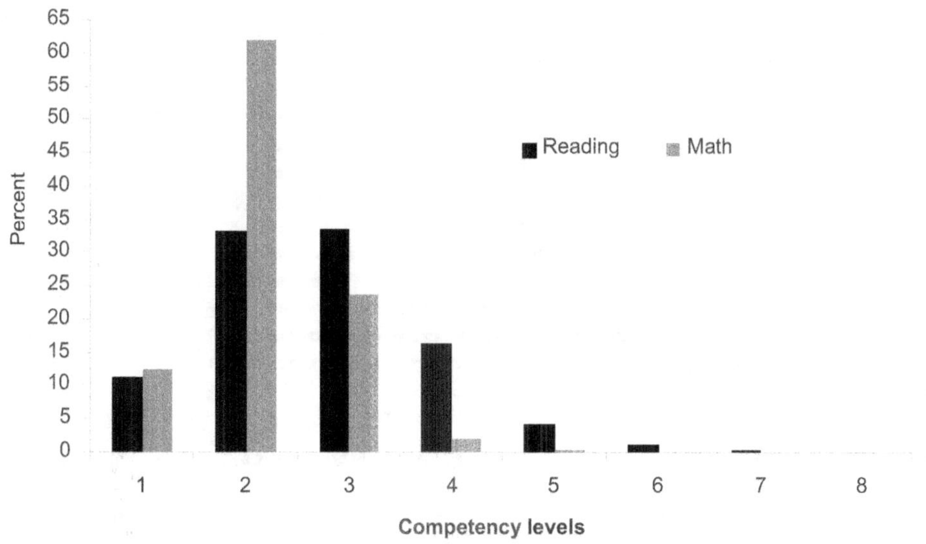

Source: SACMEQ II report 2005.

Compared to other countries, Malawi fares poorly, being at the bottom of all the SACMEQ countries in English reading and next to last in mathematics (figure 4.3). Students were among the lowest achievers in the region, indicating that Malawi provided the lowest quality of primary schooling.

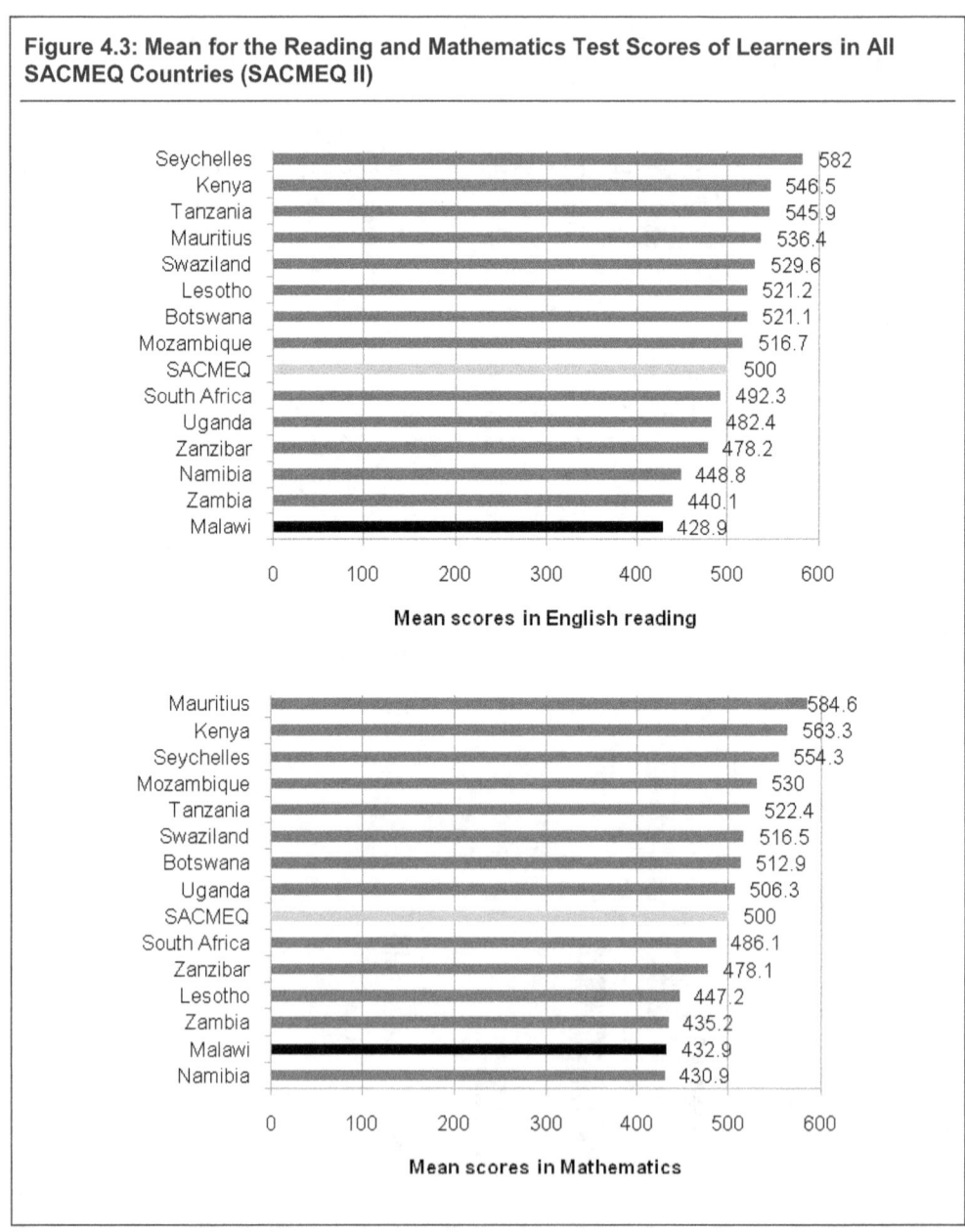

Figure 4.3: Mean for the Reading and Mathematics Test Scores of Learners in All SACMEQ Countries (SACMEQ II)

Source: SACMEQ II report, 2005.
Note: SACMEQ scores are scaled so that the average of all students is 500 and the standard deviation is 100.

There is a strong need to further investigate these results and better understand why competency levels are so poor and have fallen over the past few years. Could it result from the rapid increase in access (of lower-achieving students from poorer households) and class size following the elimination of school fees in 1994? Yet, an increase in school enrollment does not systematically lead to a deterioration of learning achievement, as illustrated by Madagascar, which has experienced significant progresses over the past years, both school coverage and quality of learning (UNESCO BREDA, 2007). The release of the third SACMEQ results will prove very insightful in that regard, by confirming or denying current trends and enabling a longitudinal analysis of potential determinants. In addition, relying on innovative assessment tools, such as the Early Grade Reading Assessment (EGRA), could prove beneficial in better understanding the quality issues at stake.

National Examination Pass Rates

National examination pass rates provide another way to look at quality issues.[12] Results on national examinations administrated at the end of each cycle or sub-cycle have the advantage of being available at the national level and represent a common test taken by all students from a given grade. One usually finds homogeneous conditions in taking the test and in the protocol of correction. These data present some limits:

- they do not cover all competencies and learning achievement acquired throughout a cycle (and therefore are not the most appropriate data for assessing learning achievement, unlike SACMEQ);
- they do not have information on students' backgrounds, as data are not made available on an individual level; and
- they do not allow for international comparisons.

PSLE Pass Rates[13]

In 2006, 93 percent of Standard 8 students sat for the PSLE, and 74 percent passed (table 4.7).[14] This means there is still one student out of four who has failed the exam. Some differences emerge according to the type of school: private schools show better results than public ones with an eight-point difference in their favor. The fact that private schools tend to be located in urban areas[15] (which may attract better and wealthier students) and have more educational inputs[16] could explain these results.

Table 4.7: Leaving School Examination Results at the Primary Level by School Type in % (2006)

	Government	Religious	Total Public	Private	Total
Sat rate (%)	93.9	93.0	93.3	95.1	93.4
Pass rate (%)	74.9	72.7	73.5	82.0	73.7

Source: EMIS 2007.

Note: Sat rate= nb of students in Std. 8 who sit the exam/nb of student in Std 8; Pass rate= nb of students in Std 8 who pass the exam/nb of student in Std. 8 who sit the exam.

Examinations at the Secondary Level: JCE and MSCE[17]

JCE and MSCE sat rates are around 95 percent (table 4.8).[18] Yet, many students failed the exam. The situation is especially concerning at the MSCE level, where only 44 percent of students who are sitting the exam pass it. JCE results are better, with a pass rate of 62 percent in 2006.

Table 4.8: JCE and MSCE Examination Results (2006)

	JCE			MSCE		
	Entered	Sat	Passed	Entered	Sat	Total
Total	61,205	58,565	36,219	44,442	42,414	18,576
% who...		95.7	61.8		95.4	43.8

Source: EMIS, 2007.
Note: JCE sat rate= nb of students in Form 2 who sit the exam/nb of student in Form 2(entered); JCE Pass rate= nb of students in Form 2 who pass the exam/nb of student in Form 2 who sit the exam.

Private schools outperform public ones. Yet, strong variations exist among public schools, with poorer outcomes associated with CDSSs and Open Day Secondary Schools (ODSSs). However, while JCE pass rates are the lowest among Open Day Schools (47 percent), the CDSSs have lower MSCE pass rates, with more than two-thirds of students who sit the exam failing it (table 4.9). In comparison, CSSs are bringing 8 out of 10 students to JCE graduation and 1 out of 2 to MSCE graduation. CSSs also bring a higher proportion of their students to graduation than private schools.

Table 4.9: JCE and MSCE Examinations Pass Rates by School Types in % (2006)

	CSS	CDSS	ODSS	Total Public	Private	Total
JCE	79.6	54.2	47.4	61.2	64.8	61.8
MSCE	53.5	33.0	43.2	41.5	50.4	43.8

Source: EMIS, 2007.

Those discrepancies could be due to some in-school factors. CDSSs are globally less well provided for than other schools. They generally have underqualified teachers,[19] a poorer learning environment, and lack appropriate teaching and learning materials and equipment.[20] More generally, CDSSs are severely under-resourced, receiving only about 15 percent of government funds allocated to national schools.[21] ODSS students are part-time learners and depend on the same teachers and use facilities of a normal school. ODSS students are not at the school on merit, but because they wish to continue with their schooling and may not be good enough. Higher pass rates for private schools could be explained by the practice of student selection, which allows the best students to enroll. This could hold also true for CSSs that attract generally the best students.[22]

Factors Influencing Examination Pass Rates

What explains the disparities captured in information so far? Some factors pertaining to class size, pedagogical organization of the class, teacher characteristics, pedagogical choices, availability of teaching and learning materials, and inspections depend on education policies. Other factors, such as student characteristics (for example gender, age, socioeconomic background) or certain school characteristics (for example, geographical situation) affect learning achievement but are not influenced by those education policies.

An analysis of quality of schooling can be performed by using national examination pass rates. It relies on multivariate analyses to distinguish among determinants those that have an impact on exam pass rates, and assess their magnitude. The purpose of such analyses is to grasp the net effect of each factor, by referring to the *all other things being equal* assumption. Results will be displayed by categories of factors: school context, classroom organization, school conditions, and teacher characteristics.

It is worthwhile to recall that data used here have several shortcomings for this analysis, although they rely on the education system's level of requirements that sanction students on a legitimate, recognized nationwide reference, and are used in some instances (as in the primary level) to rank students according to their grades. These shortcomings are as follows:

- National examination pass rates are a somewhat imprecise measure of learning achievement, as they do not really explain what students have really acquired.[23]
- The unit of observation being *pass rates at the school level*, data do not provide information on students' socioeconomic background and initial competency level, limiting the analysis of situations that assume the existence of differences arising according to the student audiences (for example, urban/rural residency, private/public schools);
- Since students are not tested at the beginning of the school year, it becomes more difficult to measure the determinants of learning as a dynamic process over the school year.
- The quasi-absence of variance in some situations (for example, women mainly located in urban zones, volunteers found only in rural areas, low STRs found in urban zones, temporary classroom mainly in rural zones, most schools having an active PTA or SMC, electrified schools with a library being mostly in urban areas) do not allow for an adequate assessment of the impact of these variables.
- Data not being available at the student level, but at the school level, leads to less data precision and variability and causes the aggregation level to be higher.

Caution is needed when analyzing the determinants of examination pass rates, as those shortcomings may lead to biased and counterintuitive results. Yet they allow, to a certain extent, the identification of certain critical issues pertaining to education quality at the school level.

Determinants of Examination Pass Rates at the Primary Level

Empirical Results

The underlying regression model of the determinants of the 2006 PSLE is based on a logistic model. Results of the regression analysis are gathered in table 4.10 (basic statistics on the model variables are in table 4A.2 of Appendix 4.2). Explanatory variables were computed using the average figures over two consecutive years (2005–2006) to grasp some retrospective features that could affect the current pass-rate level (for 2006).

Two models are presented. The first model involves contextual factors (geographical situation and the type of school), which are somewhat exogenous to education policies. The second model builds on the first by including variables related to conditions in classrooms, schools, and teacher characteristics; factors that are dictated by policies.

Marginal effects have been reproduced in the table. Marginal effect refers to the percentage point change in the examination pass rate in response to a one percent increase/decrease in the share of the corresponding variable at the expense of a one percent decline/increase in the share of the reference.

For instance, a 10 percent increase in the proportion of volunteers within a school at the expense of civil servant teachers entails a 1.98 percentage point drop in PSLE pass rates from its average level, all other things being equal. For continuous variables, the marginal effect corresponds to the percentage point change in the pass rate in response to an increase of one unit of the corresponding variable above the sample mean of the corresponding variable.

The explanatory power of Model 2 is 26.4 percent, which is good for such a model specification, although limited in absolute terms.[24]

CONTEXTUAL FACTORS

Some correlations exist between location and student achievement.[25] Indeed, urban schools tend to perform better than rural ones. Yet, one should not infer that rural schools are perform less well than urban ones: indeed, the variable may be capturing specific effects that were not grasped by the model, such as students' background and initial learning level. Such a result could also simply mean that rural schools have a more challenging environment than urban schools (for example, higher STRs, less access to facilities).

Disparities are also observed across divisions: All divisions, except Shire Highlands, are bringing relatively fewer students to graduation than the Central Western division. The fact that location division dummy variables are almost all statistically significant—even when controlling for conditions in classrooms, schools, and teacher characteristics— suggests that other unobserved differences across locations are at work. It would be interesting to further investigate the factors associated with better results in the Central Western division, and by the same token, why the Northern and Central Eastern divisions are faring poorly compared to the others.

Table 4.10: Determinants of PSLE Results at the National Level (2006)—Marginal Effect

	Model 1	Model 2
R2	15%	26%
Average pass rate	75.5	73.5
Number of observations	3 198	3 163
	Marginal effect	Marginal effect
Contextual factors		
Division		
Northern	–0.181 ***	–0.179 ***
Central Eastern	–0.138 ***	–0.143 ***
Central Western	Ref	Ref
Southern Eastern	–0.051 ***	–0.065 ***
Southern Western	–0.041 ***	–0.044 ***
Shire Highlands	–0.007	–0.004
Location		
Urban	Ref	Ref
Rural	–0.160 ***	–0.053 ***
Type of school		
Government	Ref	Ref
Religious agency	0.005	0.011
Private	0.073 ***	0.069 ***
Classroom/pedagogical organization		
STR>60:1(Ref: STR<=60:1)		–0.043 ***
% of repeaters		0.015 ***
Week teaching time (hour)		0.001 ***
At least 1 book for 2 students (Chichewa) (Ref: less than one book per two students)		0.013 ***
At least 1 book for 2 students (English)(Ref: less than one book per two students)		0.014
At least 1 book for 2 students (Mathematics)(Ref: less than one book per two students)		–0.008
School conditions		
Overlapping shift (Ref: Single shift)		–0.012 ***
Type of classroom		
Proportion of Permanent classrooms		Pseudo–ref
Proportion of Temporary classrooms		–0.042 ***
Proportion of Open air classrooms		0.008
School facilities		
Has a library		0.040 ***
Has latrines		0.062 ***
Has electricity		0.071 ***
Has water		0.010
Parent-teacher association/school management committee is active (Ref: not active)		0.009
Teacher characteristics		
Proportion of female teachers		0.216 ***
Proportion of teachers who are		
Civil servants		Pseudo–ref
Temporary		–0.051
Month–to–Month		–0.041
Volunteers		–0.198 ***
Proportion of teachers with		
PSLE		–0.008
JCE		–0.128 ***
MSLE		Pseudo–ref
Higher education diploma/degree		0.097

Sources: Econometric models using EMIS 2005, 2006, 2007. Pseudo-reference is used and it is not a reference per se because variables refer to percentage and not to a regular categorical variable.
Notes: Reading: A 10-percent point drop in the share of teachers with a JCE to the benefit of MSCE teachers would increase the pass rate by 1.52 percent (from its current average level). The marginal impact of the variable is positive, indicating that the higher the level of marginal effect, the better its performance as measured by the PSLE pass rate.
***: significant at 1%, ** at 5%, * at 10%

Private schools have better results than public ones—whether government based or religious—even when controlling for factors such as location, classroom organization, school conditions, and teacher characteristics. Unobserved factors are likely too. Indeed, data do not allow a control for student characteristics and some teacher features. Private schools may attract students from higher socioeconomic and cultural backgrounds (which are often correlated with better scoring). In addition, it is believed that teachers in private schools display greater dedication since they are accountable to their immediate bosses whose bait for higher enrollment and/or prices is a good pass rate.

Classroom/Pedagogical Organization

Class size has a significantly negative effect on student performances. Classes of big size—proxied here by an STR of more than 60:1—are showing worse results than smaller size classes. This could imply that teachers might be finding it difficult to adapt their pedagogy and devote enough time to each student when dealing with a sizable number of students. The national policy to bring down the STR to 60:1 could have a positive impact on student learning achievement.

The **availability of books has little significant impact on learning achievement**. Indeed, **only Chichewa books tend to have a positive impact**. More generally, issues related to book use at school and class levels may be at stake. Indeed, there is some evidence that books are being kept in head teacher's offices to prevent them from deterioration. The books might be available at schools but not in students' hands, thus having no effect on learning.

Instructional time has a significant and positive impact on pass rates. Teaching time is a key element in learning outcomes. In Malawi, the total instructional time in primary schools amounts to 721 hours, far below the theoretical 910 hours. On average, a student is taught 18.5 hours per week, or 3.7 hours per day. This ranges from around 3 hours in the lower grades to close to 4 hours in the upper ones. This figure is overevaluated, as teacher absenteeism is not recorded here. A Public Expenditure Tracking Survey (PETS) conducted in 2004 estimated teacher absenteeism at 20 percent on any given day, which would mean an estimated average volume of annual instructional time of only 577 hours. In addition, late entry, strikes, and casual holidays are all bringing down teaching time. Student absenteeism, whether linked to sickness, household chores, or productive labor, may further reduce the number of hours a student is being taught. Addressing this issue, as well as that of teacher absenteeism, is crucial to improving learning outcomes.

A lower percentage of repetition at the school level tends to have a significant and positive effect on learning achievement. There is an array of literature on the effect repetition has on dropouts (see box 4.1). Students remaining in the system are certainly the best ones, allowing for a higher level of pass rates. This result could be a simple reflection of the selection process in place at the school level.

Conditions in Schools

Overlapping shift is having a significant negative impact on pass rate levels. Teachers might find it difficult in such an organizational mode to adapt their pedagogy and teaching.

Variables related to school environment show significant effects on quality outcomes. First, econometric model results show that **using temporary classrooms tends to bring down the level of PSLE pass rates**. However, open-air classrooms did not seem to have a negative effect on PSLE pass rates, compared to permanent classrooms. This could be linked to the fact that open air classrooms tend to be used at lower grades, not upper grades.

In general, the availability of facilities has a positive effect on examination pass rates. Endowments, such as latrines, libraries, and electricity are positively correlated with pass rates. Electricity has the most important impact, with a marginal effect of 0.071 (All other things being equal, schools with electricity show an average pass rate that is 7 percent higher than schools without) against 0.062 for latrines and 0.040 for libraries. The availability of water does not seem to be as critical because its net effect is not statistically significant.

Schools that have an active Parent Teacher Association (PTA) and/or a School Management Committee (SMC) do not have better results. Yet, the majority of schools have an active PTA and/or a school management committee.[26] And these groups could be more active in schools that face problems. The data do not allow for further examination of this issue.

TEACHER CHARACTERISTICS

Female teachers tend to display better results than their male peers. All other things being equal, the higher the proportion of female teachers in a school, the higher the PSLE pass rate. The impact is quite important: a 10 percent increase in the proportion of female teachers within a school entails a 2.2 percent increase in the PSLE pass rate. However, other unobservable variables are not taken into account, such as the students' initial levels and geographic location (female teachers are mostly located in urban zones).

Volunteer teachers do not fare as well as their counterparts, ceteris paribus. The marginal net effect is quite substantial: A 10 percent increase in the proportion .of volunteers within a school entails a 2 percent drop in PSLE pass rates. Yet, care is needed when analyzing these results because volunteer teachers tend to be located in the most remote zones, which are known to have more difficult environmental and schooling conditions.

Teachers with a JCE seem to be less effective than their peers with an MSCE. The current policy of upgrading initial teacher qualification to the MSCE tends to be supported by the evidence. Yet, the magnitude of the gain in pass rates must be balanced against the implied costs of raising teacher qualification. It is reasonable to think about tradeoffs.

The analysis conducted so far, though instructive, remains somewhat limited, given the initial data constraints and the relatively modest explaining power of the model (although it is higher than what is observed for similar analyses conducted in other African countries). Nevertheless, the analysis shows that other factors, which could not be captured by the current model specification, can affect student results.

Such factors could be termed the "classroom effect" or the "teacher effect," and refer to teacher motivation, charisma, talent, pedagogical skills, and interaction with students. International evidence suggests that the teacher effect can significantly influence student learning. It would be useful to identify and visit strong schools to have a better understanding of what works and what does not and reproduce good practices in poorer-performing schools. Producing more adapted methodology (such as the value-added approach) and data to adequately grasp determinants of learning achievement could also be helpful.

Determinants of Pass Rates at the Secondary Level

A similar logistic model was used to assess the determinants of 2006 MSCE results.[27] As with the analysis on PSLE pass rates, two models were run. The first model included only contextual variables, the second one added variables related to conditions in classrooms and schools, as well as teacher characteristics (factors that are dictated by policies). Marginal effects are presented in table 4.11. The explanatory power of the second model reaches 39 percent, which is very good for such a model specification. Yet again, data suffers from significant flaws that limit the overall relevancy of the analysis (see the beginning of section II.2), although the issue of limited data variation is less marked at the secondary level than the primary level.

Empirical Results

CONTEXTUAL FACTORS

The geographical situation shows no significant impact on MSCE results. Indeed, no significant differences are observed between schools located in rural areas or urban ones. This may be related to the fact that unlike primary schools, secondary schools are not located in the most remote rural zones. In addition, no strong pattern arises across divisions, except in the Southern Western division, which seems to fare worse than the others (significant negative marginal effect). This feature remains even when controlling for conditions in classroom and school and teacher characteristics, suggesting that other unobserved differences are at work here.

CSSs (and to a lesser extent, private schools) tend to have far better results than CDSSs, even when controlling for factors such as classroom organization, school conditions, and teacher characteristics. Unobserved factors are also likely. Unfortunately, available data do not allow for control of student characteristics and for some teacher features. CSSs and private schools may indeed attract students from higher socioeconomic and cultural backgrounds (which are often correlated to better scoring). Enrollment strategies may also differ from one type of school to the other, further exacerbating social selection.

CLASSROOM/PEDAGOGICAL ORGANIZATION

Class size, proxied by the STR, is not statistically significant. The STR in the secondary level is generally low, averaging 21:1; being slightly higher in CSSs (25:1) than in CDSSs (20:1) and private schools (21:1). It seems that there should be some leeway to increase the STR without harming student learning conditions.

The **availability of books has a positive, statistically significant impact on MSCE pass rates.**

Table 4.11: Determinants of MSCE Results at the National Level (2006)—Marginal Effect

		Model 1	Model 2
	R^2	32	38
	Average pass rate	38.9	38.0
	Number of observations	736	714
		Marginal effect	Marginal effect
Contextual factors			
Division			
	Northern	–0.010	0.007
	Central Eastern	–0.033	–0.023
	Central Western	Ref	Ref
	Southern Eastern	0.023	0.032
	Southern Western	–0.041**	–0.040**
	Shire Highlands	–0.036	–0.022
Location			
	Urban	Ref	Ref
	Rural	–0.053	–0.013
Type of school			
	CSS	0.255 ***	0.150 ***
	CDSS	Ref	Ref
	Open Day school	0.014	–0.008
	Private	0.186 *	0.136 ***
Classroom/pedagogical organization			
	STR		–0.00004
	% of repeaters		–0.025
	Books per student		0.003**
School conditions			
Proportion of classroom			
	Permanent		Pseudo–ref
	Temporary		–0.006
School facilities			
	Has a library		0.012
	Has a lab		0.071***
	Has latrines		–0.015
	Has electricity		–0.010
	Has water		0.0004
Parent teacher association/school management committee is active (Ref : not active)			0.0006
Teacher characteristics			
	Proportion of female teachers		0.214 ***
Proportion of teachers who are			
	Grade unknown		0.039
	I level		Pseudo–ref
	H/G/F level		–0.062
	K/L/M/I level/primary (equal to PT4-PT1 grades)		–0.074 **

Sources: Econometric model using EMIS 2006, 2007.

Notes: Reading: a 10 percent increase in the share of female teachers at the expense of male teachers would increase, all other things being equal, the MSCE pass rate by 2.14 percent (from its current average level). The marginal impact of the book per student variable is positive, indicating that the higher the number of books per student, the better the MSCE pass rate.

***: significant at 1%, ** at 5%, * at 10%

CONDITIONS IN SCHOOLS

Variables related to school facilities have a limited effect. Whether a classroom is permanent or temporary does not affect MSCE pass rates (it is not statistically significant). Similarly, the fact that a school has a library, latrines, water, or electricity does not help bring more students to graduation. Yet, having a lab tends increase the level of the MSCE pass rate (a marginal effect of 0.071). However, schools that possess a lab are usually CSSs.

TEACHER CHARACTERISTICS

Female teachers tend to display better results than their male peers. All other things being equal, the higher the proportion of female teachers in a school, the higher the MSCE pass rate. Again, it is important not to assume that male teachers are less efficient, because many other unobservable variables are not taken into account, such as the students' initial level.

PT4 to PT1 grade teachers lead to poorer performances at the school level compared to Grade I teachers. All things being equal, the higher their proportion the lower the examination pass rate. It is important to note that those teachers were initially intended to teach in primary school, and may be lacking the necessary competences to teach in secondary schools. And, they may be posted in schools that face harsher working conditions. The great majority of CDSSs employ these teachers, and these schools are known to be less well endowed with quality educational inputs.

A third model was run with the grade variable replaced by the academic qualification of teachers. Indeed, the strong correlation existing between the variables led to some bias. The results (not shown) indicate that MSCE holders are performing less well than higher education graduates in education, ceteris paribus.

Beyond the limits pertaining to the data in hand, the factors that have been analyzed cover most school costs (for example, teacher salaries, pedagogical materials). That these factors explain just a minor part (from 20 to 40 percent) of school differences in student learning outcomes, tells us that many other factors are at stake. Additional in-depth analyses of learning outcomes are required for clear policy orientations.

However, these results highlight the need to question aspects of education management by looking more specifically at: i) administrative management concerning the allocation of resources (human, material, and financial) from central to decentralized and to school levels; and ii) pedagogical management that deals with the transformation, at school level, of the allocated resources into student learning achievement. These two aspects are reviewed in the following sections.

Administration Management

This section briefly presents the institutional processes pertaining to human resource allocation, before turning to a description of teacher characteristics and the consistency of their deployment across schools. A similar analysis will then be undertaken for the allocation of books and funds. The section ends with an overview of possible economy of scale (based on the size of the schools).

Administrative Management Issues: Are Resources Being Allocated According to Needs?

Primary Level

Institutional Aspects of Public Teacher Management: Recruitment and Deployment of Teacher

Teachers in Malawi can be classified into four categories: civil servants, month-to-month teachers, temporary teachers, and volunteers. Recruitment and allocation processes depend very much on their status.

Civil Servants are those who are in normal service, recruited through interviews by the Teaching Service Commission (TSC). They are allocated through a planned deployment system, which is decentralized to local education authorities. After they finish training, the newly qualified teachers are allocated to primary education districts by the Directorate of Basic Education in liaison with the Human Resources and Management division of the Ministry of Education. This allocation is theoretically based on district needs as indicated by STRs and available vacancies. The ministry's policy is to post a teacher where a vacancy exists, either by new deployment or redeployment. Yet, teachers can request a posting to another district based on various reasons, some of which are "following husband," "to be close to a big hospital," and "attending a part-time course," among others. Movements of teachers from one district to another, within and outside the division, are coordinated at the division level in consultation with the Ministry of Education's headquarters. No newly qualified teachers have been allocated to the urban education districts of Blantyre, Zomba, Lilongwe, and Mzuzu since 2007. Teachers have to sign a bond that ties them to work in the rural areas for at least five years.

Month-to-month teachers are former civil servants who have retired from teaching after reaching 55 years (the former retirement age[28]) and who have been reengaged on a contract basis to fill staffing gaps that exist in rural schools. The process of re-engagement involves a declaration of vacancies by the district, through which possible candidates are identified based on their records of service and a health report from a reputable hospital. Ministry of Education headquarters thereafter follow the reengagement process with the Department of Human Resource Development. Month-to-month contract teachers are qualified teachers, but cannot be promoted. They are not supposed to hold positions apart from teaching and are sent where the needs are highest, especially in rural areas. They are reemployed on a new contract after certifying that they are physically fit.

Temporary teachers were recruited largely to meet the teacher shortage that resulted from the 1994 enrollment boom (which was a consequence of Free Primary Education). Most of these teachers were recruited untrained in 1994–1996, and have been trained over the years through the Malawi Integrated In-Service Teacher Education Programme (MIITEP). Yet, there are still some untrained temporary teachers in the system.

Volunteer teachers are locally recruited, typically hired by SMCs, PTAs, or religious agencies. They also include teachers recruited by foreign organizations, such as the Peace Corps, VSO, and the Japanese Volunteers. Volunteer teachers are meant to address teacher shortages in rural schools where qualified teachers do not usually stay. These teachers are not recorded in the payroll, and are normally local people educated to MSCE or at least the JCE level. They are encouraged by the community to work as teachers to make up for the shortages that exist. In some cases, they receive payment from the community, and in few cases receive money from fellow teachers. Some of these teachers may aspire to becoming regular teachers. Volunteer teachers are included in in-service trainings, and head teachers are expected to provide them with some guidance on teaching skills.

Characteristics of Teachers in Government-Funded Schools

TEACHER STATUS

In 2007, the total number of teachers was 42,330, well below the 2000 level of 47,840.[29] Ninety-six percent worked in government-funded schools.[30] The great majority of government-funded school teachers are regular civil servants (89 percent), while temporary and month-to-month teachers account for 1.5 and 3.4 percent, respectively. Volunteer teachers make up 6.5 percent of the total teaching force working in government-funded schools.

Table 4.12: Teacher Status by Location (in %), Government-Funded Primary Schools (2007)

Teacher status	Urban	Rural	Total (%)	Total (in numbers)
Civil servant	97.6	87.2	88.6	35,982
Temporary	2.3	1.4	1.5	628
Month-to-month teacher	0.1	3.9	3.4	1,369
Volunteer	0.0	7.5	6.5	2,633
Total	100.0	100.0	100.0	40,612

Source: EMIS, 2007.

Female teachers account for 38 percent of the teaching force. They are overrepresented in urban settings;[31] a reason often evoked is to "follow the husband." In Malawi, a female teacher cannot be denied the opportunity to join her husband, no matter where the husband is.

Table 4.13: Teacher Distribution by Gender and Location (in %), Government-Funded Primary Schools (2007)

Teacher distribution	Female	Male	Total
Urban	29.8	3.5	13.4
Rural	70.2	96.5	86.6
Total	100.0	100.0	100.0

Source: EMIS, 2007.

TEACHER QUALIFICATIONS

The distribution of teacher qualifications as depicted in the table 4.14 shows that most public primary teachers hold a MSCE (55 percent) or a JCE (47 percent), while Primary School Leaving Certificate of Education (PSLCE) and diploma/degree holders are rare. The MSCE holders are more in demand than JCE holders. On average, male teachers working in government-funded schools have slightly more academic education than their female counterparts. Higher academic qualifications are also observed in urban settings, where 61 percent of teachers hold an MSCE compared to 54 percent in rural areas.

Table 4.14: Teacher Qualifications and Training Status by Location and Gender (in %), Government-Funded Primary Schools (2007)

	Urban	Rural	Female	Male	Total
Academic qualification					
PSLCE	0.1	0.8	1.0	0.6	0.7
JCE	39.0	45.4	49.6	41.6	44.6
MSCE	60.8	53.6	49.4	57.7	54.6
Diploma/degree	0.1	0.1	0.1	0.2	0.1
Training status					
Trained	97.2	90.5	94.2	89.7	91.4
Untrained	2.8	9.5	5.8	10.3	8.6
Total	100.0	100.0	100.0	100.0	100.0

Source: EMIS, 2007.

Almost all teachers are qualified[32] (91 percent) with a small amount (9 percent) still untrained. The untrained are mostly volunteers (75 percent) and temporary teachers (13 percent)[33] and as a result mostly located in rural areas (96 percent). Teacher mobility can create additional qualification imbalances between rural and urban areas, usually in favor of the urban. A majority of trained teachers (56 percent) went through the MIITEP, followed by the two-year program (26 percent) and the one-year program (13 percent). Teachers with the Malawi Special Teacher Education Programme (MASTEP) qualification are quite rare now. See Appendix 4.4 for a brief description of training practices in Malawi.

Table 4.15: Types of Training among Trained Teachers (in %), Government-Funded Primary Schools (2007)

MASTEP	MIITEP	2 Years of Training	1 Year of Training	Total
5.2	55.5	26.3	13.0	100

Source: EMIS, 2007.

TEACHER ATTRITION

Being a primary school teacher is a relatively stable profession in Malawi; many teachers remain in the system until retirement. In 2007, 4,529 primary school teachers (working in government-funded primary schools) left their schools, corresponding to an attrition rate of 3.2 percent. Among those, 14.3 percent retired, 37.2 percent passed away, and 7 percent suffered from prolonged illnesses. The two latter reasons could be related to the HIV/AIDS pandemic. Indeed, with a prevalence rate of 12 percent (see Chapter 1), HIV has a major impact on the labor force in Malawi. Teachers also left because they were dismissed (10.7 percent), often for misconduct with students, or because they preferred office work (7 percent). Nine percent of teachers resign. This is quite limited if one considers the already limited level of attrition in public schools.

Table 4.16: Reasons for Attrition among Government-Funded Primary Schools

	Urban	Rural	Male	Female	Total
Total attrition rate (%)	**3.8**	**3.2**	**3.5**	**2.9**	**3.2**
Causes (%)					
Died	38.5	36.5	35.2	39.9	37.2
Dismissed	5.8	11.5	10.5	10.7	10.7
Prolonged illness	11.5	6.1	5.8	9.3	7.0
Resigned	8.2	8.6	9.2	7.1	8.5
Retired	10.1	14.9	17.6	7.3	14.3
Transferred to a non-teaching post	3.4	7.7	7.2	6.6	7.0
Reason not known/Other	22.6	14.8	14.5	19.1	16.3
Total	100.0	100.0	100.0	100.0	100.0

Source: EMIS, 2007.

Although available data do not distinguish between teachers who are qualified and those who are not, retaining qualified teachers in rural schools is a major, well-known issue. This is linked to motivation and job satisfaction. The Ministry, with DFID support, intends to introduce a Special Allowance for teachers who work in rural areas as an incentive to keep them in school. The scheme is still under discussion as the Ministry looks for ways to sustain it in the future without donor support.

STR AVERAGE

Malawi's STR has deteriorated over the past decade, rising from 63:1 in 2000 to 86:1 in 2007 (or 80:1 if volunteer teachers are included). This comes from a conjunction of parallel phenomena: the increase in student enrollment and student retention and a reduction in the number of teachers.

Table 4.17: STR by Location in All Government-Funded Schools (1999 and 2007)

	1999	2007	2007
		Without Volunteers	With Volunteers
Students per teacher	63	86	80
Students per qualified teacher	118	91	88

Sources: EMIS 1999 (CSR, 2004), EMIS 2007.

As indicated by figure 4.4, Malawi has the highest STR amongst the SADC countries, and is well above the SADC average STR of 40:1.

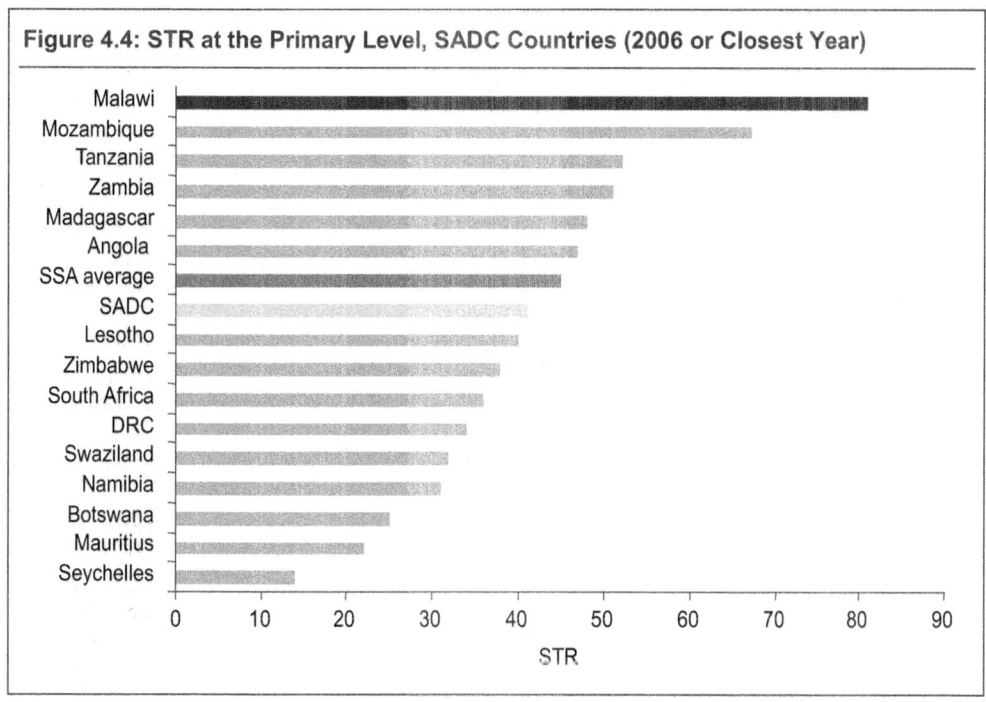

Figure 4.4: STR at the Primary Level, SADC Countries (2006 or Closest Year)

Source: World Bank data 2009.

In looking at the SqTR, trends show an improvement, as indicated by the decrease in the ratio from 118:1 in 1999 to 91:1 in 2007 (or 88:1 with volunteers). This improvement stems from the continuous training efforts used by the Ministry.

There are also notable differences in the STRs by grade, ranging from a very high level in Standard 1 (110:1) to a low 20:1 in Standard 8. This downward trend points to the high number of dropouts as students move up to the next grade. Lower STRs at upper standards also derive from the continuing use of specialized teachers: they often teach only certain subjects and consequently have abundant free time.

Although class size has decreased over the years (from 94 students per classroom in 2000 to 76 in 2007), the level remains quite high, especially at lower standards. This situation is puzzling because schools provide only 3–4 hours of sessions a day. It is also unclear why, in some cases, two teachers may teach a classroom of 90 students. As pointed out in the NESP appraisal report, "with only 15 percent of classrooms used in [overlapping] shifts, average class size could be cut nearly in half by universalizing double-shifting which, ceteris paribus, should by itself boost achievement at no additional cost except that of teachers which appears to be the most binding constraint" (Bellew, 2008).

Table 4.18: STRs and Class Size, Standards 1–8, in Government-Funded Public Schools (2000 and 2007)

	Std 1	Std 2	Std 3	Std 4	Std 5	Std 6	Std 7	Std 8
STR								
2000	100	76	64	52	45	39	33	28
2007	110	88	70	55	48	38	30	20
Class size								
2007	121	97	92	73	66	55	48	43

Sources: EMIS 2000 (CSR 2004), EMIS 2007 (2007 includes volunteer teachers).

Space availability may be at stake, as reflected by the high proportion of classes still held under trees (17 percent). This, along the high STRs, illustrates difficulties faced by the education system to meet its infrastructure and teacher needs.

Consistency in Teacher Allocation: How Well Are Teachers Being Allocated to Schools?

A more empirical analysis of teacher deployment can be made by quantitatively assessing its consistency. This analysis deals with equity in schooling conditions across schools because the allocation of teachers according to the number of students at school level is the way to ensure equity in terms of STRs.

QUANTITATIVE ANALYSIS

The analysis examines the relation between the number of students enrolled in a school and the number of teachers deployed to that same school. Theoretically, it is expected that the number of teachers allocated to a school is proportional with the number of students in that school. A consistent deployment of teachers would imply that schools of the same size have the same number of teachers.

The relationship between the number of students and the number of teachers (government-paid only) in all Malawi public school is plotted in figure 4.5. It shows a global positive relationship between the two variables, but wide variations can be observed across schools. For instance, schools with 200 students can have from 3 to 10 teachers. These features entail great STR variations, and by extension, huge disparities in schooling conditions across schools.

The statistical analysis offers a global measure of the consistency of teacher allocation. This measure refers to the R^2, known as the coefficient of determination,[34] which is calculated on all schools throughout the country. It allows for an assessment of the extent to which the number of teachers is proportional to the number of students enrolled. In Malawi, the R^2 equals 58 percent.[35] This means that 58 percent of the observed variations in teacher numbers are explained by differences in the numbers of students.

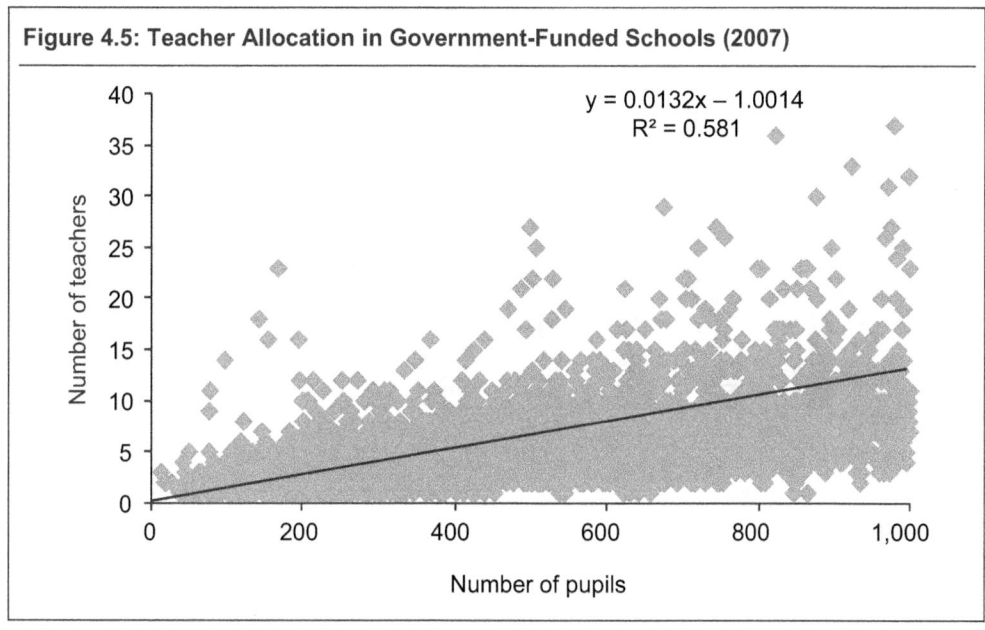

Figure 4.5: Teacher Allocation in Government-Funded Schools (2007)

$y = 0.0132x - 1.0014$
$R^2 = 0.581$

Source: Authors' construction based on data from EMIS 2007.
Note: Volunteer teachers are not included.

The complementary measure (1-R^2), called the degree of randomness, measures the proportion of situations where the number of teachers is not explained by the number of students in the school. The degree of randomness in 2007 was 42 percent, well above the average of a sample of African countries (31 percent), for which such information was available. In addition, it seems the situation has deteriorated; in 2000, the randomness factor was 34 percent. These results highlight the strong need for better teacher allocation in Malawi to ensure more consistent and more equitable deployment.

CONSISTENCY OF TEACHER DEPLOYMENT AT THE SUBNATIONAL LEVEL

To get a more accurate picture of the process of teacher deployment, the analysis can be pursued by focusing on the situation that prevails in urban and rural areas and at the division level. It is interesting to see the extent in which over- and underendowments of teachers (vis-à-vis the average situation) are randomly allocated or if certain locations and divisions appear to be favored.

The deployment of primary teachers appears uneven, with teachers concentrated in urban schools, and a scarcity of teachers in rural remote schools. Indeed, urban government-funded primary schools have an average STR of 46:1, while rural schools have an average STR of 93:1 (or 86:1 with volunteers). Figure 4.6 shows that the degradation of the STR has essentially affected rural zones. The deployment of qualified teachers is also skewed towards urban zones: While urban areas have maintained an SqTR of 47:1, rural areas remain seriously deprived of sufficient qualified teachers (an SqTR of 99:1 or 95:1 if volunteers are included).

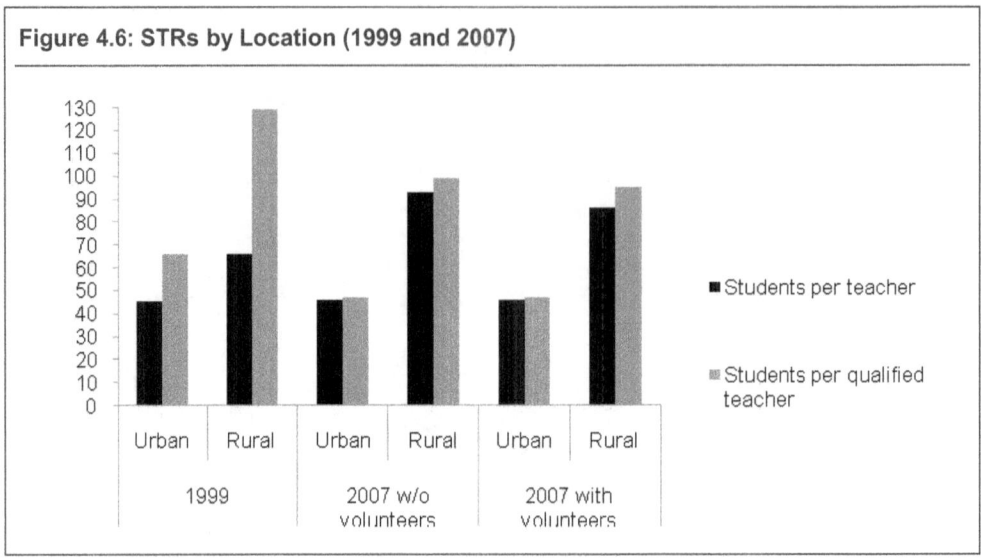

Figure 4.6: STRs by Location (1999 and 2007)

Sources: EMIS 2007, CSR 2004.

Teacher allocation across divisions is also quite uneven, marked by wide disparities in STRs—from 75:1 in the Northern division to 105:1 in the Shire Highlands. Including volunteer teachers further widens the gap between divisions (from 66 to 104), without however affecting the ranking of divisions according to the level of their STR.[36] Over the years, the dispersion across divisions has increased (from 12 in 1999 to 27 in 2007), at the expense of certain divisions, such as Shire Highlands and South Eastern, which have seen their STRs burst to 105:1 and 104:1, respectively. While the Southern Eastern division relied on volunteers to make up for the shortage of teachers, the Shire Highlands did not. As a result, the Shire Highlands has the highest STR.

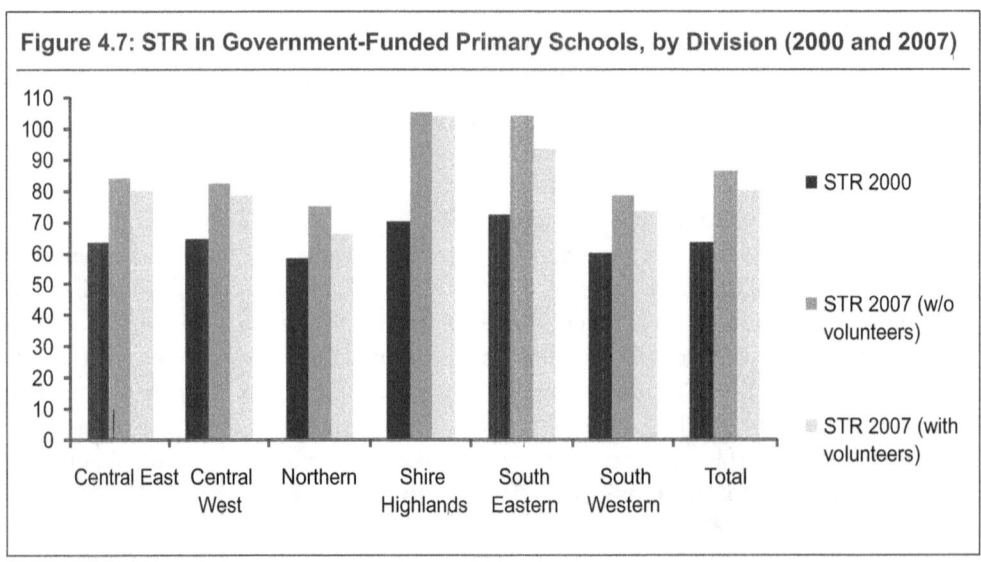

Figure 4.7: STR in Government-Funded Primary Schools, by Division (2000 and 2007)

Source: EMIS 2007.

To further analyze the degree of inconsistency in allocating teachers within divisions, a regression was run for each of the six divisions. The degree of randomness differs substantially from one division to the other, with higher inconsistencies in teacher allocation observed in the Shire Highlands and Northern divisions, and to a lesser extent in the Central Eastern division (see table 4.19).

Table 4.19: Degree of Randomness at Division Level, Government-Funded Schools (2007)

Division	Degree of randomness (1-R^2) (in %)
Central East	44.8
Central West	38.3
Northern	32.3
Shire Highlands	52.4
South Eastern	48.6
South Western	34.3
Malawi	**41.5**

Source: EMIS, 2007.
Note: Calculations include volunteer teachers.

Disparities in teacher deployment are also striking at the district level, with important disparities found between urban and rural districts. While in all urban districts the STR falls below the 60:1 policy target, in rural districts ratios above 100:1 are not uncommon (Map 4.1). This is the case in Mangochi (129:1), Machinga (117:1), Dedza (110), Ntcheu (102:1), and Mulanje (110:1), which are very far from the policy target (see table 4A.5 in Appendix 4.3 for details). This situation already prevailed in 2000 (CSR, 2004), meaning that little improvement has been made since.

Improving the supply of teachers and their deployment is necessary if each student is to benefit from equitable monitoring. Teachers are in acute short supply in many rural districts and the issue of their qualifications remains rampant, although important improvements could have been recorded. The Education Sector Development Plan is planning a series of measures to overcome these problems, such as introducing distance and parallel modes of training (including in-service training and continuous professional-development programs); providing hardship funds for teachers working in remote zones; and reallocating CDSS primary teachers to primary schools.

Allocation of Material Resources: Book Allocation Process and Book Allocation Empirical Results

The allocation of textbooks in primary schools is set by the guidelines on Teaching and Learning Materials (formerly the Draft National School Textbook Policy of 2006), which states in its foreword that "The education system must have a continuous supply of quality, relevant and accessible teaching and learning materials to a ratio of 1:1." As such, the intention is to allocate one textbook per learner for each subject taught. Replacement of textbooks is planned every three years.

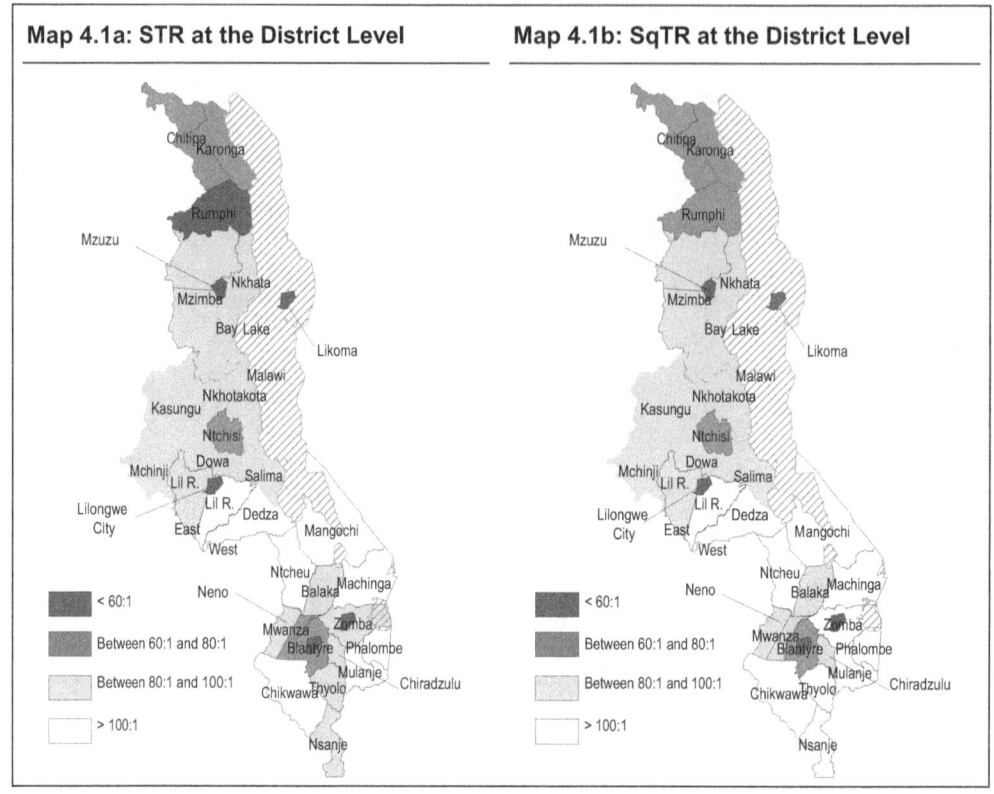

Source: EMIS 2007.

Textbooks are distributed free of cost to all public schools. There is no official policy on the distribution of textbooks to private schools, which represent a little over four percent of primary schools in Malawi. The current practice is for private schools to take textbooks from public schools. This results in a negative skewing of the public distribution figures. There are, however, plans underway to supply textbooks to private schools based on a cost-recovery mechanism. Reliance on donors is a critical problem for the distribution of textbooks to schools. There is a severe lack of government funds for textbooks, especially at the secondary level where local school initiatives such as the Textbook Revolving Fund represent the main source of funds for textbooks.

The process of delivering textbooks to primary schools is chain-like in structure. Firstly, procurement requirements are calculated and compiled by the Basic Education Department at the Ministry of Education headquarters. A distribution plan is formulated for each school. Then, the procurement requirements and distribution plans are submitted to a procurement agency that handles bids and the final identification of supplier(s). Suppliers are mostly located outside of Malawi due to capacity constraints in the country's printing industry. Once the books are printed, they are sent to regional warehouses from which private distributors deliver them directly to schools. The district education managers facilitate the process of distribution and the supplies unit is tasked with the responsibility of monitoring the process.

There are formidable challenges associated with the distribution of textbooks to and within schools. Firstly, the remote location and poor accessibility to some schools hinders the effective delivery of books. This is exacerbated by the targeted timing of delivery, which coincides with the wet season in Malawi. Further, noninvolvement on the part of district education managers at times negatively affects the distribution. At the school itself, there are further problems with distribution and utilization of books. Although the school may have received the requisite number of books to achieve the desired 1:1 student-textbook ratio, the target is not met for a number of other reasons. For example, teachers may be reluctant to let children use the books because of possible future absenteeism, dropping out, and lack of care for the books. Also, it is reported that some head teachers hoard textbooks to offset the possibility of a future shortage.

Finally, textbooks in primary schools have been undergoing a major overhaul with the introduction of the Primary Curriculum and Assessment Reform (PCAR). Primary school textbooks are being replaced to reflect the upgraded curriculum. This process began in 2006/07 with half of the new Standard 1 textbooks and was continued in 2007/08 with the remaining half of Standard 1 books, along with those for standards 2, 5, and 6. The target for 2008/09 is replacement of standards 3 and 7. These developments represent a significant change in the system that is current and ongoing and may not be reflected in the existing data.

Empirical Results

The allocation of English, Chichewa, and Mathematics books tends to follow the same pattern: On average, there are 0.5 books per student, with upper standards being better endowed than lower ones (table 4.20). Yet, almost a third of students in Standard 8 do not have a book, most share books in groups of two or three.

Table 4.20: Book Allocation by Standards in Government-Aided Schools (2007)

	Std1	Std2	Std3	Std4	Std5	Std6	Std7	Std8
Chichewa								
Books / students	0.05	0.5	0.4	0.4	0.4	0.5	0.6	0.7
Student-book ratio	18.3:1	2.1:1	2.6:1	2.4:1	2.2:1	1.9:1	1.7:1	1.5:1
% students without book	94	52	62	58	54	49	43	32
% of schools with less than 1 book for 2 students	95	45	39	46	52	61	68	75
English								
Books / students	0.06	0.5	0.4	0.4	0.5	0.5	0.6	0.7
Student-book ratio	17.4:1	1.9:1	2.4:1	2.3:1	2.2:1	1.9:1	1.6:1	1.4:1
% students without book	94	46	58	56	54	46	37	28
% of schools with less than 1 book for 2 students	95	51	41	47	51	59	68	74
Mathematics								
Books / students	0.06	0.6	0.5	0.5	0.5	0.6	0.7	0.7
Student-book ratio	17.2:1	1.6:1	2:1.	2.1:1	2:1	1.7:1	1.5:1	1.4:1
% students without book	94	30	51	52	49	40	34	29
% of schools with less than 1 book for 2 students	95	58	47	49	55	65	70	75

Source: EMIS 2007.

The degree of coherence in book allocations at the school level (the R^2) tends to rise up to Standard 5, and decreases thereafter (table 4.21). General book allocation consistency remains low, varying between 20 percent (Mathematics, Standard 2)[37] to 38 percent (Chichewa, Standard 5). In the best case, 38 percent of the books are allocated according to the number of students enrolled in the school. In most cases, the allocation process depends on factors other than the number of students. A similar analysis conducted at division level (see results table 4A.6 in Appendix 4.3) show great variations in book allocation consistency across divisions, with a somewhat more consistent allocation process in the South Western division (higher R^2 values for all standards) but a poorer one in the Central Eastern and Shire Highlands divisions.

Table 4.21: Book Allocation Coherence by Standards in Government-Aided Schools (2007) (in %)

R^2	Std1	Std2	Std3	Std4	Std5	Std6	Std7	Std8
English	0	24.7	26.3	34.2	36.8	28.5	28.1	19.9
Chichewa	1.3	22.0	26.8	32.9	38.2	34.3	34.7	23.8
Mathematics	0.9	20.0	24.3	33.8	35.2	35.6	26.0	23.7

Source: EMIS, 2007.

ORT Funds

ORT funding for primary education is allocated through the National Local Government Financing Committee to local district, town, and city assemblies. Allocation of funds is based on a formula,[38] which was developed so that similar districts would receive the same funding per annum and districts that are not similar would receive different funding based on their characteristics (to fulfill principles of horizontal and vertical equity). At the school level, funding allocation is based on student enrollment. Schools are categorized in five enrollment bands as follows: 10–500; 501–1500; 1501–2500; 2501–3500; 3501–4500+.

ORT funding is used for day-to-day operations for the education districts, utility bills, teachers' leave grants, expenses for special needs education, and maintenance work. Funds are also used to procure additional teaching and learning materials and aid in the minor maintenance and rehabilitation of schools. As shown by the figure 4A.4 in Appendix 4.1, the allocation of ORT funds across districts is very consistent— 87 percent of the funding is allocated based on school enrollment at the district level. Yet, there is some evidence that when allocating funds, the principle of adequacy is not always considered, as what is shared is what is available. Some evidence also suggests that at the school level, funding is still inadequate although there has being a great improvement compared to 2005, when schools received no direct funding from the government to enable them operate effectively. Under the Direct Support to Schools Initiative, schools have been receiving amounts ranging from MK81,000 to MK148,000.

Secondary Level

Secondary schools in Malawi can be put in the following categories: CSSs,[39] CDSSs, ODSSs, and private secondary schools. CDSSs currently account for the majority of schools (55 percent) and enroll almost half of the students (47 percent). The remaining students are in CSSs (26.5 percent) and private schools (22.8 percent). A small proportion of students attend ODSSs (3.3 percent).[40]

Institutional Aspects of Teacher Management: Recruitment and Deployment Patterns

Teacher recruitment is done through two routes: when students graduate from colleges and universities and from direct application to the Ministry of Education. Once diploma and degree holder results are out, deans of education send names of successful students to the Ministry of Education. The secondary school directorate allocates them to divisions, which in turn deploy them to secondary schools as per demand according to subject combinations within the division. Non-education degree and diploma students apply directly to the ministry for teaching posts. The secondary and human resource departments scrutinize the applicant's qualifications to check his or her suitability to teach. The human resource department then formalizes the recruitment process.

Main Teacher Characteristics

There are 10,258 secondary school teachers in Malawi, of which 8,026[41] are working in government-funded schools. Among public secondary schools, the CDSSs have the highest number of teachers (60 percent), followed by the CSSs (33 percent) and the ODSSs (7 percent). Female teachers are one-fifth of the public teaching force. They tend to be concentrated in urban and other semi-urban centers because they often "follow their husbands" (that is transfer from one school to another is determined by the husband's duty station.)

TEACHER QUALIFICATIONS

Underqualified teachers (60 percent) in secondary schools still remain a big challenge. Most of these teachers work in CDSSs, which have an unqualified teaching force of 81 percent, compared to 27 percent in CSSs. Formerly, teachers who were trained to teach primary were also sent to secondary schools, especially CSSs, following the expansion of the secondary school subsector.

These teachers (for example, PT1–PT4 teachers) make up the majority of the teaching force in CDSSs. Not surprisingly, CDSS teachers have lower academic qualifications than their peers in CSSs (see table 4.22).

Table 4.22: Teacher Characteristics in Government-Funded Secondary Schools by Type of School (2007) (in %)

	CSS	CDSS	Open School	Total
Number	2,662	4,813	551	8,026
%	33.2	59.9	6.9	100.0
% female	25.8	20.1	22.1	22.1
Academic/Qualification (%)				
PSLCE	1.2	0.3	0.4	0.6
JCE	1.3	0.3	0.0	0.6
MSCE	12.4	78.1	32.8	53.2
Education diploma/degree	72.6	18.9	57.0	39.3
Non-education diploma/degree	12.5	2.4	9.8	6.3
Grade (%)				
POE (I)	38.3	13.4	37.8	23.1
POB (I)	20.1	3.1	15.3	9.4
POC (I)	9.4	1.2	5.3	4.1
P8 (H)	5.9	1.2	4.5	3.0
P7 (G)	9.6	1.8	6.1	4.6
P6 (F)	1.7	0.3	0.4	0.7
P5 (F)	0.2	0.0	0.0	0.1
PT1 (L) to PT4 (I)	14.8	79.0	30.6	55.0
Training (%)				
Trained	72.9	19.3	57.9	39.8
Untrained	27.1	80.7	42.1	60.2
Total (%)	100	100	100	100
STR	21:1	21:1	13:1	20:1
SqTR	29:1	107:1	22:1	51:1

Source: EMIS, 2007, based on teachers from which data are available (7,868 teachers).

TEACHER ATTRITION

Teacher attrition rates are 4.3 percent in government secondary schools and 21.6 percent in private secondary schools, for a total attrition rate of 8 percent. Retaining teachers, especially in private schools seems quite tricky; among those teachers who have left the private schooling system, 42.5 percent have resigned. In public schools, the issue is less rampant. Death is another major cause of attrition (29 percent) in public schools. The HIV/AIDS scourge is largely responsible and also causes absence due to prolonged illness. Both death and prolonged illness account for a third of attrition in public schools. Retirement and transfers to an office post further deplete public schools of their teachers.

Table 4.23: Teacher Attrition by Reason at the Secondary Level (2007)

Attrition (%)	Government-Funded Schools	Private	Total
Total attrition rate	4.3	21.6	8.1
Causes			
Died	29.2	3.9	14.6
Transferred to a non-teaching post	16.0	11.6	13.5
Resigned	17.5	42.5	32.0
Dismissed	1.7	25.3	15.4
Retired	7.4	2.1	4.3
Prolonged illness	5.4	1.9	3.4
Reason not known/other	22.6	12.6	16.8
Total	100	100	100
Number	349	482	831

Source: EMIS, 2007.

Note: Does not take into account transfers to other teaching positions.

Average STR

Student-teacher ratios are low overall (20:142). While no major differences exist between CSSs and CDSSs, ODSSs display an extremely low STR that averages 13:1. Most teachers in open schools are also teaching in CSSs or CDSSs, and have been placed in ODSSs to fill a need. The SqTR, however, is generally high in public secondary schools (51:1). This is largely because the subsector has been flooded by underqualified teachers who have been moved from primary school.

Yet, strong differences appear across types of schools: the SqTR ranges from 22:1 in ODSSs to 29:1 in CSSs, and 107:1 in CDSSs. This also highlights the serious shortage of qualified teachers in CDSSs. The fact that most CDSSs are staffed with underqualified teachers raises some serious equity and efficiency concerns. Upgrading underqualified teachers in secondary schools through distant and residential programs would be required to improve levels of SqTRs.

Table 4.24 gathers information on the allocation of teachers by geographical location. While few differences appear between rural and urban areas in the STR, stronger differences emerge in teacher qualification. In 2007, the SqTR was 33:1 in urban settings compared to 58:1 in rural ones. Yet, this is a significant improvement from 1999, when the SqTR averaged 59:1 in urban areas and 131:1 in rural ones.[43]

STRs across divisions generally show a similar pattern, except for the Shire Highlands, which displays a slightly higher STR than the other divisions. More marked variations between divisions are observed for the SqTR. The shortage of qualified teachers is also pervasive in the Central Western division, as indicated by the high value of its SqTR.

Table 4.24: STR by Types of Schools and Location, Government-Funded Secondary Schools (2007)

	Average Number of Students	Average Number of Teachers	Average Number of Qualified Teachers	STR	SqTR
Type of school					
CSS	393	18.9	13.8	20.8	28.6
CDSS	172	8.4	1.6	20.6	106.6
ODSS	158	12.5	7.2	12.6	21.7
Location					
Urban	370.5	20.6	11.1	17.9	33.2
Rural	195.1	9.4	3.4	20.8	57.9
Division					
Northern	161.5	8.5	3.4	19.0	47.6
Central Eastern	214.4	10.1	4.1	21.2	52.6
Central Western	258.3	12.7	4.4	20.3	58.4
Southern Eastern	201.9	11.1	4.9	18.2	41.5
Southern Western	231.3	12.0	4.8	19.2	47.7
Shire Highlands	239.8	9.6	4.0	24.9	59.3
Average	213.1	10.5	4.2	20.2	51.1
(min-max)	(12-1447)	(2-59)	(1-50)	(2.6-55.7)	(4.3-391)

Source: EMIS, 2007.

Consistency in Teacher Allocation

Figure 4A.5 in Appendix 4.1 provides a visual analysis of the allocation of teachers across schools. It shows some substantial variations in the number of teachers across schools of similar size. As an example, a school of 220 students can have between 9–15 teachers. Yet, compared to the situation prevailing in primary schools, the allocation of teachers across public secondary schools is more consistent, as indicated by the value of the R^2 of 72 percent. This value indicates that 72 percent of the variation in teacher allocation to schools is explained by the number of students. This is a great improvement from 2000, when 41 percent of teacher deployment variation was explained by school size. However, despite a high R^2 value, there remains room for improvement throughout the system, as 28 percent of teacher allocation still depends on factors other than school enrollment.

ORT Funds

As with primary schools, ORT funding to secondary schools is used for day-to-day operations, utility bills, teachers' leave grants, some capital purchases, and maintenance work. In July 2008, all secondary schools began retaining both tuition and boarding fees to be used at the school level. The retained fees will increase the ORT received from Treasury.

ORT funding to secondary schools concerns the CSSs and the initial list of approved CDSSs. These schools receive an allocation based on a set formula.[44] CDSSs, which came onto the approved list later, receive a lump sum of MK500,000 per annum if they have forms 1–4, and MK300,000 if they are have junior secondary forms 1–2. These amounts are considered the bare minimum. Funds to schools are channeled through cost centers. CDSSs that are not cost centers obtain their funds from the education divisions at the rate of approximately MK10,000 per month. Grant-aided secondary schools receive funds according to an agreement between religious agencies and the Ministry of Education. This agreement stipulates that single-stream schools receive MK42,500 per month, double-stream MK82,500 per month, and triple-stream MK122,500 per month.

Table 4.25: Recap of the Funds Allocated to Secondary Schools

Type of School	Funding Level
CSSs	Formula*
CDSSs approved/cost center	Formula
CDSSs not approved/cost center	MK300,000 if form 1 to 2 MK500,000 if form 1 to 4
Grant-aided	MK42,500 if single-stream MK82,500 if double-stream MK122,500 if triple-stream
CDSSs/not cost centers	MK10,000

Source: EMIS, 2007.
* CDSSs in this group are not included in the formula because of inadequate funds from Treasury; if these CDSSs were included, the original list of schools would receive much less than they normally did.

As noted in the formula, the number of students is not taken into account when allocating funds, as the funds rely more on the types of expenses borne by the schools. Those schools (for example, CSSs) who have more facilities and higher utility bills will get more money, as they also have more maintenance work than less well-endowed schools (for example, CDSSs). This creates a situation wherein the allocation of funds is weakly linked to the variation of the number of students enrolled at school and where 68 percent of the allocation of funds is explained by factors other than the number of students at school level. This current allocation formula, although it allows for those schools with services to take care of them, exacerbates iniquity across types of schools, to the detriment of CDSSs, which are already less well endowed than CSSs.

Economy of Scale in School Production

When analyzing global or average situations, it is implicitly assumed that resources per student do not depend, on average, on the size of the school in which students are enrolled. This hypothesis does not always hold, as the average cost per student may happen to decrease with the number of students enrolled. Certain fixed costs, such as the remuneration of specialized teachers and of administrative and support staff at the school level, are spread out over the rising enrollment. Economy of scale in service delivery may occur, with cost per student falling as the enrollment increases.

Economies of Scale at the Primary Level

Earlier in this chapter, the relationship between the number of teachers and students in primary schools was analyzed. Some extreme observations have been removed to come up with the following relationship:

(1) Number of teachers=0.046 + 0.011 × number of students

Multiplying both sides by the teacher mean wage (for example, MK189,395) results in the total wage bill (staff in primary schools are mainly teachers) at school level:

(2) Wage bill = 8,712 + 2,083 × number of students

In equation (2), the intercept 8,712 represents the school's fixed costs or structural costs. The multiplicative coefficient of the "number of students" variable corresponds to the marginal cost per student (what it costs on average in terms of the wage bill to increase the number of students by one unit). From equation 2, it is possible to compute the wage unit cost (per student), which refers to the wage spending divided by the number of students enrolled:

(3) Wage unit cost = 2,083 + 8,712/number of students

Equation (3) makes clear that the teacher wage unit cost corresponds to the addition of the marginal costs and the allocation of fixed costs between students enrolled. The bigger the school size (for example, the number of students enrolled) the bigger this latter component (fixed costs are being allocated among a bigger number of students). Economies of scale can potentially occur in the school production. Table 4.26 and its related figure 4.8, represent the relationship between the size of enrollments (school size) and unit costs (personnel cost per students) at the primary level.

Table 4.26: Relationship between the Wage Unit Cost and the Number of Students at the Primary Level

Number of students	80	150	200	325	550	**624**	835	1,200	1,450	2,275
Wage unit cost (MK)	2,192	2,141	2,127	2,110	2,099	**2,097**	2,093	2,090	2,089	2,087

Source: EMIS 2007; simulation from regression.

A negative, somewhat limited relationship between wage unit costs and school size prevails; this phenomenon is more marked for schools of small size, which enroll 550 students and less. Yet, the dispersion of unit costs among schools is quite narrow, varying from MK2,192 in schools with 80 students to MK2,087 in big schools enrolling 2,275 students; the difference corresponding to MK105 (US$0.75).

The magnitude of economies of scale is quite modest at the primary level,[45] which implies that large schools are not cheaper to run than small schools, but they may be located farther from the average student home. The current network of public schools tends to stress size over proximity. The average school enrollment is 642 in government-funded schools (600 in public schools, 667 in religious ones) compared to 194 in private schools. Among government-funded schools, 25 percent enroll less than 325 students and 10 percent less than 200 students. This is a real contrast with private schools, wherein 66 percent enroll less than 250 students each.

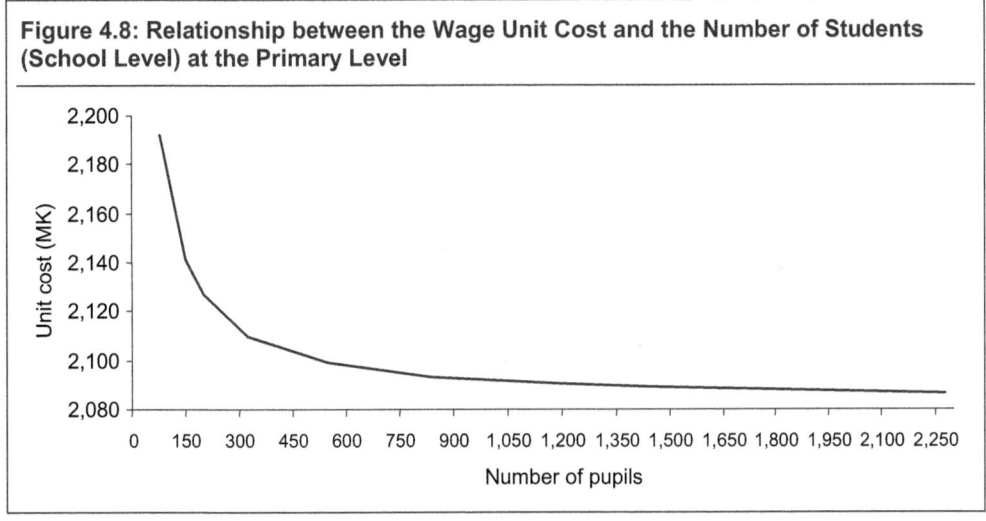

Figure 4.8: Relationship between the Wage Unit Cost and the Number of Students (School Level) at the Primary Level

Source: EMIS 2007, simulation from regression.

Economies of Scale at the Secondary Level

A similar exercise has being conducted for secondary schools, relying on costs related to teaching and support staff.[46] The general shape of the relationship is quite similar to the one observed at the primary level, although unit costs at the secondary level are 8.9 times higher than those at the primary level (MK19,316 on average compared to MK2,179 at the primary level); implying a relatively higher cost to deliver secondary services. Unit cost dispersions are also wider, ranging from MK26,705 in schools with 30 students to MK17,465 in schools with 800 students (for example, corresponding to a dispersion of MK9,240). The level at which the unit spending tends to stabilize is reached at around 100–150 students.

Table 4.27: Relationship between the Wage Unit Cost (Teachers Only) and the Number of Students at the Secondary Level

Number of students	50	110	170	**212**	275	410	530	800
Unit cost—all school staff (MK)	22,865	19,723	18,799	**18,464**	18,152	17,807	17,648	17,465

Source: EMIS, 2007; simulation from regression.

The average enrollment in secondary schools is relatively small (212). This is in sharp contrast to the primary level, where schools have been enrolling an average of 642 students. Variations arise across types of school, with CSSs enrolling an average of 393 students compared to 172 students in CDSSs and 158 in ODSSs. Unit costs at enrollment of more than 150 students (MK18,247) are 13 percent less than those for enrollment of 150 students and less (MK20,672). Yet, about a fifth of the students are currently enrolled in schools serving less than 150 students. Scale economies are clearly possible at the secondary level, by favoring *bigger* schools of more than 150 students. This result has major implications because the number of students who need to access secondary school will increase as more children complete primary school.[47]

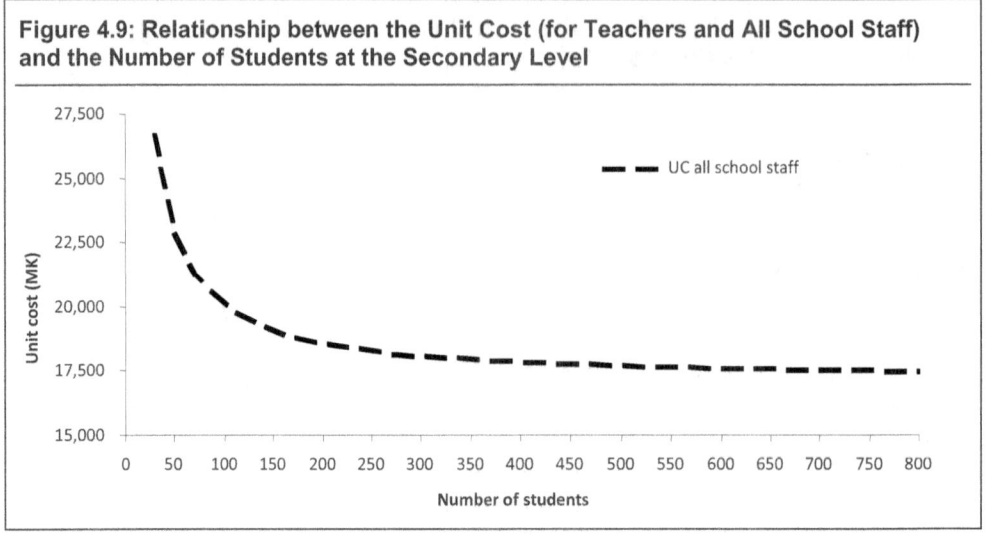

Figure 4.9: Relationship between the Unit Cost (for Teachers and All School Staff) and the Number of Students at the Secondary Level

Source: EMIS, 2007; simulation from regression.

Pedagogical Management: Transforming Inputs into Learning Outcomes

At the center of pedagogical management stands the issue of transforming mobilized inputs into concrete results, a process that should be as efficient as possible. How do schools perform in that regard? Do better endowed schools fare better?

At the Primary Level

Data used refers to PSLE pass rates analyzed earlier in this chapter (adjusted for local wealth conditions to control for some wealth-related disparities) and to unit costs based on teacher and book expenditures, both computed at the school level. Figure 4.10 illustrates the relationship between unit costs and PLSE pass rates for each government-funded school. It shows that the relation is weak in two respects:

- For a given pass rate result, a strong dispersion in unit costs prevails. Indeed, a pass rate of 60 percent can be obtained by investing between MK1,372 to MK7,879 per student. This implies that students enrolled in schools unevenly endowed can acquire a similar level of learning.
- For a given unit cost, a great variability of pass rates results can be found across schools.[48] Ultimately, schools that cost the most do not always present the best national examination results. Conversely, less endowed schools do not always display the worst results. These patterns are not unique to Malawi; they can be found in most African countries.

The particularly weak relationship between PSLE results and spending per student raises questions about the supervision process. As resources are scare, it seems important to improve inspection and supervision mechanisms to increase accountability and eventually improve the transformation of resources into student learning outcomes.

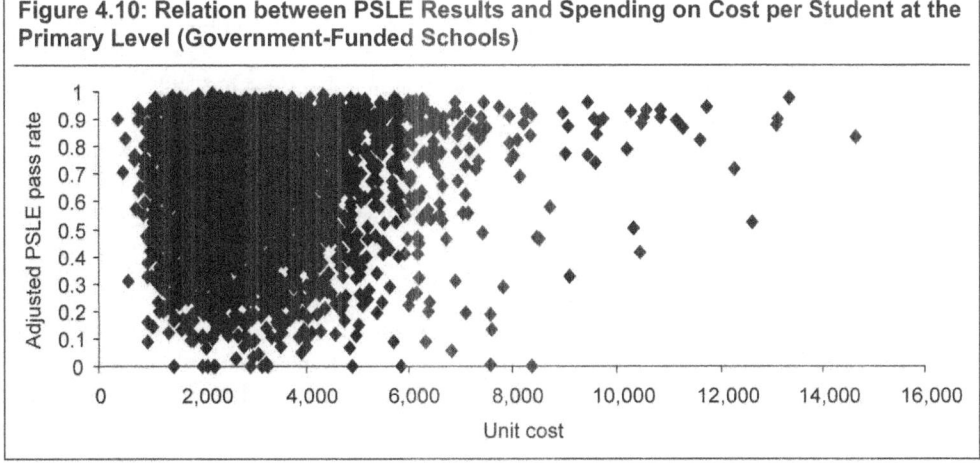

Figure 4.10: Relation between PSLE Results and Spending on Cost per Student at the Primary Level (Government-Funded Schools)

Sources: EMIS 2007, budget law 2008.
Note: Unit costs include school teachers and books related expenses.

At the Secondary Level

A similar exercise, conducted for the secondary level, reveals similar patterns: i) a great variability of costs for JCE and MSCE pass rates across secondary schools; and ii) a weak link between exam-rate results and unit costs (related to staff-wage expenses). For example, for a given unit cost of MK17,896, one school presents a JCE pass rate of 38 percent while another brings 71 percent of its students to graduation. Better endowed schools do not perform systematically better, while schools showing poor results are not always the ones with the lowest level of unit costs. As with the primary level, flaws appear in the process of transforming resources into results.

The strong randomness in the relationship between schools inputs and their pedagogical outcomes measured by examination result pass rates shows the existence of strong weaknesses in the pedagogical supervision of the system and the absence of management based on results. It is a domain for which improvement should be sought, as results are not used to regulate observed deviations. Such a policy would entail radical changes in the way the system is managed. What will help improve the quality of the system is an optimal allocation of resources that takes into account the progress made in school results and looks at it in relation to resources used.

Beyond the issue of resource allocation, the way resources are used seems to be a major influence on the level of learning outcome. Improving supervision and accountability mechanisms at the local level are effective interventions. Also, training PTAs and SMCs, together with teaches, on certain school management issues would make schools accountable to the community for the performance of students and the use of resources.

Notes

[1] We have relied here on EMIS data to allow for a consistent comparison in time and grades with 1999 figures. Yet, there are some evidences that EMIS data underestimate the level of repetition, as some students may be recorded as new entrants when they have dropped out from school and

returned to the same grade the following year. See Chapter 2 for additional information on repetition issues.

[2] Selection into Form 1 is not automatic but is based on merit and the availability of secondary places, which may become more limited as the number of primary school completers increases. Higher repetition rates at Standard 8 may be linked to the need for some learners to increase their chances to get into the secondary level.

[3] The repetition rate was 5.4 percent at the lower secondary against 7.2 percent at the upper secondary in 2006.

[4] The quality of data on repetition before 2004 is weak for the secondary level. As a result, the analysis was conducted on data from 2004 onward.

[5] In Chapter 2, an analysis of survival patterns was conducted using household survey data. The survival rate is complementary to 100 percent of the dropout rate. Dropouts may be overestimated at early grades as children who are leaving school in the middle of the year to reintegrate into it the following year are considered dropouts instead of repeaters, as repetition refers to administrative decisions made at the school level.

[6] This CSR uses a cross-section schooling profile that relies on administrative data for global enrollment and an IHS 2004 repetition structure.

[7] Dropout and repetition related coefficients are also useful to characterize the magnitude of the wastage. They are computed as follows: While the numerator of the dropout-related coefficient (also known as the efficiency coefficient with no repetition) includes only student-years associated with dropping out, the numerator of the repetition-related coefficient (also known as the efficiency coefficient with no dropouts) includes only student-years associated with grade repetition. The overall coefficient (the IEC, the product of the two) takes into account the student-years associated with both dropouts and grade repetitions.

[8] The computation of the coefficient is based on the following assumptions: i) it measures output as the number of graduates; ii) it assigns no value to skills acquired by dropouts; and iii) repetition is considered wasteful.

[9] A standardized indicator is needed to allow comparisons with other countries, such as an efficiency coefficient based on a primary education cycle of six years.

[10] Improving all aspects of the quality of education and ensuring excellence of all so that recognized and measurable learning outcomes are achieved by all, especially in literacy, numeracy, and essential life skills.

[11] Yet, this finding may not totally reflect declining quality so much as an increase in lower-achieving students in the system following the implementation of the fee-free policy in 1994. Indeed, abolishing school fees usually boosts school participation for students from a lower socioeconomic background, who usually face more educational challenges.

[12] See Chapter 2 for more about examinations. They are also used to select students for public secondary schools by ranking them and deciding what type of secondary schools they will be able to attend.

[13] EMIS data are used here. Sampling had to be restricted to schools that had presented candidates in 2006. The resulting dataset pertains to 3,539 schools out of 5,294 (all school types considered). For each school, information is available on exam pass rates as well as on the characteristics of schools and teachers.

[14] In 2006, 144,338 students sat for the exams and 106,363 passed.

[15] Forty percent of private schools are located in urban zones compared to 3.2 percent of government-funded schools.

[16] The STR is 24:1 in private schools against 80:1 in public schools. Also, a private school is more likely to have access to facilities, such as water, electricity, and a library. Teachers are generally younger (35 years old compared to 39 years old in public schools) and also more qualified (in

terms of academic qualifications). However, very few teachers in private schools (17 percent) are trained in comparison to teachers in government-funded schools (91 percent).

[17] Just as for the PSLE computation, JCE and MSCE computations are required to work on a sample of schools that had students who registered for the examination, and for which the number of students who passed the exam was above or equal to those who sat it. This led to a sample size of 968 schools and 824 schools, respectively (out of 1,046), for JCE and MSCE pass rates analyses.

[18] There is little difference between the number of students who entered the exam and the number of students enrolled in Standard 8.

[19] While 81 percent of CDSS teachers are untrained, only 27 percent of CSS teachers are. This is because numerous teachers trained to teach at the primary level are loaned to secondary schools, especially in CDSSs, because there is a shortage of appropriate teachers for the secondary school subsector. They represent 79 percent of the teaching force in CDSSs, compared to 15 percent in CSSs.

[20] The learning environment is also not quite conducive to teaching and learning; most classrooms lack desks, classrooms themselves are in poor shape, teaching and learning materials including textbooks, equipment, and facilities (both in normal classrooms and laboratories) are grossly inadequate, or nonexistent in some cases.

[21] EMIS data provide some information on fund flow at the school level. They show that while CSSs receive 86 percent of government funding, CDSSs only get 13 percent. Although this could be explained by the fact that CSSs have more current expenditures to cover than CDSSs (for example, boarding facilities, utilities), this allocation of government funds tends to reinforce iniquities between types of schools.

[22] Indeed, PSLE results are used to rank students, with the best one entering CSSs.

[23] In addition, pass rates are sometimes used to regulate students flows from one cycle to the next.

[24] In many similar exercises conducted in various countries, the explanatory power of such models tends to reach a best 10 percent (Swaziland: 5.3 percent; Niger: 7.9 percent; Mali: 7.6 percent). Information comes from most recent country-specific CSRs.

[25] Schools are classified simply as either rural or urban, and only considered urban if they fall within the urban administrative area. As a result, 95 percent of schools are considered rural, and this broad category includes many in peri-urban areas and those in small towns, along with the most isolated rural schools.

[26] PTAs and SMCs have currently have little to do with general school oversight, including monitoring learning outcomes. Indeed, PTA activities are mainly linked to school construction and maintenance, and to some extent to teacher pay and the purchase of school supplies (Bellew, 2008).

[27] The model was computed by relying only on 2007 (for the exam data) and 2006 data. Basic statistics on the model variables are in table 4A.3 of Appendix 4.2.

[28] Since June 2006, the retirement age has been raised to 60 years old.

[29] Following low teacher training outputs (about 2,500 a year over the past years), the supply of teachers has been inadequate to meet teacher needs. The current accumulated shortfall of primary school teachers is estimated at 13,000 (Bellew, 2008).

[30] Volunteers are also included in this analysis, although they are not paid by the government. By extension, government-funded teachers or public teacher will be referred to as well.

[31] Female teachers have above-average allocations to Central West and South West education divisions, while the Shire Highlands tend to have the fewest. The first two divisions are urban, around Lilongwe and Blantyre where most commercial activities take place. Shire Highlands is rural.

[32] A **qualified teacher** is defined as one who has not just an academic qualification, but has also trained as a teacher for the appropriate level. A primary qualified teacher who is sent to teach at a secondary school is considered unqualified.

[33] Note that almost 11 percent of the untrained teachers are civil servants.

[34] The value of the indicator ranges between 0 and 100 percent (or 0 and 1). The 100 percent value corresponds to a functional relationship where all the observations are located on the mean relationship (regression line), meaning that all schools are being treated equally (perfect equity) and the number of teachers depends only on the number of students enrolled at school level. On the other hand, a 0 value, indicates an absence of relationship between the number of teachers and the number of students they are teaching.

[35] The inclusion of volunteer teachers slightly improves the R^2 from 58.1 percent to 58.5 percent.

[36] In some cases, their recruitment has helped ease the pressure. This is particularly the case in the Southern Eastern and Northern divisions, where the recruitment of volunteers has caused a decrease in the STR of 11 points and 9 points, respectively. Yet, the use of volunteer teachers has not been systematic, as in the Shire Highlands and to a lesser extent in the Southern Western division.

[37] The analysis at Standard 1 is not relevant as most students do not have books.

[38] The formula is based on district characteristics that are divided into three major components: demographic data, economic data, and social factors. There are variables under each component, which are used by the district assembly as a basis for allocating funding and to maintain objectivity. These variables include: the proportion of children under 14 years; land area; number of schools; road length requiring reshaping; education in an urban setting (utility bills); number of special needs centers; STRs; Primary school enrollment, and the number of primary school teachers. There are four main areas of expenditure for the district assemblies with respect to primary education: These are leave grants, operations, maintenance, and special needs education. These variables are weighted and standardized on a 100-point scale in the formula. The total weighted points for each variable determine how much funding should go to each type of major area of educational expenditure at the local assembly level.

[39] CSSs comprise four government national schools, grant-aided secondary schools, district boarding secondary schools, and day secondary schools. Grant-aided schools are considered public in the current analysis as teachers are being funded by the government.

[40] Open-day schools are providing students with night sessions. CSSs, private schools, and ODSSs account for 13.5 percent, 27.1 percent, and 4.2 percent of the schools, respectively.

[41] From that figure, discount the 269 teachers who are working in two schools, usually a CDSS or a CSS and an ODSS.

[42] With such a level, Malawi is among SADC countries with the lowest STRs, ranking below the average STR of the region (23:1).

[43] Similarly, the indicators for STR were 28:1 in urban areas and 36:1 in rural areas (CSR, 2004).

[44] The formula is based on school characteristics, which are divided into three components: basic school capacity, curriculum enhancement, and auxiliary or support factors. There are variables under each component that are referred to as expenditure drivers/generators. The purpose of all these variables is to base funding allocation on what things will cause the school to spend so that there is objectivity in allocating funds.

[45] The unit cost for schools with 550 students and less is MK2,118 against MK2,093 for schools enrolling more than 550 students (a 1.2 percent difference).

[46] Unit cost = 17105+288003/number of students. Teacher mean wage amounted to MK343,000 in 2007, while the wage related to all staff was MK292,895.

[47] Yet the level of fixed costs (such as the one related to infrastructure costs) may be a constraint on the expansion of the secondary level.

[48] For instance, for a given unit cost of MK3,287 PSLE pass rates may vary from 50 to 100 percent.

CHAPTER 5

Equity and Disparities

Summary of the Chapter

Schooling access suffers from disparities according to gender. Considering present enrollment, gender parity indexes (calculated by dividing the GER of the girls by the GER of the boys), ranged from 1.04 in the first four standards of primary education to 0.50 in higher education and 0.38 in TEVET. Five and a half times more girls than boys are enrolled in non-formal educational programs. Boys are more likely to repeat standards than girls. However, more girls drop out in primary and secondary education and they do not perform as well as boys (as shown by SACMEQ data and results on national examinations).[1]

Nevertheless, access to education suffers more from type of location and income disparities than from gender. The difference in the primary completion rate (proxied by the access rate to Standard 8) is 14 percent between boys and girls, yet 34 percent between urban and rural students. And the disparity is still greater—44 percent—between the richest 20 percent of the population and the poorest 20 percent. For secondary completion, the difference is 9 percent between boys and girls, 26 percent between urban and rural students, and 29 percent between rich and poor. Furthermore, in higher education, the students from the richest 20 percent represent 91 percent of the total number of students while those from the poorest 40 percent account for only 0.7 percent.

The Northern region's GERs in primary (134 percent) and secondary education (28 percent) are much higher than the national averages (101 percent and 16 percent, respectively). The primary completion rate in the Northern region is 1.8 times higher than the national value. It rises above 50 percent in a few districts (Mzimba, Rumphi, and Nkhatabay), and falls under 30 percent in six others (Dedza, Mangochi, Ntcheu, Machinga, Phalombe, and Thyolo). The secondary completion rate (proxied by the access rate to Form 4) is the same in the Northern region as the Southern (12 percent), whereas the Central is lower (9 percent). At the district level, Blantyre has the maximum value (30 percent), while 19 districts have less than 10 percent, 3 of them being under 5 percent: Chitipa, Balaka, and Machinga. SACMEQ shows that pupils in large cities have a better chance of reaching a minimum mastery level than those in other areas and have better national examination results than students in rural areas. Moreover, pupils in the South Eastern and South Western education divisions are faring better than those in Central Eastern and Northern regions.

Seventy-three percent of public resources are appropriated by the most educated 10 percent of students, which makes Malawi one of the least equitable countries in Africa. Moreover, due to social selectivity and the distribution of public resources by education levels, urban people appropriate 8.4 times more resources than rural, and the richest 20 percent of households get 11.4 times more public education spending than the poorest 20 percent.

* * *

Chapter 5 examines education equity and focuses on disparities across gender, location, region, and household income. Equity entails putting measures in place aimed at reducing the existing regional, district, and socioeconomic disparities in educational access, retention, and learning at all levels of the system. An equitable distribution of education resources plays an important role in reducing poverty and increasing access for more disadvantaged groups. Furthermore, education as an investment contributes to the positive economic and social status of individuals in their adult lives. It constitutes the largest government expenditure and has the widest outreach because almost all families in Malawi have children, or are guardians for children, and as such, have the potential to benefit from public subsidies through education. In this way, the education sector can become an effective fiscal instrument for alleviating poverty and redistributing income. Consequently, this chapter also examines who benefits from public spending on education.

Disparities among Social Groups

This section focuses on the schooling distribution according to socioeconomic criteria. Table 5.1 shows the social structure (by gender, location, and wealth quintile) of people aged 5–24 years, according their highest level of education. It should be contrasted with the comparison group that shows the entire population of people in this age group.

Table 5.1: Social Structure by Highest Level of Education and Comparison Group, 5–24 Years Old (in %)

	Comparison Group (5–24 years old)	Highest Level of Education Attended				
		Never Attended School	Non-Formal Education	Primary	Secondary	Higher Education
Gender						
Boys	49	50	14	48	53	52
Girls	51	50	86	51	47	48
Total	100	100	100	100	100	100
Location						
Urban	12	5	11	11	33	76
Rural	88	95	89	89	67	24
Total	100	100	100	100	100	100
Wealth Index						
Q1	20	29	21	20	7	0.7
Q2	20	25	19	20	10	0.0
Q3	19	21	32	20	14	3.5
Q4	20	16	24	21	19	4.5
Q5	21	9	5	20	50	91.3
Total	100	100	100	100	100	100

Source: Calculation from MICS 2006 data.
Note: In this table, both individuals who are currently attending as well as those who have dropped out are considered. For instance, 89 percent of those who have reached primary education are rural: This proportion refers to those who are currently enrolled in primary (whatever the grade) and those who dropped out during primary.

A similar gender trend as the one observed in the comparison group applies to those for whom primary education is the highest level attended: 52 percent of those who have attended only primary are girls. More boys than girls attend secondary and higher education, but the difference is still very slight. Alternatively, more girls (86 percent) attend non-formal education than boys.

The majority of Malawians (88 percent) live in rural areas and rural children represent most of those who have had no education (95 percent) or attend non-formal education (89 percent). Most primary students live in rural areas; the percentage decreases a bit in secondary education. It is worth noting that the four major cities in Malawi (Lilongwe, Blantyre, Mzuzu, and Zomba) are the only areas considered urban and the rest of the country is classified as rural. However, despite the small urban population, far more students in these areas go on to higher education (76 percent) compared to rural students.

Among the group reaching higher education, 91.3 percent belong to the richest 20 percent of households, while only 0.7 percent come from the poorest 40 percent.

Table 5.1 shows educational attainment among the 5–24-year-olds, but the children who are currently attending school also need to be looked at. This can be done by displaying enrollment indicators and schooling profiles, using either administrative data or households surveys.

Gender Disparities

Schooling Coverage at Different Levels of Education

Table 5.2 displays GER gender parity indexes across the educational system, from preschool (ECD Level 2) to higher education (including adult literacy programs), from 2000–2007.

Parity indexes have increased since 2000, meaning improved enrollments for girls at all educational levels. However, gender disparity varies from one level to another; the parity index starts at 1.04 in the first four standards and decreases down to 0.67 in the two last forms.

Table 5.2: Gender Parity Indexes at Different Education Levels, 2000–2007

| Year | Pre-school (level 2) | Primary | | | Secondary | | | TEVET | Higher Education | Adult Literacy |
		Std1–Std4	Std5–Std8	Std1–Std8	Form 1–2	Form 3–4	Form 1–4			
2000		1.00	0.82	0.94	0.69	0.65	0.67		0.34	6.43
2001		1.00	0.83	0.95	0.74	0.67	0.71		0.33	5.94
2002		1.01	0.90	0.97	0.77	0.70	0.74		0.36	5.39
2003		1.01	0.93	0.99	0.81	0.67	0.75		0.42	5.40
2004		1.04	0.92	1.01	0.81	0.69	0.76		0.45	6.55
2005		1.04	0.94	1.01	0.80	0.68	0.75		0.44	5.67
2006		1.04	0.96	1.02	0.88	0.67	0.79		0.41	5.51
2007	0.87	1.04	0.96	1.02	0.85	0.67	0.77	0.38	0.50	-

Source: Primary, secondary, TEVET, and higher education data from EMIS 2007 (MOEST) and preschool and adult literacy data from the Ministry of Women and Child Development
Note: Parity indexes on enrollment coverage are computed by dividing GER for girls by GER for boys. The GER measure is replaced by the number of students or learners by 100,000 inhabitants, if relevant.

For gender disparities in primary and secondary education, international data are available to compare Malawi with other African countries. With parity of 1.02 for primary education, Malawi stands above the SADC average (1.00) and the SSA average (0.9). In lower secondary (Form 1–Form 2), Malawi is behind SADC average (0.9), while it remains above the African average (0.8). Finally, for upper secondary Malawi stands behind the African average of 0.8, which is also the SADC average.

It was not possible to find data and produce trends of parity index for technical and Vocational Training (TEVET). However, 2007 data show that the enrolment of girls is very low compared to boys: for every 100 boys enrolled, there are only 38 girls. This could be explained by the fact that most courses offered under TEVET are in subjects associated with traditional male occupations. Female students were introduced to the so-called non-traditional courses in 2002.

In higher education, the trend is similar with a parity index of 50. However, there has been a significant increase in number of girls every year, as the same figure was around 0.34 in 2000. Many more girls attend non-formal education than boys (enrollment in adult literacy programs is 5.5 times higher for girls than boys [2006]) and this is a consequence of the decreasing enrollment of girls in formal education.

Figure 5.1 confirms those trends for primary and secondary education, displaying a simplified schooling profile per gender, from MICS data. It illustrates that there is a high access (96 percent) to Standard 1 for both boys and girls in Malawi. However, less than 50 percent of boys reach Standard 8 and the percentage for girls is much lower (31). Access to lower and upper secondary education is low for boys and even lower for girls.

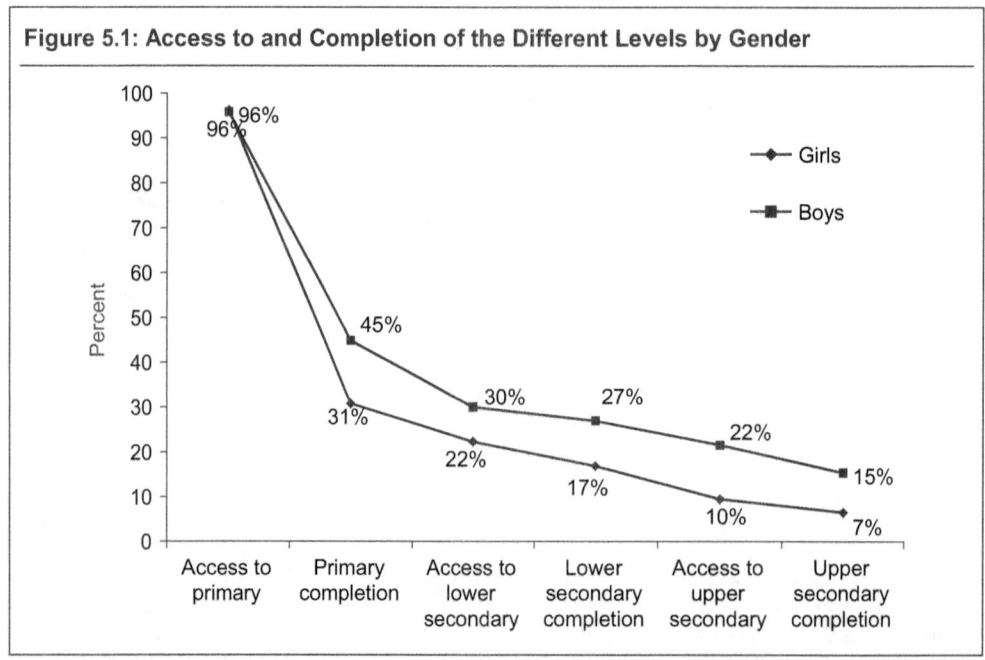

Figure 5.1: Access to and Completion of the Different Levels by Gender

Source: Calculation according to MICS 2006 database.

As noted in Chapter 2, issues of teenage pregnancy, early marriage, and lack of tuition fees affect girls' completion of primary education. Differences in access to lower secondary education can first be explained by the primary completion rate figures but also by some government policies, particularly on availability of space in boarding schools for boys and girls. Generally all government co-education boarding schools in Malawi have an access ratio of two boys to every one girl. This difference contributes to the lower access girls have to secondary education, although secondary day schools have a ratio of 1:1 during selection. In addition, the selection policy from primary to secondary is bottlenecked due to limited space in public secondary schools. Most children who pass national examinations at the end of the primary school cycle do not make it to secondary school because there aren't enough spaces.

On Internal Efficiency

In general, boys are more likely to repeat than girls (see tables 5A.1 and 5A.2 in Appendix 5.1). While girls are more likely to remain in school than boys during the first years of schooling, girls drop out at a higher rate after Standard 4. Marriage and pregnancy are the two main causes.[2] For boys, family responsibilities and the need to work are the main reasons for dropping out. (See tables 5A.3 and 5A.4 in Appendix 5.1 for more information.)

On Learning Outcomes

SACMEQ

There are gender differences in pupils reaching a minimum or desirable level of mastery in reading. Looking at the minimal level of mastery in table 5.3, girls fare worse than boys. A similar pattern is also shown for pupils reaching a *desirable* level of mastery. Under this category, both boys and girls performed badly, but boys still scored slightly higher than girls.

Table 5.3: Percentage of Pupils Reaching Minimum and Desirable Levels of Reading Mastery (SACMEQ II)

	Pupils Reaching *Minimum* Level of Mastery in Reading (in %) (SE)	Pupils Reaching *Desirable* Level of Mastery in Reading (in %) (SE)
Gender		
Boys	10.5 (1.21)	0.5 (0.20)
Girls	6.6 (1.09)	0.1 (0.10)
Total	8.6 (0.95)	0.3 (0.12)

Source: SACMEQ II report, 2005.
Note: SE = sampling error.

National Exams

PSLE: Table 5.4 displays PSLE results for 2006 by gender. In 2006, 93 percent of students sat for the exam and there was little difference between boys and girls. The total pass rate was 73.7 percent in 2006, meaning that is one pupil out of four who failed the exam. More boys passed than girls, which is consistent with the SACMEQ findings showing that boys are scoring higher in English, reading, and mathematics than girls.

Table 5.4: Leaving School Examination Results at the Primary Level by Gender (2006)

	Entered			Sat			Passed		
	Male	Female	Total	Male	Female	Total	Male	Female	Total
Total	87,182	67,388	154,570	81,805	62,533	144,338	63,365	42,998	106,363
% who…				93.8	92.8	93.4	77.4	68.8	73.7

Source: EMIS 2007.

JCE and MSCE: As can be seen in table 5.5, girls perform less well than boys at both of these secondary-level exams. This is striking at the JCE level, with 52 percent of girls passing the exam compared with 69 percent of boys. At the MSCE level, barely a third of girls sitting for the exam passed compare to almost half of the boys.

Table 5.5: JCE and MSCE Examination Results at the Secondary Level by Gender (2006)

	Entered			Sat			Passed		
	Male	Female	Total	Male	Female	Total	Male	Female	Total
JCE Total	34,790	26,415	61,205	33,490	25,075	58,565	23,230	12,989	36,219
% who…				96.3	94.9	95.7	69.4	51.8	61.8
MSCE Total	26,749	17,693	44,442	25,703	16,711	42,414	12,522	6,054	18,576
% who…				96.1	94.4	95.4	48.7	36.2	43.8

Sources: EMIS 2006, 2007.

Disparities According to Family Income Level

Children from the richest to the poorest quintiles access Standard 1 equally (see figure 5.2). However, significant differences appear to be more pronounced between quintile 5 and the rest of the quintiles when it comes to primary and secondary completion and access to secondary education. Sixty-seven percent of children from the richest households (quintile 5) complete primary education as opposed to only 23 percent from the poorest groups. And less than 10 percent of children from the poorest groups less have access to secondary education. The poorest group also has very low completion rates for lower and upper secondary education: 8 percent and 2 percent, respectively. In contrast, more than half the children from the richest households have access to secondary education and complete lower secondary education.

Figure 5.2: Access to and Completion of the Different Levels by Wealth Quintile

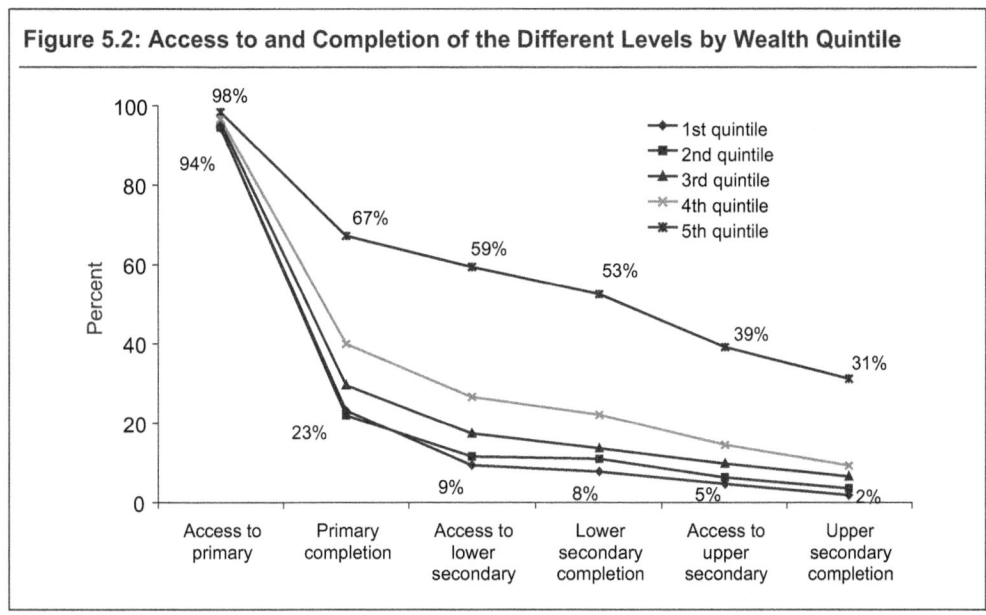

Source: Calculation from MICS 2006 database.

In conclusion, income disparities are much more important than gender disparities. For instance, according to MICS raw data (see table 5.6), the difference in primary completion is 14 percent between boys and girls (in favor of boys), but it increases to 44 percent between the two extreme income quintiles.

Table 5.6: Differences of Access and Completion Rates in Primary and Secondary Education

Difference according to ...	Access to Primary (Std 1)	Primary Completion (Std 8)	Access to Lower Secondary (Form 1)	Completion of Lower Secondary (Form 2)	Access to Upper Secondary (Form 3)	Completion of Upper Secondary (Form 4)
Gender (boys-girls)	0%	14%	8%	10%	12%	9%
Income (q5–q1)	4%	44%	50%	45%	35%	29%

Source: Calculation from MICS 2006 database.

Location Disparities

Disparities in School Coverage by Type of Location (Urban-Rural)

Figure 5.3 shows that students from urban areas have better access to all levels of education than students from rural areas, except in primary education where access rates to Standard 1 are equal. In rural areas the primary completion rate is only 32 percent (less than half the amount for urban), the lower secondary completion is only 16 percent, and the upper secondary completion rate is 6 percent.

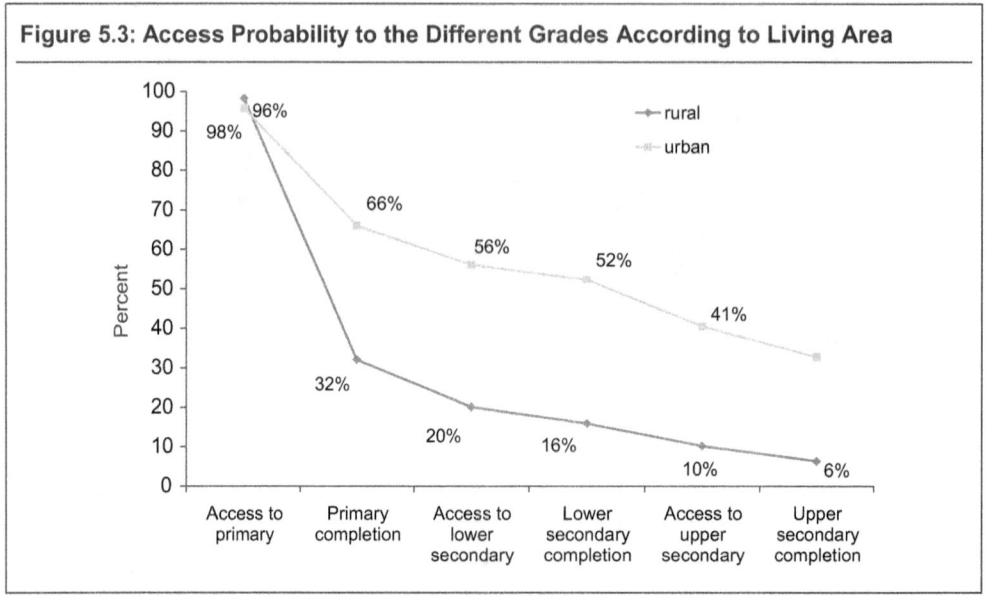

Figure 5.3: Access Probability to the Different Grades According to Living Area

Source: Calculation according to MICS 2006 database.

For primary and lower secondary levels, some international data are available for comparisons of Malawi with other African countries in terms of rural and urban disparities. Figure 5.4 shows that on average the primary completion rate for urban students is 2.8 times higher than for rural students, ranking from 1.17 (Côte d'Ivoire) to 8.6 (Niger): The situation for Malawi appears to be in the middle in terms of equity when compared to other African countries.

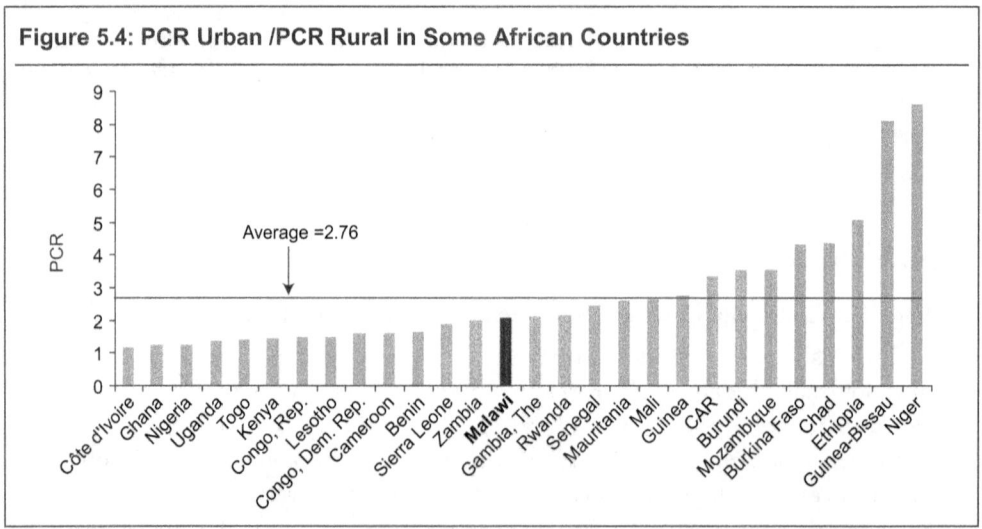

Figure 5.4: PCR Urban /PCR Rural in Some African Countries

Sources: Calculation from MICS 2006 for Malawi, World Bank data base for the other countries.
Note: Data are from 2007 or thereabouts.

Figure 5A.1 in Appendix 5.2 shows that the completion of lower secondary by urban students appears to be more favorable in Malawi than in other African countries. Malawi's urban rate is 3.2 times higher than the rural, while the African average is 5.2, ranging from 1.5 (Ghana) to 8.7 (Guinea Bissau).

Disparities by Region

Identifying regional disparities may help to specifically target areas for which education coverage within primary and secondary education is lower than the national level.

As figure 5.5 shows, there are no disparities in access to Standard 1 among Malawi's three regions. However, some significant differences begin to appear in other levels. More children from the Northern region complete primary and lower secondary education and have access to lower secondary. Nevertheless, the differences in access among the regions decrease for upper secondary and there is almost parity among the regions when it comes to completion of upper secondary education.

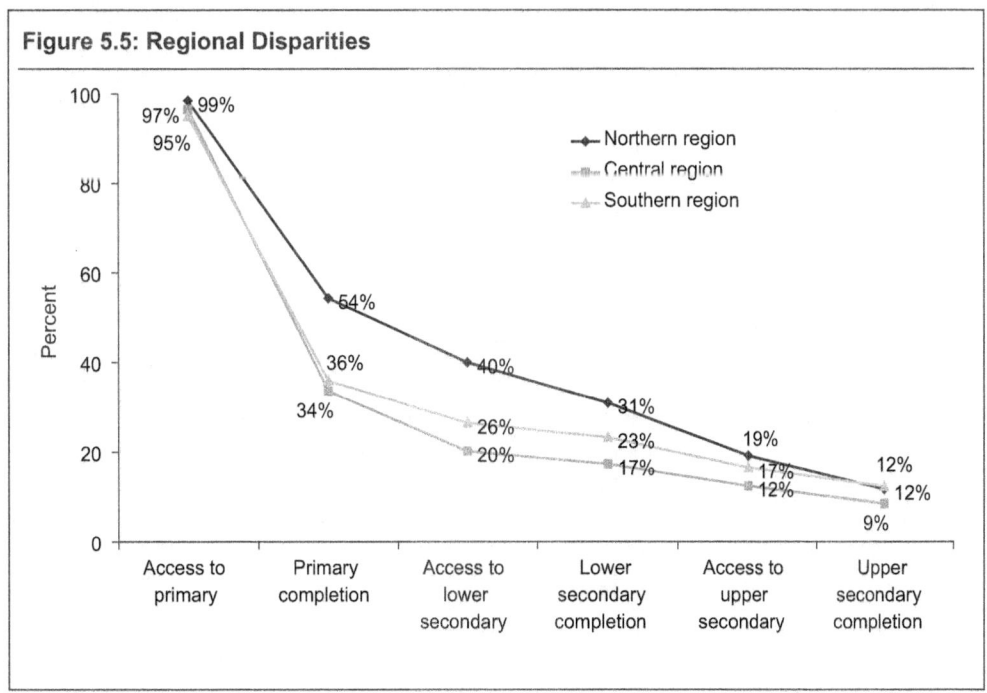

Figure 5.5: Regional Disparities

Source: Calculation from MICS 2006 database.

Table 5.7 provides additional information on survival within each cycle and transitions between cycles by region.

Table 5.7: Survival Rates and Transition Across Levels (in %)

	Survival Rate in Primary	Transition Primary → Lower Secondary	Survival Rate in Lower Secondary	Transition Lower → Upper Secondary	Survival Rate in Upper Secondary
Northern region	55	74	78	62	61
Central region	35	60	86	72	68
Southern region	38	74	88	71	75

Source: Calculation from MICS 2006 database.

There are variations among the regions in survival rate at primary. The primary survival rate in the Northern region is 1.5 times higher than in the Central and Southern regions.

In addition, EMIS data (2007) show that the Northern region has better education indicators compared to other regions, such as a pupil/qualified teacher ratio. Survival rates in lower secondary seem to be the reverse of survival rates in primary when examined by region. The Southern region has the highest survival rate for lower secondary, while Central is a close second, and the Northern region is worse. This means that more children that enroll in secondary school are retained in Southern and Central regions than in the Northern region.

The Southern and Northern regions have equal transition rates from to primary to lower secondary and the central region has a lower transition rate. This may indicate that the Central region has fewer secondary school places compared to the other regions. In Malawi, secondary school selection is determined by the availability of places.

Transition rates between lower and upper secondary show significant differences among the regions and surprisingly, the results are the reverse of the transition rate between primary and lower secondary. The Central region has the highest transition rate for lower and upper secondary, closely followed by the Southern region. The Northern region has the lowest transition rate. The results indicate that it is likely that more children in the Central and Southern regions pass the JCE at the end of two years of secondary education. In Malawi, the JCE determines who progresses to upper secondary education. Survival in upper secondary is highest in the Southern region, lower in the Central region, and lowest in the Northern region. This means that more children in the Southern region do not leave school and are retained in secondary education.

Disparities by District

Primary Education: The majority of the districts have a GER above 100 percent, meaning that they have more children in school than the numbers of primary school-official age children (see table 5A.5 in Appendix 5.2). However this could also mean that most children in these districts are overage or underage. On the other hand, some districts have a GER that is less than 100 percent.

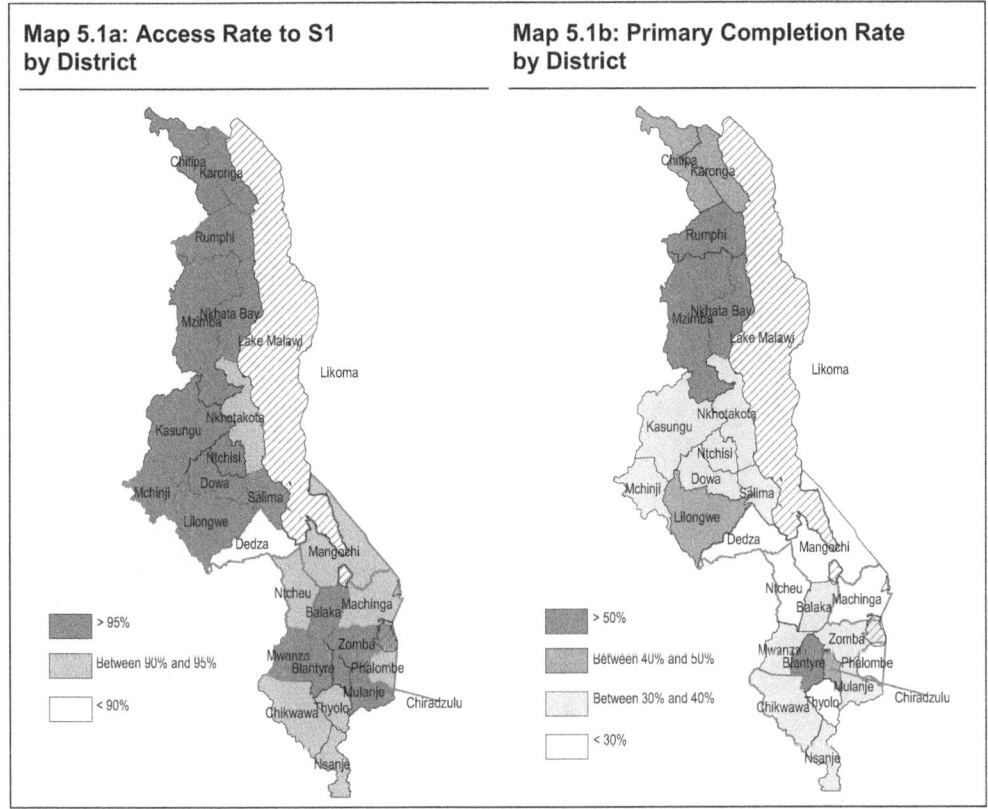

Source: from MICS 2006 estimates.
Note: Related figures are reported in Appendix 5.3.

Only a few districts (Mzimba, Rumphi, Nkhatabay, and Blantyre) have primary completion rates above 50 percent. Most districts have primary completion rates below 40 percent. Maps 5.1a and 5.1b provide additional representations of the access rate to Standard 1 and the primary completion rate according to MICS data.

In most districts, access to Standard 1 is above 90 percent (which is consistent with administrative data). The only exception is Dedza which stand at 88 percent. Eight districts range between 90 and 95 percent (Nkhotakota, Mangochi, Ntcheu, Machinga, Phalombe, Thyolo, Chikwawa, and Nsanje).

In all other districts, access to Standard 1 is above 95 percent. There is more variation in the primary completion rate. A few district have rates above 50 percent (Rumphi, Nkhatabay, and Mzimba), while six districts have a very low level of completion: Dedza (18 percent), Mangochi (25 percent), Ntcheu (29 percent), Machinga (24 percent), Phalombe (22 percent), and Thyolo (27 percent).

Secondary Education: The access rate to Form 1 and the secondary completion rate (proxied by the access rate to Form 4) derived from MICS are displayed in maps 5.2a and 5.2b.

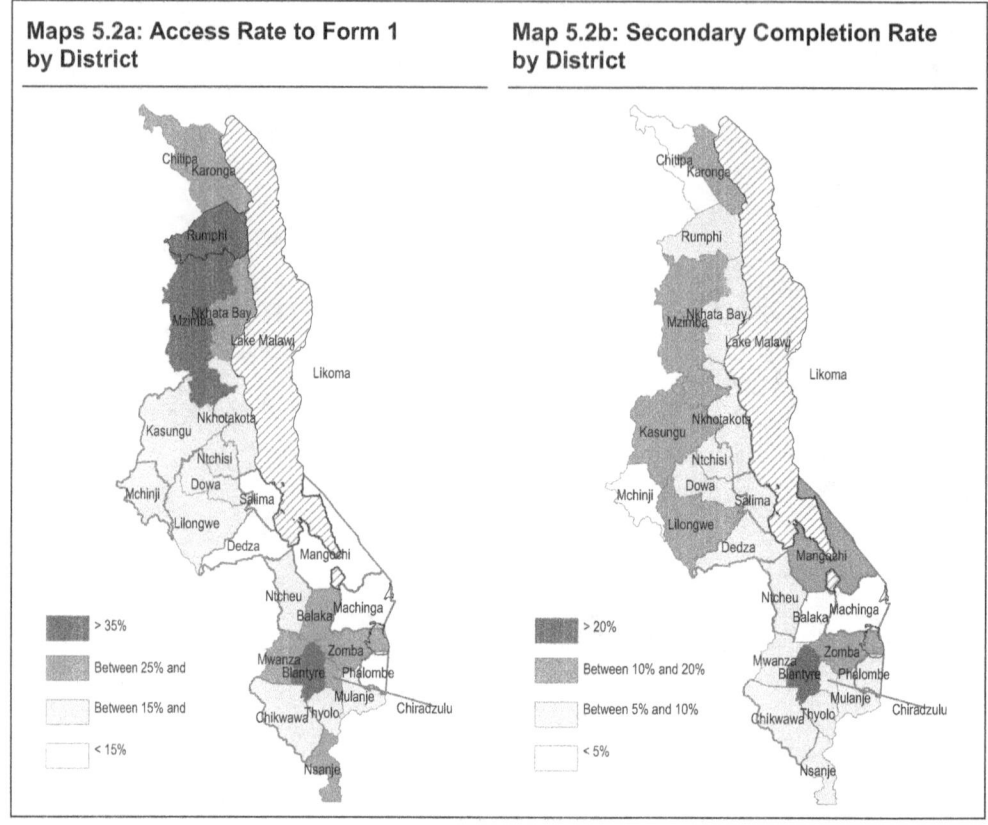

Source: from MICS 2006 estimates
Note: Related figures are reported in Appendix 5.

Map 5.2a shows that the access rate to Form 1 is particularly high in the districts of Rumphi (43 percent), Mzimba (45 percent), and Blantyre (47 percent); it remains particularly low in the districts of Salima (14 percent), Mangochi (15 percent), Machinga (15 percent), Phalombe (14 percent), and Dedza (11 percent).

The secondary completion rate is very low, with the Northern region being at the same level as the Southern (12 percent), and the Central falling even lower (9 percent). This implies a better retention in the Southern region and a lower one in the Northern. At the district level, Map 5.2b shows that Blantyre has the maximum value (30 percent), while 19 districts have less than 10 percent, three of them being under 5 percent: Chitipa (4 percent), Balaka (4 percent) and Machinga (2 percent).

On Learning Outcomes

SACMEQ

Pupils' achievements also tend to vary across locations: pupils in large cities stand a better chance of reaching the minimum mastery levels than those in other areas. More pupils from large cities (20.5 percent) reached a minimum level of mastery compared to small towns and rural or isolated areas (8.1 percent and 6.5 percent, respectively). Likewise, large cities had a slightly higher number of pupils who reached a desirable level of mastery than small towns and remote or rural areas, although all areas did not perform well. Disparities can also be seen across divisions. Pupils in South Eastern and South Western divisions fared better, while children living in the Central Eastern and Northern divisions lagged behind. (See table 5.8.)

Table 5.8: Percentage of Pupils Reaching Minimum and Desirable Levels of Reading Mastery (SACMEQ II)

	Pupils reaching *Minimum* Level of Reading Mastery, % (SE)	Pupils Reaching *Desirable* Level of Reading Mastery, % (SE)
Location		
Rural/isolated	6.5 (0.97)	0.2 (0.12)
Small town	8.1 (1.83)	0.0 (0.00)
Large city	20.5 (4.34)	1.7 (0.74)
Division		
North	4.8 (1.75)	0.3 (0.33)
Central East	3.1 (1.56)	0.0 (0.00)
Central West	9.8 (2.16)	0.4 (0.27)
South East	11.8 (2.22)	0.0 (0.00)
South West	13.9 (3.16)	1.3 (0.55)
Shire Highlands	7.5 (2.09)	0.0 (0.00)
Total	8.6 (0.95)	0.3 (0.12)

Source: SACMEQ II report 2005.
Note: SE = sampling error.

National Exams

Primary School Leaving Examination (PSLE) Pass Rates: Table 5A.6 in Appendix 5.2 shows PSLE results for 2006 by school status, type of location, and division. Discrepancies arise across geographical locations: sat rates are lower in rural schools (93 percent) than in urban ones (98 percent) and the Central Eastern and Northern divisions display below-average sat rates.

Urban-based schools show better pass rates than those in rural areas. Children in urban areas have a better socioeconomic status compared to those in rural areas. As such, they have more learning opportunities, such as private tuition, libraries, and reading materials at home. They may also have more free time to study compared to a rural child who has to do household chores or other productive work. Motivation issues may also be at stake.

Wide variations arise across divisions: from a pass rate of 64 percent in the Northern division to 82 percent in the Central Eastern one. Some education divisions— such as the Central Western—have considerably large urban and semi-urban populations, which could explain such differences.

Examinations at the Secondary Level: Junior Certificate Examination (JCE) and Malawi School Certificate Examination (MSCE): Rural schools perform far less well than urban ones; girls attending rural schools are particularly at risk of failing the exams. Variations across divisions can also be observed: JCE pass rates range from 51 percent in the Central Eastern education division to 68 percent in the Shire Highlands education division. For the MSCE pass rate, they vary from 39 percent in the Central Eastern division to 48 percent in the South Eastern division.

The situation for girls is particularly critical in the Central Eastern division, with only 39 percent and 29 percent of female students passing the JCE and MSCE exams, respectively. Wider disparities between boys and girls can be found within CDSSs. See table 5A.7 in Appendix 5.2 for more information.

Equity in Distribution of Public Resources for Education

For a given cohort (generation), each child will benefit from different amounts of public education resources, due to the different pathways. Those who will never attend school will not benefit from any public resources allocated to the education system, while students will benefit from an increasing amount of resources, according to the number of years they spend in the system. In order to estimate the share of public resources granted to each group of individuals according to their highest education level, it is necessary to determine the distribution of individuals and the respective amount of public resources used for their studies (see table 5.9).

Table 5.9: Distribution of Public Education Spending According to the Highest Level Attended (Pseudo-Cohort of 100 Children)

	Cohort		Public Spending					Cumulative Distribution	
			Per individual			Per cohort			
Level	Access Rates (%)	Highest Level Attended (%)	Public Unit Cost	Number of Years	Accumulated Cost During Studies	Accumulated (in MWK)	% of Total	Cohort (%)	Public Spending (%)
No school		0.1	0		0	0	0.0	0.0	0.0
S1	99.9	3.1	3,019	1	3,019	93	0.1	3.2	0.1
S2	96.8	9.2	3,019	1	6,039	556	0.7	12.4	0.9
S3	87.6	11.3	3,019	1	9,058	1,023	1.4	23.7	2.2
S4	76.3	10.5	3,019	1	12,078	1,262	1.7	34.2	3.9
S5	65.8	13.3	3,019	1	15,097	2,013	2.7	47.5	6.5
S6	52.5	6.8	3,019	1	18,117	1,234	1.6	54.3	8.2
S7	45.7	11.0	3,019	1	21,136	2,326	3.1	65.3	11.2
S8	34.7	17.7	3,019	1	24,155	4,267	5.6	83.0	16.9
F1	17.0	0.0	30,292	1	54,447	—	0.0	83.0	16.9
F2	17.0	3.9	30,292	1	84,739	3,305	4.4	86.9	21.2
F3	13.1	0.0	30,292	1	115,031	—	0.0	86.9	21.2
F4	13.1	11.8	30,292	1	145,323	17,148	22.7	98.7	43.9
Higher*	1.30	1.3	780,479	4	3,267,240	42,474	56.1	100.0	100.0

Sources: Calculation from EMIS 2007 database, UN Population, and results from Chapter 3

* The GER is used here for higher education, with 18–21-year-olds as the reference population group, and assuming a four-year duration of the cycle.

Construction of the table: For each level the proportion of individuals for whom the level was the highest attended was computed. For example, the access rate to Standard 1 is 99.9 percent and the access rate to Standard 2 is 96.8 percent, so for 3.1 percent (99.9 – 96.8) of pupils Standard 1 was the highest level they attended. For each highest level attended, the resources accumulated by an individual were computed. For instance, a pupil having Form 2 as highest level attended accumulated 8 (number of years of primary education) x 3,019 (public unit cost for one year in primary) + 2 (number of grades attended in secondary education) x 30,292 (public unit cost for one year in secondary) = MK84,736. Finally, a computation was done of the accumulated public spending for all the individuals with the same highest level attended by multiplying the percentage of cohort that end up at this level per the cumulated cost for one pupil with that highest level attended. The distribution of public spending according to the highest level attended was obtained. Finally, a computation was made of the cumulative distribution of individuals and the public education resources spent for them. For example, the 34 percent of the cohort who leave school in Standard 4 or before get only 3.9 percent of the public resources dedicated to education.

Table 5.9 shows the very inequitable distribution of public resources devoted to education. As an example, the 83 percent of individuals leaving school in primary education appropriate only at 16.9 percent of public spending, while the few (1.3 percent) who reach higher education benefit from 56 percent of those resources. The 11.8 percent that leave with a complete secondary education will benefit from 22.7 percent of public resources.

The education Lorenz curve (resources' concentration curve) can be computed from the two last columns of table 5.9 (see Figure 5.6).

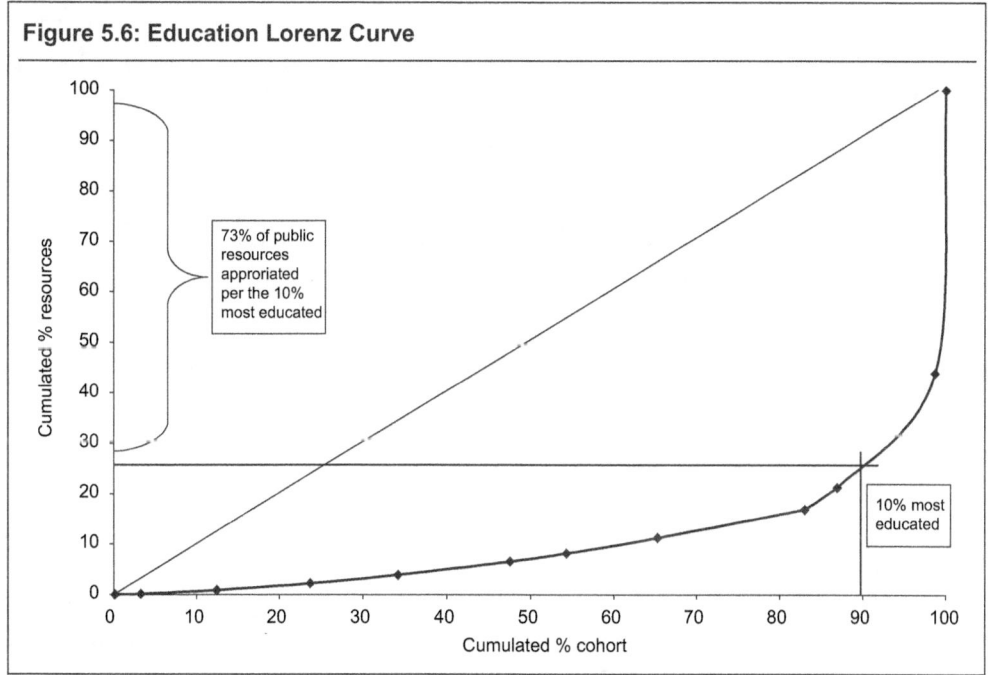

Sources: Calculation from EMIS 2007 database, UN population, and results from Chapter 3.

The diagonal line of this figure would correspond to the situation of perfect equality in access to education public resources among all individuals. The curve itself is the present situation of Malawi and it differs significantly from the diagonal reference. In order to estimate the importance of this deviation, two indicators can be computed:

- The first one is the Gini index, computed by dividing the surface of the area between the diagonal and the curve by the surface of the area of the triangle defined by the curves and reference axis. This indicator ranks from 0 and 1 and its value is as little as the distribution of resources is equalitarian. In Malawi, the Gini index is equal to **0.78** for 2007;
- The second indicator is the share of public resources appropriated by the 10 percent most educated[3] (i.e., those who complete the most schooling). This indicator reaches **73 percent** in Malawi.

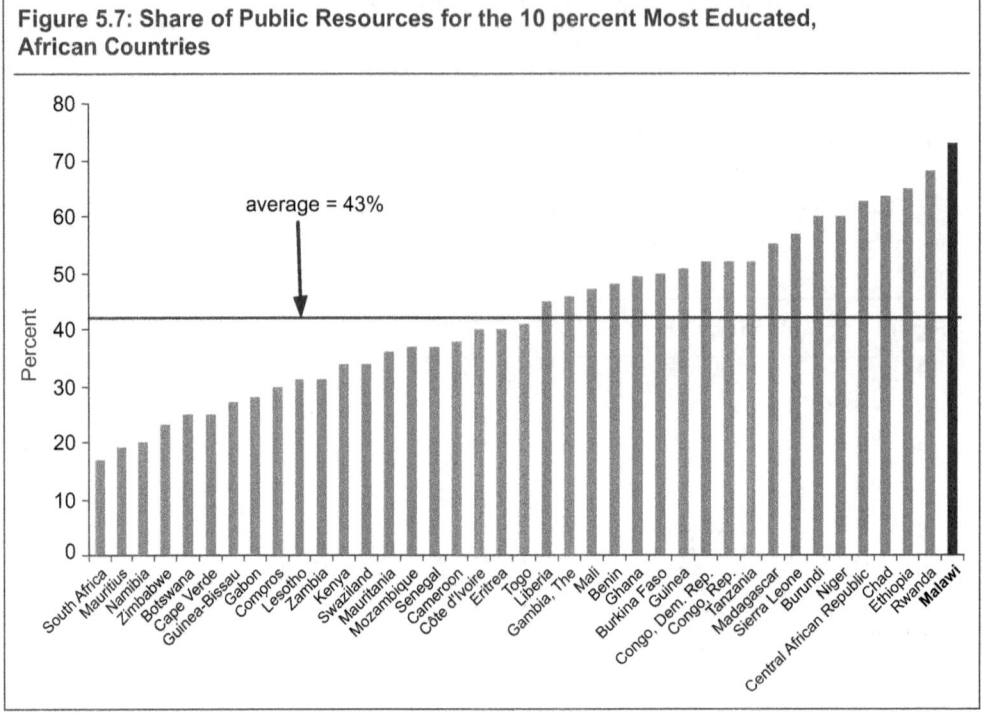

Figure 5.7: Share of Public Resources for the 10 percent Most Educated, African Countries

Source: World Bank database.

Once again, it can be useful to use international comparisons. Figure 5.7 displays the share of public resources appropriated by the 10 percent most educated that can be observed among African countries.

The average value of the indicator is 43 percent. To this point of view, Malawi appears to be the country that provides the most inequitable distribution of public resources dedicated to education.

Analyzing benefit incidence can then become possible, according to the different variables studied in this chapter. Thanks to the data on schooling disparities across social groups (boys/girls, urban/rural, and richest/poorest) and the concentration of resources by highest level attended, it is possible to compute the public resources distribution by social group (see table 5.18).

Urban people (12 percent of the global population) benefit from 53 percent of the public resources for education. Consequently, urban people benefit on average per individual from 8.4 times more resources than rural people.

The richest 20 percent (quintile q1) benefit from 68 percent of the public resources for education, while the poorest 20 percent only receive 6 percent. As a consequence, the richest benefit from 11.4 times more public spending than do the poorest.

Table 5.18: Benefit Incidence

	No Ed. (%)	Primary (%)	Secondary (%)	Higher (%)	Total (a) (%)	Pop. (b) (%)	(a)/(b)	Appropriation Index
Gender								
Girls	0	9	13	27	**48**	51	0.95	1.00
Boys	0	8	14	29	**52**	49	1.05	1.11
Location								
Rural	0	15	18	13	**47**	88	0.53	1.00
Urban	0	2	9	43	**53**	12	4.45	**8.41**
Wealth Index								
q1	0	3	2	0	**6**	20	0.28	1.00
q2	0	3	3	0	**6**	20	0.30	1.07
q3	0	3	4	2	**9**	19	0.48	1.70
q4	0	4	5	3	**11**	20	0.56	1.98
q5	0	3	14	51	**68**	21	3.24	**11.46**

Sources: Calculations from MICS, EMIS 2007, and results from Chapter 3.

How to read the table: Children coming from the poorest households (q1) represent 20 percent of those with primary education as the highest level attended (table 5.1); yet 17 percent of public education resources go to individuals who have attended primary as the highest level (table 5.17). As a consequence, individuals from the poorest households with primary as highest level attended get 20 percent x 17 percent = 3.5 percent of all public education resources. This percentage can be computed for all categories, at each highest education level. For each category, the sum of resources accumulated needs (column a) to be compared to the category's weight among the population (column b). For instance, children from the richest households represent 21 percent of the population, while they get 68 percent of the public resources dedicated to education.

Notes

[1] The 2006 scores average 68.8 percent for girls compared to 77.4 percent for boys in the PSLE; 52 percent for girls against 69 percent for boys in the JCE and 36 percent for girls compared to 49 percent for boys in the MSCE.

[2] The government introduced a re–admission policy in 2007 to enable teenage mothers go back to school after delivery.

[3] computed by linear interpolation

CHAPTER 6

Technical, Entrepreneurial, and Vocational Education and Training

Summary of the Chapter

The technical, entrepreneurial, and vocational education and training (TEVET) system in Malawi is highly diverse, fragmented, and uncoordinated, with multiple private and public provider systems. Access to the regular TEVET programs—regulated and administered by the TEVET Authority (TEVETA) and provided mainly as four-year apprenticeship training—is very low compared to the demand. The training in the formal system is mainly limited to traditional technical trades. However, additional skill development opportunities are provided by other ministries, NGOs, and church-run schools in the private training market and, not least, by companies that include the informal sector (mastercraftsman training).

As far as the formal TEVET system is concerned, access is biased against girls, those from poorer districts who have left school, and those with lower educational attainment. Regarding the gender bias, the number of women in the public technical colleges (TCs) is slowly increasing to 30 percent, which is the result of a positive discrimination policy administered by TEVETA. Access to regular TEVET programs has recently been limited to MSCE holders, effectively excluding the majority of the country's youth from the publicly subsidized general TEVET system.

TEVET is funded by multiple sources, including public expenditure, household contributions, and investments from Malawi's business sector. Unit public allocation to TCs is not related to actual training costs, enrollment, or other performance indicators. Private contributions to TEVET are high for students without access to the regular TEVET programs, with annual tuition fees of up to MK120,000. The TEVET Fund has been successful at mobilizing more private sector resources for TEVET. Levy income from private companies contributed 84 percent of the entire TEVET Fund in 2007.

The quality of TEVET is negatively affected by multiple factors, including inadequate equipment and facilities, a shortage of training material due to financial constraints, a high trainee/teacher ratio, and in particular, deficient practical competences of TEVET teachers coupled with the absence of a systematic TEVET teacher training system. A low quality of training leads to low pass rates in national examinations (50–67 percent). The most important impediment to sustainable quality improvement is the co-existence of the three local qualification systems: trade testing; Malawi (Advanced) Craft (MAC); and Competency-Based Education and Training (CBET), which is implemented by TEVETA. This prevents the development of a unified employer-involved quality assurance system and forces teachers to train on the basis of parallel curricula.

The lack of clarity about the division of roles and responsibilities between the main actors (TEVETA; the Ministry of Education, Science and Technology [MOEST]; and the Ministry of Labor) and major stakeholders (such as the private sector) is one of the most important reasons why a further implementation of the agreed TEVET sector reform has been very slow. It also affects the status of the public TCs, whose current scope of responsibility is not appropriate for the diverse funding and program structure they have to manage.

* * *

Introduction

The training supply in Malawi is diverse, fragmented, and uncoordinated, and provided through various public and private provider systems. The most important provider types are briefly described in Table 6.1.

Table 6.1: Synopsis of Different TEVET Provider Types in Malawi

Provider Type	Brief Description	Provision/Qualifications
Public formal TEVET: TEVET in public Technical Colleges	Provided in seven TCs, long-term pre-employment training courses form the core of the formal public training supply. These can be further divided into "regular" programs, which are the courses recruited for, sponsored by, and regulated by TEVETA, and which are mainly provided through apprenticeship. The so-called "parallel" programs, on the other hand, include mainly apprenticeship and non-apprenticeship courses offered by the public colleges on their own account and responsibility. Parallel programs also include a range of short-term courses. For regular students, boarding is provided. TCs receive base funding from the public budget and program funding from TEVETA and charge trainees tuition fees.	Technical colleges are under the Ministry of Education. Training is geared towards TEVETA CBET qualifications in the case of regular programs, and Malawi (Advanced) Craft and other qualifications in parallel programs.
Private provision: TEVET provided by NGOs and private commercial schools	This is by far the largest provider type, although the total number of institutions and enrollment is unknown. A preliminary provider directory from 1999 identified a total of 130 private and NGO-training providers enrolling close to 10,000 students. Training institutions cater for a range of training fields that is much wider than the occupational groups provided in the public TCs. Training duration varies, however, many institutions offer formalized courses. Private commercial institutions offer mainly cheap-to-train commercial trades (for example, accounting, management, secretarial, IT) and are concentrated in urban areas. However, the private training market also stretches into rural areas, and includes more traditional technical trades. Training courses are financed by a combination of donor and private financing (fees) in the case of NGOs, and are usually fully privately financed (through fees) in the case of private commercial providers.	Schools are self-managed. Many, but not all, programs aim at preparing students for Trade Test, Malawi Craft and Advanced Craft certification examinations, and other international qualifications. Schools also issue school certificates.

(Table continues on next page)

Table 6.1 (continued)

Provider Type	Brief Description	Provision/Qualifications
Providers of sector-specific training	These are mainly public training institutions providing specialized training. Examples include the Malawi Institute of Hospitality (MIT), Marine Training College, Police Training Schools, and others. Schools offer both long-term, pre-employment training as well as short-term skills and upgrading. Although often sponsored by sector ministries, some schools are self-financing and charge significant fees.	Sector ministries Some institutions (for example, MIT) conduct TEVETA approved examinations.
TEVET for special target groups	Public, parastatal, or NGO training provisions to cater for special target groups, such as small and micro businesses, start-ups, handicapped, etc. Examples include the Malawi Enterprise Development Institute, Magomero Vocational Training School, and others.	Self-managed or under the auspices of sector ministries, and usually issuing their own certification.
Company-based training	The overall extent of employer-based training is unknown. Some large private and parastatal companies maintain own training centers. Other companies pay for staff attending external training courses provided by training institutions against fees. The larger part of company-based training is provided as on-the-job training. Training is financed by companies. However, recently parts of the cost of company-based training have been reimbursed by TEVETA to companies that have paid the TEVET levy.	Provided and managed by companies. Company-owned training centers issue own or TEVETA registered certificates, external training is geared, if provided at all, for various certificates available in the training market
Traditional apprenticeship	Traditional apprenticeship, also called *mastercraftsman training*, is a wide-spread system of on-the-job training provided in the informal sector. The system is self-financing with trainees accepting no or low wages during the training period. The extent and quality depends largely on the qualifications and background of the masters and the economic prospects of the individual businesses. Trades in which the system is common include baking, basket weaving, bicycle repair, boat building, construction, mechanics, welding, battery charging, tin smithing, woodwork, radio and electrical repair, tailoring, shoe repair, net mending and others. Traditional apprenticeship is dominated by typical male trades. Trainees from the traditional apprenticeship system have the option to undergo trade testing, if the Trade Testing system covers the relevant trade. Systematic information on the use of this option is not available, but according to information from the Trade Testing Directorate in the Ministry of Labor a considerable portion of the external trade-testing candidates comes from the informal sector.	Self-organized by informal mastercraftsmen. Participation in Trade Test examinations is optional.

Source: Authors.

The introduction of the concept of Technical, Entrepreneurial and Vocational Education and Training (TEVET) in the TEVET Act of 1999 aimed at re-orienting training to the needs of the labor market. It was connected with the political will to broaden public attention to the entire spectrum of formal, non-formal, and informal vocational learning, and to create mechanisms for integration and effective coordination of the different TEVET subsystems.[1] However, coordination to date is still highly unsatisfactory and consequently, information and knowledge about the different provider systems remains deficient or entirely absent.

This chapter provides an overview of the basic features and issues of the Malawian TEVET system, as they pertain to enrollment, equity of access, financing, and quality and management issues. Due to the data deficiencies, most of the analyses are focused on the formal public TEVET supply and those TEVET schemes administered or facilitated by the TEVET Authority (TEVETA).

The TEVET system is supposed to specifically prepare (or upgrade) people for employment. The ultimate benchmark of success and appropriateness of a TEVET system is therefore its external efficiency and responsiveness to the needs of the labor market. This issue, however, is not taken up in this chapter but in Chapter Eight, which is devoted to the external efficiency of education.

Enrollment

The total enrollment in the TEVET system is unknown. It is apparent, however, that the publicly financed programs provided in TCs under the auspices of MOEST and TEVETA only cater to a small fraction of the entire training supply in Malawi. It should also be emphasized that even in the formal TEVET segment, data are subject to a high degree of uncertainty.[2]

Regular Apprenticeship Training

The core of the public formal TEVET supply under the auspices of the MOEST is provided by seven public technical colleges (TCs). The colleges offer two- to four- year training programs that intend to provide initial (pre-employment) vocational training to school leavers. The dominant training program is the National Apprenticeship Program, managed and subsidized by TEVETA. Training under the apprenticeship program is organized as cooperative training between the colleges and companies, with one year of initial full-time training in a TC followed by three years split into two terms of in-company training and one term of college instruction each year.

At the moment, the regular apprenticeship system only provides for an annual intake capacity of around 700 apprentices against some 10,000 applications. In 2007, this intake represented 0.21 percent of the relevant age group (16 years) and 3.9 percent of the MSCE graduates of the previous year. Major restrictions, according to TEVETA, include capacities in the TCs—notably limitations in boarding places, the availability of teachers and instructors, and most importantly, the availability of apprenticeship places provided by the industry. Figure 6.1 shows the development of annual intake into the regular TEVETA-managed apprenticeship system from 2001 to 2008. In 2006, all training capacities in the TCs were redirected to regular TEVETA-managed programs,[3] which accounts for the steep increase from that year on.

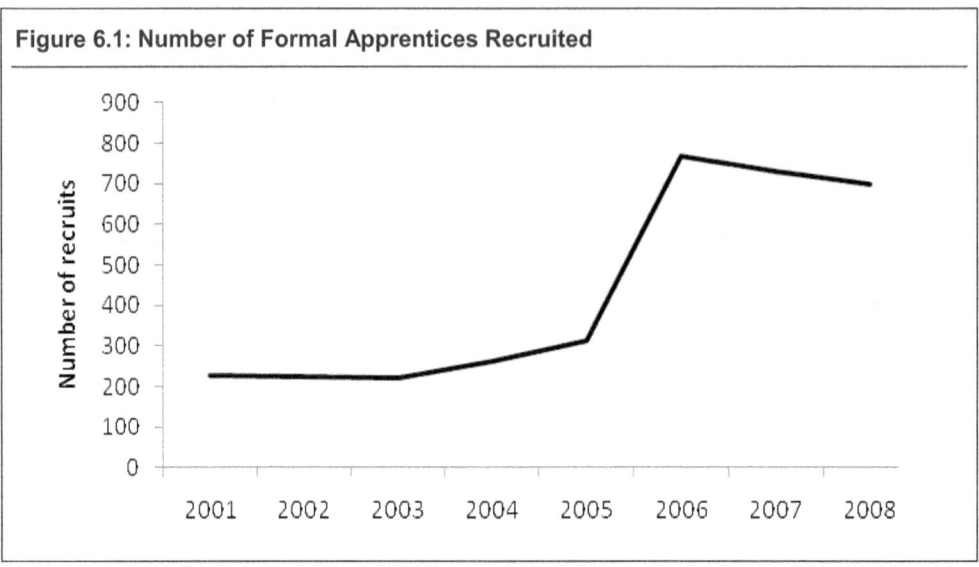

Figure 6.1: Number of Formal Apprentices Recruited

Source: TEVETA.

Enrollment in Technical Colleges

Although the regular apprenticeship programs are the only ones that are publicly managed and funded, total actual training activities in TCs are substantially higher. In addition to the TEVETA-administered apprenticeship places, TCs also enroll "parallel" students. Some of these students attend programs that follow the same apprenticeship delivery structure, however they are geared for other certifications. Others attend various short and long-term programs in non-apprenticeable trades.

Data on the quantity of parallel students are not reliable. Since the parallel student intake is not legally provided for, and financed by training fees in a parallel account system, colleges tend to underreport the number of students enrolled in parallel courses.

The only comprehensive records of parallel students available are for 2007 (see table 6.2 and table 6A.1 in Appendix 6). They show that the number of parallel students in that year was 65 percent higher than the number of regular students, and that more than 60 percent of the entire training supply was in the public colleges. While colleges have always recruited parallel students, it is generally assumed that the intake increased significantly after 2004, reflecting the growing number of JCE graduates in need of further education opportunities. It is also assumed, therefore, that the total annual enrollment in public colleges has been well above 4,000 trainees in recent years.

Table 6.2 Number of Regular and Parallel Students in Technical Colleges (2007)

	Male	Female	Total
Regular	1,288	522	1,810
Parallel	2,179	818	2,997
Total	3,467	1,340	4,807

Source: Malawi Education Statistics 2007.

Parallel students have to pay substantially higher tuition fees compared to regular (TEVETA-sponsored) students. It is hardly surprising that the relative parallel student intake is substantially higher in urban (Lilongwe, Soche, Mzuzu) than in rural areas (Livingstonia, Nasawa, Namitete, Salima). See table 6A.1 in Appendix 6 for more information.

Even taking parallel students into account, the overall enrollment in formal TEVET is extremely low in Malawi compared to its SADC neighbors (see figure 6.2). Per 100,000 inhabitants, Malawi records only 35 students. These figures are substantially higher elsewhere in the region, between 110 and 130 in Lesotho, Mozambique, and Madagascar, and far higher in other countries. Botswana and Mauritius lead the group of countries (for which data were available) with 1,228 trainees and 1,561 trainees per 100,000 inhabitants, respectively. Even if the other public TEVET providers for whom enrollment is not recorded here were included in this calculation, it appears unlikely that Malawi would be able to climb up substantially in this comparative rating.

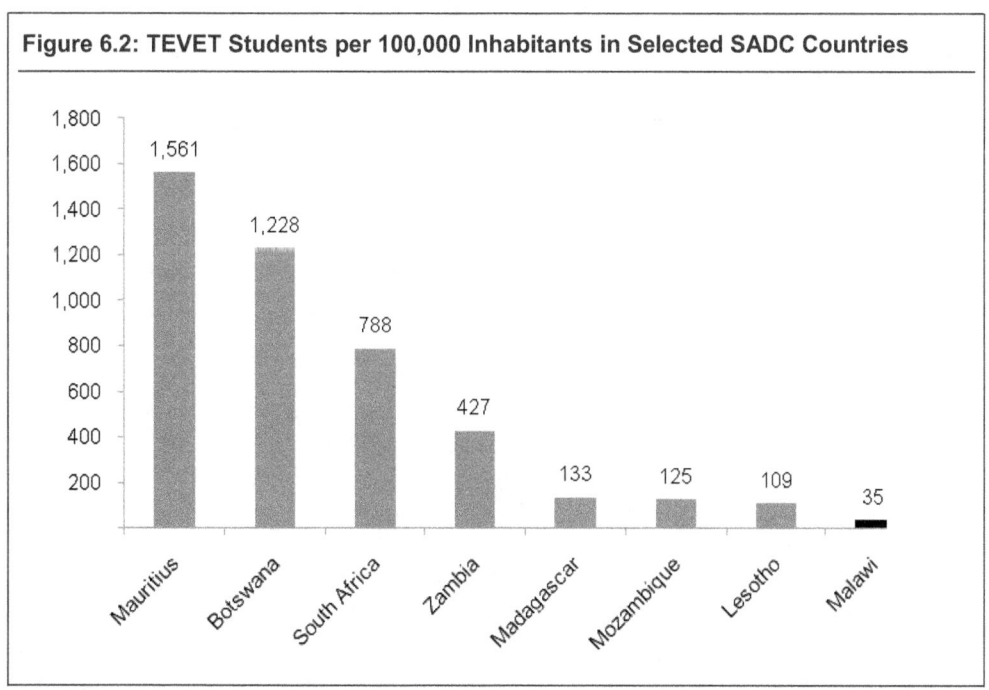

Figure 6.2: TEVET Students per 100,000 Inhabitants in Selected SADC Countries

Source: Calculation using World Bank database.

TEVET Supply

Although enrollment data are lacking, or were not available for this study, the supply of TEVET in the many other provider systems, including NGOs, church-run institutions, private commercial training schools, other government-run schools, and training centers owned by companies, is presumably many times greater than the TEVETA/MOEST-controlled programs. Table 6.1 provides an overview of these other provider systems. In a TEVET provider directory of 1999, a total of 162 training institutions were identified apart from the seven TCs. The total number of trainees enrolled was recorded at 22,940.[4] However, the directory did not identify all institutions at that time and the total number of institutions is likely to have increased since (in particular in the private commercial training market). Furthermore, company-based training and traditional apprenticeships (mastercraftsman training, see table 6.1), account for a significant number of young people and workers in training. Hence, the overall access to TEVET in Malawi is presumably much larger than indicated in the TC enrollment estimates under the MOEST.

It is worth noting that TEVETA, with its private sector and informal sector training programs, appears to be increasingly integrating non-traditional target groups (for example employees, workers, informal sector operators) and TEVET provider systems into the TEVET system. TEVETA provides incentives for levy-paying companies to invest in staff training, supports industry with training needs assessments, and subsidizes the special training initiatives of business associations and companies. Within its informal sector training program, it has tailored skill development programs to informal sector operators and workers.

Equity

Data allowing for some analysis of equity in the access to TEVET are again available only for selected segments of the entire training supply, primarily for the formal TEVET provision.

Female Participation

Data on the gender equality of access to TEVET show that girls are underrepresented in all segments of the system for which records are available. As shown in table 6.2, less than 30 percent of girls are enrolled in TCs.

However, the participation rates of girls clearly show an upward trend. Figure 6.3 indicates that an increasing number of girls are participating in the Malawi Craft and Advanced Craft Examinations (from 11 percent in 2003 to 23 percent in 2007). The growth is more pronounced in the lower level Malawi Craft Examination and reached a 25 percent participation rate in 2007. The lower share of female examination candidates for the higher level Advanced Craft Certificate can be explained by the fact that girls are more likely to fail in the lower level Malawi Craft Certificate. As indicated in figure 6.4, less than 50 percent of females pass the examinations. In comparison, the overall pass rate of males from 2003–2007 was above 70 percent. At 10.2 percent, female participation rates are even lower for the trade testing system. However, pass rates are more or less the same for both sexes in this examination system.

Considering that the recorded participation rates refer to provider and testing systems that are all dominated by traditional "male" occupations, the absolute rates as well as the positive trends indicate an encouraging development. In fact, disaggregated data from Malawi Craft Examinations and the trade testing system show that girls have now made it well into core technical trades, such as painting and decoration, machine woodwork, electrical installation, auto electrical, sheet metal work, or plumbing (see also table 6A.15 in Appendix 6.2). One explanation for this is the systematic "affirmative action policy" TEVETA has employed over the years in the recruitment of apprentices. Through pro-active recruitment of girls, TEVETA has continuously managed to raise the female participation rate well above the application rate. Since 2004, it has more or less managed to permanently reach the target enrollment rate of 30 percent.

Data indicating the gender division in other provider systems were not available for this study. It is not unlikely that overall the female participation rate is higher for those than in the public formal system, as the range of trades is wider and includes more occupational fields that are traditional for female students, such as hospitality, secretarial, and other commercial trades.

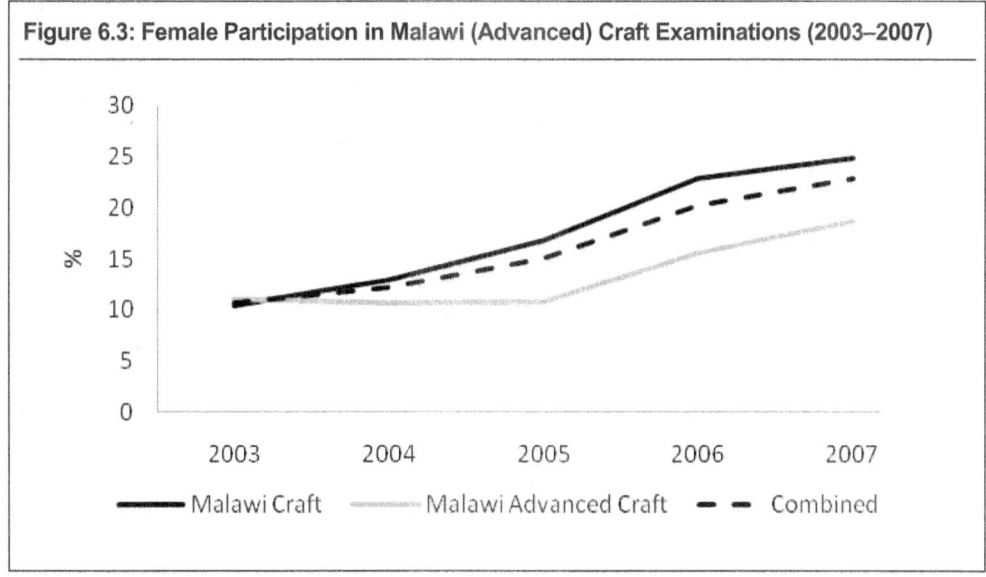

Figure 6.3: Female Participation in Malawi (Advanced) Craft Examinations (2003–2007)

Source: MANEB.

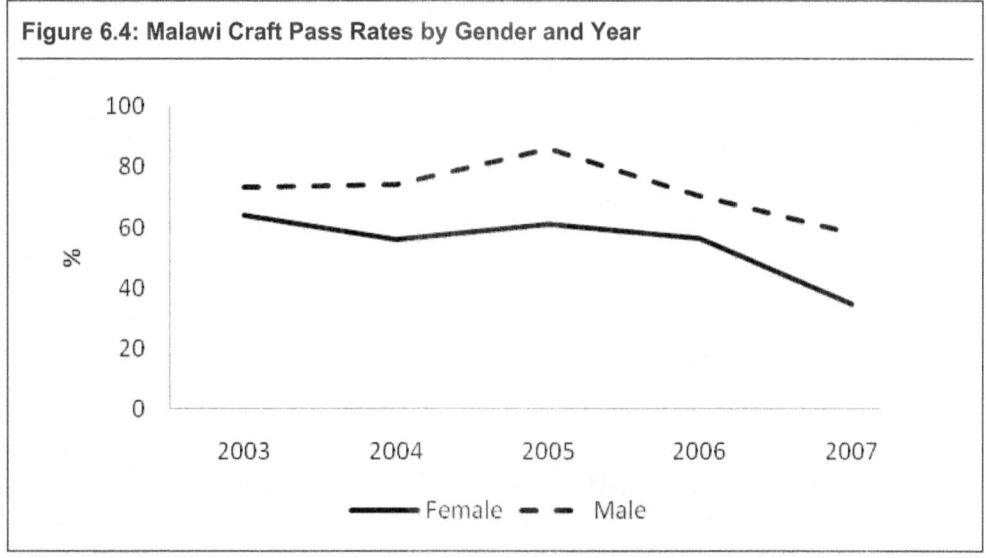

Figure 6.4: Malawi Craft Pass Rates by Gender and Year

Source: MANEB.

Regional Distribution

With a limited number of formal TEVET institutions, it is government policy to draw students from all over the country into the different training institutions, which are located in various urban and rural centers in all three regions. Information on the regional access distribution to TEVET can best be obtained from the origin of students enrolled in any of the TCs. If the regional shares of students admitted by TEVETA into the apprenticeship programs are compared with the shares of each region of the entire Malawian population, data for the last four years show that students from the Northern region were over-represented in the admission to regular TEVET programs, whereas the Central and Southern regions were under-represented. The privileged situation of students from the Northern part of Malawi reflects a typical phenomenon in the country's education system and has to be seen as a direct consequence of the region's higher overall educational attainment rates. The more students complete secondary education, the more they are eligible to apply for regular TEVET.

Access by Social Status of Districts

Information on access to TEVET by social status is difficult to obtain as neither TEVETA nor schools usually collect systematic information on the social status of students. Household survey data suggest a highly unbalanced distribution of TC students to the disadvantage of lower-income groups. However, the number of cases in the survey for TC students was too low to provide a reliable indication. Instead, the participation of students from districts with a relatively high poverty incidence was used as a proxy. In figure 6.5, the relative admission share to regular TEVET programs in each district[5] is related to the poverty status of the district.[6] The figure shows that the majority of relatively better-off districts have above-average admission rates to TEVET programs, indicating that students from richer districts are more likely to be admitted to regular TEVET programs. On the other hand, poorer districts show relatively lower admission rates. In order to use TEVET as an instrument to support social and economic development, the relations should be reversed towards an over-proportionate access to TEVET programs in districts where more poor people live. A comparison of the trend lines for 2005 and 2008 indicates a positive trend in this direction with recent achievements towards integrating more students from poor districts into the TEVET system.

However, apart from some preferential access for women and people with disabilities, places in the regular TEVET programs are awarded on the basis of merit.[7] There is no provision for the social background of candidates, which may be a concern because the regular programs are the only highly subsidized and therefore low-fee general TEVET programs.[8]

Access by Educational Attainment

The current formal TEVET system in Malawi is concentrated on high educational achievers. Access to regular (that is, subsidized) training has been limited to MSCE holders since 2006. Parallel programs still cater to those who have left school with a JCE and higher certificates. However, no information is available on the actual participation of school-leavers below MSCE in these programs.

Figure 6.5: Poverty and TEVET Admission by District (2005 Compared to 2008)

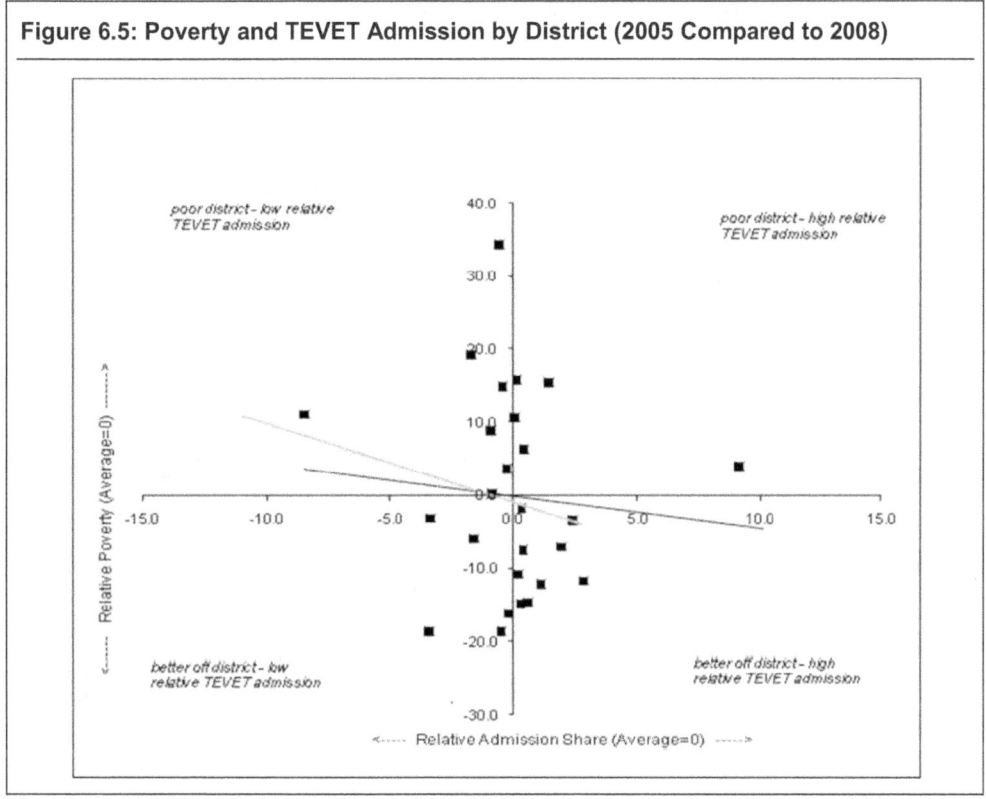

Source: Calculations from Malawi Education Statistics and MICS 2006.

School dropouts naturally constitute a core target group for public skill development programs that have no access to the formal TEVET system. People who have left school have to find training opportunities in other non-formal programs offered by NGOs, some line ministries, or TEVETA—or in the private training market, which involves high costs (see also section IV.4).

Costs and Financing

TEVET in Malawi, including the public TEVET system, is funded by multiple sources. Although again, a comprehensive picture of all contributions is not readily available, it can be assumed that public expenditure is one, but most likely not the most important, funding source. Apart from public expenditure from the MOEST budget, TEVET is also financed by other line ministries, companies, and donors as well as private households. To a lesser extent, training institutions are also recovering parts of their cost through income-generating activities. The matrix in table 6.3 summarizes the different sources by the type of training they are funding.

Table 6.3: Sources of TEVET Funding by Training Provider System

Type of Training Sources	Training in Public TEVET Institutions	Training by Non-Public Providers	Training by Employers (in-house, apprenticeship, and external)
Public Budgetary Provision	Base funding of TCs; funding of sector-specific training (for example, water, agriculture, medical) and training for specific target groups (for example, handicapped)	Subsidies to (parastatal) providers with earmarked target group (for example, MEDI)	
TEVET Levy Fund (paid by public and private employers)	Subsidy for training material of formal TEVETA-sponsored apprentices, selected grants for capital investment, bursaries to students	Funding of special programs conducted by private institutions targeting mainly the informal sector	Part-reimbursement of cost-of-staff training programs for levy-paying companies
Private Households	Tuition fees and boarding fees	Tuition fees In the case of private commercial providers, these are cost-recovery fees	Acceptance of no or lower wages in case of traditional apprenticeship training
Income-generating activities	Common in public TEVET institutions	Common in NGO TEVET institutions, occasionally as well in private commercial institutions	
Companies	Indirectly co-financing through TEVET Levy, and offering apprentices places	Indirectly co-financing through TEVET Levy	Direct financing of company-training centers and sponsorships of (in-house and external) staff training programs
Foreign donors	No significant contribution at the moment; some special programs are funded with donor support	Some foreign NGO and churches involved in funding of NGO training; some special programs are funded with donor support; also program funding of TEVETA	

Source: Authors.

Public Expenditure

Public expenditure for TEVET involves, as indicated above, an allocation to the TCs under Vote 250 (Ministry of Education budget)[9], allocations to various TEVET institutions under different ministries, as well as allocations to fund supportive and regulatory functions. The latter category comprises ministerial overheads for the MOEST Department in charge of technical education and training, the government contribution to the TEVET Authority (TEVETA), testing and examination (that is, Trade Testing in the Ministry of Labor), as well as allocations to MANEB (Malawi National Examination Board) to fund activities related to Malawi (Advanced) Craft examinations.

Table 6.4 provides an overview of identified TEVET-related public allocations in the revised 2007/8 budget. It shows that during the recent fiscal year a total of at least MK760 million in recurrent expenditure was committed to directly support TEVET and skills development in Malawi.

Table 6.4: Total Public Spending for TEVET 2007/08 (MK)

RECURRENT	
Ministry of Education	
Allocation to TCs	168,724,305
Administrative cost, TVT department	10,645,000
MOEST subsidy to TEVETA	60,000,000
Staff Development Institute	40,832,395
TEVET share of global admin. cost MOEST	7,636,322
MANEB, share of TEVET	2,912,738
UNESCO National Commission, TEVET share	76,426
Ministry of Labor (MOL)	
Trade Testing department	32,448,940
By other ministries	
Natural Resources College	6,000,000
Limbe Police Training School	26,611,680
Mtakataka Police Training School	22,442,527
Malawi Armed Forces Colleges	272,339,089
Malawi College of Forestry and Wildlife	18,489,195
Civil Aviation Training School	9,796,137
Marine Training College	14,831,550
MEDI	60,000,000
Works Training Unit	5,739,295
Total MOEST	290,827,186
Total Trade Testing Services	32,448,940
Total other ministries	436,249,473
Grand Total	**759,525,599**
CAPITAL	
Village Polytechnics (MOL), donor contributions	77,920,000
Trade testing modernization (MOL), donors	303,156,000
Trade testing modernization MOL, government of Malawi	24,843,000
Total identified budgeted	405,919,000
Total identified executed	24,843,000

Source: Government of Malawi, Revised Budget 2007/8.

A total of MK405 million were allocated to TEVET as capital expenditure, of which, however, only the government allocation to the modernization of trade testing was actually executed.

Public recurrent unit spending for TEVET can only be calculated for TEVET provided in the seven public TCs. Table 6.5 shows that according to the 2007/8 revised budget data, the average recurrent unit spending per year amounted to MK35,100 if only allocations to TCs are taken into account. If the entire MOEST expenditure for TEVET[10] is considered, the total recurrent per capita expenditure amounts to

MK51,408. This represents 70 percent more than the average expenditure for secondary education (see Chapter 3).

The recurrent unit allocation to TCs rises to MK93,218 if only the regular students are taken into account (that is, those admitted through formal recruitment channels and for whom the public allocation is meant). Considering the entire MOEST allocation to TEVET, it even amounts to MK136,529, four and a half times the amount allocated to general secondary education and 45 times the recurrent unit expenditure for primary education (see again Chapter 3).

Overall public unit spending on TEVET, including public administration, testing, and examination costs as a percentage of GDP per capita amount to 141 percent, which puts Malawi into the upper third of a group of African countries, for which comparable data are available (see figure 6A.1 in Appendix 6.1).

Table 6.5 reveals huge differences in the public recurrent unit allocation by TC, ranging from MK12,000 to MK102,000 per student/year. The differences can partly be explained by the factor capacity. The analysis shows that public unit expenditure is lower with rising overall enrollment. At least in the case of Lilongwe Technical College, the relative low unit expenditure appears to also be a function of the college's high capacity to recruit parallel students, which is also related to its urban location.

Generally, allocations of public funds, which are supposed to provide base funding to the colleges, are based on standard formulas and historical budget figures. The allocation is more or less disconnected from actual enrollment or other performance indicators.

Table 6.5: Summary per Trainee of Public Allocations to TCs, 2007/08

Institution	Budget Allocation (in MK)	Total Enrolled students	Unit Public Expenditure (in MK)	Regular Students Only	Unit Expenditure (regular trainees only) in MK
Lilongwe	28,031,679	2,288	12,252	574	48,836
Soche	23,530,614	435	54,093	155	151,810
Mzuzu	15,652,396	486	32,207	236	66,324
Namitete	18,723,328	217	86,283	73	256,484
Livingstonia	35,346,919	348	101,572	176	200,835
Salima	23,095,926	680	33,965	492	46,943
Nasawa	24,343,443	353	68,962	104	234,072
Total	168,724,305	4,807	35,100	1,810	93,218

Source: Government of Malawi, Revised Budget 2007/08.

Not surprisingly, the functional distribution of the public budget allocation (see table 6.6) shows that the staff and management cost in TEVET are less important than in general education.

On average, management and support services account for 57 percent of the budget, personal emoluments alone for 35 percent. Boarding and feeding represents the next important item in terms of cost, followed by teaching services, which include training materials.

Table 6.6: Expenditure in TC 2007/08 (Revised Budget) by Subprograms (in %)

Subprogram	Average Percentage Across TCs
02: Mgmt. & support services (incl. PE)	56.6
06: Staff development	2.8
15: HIV/AIDS intervention	3.3
19: Special needs	0.2
26: Sports and culture	0.3
30: Boarding and feeding	19.6
31: Teaching services	17.3
Total	100.0
of which PE	34.9

Source: Government of Malawi, Revised Budget 2007/08.
Note: Detailed figures by technical college can be found in table 6A.6 in Appendix 6.2.

It is important to emphasize that due to the income and expenditure structure of the TCs (which are discussed in further detail in section IV.2), the expenditure structure represented in the budgets does not describe the actual expenditure and cost structure of TEVET in Malawi. Colleges use other incomes to supplement their budgets. Notably, the PE budget depends on the posts that are actually filled. If this rate is low (typically in more rural locations) additional staff is recruited directly by the college and paid out of the PU (own income) account, which is not reflected in the government budget. Inaccuracies are further aggravated by the fact that the budget allocation, on which the description above is based, is usually subject to substantial cuts in execution. For example, in the budget year 2005/6 the average execution rate for a sample of colleges was only 64.5 percent (see also Table 6A.7 in Appendix 6).[11] Finally, the problem colleges usually face is that actual costs during the academic year often cannot be fully anticipated during the budget preparation process. Substantial budgetary and accounting creativity is required from the colleges in their day-to-day financial management. One of the uncertainties refers to prices of training material and food. In a recent discussion on the issue of boarding in TCs, principals pointed to the drastically high cost of providing meals to students in view of rising food prices. The other major determinant of costs and spending is the actual number of parallel students and their distribution by training field, which affects costs for training material.

The TEVET Levy Fund

Funds channeled through TEVETA into formal and non-formal training as well as regulatory and supportive functions in the TEVET system are increasingly important on the national scale. As shown in table 6.7, TEVETA income almost tripled between 2002/3 and 2006/7. Levy income from the private sector is by far the most important source of income. With its income structure, TEVETA is in fact a system for channeling industry funds into the national TEVET system.

Table 6.7: TEVETA Income from 2003–2007 (MK)

	2002/3	2003/4	2004/5	2005/6	2006/7
Levy from public sector	30,000	30,000	25,000	44,850	23,373
Levy from private sector	**41,589**	**97,153**	**160,331**	**211,100**	**248,659**
Other income*	25,039	22,230	19,771	14,234	12,421
Donor support	5,351	19,546	14,930	25,480	13,224
Total income	101,979	168,929	220,033	295,663	297,676

Source: TEVETA Secretariat.
*Includes interest income, rental income, contributions from other partners, and miscellaneous.

It is encouraging that after substantial resistance in the early 2000s, levy income from the private sector is steadily increasing. Although still at a very low level, it is now much higher than the public expenditure for TCs. Institutional donor support to TEVETA was significant during its first years. A diversified range of donors now contributes mainly to earmarked programs.

Box 6.1: More about the TEVET Levy Fund

TEVETA's income is derived in large parts from the TEVET levy. This levy is based on the TEVET Act of 1999 and was introduced in 2000/01. It is set at one percent of the gross emoluments of employers. Private and public employers are levied. Levy collection is done by TEVETA. Base data on companies are provided by the Registrar of Companies. Individual TEVETA inspectors (currently there are five) assess all companies and invoice them accordingly. The levy for each company is calculated on the previous year's payroll. In 2007/8, approximately 550 companies were obliged to pay the levy. According to information from TEVETA, compliance is high. The TEVET secretariat reports problems with the government contribution (GOM's contribution to the TEVET levy fund in its function as employer) since the contribution is transferred through the MOE budget. The contribution is paid in monthly installments.

TEVETA expenditure can be divided into:

- funding and subsidies for training activities, in particular subsidies for the regular TEVET programs, support to different private sector training programs, and funding of training courses for informal sector operators
- funding of TEVETA's regulatory function of the TEVET system, including quality assurance (such as standard setting, curriculum development, and assessment), research, and monitoring
- funding of governance and administration, which covers staff costs for the TEVETA head office and the regional offices, costs related to the TEVETA Board, and the management of the levy fund.[12]

Table 6.8 shows that although increasing in absolute terms (see Appendix 6), the relative share of administration costs (TEVETA Secretariat and Regional Service Centers) of the expenditure is decreasing—from almost 60 percent in 2002/3 to 27.6 percent in 2006/7. In Africa, national training funds are sometimes blamed for their high administration costs, so this appears to be an encouraging trend.

Table 6.8: TEVETA Expenditure Structure 2002/03 to 2006/07 (in %)

	2002/03	2003/04	2004/05	2005/06	2006/07
Private sector training	2.7	5.6	4.9	6.2	12.6
Apprenticeship, other training	20.4	13.6	17.9	19.6	21.1
Informal sector outreach program	3.6	5.5	5.6	6.1	2.5
Total training support	*26.7*	*24.7*	*28.4*	*31.9*	*36.2*
Quality assurance services	6.2	9.8	8.2	11.1	10.7
IEC activities	3.2	4.8	5.9	1.8	3.5
Planning, monitoring, and evaluation	1.0	2.6	4.9	6.1	4.6
Total regulatory functions	*10.4*	*17.2*	*19.0*	*19.0*	*18.8*
TEVETA Secretariat	37.9	38.0	34.1	31.7	28.6
Regional service centers	21.6	15.0	10.7	10.5	9.0
Total administration and management	*59.5*	*53.0*	*44.8*	*42.2*	*37.6*
Fund management	3.3	5.1	7.7	6.8	7.4
Total expenditure	100.0	100.0	100.0	100.0	100.0

Source: TEVET Secretariat.

However, direct training subsidies for apprenticeship training and private-sector training are increasing absolutely as well as relatively. Only the informal sector outreach program experienced a drawback in 2007 relative to the prior years. TEVETA activities related to the regulatory function of the national TEVET system, which includes quality assurance services, information, evaluation, and communication (IEC) activities as well as planning, monitoring, and evaluation, are also increasing. Their share is now 18.8 percent of the total budget, compared to 10.4 percent in fiscal year 2003.

Contributions from Private Employers

The overall volume of TEVET investment by parastatal and private employers is unknown. However, it appears that its extent is rather significant. Systematic information is only available for the employers' contribution to the TEVET levy fund, which has increased (nominally) from MK42.6 million in 2002/3 to MK248.7 million in 2006/7. An indication of a rather substantial investment for staff training is given by the Malawi Investment Climate Assessment of 2006, which found that 52 percent of the surveyed companies provide internally or externally organized staff training.[13]

Contributions from Private Households

Private households contribute significantly to the cost of TEVET in Malawi, mainly through fees (tuition and examination), boarding fees, the cost of living of trainees (if boarding is not an option), as well as opportunity costs if a trainee would have otherwise been employed and earned an income.

Data from the 2004 Integrated Household Survey (IHS) suggest that the average annual household spending per student in TEVET is double that for students in secondary education.[14] The data also show a significant rural / urban difference in TEVET-related household expenditure, with urban households spending almost four times as much as rural households. This reflects the concentration of private commercial TEVET institutions in urban areas.

Tuition fees vary substantially between public, private non-commercial, and private-for-profit institutions, and depend on the training program. In the formal TEVET programs provided in the TCs, private contributions are highly differentiated according to the status of the students—whether they are regular (TEVETA-sponsored) apprentices or parallel students recruited directly by the colleges. In private for-profit institutions, as well as in non-subsidized public and non-commercial institutions, fees are usually charged on a cost-recovery basis. This normally equals the full training cost (after the deduction of institutional income through production). Fees in this TEVET market segment vary substantially. Tuition fees per annum of between MK22,500 and MK120,000 were established in recent visits to training institutions.

TEVET programs provided by NGOs and church-related institutions are usually less expensive for private households. However, with few exceptions, all institutions charge at least a commitment fee. Fees in visited institutions ranged from MK10,000 to MK28,000 per annum. In non-governmental institutions, boarding is normally not available (again with a few exceptions).

If training is geared towards formal qualification, additional examination fees are charged. These currently range between MK750 (Trade Test 1) and MK2,500 (Malawi Advanced Craft). See table 6A.9 in Appendix 6.

The Total Income of Technical Colleges and Full Unit Cost

It was not possible to calculate the unit cost of training in any of the different TEVET provider systems in Malawi by taking the contributions of all funding sources into account. Such a calculation would have required the comprehensive budgets of individual institutions and training institutions were generally not prepared to provide access to such financial data. Even the MOEST lacks any information about income and the comprehensive budget of the technical colleges, which operate under it.

Principally, TCs obtain funding from the following sources managed through three different accounts (box 6A.1 in Appendix 6.1):

- MOEST (up to 2005 MOLVT) subsidy to recurrent cost
- capital budget subsidy from MOEST (formerly MOLVT)
- contributions made to the recurrent cost of regular apprenticeship training by the TEVET Fund; this contribution, which currently represents a lump sum across all trade subsidy, is accounted for separately and not included in the public budget of TCs
- possibly, albeit rarely, capital budget subsidies from TEVETA
- income from training fees for regular and parallel trainees[15]
- income from commercial activities, which include "training consultancies" (different tailor-made training programs fully paid by clients, which are companies or other organizations), and other commercial activities (production).

Lilongwe Technical College is the only public TEVET institution under MOEST that has provided some information about its income structure. In 2007/8, it received 37 percent of its total budget from MOEST subsidies. Less than 7 percent were subsidies from TEVETA and around 56 percent was generated through fees and other commercial income of the college. In total, this added up to a consolidated annual recurrent unit spending of MK46,511, almost four times higher than the public subsidy (see table 6.5). Lilongwe Technical College's data may not be generalized, however, as the college is able to recruit a particularly high number of parallel students and has an overall high enrollment that presumably results in a much better capacity utilization than other public TCs. Scattered information from other (including non-public) training institutions that were visited indicates a unit spending of around MK100,000 to MK200,000 per annum,[16] which is generally much higher.

TEVETA has started to update unit cost data by assessing the cost for training materials for different occupational areas, in accordance with the CBET curricula, to form a future revision of the TEVETA per capita subsidies for regular apprenticeship students. The total annuals found in the study range from MK22,000 to MK131,000 per student, which in most cases represents substantially more than the current lump sum subsidy of MK12,000 per term across trades (Maganga, 2008).

Internal Efficiency and Quality

In the following section, available data on the external efficiency of the TEVET system will be examined, as well as the factors affecting TEVET quality, which can be considered a cause of the efficiency problems observed.

Internal Efficiency Indicators

Examination Results, Dropouts, and Repetition

Examination results are among the few systematically recorded indicators for TEVET's internal efficiency in Malawi. Information is available for the MANEB-based Malawi (Advanced) Craft (MAC) system and for the Ministry of Labor-administered National Trade Testing (NTT) system, both of which only target traditional technical trades.

The overall pass rate for MAC examinations over the last five years for which data were available (2003– 2007) was 67.2 percent, almost the same as for the lower level Malawi Craft (67 percent) and the higher level Malawi Advanced Craft (67.7 percent), which indicates that more than 30 percent of the candidates do not reach their educational goals after two and four years of training, respectively. The situation is even more worrisome for the trade testing system, where only an average of 52.8 percent of students passed the tests over the last five years.[17]

Results in the MAC examinations vary substantially by training institution, with differences between the rates of individual institutions of 27 percent (Malawi Craft) and 20 percent (Malawi Advanced Craft). The situation is similar for the trade testing system. Overall, however, those who have completed training programs in TEVET institutions have a much better success rate (57 percent) than external candidates (40 percent).[18]

Substantial differences in examination results occur also between the different trades (figure 6.6). Again, the findings would merit a more thorough analysis, but it can seen that pass rates are particularly low in the trades such as electrical and mechanical, for which training delivery is more expensive.

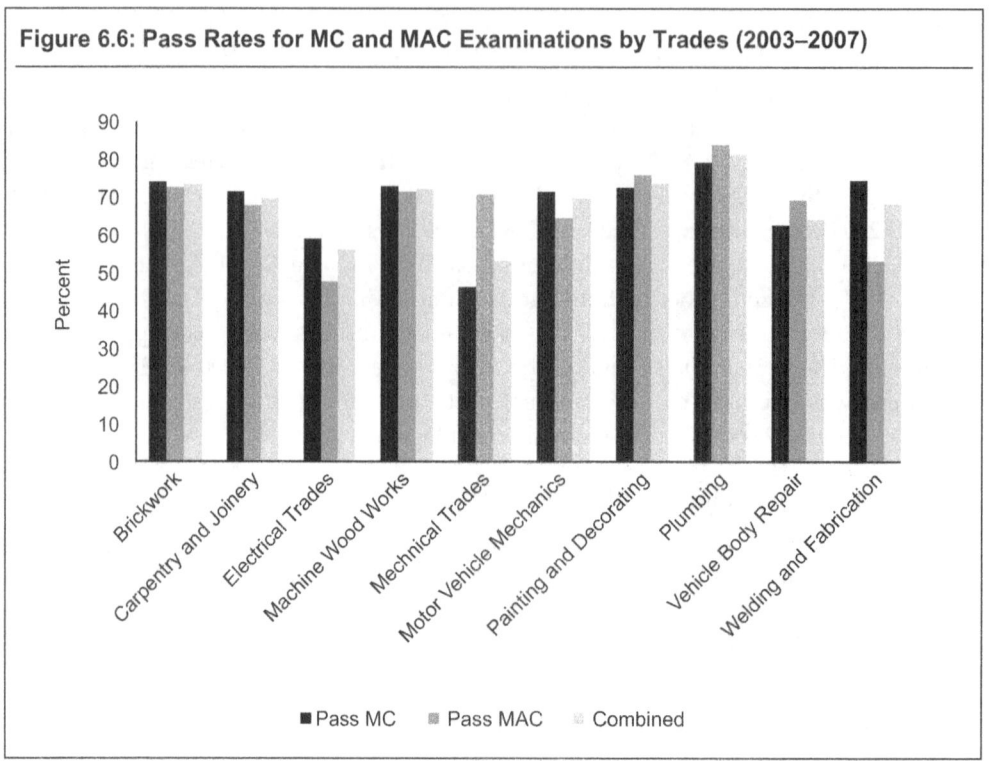

Figure 6.6: Pass Rates for MC and MAC Examinations by Trades (2003–2007)

Source: Malawi National Examination Board.

Information on dropout rates is only available for the regular apprenticeship system, and the rates are generally low, around 6–8 percent. TEVETA assumes that dropouts mainly occur because alternative options open up for students, such as more attractive educational paths (such as admission to a university), and occasionally employment opportunities. Regular apprenticeship training is highly subsidized and poor students receive scholarships, so social reasons are unlikely to cause students to drop out of the system. This situation is most likely very different for parallel students, however relevant data are not recorded. More information and analysis are urgently needed.

Quality

There is a general perception in Malawi that TEVET is of low quality and relevance. While Chapter 8 will look more closely at relevance indicators, this section points to some of the most important factors affecting the quality of training delivery in Malawi.

The system is faced with a number of challenges that affect the training delivery, including unqualified teachers and managers in the training institutions, the low preparedness of students coming from the education system, outdated training equipment, a lack of learning and teaching material, and the problem of parallel qualifications and curricula. Relevance (that is, the responsiveness of training to the needs of the labor market), is again affected by the quality of the training and the responsiveness of curricula to the needs of the economy.

Parallel Qualifications and Curricula

One of the major problems of quality assurance in the Malawian TEVET system is the co-existence of three different Malawian, and a range of foreign, qualification assessment systems (see box 6.2). The situation seriously affects the quality of training because of the following:

- Teachers and instructors have to teach according to different curricula or parallel training plans, often in the same class or group, in order to prepare students for different qualifications.
- The murky state of the TEVET qualification system prevents the needed revision and updating of the curricula. Only the new CBET qualifications, recently defined with the involvement of employers, reflect the skill requirements of today's labor market. However, the coverage of this new system is limited because it is restricted to regular training programs. The other two Malawian qualification systems (MAC and in particular, NTT), have not been revised or updated for many years, pending a final decision on the integration path towards one unified Malawian TEVET qualification system.

Box 6.2: The Malawian TEVET Landscape—A Jungle of Qualifications and Programs

In various attempts over the last decades to consolidate and nationalize TEVET qualifications in Malawi, new qualification systems and principles were added without removing the old ones. Furthermore, as a result of the limited scope and credibility of Malawian qualifications, a significant range of foreign qualifications have also been established in the market.

At the moment, three different national assessment and certification systems co-exist:

1. The three-level National Trade Testing (NTT) System is administered by the Trade Testing Department of the Ministry of Labor. It is the oldest system in Malawi, well known by industry, and recognized in the public salary and national minimum wage scale. Assessment comprises a theory and a practical part, but it is generally perceived to have an emphasis on practical competence. Trade testing is an open assessment and certification scheme, therefore admission to the trade testing system does not require prior attendance in a specified training program. So-called external candidates who work in industry and may never have attended formal training sit for testing along with trainees from various public and private training institutions.

2. The two-tiered Malawi Craft/Advanced Craft system is administered by the Ministry of Education and its examination body, MANEB. The system was developed in the 1980s in an attempt to indigenize the British City & Guilds qualifications, which were previously used as the target qualifications of the National Apprenticeship System. Malawi Craft/Advanced Craft struggled for a long time to receive formal recognition in the public salary and minimum wage scales, which seriously affected its appeal to students. Unlike the NTT system, the Malawi Craft/Advanced Craft system is program-based. Qualifications require the completion of two (Malawi Craft) or four (Malawi Advanced Craft) years of formal training, provided mainly in public and private institutions and implemented as apprenticeship training.

(Box continues on next page)

Box 6.2 (continued)

3. The new four-level credit-point based CBET system was introduced in 2005 by TEVETA and is currently only used as the target qualification of formal TEVETA-sponsored apprentices and recently, also selected non-apprenticeable training programs for TEVETA-sponsored trainees, for instance for secretarial studies and tailoring. The original intent behind the introduction of the CBET system was to create a unified, integrated TEVET qualification system for Malawi that was in line with the envisaged SADC qualification framework. CBET was meant to eventually replace the Malawi Craft/Advanced Craft and NTT systems. However, although modular and competency-based according to the design principle, CBET certification at the moment requires attendance in a specified training program. In most cases, a CBET qualification requires a certain amount of regulated industrial modules, making it in effect inaccessible to non-TEVETA students. The CBET qualification has recently been gazetted, however is not yet recognized by public salary and minimum wage scales.

In addition to these three, a substantial number of external, foreign qualifications are offered in the Malawi training market. City & Guilds, administered in Malawi by the British Council, is one of the most common, but various others are also offered, in particular in the commercial, accountancy, and IT occupational areas, such as Pitman, PAEC, and CISCO. Furthermore, many training institutions, in particular in the non-public training market, offer in-house certificates after attendance in various long- and short-term training programs.

Principally, a range of local qualifications complemented with international ones are a common pattern reflecting the multiple needs in the labor market. In Malawi, however, the parallel national qualification structure in the mainstream segment of TEVET engenders substantial irritation and a lack of transparency in the labor market. It also causes unnecessary efforts and costs for students.

Training institutions have in the past reacted to the situation with a pragmatic approach. They may offer students preparation for multiple testing, often within the same training programs. The so-called "parallel" apprenticeship students in the public TCs, for example, follow the Malawi Craft/Advanced Craft curriculum, undergo the MANEB examinations, and almost always sit at the same time for the National Trade Tests to maximize their employment chances after graduation. In the course of a four-year apprenticeship program, the normal students collect five different qualifications in two different qualification systems. If resources allow, individual students also try to additionally master the external (and costly) City & Guilds examinations, assuming this will provide an added advantage in the labor market. The situation is also complicated in the case of the TEVETA-sponsored apprenticeship trainees since 2005. They are trained, mainly in public TCs (and often in the same classes with the parallel students), and assessed according to the new CBET system and explicitly discouraged to sit for the other available exams. However, as colleges explained to us, these students also prefer to secure at least NTT qualification and thus "secretly" register as external candidates in the trade testing centers.

Source: Authors.

In order to solve the issue of parallel qualifications, the government has made preparations to hold consultative meetings with all concerned stakeholders.

Parallel Students

As previously indicated, enrollment in parallel programs has increased substantially in recent years. Colleges take in additional parallel students to accommodate an increasing demand for training and to supplement institutional income. However, (as indicated in figure 6.7), the parallel intake has created an additional burden for the teaching staff of most TCs. Furthermore, as visits to training institutions suggest, training resources such as equipment and tools, training materials, and even kitchen facilities are not proportionately increased, which leads to a lower per trainee availability of already scarce resources.

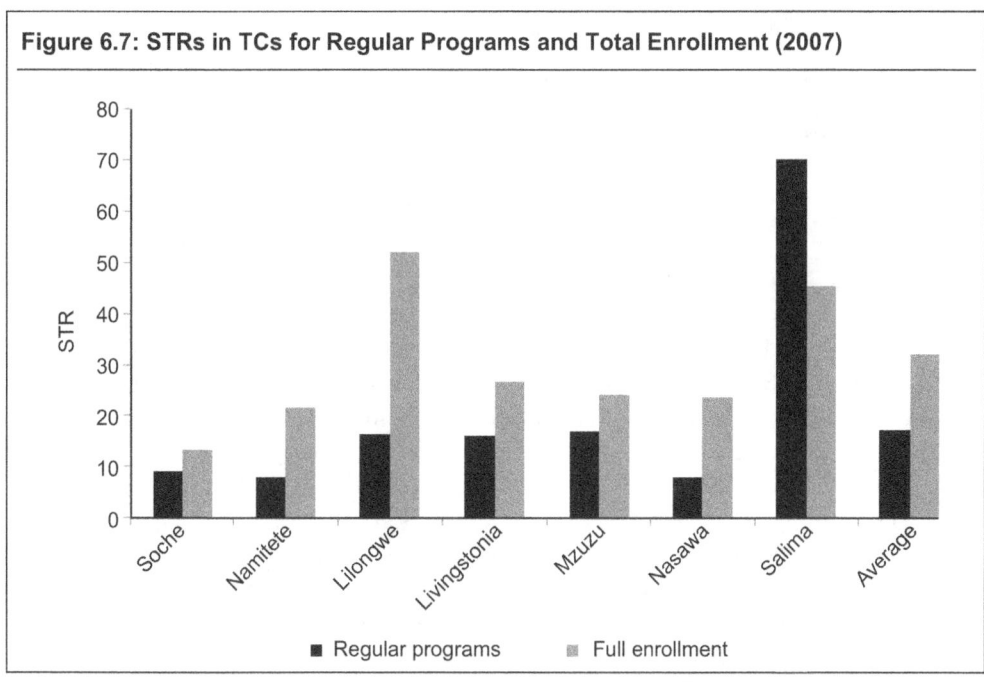

Figure 6.7: STRs in TCs for Regular Programs and Total Enrollment (2007)

Source: MOEST Teachers Records; Education Statistics 2007.
Note: The STR for regular programs pairs regular students with formally recruited teachers, while the STR for full enrollment puts together all (regular and parallel) students with the total number of teachers and training, including establishment and part-time teachers hired through the PU account.

The Availability and Qualifications of Technical Teachers/Instructors and Managers

The quality of training delivery is also negatively affected by the inadequate availability and lack of appropriate qualifications and competences of technical teachers and instructors.

Data on employed teachers and vacancies in public TCs suggest a severe shortage of teachers. Available data for the second term of the academic year 2007 show that only 55 percent of all teaching positions listed in the establishment were actually filled. Rates of establishment posts filled between the individual training institutions vary enormously, ranging from 24 percent for Salima Technical College to 85 percent for Lilongwe. Some, however not all, of the vacancies are filled with contract teachers hired directly by the colleges through the PU budget. The establishment is based on the capacities for formal students, while actual enrollment is much higher through parallel students.

Figure 6.7 shows huge differences in the student/teacher ratio in the individual TCs. Salima Technical College appeared to face a serious situation in 2007: The overall ratio (that is, government-employed plus PU teachers against the entire enrollment of regular and parallel students) was above 30:1 on average, far above the recommended rate of 7:1,[19] and a rate at which practical training can no longer be meaningfully delivered.

Available TEVET teachers are often inadequately qualified and overwhelmingly not appropriately competent. Malawi so far does not have a TEVET teacher training institution.

Table 6.9: Qualifications of Teachers in TCs (2007)

Highest qualification	% of all regular teachers in TCs
Bachelor of Science in Technical Education	50.9
Diploma in Technical Education	36.6
Certificate in Technical Education	10.7
Others	1.8
Total	100.0

Source: Education Statistics 2007.

Instructors in TEVET institutions are usually graduates from the Malawi Polytechnic (MP) or graduates from technical colleges. The MP offers tertiary education in technical and vocational education intended for teachers of practical subjects in secondary schools. However, the MP's training is rather theoretical and does not create competent hands-on teachers for the TEVET system. The consequence is an overemphasis of theoretical training in technical colleges.

Table 6.9 shows that among the teachers formally recruited by government, 86.5 percent can be classified as qualified according to existing standards, which require at least a diploma. For underqualified (regular) teachers, the GoM as well as TEVETA provide upgrading courses, partly in cooperation with foreign partners. A major effort to further develop TEVET teacher training is currently being undertaken jointly by TEVETA and the MP with assistance from the Canadian International Development Agency (CIDA).

During interviews, however, colleges complained that often these teachers, who are recruited and placed by the government, were inappropriately qualified because they were qualified for technical or academic subjects that are different from the ones actually needed in school.

No information about competences and qualifications is available for the 30 percent of teachers in TCs who are directly recruited by the colleges.

Equipment and Facilities

Equipment is not sufficiently available and is often outdated, which is another cause for low training quality. Most of the equipment found in public TCs was donated by the British government in the early 1980s, when the apprenticeship system was introduced. In an attempt to address the problem, the government has plans to purchase modern training equipment for all public colleges, and procurement plans for fiscal year 2008/9 worth some US$4 million are under preparation. Some equipment has also been procured by TEVETA, or donated by private companies and occasionally foreign donors.

Apprenticeship Management

Industrial attachment is a basic principle and mandatory in the apprenticeship training system from year two onwards. It exposes trainees to modern equipment that is not available in training institutions and to work ethics and routines. Since the curricula are based on the cooperative training approach between colleges and companies, failure to secure apprenticeship places seriously affects the training quality and relevance. TEVETA records show that overall, regularly recruited students were successfully provided with attachment places in recent years. Since 2001, attachment rates have been well above 80 percent and have sometimes reached 90 percent[20]. Students who do not find apprenticeship places are usually able to undergo the practice modules required in the colleges; however, they lack the advantages of industrial exposure.

The situation looks substantially different in the case of parallel students. They have to find attachment places mainly on their own. Places, however, are rare and already a restricting factor in the regular apprenticeship system. The attachment places that parallel students manage to obtain are more often found in smaller companies, which may have less training resources and equipment. Although precise figures are not available, the TEVETA Labor Market Survey, as well as information provided by TCs, suggests a much lower attachment rate for parallel students. Furthermore, the industrial attachment practice is not managed and supervised by TEVETA, as it is in the case of regular students.

Quality Assurance

To date, the Malawian TEVET system lacks an appropriate and comprehensive quality assurance mechanism. Quality assurance in TEVET usually comprises appropriate assessment systems and accreditation (preferably oriented towards facilitating quality management at school level), as well as quality control mechanisms within provider systems.

TEVETA is currently in the process of building up a modern, competency-based assessment system. Implementation has just started and so far only covers the minority of regular apprentices.

The two most important assessment systems, MAC and NTT, are inadequate. The MANEB examinations system is based only on theory examinations and leaves the practical assessment to teachers, who lack appropriate practical competence. The trade testing system, on the other hand, although oriented in both practical and theory, is severely under-resourced and based on mainly outdated training standards. It is not yet linked to the new CBET Standards.

The accreditation of training providers does not yet exist, although TEVETA is working on the conceptualization of a modern accreditation system. Currently, the registration of all TEVET providers in Malawi, combined with institutional assessments, can be seen as a first step.

The Ministry of Education furthermore maintains its own system of quality control of the TCs that it administers. The ministry is supposed to ensure that colleges have enough qualified trainers, sufficient tools and equipment, appropriate facilities, and that colleges follow the training programs in accordance with public policies. Responsibilities in the MOEST rest with the Department of Education, Methods and Advisory Services. However, recently the system has not been effective, mainly due to a shortage of qualified inspectors and limited financial resources. Only one college has been visited by MOEST inspectors since 2006.

Governance Issues and Institutional Set-up

Governance and management of TEVET usually poses a substantial challenge to policy-makers. Skill development cuts across the interest of various governmental sectors and cannot successfully be implemented without the participation of industries and employers. To make sure that training programs are aligned to what the different labor market segments need, people who represent and know the formal and informal worlds of work need to be incorporated into the planning, implementation, and supervision processes in the TEVET system. The institutional set-up for TEVET management needs to be built in a way that can:

- facilitate coordination and cooperation between different government sectors, such as education, labor, agriculture, health, public works, and others
- regulate training delivery in all different sectors and by different provider systems in a way that guarantees a coordinated and articulated training approach
- ensure that non-government stakeholders (in particular industry), the informal sector, and civil society also articulate their interests and views and influence TEVET development appropriately.

Malawi has struggled for many years to find the appropriate institutional set-up as the numerous changes in ministerial responsibility for TEVET over the last decades demonstrate. However, management problems still constitute one of the major obstacles to TEVET development and to the provision of appropriately skilled human resources to the Malawian economy. As the scope of this analysis is limited, the following section concentrates on three relevant topics: governance, the management of training institutions and stakeholder involvement.

Governance and Regulatory Functions

The latest major reorientation of the TEVET system led to the establishment of TEVETA in the late 1990s, which came about after several years of diagnostic work and discussion within Malawi. TEVETA was formed with the aim to:

- facilitate the move from an essentially supply-driven to a demand-responsive TEVET system
- integrate the fragmented TEVET provider systems
- overcome the situation of parallel qualification systems with the creation of one new CBET qualification framework
- develop modern methods of quality assurance and regulation and to promote the sustainability of TEVET through the transformation of the previous Industrial Training Fund into the levy-based TEVET Fund.

The authority was formed as an autonomous body that reflected the need of responsiveness to different stakeholder groups—mainly the education sector; the labor sector; and the private business sector, both formal and informal. It is based on the TEVET Policy approved in 1998 and the TEVET Act adopted in 1999. According to these documents, TEVETA's main role in the Malawian TEVET system is policy development, regulation, quality assurance and facilitation, while the Authority is not supposed to be directly involved in training delivery.[21]

Initially funded with substantial donor support, TEVETA has achieved important reform steps, including the establishment of the TEVET Fund; the commencement of a new CBET-based qualification framework; and the promotion of non-formal training activities, with special emphasis on private and informal sector training, as well as research initiatives to fill some of the striking knowledge gaps.

TEVET delivery remained with the line ministries in the case of public TEVET institutions, as well as various private providers. Gradually, but far from comprehensively, different providers have adopted the new CBET qualifications that are managed by TEVETA.[22] For formal TEVET provided in the public TCs, responsibility was moved from the Ministry of Labor and Vocational Training to the MOEST in 2006.

Through their responsibility for the most popular Malawian TEVET qualifications, the Malawi National Examinations Board (MANEB) under MOEST and the Directorate of Trade Testing in the Ministry of Labor still assume core regulatory functions in the TEVET system. As an open system allowing for recognition of prior learning, trade testing constitutes an important element of the TEVET reform, and would need to align its trade standards with the new CBET standards. However, further development and updating of the trade testing system has come to a standstill. While trade testing is the most important assessment system in Malawi in terms of candidates passing through and acceptance with industry, it is underfinanced and mainly relies on outdated trade standards.

Management of Public TEVET Institutions

The problems inherent in the TEVET system translate into the numerous challenges TEVET institutions are facing in the day-to-day delivery of training. These include a shortage of appropriately competent teaching staff; the unavailability and shortage of learning, teaching, and training material; the need to train towards various parallel qualification systems; and a shortage of apprenticeship places for students, which leads to a higher demand on practical training within the institutions.[23] In particular, the public TCs are substantially restricted in their ability to flexibly and creatively cope with these challenges. Some of the problems they are facing include the following:

- TCs are forced to operate with three different accounts reflecting the different revenues they receive from treasury, TEVETA, and their own income. Only the funds in the PU account can be flexibly and independently used to cover unexpected expenses, which creates incentives to increase the parallel student intake irrespective of capacity.
- The TCs are obliged to maintain boarding facilities for regular students, which in the past has caused substantial drains on the available budget when food prices rose unexpectedly. Boarding management consumes a substantial share of the institutions' management capabilities.
- If not financed through the PU account, colleges are dependent on a rather inflexible public procurement system, which causes delays in providing training material.
- Due to competing employment opportunities for well-qualified technical teachers, the staff turnover in technical training institutions tends to be high. However, TCs lack the opportunity to directly recruit new staff. Apart from part-time teachers paid from the PU account, recruitment is centrally done by the Teaching Services Commission in the MOEST, and it take a year or more from the time a vacancy is reported until a post is filled.[24] Furthermore, college

managers complain about the frequent recruitment of teaching staff with qualifications that are different from the ones required.

In the beginning of the decade, a discussion was initiated and a first draft policy paper prepared about granting TCs more operational autonomy. This discussion came to a standstill when the colleges were transferred to the MOEST. Considering the enormous restrictions imposed on the technical colleges through being part of the central procurement and staff recruitment system and by needing to accommodate three separate financial management systems, the discussion about merits and risks involved in granting more autonomy to TCs should be taken up again.

Stakeholder Involvement

Stakeholder involvement in Malawi's TEVET system is institutionalized in different ways; however, the fragmented structure in the TEVET system does not always facilitate appropriate dialogues.

TEVETA appears to have developed a significant communication and involvement with employers, in particular with private firms in the formal and informal sector and their representative associations. Apart from sitting on TEVETA's Board and contributing through the TEVET levy the bulk of the Authority's budget, companies, or associations are increasingly involved in standard setting and the implementation of programs that are tailor-made for them. Companies are regularly approached by TEVETA in the context of training needs assessments and are eligible to benefit from the private-sector training program.

Naturally, MOEST is heavily involved with its TCs, although it lacks any day-to-day or regular contact with employers. This is partly caused by the fact that the responsibility for organizing and supervising the industrial attachment part of the mainstream TEVET system is administered by TEVETA.[25]

Of the examination bodies, only the Directorate of Trade Testing used to maintain close relationships with industry—for example, through the Trade Advisory Groups, which were instrumental in revising testing standards. However, this participation has practically dried up since the future of the trade testing system is unclear.

Currently, the actual stakeholder influence (mainly of employers and civil society) on the public formal TEVET sector is mainly exerted through TEVETA. In fact non-governmental stakeholders dominate the TEVETA Board, holding most of the 10 regular seats, while the government is only represented with four ex-officio members. Considering the important stake government has in the provision and financing of TEVET in Malawi, the board structure may require a restructuring aiming at creating ownership of TEVETA among key government sectors (for example, MOEST, MOL, MOF) through inclusion in the decision-making structures.

Notes

[1]What is labeled as formal, non-formal, or informal training varies among countries and users. Usually, the term "formal training" is used to describe training programs that are structured, provided in an accredited training institution, and lead to a recognized, national qualification. On the other hand, "non-formal training" refers to training also provided in a structured mode of delivery and following a prescribed curriculum, yet normally not leading to recognized national

qualifications but rather to institutional certificates. *"Informal training"* usually describes all kinds of non-structured learning and mainly includes on-the-job training, including traditional apprenticeships, or self-learning.

In Malawi, like in many other countries, these definitions do not sufficiently capture the reality of the TEVET landscape. Definition problems arise for example with respect to training programs geared towards international, but not nationally recognized, certification, as for example the City and Guilds qualifications. Also, many of the courses provided in NGOs that would normally be classified as non-formal, as well as informal, on-the job-learning, lead to Trade Testing Certificates, which is a recognized national qualification system. In these cases, the training would lead to formal qualifications but is delivered in a non-formal way.

[2] TEVETA is systematically recording data on regular student intake and enrollment. The system of data collection from TCs by the MOEST, however, remains rather weak and records reveal a high level of inconsistency. This is most likely due to the fact that the questionnaires meant to capture student returns that sent out to colleges are not clearly defined, or understood by the colleges. For example, return data are unclear with respect to the questions, whether students enrolled, or only those who are actually physically present in the college, are captured. There is a difference, as a significant number of students regularly undergo industrial attachment.

[3] Between 2003 and 2006, the Ministry of Labor (which at that time had the responsibility for TCs), also recruited parallel students in addition to the regular apprenticeship intake administered by TEVETA.

[4] The summary of records of the 1999 TEVET Provider Directory can be found in table 6A.2 in Appendix 6.

[5] Relation of the district's share of TEVET student intake to the total TEVET intake to the district's share in the total population.

[6] Poverty status is measured by the percentage of the population belonging to the lowest income quintile as compared to the national average.

[7] The admission is done through a fully computerized and transparent selection process.

[8] "General" as compared to the TEVET programs that prepare for specialized state employment, such as policy training, teacher education, etc.

[9] Until 2005, the colleges were under the Ministry of Labor.

[10] See table 6.5 for the entire MOEST TEVET-related budget without the Staff Development Institute.

[11] The execution rate is likely to have recently improved as resources have been directly disbursed by treasury since 2006.

[12] Further details on TEVETA spending are included in Appendix 6.

[13] Africa Private Sector Group, Malawi. Investment Climate Assessment (ICA), June 23, 2006

[14] See also Chapter 3.

[15] The tuition part of the fee from regular apprentices (MK 2,000) has to be transferred to a government account.

[16] It should be noted that the unit cost for training institutions in the case of training provided by apprenticeship is generally lower than for other institutional training schemes, because parts of the training are provided by companies. In the case of a four-year apprenticeship training in Malawi, a student should not spend more than a total of two years in the technical college on a net basis.

[17] Interestingly, pass rates are almost identical for men and women. For further details on trade testing see Appendix 6A.13.

[18] Further characteristics of the trade testing system and its results can be found in Appendix 6A.13.

[19] This ratio includes workshop assistants.

[20] The low attachment rate currently recorded for 2007 can be explained by the fact that most students spent most of their first year in college, so the actual attachment is just taking place during the first year.

[21] For the definition of TEVETA's roles, see TEVET Act, paragraph 11 (a); and TEVET Policy, paragraph 4.1.1.

[22] One example outside the system of public TCs is the Malawi Institute of Tourism (MIT) of the Ministry of Tourism. Some private providers, for example Rumphi Technical College, have started to recruit regular students sponsored by TEVETA.

[23] This is a particular concern for parallel students.

[24] In 2005 and 2008, the Teaching Service Commission in the MOEST was not appointed at all, so no new staff were recruited.

[25] Although comprehensive information is lacking, relationships among other sector ministries with TEVET institutions and relevant employers appears to be better overall.

CHAPTER 7

Higher Education

Summary of the Chapter

University enrollments almost doubled from 2003–2008, partly because of the enrollment of non-residential students and the establishment of private universities (which contributed 12.4 percent to the total enrollment in 2008). Female enrollment has remained at around 30 percent in public institutions and around 40 percent in private institutions.

However, Malawi still has the lowest university enrollment (51 per 100,000 inhabitants) when compared to some SSA countries whose average is 337. Limited infrastructure constrains the growth of university education.

Malawi universities offer 18 fields of study. Education, applied science, commerce, social sciences, and the humanities account for the highest enrollment. Science and engineering are each around 4.3 percent of total enrollment. Information and communication technologies (ICT) is around 2.7 percent.

Post-graduate studies account for less than 10 percent of total enrollment. The highest enrollments are in the social sciences and science. Private colleges are not yet offering post-graduate programs. Areas critical to the implementation of the Malawi Growth and Development Strategy (MGDS) are not well covered.

The amount of the education budget allocated to higher education (27 percent) is higher than the average (21 percent) for SSA countries. The subventions account for over 80 percent of the income of public universities, while student fees and other income contribute less than 10 percent each. Government subsidization of higher education is a source of great inequity because over 90 percent of university students come from the wealthiest 20 percent of Malawi households. Student fees are the main source of income for private universities.

Emoluments and benefits consume more than 50 percent of expenditures in public institutions. Very little is spent on teaching materials, equipment, books, and periodicals. Emoluments take up less than 40 percent of the total expenditure in private universities (which also spend more on teaching materials than public institutions).

Malawi's higher education recurrent unit cost of 21.5 times the GDP per capita is the highest among all the SSA countries (for which the average is 3.14 times the GDP per capita). This is because the average student/lecturer ratio of 11:1 for both public and private institutions is very low compared to other countries in SSA (the average is 20:4) of similar GDP. Lecturer's salaries, expressed at 63.9 times the GDP per capita, are also higher compared to other SSA countries with a similar GDP (the average is 23.8 times GDP per capita). This also contributes to a very high unit cost.

The National University Student Loan Trust for needy students does not apply a "Means Test" and as result almost all applicants access it. The system is not equitable because those who take out loans are among the wealthiest, and also because non-residents and students in private universities are not eligible. The absence of a legal framework means that the loan recovery mechanism has not been established. In the meantime, a serious backlog of loans is building up. The loans have hidden subsidies, which will result in low repayment and recovery ratios. As a result, the Loan Trust will require continued allocation from the government.

Graduates at both the graduate and postgraduate level are very well absorbed into the labor market, where their salaries expressed as GDP per capita are much higher than those of countries with a similar GDP.

* * *

This chapter provides an in-depth analysis of the higher education subsector (following the brief analysis that was done in the 2004 CSR). The analysis highlights the status of higher education, some key challenges the sector faces, and goes on to propose policy options for improvement. A challenge in conducting this analysis was data collection, which was done mainly by the institutions themselves, most of which have yet to establish management information systems. As a result, some data were inadequate and at times completely absent. There are gaps and inconsistencies in data, yet these should not invalidate the findings of this report. The analysis focuses on the following areas:

- the structure of the higher education system;
- the distribution and nature of enrollments, including the level and field of study and the equity dimension;
- financing and expenditure patterns (for example, the fee structure and sponsorship of students);
- staffing patterns;
- the internal efficiency of the sub-sector; and
- management and policy issues.

The chapter concludes with recommendations. Only public and private institutions that offer degrees and post-graduate studies are covered in this study. Other institutions that offer diploma programs are mentioned in Chapter 6.

The Genesis and Growth of Higher Education in Malawi

Public Universities

University of Malawi

In October 1964, the first public university in Malawi was established by the University of Malawi (Provisional Council) Act. Over the years, the university has expanded and currently has five constituent colleges: Chancellor College in Zomba, the Polytechnic, College of Medicine, Bunda College of Agriculture in Blantyre, and the Kamuzu College of Nursing in Lilongwe.

Mzuzu University

Noting the insatiable demand for higher education in Malawi, the government decided to establish a second public university in the Northern region. The Mzuzu University campus at Choma in Mzuzu opened in 1999.

Private Universities

The two public universities are not able to absorb the majority of secondary school graduates in Malawi. Private universities in Malawi are a welcome development as they augment the efforts of the public universities in increasing enrollments. There are currently four private universities in Malawi: Shareworld University (with campuses in Blantyre, Lilongwe, and Mzuzu), which started offering degree programs in 2006; Catholic University of Malawi in Blantyre, which was established in 2006; Livingstonia University in Rumphi, which was established in 2003; and Adventist University of Malawi at Lake View in Ntcheu, which was established in 2007. At the time of this writing, three of the private universities were accredited.[1]

Higher Education Enrollments and Fields of Study

Enrollments

Malawi's higher education system is still very small compared to those of other countries in the region. The public universities enroll the majority of students. Total university enrollment constitutes roughly 0.3 percent of students of eligible age.

Table 7.1 shows the total university enrollment for 2003–2008 and enrollment per 100,000 inhabitants by gender. The data show an increase in enrollment per 100,000 inhabitants, for both males and females. The number of female students is much lower than the number of male students, which indicates a persistent gender disparity.

Table 7.1: Enrollment, Actual Number, and Number per 100,000 Inhabitants

Year	Male (actual number)	Female (actual number)	Total (actual number)	Male (per 100,000 inhabitants)	Female (per 100,000 inhabitants)	Total (per 100,000 inhabitants)
2003	3,262	1,397	4,659	53	22	37
2004	3,877	1,706	5,583	61	26	44
2005	4,208	2,051	6,259	65	31	48
2006	4,947	2,410	7,357	74	36	55
2007	5,686	2,788	8,474	83	40	61
2008	5,964	3,118	9,082	84	44	64
			Average	70	33	51

Source: Data from higher education institutions.

Figure 7A.1 in Appendix 7.1 compares higher education enrollments per 100,000 inhabitants (5A programs under the 1997 International Standard Classification of Education[2]). Malawi, with an average of 51 for 2005–2006, has the lowest number of enrolled university students per 100,000 inhabitants in the selected Sub-Saharan countries for which data was available.

However, the annual rate of change in enrollments per 100,000 for Malawi is about 10.53 percent and is one of the highest (as shown in figure 7A.5 in Appendix 7.3), being well above the SSA average of 8.21 percent.

Figure 7.1 shows the growth of enrollments for both public and private universities in Malawi for 2003–2008. Enrollment increased from 4,659 in 2003 to 9,082 in 2008.[3] Evidently the bulk of university enrollment comes from the two public institutions. The contribution of private universities is still quite small in spite of their number. Their enrollment share increased from 0.9 percent in 2003 to 11.0 percent in 2008. Enrollments in these institutions are still low because the majority of the private universities are still in their infancy and because they offer a limited number of fields.[4] Constraints to increased enrollment and in general, access to higher education in Malawi are discussed in Section II.7.

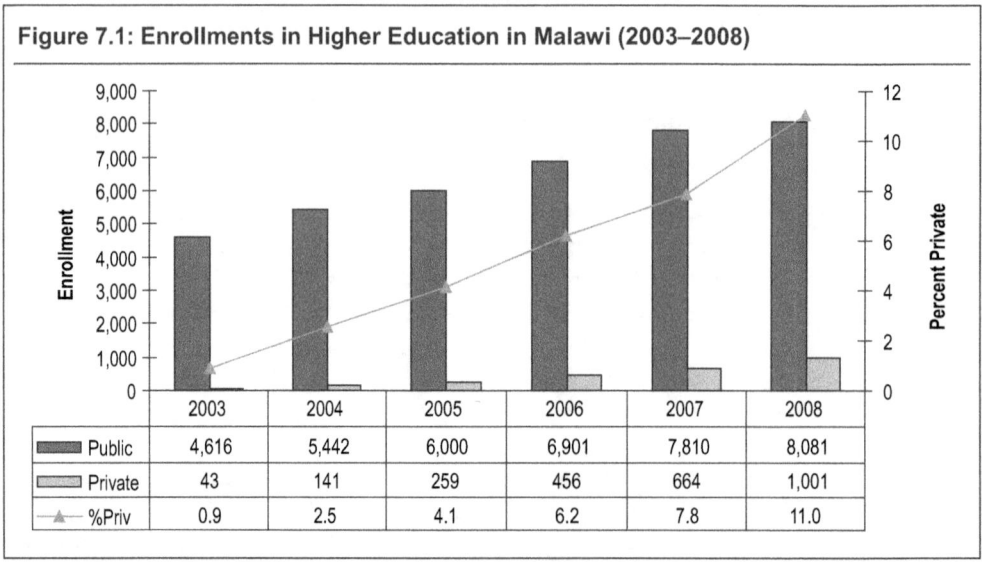

Figure 7.1: Enrollments in Higher Education in Malawi (2003–2008)

	2003	2004	2005	2006	2007	2008
Public	4,616	5,442	6,000	6,901	7,810	8,081
Private	43	141	259	456	664	1,001
%Priv	0.9	2.5	4.1	6.2	7.8	11.0

Source: Data from higher education institutions.

Enrollments in public institutions are limited by bed space as required in the University of Malawi Act. Bed space has not increased significantly over time due to lack of funding. The enrollment increase at UNIMA colleges and MZUNI can be attributed to the enrollment of non-residential[5] students. These students are selected by the colleges themselves, unlike the residential students who are selected centrally by the university office. The Kamuzu College of Nursing and the College of Medicine do not enroll non-residential students because of the nature of their training.

As shown in figure 7.2, the impact of non-residential students on enrollments has been quite significant, particularly at Chancellor College, the Polytechnic, and MZUNI. For instance, non-residential students comprised 51.9 percent of the total enrollment at the Polytechnic in 2006 and 57.7 percent at MZUNI in 2008. Figure 7.2 shows that the percentage of non-residential students at Polytechnic started to decline after 2006 and this roughly coincides with the fall in enrollments for this institution as shown in figure 7A.6 in Appendix 7.3. Similarly, at Chancellor College the fall in the enrollment of non-residential students in 2008 is reflected in the fall of total enrollments for that year.

A number of external institutions provide access to university education through distance education. The number of students accessing university education through this route is unknown but could be quite substantial. This is an area that needs further investigation in order get a complete picture of higher education enrollments in Malawi.

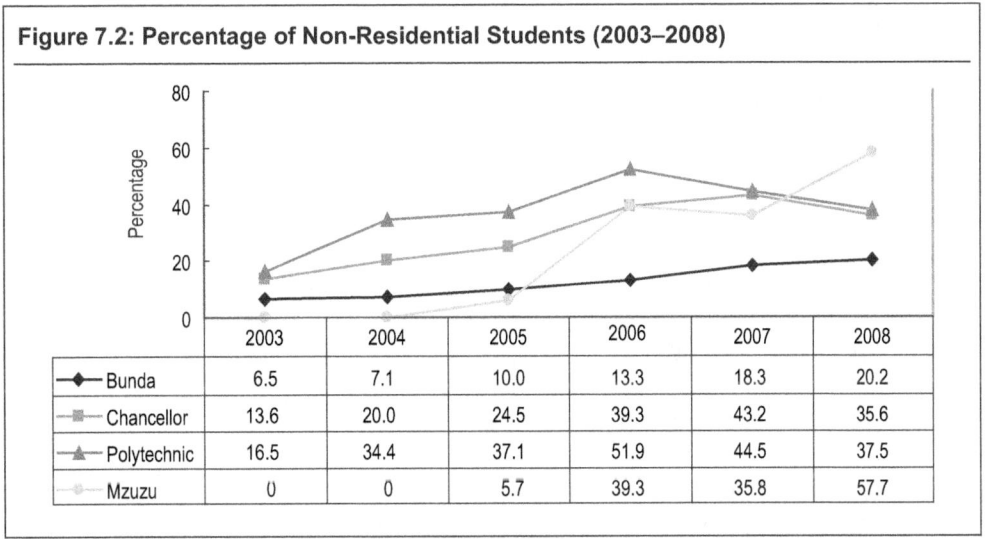

Figure 7.2: Percentage of Non-Residential Students (2003–2008)

	2003	2004	2005	2006	2007	2008
Bunda	6.5	7.1	10.0	13.3	18.3	20.2
Chancellor	13.6	20.0	24.5	39.3	43.2	35.6
Polytechnic	16.5	34.4	37.1	51.9	44.5	37.5
Mzuzu	0	0	5.7	39.3	35.8	57.7

Source: Data from higher education institutions.

Distribution of Enrollments by Field of Study

This section provides a breakdown of the fields of study in both public and private institutions for 2008 (this year being the one with the most recent available data) to determine to what extent the areas offered are relevant to the human resource needs of Malawi. These show the trends from 2003 to 2008.

Table 7.2 shows the distribution by field of study and type of institution for 2008. The data for both types of institutions show that education[6] is the field with the highest number of students at 23.1 percent. Enrollment in education has been enhanced by private universities, three of which offer degrees in education. Education accounts for the highest number of students in private universities, constituting 31.5 percent of the total enrollment. However, while education still has the highest enrollment of all fields, the percentages at Chancellor College, the Polytechnic, and Mzuzu University are decreasing as enrollments in new and other fields are increasing.

Enrollments in private universities are small at this stage because they offer only six out of the 18 fields of study currently available in Malawi (see table 7.2). They also offer the "soft" fields of education, humanities, commerce, developmental studies, and ICT. None offer the sciences, engineering, and health-related programs at the degree level, presumably because of the cost related to establishing such programs. There are plans to offer law at Catholic University and Shareworld University.

Table 7.2: Fields of Study (2008)

Field of Study	Public Institutions		Private Institutions		Both Types		
	Enrollment	% Distrib.	Enrollment	% Distrib.	Enrollment	% Distrib.	%Priv.
Education	1,785	22.1	315	31.5	2,097	23.1	15.0
Commerce	665	8.2	212	21.2	877	9.7	24.2
Social science	604	7.5	253	25.3	857	9.4	29.5
Humanities	621	7.7	153	15.3	774	8.5	19.8
Applied science	730	9.0	—	—	730	8.0	—
Medicine	529	6.5	—	—	529	5.8	—
Environmental science	472	5.8	—	—	472	5.2	—
Nursing	467	5.8	—	—	467	5.1	—
Engineering	394	4.9	—	—	394	4.3	—
Science	390	4.8	—	—	390	4.3	—
Agriculture	371	4.6	—	—	371	4.1	—
Developmental studies	287	3.6	55	5.5	342	3.8	16.1
ICT	236	2.9	13	1.3	249	2.7	5.2
Built environment	186	2.3	—	—	186	2.0	—
Health science	151	1.9	—	—	151	1.7	—
Law	103	1.3	—	—	103	1.1	—
Tourism	58	0.7	—	—	58	0.6	—
Other	32	0.4	—	—	32	0.4	—
Total	8,081	100.0	1,001	100.0	9,079	100.0	11.0

Source: Data from higher education institutions.

Trends in enrollment have changed since 2001, when enrollment in agriculture was second only to education. Agriculture is now in ninth position. Enrollment in agriculture at Bunda is also falling. The tracer study (Pfeiffer and Chiunda, 2008; see Appendix 9) revealed that agriculture graduates took longer than other graduates to secure employment and this may account for the field's decrease in popularity. Engineering, Science, and ICT—which are necessary for the diversification of the economy—still have low enrollments. In fact, the number of students enrolling in engineering at the Polytechnic, and science at Chancellor College has changed little during the period under review. Engineering has actually seen a slow decline in enrollment. Given the importance the implementation of the Malawi Growth and Development Strategy (MGDS) has placed in these fields, there is a need to examine the trends with a view to increasing enrollment in these important areas.

A positive development is the increase in enrollment in applied science, medicine and environmental science. Enrollment in Applied Science at the Polytechnic has been increasing since 2003. Enrollments in Medicine have also been increasing over the same period. Tourism (which has the potential to improve that industry in Malawi) and health science were introduced in the last three years and have the potential to increase in enrollment. So far, there have been no graduates from these fields, so employability cannot yet be tested.

Table 7.2 also shows the contribution of private universities to the programs they are offering. While most private universities indicated that education was one of their priorities during visits to the institutions, the table shows that their biggest contribution is to the social sciences. They currently contribute 15.0 percent to the total education enrollment.

Duplication

There is duplication in some of the fields offered by the universities. Education, for instance, is offered in six of the higher education institutions. This may not necessarily be negative given the acute shortage of secondary school teachers in Malawi, although there is no accurate data to suggest what percentage of education graduates from universities teach in schools.

Given the critical shortage of science teachers in Malawi, it is instructive to examine the distribution of enrollments in education between the Bachelor of Arts Education and Bachelor of Science Education degrees. The total enrollment in the Bachelor of Science Education comprised only 22.9 percent of the total education enrollment and 5.3 percent of the total university enrollment for 2008. The Bachelor of Science (Technical Education) offered at the Polytechnic comprised only 9.3 percent of the total education enrollment. The low enrollment in the Bachelor of Science Education is symptomatic of the problems facing science education in the country. Malawi needs to look at innovative ways of addressing the challenges it faces in science education if it is to improve in this field. Science and technology, together with ICT, are recognized as being critical to the development of Malawi in the MGDS.

Bunda College and MZUNI both offer degrees in Forestry and Fisheries, with Bunda also offering a post-graduate program in this field. Humanities programs are offered at Chancellor College, Shareworld University, and Adventist University of Malawi. Social sciences are offered at Chancellor College and Catholic University. Chancellor College also offers postgraduate programs in social sciences. The Polytechnic offers a Bachelor of Arts in journalism, while Chancellor College offers a Bachelor of Arts in media studies in the Faculty of Humanities.

The bulk of the humanities programs are offered by Chancellor College while Shareworld and Adventist University contribute 21.0 percent of the enrollment. Most students are studying for the Bachelor of Arts in humanities. A smaller percentage (3.2) are studying for the Bachelor of Arts in human resources management, which is offered at both Chancellor College and Shareworld.

Environmental science is an important field for a country like Malawi, given the scale of environmental degradation that is occurring and the number of fishing activities in Lake Malawi. Two programs in this field are the Bachelor of Science (Forestry) and the Bachelor of Science (Fisheries), both of which are offered at Bunda College of Agriculture and MZUNI. Enrollment in fisheries comprises 12.5 percent of the total field of study, while forestry is 37.9 percent. For both programs, enrollment in the individual institutions increased very little from 2003–2008.

A closer examination of the field of commerce shows that 45.5 percent of students in this field are studying for the Bachelor of Business Administration, which is offered at the Polytechnic, Shareworld, and Adventist universities. The two private institutions contribute only 16.3 percent of the enrollment. Accountancy, which is offered in the Polytechnic is the second largest program and accounts for 26.8 percent of the enrollment in commerce. In social science, the Bachelor of Social Science has the highest enrollment at 75.6 percent. This is offered at Chancellor College and Catholic University.

In agriculture, most students (41.2 percent) are studying for the Bachelor of Agriculture. The Bachelor of Irrigation Engineering is an important program for

Malawi's objective to ensure food security. It began in 2005 and has only 17.8 percent of the agriculture faculty enrollment. Given the importance placed on irrigation, water development, and food security in the MGDS, we need to examine strategies to increase enrollments in this program.

We have already observed that enrollments in engineering are among the lowest. An examination of the distribution of programs shows that both civil and electrical engineering programs have the highest enrollments within the field, with a percentage of 37.8 and 30.2, respectively. Mechanical engineering has only 12.4 percent of the total engineering enrollments. This is a vital field where efforts should be made to increase enrollment given the importance attached to manufacturing in the MGDS.

Another necessary field of study for Malawi is that of built environment, which is offered in the Polytechnic only. The school offers Bachelor of Science degrees in architecture, land surveying, quantity surveying, land economy, and physical planning. The bulk of the students in this field are in architectural studies and quantity surveying (33.3 percent and 39.8 percent of the total faculty enrollment, respectively). The Bachelor of Science in land economy and the Bachelor of Science in physical planning were only established in 2008 and currently have very low enrollments. These areas need to grow in order the address the shortage of human resources in these fields.

The question is whether this duplication is desirable. The discussion on enrollments has shown that growth in enrollments is likely to come from non-residential students. Unless some programs are duplicated in the institutions, then access to them might be difficult without increasing bed space in the institutions. If fields are still demanded by the labor market then there is no harm in duplication of fields in order to ensure access to them. The tracer study findings suggest that no fields are saturated yet on the Malawi labor market. However, the demand for skills on the labor market needs to be monitored to ensure that if fields become saturated, then they do not continue to be duplicated or proliferated in the universities.

Postgraduate Enrollments

Postgraduate programs are important because they promote research, which is critical to the development of new information and knowledge. Enrollments at this level are relatively low in relation to the total enrollment in public institutions, partly because not all institutions offer postgraduate programs, and in some few programs are offered. As Figure 7.3 shows, Bunda College of Agriculture (which started offering postgraduate programs in 2005) and Chancellor College (which has been offering postgraduate programs for some time) offer the vast majority of programs at the master's level. The number of postgraduate students has remained below 12 percent of the total enrollment for both institutions with fluctuations. The Polytechnic, in spite of its age, size, high undergraduate enrollment, and the diversity of programs it offers, has a very small postgraduate enrollment. It offers only two postgraduate programs: a Master of Business Administration and a postgraduate diploma in management. Such enrollments have been steadily increasing—from 1.8 percent of the total student enrollment to 2.8 percent in 2008.

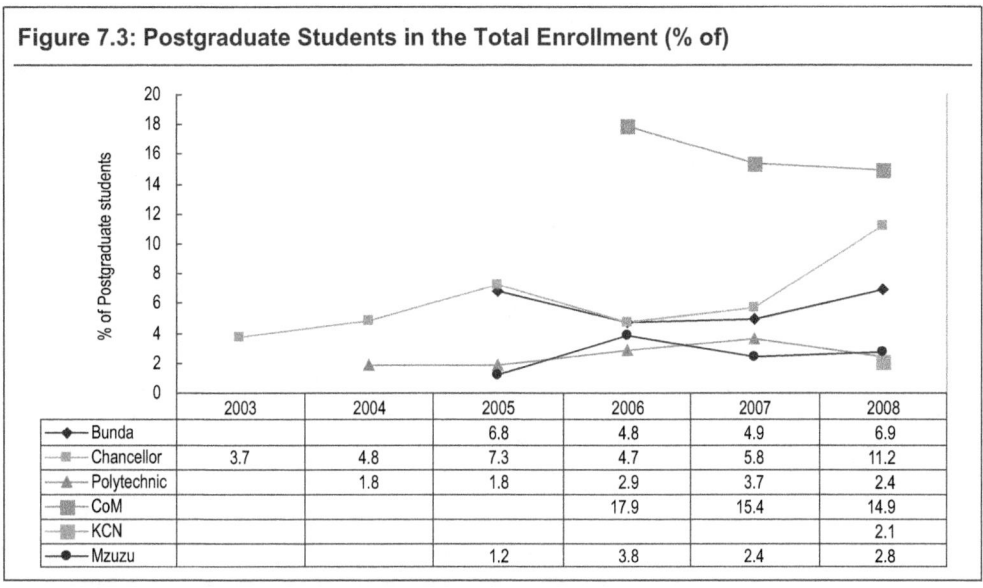

Figure 7.3: Postgraduate Students in the Total Enrollment (% of)

	2003	2004	2005	2006	2007	2008
Bunda			6.8	4.8	4.9	6.9
Chancellor	3.7	4.8	7.3	4.7	5.8	11.2
Polytechnic		1.8	1.8	2.9	3.7	2.4
CoM				17.9	15.4	14.9
KCN						2.1
Mzuzu			1.2	3.8	2.4	2.8

Source: Data from higher education institutions.

Only Chancellor College and MZUNI offers PhD programs in English and theology (humanities), in biology and chemistry (sciences), and in economics (social sciences). The overall enrollment in the PhD programs is less than five percent of the total enrollment in postgraduate programs.

Postgraduate Fields of Study

Table 7.3[7] shows the fields of study and the total enrollment in those fields from 2003–2008. The data show that the social sciences have had the highest enrollment at the postgraduate level. This field includes the Master of Arts in developmental studies, economics, and African social history.

The next most popular field of study is the humanities. The programs in that field are the Master of Arts in philosophy, human resource management, English, theater, mass communication and development, theology, and history. PhDs are offered in English and theology.

The third largest field is the sciences. The programs in this field are the Master of Science in mathematics, mathematical science, geography, chemistry, applied chemistry, environmental chemistry, and biology. PhDs are offered in biology and chemistry. It is doubtful that the current postgraduate programs will respond to the human resources needed for the development of Malawi. Engineering is clearly missing from the postgraduate program in spite of the importance technology has been accorded in the MGDS and the technological advancement taking place across the globe. Malawi is not likely to develop at a fast pace without adopting technology and conducting research into innovations that directly address its technological needs. The planned University of Science and Technology will hopefully address this situation.

Table 7.3: Postgraduate Students by Fields of Study and College (2008)

Year	Chancellor College				Bunda			CoM	KCN	Polytechnic		MZUNI
	Education	Humanities	Sciences	Social Science	Agriculture	Developmental Studies	Environmental Sciences	Public Health	Medicine	Nursing	Management	Business	Education
2003	0	16	30	12	25	0	6	0	0	0	14	0	
2004	0	37	35	12	19	7	7	0	0	0	19	17	
2005	0	42	45	60	11	20	19	0	0	0	20	17	
2006	0	34	36	35	4	17	16	50	6	0	18	49	
2007	29	27	20	74	8	20	13	51	10	0	31	51	
2008	41	74	68	92	10	34	17	61	18	10	56	0	13

Source: Data from higher education institutions.

PhD programs are only offered at Chancellor College in theology, English, chemistry, biology, and economics. Enrollment in the programs comprised 4.8 percent of the postgraduate enrollment at Chancellor College and 2.3 percent of the whole postgraduate enrollment for 2008.

A key output under Sub-Theme 2c of the MGDS is improving the quality of higher education and the two main activities for achieving this are:

- providing training at the PhD level to existing staff, providing training to new staff, and establishing external quality control and accreditation; and
- developing comprehensive policies on research and development.[8]

Both of these activities require expanded postgraduate programs. The main constraints to providing and expanding postgraduate studies have been the lack of funding to support such programs and the small number of lecturers with postgraduate qualifications in the institutions.

Enrollment Policy

The University of Malawi selects its residential students centrally on merit. For entry, students are required to have a minimum of six credits in MSCE in subjects relevant to the faculty in which they intend to enroll. In addition, aspiring students have to pass an aptitude entrance examination test administered by the university. MSCE grades and the results of the aptitude test each contribute 50 percent to this selection process. Selection for each college is dependent on the bed space that is available in the college. Those who qualify but are not chosen by the centralized selection system can be selected at the college level as non-residential students. The College of Medicine administers its own aptitude test for those MSCE graduates who want to enroll in the pre-med program. Those with A-level qualifications enroll directly into the degree program. UNIMA, unlike MZUNI and private colleges, has an affirmative action policy for enrollment of women. The impact of this policy has been minimal because institutions that do not apply this policy have similar or higher enrollment numbers for women. MZUNI and the private colleges do not administer entrance examinations to aspiring students.

Constraints on Increased Access

On average, all higher education institutions receive more applications than they can accommodate. In 2007, MZUNI received over 6,000 applications for 800 places. Adventist University selected 40 students out of 300 applications. In 2008, UNIMA received approximately 4,000 applications. Of these, approximately 3,500 passed the entrance examination and 980 were selected, reflecting an absorption rate of 28 percent of those who passed and 24.5 percent of those who applied. Each year, universities have absorbed less than 40 percent of the MSCE graduate from the previous year. As a result, a backlog of students from previous years is building up, until such time as new strategies are adopted to enroll a large of students.

The current infrastructure at both public and private universities has been the single largest constraint on expanding enrollment in higher education. In the public institutions, the existing infrastructure was designed for small classes and programs that did not require extensive facilities. It is difficult to adapt them in order to increase enrollments and accommodate the diverse programs and levels of teaching universities have started to offer over the last few years. In addition, there has been insufficient funding allocated to maintain the infrastructure, which is in very poor condition. There is limited student accommodation; insufficient classrooms, laboratory, and library space; and dilapidated buildings. Libraries are poorly resourced and ICT is not yet widespread because of its cost. This, together with inadequate and in some cases obsolete teaching and learning materials, has limited the expansion of public higher education enrollment and to some extent affected the quality of education.

While the introduction of non-residential students has increased enrollment, the shortage of facilities limits the growth of enrollment in public institutions. The expansion of the non-residential programs will also be limited by the availability of decent low-cost accommodations that are close to the institutions, as well as the escalating cost of commuting. Because of their isolated locations, it will be difficult for the private universities to introduce non-residential programs. That means that enrollment in these institutions will necessarily be limited by bed space and the resources needed to increase accommodation facilities, especially given that they rely mainly on student fees for their operations. The universities should therefore explore the use of distance education as a way of reaching more eligible students, as has happened in some countries in the region. Examples of these are Tanzania's Open University, which has enrolled over 10,000 students and the Zimbabwe Open University, which has enrolled over 18,000 (Bloom, Canning, and Chan, 2006). Malawi needs to seriously consider establishing an open university—rather than having each institution establish its own distance education program, as appears to be the current plan.

In addition, Malawi should explore ways in which it can benefit from the SADC Protocol on Education and Training,[9] which provides for the education and training of students from member countries in institutions that are available in the region. This could be an expedient and less costly option of addressing those areas for which Malawi does not currently have adequate capacity (especially at the postgraduate level), given that under the protocol the students are expected to pay local fees and not external fees.

The rigid curriculum offered in public institutions that require students to take courses over a four-year period limits enrollment because once enrolled, students are forced to stay in college for the next four years before they can acquire a qualification. Changing the curriculum to a credit-hour system, as practiced in some of the private universities, could introduce flexibility in how long students are required to study before they can graduate. It would also provide flexibility for how students finance their studies in that they can take courses as and when they have the resources while accumulating the required credit hours to graduate.

Staffing at both the undergraduate and graduate level has also had a negative effect on enrollments. Student/lecturer ratios in some departments and faculties are very low, and if adjusted could result in higher enrollments. The fact that all institutions have to rely on staff associates who are not technically qualified to teach at this level is evidence that institutions are not able to recruit adequately qualified teaching staff. Both public and private universities have used adjunct staff in order to address their staffing gaps. The lack of staff also means that the infrastructure is under-utilized, as evidenced by the fact that most of the infrastructure lies idle during the evenings, weekends, and college breaks. This is also as a result of the rigid structure of the curriculum mentioned above.

Financing

Sources of Financing for Public and Private Universities

The main source of financing for the public institutions of UNIMA and MZUNI is subvention from government for both capital and recurrent expenditures. Government recurrent expenditure on higher education in 2008 made up 27.1 percent of the total government recurrent expenditure on education, which is high compared to other SSA countries.[10] Figure 7.4 shows income from government subvention, tuition fees, and other income for the UNIMA colleges for 2004/05 to 2007/08. Figure 7.5 shows the same for MZUNI for 2002/03 to 2004/05.[11] Details of the actual figures are shown in Appendix 7.4.

The figures show that subventions from the government to all institutions have been increasing at different rates during the period. Allocations for 2007/08 are much higher than allocations for previous years. The level of subventions also varies by institution, and is related to enrollment. Although the subvention from government to the public institutions has been increasing with the number of students enrolled, the allocations are not adequate to meet the requirements of the institutions. Generally, public universities receive about 50 percent of what they request from the government and have to augment this with tuition fees and other income. As can be seen from figures 7.4 and 7.5, these sources of income are much lower than the government subvention.

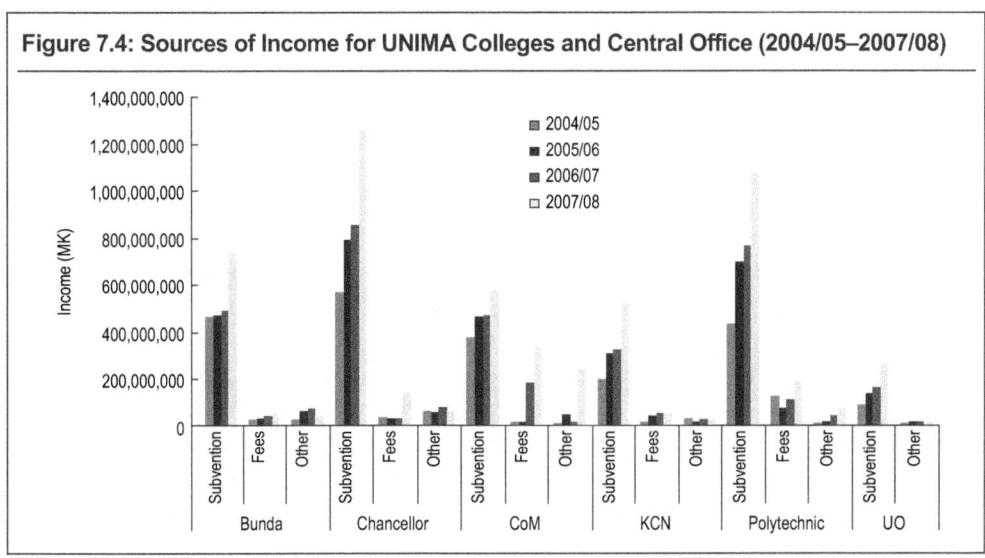

Figure 7.4: Sources of Income for UNIMA Colleges and Central Office (2004/05–2007/08)

Source: Audited Financial Statements: 2004/05–2007/08 from the University Office.

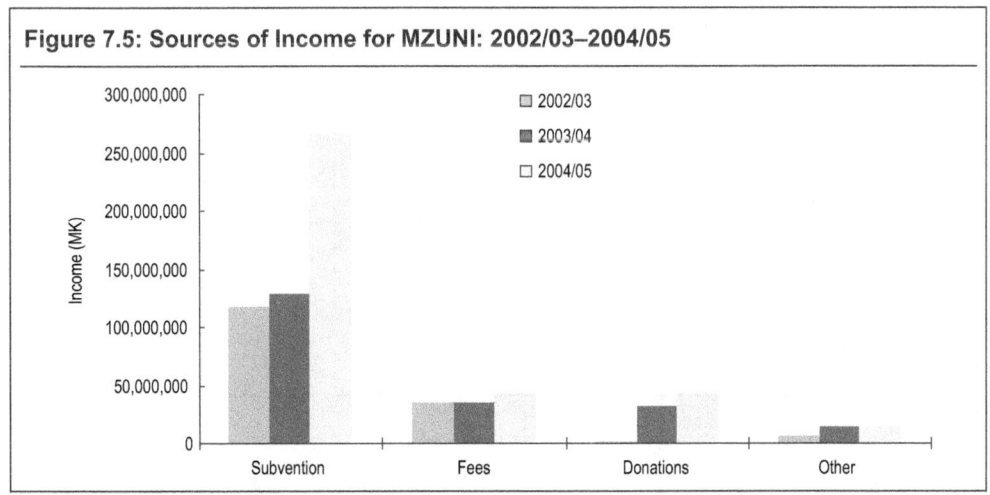

Figure 7.5: Sources of Income for MZUNI: 2002/03–2004/05

Source: MZUNI audited financial statements: 2002/03–2004/05.

Figures 7A.2 and 7.A.3 in Appendix 7.1[12] contain the percentage of subvention to total income for all the colleges. Figure 7A.2 shows that for most colleges, government subvention is above 80 percent, except for the College of Medicine, whose percentage is 49.6 percent of total income in 2007/8. The subvention percentage for MZUNI was 73.5 percent in 2002/03. It fell to 61.4 percent in 2003/04 and rose again to 72.8 percent in 2004/05. This emphasizes the extent to which public institutions are highly dependent on government subvention. The percentage of subvention to total income for the College of Medicine declined from 93.5 percent in 2004/05 to 49.6 percent in 2007/2008. Currently, less than 12 percent of the government subvention goes to the university office responsible for carrying out some key functions of the university before decentralization. This percentage has increased from 4.2 percent in 2004/05 to 5.9 percent in 2007/08.

Figures 7A.2 and 7A.3 in Appendix 7.1 also show that fees make up a very low percentage of the total income of the institutions. The percentages have also varied by institution and by year. On average, the Polytechnic and the College of Medicine have averages in excess of 10 percent, while averages for the remainder are below 10 percent (the lowest being Chancellor College which has averaged 5.6 percent). The percentage of fees for MZUNI has decreased from 21.8 percent in 2002/02 to 11.7 percent in 2004.

It is worth noting that there has been a dramatic increase in the percentage of fees for the College of Medicine (from 4 percent in 2004/05 to 29.2 percent in 2007/08) in spite of its low enrollment when compared to institutions like Chancellor College and the Polytechnic. The high percentage of tuition fees revenue for the College of Medicine has to do with its fee structure, which is different from other UNIMA Colleges. The College of Medicine's fees range from MK25,000 to MK720,000, compared to MK25,000 for UNIMA and MK55,000 for MZUNI. Non-residential students pay MK100,000 at UNIMA while those at MZUNI pay a tuition fee of MK28,000[13] per year. Table 7.4 compares fees for public and private institutions.

Table 7.4: Comparison of Fees in Public and Private Universities (in MK)

	PUBLIC UNIVERSITIES			PRIVATE UNIVERSITIES			
		University of Malawi					
Type of Student	Mzuzu University	Bunda, Chancellor College, Malawi Polytechnic, KCN	College of Medicine	Catholic University	Livingstonia	Adventist University	Shareworld University
Regular students	55,000	25,000	25,000–720,000	320,000	230,000	216,000	260,000–390,000
Non-residential	150,000	100,000					

Source: Data from higher education institutions.

The fees are much lower than the unit cost for university education in Malawi. An assessment carried out by UNIMA in 2006 suggested that the economic cost for UNIMA and MZUNI operations was MK1,275,126 and MK1,083,088, respectively.

The two acts of Parliament that created the two public universities allow them to set their own fees, but these have to be approved by the Ministry of Education. The last fee increase was approved in 2005. As a result, fees have remained low and the student contribution has remained at the levels shown in Figures 7.6 and 7.7. The universities have submitted a proposal for a fee increase to the government. The proposed increase is much higher than the maximum of MK60,000 by 2017 suggested in the NESP. At this level, it is difficult to see how universities can continue their operations without increased government subventions.

The government intends to reduce the percentage of allocation to higher education, as indicated in the National Education Strategic Plan (NESP), which predicts that government subvention to higher education will fall from 14.7 percent in

2008 to 10.4 percent in 2017[14]. However, the proposed reduction in the percentage does not necessarily mean a reduction of the subventions in real terms. If the GDP increases as anticipated, then the percentage allocated to education in the budget will increase. In turn, the allocation to higher education in real terms may also increase even if its share related to the global education sector may decrease.

Tuition fees are the main source of income in the private colleges. The fees range from MK230,000 at Livingstonia to MK390,000 at Shareworld, as shown in table 7.4. The tuition fees at Adventist University are charged per credit hour[15]. This has increased from MK2,000 in 2004 to MK 4,000 in 2008. Students at Adventist also pay boarding fees in addition to the tuition fees. Livingstonia University has relied a great deal on support from private organizations. Other resources are generated from linkages with external universities in the United States. The other church-related universities also receive minimal funding from their church organizations (less than three percent of their total income). Shareworld University relies solely on tuition fees, which range from 260,000 to 390,000. The fees in private institutions are therefore significantly higher than those in public institutions, with the exception of the College of Medicine. The tuition fees of private universities, which rely almost solely on this income source, are well below the determined economic costs for the public institutions. This raises the question of how the institutions are managing to provide education at costs so well below assessed economic unit costs for Malawi.

The third source of income is funds generated by the institution through consultancy services. Figure 7.4 indicates that the UNIMA colleges have been able to generate their own resources at varying levels. The data show that College of Medicine generated the highest percentage of its income (21.2) while Chancellor College had the lowest (4.4) in 2007/08. The MIM report[16] suggested that there is scope for universities to generate higher levels of their own resources. The departments/faculties can retain a certain percent of the income it generates but the percentages vary from college to college. A substantial amount of resources generated in the departments are not accounted for because of lack of a coordinated system to monitor the income.

MZUNI also receives donations generated by a fund-raising committee that has been created for this purpose. From 2003/04–2004/05, donations have provided more income than other sources generated within the institution. While donations made up only 0.8 percent of total income in 2002/03, they increased to 15.4 percent in 2003/04; other resources contributed 3.9 percent in 2002/03 and increased to 6.8 percent in 2003/4.

Given the government's intention to reduce the percentage of the education budget allocated to higher education and the noted delay in increasing tuition fees, universities need to consider generating their own resources if they are to survive.

Expenditure

The actual expenditures for both UNIMA colleges and MZUNI for other recurrent transactions (ORT) for 2003–2008 are shown in tables 7A.10[17] and 7A.11 in Appendix 7.4.

Expenditure Trends

Tables 7A.1, 7A.2, 7A.3, and 7A.4 in Appendix 7.2 show the percentage of selected categories of expenditure for UNIMA, MZUNI, Livingstonia University, and Catholic University, respectively.[18] The data show difference in their expenditure patterns, which could be attributed to differences in management structure, practices, programs offered, and the age of the institutions. The analysis shows that for the four institutions, emoluments and benefits of staff consumed that largest share of the expenditures. While the percentages for these categories fluctuated over the period, they were at their highest in 2006/07 for the public institutions. UNIMA has a higher percentage of its expenditure in this category than MZUNI.

For MZUNI, the second highest expenditure item is student provisions/allowances, which decreased from 17.4 percent in 2003/04 to 9 percent in 2006/07 with increased enrollments. This is substantial for an expenditure that is not considered a core business of the university. The public institutions are hoping to reduce this category through outsourcing (expected to start in 2009). For UNIMA, except for Bunda, the second largest expenditure category was common services, which includes general administration.

UNIMA's student provisions/allowances fell into third place. The costs captured in the data do not include all the additional administrative costs incurred by the central office. If this was taken into account, the percentage for general administration would be higher for UNIMA.

Provision of common services was the third highest expenditure for MZUNI, but this expenditure has decreased over time. Lease financing and the purchase of assets was MZUNI's fourth largest expenditure category (except for 2004/05), closely followed by the expenditures for teaching materials/equipment. The increase in teaching materials/equipment is a step in the right direction because this is a core function expenditure.

Quality-related inputs such as teaching materials have shown low expenditure and the category has remained below one percent at UNIMA. Books and periodicals have also been a low priority in both public institutions, especially at UNIMA where again the percentage allocation has remained below one percent, with no expenditure at all in 2003/04. An analysis of the expenditure patterns for the individual colleges shows that all colleges have spent very little or nothing on these two important categories despite the great shortage of teaching materials, books, and periodicals in these institutions.

Allocations to staff development are low for the two public institutions, falling below two percent. Publications and research allocations are also low and not conducive to promoting research in the institutions. However, visits to the institutions have revealed that some research is going on, in some cases with funding from external sources. But reliance on donor support for research is not sustainable and the work so supported may not necessarily address the research needs of Malawi.

It has not been possible to carry out an in-depth analysis of expenditure patterns in private universities because of a lack of data. Tables 7.5c and 7.5d show the expenditure patterns for Livingstonia University and Catholic University for which expenditure was made available. The tables show that the expenditure patterns are somewhat different from that of public institutions. One major difference is the percentage spent on remuneration, which is much lower than in public institutions. Livingstonia also tends to spend a higher percentage of its income on student provisions, although this has been decreasing over the years. Student provision/allowances for Livingstonia University exceeded the percentage of emoluments in 2003/04 and have remained above 20 percent. Teaching materials and equipment have been receiving a much higher allocation at Livingstonia than at UNIMA. Yet books and periodicals were allocated 3.1 percent in 2003/04 but little or nothing in subsequent years. Catholic University has spent small percentages on teaching materials/equipment and on books and periodicals over the last two years. The other private colleges spend a much lower percentage of their revenue on emoluments, however an increase has been observed in this category of expenditure. For instance, at Adventist University the percentage has increased from 10.1 percent in 2004 to 27.4 percent in 2008.[19] The expenditure at Catholic is in the same range of the public universities and set to get even higher according to the budget estimate for 2008/09, when the numbers will reach 74.5 percent. Shareworld spent only 31.7 percent of its expenditure on emoluments and benefits.[20]

Livingstonia University provides meals for students, which might explain the large percentage of expenditure on student provisions/allowances. At Adventist University, the students pay accommodation fees that are used to finance their meals and these fees are reviewed upwards annually. At Catholic University, parents have taken charge of student meals and the food has been completely outsourced to a private company, with the university only providing a supervisor to ensure quality of service. This is reflected in the reduction in the percentage of the expenditure on student provisions/allowances, which has decreased from 17.2 percent in 2006/07 and is anticipated to drop to 0.9 percent in the current financial year. Shareworld is not a residential institution but does assist students in finding accommodation with private lodge owners and therefore does not incur any serious costs for this category.

Surpluses and Deficits

Table 7.5 shows the surpluses and deficits of the expenditures for the UNIMA colleges. The data show that all colleges, including the University Office, have incurred some deficits in their expenditure. Of particular note is Bunda College, which has deficits for 2005/06–2007/08. Its trend shows a surplus of MK1,815,000 in 2004/05, leading to an increased deficit of MK-222,461,001 in 2007/08. The deficit for 2006/07 was 34.6 percent of the total income for that year. The deficit for 2007/08 was 26.7 percent. This is a substantial over-expenditure and it suggests either serious underfunding or lack of financial controls and oversight. Chancellor College had an over-expenditure of 18.8 percent in 2006/07 but this was reduced to -2.3 percent in 2007/08. The College of Medicine, which incurred an 18.7 percent surplus in 2005/06 incurred a deficit of 5 percent in 2007/08. Both Kamuzu College of Nursing and the Polytechnic incurred surpluses of 11.6 and 7.6 percent in 2007/08, having sustained respective deficits of 7.5 and 10.6 percent in the previous year.

Table 7.5: Surplus and Deficit in Expenditures

Year	Bunda Surp/Defct	Bunda % Expend	Chancellor Surp/Defct	Chancellor % Expend	CoM Surp/Defct	CoM % Expend	KCN Surp/Defct	KCN % Expend	Polytechnic Surp/Defct	Polytechnic % Expend	UO Surp/Defct	UO % Expend
2004/05	1,815000	0.4	19172000	2.9	63506000	16.0	–1123000	–0.5	37669000	6.6	–9,317,000	–9.3
2005/06	–72,678,000	–12.9	–25143000	–2.9	86108000	18.7	13020000	3.6	–82506000	–10.6	1,646,000	1.1
2006/07	–206,594,000	–34.6	–180401000	–18.8	–57399000	–8.6	–29928000	–7.5	–96082000	–10.6	2,477,000	1.4
2007/08	–222,461,001	–26.7	–33619456	–2.3	–57399000	–5.0	62055000	11.6	101858616	7.6	27,029,000	10.9

Source: Audited financial statements: 2004/05–2007/08 from the University Office.

The deficits suggest that colleges go through periods of underfunding from government, which constitutes the greatest percentage of their income. Colleges therefore need to enhance their alternative sources of income, such as tuition fees, and own resources. Government should be more responsive to requests from the universities to increase tuitions fees in line with economic costs. The findings of this report and other reports on Malawi have shown that university students come from the 5th quartile of the population and therefore have some capacity to pay higher tuition fees. There is also need for a review of the Loan Trust to ensure that it targets the really needy in order to create savings that can be used for other important core university functions, or to increase the number of needy beneficiaries.

Unit Costs

Unit costs have been calculated using the total actual expenditure provided by the institutions and the book allowances of MK10,000 that students receive from the Trust Fund. It is assumed that the students do indeed use this money to purchase textbooks, and that non-residential students also spend the same amount on textbooks, although this is not provided to them from the Loan Trust. Other costs met by the students like travel, upkeep, and accommodations (in the case of non-residential students) other than those provided in the institution as part of the fees are not included in the analysis because of the difficulties associated with accurately determining them. Such costs will vary by student and situation. As a result, the unit cost determined in this analysis will necessarily be lower than the actual unit cost.

The average unit costs for higher education in Malawi were discussed in Chapter 3, where it was shown that they are the highest in the region. (See figure 3.4 in Chapter 3.)

Figure 7.6 shows the unit cost as GDP per capita for the public and private institutions.[21] The figure shows that the unit cost for Malawi is very high compared to other countries[22] and that unit costs for public institutions are much higher than those for private institutions. The data show variations in unit costs across institutions with the College of Medicine having the highest unit costs for each year.

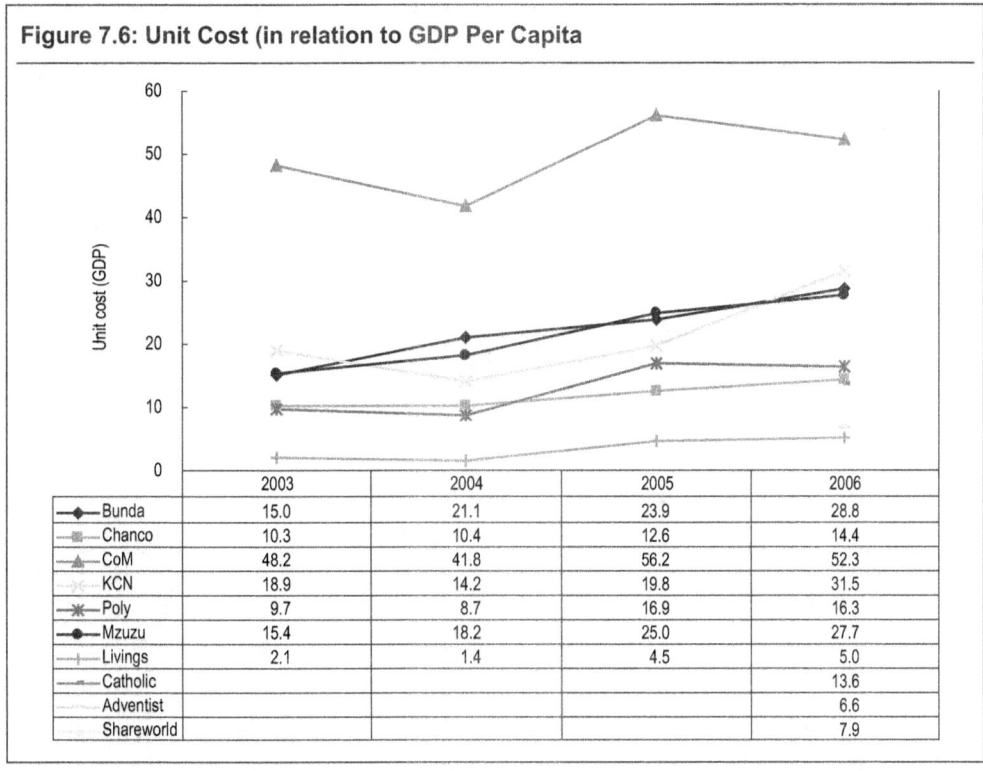

Figure 7.6: Unit Cost (in relation to GDP Per Capita

	2003	2004	2005	2006
Bunda	15.0	21.1	23.9	28.8
Chanco	10.3	10.4	12.6	14.4
CoM	48.2	41.8	56.2	52.3
KCN	18.9	14.2	19.8	31.5
Poly	9.7	8.7	16.9	16.3
Mzuzu	15.4	18.2	25.0	27.7
Livings	2.1	1.4	4.5	5.0
Catholic				13.6
Adventist				6.6
Shareworld				7.9

Source: Data from higher education institutions.

Unit costs for all institutions have varied from year to year but have shown an upward trend. Of particular note is the low unit cost for private universities compared to public universities, and in particular Livingstonia University. One possible reason for the low unit cost is the nature of the programs that are delivered in these institutions. For instance, Livingstonia University provides only education degrees and receives a lot of support from well wishers in cash and in goods and services. The unit cost is low because the college uses its small staff team to play various roles and handle other responsibilities.

Because private universities rely entirely on fees they are more likely to manage their resources better than public institutions, which receive much of their money from government. The increasing trend of unit cost with enrollments would suggest that economies of scale are not being realized in the institutions. MZUNI's unit costs are higher than for UNIMA. This could be explained by the fact that MZUNI is still establishing new programs.

It is also worth noting that even though non-residential students in public universities pay higher fees than residential students, the fees of MK100,000 are much lower than the unit cost for this level of education. Therefore, their education is also indirectly subsidized by the government.

Unit Cost by Expenditure Category

This section analyzes the actual expenditure cost per student for selected expenditure categories. These are emoluments, student provisions/allowances, teaching materials/equipment, and common services. A comparison of tables 7.7a and 7.7b shows that the unit costs for emoluments and benefits in both institutions have increased substantially for the period under review, with MZUNI having higher unit costs than UNIMA except in 2003/04. This shows a problem of staff usage in the institutions. With good management and efficient utilization of staff, unit costs on emoluments should be expected to decrease. The increase in this unit cost is also related to increases in salaries and benefits during this period. An analysis of the enrollment data for MZUNI shows that the institution offers courses to very small classes, especially in the newly introduced programs. Economies of scale that can be achieved from having large classes are obviously not being realized. A policy on the minimum number of students that are required before a class can be offered is needed. For example, Catholic University requires a minimum of 12 students before a program can be offered.

Table 7.6a: Unit Cost Per Expenditure Category: UNIMA (in MK)

	2003/04	2004/05	2005/06	2006/07
Emoluments and benefits	254,822	239,538	329,891	404,965
Student provisions/allowances	26,955	37,788	44,591	47,594
Teaching materials/equipment	2,258	3,212	2,428	6,519
Books and periodicals	209	4,104	1,210	1,374
Common services (represents general administration)	56,639	45,077	85,214	96,899

Source: Data from UNIMA colleges.

Table 7.6b: Unit Cost per Expenditure Category: MZUNI (in MK)

	2003/04	2004/05	2005/06	2006/07
Emoluments and benefits	222,496	306,233	395,920	508,378
Student provisions/allowances	96,990	90,346	93,668	90,948
Teaching materials/equipment	9,460	24,668	77,093	88,148
Books and periodicals	20,226	12,039	12,737	14,307
Common services (represents general administration)	33,774	48,132	14,013	19,636

Source: Data from MZUNI.

Student provisions/allowances for both institutions are relatively high compared with other categories for both institutions and again those for MZUNI are higher than those for UNIMA. It is interesting to note that this unit cost is higher than the total fees paid by students, which combines both tuition and provision of MK25,000 at UNIMA and MK55,000 at MZUNI. These figures emphasize the levels of subsidization in higher education and call into question whether the concept of cost sharing is really being achieved in these institutions.

Unit costs for teaching and learning materials and equipment show an increasing trend for both institutions, with MZUNI providing a higher allocation per student than UNIMA. For instance MZUNI provided 3.6 percent in 2003/04 and increased this to 8.3 percent in 2006/07 for learning and teaching materials. Their allocation to books and periodicals has remained above 1.4 percent for the period. This could be because MZUNI is still introducing new programs and has to allocate more to this item. Unit costs for research and publications are also very low. The level of funding is against a background where most of the equipment is old, obsolete, and unserviceable. This is particularly so in the fields of engineering and science. The capital budget to public institutions has been non-existent, although some commitment to this has been made in the National Education Sector Plan (NESP). The libraries are also old and inadequate for the level of enrollments in the colleges.

Donor funding to institutions for equipment has been limited, leaving institutions totally dependent on government subventions for these items. The World Bank has provided some learning and teaching resources to Chancellor College, the Polytechnic, and MZUNI as part of the rehabilitation and staff development program. SIU has also provided some resources to UNIMA colleges through direct financing and linkages with external universities. Universities should therefore prioritize those categories that are directly related to their core functions.

Recommendations from the MIM report suggested that UNIMA should devise ways to reduce unit costs given the high percentage allocation to higher education in the education budget. This has not apparently been the case since unit costs for both institutions are increasing with MZUNI having a much higher unit cost in 2008 than UNIMA. Steps have been taken in the public institutions to reduce unit costs by outsourcing some non-professional services in the UNIMA colleges like cleaning, security, and ground maintenance. This is a step in the right direction. The impact of this initiative on unit costs has not been felt because the reforms started in 2008 and outsourcing of student provisions will only start in 2009.

Student Financing

The National University Student Loan Trust (NUSLT), which should lend and recover the loans from graduates, was established in 2005. Before then, students received grants and loans, which were never recovered. The Malawi model, like many others in the world, is the mortgage-type loan with a fixed rate of payment over a period of time. Other countries use the income contingency system, which is based on a percentage of the salary of the borrowers when they are in employment until the loan is repaid.

The main objective of the NUSLT is to improve access, especially for the "needy"[23] from poor backgrounds, thereby ensuring equity. This also constitutes a form of cost sharing, which would in turn be a source of revenue for the universities. A silent and not often mentioned objective is the increase in motivation and serious pursuit of learning among students who are paying for their education (albeit in the future).

Unlike loan schemes in other countries, this system does not apply a "means test." It is reported that about one percent of the applicants are turned down based on the information provided by the guarantor. Non-residential, mature entry students; those in non-degree programs in the public universities; and those in accredited private universities are not eligible for loans from the Trust. Like many other student loan systems, the National University Student Loan Trust (NUSLT) is solely financed by the government, although the Trust is empowered to solicit additional resources for the Fund.

The loan provides for the fees that comprise tuition and accommodation and are paid directly to the institution. A book allowance of MK10,000 is part of the loan and is paid directly to the student. The total loan disbursement for the four-year programs in Malawi universities is MK140,000 for a student at UNIMA and MK224,000 for MZUNI. Since the scheme's inception, more than MK400,000,000 has been disbursed, but recovery has not yet started.

The loan agreement requires that loan repayment start three months after completion of studies and is payable over a period of six years in equal monthly installments. The loan is interest free. This payment rate translates to MK1,944 monthly for UNIMA graduates and MK3,111 monthly for MZUNI graduates over the 72 months of the payment period. Results from the tracer study [24] showed that the arithmetic mean of the monthly salaries for university graduates was MK83,681 and a median of MK65,000. The computed payment rates amount to 3 percent and 4.7 percent of the median salaries for UNIMA and MZUNI graduates. This suggests that for those in employment the monthly repayment amount is manageable and could even be increased for quicker recovery, which would result in a better loan repayment ratio. In addition to this, the tracer study on higher education graduates showed that it takes up to 5.5 months for those seeking employment to get a job. This of course varies with the field of study. On average the study found that 75 percent of graduates secure employment after six months. The grace period of 3 months is therefore too short and needs to be adjusted.

Article 6 of the agreement requires the participation of employers of graduates in deducting and remitting the monthly repayments to the Trust. In the event of the borrower defaulting on payment, Article 7 provides for the Trust to *"use any lawful means as it deems necessary to recover the loan."* The agreement also makes the guarantor responsible for the payment of the loan in case of death of the borrower in Article 8(2) of the Agreement. However, there is no legal framework to enforce these provisions. Countries like Zimbabwe and South Africa have such legal frameworks, which have proved effective in improving loan repayments. A legal framework that spells out the responsibilities and obligations of all parties and the applicable sanctions is a critical prerequisite to the success of this scheme.

The agreement further holds the guarantor responsible for lack of payment of the loan in the event of the borrower failing to pay even as a result of death. There is a need to provide for deferment of the loans in periods of unemployment and genuine economic hardship and cancellation in the case of death of the borrower.

The recovery ratio of the total loans disbursed will be affected by repayment ratio[25] and administrative efficiency in the recovery of the loans including the ability to reduce the level of defaulters. A number of studies that have been conducted on student loan schemes (Shen and Ziderman, 2008) have shown that the recovery ratio is affected by interest subsidy and payment periods. The interest rate subsidy creates high hidden costs that result in low repayment, while long payment periods also increase the hidden grant to the borrower. Both these have the effect of lowering the repayment ratio.[26] Countries that have completely interest-free loans in Africa, like Egypt and Ethiopia, have recovery rates of 11.95 and 35.24, respectively. Namibia, however, has a small built-in subsidy ratio of 0.21[27] has a repayment ratio of close to 100 percent. Because the student loans in Malawi are interest free and payable over a period of six years, the government has built-in subsidies that will reduce the loan repayment ratio. Other factors that will affect the loan repayment ratio are payment arrears (as already noted, a backlog of loans exists), non-payment of the loans, and administrative costs. Administrative costs for the Trust were 9 percent in 2007/08 and 25 percent in 2008/09.

The design and the built-in subsidies in the Loan Trust will likely result in low repayment rates. It is unlikely that the Trust will act as a revolving fund because of this and the anticipated increase in enrollment. The Government is going to have to continue to support the scheme financially. It is projected that student loan outlays will increase from MK406 million in 2008 to MK819 million in 2017, to cater for the increase in beneficiaries who are expected to increase from 7,883 in 2008 to 15,017 in 2017, and also increases in tuition fees. Fees are expected to increase to MK60,000 at UNIMA and MK80,000 at MZUNI during the same period. Beneficiaries will probably decrease from the current 100 percent of applicants to 75 percent in 2017. There are plans to institute a means test system to be used for screening applicants.

While the NUSLT objective of cost-sharing is being met, the level of the sharing is still too small compared to the actual unit cost of providing tuition at this level. The level of cost sharing is further diminished by the hidden subsidies in the loans as discussed above.

Internal Efficiency

Staffing

The public universities face difficulties in securing adequately qualified staff at both undergraduate and postgraduate levels. Table 7.7 shows the staffing by qualification and designation of the institutions that provided data for 2008.[28] The data show that public institutions use staff associates and assistant lecturers[29] in order to meet the staffing gap in their requirements.

Table 7.7: Staff Profile in Public and Private Universities

Staff Designations	Professor	Assoc. Professor	Senior Lecturer	Lecturer	Assistant Lecturer	Staff Associate	Instructor	Total	%Staff Associate and Assistant Lecturer	%Professor	Administrative Staff	Support Staff
Bunda	12	10	24	79		20		145	13.8	8.3	9	210
Chancellor College	12	10	24	119	30	6		201	17.9	6.0		
College of Medicine	6	8	25	62	38			139	27.3	4.3	14	278
Kamuzu College of Nursing	0	1	11	25		12		49	24.5	0.0	9	114
Polytechnic	1	2	33	94	39	43	2	214	38.3	0.5	15	
MZUNI	2	6	24	54	8	35		129	33.3	1.6	13	209
Adventist								14				11
Catholic	2	0	9	8	2	6		27	29.6	7.4	10	60
Livingstonia								14				
Shareworld	1	1	7	10		1		20			10	18

Source: Data from higher education institutions.

The percentage of such staff ranges from 13.8 percent at Banda to 38.3 percent at the Polytechnic. Kamuzu College of Nursing and the College of Medicine have staff associates and assistant lecturers as close to 25 percent of their total staff. Given that Nursing and Medicine are very specialized areas, the use of under-qualified staff in their institutions should be a matter of concern. One third of the staff at MZUNI are staff associates. The number of professors range from 0 percent at the College of Nursing to 8.3 percent at Bunda. MZUNI has only two professors out of the total staff of 129.

Table 7.8 shows the qualifications of the staff in the public institutions for which such data was provided. The data emphasizes the lack of staff with senior qualifications in the public institutions. Of particular note is the percentage of staff with PhDs at the Polytechnic (5.6 percent) and MZUNI (11.6 percent). The low percentages of staff with PhD qualifications and professors reduce the capacity of these institutions to support postgraduate programs and conduct research, especially in areas associated with economic growth, such as mathematics and engineering. A key action in the MGDS in relation to increasing enrollments at the university level is recruiting and training more adequate staff to 50 percent of current levels, with 70 percent at Masters level, 30 percent at PhD level. This will assume a total elimination of assistant lecturers and staff associates, who comprise roughly 25.9 percent of the current teaching staff in the public universities. It will also necessitate substantial resources, both in terms of upgrading of the staff and in emoluments for the additional and more highly qualified staff. Given the government's intention to reduce the percentage of the allocation to higher education over time, it is difficult to see how this can be attained unless other sources of financing higher education are mobilized.

Table 7.8: Qualifications of Staff in Public Institutions

Staff Qualifications	PhD	Masters	Degree	Diploma	Total	% PhD	% Masters
Bunda	47	81	16		144	32.6	56.3
Chancellor College	59	125	53	1	238	24.8	52.5
Polytechnic	12	101	89	14	216	5.6	46.8
MZUNI	15	69	45		129	11.6	53.5
Total	133	376	203	15	727	18.3	51.7

Source: Data from higher education institutions.

Student/Staff Ratios

Table 7.9 shows the student/staff ratios for both academic and support staff and compares the current ratios to those in 2001. There have been marginal improvements in some colleges, but the ratios, averaging 11:1 are well below those of other countries in the SSA, which averaged around 20.4 for 2006.[30]

Kamuzu College of Nursing managed to double its student to lecturer ratio while the College of Medicine increased its ratio from one in 2004 to four in 2008. This college presents a rather special case because some of its programs need an almost one-to-one ratio between the student and the lecturer.

Table 7.9: Student/Staff Ratios for 2008

Institution	Students	Lecturers	S/L Ratio 2008	S/L Ratio 2001	Support Staff	S/SS Ratio 2008	S/SS Ratio 2001
Bunda	886	145	6	6	219	4	6
Chancellor	2,446	201	12	8			23
CoM	529	139	4	1	292	2	3
KCN	467	49	10	5	123	4	2
Poly	2,305	214	11	8			18
MZUNI	1448	129	11	8	222	7	3
Adventist	270	14	19		11	25	
Catholic	363	27	13		70	5	
Livingstonia	147	14	11		0		
Shareworld	221	20	11		28	8	
Mean			11	6			9

Source: Data from higher education institutions.
Note: The student/support staff ratio includes administrative staff as well.

The 2004 CSR noted that the student/support staff ratios were very low and contributed to high emoluments. The current data show improvements in the student/staff ratios for Chancellor College, Kamuzu College of Nursing, the Polytechnic, and MZUNI but not for Bunda. Yet the improved ratios are still low, meaning that the institutions still have the capacity to increase enrollments without necessarily increasing their staff. This suggests inefficiencies in how staff are managed and utilized. Better utilization of staff could go a long way towards reducing the current high unit costs.

Improvements at MZUNI have been made through a freeze in the hiring of support staff and an outsourcing of new non-core areas. In 2008, all UNIMA constituent colleges retrenched support staff in of ground maintenance, cleaning, and security. Available data show that the Polytechnic retrenched 117 workers, College of Medicine 39 workers and Kamuzu College of Nursing 52 workers. The effects of this downsizing on ratios and emoluments will probably not be felt until 2009/10. There are plans in some colleges to outsource catering, which is one of the biggest drains on the expenditure budget.

The data from the private colleges is difficult to interpret because some have included their adjunct staff and some have not. The ratio for Catholic University (which included its adjunct staff is more in line with the average for the region). Those that did not provide information on adjunct staff have high ratios that would otherwise be reduced if adjunct staff were included.

Graduate Output

University output increased from 983 in 2003 to 1,447 in 2007 (an increase of 47.2 percent), in line with increased enrollments. The breakdown of the output by field is shown in table 7.10. The data show that by far the largest number of graduates was in education and that ICT had the lowest number. Commerce, which had the second highest enrollment after education, also provided the second highest output of graduates at 9.2 percent, followed by environmental science with 8.5 percent. Social science, applied science, and nursing contributed around 5 percent each. The humanities contributed only 3.6 percent of the graduates and falls in the same category as engineering and agriculture whose contribution is just around 3.0 percent. Law, medicine, and developmental studies contributed less than 2 percent to the graduate output.

Table 7.10: Cumulative University Graduate Output (2003–2007)

Field	Male	Female	Total	% Female	% Total
Education	1,440	501	1,941	25.8	19.5
Commerce	626	292	918	31.8	9.2
Environmental science	625	219	844	25.9	8.5
Nursing	125	428	553	77.4	5.5
Applied science	394	127	521	24.4	5.2
Social science	292	202	494	40.9	5.0
Humanities	226	133	359	37.0	3.6
Engineering	323	33	356	9.3	3.6
Agriculture	197	104	301	34.6	3.0
Built environment	197	32	229	14.0	2.3
Science	168	50	218	22.9	2.2
Law	127	41	168	24.4	1.7
Medicine	70	38	108	35.2	1.1
Developmental studies	71	28	99	28.3	1.0
ICT	66	8	74	10.8	0.7
Total	7,012	2,956	9,968	29.7	100.0

Source: Data from higher education institutions.

Table 7.10 shows that the percentage of female graduates is lower than the enrollment of women for the period. For instance, female enrollment in Engineering was 32.7 percent yet the percentage of women who graduated is only 3.6 percent. This suggests that pass rates for women and/or their retention in the system are lower than those for men. Although the graduate output has generally shown an upward trend, it has fluctuated both by institution and by field. Care should be taken in interpreting these results because the comparison is not of the same cohorts.

Figure 7.7 shows the graduate output and trends for each institution by year. Chancellor College and the Polytechnic account for the largest number of graduates in any given year, with percentage contributions of 31.5 and 35.2 percent, respectively. Livingstonia is the only private university that did not have graduates from 2003–2006. In 2007, it graduated .5 percent of students. Bunda contributed 11.8 percent, MZUNI 11.3 percent, and KCN 8.1 percent. The College of Medicine contributed 1.6 percent. The data for each institution show fluctuations in output from year to year. The Polytechnic's upward trend began to decrease in 2007. The KCN also showed a somewhat consistent upward trend, but for the rest of the institutions there has been some variation in the annual graduate output, which is consistent with the variations noted in enrollment.

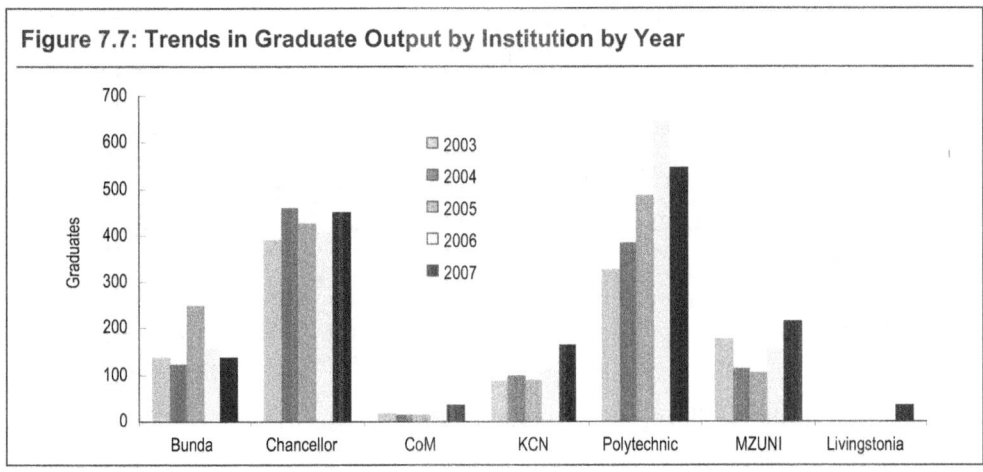

Figure 7.7: Trends in Graduate Output by Institution by Year

Source: Data from higher education institutions.

Figure 7.8 shows graduate output and trends by field of study. As can be expected, the highest percent of graduates is in education and the numbers have increased since 2004. Given the shortage of secondary school teachers in Malawi, this is a welcome trend. However, it is not known how many of the education graduates actually end up teaching, as the Tracer Study did not track these graduates. This is an area for further review and analysis. The number of commerce graduates has fluctuated annually and reached its highest level in 2005 before starting a downward trend. Graduate output in the environmental sciences reached a maximum in 2005 and declined in the following two years. Graduate output in science was at its lowest in 2005 and is now showing an upward trend, but the output is still quite small for such an important field. The social science graduates reached a peak in 2005 and the numbers have since started falling.

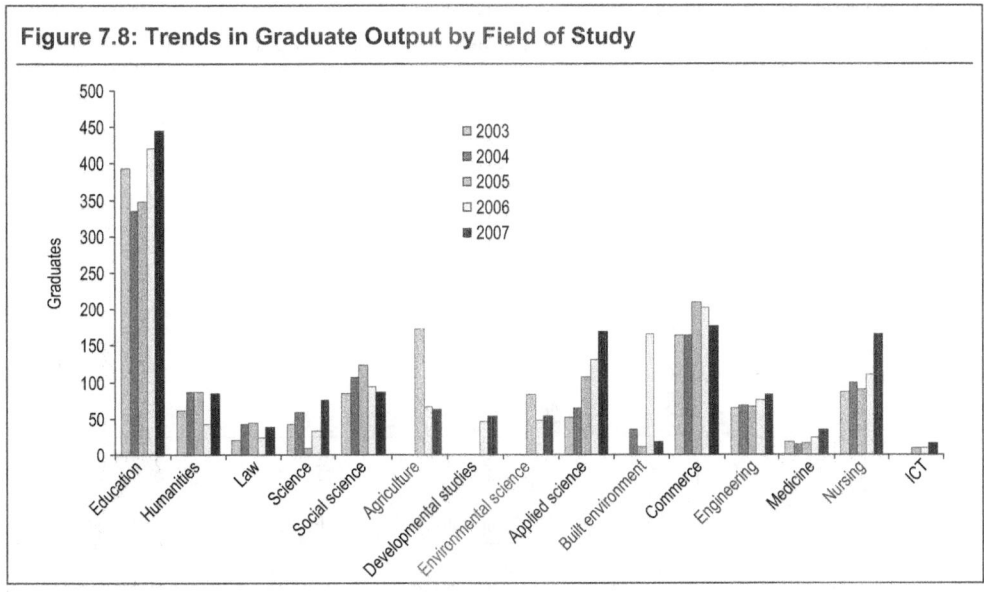

Figure 7.8: Trends in Graduate Output by Field of Study

Source: Data from higher education institutions.

Graduate output in agriculture fell significantly from a high of 173 in 2005 to 62 in 2007. As enrollments have been falling, the output is not expected to increase much in this important field. Applied science and nursing are showing an upward trend, which is good because of the need for such graduates in Malawi. Although graduate output in engineering is increasing, the total output and the rate of increase have remained small over the period. ICT is currently offered in MZUNI and Shareworld, yet Shareworld has not graduated any students. As a result, the output is still very small and it decreased in 2007.

As can be expected from enrollments, there are few graduates are the postgraduate level. The total cumulative output for the postgraduates from 2000–2008 was 332 compared to the cumulative total of 9,968 at the undergraduate level. The breakdown was:

- Chancellor College—188
- the Polytechnic—40
- Bunda—49,
- the College of Medicine—33
- MZUNI—11

The cumulative Masters output for the six-year period is only 321 graduates. As noted in figure 7.13, the output has fluctuated over the years for both genders. The fields with the highest output include:

- Economics—47
- Science—46
- Arts—21
- Environmental science—12
- Theology and religious education—8
- Policy planning and leadership—8

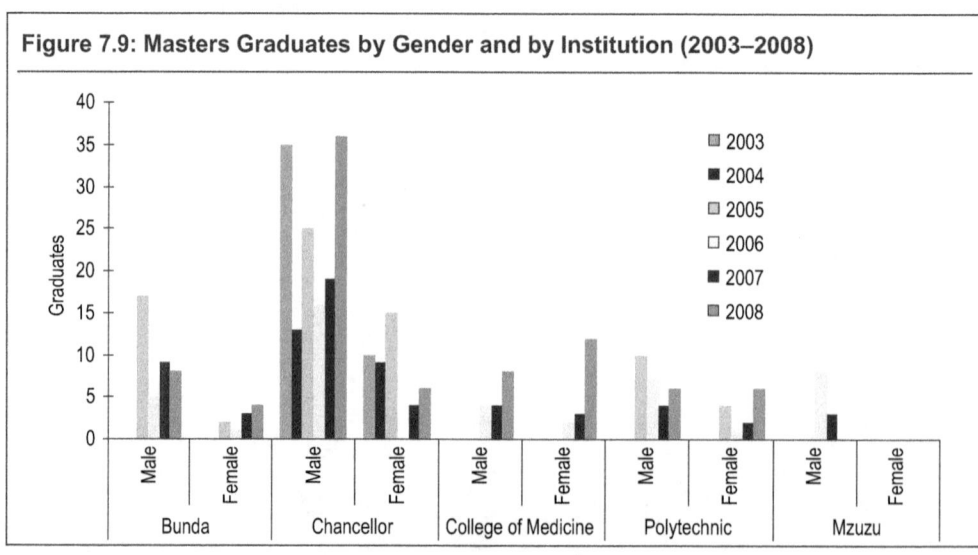

Figure 7.9: Masters Graduates by Gender and by Institution (2003–2008)

Source: Data from higher education institutions and the UNIMA University Office.

The constraints that inhibit the Polytechnic from offering postgraduate programs in engineering, applied science, and built environment need to be addressed as these studies would help Malawi develop in science and technology and improve its key economy indicators.

The cumulative output at the doctoral level for the period under review was 10 males and one female. Theology had six graduates. Education, biology, chemistry, rural development and extension, and dramatic literature had one graduate each. The bias is towards the arts rather than the sciences. The participation of women at this level is the lowest compared to the other levels.

According to the findings of the Tracer Study, the fields offered by the institutions are relevant to the needs of the labor market and the majority of the graduates are able to secure employment within six months of graduation (except for agriculture graduates who take a bit longer). Certainly, there does not seem to be a backlog of graduates who are unemployed. The external efficiency of higher education is discussed in Chapter 8.

Equity in Higher Education

Chapters 4 and 5 have already provided information on equity issues in accessing and financing higher education. This section will provide a more detailed analysis of some aspects of equity in higher education.

Gender Enrollment

It has already been noted that female enrollments in higher education are much lower than those for males. This is so for both public and private universities. However, the percentage women enrolled in private universities surpasses that of the public institutions, as shown in Figure 7A.4 in Appendix 7.1.

There are a number of reasons why female enrollments are low in higher education. The first is that dropout rates for females increase throughout the education cycle, as discussed in Chapter 2. This reduces the number of women who sit for the MSCE examination. The second is that the percentage pass for female-to-female[31] is lower than that for male-to-male. As a result, there is a double screening in the numbers of women who eventually qualify for university entry.

A positive trend, however, is that the female–to-female percentage of those enrolled was below the male–to-male percentage in 2004 and 2005 but is now higher. The establishment of private universities, which have higher female enrollment percentages, has probably contributed to the increase in female-to-female enrollment percentages.

Bed space also limits the enrollment of more females as the institutions have more male bed space than for females (except at KCN where the reverse is true). In 2008, the total bed space for all the UNIMA colleges was 2,761 for males and 1,383 for females. The introduction of non-residential programs has increased enrollments for both genders but the enrollment statistics show that the percentage of non-residential female students is consistently lower than that of males, and also lower than that of residential female students. On average, non-residential females comprise 23.2 percent of the total non-residential enrollment at Bunda, 24.3 at Chancellor College, and 26.2 at the Polytechnic. This may be attributed to financing problems, having to live alone in rented accommodations, and daily commuting. Increasing bed space for women could assist in increasing the percentage of women in residence who automatically receive support from the Trust. MZUNI has taken the positive step of converting a male hostel into a female hostel.

Financing should not really be a constraint for women who are enrolled in residential programs given the existence of the Loan Trust, but it is certainly a constraint for those who enroll in the non-residential programs because they are not eligible for loans. This situation needs further examination in order to improve female participation in higher education.

Although dropouts are generally low in higher education, some programs like nursing experience relatively high dropout rates, particularly during the first year, and this would affect the percentage of women overall. Data on dropouts from the universities have been very limited and it has not been possible to do an in-depth analysis of this phenomenon.

Field of Study

This section examines the participation of women in the fields of study in the university system. Table 7.11 shows enrollment statistics for 2008 in the various fields.

Table 7.11: Enrollment of Women by Fields of Study (2008)

Field	Male	Female	Total	% Female
Nursing	102	365	467	78.2
Health Science	66	85	151	56.3
Social Science	523	334	857	39.0
Humanities	480	294	774	38.0
Agriculture	235	136	371	36.7
Education	1,354	743	2,097	35.4
Environmental Science	312	160	472	33.9
Developmental Studies	230	112	342	32.7
Medicine	358	171	529	32.3
Commerce	607	270	877	30.8
Law	74	29	103	28.2
ICT	184	65	249	26.1
Science	295	95	390	24.4
Tourism	44	14	58	24.1
Built Environment	146	40	186	21.5
Applied Science	587	143	730	19.6
Engineering	346	48	394	12.2
Other	30	2	32	6.3
Total	5,976	3,106	9,082	34.2

Source: Data from higher education institutions.

The data basically reinforce the fact that the percentage of females in higher education is lower than that of males but it also shows where their enrollment is concentrated. Nursing, with 78.2 percent, has the highest number of females enrolled, followed by health sciences with 56.3 percent. The next eight fields are around 30 percent and this includes education, which although recording the highest number of female students has a percentage of only 35.3 women to men. Female percentages for most of the fields fall below 40, except the health-related fields, social science, and the humanities—as shown in figure 7A.10 in Appendix 7. Of note are the fields where female percentages are below 30. These include ICT, tourism, built environment, engineering, and applied sciences.[32]

Strategies are needed to enhance the participation of women in higher education and in male-dominated fields. One possible avenue is already practiced at the College of Medicine, which provides a pre-med program to prepare students for degree-level work. Similarly, the universities could offer a preliminary year for preparing female students to enter the male-dominated fields.

As expected, the enrollment of women at the postgraduate level is even lower than at the undergraduate level. The data in table 7A.13 in Appendix 7.5 show that the percentage of women enrolled in postgraduate studies has grown from 19 in 2003 to 29 in 2008. Of the eight students who are enrolled at the doctoral level, only two are female.

Socioeconomic Status

A comparison of enrollments in the whole education system as a function of socio-economic status was discussed in Chapter 5 and in this chapter under student financing. Table 5.1 in Chapter 5 showed that children from the 5th quintile comprised 91.3 percent of the enrollment in higher education, while children from the 1st quintile comprised only 0.7 percent. This means that government is subsidizing the well-off through subventions to the universities and the Loan Trust at the expense of those who really need financial help. Just who benefits from the Loan Trust is something the government needs to address. Restricting loan access to only residential students is glaringly inequitable in that it leaves out non-residential Malawians in public institutions and those enrolled in accredited private institutions. Issues of public spending on education and its inequities are discussed in greater detail in Chapter 4.

Data on handicapped students were not available, but visits to both public and private higher education institutions revealed that higher education institutions did not have the facilities to cater for people with physical disabilities. It is noted that some schools enroll students with physical disabilities. This is an area that needs further investigation to provide a clearer picture of the plight of physically challenged students in higher education. In their strategic plans, UNIMA indicated that they would like to increase access for this group but this will depend to a large extent on resources for making facilities handicapped-accessible.

Governance and Management

The governance and management of higher education institutions refers to the way in which these institutions are formally organized and operated. Kegan and Eckel (2004: 371-398) note that governance is a 'multi-level concept' which includes several different bodies and processes, both internal and external. The notion of 'good governance' is as applicable to universities as it is elsewhere and has a direct correlation to the quality of education provided by these institutions. Universities in Malawi, both public and private, have a number of governance and management issues that need to be addressed to improve performance (Malawi Institute of Management, 2004).

Academic freedom is a feature of university operations in Malawi, meaning that scholars are permitted to pursue teaching, learning, and research without restraints imposed by the institutions that govern them. This is a fundamental tenet of good governance in higher education systems, and Malawi has satisfied this condition. There is, however, scope for discussions on the extent to which the government and universities can collaborate on shaping the higher education curriculum to be responsive to the needs of the Malawian economy.

Shared governance is characterized by the delegation of responsibilities to those who are best equipped to handle them. At a systemic level, it refers to the participation of higher education institutions and their advocates in the formulation of higher education policy. In Malawi, universities are in the unique position of being subvented organizations, which although falling within the ambit of the Ministry of Education, maintain some level of autonomy on internal management and policy issues. In this way, shared governance at the system level is achieved, although a clearer articulation of the relationships between government and universities is needed.

At the institutional level, shared governance refers to the participation of the faculty (and in some cases, students) in the management of the university, including educational policy formulation, academic appointments, and administrative matters. The decentralization of several functions important to the colleges has been the first step towards achieving shared governance at the institutional level. For example, the University Office consolidates the budgets for universities and lobbies for more resources but the actual financial administration has now been completely devolved to the colleges, placing them squarely in charge of the implementation of their subventions. Further, recruitment of staff and staff development have also been decentralized to the colleges.

However, the quest for shared governance at the higher education level is stymied by a lack of resources at the institutional level to effectively carry out the devolved functions. Universities also lack clear guidelines on the internal management of these functions. This has resulted in situations where staff have failed to make crucial decisions and to adhere strictly to the enrollment regulations. A clear assignment of rights and responsibilities for faculty, administrators, students, and external supervisors is needed to achieve a system of shared governance that works. Further, it is critical that a monitoring and evaluation framework for the decentralization process be put in place.

One positive move on the part of the public universities towards management reform has been the outsourcing of non-educational functions so that attention can be concentrated on the core functions of these institutions. (See section IV.2.) This should go some way in reducing the student provisions/allowances bill, which was the second highest expenditure recorded at MZUNI and the third highest at UNIMA colleges. It is perhaps too early to assess the impact of this initiative on efficiency and cost savings but anecdotal evidence suggests that there are improvements in the efficiency of service delivery, reduced industrial action, and less administrative work for the administrators. However, negatives have been noted, such as outsourced service providers being erratic in their performance. Some form of a quality assurance committee at the level of the university is therefore needed to sustain this intervention.

Financial stability presents another major issue of governance that needs to be addressed in higher education. Uncertainty over future financing and fluctuations in funding hinder the effective governance and management of higher education institutions, since they render medium-term planning difficult. It has been seen that the subventions to universities in Malawi from government do not display a consistent pattern, and the uncertainty surrounding fee-setting has placed universities in the precarious position of being unable to determine their future levels of funding, and therefore the nature and scope of their operations.

It should also be noted that the financing providers can affect the autonomy of higher education institutions. In Malawi's case, there is the particular danger of public universities being supported largely by the government, and some private universities being primarily funded by religious organizations. In such a situation, it becomes even more critical to clarify the expectations of all stake-holders in the higher education sector.

In Malawi, the higher education sector is in its infancy and is rapidly expanding. It has been difficult to regulate the emergence of new universities in relation to the standardization of salaries, the coordination of quality and quality assurance, student admissions, and financing mechanisms. To resolve these problems, the pending Higher Education Act will create the National Council for Higher Education (NCHE), which will be empowered to oversee higher education institutions and look at quality and quality assurance mechanisms. An important function of the NCHE will be to protect the Malawian student as a customer by instituting a semi-autonomous accreditation and quality assurance agency under its supervision.

Finally, the desired levels of autonomy to be attained by higher education institutions do not preclude the need for accountability on the part of universities. There is currently a council for oversight in existence, but again there is a need to clearly define the roles of this body. Guidelines need to be developed, requiring universities to periodically report on their activities and have their performance assessed in a transparent manner by a suitably composed body. The forthcoming NCHE may wish to undertake the fulfillment of this important principle of good governance.

Notes

[1] Accreditation of private universities is done by the Department of Human Resource Management and Development, which is part of the Office of the President and Cabinet.
[2] Under the ISCED program, 5A refers to first degree, second degree, and further degree and Research. This is primarily university education.
[3] Details of annual enrollments by type of institution and by gender are shown in Appendix 7.3.
[4] For example, Livingstonia University only offers a Bachelor of Education degree and the first year's enrollment has remained below 160 since the program's inception in 2003. Catholic

University only offers two degree programs in social sciences and education. The Adventist University of Malawi offers education and business studies, while Shareworld offers seven programs but has small enrollments. It has attempted to increase its enrollments by opening centers in Lilongwe and Mzuzu to make its programs more accessible.

[5] sometimes referred to as "parallel" students

[6] Education enrollment statistics have been combined with statistics on enrollment in education and media studies eoffered at the Polytechnic. The Polytechnic had the largest enrollment in the previous CSR (2001 data).

[7] See also figure 7A.7 in Appendix 7.3 for enrollments by field of study.

[8] See Page 97 of the MGDS document.

[9] Protocol which was signed in Blantyre by SADC Heads of states on September 8, 1997 provides for SADC member states to use training facilities that are available in member states for training personnel and also for establishing Centres of Excellence where specialized training can take place for member states.

[10] See figure 7A.8 in Appendix 7.3.

[11] The data for these two figures were extracted from the available audited financial statements for the two institutions.

[12] See Appendix 7.4 for detailed tables of the percentages.

[13] The fee includes: tuition, registration, caution, medical, and student union charges.

[14] The subvention only comprises around half of the total public expenditure to higher education because salaries are not counted, as well as some other government expenditures.

[15] Students are expected to take at least 17 credit hours per semester.

[16] The Malawi Institute of Management was commissioned to carry out an in-depth study of UNIMA in 2002 and produced a report with recommendations on how to improve public university education in the country. Implementation of some of the recommendations is underway.

[17] Table was compiled using data from the individual colleges.

[18] Expenditures for Catholic University start from 2006/07 and those for 2008/09 are budget figures and not actual expenditures.

[19] Adventist University has a policy of not allowing emoluments to exceed 50 percent of total expenditure.

[20] The percentages for Adventist and Shareworld are based on revenue calculated from tuition fees and student enrollment, while those for Livinsgstonia, Catholic, and the public universities are based on actual total expenditure.

[21] See Appendix 7.4 for a table of unit cost calculations. Unit costs for Livingstonia were calculated using expenditure data for the period. Unit costs for the other institutions were based on the tuition fees for 2008, seeing as the institutions rely almost entirely on the tuition fees paid by the students.

[22] See Figure 3.4 for a comparison.

[23] This is the term used in the policy document for the NUSTF.

[24] As part of the CSR process a tracer study for both TEVET and hgher education was commissioned to provide data on the fate of the graduates of the system.

[25] Recovery ratio measures the ratio of total repayments to the total loan disbursements.

[26] The loan repayment ratio is a measure of how much of a loan an average borrower is required to pay (See Shen and Zinderman, Student Loans Repayment and Recovery).

[27] Average for eight selected SAA countries is 58.26 percent (Egypt, Ethiopia, Ghana, Kenya, Mauritius, Namibia, Nigeria, and South Africa). The repayment period for Namibia is equal to the period of time of study, which in this case is three years.

[28] A few institutions provided staffing data for the whole period but most did not so it has not been possible to do an analysis of how student/staff ratios have changed over this time.
[29] Assistant lecturers are those with an Honors degree, while staff associates have a first degree.
[30] See figure 7A.9 in Appendix 7 for the comparison.
[31] This refers to the percentage of females passing against the number of females who entered the examination.
[32] These are Certificate and Diploma Security Studies offered at MZUNI.

CHAPTER 8

External Efficiency

Summary of the Chapter

Education has a direct influence on people's social behavior. People with more education have different ways of responding to certain situations (for example, pregnancy, malarial treatment for children, and HIV/AIDS) than those with less education, independent of household income.

The primary level accounts for almost half (48 percent) of the total impact of education on social behavior. Therefore, changes need to be implemented so that all Malawian children achieve at least the primary cycle.

Education has a direct connection to the labor market. With each additional level of income that a Malawian gains, he or she also gains an increasing average annual income. And the income gain for higher education is particularly huge. It shows there is a severe shortage of academically trained Malawians.

Tracer studies indicate a generally high satisfaction with higher education outcomes among graduates and employers. The average time span between graduation and job entrance is relatively low. Unemployment rates for academically trained people are among the lowest in Africa.

TEVET completers also have a high acceptance in the labor market, with the best employment rate of all African countries for which comparative data were available. The average TEVET graduate's monthly income of MK16,700, however, remains relatively low compared to higher education graduates. The income prospects of TEVET graduates who venture into self-employment appears to be higher than those of the wage-employed. No significant correlation exists between the duration of training and income, which raises a concern about the appropriateness of the long duration of the regular public regular TEVET program.

The rates of return (ROR) to education in Malawi are very high, in particular at higher education levels, which reflect Malawi's low overall access to education. Private ROR of 54 percent for TEVET and 171 percent for higher education also indicate severe shortages of skilled and highly educated human resources, demonstrating the country's urgent need to ensure greater access rates to stimulate growth.

* * *

Chapter 8 looks at external efficiency, meaning the impact of education and training on economic and social development and on peoples' lives. It first analyzes the effect education has on social behavior and human development in Malawi, and then examines available information on the relevance that education and training have to the labor market.

Education and Human Development in Malawi

This first section focuses on the social impact of general and tertiary education. It is important to emphasize that the effect education has on behavior is inextricably linked to the fact that a better income causes different social behaviors. Beyond that, higher levels of education create their own behavioral changes, independent of the impact on income. See figure 8.1.

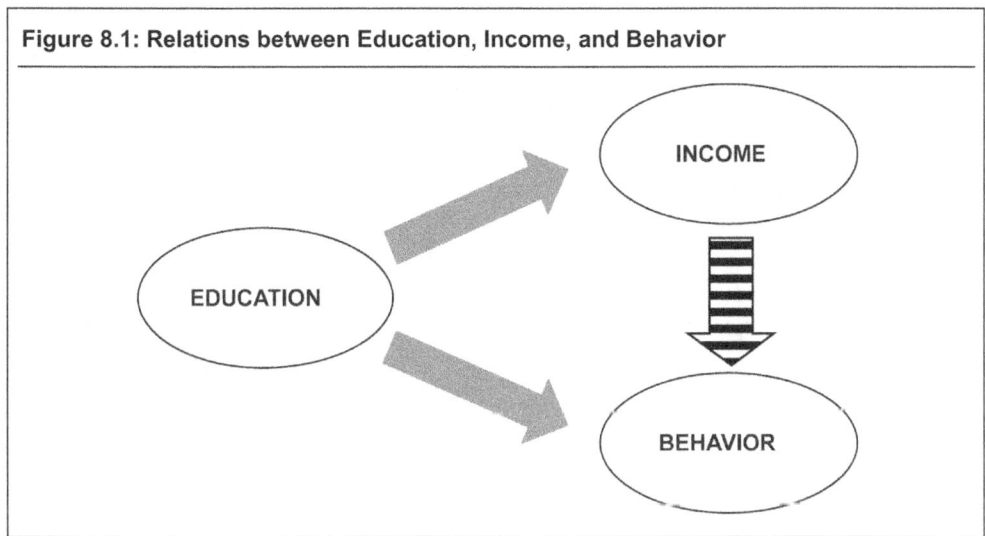

Figure 8.1: Relations between Education, Income, and Behavior

Looking at the relationship education has to income and behavior allows us to see the connection between schooling and a number of social outcomes, particularly for women—such as behavior during pregnancy, birth history, or knowledge about HIV/AIDS. This last is one of the major national challenges in Malawi. The data allow us to identify the behavioral changes that can be attributed to each grade and of each level of education. A cost/benefit analysis can be conducted for the levels of education, since it is known that one year of spending for school is not the same at the primary, secondary, or higher education levels.

The Impact of Education on Social Behavior

Figures used to analyze the impact of education on social behavior are primarily from the Multi Indicator Cluster Survey (MICS) that was conducted in Malawi in 2006. The National Statistical Office (NSO) carried out the survey in collaboration with the United Nations Children's Fund (UNICEF). The NSO provides statistically valid estimates at a district level on a number of indicators related to the wellbeing of children and women. Econometric models were used to conduct the analysis. These models included control variables such age, sex, geographical location, a wealth index, and a health supply index to assess the effects of education ceteris paribus (that is, the simulated net impact). Table 8.1 summarizes these results.

Table 8.1: Simulated Net Impact of Education on Social Behaviors in Malawi

				Highest Grade Completed in School							
			Non-	Primary				Secondary		Higher Ed.	
		Average	Educated	2	4	6	8	10	12	14	16
Use of tetanus toxoid during pregnancy (%)		86.2	81.6	82.3	83.2	84.4	85.7	87	88.2	89.3	90
Use of Vitamin A during pregnancy (%)		88.2	84.8	84.6	84.9	85.7	86.8	88.1	89.7	91.2	92.8
Use of antimalaria treatments for kids (%)		18.9	10.7	11.8	13.1	14.6	16.2	18	20	22.2	24.7
Woman's age at her first birth	20–29 years old	19.4	17.8	18.1	18.4	18.7	19.0	19.3	19.8	20.3	21.0
	40–49 years old	20.0	19.9	19.9	19.9	19.9	20.0	20.0	20.0	20.1	20.2
	15–49 years old	19.5	18.7	18.7	18.7	18.8	19.1	19.4	19.8	20.3	20.9
Probability of antenatal consultation (%)		95.8	91.9	92.8	93.7	94.6	95.6	96.5	97.5	98.4	99.4
Prob. of using iron tablets during pregnancy (%)		86.1	76.9	80.0	82.6	84.8	86.6	88.1	89.2	90.0	90.5
Prob. of assistance at delivery (%)		66.4	42.7	46.6	52.6	59.9	67.3	74.1	79.2	81.6	80.5
Time span between births (years)		3.4	3.0	2.9	2.8	2.8	3.0	3.2	3.4	3.8	4.3
Total number of live birth in a lifetime	Women 15–49 y.o.	2.3	4.4	3.5	2.9	2.4	2.1	1.8	1.7	1.6	1.5
	Women 49 y.o.	6.9	8	8	7.9	7.7	7.4	7	6.5	5.9	5.3
HIV/AIDS knowledge [Score on a scale from 0 to 11]		8.1	7	7.4	7.7	8	8.3	8.5	8.7	8.9	9.1
Probability of stillbirths (%)		4.5	9.1	7.4	6.0	4.9	4.1	3.5	3.0	2.8	2.7
Probability of female literacy (%)		77.4	2.8	19.5	58.0	84.8	96.9	100.00	100.00	100.00	100.00

Source: Calculations from MICS 2006 data.

Note: Except for the column "average," figures in the table are not simple descriptive statistics of the different phenomenon according to the highest education level completed. They result from econometric models and identify the net impact of education with everything else (gender, age, area living, income level, health facilities) constant. For instance, the simulated net probability of using antimalaria treatments for children, for an individual with higher education (16 years completed) is 24.7 percent. That means 24.7 percent is the rate for a simulated individual (who does not really exist) who would have same age, area of living, gender, income level, and health facilities as an average Malawian but who would have attended higher education.

Ten different social behaviors and competencies were analyzed. In all cases the strong influence of education could be established. The individual results are attached in Appendix 8.1.

Antenatal consultation is common in Malawi, but education has clearly improved the likelihood of having it. While the possibility of consulting a health specialist during the antenatal period is 92 percent for a non-educated woman, this number rises to 96 percent for a PSLE-graduated (end of primary cycle) woman and to 99 percent for a woman who is a higher education graduate.

Similar patterns were found in the probability of women using iron supplements during pregnancy. Evidence from MICS data show that at a national level, 86.1 percent of women take iron supplements during pregnancy, but that only 76.9 percent of non-educated women do so. For a PSLCE-holder, this probability increases to 86.6 percent, and to above 90 percent for a university graduate.

Education level also increases with the number of women who seek and receive help during childbirth. On average, 81 percent of women with a university degree have assistance during childbirth. This number decreases to 66 percent of all 15–49-year-old Malawian women and 43 percent for the non-educated. Education can also help reduce the number of stillbirths. The data indicate that the numbers range from 9 percent for a non-educated woman to 3 percent for a woman who has completed secondary Form 4 (grade 12).

The MICS asked mothers with children under the age of five who had had a fever in the two weeks prior to the survey whether the child had been taken to a health facility during the illness, and if so, what the medicine was given. An analysis of the data indicate that at the national level, the average probability of using antimalarial treatment for children under five is very low, which is a concern in itself. However, one important finding was that mothers with a low level of education are less likely to provide appropriate antimalarial treatment to their children. While a child of a non-educated mother has a 10.7 percent chance of receiving antimalarial treatment, the chance rises to 16 percent for the child of a mother who has completed Standard 8, and to 20 percent for a child with a mother who has completed Form 4.

Age at first birth is slightly higher in Malawi for older women than for younger ones. But in contrast to the younger generation, the behavior of older women was less likely to be influenced by the duration of schooling. For the older generation [40–49] no difference has been noted according to the level of education. In the younger generation, a non-educated woman is likely to have a first child at an average of 17.8 years, whereas this age is 19 years for a woman with a PSLCE and 19.8 at the end of the upper secondary cycle.

Compared to other countries, age at first birth is relatively low in Malawi. With an increasing level of education, the interval between two consecutive births is expected to be longer. In Malawi, this assertion is especially true for the secondary and higher levels of education, which indicates that primary cycle schooling alone does not have a strong positive effect on birth spacing. Women need more years of schooling to start significantly increasing the time span (currently an average of 3.4 years) between births.

Education also helps to reduce the total number of births women may have. The average number of live births of a 49–year-old woman is rather high in Malawi (6.9 births). A non-educated woman gives birth approximately eight times in her life, and this figure does not vary substantially for women who have had primary education. Everything else constant, eight years of schooling helps reduce this figure by about 0.6 points only, while 12 years of education correspond to a reduction of 1.5 points. After 16 years of education (secondary school plus four years of higher education), the average number of births drops by 2.8, which means an average number of 5.3 children for each highly educated woman. Despite the impact of education, these figures for Malawi remain high compared to other countries with similar characteristics.

The fight against HIV/AIDS is a major national challenge in Malawi given its high prevalence in the country. The MICS was an opportunity to ask both men and women about their knowledge of the disease. The results indicate that people with a lower level of education score lower in their knowledge about HIV/AIDS than do the more educated. There is no doubt that schooling can help strengthen people's understanding of the disease.

Literacy is probably the most important outcome expected from education, especially in the primary cycle. The MICS required respondents to read a short sentence in English, Chichewa, or Tumbuka. Although literacy comprises more than just reading skills, this indicator was used here to analyze the net impact of education on literacy.

Logistic regression was used to estimate the probability of being literate at given grade completed, all other things (age, wealth index, health supply index, geographical location) being equal. Results indicate the strong positive effect that education has on literacy: 97 and 98 percent respectively for women and men who have completed Standard 8, while less than 3 percent for both if non-educated.

Comparison of Outcomes by Level and Cost-Benefit Analysis

The social outcomes of education can be analyzed from an economic viewpoint that compares the effect each level of schooling has on the total social outcomes. Such a distinction is pertinent for at least two reasons:

1. For policy makers it would be useful to know which level of schooling is the most effective to quickly support poverty reduction in the country, or human development in general. Choices, especially regarding public investments, may be made accordingly.
2. The duration of schooling is not the same for every level.

In Malawi's case, the primary cycle ranges from standards 1–8, while secondary education takes only half of this duration (two years for each lower secondary and upper secondary level).

The tertiary cycle spans at least four years. Different levels of education involve different costs. Since it is possible to identify how far each level affects human development, it is useful to examine the cost of each year of schooling and its benefits (see table 8.2).

On average, the primary cycle represents almost half (48 percent) of the total social impact of the behaviors in table 8.2, while secondary as well as higher education (four years duration) each account for 26 percent. One year of schooling equals 6 percent for the primary cycle, 6.5 percent for the secondary cycle, and 6.4 percent for higher education. Therefore, we can say that in Malawi each year of schooling means an approximately 6 percent increased impact on social behavior.

The primary cycle has a high impact on competencies and social indicators like literacy, stillbirth, HIV/AIDS knowledge, and assistance at delivery. For these indicators, up to two-thirds of the total impact has been made by the completion of Standard 8. Conversely, the primary cycle has a low effect on behaviors such as using vitamin A for children under five, total live births, a woman's age at first birth, or birth interval. For these indicators, its contribution is less than 25 percent.

Finally, we confront each cycle's contribution with its costs as shown in table 8.2. Costs here represent units of gross domestic product (GDP) per capita (estimated to be MK36,358 in 2008). They were obtained by multiplying the unit cost of each cycle by its duration. Results in the last row of the table indicate a very high efficiency in the primary cycle compared to secondary, and especially tertiary, education. All costs being equal, the efficiency of the primary cycle in enhancing human development is 9 times higher than that of the secondary cycle and 243 times higher than that of tertiary education.

Table 8.2: Impact of a Mother's Education on Various Adult Behaviors (Share for the Different Cycles) (in %)

		Primary (vs. Non-educated)	Second. 1 (vs. primary cycle)	Second. 2 (vs. second. 1)	Higher Ed (vs. second. 2)	Total
High contribution of primary cycle	Enhancing literacy	96.9	3.1	0.0	0.0	100
	Reducing stillbirth	78.1	9.8	.6.7	5.4	100
	Encouraging use of iron tablets	71.4	10.6	8.2	9.8	100
	Knowledge about HIV/AIDS (on 0–11 scale)	67.5	11.4	9.2	11.9	100
	Assistance at delivery	65.3	17.9	13.5	3.4	100
Medium contribution of primary cycle	Antenatal care	49.0	12.6	12.7	25.7	100
	Use of tetanus toxins	48.5	15.4	14.5	21.6	100
	Antimalarial treatments	39.7	12.8	14.2	33.3	100
Moderated contribution of primary cycle	Use of vitamin A for children under five	24.3	17.1	19.1	39.5	100
	Total live births [49 y.o.]	21.6	14.3	17.8	46.3	100
	Age at first birth	17.0	14.6	18.7	49.8	100
	Birth interval	0.0	16.2	23.2	60.6	100
Average social impact		48.3	13.0	13.1	25.6	100
Unit cost as percentage of GDP per capita)		8.3	83.3		2,146.7	—
Total spending (unit of GDP per capita)		0.66	3.33		85.87	—
Efficiency (= impact/spending)		0.727	0.078		0.003	—

Source: Calculation from MICS 2006 data and data from Chapter 3.

Relevance of Education for the Labor Market

It is important to look at the relevance of education and training for the labor market (that is, the value the employment sector ascribes to educational background and qualifications). We must also ascertain whether the skills and competences of graduates, particularly of TEVET and higher education, match the requirements of employers and the development needs of the economy. Major primary data sources for this analysis were the 2004 Integrated Household Survey (IHS) as well as two tracer studies conducted in 2008, which when combined add substantial value to the understanding of the external efficiency of TEVET and HE, despite their different emphases and sample frames. These studies are:

- The Malawi Labor Market Survey (LMS) commissioned by TEVETA (JIMAT, 2008). The study comprises five individual surveys: a tracer survey of TEVET graduates, a skills demand survey of formal companies, an informal sector survey, an informal sector employees survey, and a tracer survey of TEVETA's informal sector training program. This study's subject is TEVET only with the tracer study focusing on formal TEVET apprentices.
- A tracer study of TEVET and higher education completers in Malawi commissioned by the GTZ and the World Bank in the context of the CSR (Pfeiffer and Chiunda, Appendix 9). Apart from higher education graduates and TEVET completers from all TEVET provider systems, the study also targeted a smaller sample of higher education dropouts.

Employment and Wages by Level of Education

With an increasing level of education, Malawians are more likely to work in better paying types of employment. Table 8.3 summarizes the distribution of the Malawian workforce by level of schooling and type of employment based on the 2004 IHS. It shows that people with no education or only primary education are overly represented in the non-formal agriculture sector or in ganyu work. Post-completion of upper primary school, employment in traditional agriculture becomes less prevalent, while the importance of the informal non-agriculture sector grows. With higher educational attainment, the likelihood of working in the public or formal private sector increases.

Unemployment declines with lower primary school attendance, compared to having no education. However, unemployment rises with increasing general education. The risk of being unemployed is particularly high for Malawians who attended upper secondary education without further education. Unemployment drops to 4.2 and 2.4 percent, respectively, for those who have gone through technical colleges and higher education. The increasing unemployment rates through secondary education are probably related to social status. The higher the educational status, the more likely it is that people belong to relatively higher income groups, which makes unemployment sustainable.

Table 8.3: Distribution of Workforce by Level of Education and Type of Employment in Percentages for 15-years-old and Over (2004)

	Non-formal agriculture (incl. ganyu)	Non-formal other than Agriculture	Formal Public Sector	Formal Private Sector	Student or Non-active	Un-employed	Total	Unemployment rate*
No school	75.0	4.1	2.1	6.8	11.1	1.0	100.0	1.1
Lower primary	66.5	4.8	2.1	8.2	17.2	1.1	100.0	1.3
Upper primary	50.5	6.2	2.3	9.7	29.8	1.4	100.0	2.1
Lower secondary	30.1	6.6	4.5	10.4	46.4	2.0	100.0	3.7
Upper secondary	20.5	7.1	12.6	18.6	34.5	6.6	100.0	10.1
Technical college	3.5	1.2	44.0	20.9	27.3	3.0	100.0	4.2
Higher	4.1	4.6	28.7	39.9	20.7	1.9	100.0	2.4
Total	55.7	5.4	3.7	9.7	23.7	1.8	100.0	2.3

Source: IHS 2004.

* The unemployment rate is based on the economically active population (that is, total without non-active, incl. students).

As can be expected, improved education leads to higher incomes. Both the annual income[1] and the income difference compared to the previous educational level increases with each level of education attained. While the gain in expected income for people with lower primary education compared to those without schooling is only 14 percent, this difference increases to almost 60 percent for those with upper primary; 89 percent with lower secondary; and 138 percent for upper secondary. Having been enrolled in a TC means 196 percent more expected income compared to upper secondary education.

Table 8.4: Annual Average Income and Expected Annual Income According to Level of Schooling

	Annual Average Income for People Working (MK)	Expected Annual Income Taking into Account Unemployment risk (MK)	Income Increase Compared to Previous Level of Education, in %
No school	7,095	7,015	
Lower primary	8,112	8,005	14.1
Upper primary	12,983	12,715	58.8
Lower secondary	24,969	24,038	89.1
Upper secondary	63,566	57,121	137.6
Technical college	176,582	169,221	196.3
Higher education	952,027	929,233	449.1

Source: IHS 2004.

Particularly high is the income jump for people with higher education, who are expected to earn almost 450 percent more than their peers who have only a TC education. The IHS data indicate very high wage premiums for technical and higher education, meaning a high labor market demand for the TEVET- and higher-education qualified workforce, and at the same time reflecting the extraordinary low enrollment rate for both educational streams (see chapters 6 and 7).

In higher education, the wage premium is extremely high compared to other countries. Recent comparable data of mean income by educational level as a percentage of GDP per capita were available for five African countries in addition to Malawi. Figure 8.2 shows that up to the lower secondary level, the mean income as a percentage of GDP in Malawi stays low in comparison to the other countries. It approaches the higher end of the group with three times the GDP per capita in upper secondary, and rises above all other countries for people with a technical training background, who can expect to earn 8.25 times the country's per capital income. However, the ratio of expected incomes to GDP per capita rises to an enormous 44.5 for people with a tertiary education background, way beyond that of other countries.

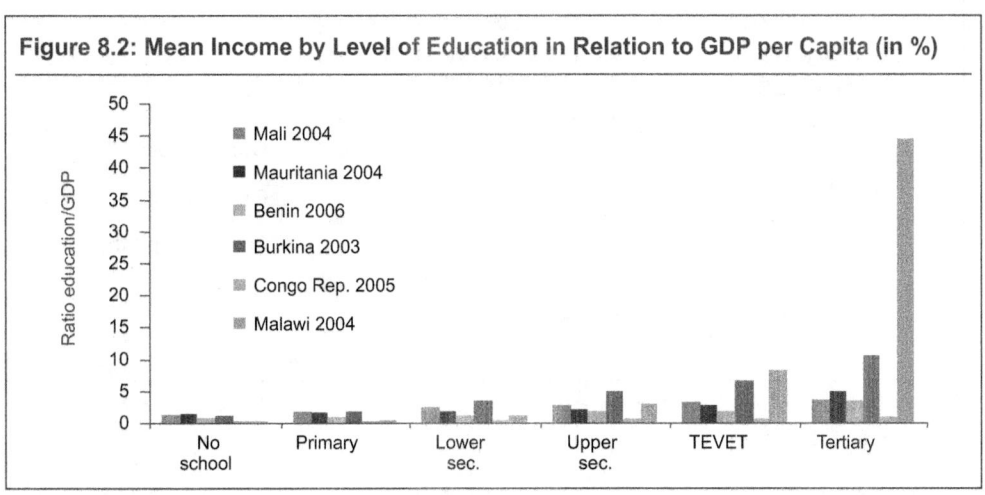

Figure 8.2: Mean Income by Level of Education in Relation to GDP per Capita (in %)

Source: World Bank database.

Labor Market Relevance of TEVET and Higher Education (Results of the Tracer Studies)

Unlike general education, TEVET and higher education (HE) are directly aimed at preparing students for employment.[2] The expected income levels presented in the previous section strongly suggest a high demand for graduates of the two educational streams, but do not necessarily provide a clear and disaggregated answer to the question of labor market relevance. Following is an analysis of existing data and information, mainly of the two 2008 tracer studies, meant to form a preliminary picture about the value and relevance of the qualifications and competencies of higher education and TEVET completers in the labor market.

Higher Education

The 2008 GTZ/World Bank tracer study of a total of 492 graduates from five different higher educational institutions[3] indicates that the higher education sector in Malawi is to a large extent successful in preparing highly qualified human resources for employment.

Overall, graduates are well employed and have success integrating into the labor market. As figure 8.3 shows, 85.3 percent of all respondents found employment after graduating from higher education, the vast majority (72.2 percent) in full-time wage employment. Self-employment is small (2.1 percent), but a substantial share of graduates are working part-time (11 percent). A relatively high amount—9.9 percent—is seeking employment, of whom the most recent graduates (2007) have the highest unemployment. The higher unemployment in the tracer study compared with the results of the 2004 IHS described in section II.1 can most likely be attributed to the fact that only graduates in the four most recent graduation years (2004–2007) were traced, which points to labor market entry problems for a still considerable number of graduates.

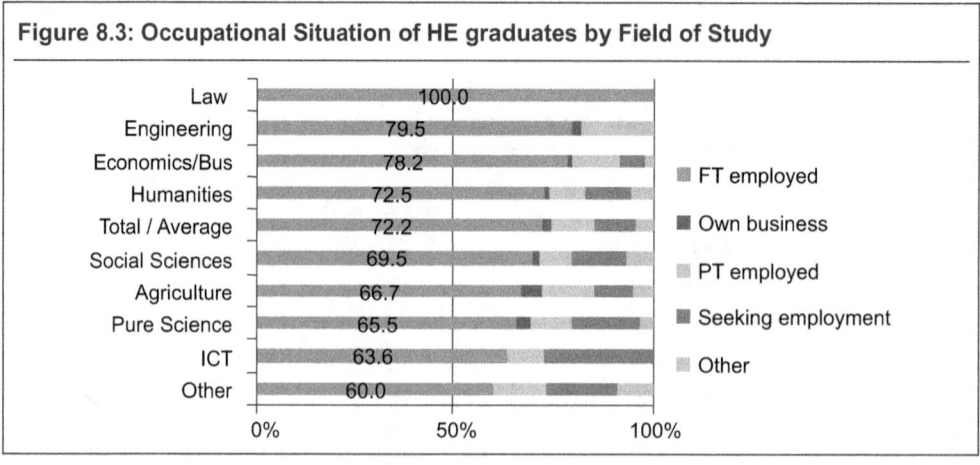

Figure 8.3: Occupational Situation of HE graduates by Field of Study

Source: Pfeiffer/Chiunda 2008 (Appendix 9).

Figure 8.3 also shows relatively clear variations in the fields of study. Law fares best by far, bringing all graduates into regular full-time employment; engineering, business/economics, and, interestingly, humanities, show above-average full-time employment rates. ICT, social science, agriculture, and pure science have below-average results. ICT also shows the highest unemployment rate, pointing to a possible saturation in the relevant labor market, which calls for further analysis.

Comparing data with other African countries shows a very high employment rate for academically trained Malawians and reflects the generally low higher education enrollment rates. Interestingly, Malawi is the only country with a markedly higher employment rate for younger rather than older academicians, suggesting an even higher recent labor market demand.[4]

The good labor market standing (of younger HE graduates in particular) is also reflected in a relatively short job search after graduation. Seventy-five percent of all graduates are employed within the first six months after graduation, and 94 percent have managed to find jobs within one year. The search process is on average much longer for those who have left university without any academic qualification (see figure 8A.1 in Appendix 8.1), which confirms the value of full academic qualifications in the market, as compared to some academic knowledge.

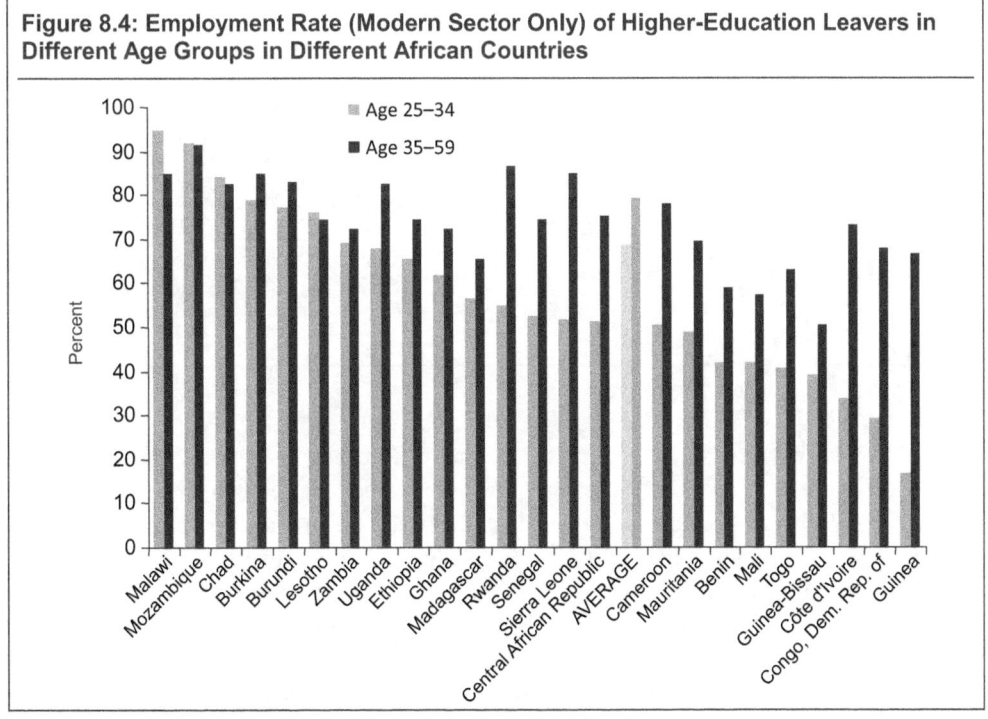

Figure 8.4: Employment Rate (Modern Sector Only) of Higher-Education Leavers in Different Age Groups in Different African Countries

Source: World Bank database.

As previously described, the income potential of HE graduates, which was also reconfirmed by the tracer study, indicates the high value the labor market attributes to academic qualifications. Not surprisingly, the income distribution of graduates in employment is characterized by a very large range of between MK9,000 and

MK640,000. The arithmetic mean per month according to the tracer study was MK 83,681 in 2008. Eighty percent of all cases are within the range of MK30,000 to MK150,000 (Pfeiffer and Chiunda, Appendix 9) with a median of MK65,000.

The mean income by study field (see figure 8.5[5]) suggests partly similar subject/occupational preferences, with a particularly high demand for lawyers and engineers. ICT and agriculture experts earn the least.[6] The high average income for the self-employed is an interesting finding that will come up once again in the analysis of TEVET graduates. However, the finding is based on a very small number of cases that only point to the insignificance of self-employment for TEVET graduates. The wage differences also, again demonstrate the superiority of qualified academics in the labor market as compared with HE dropouts.

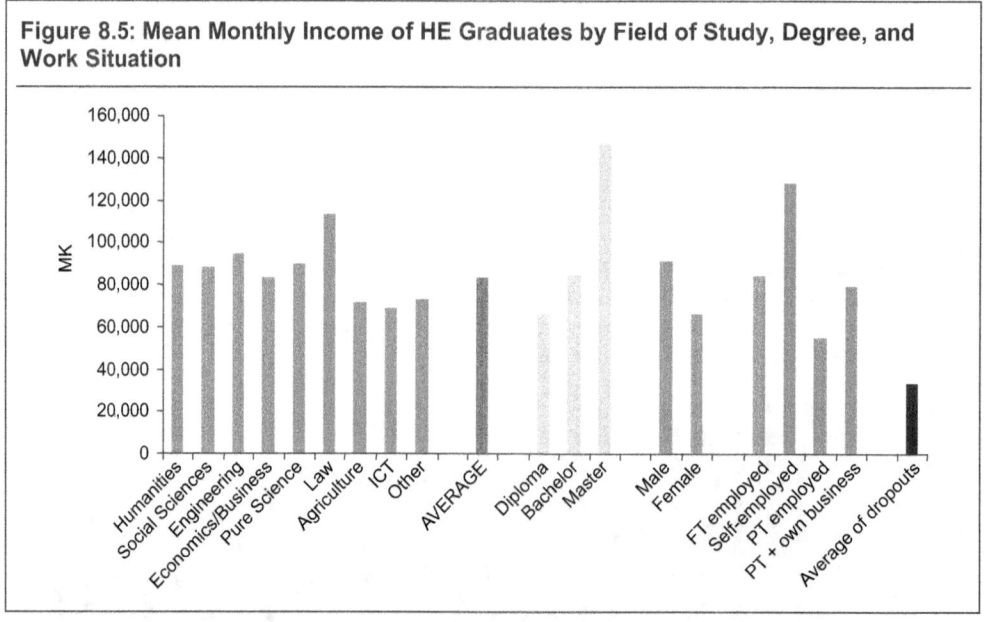

Figure 8.5: Mean Monthly Income of HE Graduates by Field of Study, Degree, and Work Situation

Source: Pfeiffer/Chiunda 2008 (Appendix 9).

Data, however, also show marked income differences by gender. Male graduates earn on average 37 percent more than their female colleagues, which can partly (but not completely) be explained by the fact that women are underrepresented in the better-paid occupational fields (Pfeiffer and Chiunda, Appendix 9).

Available wage data also point to the good career promotion performance of academically trained people. On average, graduates improved their wages by 15–20 percent per year (Pfeiffer and Chiunda, Appendix 9).

With the positive labor market position of HE graduates, it is hardly surprising that they are overwhelmingly highly satisfied with their studies. More than 70 percent of HE graduates in the tracer studies said they were satisfied or very satisfied with their studies, and only 8.2 percent were not or not at all satisfied. Also with respect to usefulness, the study found a very positive evaluation (Pfeiffer and Chiunda, Appendix 9).

Table 8.5: Months Needed by HE Graduates to Properly Carry out Professional Tasks

Months	%
1	18.2
2–3	29.8
4–6	26.4
More	25.6

Source: Pfeiffer and Chiunda, Tracer Study of TEVET and Higher Education Completers in Malawi, See Appendix 9.

Still positive (although less enthusiastic) are employers about the performance of HE graduates. The best scores were for basic professional abilities and knowledge, least for special professional knowledge. Ten percent of employers were generally unsatisfied, indicating that a share of HE graduates do not exhibit the expected level of knowledge and competence (Pfeiffer and Chiunda, Appendix 9). A large number of employers (74.4 percent) said that a graduate would normally need six months or less for professional adaptation (see table 8.5), which is a good result in international comparisons.

TEVET

As is the case for higher education, TEVET also appears to be relevant to the needs of the labor market. According to the GTZ/World Bank tracer survey (Pfeiffer and Chiunda, Appendix 9), which followed completers from various TEVET programs and provider systems, 93 percent of all completers indicated that the training was somewhat or very useful, despite a range of complaints about organizational issues during the program. The TEVETA Labor Market Survey (JIMAT, 2008), which only included participants in the formal TEVET apprenticeship program in its sample, confirms this general perception. Both studies also show that completers usually work in the professional field, for which they were trained. The GTZ/World Bank study shows an 80 percent matching rate. Also, the TEVETA study verified for former formal apprentices a high correspondence between field of training and work (Pearson coefficient of 0.927).

Table 8.6: Direct Results of Training Indicated by TEVET Graduates

Results of Training	% of Respondents
I got a job.	3.3
I have been able to make better products.	38.9
I have been hired more frequently to provide my services.	30.8
I managed to open my own business.	24.3
No change	14.5
Total (n=1000)	

Source: Pfeiffer and Chiunda, Tracer Study of TEVET and Higher Education Completers in Malawi, Appendix 9.

Both tracer studies suggest that TEVET completers have generally good chances to find employment. Only 15 percent of completers in the GTZ/World Bank study and 9 percent of completers in the TEVETA LMS remained unemployed. This appears to be a remarkable result by African standards. A recent tracer study of TEVET completers in Mozambique, for example, showed that 74 percent of 2005 graduates were not able to find employment in the profession for which they had been trained.[7]

Table 8.7: Employment Status of TEVET Completers

Current Employment Status	% of Total (Pfeiffer/Chiunda)	% of Total (JIMAT)*
Wage employment full-time	38.3	85.4
Wage employed part-time	8.0	
Self-employed (own business)	28.7	5.7
Self employed and wage employed	4.1	
Unemployed but looking for employment	15.2	8.9
Unemployed, not looking for employment	1.4	
Continuing studies	4.4	

Source: Pfeiffer and Chiunda, Tracer Study of TEVET and Higher Education Completers in Malawi (Appendix 9); JIMAT 2008.
* JIMAT figures were modified by extracting "students on attachment" from the sample, as these are not considered still under training.

One interesting finding of the GTZ/World Bank tracer study is the relatively high share (29 percent) of self-employed among TEVET completers. This figure is much lower (6 percent) in the JIMAT study, indicating that the informal sector as an employment destination is much less important for formal TEVET graduates than for others, including those who have been trained in private and by NGO training institutions.[8] It may also point to the increasing importance of organized skills development for the informal sector. While the Gemini study in 2000 (Malawi National Gemini Baseline Survey, 2000) still showed a rather negligible amount of skill development other than through traditional apprenticeship in the informal sector in Malawi, the TEVETA LMS in 2008 established a 35 percent rate of business owners who had previously undergone some kind of skills training in a TEVET institution. Forty percent of all business owners hold a formal qualification according to these findings (JIMAT, 2008).

As in higher education, Malawi again fares extremely well with respect to the employment rates of TEVET completers and leavers in comparison to other African countries (see table 8.8). Again, the difference between the age groups is relatively small, indicating the relatively stable labor market performance of people with a TEVET background over the years.

Table 8.8: Employment (of All Kinds) Rate of TEVET Graduates or Leavers, Aged 25–34 and 35–59 in Different African Countries (in %)

Country	Job Insertion, TEVET, 25–34	Job Insertion, TEVET, 35–59	Year	Difference Between Age Groups
Malawi	93.9	97.8	2004	−3.9
Uganda	92.8	96.6	2002	−3.8
Rwanda	92.7	90.4	2001	2.3
Lesotho	91.2	97.0	2002	−5.8
Mozambique	90.6	96.9	2002	−6.3
Ethiopia	89.7	94.7	2004	−5.0
Ghana	89.5	93.8	2003	−4.3
Benin	83.0	93.0	2006	−10.0
Mauritania	79.3	91.3	2005	−12.0
Burkina Faso	78.0	88.4	2002	−10.4
Mali	72.8	74.2	2004	−1.4
Sierra Leone	72.3	88.6	2003	−16.3
Togo	71.0	80.0	2006	−9.0
Cameroon	70.9	81.6	2001	−10.7
Côte d'Ivoire	69.8	67.8	2002	2.0
Senegal	60.5	77.5	2001	−17.0
Central African Republic	60.3	79.7	2003	−19.4
Congo, Rep.	59.6	70.2	2003	−19.0
Guinea	56.6	83.2	2002	−26.6
Chad	49.4	97.6	2002	−48.2
Average	76.19	87.47		−11.28

Source: World Bank database.

Another indicator for the good value of TEVET qualifications is the duration between completion and entrance into employment. Both tracer studies show good results in this regard. Yet the data in figure 8.6 suggest that apprenticeship training in fact eases labor market entry, because students have built up relations with future employers during the training time. According to the TEVETA LMS, 86 percent of all employed former apprentices found jobs within the first six months, while only 64 percent of the mixed group of TEVET graduates did so.

In view of the findings that TEVET completers are in demand in the labor market, the low-income level noted by both tracer studies is a cause of concern. While international comparative data show that the expected income of Malawians with a TEVET background in relation to the country's GDP per capita. is relatively favorable (see figure 8.2), expected income remains very low compared to the expected incomes after completion of higher education. This is of particular concern because of the level and duration of formal TEVET programs, which are post-secondary and often last four years. The GTZ/World Bank study established a mean monthly net income of only MK16,730, again with an extremely skewed distribution. Fifty-three percent of all completers earn MK10,000 or less (see figure 8.7). There is no significant difference by gender.

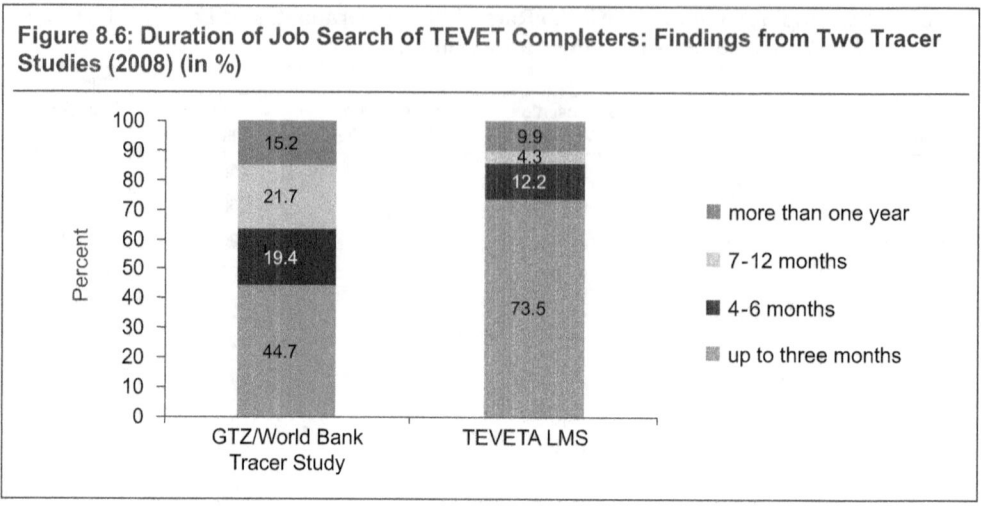

Figure 8.6: Duration of Job Search of TEVET Completers: Findings from Two Tracer Studies (2008) (in %)

Source: Pfeiffer/Chiunda 2008 (Appendix 9).

Interestingly, with an average MK20,724 monthly net income, self-employment pays better than wage employment. It is hardly surprising that self-employment has turned into an attractive option for TEVET completers. This is confirmed by the TEVETA LMS, where 57.6 percent of the traced former apprentices indicated that they want to be self-employed (JIMAT, 2008).

The income of former apprentices merits special attention and further research. Sixty-four percent, as the TEVETA study shows, are in the wage range below MK10,000. It is worth noting that 53 percent of all apprentices traced by JIMAT receive an allowance of between MK6,000 and MK10,000 during the second year of their apprenticeship (JIMAT, 2008). So apprentices hardly earn more after graduation than they receive in the first half of their studies.

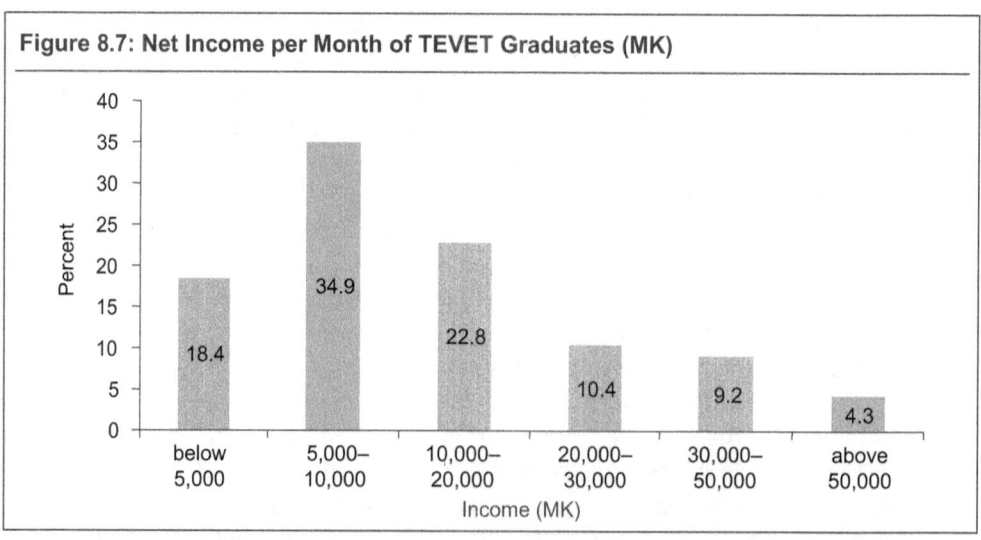

Figure 8.7: Net Income per Month of TEVET Graduates (MK)

Source: Pfeiffer/Chiunda 2008 (Appendix 9).

A wage differential should be expected with respect to the duration of training, however Pfeiffer and Chiunda (see Appendix 9) established only a rather weak correlation between duration of training and monthly income. In actual fact, the average income prospect of a graduate from a four-, post-MSCE apprenticeship program is similar to that of graduate from a one-year, non-formal training course, and substantially below that of a university graduate with a similar length of post-MSCE education.

The low average income of TEVET completers is sometimes explained by the low stipulated minimum wages for TEVET graduates, which cover the most common qualification systems—trade testing and Malawi (Advanced) Craft. These wages range between MK2,338 for a Trade Test 3 holder and MK4,500 for a Malawi Advanced Craft holder and have not been adjusted since 2003.[9] Systematic data on 2008 overall wage levels are not available. In 2008, Ministry of Labor company inspections in Blantyre established a mean wage range between MK4,500 and MK5,900 for laborers, and between MK7,000 and MK20,500 for production workers (Ministry of Labor, 2008). It appears that although TEVET completers find jobs, the demand for TEVET-level skilled human resources is apparently not sufficiently high to push wages well above formal production workers, and significantly above the politically induced low minimum wages.

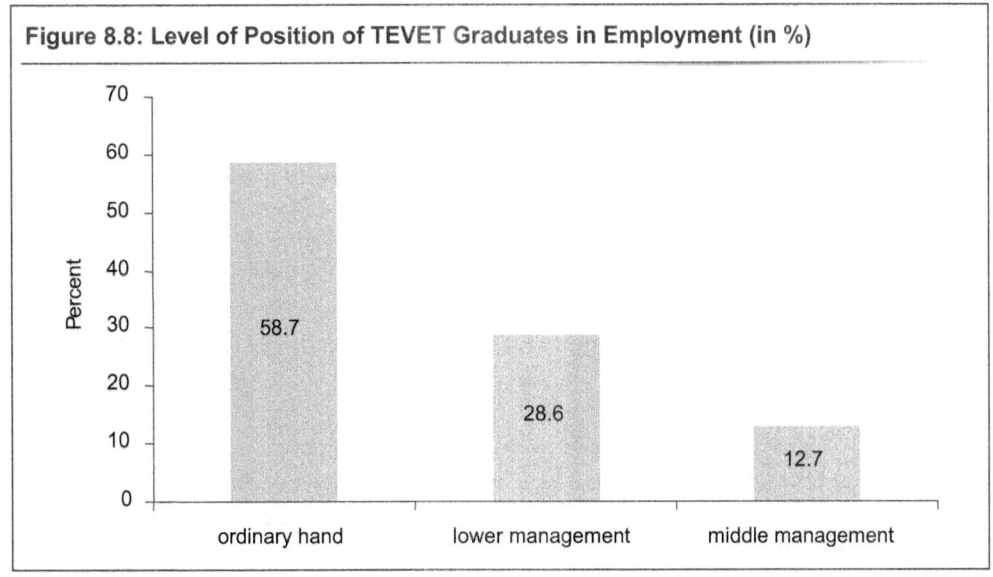

Figure 8.8: Level of Position of TEVET Graduates in Employment (in %)

Source: Pfeiffer/Chiunda 2008 (Appendix 9).

A possible explanation for the relatively low wage level of TEVET graduates (particularly in comparison to their peers with higher education) could be that TEVET completers basically replace unskilled labor. This assumption is supported by both tracer surveys, which find that most TEVET graduates remain so-called "helping hands" in the company for which they are working. In the GTZ/World Bank study, this percentage is close to 60 percent, while the situation for former apprentices is even worse, as the JIMAT study shows: Seventy-five percent of the employed were helping hands. A comparison with positions at first employment and at the time of the study demonstrates that only a small amount (some 14 percent) were able to advance over time (table 8.9).

Table 8.9: Position of TEVET Completers at First Employment and Time of Study (in %)

Position	At First Employment	At Time of Study
Ordinary hand	89.4	74.8
Supervisor	5.0	11.0
Foreman/middle management	2.8	11.5
Other	2.8	2.8

Source: JIMAT 2008.

As responses to open questions in the tracer studies show, low wages are one of the main reasons for lack of interest in TEVET among young Malawians. Further research into the wage determination of TEVET completers is recommended.

Although the two studies provide some insight into the relative value of the different TEVET certificates in the labor market, there are some doubts about the validity of replies in both surveys.[10] The GTZ/World Bank study shows a significant market preference for certificate holders of any kind compared to those without certificates. City and Guilds graduates tend to be better remunerated, however, the overall findings do not provide evidence that preferences for certain certificates also lead to better pay. The TEVETA LMS included questions about the qualification preferences in its employers' survey, and the results suggest a rather undecided picture: 58 percent of employers indicated they did not have preferences and 51 percent said they did not differentiate between the qualifications in wage setting. Of those who do, the highest wages are clearly paid to City and Guilds holders, a finding that corresponds with the GTZ/World Bank study.[11] The JIMAT study also provides some indications of the preference of employers for trade testing over Malawi Craft and Advanced Craft, and hence supports the general assumption in this regard.

In figure 8.9, significant income variations can be seen by field of study. In general, the food and hospitality sectors tend to pay less, while some fields, including more modern trades, pay better. Income differences, however, appear to be an issue of trade-specific characteristics (for example, company sizes, economic sectors) rather than of human resource shortages.[12] The TEVETA LMS interviewed companies about their unmet skills demand by occupation. The findings are presented in figure 8.11 in Section II.4. There appears to be no obvious correlation with the level of demand and average salary of TEVET graduates. For some occupations, where (according to the TEVETA LMS), the current unmet demand is particularly high,[13] salaries are also above the mean average, such as for steel fixing, refrigeration, and fabrication and welding. Other occupational fields, such as plumbing, electrical installation, and painting and decoration recorded a large demand but pay a below-average salary.

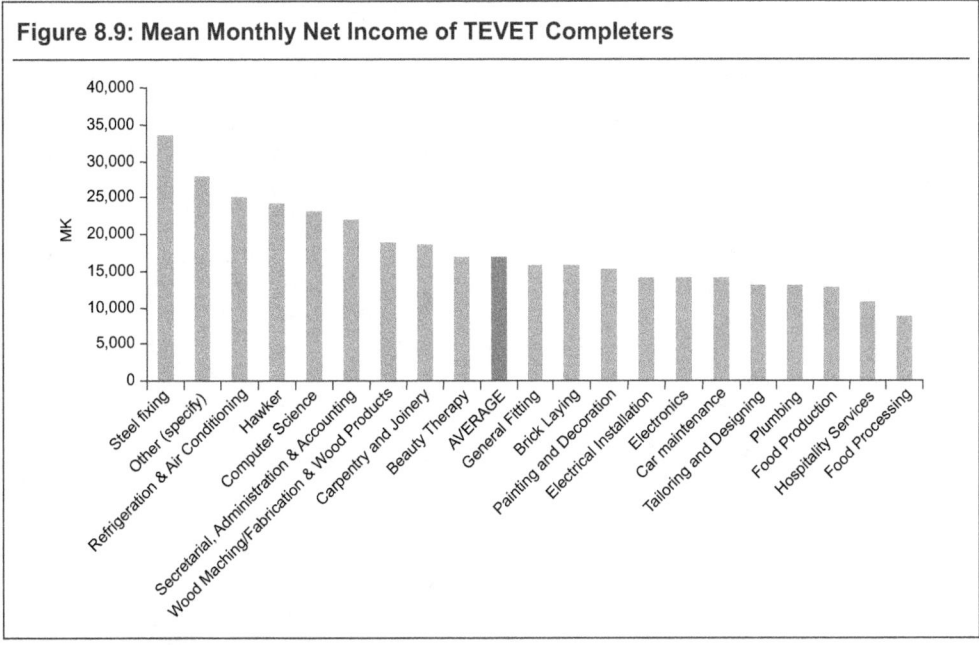

Source: Pfeiffer/Chiunda 2008 (Appendix 9).

Rates of Return to Education

A comparative view of the rates of return to different levels of schooling provides evidence of the economic value added to each additional educational level attained. Rates of return (ROR) are assumed to reflect the increased labor productivity induced by education. Private ROR describe the average extra income gained by an individual through additional education in relation to the cost of this education for the individual (including the foregone earnings due to longer studies). The social ROR informs about the gain of society at large. It is calculated by relating the additional expected income to the total cost involved in the education, both private and public. An analysis of the rates of return to each level of schooling in Malawi helps us understand whether investments in education for both private households and society are beneficial, and may serve as a tool to analyze the appropriateness of educational investment.

The growing income differential in relation to an increasing level of schooling corresponds with increasing private rates of return to education. Table 8.10 shows very high ROR to education in Malawi, established already in ROR to education analyses in previous years.[14] Returns to education appear to be high by African standards. Table 8.11 compares returns in Malawi to those recently calculated with the same methodology for Benin and Congo. The high returns reflect that education is still a rare privilege in Malawi, for which the labor market is prepared to pay a high premium compared to its costs.[15]

Table 8.10: Private and Social Rates of Return to Education

Rates of return	Additional Annual Income Compared to Lower Level (MK)	Public Cost per Student in the Level (MK)	Private Cost per Student (direct + foregone earnings, MK)	Total Social Cost (public + private, MK)	Private ROR	Social ROR
Lower primary	990	8,384	20,176	28,559	5%	3%
Upper primary	4,710	7,990	31,643	39,633	15%	12%
Lower secondary	11,323	52,900	52,598	105,498	22%	11%
Upper secondary	33,083	56,256	75,462	131,718	44%	25%
TC (compared to upper secondary)	112,100	111,912	207,492	319,404	54%	35%
Higher	872,112	3,233,722	508,857	3,742,579	171%	23%

Source: Own calculations based on IHS 2004 data and data from Chapter 3.
Note: Public and private direct cost are computed by multiplying the **annual** unit cost (as calculated in Chapter 3) by the average number of years of schooling within the level of education (see Appendix 8.3 for more details).

Table 8.11: ROR in Malawi Compared to Selected Other African Countries

	Malawi (priv.)*	Malawi (soc.)*	Benin (priv.)*	Benin (soc.)*	Congo (priv.)*	Congo (soc.)*
Lower primary	5%	3%				
Upper primary	15%	12%	4%	3%	3%	3%
Lower secondary	22%	11%	1%	1%	3%	2%
Upper secondary	44%	25%	9%	7%	4%	2%
TC (compared to upper sec.)	54%	35%	2%	2%	3%	2%
Higher education	171%	23%	5%	3%	4%	1%

Source: Malawi IHS 2004; CSR Benin; CSR Republic of Congo.
* In Benin and Congo, TEVET is post-primary. The ROR represents the return from primary education to TEVET.

Rates of return for Malawi were calculated based on IHS 2004 data. A detailed description of the methodology used is attached in Appendix 8.3.

Interesting is also the enormous gap between the returns to higher education and the educational levels below. It indicates a severe shortage of academically trained human resources. The high income of academics may also be related to the privileged status that academics enjoy in the public sector, where a large portion of them are employed. Furthermore, the regional labor market for academics, in which Malawian HE graduates compete, is likely to induce an additional push in wages. While the income level for academically trained people in Malawi is high relative to the average income level of the country, expected incomes in absolute terms may still be relatively low compared to the incomes of academics in neighboring countries that have a much higher per capita income than Malawi.

The difference between private and social ROR makes for another interesting finding. Social ROR are per definition lower than private ROR, once the public cost involved in providing education is factored in. Again, overall social ROR to education in Malawi are very high at all levels. However, there is an enormous difference between the private and social ROR in higher education. For an average academic, the private return is 7.5 times higher than the social return, because a much higher share of the total cost of higher education, as compared to all other educational levels, is borne by the government (see table 8.10).

Skill Needs in the Labor Market

The evidence from the rate of return analysis and the tracer studies presented in this chapter indicates a high demand for skilled and academically educated human resources. This finding is also supported by a few other business surveys. However, too little is still known about the concrete structures and patterns of unmet current and future skill demands in terms of occupations, competencies, and qualification levels. The tracer studies, which need to be analyzed in further depth, provide valuable insight into demand structures for those occupations in which training is actually offered in the TEVET and higher education systems. However, by their very nature the tracer studies are silent about emerging occupations and other economic sectors not currently targeted within the professional education system. This section sketches some preliminary ideas on skill demands in Malawi.

Basic information on the employment structure in Malawi raises questions about the appropriateness of the training offered by the formal TEVET system. In 2006, 76 percent of all employed Malawians worked in agriculture, and only 6 percent in the manufacturing and construction sectors, which is where most graduates from the formal TEVET programs seek jobs. Only recently do the developing training programs for commercial trades[16] and one public TEVET institution—the Malawi Institute of Tourism—cater for the hospitality, trade, and service sector. This sector employs (apart from the civil service with 10 percent of all employed) the majority of the non-agriculture work force in Malawi. The entire spectrum of TEVET offers in Malawi still needs to be assessed once the results from the current TEVET provider registration process by TEVETA are available. However, it is evident that the formal public TEVET system, with its traditional range of technical trades, caters for only a small fraction of the labor market. Subject to further verification, the service sector is likely to be increasingly catered to by the private commercial training market. However, the lack of TEVET level-training related to the agricultural sector appears to be significant in an agriculture-dominated economy, such as Malawi's.

Available recent enterprise surveys clearly point to unmet education and skills demand. In the 2007 Malawi Business Climate Survey of the Malawi Chamber of Commerce and Industry (MCCI), the lack of availability of a local skilled workforce rated as a major obstacle to doing business by the surveyed companies. "There is a general feeling that training of the workforce is to a great extent not in line with the changing needs of the industries" (MCCI, 2007). Notably, this problem was raised by companies in the manufacturing sector, where it ranked as the top obstacle to doing business. The Africa Private Sector Group in its Malawi Investment Climate Assessment (ICA) 2006 came to similar conclusions. In this survey, which mainly targeted manufacturing enterprises (and to a lesser extent the service sector), close to 50 percent of businesses perceived the skills and education of available workers to be a major or very severe obstacle (see table 8.12). This perception was higher for formal companies and less pronounced in the informal sector. For comparison, labor regulations were only indicated to be a serious problem by 13 percent of all companies.

The perception of skill and educational shortages is higher for larger companies. It is also higher in foreign-owned firms than in domestically owned, and higher for exporter than for non-exporters.

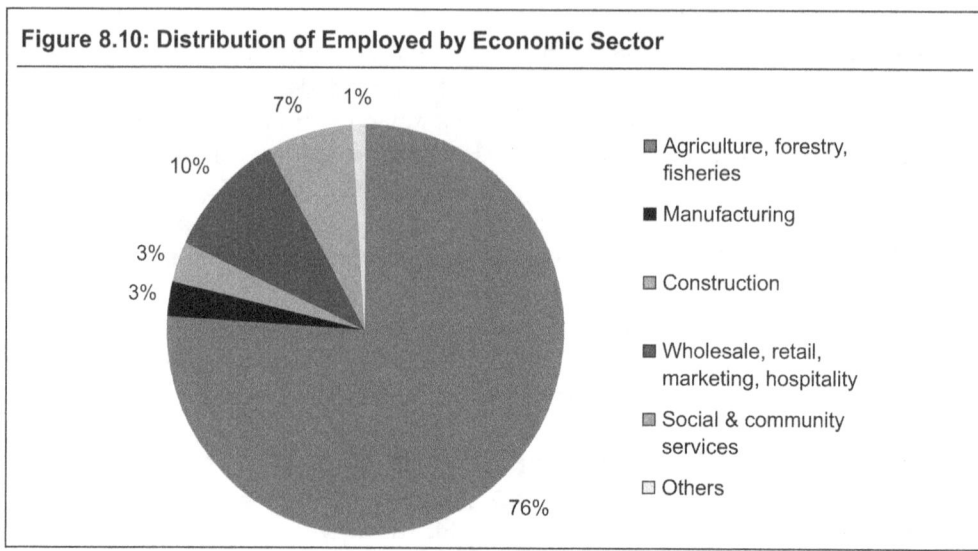

Figure 8.10: Distribution of Employed by Economic Sector

Source: Malawi Poverty & Vulnerability Assessment 2006.

Table 8.12: Percentage of Firms that Report Labor Regulations and Skill Levels of Workers as a Major or Severe Constraint in Malawi

Firm Category	Labor Regulations	Skills and Education of Available Workers
Small	10.9	35.9
Medium	15.0	55.0
Large	13.2	62.3
Domestically owned	12.7	46.6
Foreign owned	12.2	58.5
Non-exporter	11.9	48.4
Exporter	15.2	54.6
Total	12.7	49.7

Source: Africa Private Sector Group, Malawi Investment Climate Assessment, 2006, p. 57.

Staff training activities by companies may also serve as an indication of skill needs. The ICA (2006) found that 52 percent of all surveyed companies provided training to their staff, either internally or externally. Not surprisingly, this rate was higher for companies that perceived skills shortage as a major impeding factor. The likelihood for employees to received company-organized training became higher in larger companies, and relatively higher in foreign-owned and exporting companies. Also, workers who are already skilled have better access to further training than their unskilled colleagues. Of the surveyed companies, 19 percent of all skilled workers received training but only 11.7 percent of unskilled workers did.[17]

The training patterns are different in the informal sector. Here, the preparedness to provide training is generally lower. Only 38 percent (compared to 52 percent in the formal training) provided training to staff. Moreover, training consisted mainly of internal training. According to the ICA, the reasons for this are two-fold: a lower perceived need for training (indicated by 61 percent of companies), and also high costs. Almost 60 percent indicated that training would be too costly.

Interestingly, only 12 percent said they feared their employees would leave after training. More recent studies (notably the tracer studies and the informal sector survey of the TEVETA LMS) point to the overall increasing importance of formalized skills development in the informal sector. As described before, the number of informal sector operators with a TEVET background appears to have increased in comparison to the 1990s. Self-employment has also become an attractive employment status for TEVET graduates. The increased attention TEVETA is according to TEVET programs that target informal sector operators and the informal sector labor market has to be welcomed in this context.

Despite the many indications for unmet skills demand, a more concrete knowledge of demand by occupations and competences is hardly available. This would be necessary, though, to sync the TEVET supply with labor market demands. More recently, only the TEVETA LMS (JIMAT, 2008) tried to identify skill demands in more concrete terms. According to JIMAT, which focused on occupational areas for which formal TEVET programs exist, unmet training needs are significant in advanced mechanics, welding and fabrication, general fitting, electronics, administration, building, calibration equipment, computer knowledge, machine maintenance, plant operators, steel fixing, advanced molding, and fire drill evacuation. A lack of practical skills was recorded as a key weakness by the majority of companies. JIMAT also found that on average across occupational fields, the demand for skilled labor as a percentage of all employed in a specific occupational field was 47.6 percent, with occupations such as water plant operators, instrumentation mechanics, mechatronics, plumbers, refrigeration technicians, painters and decorators, roofers, drivers, electricians, plant operators, and welders showing an above-average shortage (unmet demand) of skilled workforce (see figure 8.11).

In view of the occupational limitations, methodological problems as well as resources needed for studies such as JIMAT's, considerable doubts remain as to whether comprehensive quantitative attempts to assess skills shortages and forecast future needs is the right approach to training needs assessment in a country like Malawi, where research capacities and resources are scarce. More qualitative assessment methods, such as sector-specific consultative meetings with employers and experts, complemented by targeted surveys of selected economic sectors, may be more promising.[18]

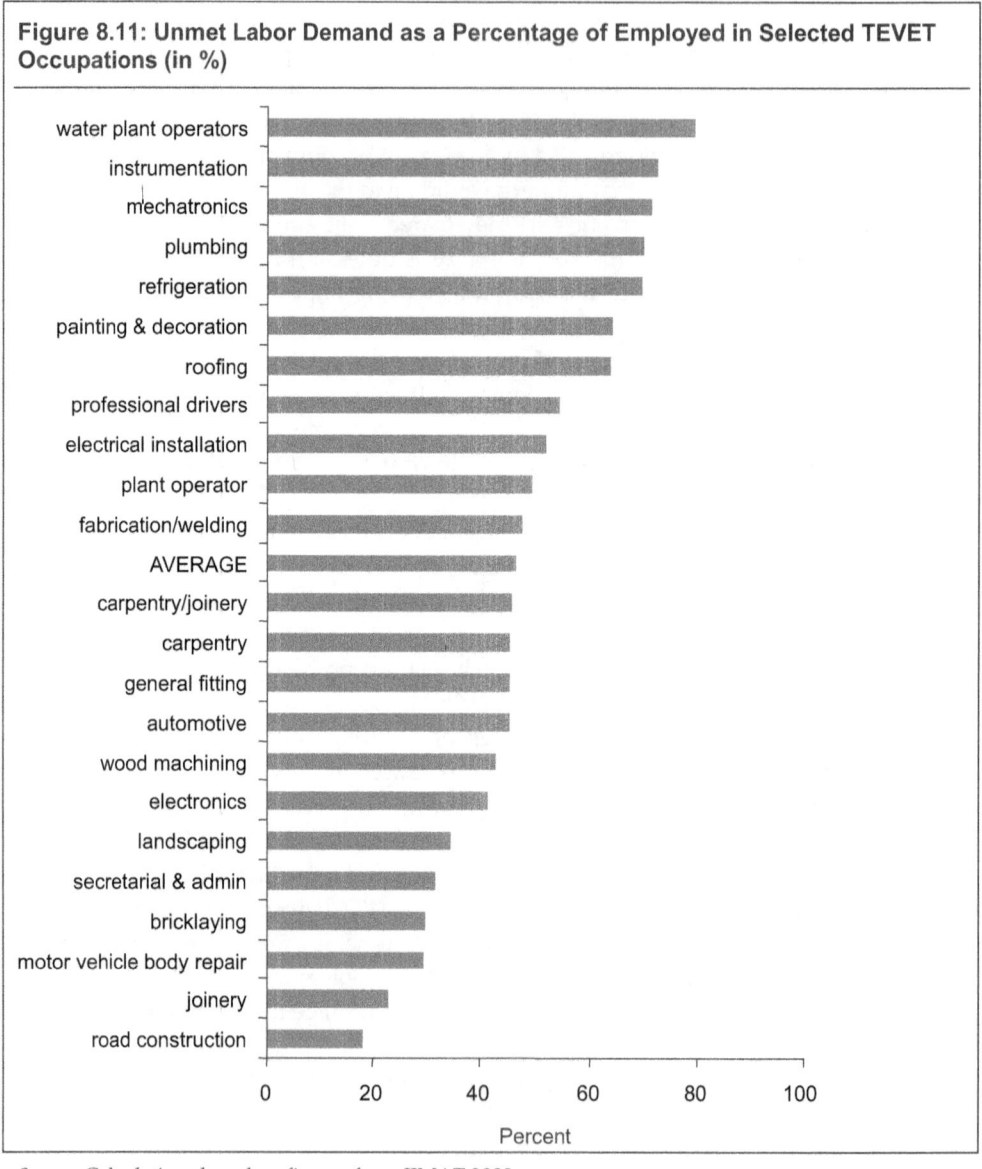

Figure 8.11: Unmet Labor Demand as a Percentage of Employed in Selected TEVET Occupations (in %)

Source: Calculations based on figures from JIMAT 2008.

Notes

[1] This refers to both the annual average income for people working recorded in the IHS, as well as the expected annual income taking the unemployment risk into account.
[2] Including self-employment
[3] The sample was drawn from Chancellor College, Polytechnical College, Bunda College, Mzuzu College, and Sharewood University.
[4] The rates indicated in figure 8.4 are slightly lower than the ones in table 8.3 because the international comparison only takes modern sector employment into account. Table 8.3 showed

that 8.7 percent of people with a higher education background are working in traditional agricultural or non-agricultural sectors.

[5] Only those who are employed are included in the calculation.

[6] The GTZ/World Bank tracer study did not include teachers and nursing training as it was assumed that these programs train for public employment.

[7] Programa Integrado de Reforma da Educacao Profissional (PIREP), Analise Estatistica do Estudo de Base Sobre Educacao Tecnica Profissional, Dezembre 2007.

[8] This JIMAT finding cannot be verified by the GTZ/World Bank study. Here, also a considerable share of the TC completers (24 percent) indicated they were self-employed. However, the results cannot be fully compared, because the GTZ/World Bank study did not only trace former formal TEVET students, but all completers of programs run by the colleges.

[9] It should be emphasized that the overall minimum wage for unskilled labor is currently MK3,280 for urban workers, equal to the minimum wage for Trade Test 2 holders.

[10] Both surveys have asked the traced graduates for their qualifications. However, the results are not clear.

[11] In the JIMAT study, the results for wages and qualifications do not distinguish among the levels of the qualifications.

[12] The 2006 Malawi Investment Climate Assessment, which mainly analyzed firms from the manufacturing sector, found strong evidence of the influence of firm size, foreign ownership, and export status on wage levels. Other factors being equal, in 2006 a foreign-owned firm payed 33 percent more than a Malawian-owned firm, an exporter 9 percent more than a non-exporting company, a medium-sized company 20 percent more than an small firm, and a large firm 30 percent more than a small firm (Investment Climate Assessment, 2006, p. 70).

[13] Measured as a percentage of current employment in the occupational area

[14] The 2006 ICA established (on the basis of its own survey data) an increase in wages of almost 15 percent for each additional year of schooling, which was reduced to 8–9 percent when data were controlled for occupation (ICA 2006, p. 68).

[15] Benin and Congo were cited because of the availability of comparable data. However, both countries have a significantly higher GDP per capita, partially explaining the lower ROR.

[16] This refers to public TCs. Supposedly the supply for so-called commercial trades is much higher in the private training market, for which no data are available.

[17] In the TEVETA LMS (JIMAT, 2008) 72 percent of all surveyed companies engaged in in-house training. This is significantly higher than in the ICA, probably because only the companies that employ skilled people were included in the sample.

[18] Also compare the recommendations in Johanson and Adams, *Skills Development in Sub-Saharan Africa*, the World Bank, 2004, pp. 57–61.

Appendixes

Appendix 1.1: Demographic and Social Development Indicators

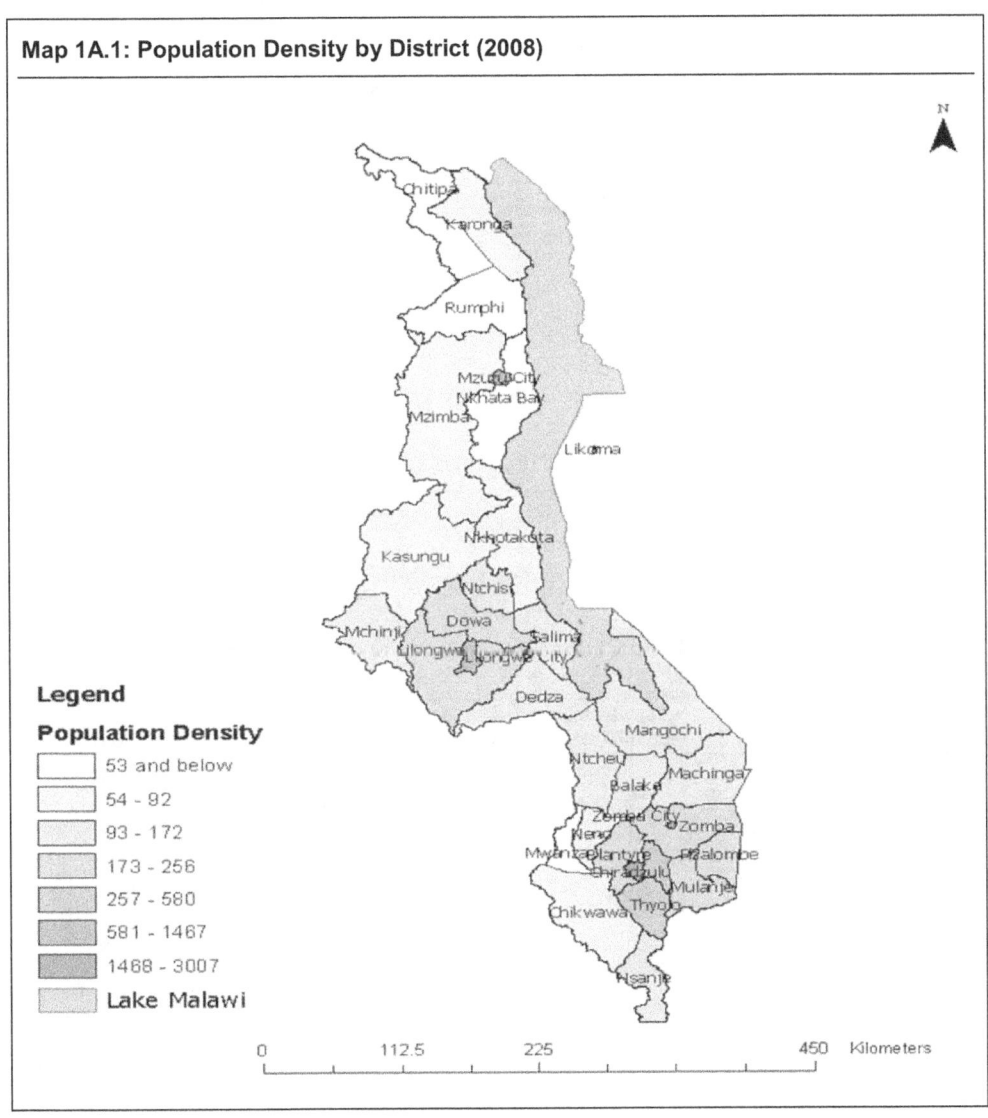

Map 1A.1: Population Density by District (2008)

Source: National Statistics Office.

Table 1A.1: 5-16-Year-Old Population as % of Total, SADC Countries (2008)

SADC Region Country	Population 5–16-Year-Olds (Thousands)	Total Population (Thousands)	Population 5–16-Year-Olds as % of Total
Malawi	**4,857**	**13,066**	**37**
Zambia	4,049	12,154	33
Congo, Dem. Rep. of	20,873	64,704	32
Angola	5,617	17,499	32
Mozambique	6,949	21,813	32
Tanzania	13,069	41,464	32
Madagascar	6,369	20,215	32
Lesotho	633	2,020	31
Swaziland	353	1,148	31
Zimbabwe	4,095	13,481	30
Namibia	632	2,102	30
Botswana	519	1,906	27
South Africa	12,216	48,832	25
Mauritius	242	1,272	19
Average	5,748	18,691	30

Source: UN Population Statistics.

Table 1A.2: Population Living Below Poverty Lines and Gini Index (2005 or Closest Year) (in %)

SADC Country	% Population Living Below US$1/Day Poverty Line	% Population Living Below US$2/Day Poverty Line	Gini Index
Angola	n.a.	n.a.	n.a.
Botswana	28.0	55.5	60.5
Congo, Dem. Rep. of	n.a.	n.a.	n.a.
Lesotho	36.4	56.1	63.2
Madagascar	61.0	85.1	47.5
Malawi	**20.8**	**62.9**	**39**
Mauritius	n.a.	n.a.	n.a.
Mozambique	36.2	74.1	47.3
Namibia	34.9	55.8	74.3
Swaziland	47.7	77.8	50.4
South Africa	10.7	34.1	57.8
Tanzania	57.8	89.9	34.6
Seychelles	n.a.	n.a.	n.a.
Zambia	63.8	87.2	50.8
Zimbabwe	56.1	83.0	50.1
SADC average	41.2	69.2	52.3

Source: UNDP Development Report 2007/08.

Table 1A.3: Orphans (0–17 Years) Due to AIDS, SADC Countries (2007)

SADC Region Country	Orphans Due to AIDS as a % of Children (0–17 Years Old)
Madagascar	Less than 0.1
Mauritius	0.1
Angola	0.6
Congo, Dem. Rep. of	0.2
Tanzania	4.7
Malawi	**7.4**
Mozambique	3.7
Zambia	9.6
Namibia	n.a.
Zimbabwe	16.2
South Africa	7.6
Lesotho	11.5
Botswana	12.1
Swaziland	10.5
SADC Average	6.5
SSA Average	3.3

Sources: UNAIDS Report on the Global AIDS Epidemic 2008; UN population data.

Table 1A.4: African Context Indexes

SADC Country	Composite Index of Social Context	Composite Index of Economic Context	Composite Index of Global Context
Angola	50.9	64.7	50.9
Botswana	61.0	66.7	61.0
Congo, Dem. Rep. of	40.4	36.7	40.4
Lesotho	47.0	56.5	47.0
Madagascar	45.8	43.8	45.8
Malawi	**39.0**	**41.5**	**39.0**
Mauritius	74.3	59.9	74.3
Mozambique	41.7	44.0	41.7
Namibia	55.7	56.4	55.7
Swaziland	81.4	75.8	81.4
South Africa	65.0	58.2	65.0
Tanzania	45.7	55.1	45.7
Seychelles	45.7	44.2	45.7
Zambia	41.3	46.6	41.3
Zimbabwe	53.2	50.8	53.2
Average for SADC countries	51.6	53.4	52.5
SSA Average	50	50	50

Source: World Bank, Africa region.

Table 1A.5: Other Social Development Indicators

	Mortality Rate (Under 5-Years-Old)	HIV/AIDS Prevalence Rate (15–49 years)	Malnutrition Prevalence, Height for Age (% of Children Under Age 5)	Adult Literacy Rate (15 Years and Older)	% Urban Population
Average SADC countries	132	14.4	33.8	75.3	35.9
Angola	260	3.7	45.2	67.4	54.0
Botswana	120	24.1	23.1	82.9	58.2
Congo, Dem. Rep.	205	3.2	38.1	67.2	32.7
Lesotho	132	23.2	46.1	82.2	19.0
Madagascar	119	0.5	47.7	70.7	27.1
Malawi	**122**	**11.5**	**49.0**	**69.0**	**17.7**
Mauritius	15	0.6	15.0	87.4	42.5
Mozambique	145	16.1	41.0	44.4	35.3
Namibia	62	19.6	23.6	88.0	35.7
South Africa	68	18.8	12.0	88.0	59.8
Swaziland	160	33.4	30.2	79.6	24.4
Tanzania	122	6.5	37.7	69.0	24.6
Zambia	182	17.0	46.8	68.0	35.1
Zimbabwe	132	20.1	17.0	91.2	36.4
Other Sub-Saharan African countries					
Benin	150	1.8	30.7	40.5	40.5
Burkina Faso	191	2.0	38.7	28.7	18.7
Burundi	190	3.3	56.8	59.3	10.3
Cameroon	149	5.4	31.7	67.9	55.5
Cape Verde	35			83.8	58.0
Central African Republic	193	10.7	38.9	48.6	38.2
Chad	208	3.5	40.9	25.7	25.8
Comoros	71	0.1	42.3	75.1	37.7
Congo, Rep.	108	5.3	31.0	86.8	60.6
Côte d'Ivoire	195	7.1	20.0	48.7	45.4
Equatorial Guinea	205	3.2	19.0	87.0	39.1
Eritrea	78	2.4	37.6	58.6	19.8
Ethiopia	127	1.4	46.5	35.9	16.3
Gabon	91	7.9	20.7	86.2	84.1
Gambia, The	137	2.4	19.2	42.0	54.7
Ghana	112	2.3	29.9	65.0	48.5
Guinea	160	1.5	26.0	29.5	33.5
Guinea-Bissau	200	3.8	30.5	64.6	29.7
Kenya	120	6.1	30.3	73.6	21.0
Liberia	235	1.7	39.5	55.5	58.8
Mali	218	1.7	38.2	23.3	31.1
Mauritania	125	0.7	34.5	55.8	40.6
Niger	256	1.1	39.7	30.4	17.0
Nigeria	194	3.9	38.3	72.0	49.0
Rwanda	203	3.0	45.3	64.9	20.2
Sao Tome and Principe	118	1.5	28.9	87.9	58.8
Senegal	119	0.9	25.4	42.6	41.9
Seychelles	13			91.8	53.4
Sierra Leone	282	1.6	33.8	38.1	41.4
Somalia	225	0.9	23.3	24.0	35.7
Sudan	90	1.6	43.3	60.9	41.7
Togo	139	3.2	26.0	73.6	40.8
Uganda	136	6.4	39.1	72.3	12.7
Average SSA	**147.2**	**6.7**	**33.7**	**62.9**	**37.9**

Sources: Data from WHO, UNAIDS, UNESCO, and the World Bank.

Appendix 1.2: Context Index, Methodology of Calculation

The World Bank has recently gathered data from different sources (e.g., the World Bank, IMF, UNESCO Institute for Statistics, UNAIDS, OECD) in order to compute a comparative context index for all Sub-Saharan African countries. This context index allows the Bank to compare the education outcomes of the countries by taking into account the cross-country differences context. This context index is made up of two subindexes: an economic context subindex and a sociodemographic context subindex, with various indicators in each subindex.

The economic context subindex includes the following indicators:

- Current revenue, excluding grants as a percentage of GDP (weight=2, data from IMF and OECD);
- Official development assistance in education as a percentage of GDP (including 20 percent of the global budget support, in case it exists, weight=1, data from OECD and World Development Indicators);
- Percentage of enrollment in private schools (weight=1, data from UNESCO Institute of Statistics); and
- GDP per capita (weight=1, data from World Bank and OECD).

The sociodemographic context subindex includes the following indicators:

- Demographic pseudo-dependency ratio (population of 5–16-year-old children as a percentage of total population, weight=2, data from UN Department of Economic and Social Affairs);
- Adult (15 years and older) literacy rate (weight=1.5, data from UNESCO Institute of Statistics);
- HIV/AIDS prevalence rate (adult 15–49 years old, weight=1.5, data from UNAIDS);
- Mortality rate for children under five years old, (per 1,000, weight=1.5, data from World Health Organization and UNICEF);
- Malnutrition (height for age) prevalence as a percentage of children under 5 years (weight=1.5, World Health Organization); and
- Urban population as a percentage of total (weight=1.5, data from the UN World Urbanization Prospects).

The ten indicators have been standardized [mean = 0 and standard deviation = 1]. The result of such a calculation for a given country represents the relative score of this country compared to the other ones. Then, the weighted[1] average of those indicators has been computed to make subindexes and the context index. Finally, the subindexes and the context index have been standardized [mean=50 and standard deviation=10] in order to avoid negative figures and to make them more reliable.

Notes

[1] Indicators that have higher relevance according to the factor analysis are higher weighted. The exact rule is based on the coefficients of each indicator relative to the data reduction factor analysis, as per the following: If the factor coefficient of the indicator is > 0.75, the weight is 2; if it between 0.5 and 0.75, the weight is 1.5; otherwise, the weight is 1.

Appendix 2.1: Education System Structure

Figure 2A.1: Structure of the Education System in Malawi

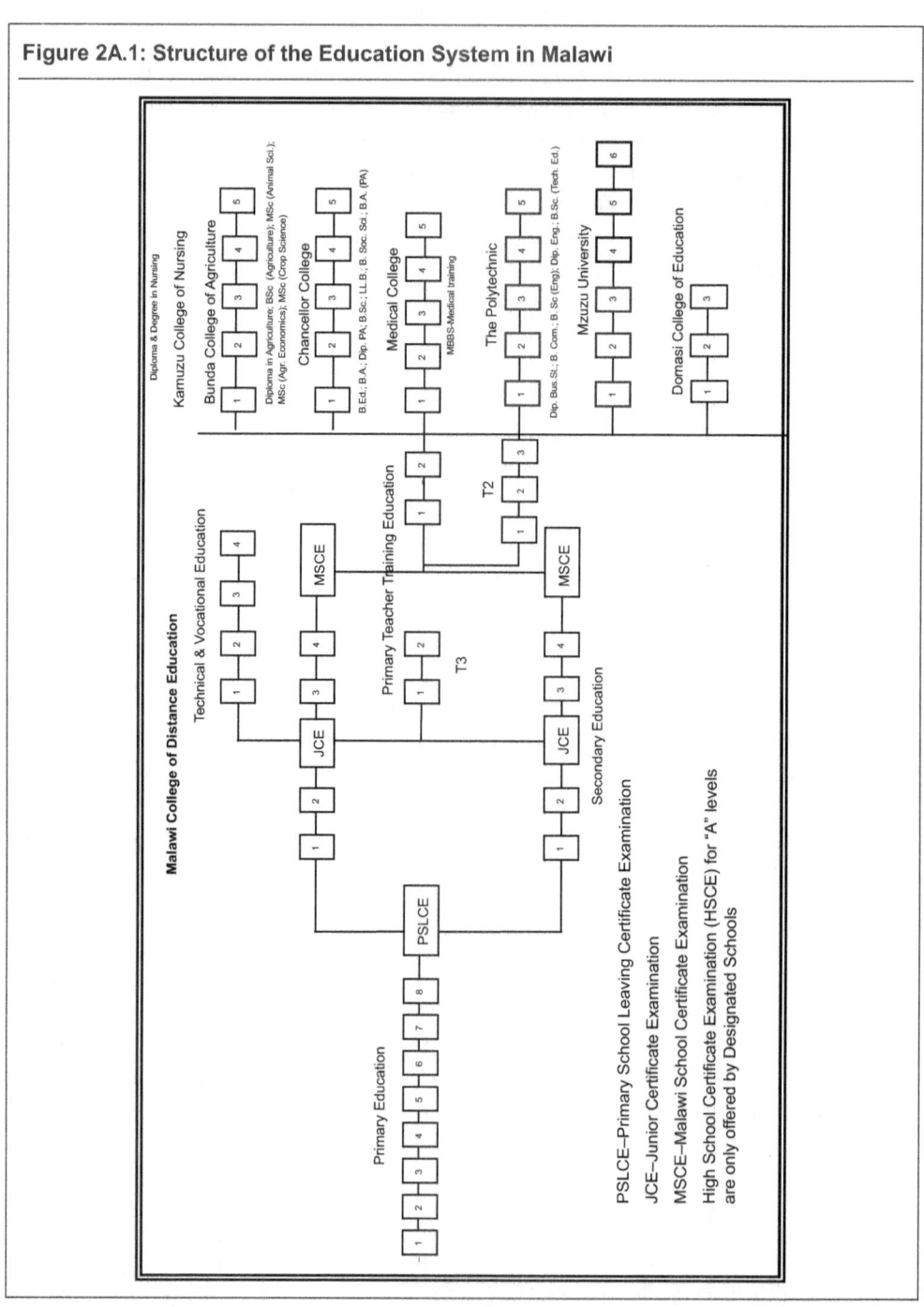

Source: Education Statistics 2007, Department of Planning, the Ministry of Education, Science and Technology.

Appendix 2.2: Enrollment Trends

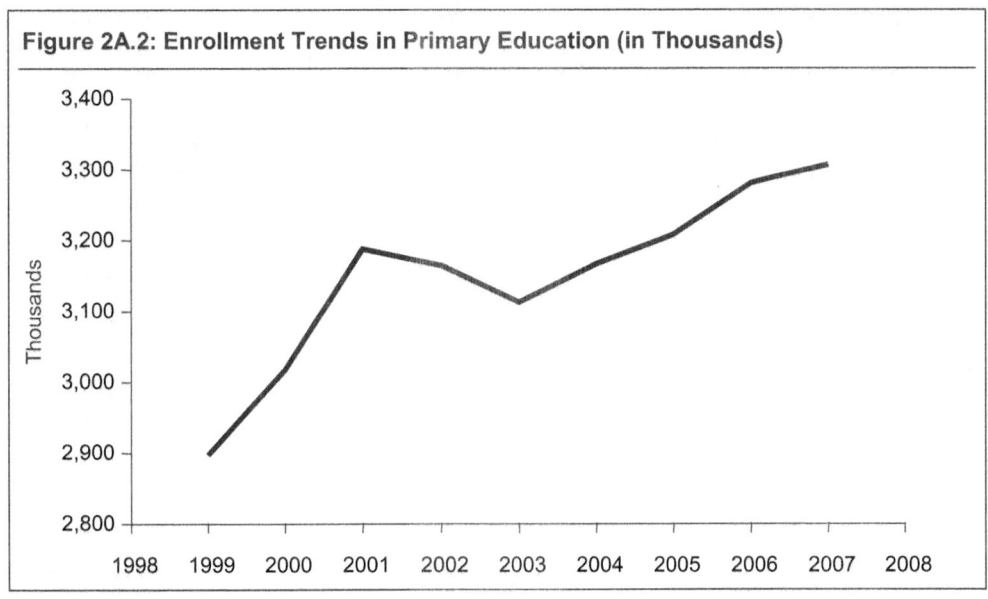

Figure 2A.2: Enrollment Trends in Primary Education (in Thousands)

Source: EMIS database.

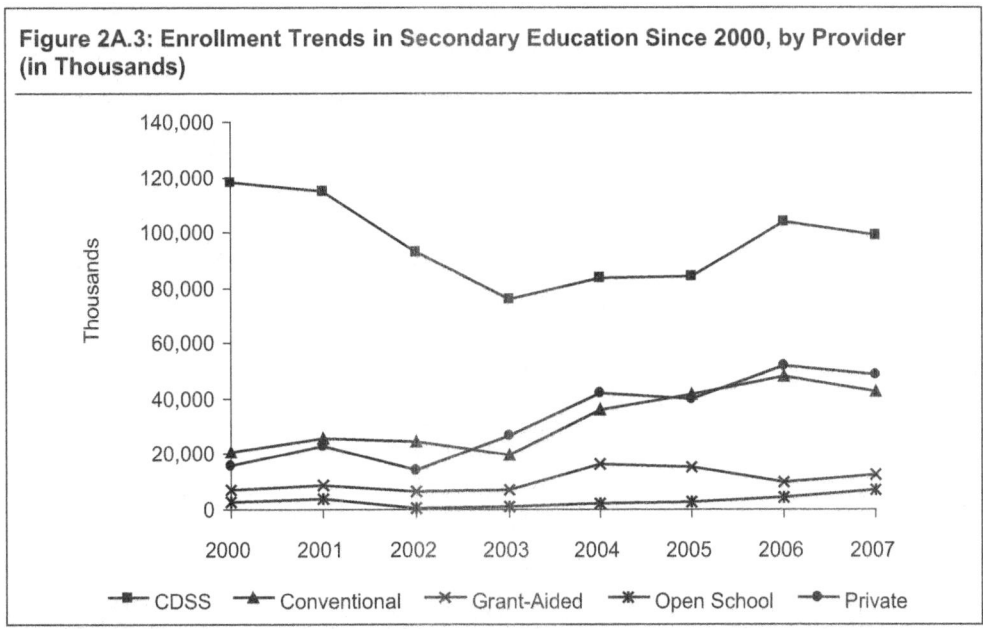

Figure 2A.3: Enrollment Trends in Secondary Education Since 2000, by Provider (in Thousands)

Source: EMIS database.

Table 2A.1: Outreach Population by Literacy Programs

	Male	Female	Total
Literacy rate* (a)	65.5%	48%	56.7%
Population 15–49 (b)	2,962,030	3,012,312	5,974,342
Illiterate population (c) = (a) x (1-(b))	1,021,900	1,566,402	2,588,303
Enrollment (d)	22,221	124,080	146,301
Outreach 100 x (d)/(c)	2.2%	7.9%	5.7%

Sources: Calculation with UN 2006 population data, MICS 2006 database, and enrollment information from the Ministry of Women and Child Development.

* Literacy here is considered in a strict sense: the share of 15–49-year-old individuals who are able to read a whole sentence without difficulty.

Appendix 2.3: Population Estimates for the Malawi CSR

Population estimates are a key issue in education planning as they are important in the calculations of almost all the education coverage indicators. These estimates are a major concern in Malawi as in cross-country analysis it has the highest and most unbelievable education indicators when computed with national population estimates. For example, when taking new entrants in Standard 1 from EMIS 2000 data and NSO's six-year populations estimate, the result is a 217 percent gross intake rate (number of new entrants in Standard 1 divided by the population of children age six). This is clearly unrealistic: It would mean that in 2000 the number of new enrolled pupils in Standard 1 was twice as much as the population of the official age to attend the first standard of primary education. The consequence at the national level is that some indicators are not computed on a yearly basis anymore as they should be, with some education planning staff admitting that the population basis does not allow such a calculation. In the context of the CSR, this issue could not be avoided and the team asked the National Statistical Office to provide the population data and projections in order to try to find, on the demographic side, an explanation of the overestimated education indicators. The CSR team also worked on both MICS Data and United Nations population estimates.

1. Population Projections from the National Statistical Office (NSO)

The NSO provided the national projections (issued from the 1998 census) by single age, gender, and districts. These data needed some strong preliminary technical work in order to analyze them with a more suitable format. First, the sum of the total population of all 31 districts gave estimates for Malawi at the global level and per single age. The global population estimates were consistent with the global official information from NSO—an estimated 10.2 million people in 1999 that would grow to 22 million inhabitants in 2023. The estimate for 2007 is 12.8 million. Staying at this global level does not allow for the estimation of any difficulties in the population projection trends (figure 2A.4).

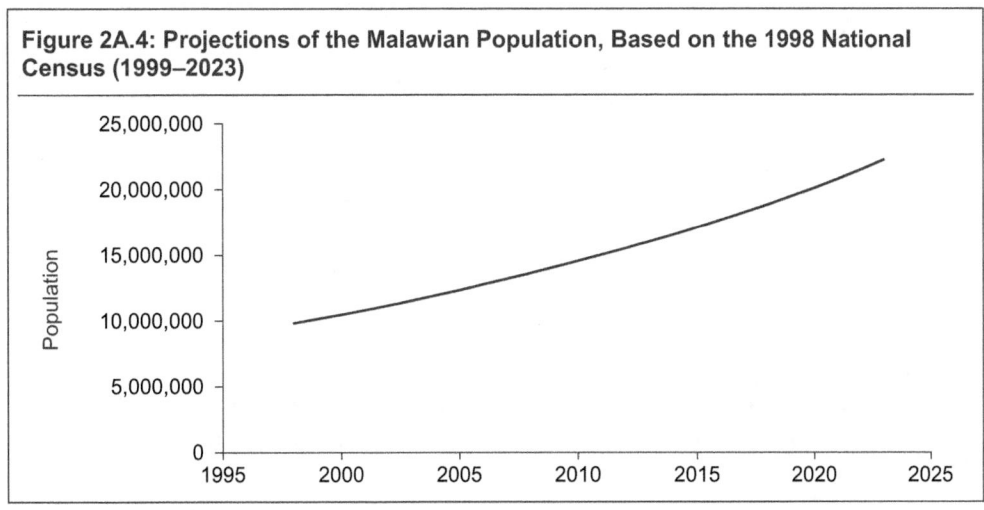

Figure 2A.4: Projections of the Malawian Population, Based on the 1998 National Census (1999–2023)

Source: NSO population projection from 1998 census.

The major problem appears when the analysis goes through the evolution by single age. According to the NSO, the trends that should be observed on each single age group would be as shown in figure 2A.5.

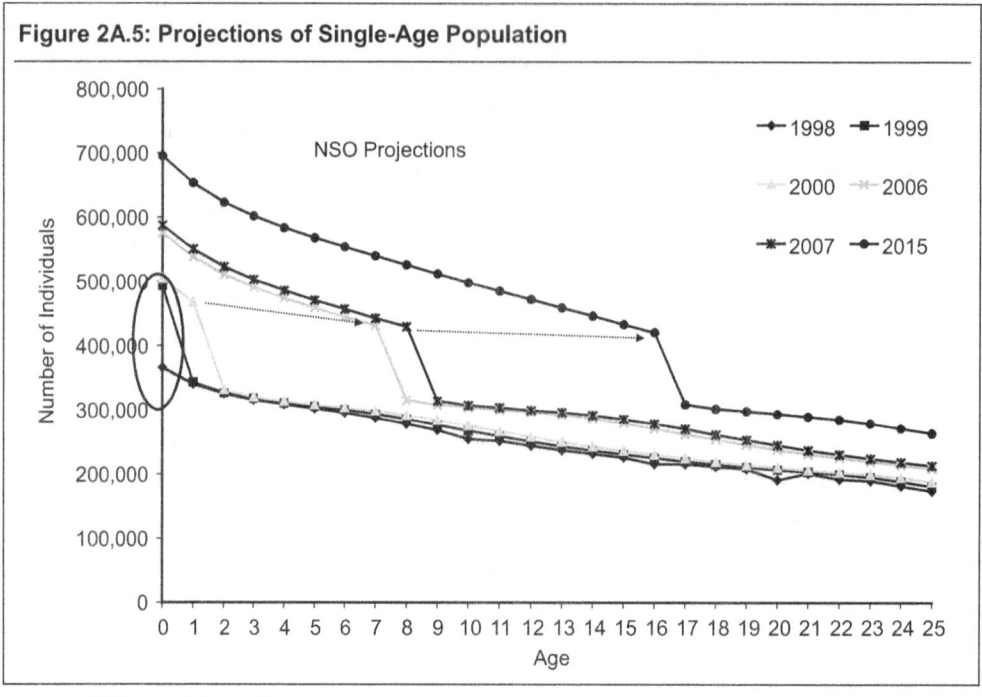

Figure 2A.5: Projections of Single-Age Population

Source: NSO population estimates.

If the data structure from the 1998 census is correct, the projections have suffered an initial "shock" that is projected from 1999 to 2023: Between 1998 and 1999, an exceptional 36 percent growth rate for the population under age one can be seen, but this is not the case for the other single age group, for which the observed growth rate stays under 10 percent. The phenomenon repeats itself from one year to another. The same 36 percent rate is encountered between 1999 and 2000 for population of age one, and then between 2000 and 2001 for the population of age two while the others rates stay realistic.

The consequence is a distorted age structure. For example, in 2007 and according to these projections, the expected number of eight-year-olds should have been 429,573, and there would be 314,773 nine-year-olds, etc. If only the school-age population for primary and secondary education is considered (see table 2A.2), the share of eight-year-olds for 2007 would be around 11 percent, while it would fall to under 8 percent for those who are nine-years-old and above. In 2006, the share of eight-year-olds would then have been 8.3 percent.

Such an evolution (the amount of eight-year-olds growing from 8.3 to 10.8 percent from one year to another) is too fragile to be taken into consideration for the calculation of education indicators.

Table 2A.2: Expected School-Age Population for 2006 and 2007, NSO Projections

	Number of Inhabitants		Share of Each Age Group (%)	
Age	2006	2007	2006	2007
6	444,769	456,942	11.7	11.5
7	431,430	442,829	11.4	11.1
8	315,246	429,573	8.3	10.8
9	308,108	314,011	8.1	7.9
10	304,349	307,138	8.0	7.7
11	300,137	303,647	7.9	7.6
12	296,590	299,450	7.8	7.5
13	292,380	295,908	7.7	7.4
14	286,497	291,721	7.6	7.3
15	279,471	285,758	7.4	7.2
16	271,246	278,676	7.2	7.0
17	262,381	270,478	6.9	6.8
Total	3,792,604	3,976,131	100.0	100.0

Source: NSO population estimates.

The NSO census unit, consulted on this phenomenon,[1] underlined that in population projections, the reported age distribution is distorted by either misreporting or underenumerating the population at any specific age. In Malawi, there would be a serious underreporting of children under age one. The projections done between 1998 and 1999 used a combination of reported ages and survivors of births from women in the reproductive age groups at given fertility rates. The numbers from 1999 on are higher because the projections have adjusted for this underreporting. However, the NSO admits that censuses suffer from underreporting, but would not assume that the underreporting is uniform in the whole population.[2]

Another explanation for this "shock" could be the specific software used to make the projections (RUP for group age and DEMPROJ for single age), and the way they compute the coefficient that displays the deceases among 0–4 year-olds.

The consequences of such a distortion for the education indicators are important: In 2007 for example, the access rates until Standard 3 would benefit from the global correction while the others (from Standard 4 to Form 4 and higher education) would not, introducing a serious bias in those indicators (overestimates of access rates to grades above Standard 3).

At this stage, it is necessary to underline that this distortion is observed within all the districts at the same time (see figure 2A.6, for example). This means that if the population estimates per specific age are biased, they are biased **all over the country**. Thus, it would seem acceptable to assume that the weight of each district in each specific age population is likely to be correct.[3]

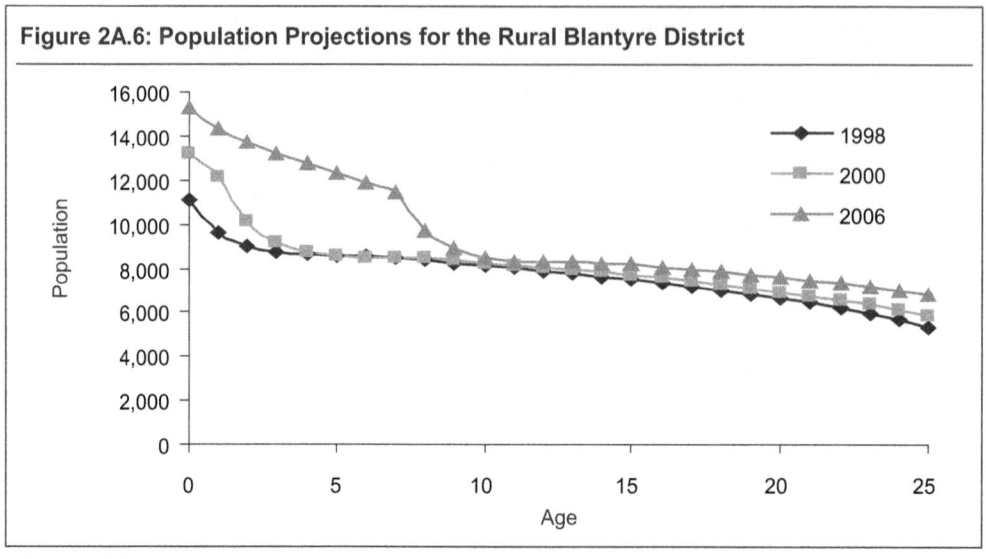

Figure 2A.6: Population Projections for the Rural Blantyre District

Source: NSO projections.

2. Estimates from the 2006 Multi Indicators Cluster Survey (MICS)

The MICS households survey is designed to obtain estimates of indicators related to the wellbeing of children and women at the district level. The MICS sample for Malawi concerned 26 districts out of 28 (in 2006), some districts being too small to obtain a sufficient number of households. It then concerned a total number of 31,200 households; according to the MICS preliminary report (NSO, 2006), "For reporting results at the regional and national levels, samples were weighted to reflect population size."

Using the MICS data, the global population for Malawi in 2006 would have been around 13.2 million. This figure is higher than the NSO projections (400,000 more individuals), yet it should be the same. MICS also provides repartition per single age but due to the misreporting of some age groups, leading to large fluctuations from one single age to another, the use of such a repartition would need preliminary work.

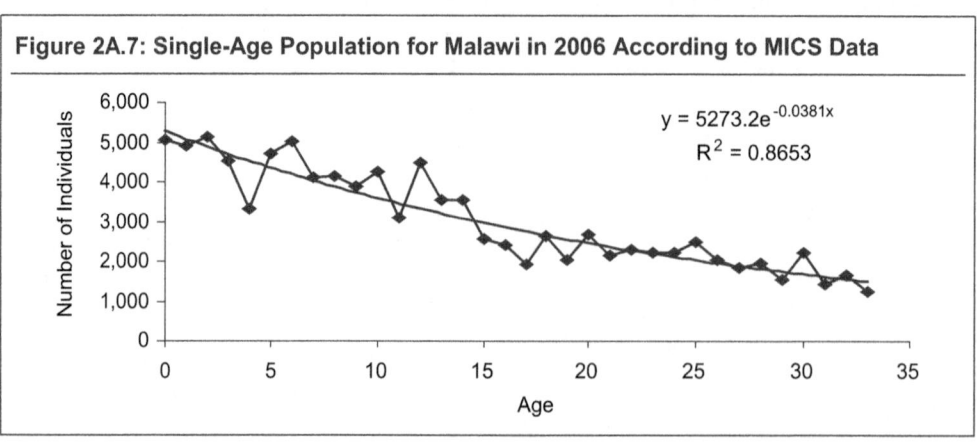

Figure 2A.7: Single-Age Population for Malawi in 2006 According to MICS Data

Source: Calculation from the MICS database.

If the MICS database and estimates can be taken as national, one should consider that, even if the figure provided by MICS is higher than the NSO projections, it might underestimate the total population of Malawi, due to the way the sampling method was conducted. The sample of households was extracted from the 1998 reported census, which as mentioned previously probably suffered from underreporting of some age groups (particularly 0–4). Thus, the inclusive probability of each household might be overestimated and the weight of each household is likely to be under the reality.

3. Projections from the United Nations Population Unit

The CSR exercise prefers to use national estimates to describe the demographic context, but when these become too problematic for being used without introducing a high bias, it is possible to use the population projections computed by the population unit of the United Nations. The 2006 revision uses, like the previous one, all relevant information about the past demographic dynamics, and involves detailed assumptions concerning fertility mortality and international migration.[4] The information used, either at the national or international level, is listed in box 2A.1.

Box 2A.1: Data Used by the UN Population Unit to Estimate and Project the Population for Malawi

Total population (2005): Estimated to be consistent with the 1998 census adjusted for under enumeration and with estimates of the subsequent trends in fertility, mortality, and international migration.

Total fertility: Based on maternity-history data from the 1992, 2000, and 2004 Malawi DHS and on estimates derived from the 1977 and 1987 censuses and the 1984 Family Formation Survey.

Infant and child mortality: Child mortality based on maternity-history data from the 1992, 2000, and 2004 Malawi DHS; estimates from UNICEF were also considered. Infant mortality estimates for the period 1995–2000 are based on results from the 1998 census. The demographic impact of AIDS has been factored into the mortality estimates.

Life expectancy at birth: Derived from estimates of infant and child mortality by assuming that the age pattern of mortality conforms to the South model of the Coale-Demeny Model Life Tables. Estimates from the 1987 and 1998 censuses and official estimates from the National Statistical Office of Malawi were also considered. The demographic impact of AIDS has been factored into the mortality estimates.

International migration: Based on refugee statistics compiled by UNHCR and on data on the number of migrant workers in South Africa.

Source: Extract from http://esa.un.org/wpp/Sources/country.aspx, March 2008

In the context of Malawi, the trend observed with the UN projections differs from the national one for an average difference per year of approximately one million people. The national population was estimated 10.9 million in 1998 (1 million more people than the number given by the national census) and should reach 20.5 million in 2023, meaning 1.5 million less than the national estimates. The total population is then supposed to be 13.5 million people in 2006, while the national estimate leads to 12.8.

Figure 2A.8: Projections of Malawian Population, Compared to the UN and NSO

[Graph showing NU projections and NSO projections from 1998 to 2028, values in Millions ranging from 0 to 25,000]

Source: NSO and UN unit for population.

Focusing on the 1998 distribution per age (Figure 2A.9), we can observe that according to the UN, the population of children under age one is 454,442—nearly 100,000 more individuals than in the national estimates. This should confirm the global underestimates of some young ages in the 1998 census, which are not corrected by the national projection. Moreover, the UN's estimates seem to have corrected a global underestimate for ages 0 to 21. On the contrary, the differences for age 22 and up seem to be very low. The underenumeration or misreporting of children under age one would have concerned not only the birth age group, but all the age groups between 0–21. This position seems more acceptable than the specific phenomenon corrected only for children under age one.

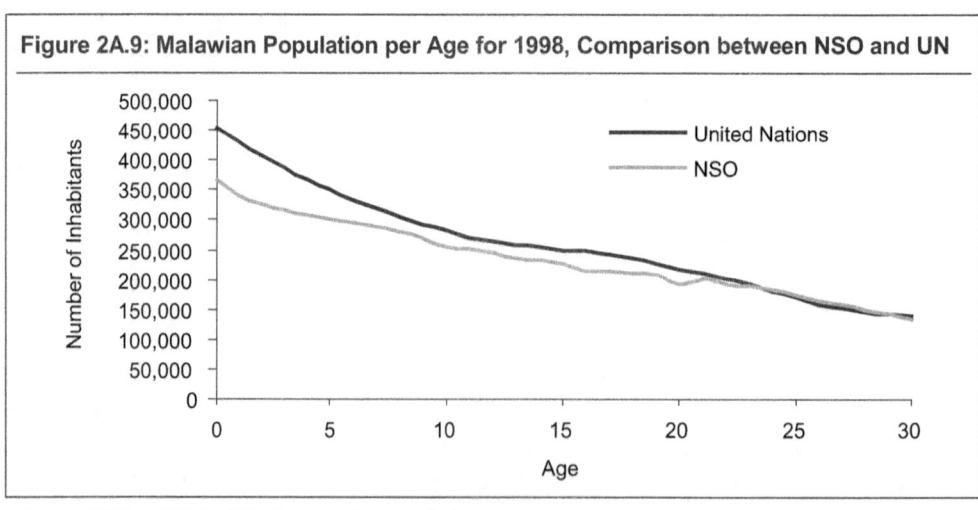

Figure 2A.9: Malawian Population per Age for 1998, Comparison between NSO and UN

Source: NSO and United Nation unit for population.

The main consequence is that the projections are more realistic, showing no major fluctuation, and average growth rates per age are more reasonable. Another consequence is that the structure per age of the population remains stable during the projected period.

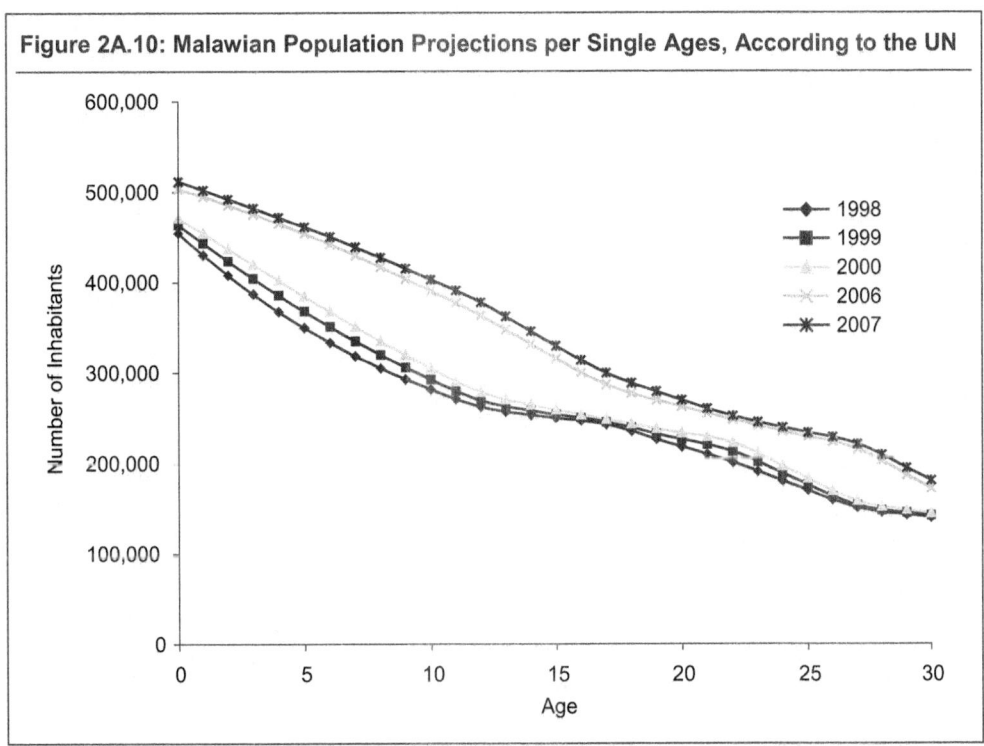

Figure 2A.10: Malawian Population Projections per Single Ages, According to the UN

Source: United Nations unit for population.

In looking at the school-age population for 2007, the choice between one of the two estimates will have major consequences on the education indicators because the differences between the two estimates particularly concerns people who were younger than 21 in 1998. As already mentioned, the national estimates for 2007 show a drop between ages 8 and 9, displaying an unrealistic evolution. Using the UN population leads to a smoothed trend. The population of primary education school-age children is 3,266,883, while the national estimate is 2,849,498. This will affect the indicators, particularly after Standard 3, since the difference for ages 6, 7, and 8 is slight.

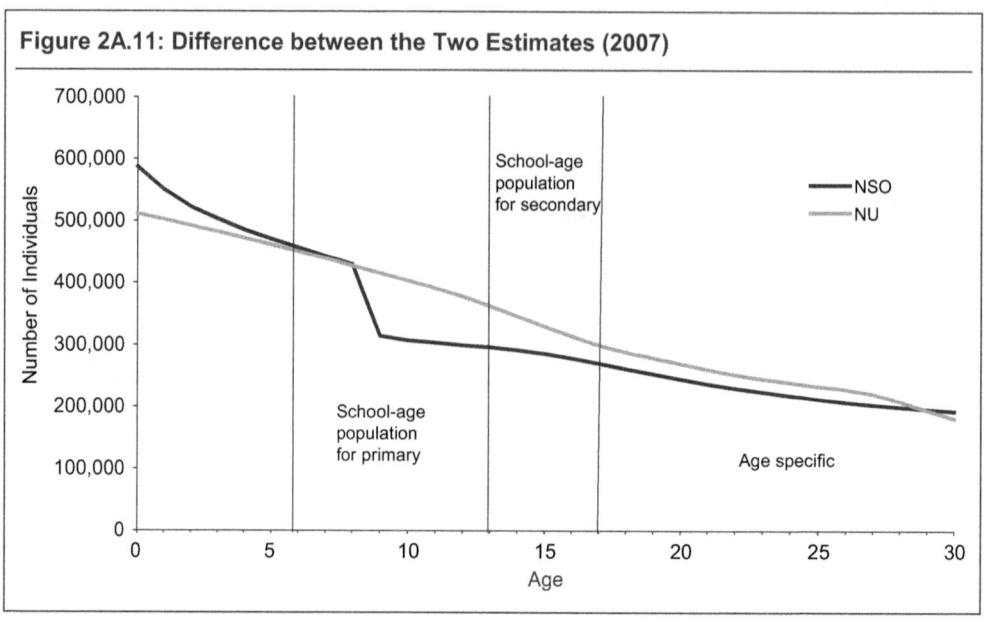

Figure 2A.11: Difference between the Two Estimates (2007)

Sources: NSO and UN.

4. Conclusion: Which Population Basis to Use in the CSR Exercise?

Table 2A.3 shows some differences between the three population estimates for 2006. It displays the MICS 2006 estimates as a median estimate between NSO and UN projections, slightly closer to the UN's, for either the global population or the specific school-age population for primary and secondary education.

Table 2A.3: Differences of Estimates (2006)

	Total Population	6–13 Years	14–17 Years
NSO projections	12,757	2,693	1,099
Estimates from MICS 2006	13,184	2,946–3,032*	1,150–1,170*
United Nations projections	13,570	3,172	1,235

Source: MICS 2006.
* Depending on the smoothing range chosen.

These differences would plead in favor of either the MICS or the UN's projections. Nevertheless, it would seem more appropriate to use the UN projections: The MICS data will underestimate the global population as it was sampled on the 1998 reported information, affected by underreporting on specific age groups. It is thus not possible to consider that 1998 is an exhaustive basis for the NSO-corrected part of this misreporting.[5] The use of the MICS estimates for the total population do not seem conceivable anymore: When looking only at the children under age one in 1998, the MICS data do not take into consideration the applied correction and should then clearly underestimate the population of age eight in 2006 (children under age one in 1998 are supposed to be around eight in 2006).

The choice of the population base has strong consequences on education indicator estimates (table 2A.4). Taking 2006 as an example, it is apparent that whether NSO or UN estimates are chosen, the calculation of apparent intake rate (primary education) leads to the same estimates as far as the reference population (six-year-olds) was corrected both by the NSO and the UN. On the contrary, the MICS estimate is much higher.

Taking into consideration the primary completion rate, the estimates vary from 38.7 percent (UN) to 46–47 percent (NSO or MICS smoothed data). This is due to the corrected estimate of 13-year-olds by the UN while the underestimates remain in both the MICS and NSO projections. As a consequence of these values, and considering that the repeaters' structure is the same for the three estimates, the difference in the GER estimate is striking: it falls from 122 percent to 104 percent when the UN's population is used.

Table 2A.4: Comparison of Some Schooling Indicators According to the Sources of Data Used for the Population Estimates (2006)

	EMIS Data with NSO Projections	MICS Data* Using EMIS Repetition Structure	EMIS Data with UN Estimates
Primary education			
Gross enrollment ratio	122%	110%	103%
Apparent intake rate	149%	157%	150%
Completion rate	46%	43%	39%
Secondary education			
Gross enrollment ratio	20%	22%	18%
Access rate to Form 1	21%	22%	18%
Access rate to Form 4	16%	16%	15%

Sources: Calculation from EMIS 2006 data, NSO projections, UN projections, and MICS data.
* The structure of repetition given by MICS is too fragile to be taken into consideration because the related question was about the grade of attendance year and not clearly about repetition.

The remaining problem with the UN's projections is that they provide information at only the national level, whereas it would be useful to have it per district and region. The proposed solution is then to use the weight of each district in each specific age group of the global population since it has been mentioned previously that this information, from NSO, should not be affected by bias. It would need to previously check the methodology of projection within the district.

Notes

[1] Jameson Ndawala.
[2] This phenomenon of underreporting might be enhanced by the fact that in Malawi, the birth registration certificate has been recently introduced and is far from being generally used by the population.
[3] It seems that the national projections have been displayed among the districts, with no district base projection. This would need to be checked with the NSO.
[4] For more technical information concerning the forecast methodology see http://esa.un.org
[5] unfortunately only for this specific age group

Appendix 2.4: Cross-Sectional Schooling Profiles According to EMIS and UN Population Data

This report uses schooling data from the national EMIS database and compares it to UN population data in order to obtain access rates for each grade of either primary or secondary education.[1] Figure 2A.12 presents the profiles for 2006 and 2007. Each point of the profile is the access rate to the corresponding standard.[2]

The stability of the profile can be first observed between 2006 and 2007, with no major change except intake (that would have decreased from 150 to 142 percent). Focusing on 2007, the global structure of the profile would show very high intake (142 percent for 2007) and a very high level of dropout as well, leading to a 55 percent access rate to Standard 6 and a 39 percent access rate to Standard 8. Moreover, the figures tend to show a higher number of dropouts between standards 1 and 2 and between standards 3 and 4.

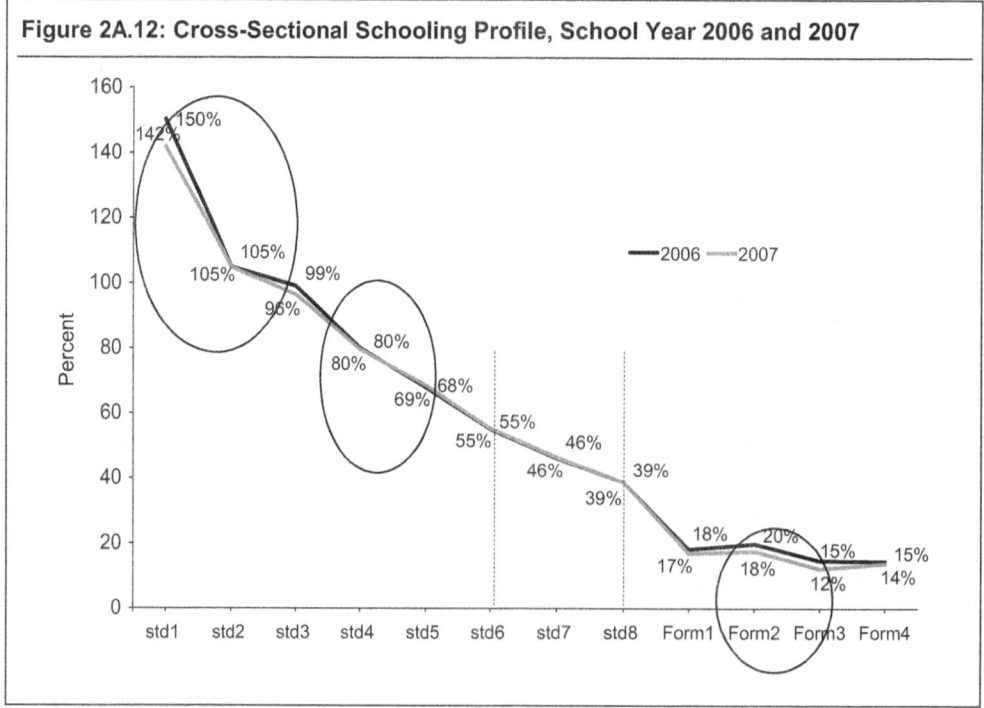

Figure 2A.12: Cross-Sectional Schooling Profile, School Year 2006 and 2007

Source: Calculations from EMIS database 2006 and 2007 and UN 2006 population estimates.

It is surprising that there continues to be such a high level of intake despite the existence of free education since 1994. There are three possible explanations: The first explanation would rely on population underestimates, but even if national estimates from the 1998 census cause problems, there is a consistency for 2007 between UN and NSO estimates for the population of six-year-olds. The second explanation would involve a multi-cohort phenomenon exposed previously, leading to a lot of children who are the official age attending the first standard of the cycle. EMIS 2007 reports that only 49 percent of non-repeaters in Standard 1 have the official age to attend that standard; 2.9 percent are under age and 47.9 percent are over age (ranging from 7 to 12 years old). Moreover, there are no birth registration certificates, so the age of children attending schools are mentioned by parents, with all the confusion this can cause school heads when they try to assess exact ages for children.

The multi-cohort phenomenon could be thus explained, and is certainly part of reality—but is not sufficient in itself—as Malawi primary education has experienced a very high level of intake (more than 150 percent) for several years (table 2A.5).

Table 2A.5: Evolution of Gross Intake Rate (Access Rate to Standard 1) since 2000

2000	2001	2002	2003	2004	2005	2006	2007
180%	181%	170%	158%	158%	150%	150%	142%

Source: Calculation from EMIS 2007 and UN population data.

The last explanation of this level could rely on an underestimate of pupils that repeat the same grade between two consecutive school years. The high number of dropouts between Standard 1 and Standard 2 can come from pupils attending part of the school year and dropping out before the end of Standard 1. There is anecdotal evidence in Malawi that many children who drop out can come back to school either the same school year or the year after, and still be considered as nonrepeaters. If they cannot be considered as repeaters because there is no official decision that makes them repeat, they should not be considered nonrepeaters as well. Being so considered could artificially inflate the number of nonrepeaters and consequently the level of intake. A methodology to correct intake, and access rates to each standard, consists of relying on an alternate repetition structure that would be provided by other information sources than EMIS. This can become possible with household survey data.

Notes

[1] The UN single-age population is used here because the new 2008 census did not provide a single age population for 2007.
[2] Each access rate is computed by dividing the number on non-repeaters of the corresponding standard by the population that is of the official age to attend.

Appendix 2.5: How to Read Educational Pyramids?

The educational pyramids give a rough idea of the school coverage for each level of education and the pupil flow from one level to another. The size of the arrows between levels grows along with the transition rates. The indicators contained in the educational pyramids are detailed below:

Access rate to first grade and access rate to last grade (per level of education)

These are calculated by relating the number of non-repeaters in the first grade and in the last grade of each level of education to the population of children of the official age for each of these grades. For example, for lower secondary education which lasts two years with a theoretical entrance age of 14 years old, we have:

$$\text{Access rate in first grade of lower secondary education} = \frac{\text{Non repeaters}_{\text{first grade}}}{\text{population}_{\text{age 14}}}$$

$$\text{Access rate in last grade of lower secondary education} = \frac{\text{Non repeaters}_{\text{last grade}}}{\text{population}_{\text{age 15}}}$$

For primary education, the access rate in the first grade corresponds to what is known as the Apparent Intake Rate (AIR). When the rate is over 100 percent (late or early entrance for some pupils), it is recapped to 100 percent (access to first grade is considered universal) in the pyramid.

Transition rate (transversal):

In the pyramid, this rate is calculated by relating for a specific year the access rate in the first grade of a level to the access rate in the last grade of the preceding level. To measure the transition rate between primary and lower secondary education for example, the following is used:

$$\text{Transition rate}_{\text{prim/sec1}} = \frac{\text{Access Rate}_{\text{first grade lower sec}}}{\text{Access Rate}_{\text{last grade primary}}}$$

This indicator is an approximation of the actual transition rate calculated by relating the number of nonrepeaters in the first grade of lower secondary education to the number of nonrepeaters in last grade of primary education the year before.

Gross enrollment ratio (GER) for each level:

Number of pupils enrolled in a given level, expressed as a percentage of the population of the official age group for this level of education. For example, for primary education, it is calculated as follows:

$$\text{GER} = \frac{\text{Enrollments in primary}}{\text{Official age groupe population}}$$

This indicator can exceed 100 percent because of repeating and early or late entrance for some children. It is an indicator of the education system's potential ability to enroll the school-age population.

Percentage of technical and vocational training:

The number of pupils following technical and vocational training is related to the total number of pupils in secondary education (general, technical, and vocational).

Figure 2A.13: Educational Pyramid

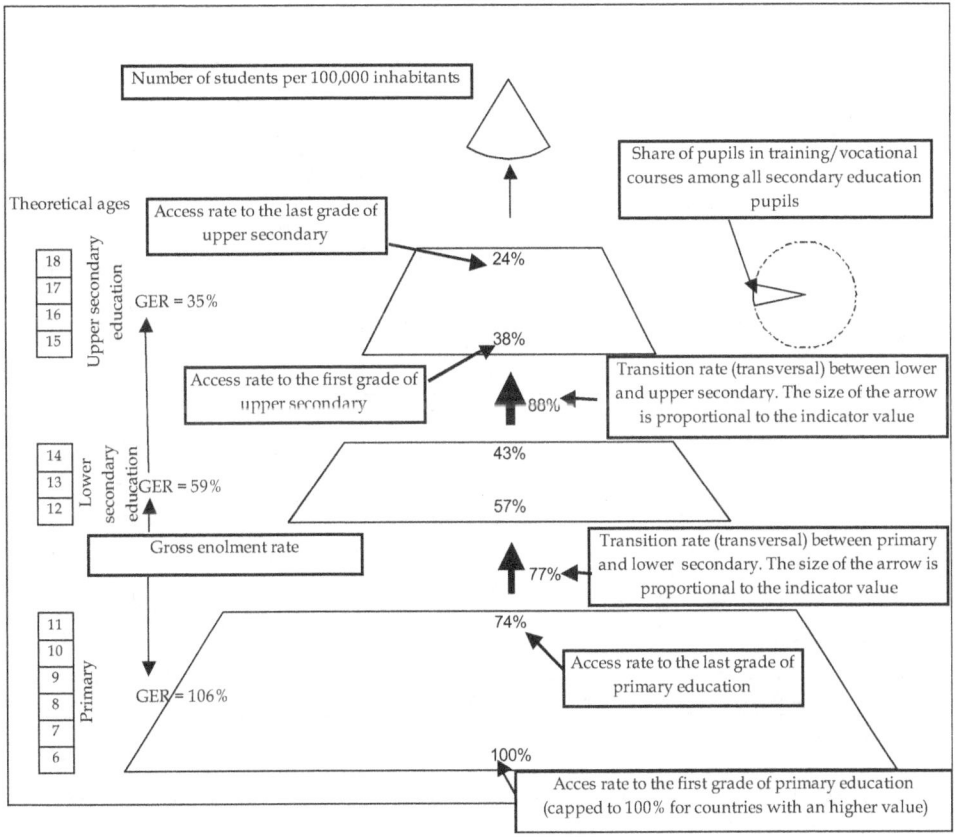

Appendix 2.6: Factors Explaining Why Some Children Never Go to Primary Education

High access probability to Standard 1 (96 percent) must not obscure the issue of the remaining 4 percent (100–96 percent) that never go to school. In order to better understand why there is a remaining access to Standard 1 problem, the information provided by both MICS and IHS data can be used, with which it is possible to comprehend the out-of-school children. Table 2A.10 provides results of a statistical model computed using data from MICS 2006, trying to relate the access probability in Standard 1 with socio economic criteria.

Table 2A.6: Model for Access Rate to Standard 1 Using Household Survey Data

Variable	Modality	Coef.	Marginal Effect[a]	Sign[b]
Dependant variable: Access Rate to Std 1				
Area (ref:urban)	Rural	– 0.047	– 0.001	ns
Gender (ref:male)	Female	0.099	0.003	ns
Income index (ref:q1)[c]	q3	0.239	0.006	**
	q4	0.389	0.009	***
	q5	0.714	0.015	***
Region (ref:northern)	Central	– 0.476	– 0.012	*
	Southern	– 0.795	– 0.022	***
Mother's level of education (ref: primary)	No education	– 1.168	– 0.037	***
	Post-primary	0.852	0.016	***
	Non-formal education	0.266	0.006	ns
Father's level of education (ref: primary)	No education	– 0.578	– 0.018	***
	Post-primary	0.888	0.016	***
	Non-formal education	– 1.897	– 0.125	ns
	Father not in household	– 0.511	– 0.013	***
	Cons.	4.450		***
Number of observation : 11 133 ; Pseudo R2==0.0872; predicted probability = 97.4%				

Source: Calculation from MICS 2006 data.

Notes:
a. The marginal effect is computed on the probability: for instance, according to this model, the probability to access school in the Southern region is 2.2 percent lower than the same probability in the Northern region, all things being equal.
b. ns= non significant, *=10 percent, **=5 percent, ***=1 percent
c. The quintile q2 is not displayed in the model because its coefficient was insignificant (no statistical difference compared to q1).

According to this model, there is no statistically significant difference in the access rate to Std 1 that would rely either on gender or area (urban/rural). Estimated access probabilities do not differ significantly between boys and girls, urban and rural. However, there are some significant differences according to other criteria, even if they remain small:

- Regarding **wealth classification**, children living in the richest 20 percent of households should have an access rate to Standard 1 only 1.5 percent above the same figure for children coming from the poorest 20 percent.
- Differences between **regions** are a little bit more important: the access rate to Standard 1 in the Southern region significantly 2.2 percent lower than in the Northern, while the same figure for the Central region is 1.2 percent lower than in the Northern region.[1]
- **The parents' education** has an increasingly positive effect on access to Standard 1. For instance, children whose mothers have no education have an access rate that is 3.7 percent less than for those whose mother has a primary education level. There is no difference regarding access to Standard 1 between children whose parents have no education and those whose parents have a non-formal education background.

IHS data also provide more qualitative information because the households were asked why children never attend school. Table 2A.11 presents the distribution of reason declared for out of school children aged from 6 to 13.

Table 2A.7: Main Reason Declared for Having Never Attended School (in %)

	6–7 Y.O.	8–9 Y.O.	10–11 Y.O.	12–13 Y.O.	Total
Still too young to attend school	69.1	23.9	8.1	1.5	47.5
No money for fees/uniform	3.9	12.7	12.9	15.4	7.7
No school nearby	4.3	9.2	9	10.4	6.4
Disabled/illness	10	29.2	50	48.5	21.3
Orphaned	3.9	11.3	10.7	10.8	6.8
Not interested/lazy	0.5	2.2	4.2	6.8	1.8
Parents didn't let me in	8.3	11.2	5.2	6.7	8.5
School conflicted with beliefs		0.3			0.1
Total	100	100	100	100	100
Number of individuals (weighted)	213,664	81,272	32,452	31,207	358,595

Source: Calculations from IHS 2004 database.

For children 6–7 years old 69.1 percent, did not enter school because their parents thought they were too young, although 6 is the official age for Standard 1 attendance. This reason is less involved for older children, but remains at the global level the main reason for children of official age not attending school (47.5 percent).

The second major reason expressed was illness and disabilities (21.3 percent), which was major for 8–9 year olds (29.2 percent) and older (around 50 percent). Being orphaned was referred to in 6.8 percent of cases.

The lack of money to pay fees and uniforms was also given as one reason for never attending school (around 13 percent for children between 8–11 and 15 percent for 12–13 year olds). This reason needs to be related to the global issue of free primary education introduced in Malawi in 1994.

Having no school nearby was also reported as the main reason for around 9 percent of children between 8–13 years old. This reason is contrary to the others, a pure supply side issue.

Notes

[1] Regional disparities are discussed in Chapter 5.

Appendix 2.7: Model Result for Retention Explanation, Based on EMIS Data

Table 2A.8: Results of Econometric Model Explaining Retention Rate at the School Level

	Coefficient	Standard Error	T-Student	Sign
% repeaters	−0.242	0.024	−10.000	***
% orphans	0.129	0.031	4.120	***
Pupil-teacher ratio	−0.001	0.000	−9.540	***
Proprietor (ref. religious authority)				
Government	−0.008	0.005	−1.550	ns
Private	0.044	0.022	1.950	*
Region (ref. central)				
Northern	0.013	0.007	2.010	**
Southern	−0.000	0.006	−0.070	ns
Distance to school (ref. <2km)				
between 2 and 2.5km	0.001	0.006	0.160	ns
between 2.5 and 3 km	−0.005	0.009	−0.540	ns
more than 3 km	0.008	0.009	0.900	ns
School has water	−0.003	0.007	−0.340	ns
School has electricity	0.010	0.014	0.710	ns
School has latrine	0.000	0.008	0.010	ns
School has library	0.007	0.011	0.610	ns
% of open-air classrooms	−0.041	0.012	−3.350	***
% of temporary classrooms	−0.027	0.009	−3.150	***
% of civil servant teachers	−0.113	0.053	−2.140	**

Number of observations: 4689; R2=0.057; ** ns=nonsignificant, *=10%, **=5%, ***=1%.

Source: EMIS data.

Appendix 2.8: Quantitative Efficiency of Education Expenditure

It is possible to estimate school life expectancy (SLE) in Malawi, combining the situation of children that never go to school with students' histories according to the distribution of final levels in general education. A cross-section schooling profile, providing access rates to each grade, allows this calculation, but for international comparison purposes, a simplified method based on the average schooling ratio (ASR), derived from the GER per cycle[1] can also be used. The result of this calculation, presented in table 2A.13,[2] gives an average duration of seven years of schooling in Malawi.[3]

Table 2A.9: ASR and School-Life Expectancy Calculation for Malawi (2007)

	Std1–4	Std 5–8	Form 1–2	Form 3–4	Higher Ed.	SLE
GER (a)	136.6%	61.4%	18.3%	14.1%	1.3%	
Duration (b)	4	4	2	2	4	
Ref.pop.	6-9y	10-13y	14-15y	16-17y	18-21y	
% repeaters (c)	22.6%	14.4%	4.4%	6.8%	0.0%	
ASR (d) = (a) x (1-(c))	105.7%	52.5%	17.5%	13.2%	1.3%	
Weighted duration (e)= (d) x (b)	4.23	2.10	0.35	0.26	0.05	7.0

Source: Calculation from EMIS 2007 and UN population estimates.

Figure 2A.14 provides an international comparison on school-life expectancy. This indicator varies between 3.1 (Niger) to 11.4 (Mauritius and South Africa) with an average value of 6.59. Malawi stands above the Africa average, but below the SADC average of 7.53.

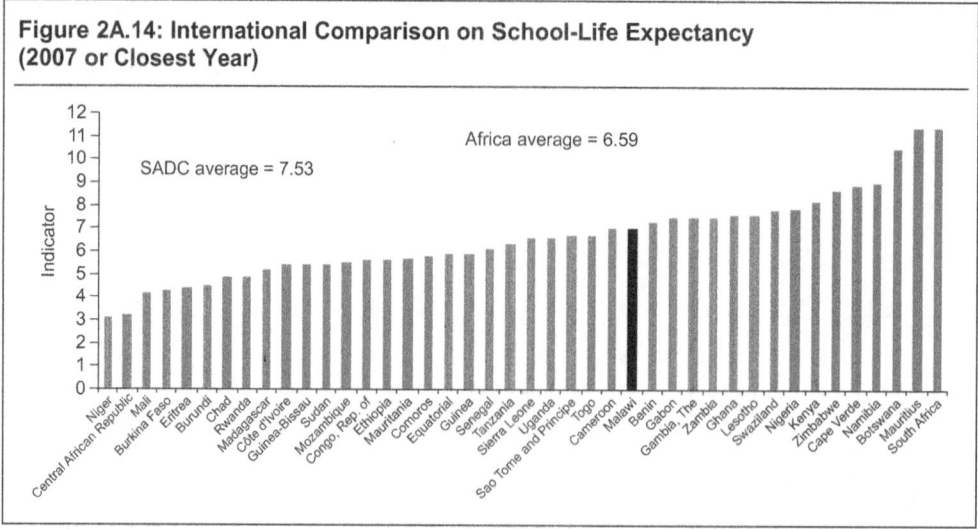

Figure 2A.14: International Comparison on School-Life Expectancy (2007 or Closest Year)

Source: World Bank database.

The issue of efficiency can be addressed in a relatively simple way, both a summary indicator of global educational coverage (school life expectancy) and an estimate of the public resources dedicated to education (Chapter 1) can be used. Both are displayed in table 2A.10, for some low-income African countries.

Table 2A.10: School Life Expectancy, Recurrent Expenditure for Education as a Share of GDP and Index, Low-Income African Countries (2007 or closest Year)

	Education Recurrent Public Expenditure as % of GDP (a)	School Life Expectancy (b)	Efficiency Index (b)/(a)
Central African Republic	1.5	3.9	2.60
Guinea	2	5.2	2.60
Rwanda	2.4	5.3	2.21
Madagascar	2.6	5.4	2.08
Niger	2.6	2.9	1.12
Guinea-Bissau	2.6	6.2	2.38
Mozambique	3	4.7	1.57
Ethiopia	3	4.6	1.53
Malawi	**4.8**	**7**	**1.46**
Mali	3.4	4.2	1.24
Togo	3.4	8.7	2.56
Tanzania	3.6	5.9	1.64
Uganda	3.7	8.1	2.19
Burundi	3.8	3.9	1.03
Gambia	4.1	6.9	1.68
Burkina Faso	4.3	4.2	0.98
Ghana	5.3	7	1.32

Sources: Calculation from Chapter 3 and EMIS data for Malawi, CSRs for the other countries.

Efficiency index as it is computed in table 2A.10 indicates the number of schooling years that the country can supply to its population by spending 1 percent of GDP. In Malawi, the result is 1.46, which is slightly below the average of the selected countries (1.77). Another way to display these results is to display on the same figure both school life expectancy and the share of public resources for education (Figure 2A.15)

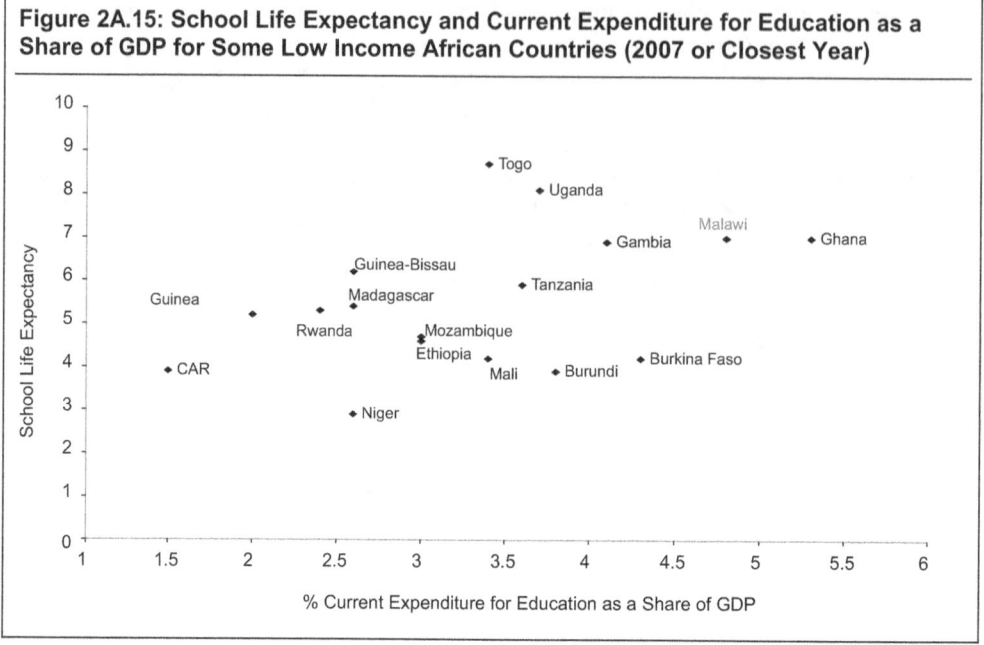

Figure 2A.15: School Life Expectancy and Current Expenditure for Education as a Share of GDP for Some Low Income African Countries (2007 or Closest Year)

Source: Table 2.16.

For a given level of mobilized public resources, there are various situations that offer different levels of schooling coverage. Thus, Malawi belongs to the countries that spend more than others, not being so efficient compared to countries spending less.

Notes

[1] For a given cycle or sub cycle, ASR=GER x (1- % repeaters).
[2] For more detailed presentation, see Pole de Dakar Méthode note n°3 : "Mesurer la couverture scolaire globale d'un pays: l'espérance de vie scolaire."
[3] Calculation with schooling profile lead to 6.2.

Appendix 3.1: Expenditure by Type and Source of Funding

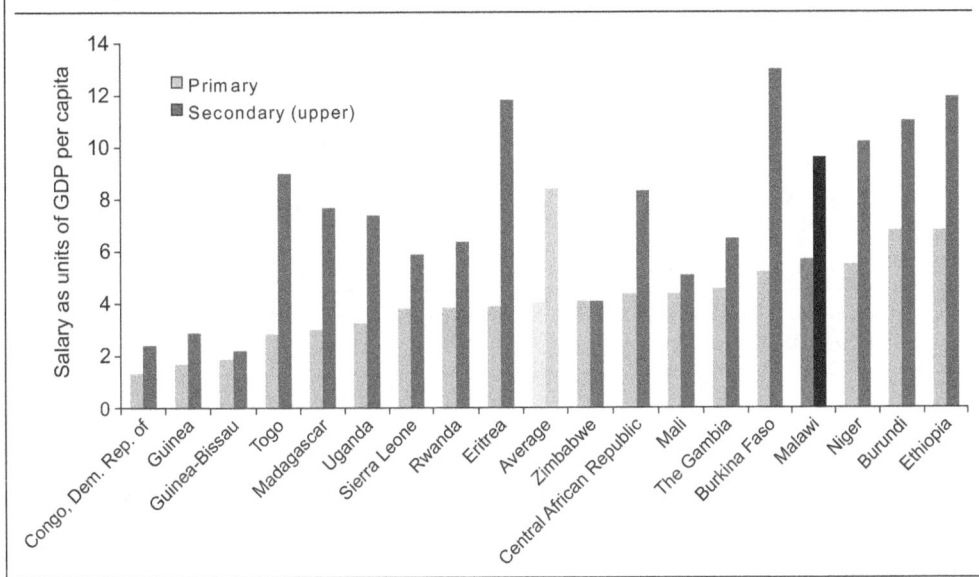

Figure 3A.1: Teachers' Average Salary (Primary and Secondary) as Units of GDP Per Capita for Countries with GDP Per Capita Lower than US$500 (2007 or last year available)

Source: Malawian salary scale and World Bank data.

Note: For comparative purposes, the secondary teachers' average salaries presented for other countries are calculated on upper secondary (the upper secondary is similar in terms of qualifications and duration to the full cycle of secondary in Malawi).

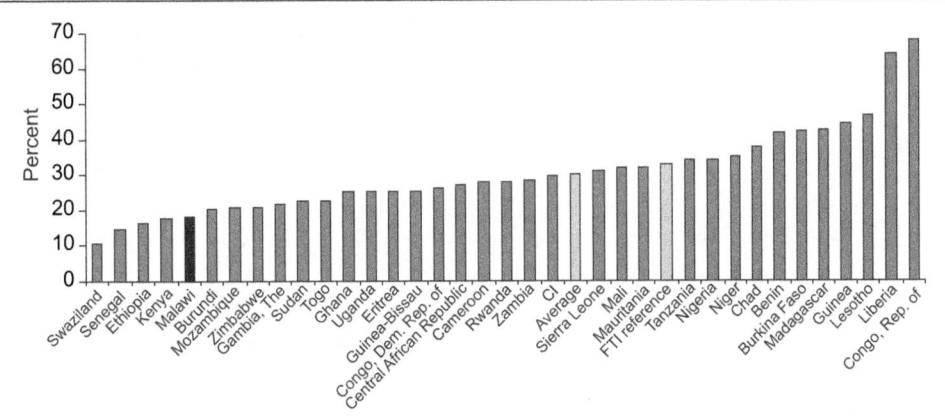

Figure 3A.2: Public Recurrent Expenditure Excluding Teachers' Salaries As a Percentage of Total Recurrent Expenditure (Primary Education) (2007 or last year available)

Source: World Bank data.

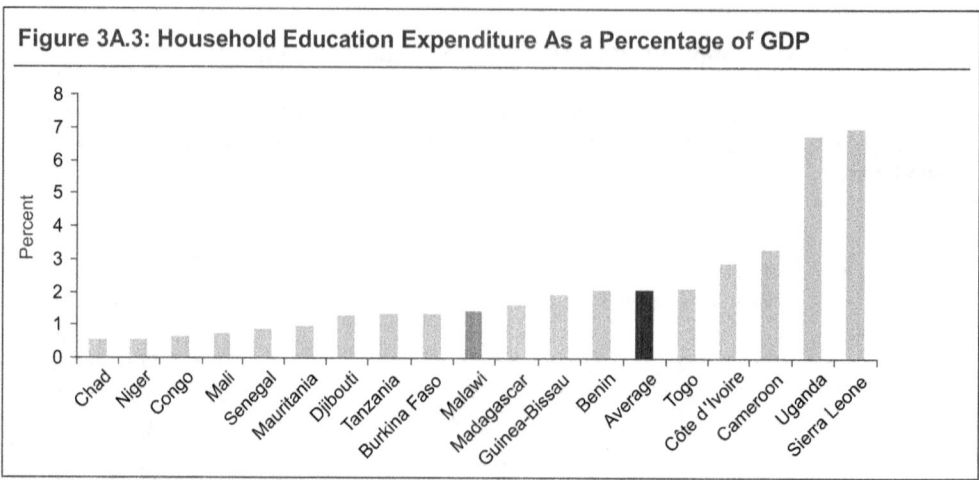

Figure 3A.3: Household Education Expenditure As a Percentage of GDP

Sources: Malawi IHS 2004 and F. Ndem, Education Household Expenditure, Pôle de Dakar, 2008.
Note: Data are from 2008 or thereabouts.

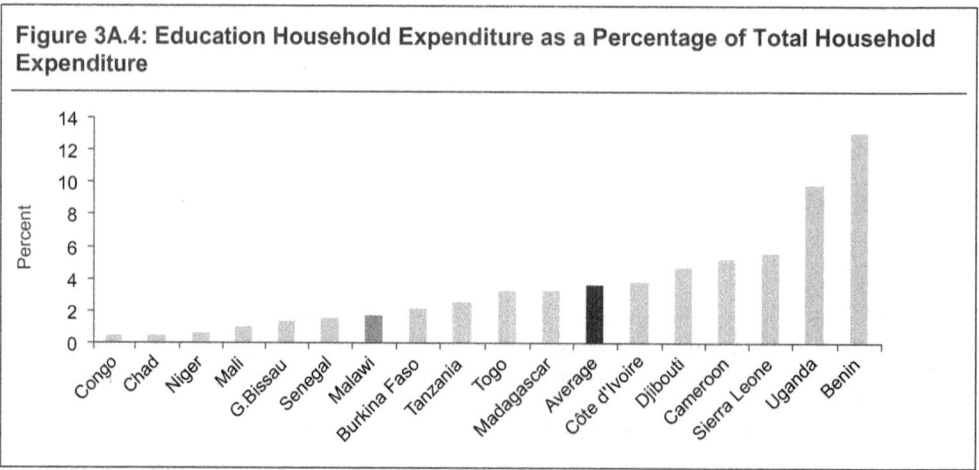

Figure 3A.4: Education Household Expenditure as a Percentage of Total Household Expenditure

Sources: Malawi IHS 2004 and F. Ndem, Education household expenditure, Pôle de Dakar, 2008.
Note: Data are from 2008 or thereabouts.

Appendix 3.2: Ministries with Some Education Activities and Education Institutions Outside of the Ministry of Education

Ministries with Some Education/Training Activities

Home Affairs
Ministry of Agriculture
Ministry of Energy and Mines
Ministry of Finance
Ministry of Labor
Ministry of Local Government
Ministry of Transportation, Public Works and Housing
Ministry of Women and Child Development
Office of the President and Cabinet

Education Institutions outside of the Ministry of Education

ARET (Agricultural Research and Extension Trust)*
College of Music*
Government Print Training School*
Institute of Journalism (under the Polytechnic)
Kamuzu Rehabilitation and Vocational Training Centre for People with Disabilities*
Malawi Army Training Colleges
Malawi College of Accountancy (self-funded)
Malawi Institute of Management
Malawi Institute of Tourism (self-funded)
Malawi Police Training School
Marine Training Centre
Ministry of Agriculture Training (in Malawi)*
Ministry of Public Works and Training—Zomba
Mpwepwe Fisheries Training School*
Natural Forestry Colleges—Dedza
Natural Resources College
School of Aviation*
School of Music (Private & Catholic Church)*
School of Health Sciences*
SDI

* Institutions without explicit expenditure in the financial government's books (have not been included in the total education expenditure)

Appendix 3.3: Recurrent and Capital Allocations to ECD and Adult Literacy

Budget allocations to early childhood development and for adult literacy are given a very low priority. Compared to the other subsectors, the allocated amounts are negligible. As an example, ECD gets an ORT allocation that is no more than MK10 million for all their recurrent activities in the entire country and this was over an extended period (i.e., from 2000–2007).

The ORT allocations to adult literacy improved somewhat from 2003/04–2006/07, after a long period of stagnation while the development allocations fell to MK30 million between 2000/01 and 2003/04 and then rose to MK45 million in 2006/07.

Both adult literacy and Early Childhood Development have very low priority ratings and their total development and recurrent expenditures only rose from MK60 million to MK 145 million from 2003/04 to 2006/07.

As a consequence, the number of children benefiting from ECD intervention is very low, although the benefits to primary education of the development of this level are well documented in education literature.

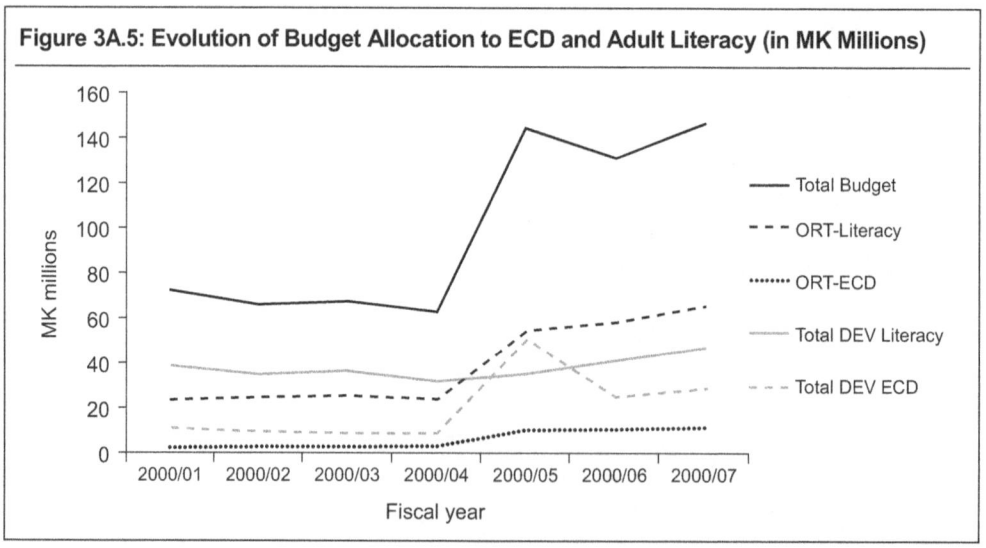

Figure 3A.5: Evolution of Budget Allocation to ECD and Adult Literacy (in MK Millions)

Source: Ministry of Women and Child Development.

Appendix 3.4: Adjustment Methodology for Comparing Distribution of Recurrent Expenditure by Level of Education

In Sub-Saharan Africa, primary education has a duration that ranges from four to eight years (the Malawian case) and secondary education varies from four (in Malawi) to seven years. The most common duration structure in Africa is six years of primary education and seven years of secondary education. To be able to compare across countries the distribution of expenditure by level of education, it is necessary to recalibrate expenditure data. The recalibration is a way of estimating what would be the distribution of expenditure by level of education if the country would have the most common structure (six years of primary and seven years of secondary). For comparative purposes and because data are not fully available in all countries, ECD, literacy, and primary teacher training are included in the primary education level and TEVET and secondary teacher training are included in secondary education. Then, the expenditure is broken down among the three big levels of education: primary education (including ECD, literacy, and primary teacher training); secondary education (including TEVET and secondary teacher training); and higher education. The recalibration of data for a country which has not the most common duration structure is done as presented in table 3A.1.

Table 3A.1: Methodology of Recalibration to a 6–7 Year Duration Structure

	% (Non-Calibrated)	Duration (in Years)	% Estimate for a 6-7 Year Duration Structure	% Calibrated*
Primary	P	Dp	P6=6 x P / Dp	P6 x (100%-H) / (T-H)
Secondary	S	Ds	S7=7 x S / Ds	S7 x (100%-H) / (T-H)
Higher	H		H	H
Total	100%		T=P6+S7+H	100%

Source: Compiled by authors.
* The last calibration is made to get back to a 100 percent total.

In Malawi's case, the calibration applies as shown in table 3A.2.

Table 3A.2: Recalibration of Malawian 2008 Recurrent Expenditure Data

	% (Non-Calibrated)	Duration (in Years)	% Estimate for a 6-7 Year Duration Structure	% Calibrated*
Primary	47.6%	8	P6=35.7%	32.5%
Secondary	25.3%	4	S7=44.3%	40.4%
Higher	27.1%		27.1%	27.1%
Total	100%		T=107.1%	100%

Source: Compiled by authors.
* The last calibration is made to get back to a 100 percent total.

Appendix 3.5: Comparative Data on Expenditure Breakdown in Higher Education

Table 3A.3: Breakdown of Public Recurrent Expenditure in Higher Education, African Countries (2007 or last year available)

	Year	Personnel Emolument	ORT	Student Welfare
Benin	2006	33%	26%	41%
Burkina Faso	2006	34%	23%	43%
Burundi	2004	37%	21%	42%
Central African Republic	2005	48%	3%	49%
Chad	2003	24%	29%	46%
Congo	2005	75%	10%	15%
Côte d'Ivoire	2007	47%	36%	18%
Djibouti	2006	53%	47%	0%
Ethiopia	2002	44%	38%	18%
Guinea	2005	59%	15%	26%
Guinea Bissau	2006	63%	37%	0%
Madagascar	2006	53%	23%	24%
Malawi	**2008**	**61%**	**27%**	**13%**
Mali	2004	24%	25%	51%
Mauritania	2004	44%	34%	21%
Niger	2002	36%	10%	55%
Rwanda	2003	65%	7%	28%
Sierra Leone	2004	78%	7%	15%
Average		49%	23%	28%

Sources: Revised 07/08 budget (Ministry of Finance and calculations) for Malawi, and World Bank data for the other countries.

Appendix 3.6: Teachers' Salaries in Primary and Secondary Education by Category of Teachers

Primary school teachers can be grouped into eight categories (Table 3A.4). H is the category with the highest average annual salary and L the category with the lowest. Volunteer teachers are paid by SMCs and are not on government payroll.

Table 3A.4: Primary Education Salaries

Category	% in Gov't.-Funded Schools (EMIS 2007)	Annual Average Salary			
		2007 (Payroll)		2008 (New Scale Mid-Point)	
		MK (000)	as Units of GDP per Capita	MK (000)	as Units of GDP per Capita
H	0.3%	533	14.9	684	19.1
I	1.4%	452	12.7	552	15.4
J	6.4%	348	9.8	384	10.7
K	21.4%	264	7.4	274	7.7
L	59.1%	159	4.4	196	5.5
Month to month	3.4%	depends on their grade when they retired			
Temporary teachers	1.5%	129	3.6	129	3.6
Volunteers	6.5%	—	—	—	—
Total	100.0%	195	5.5	225	6.3

Source: EMIS 2007, salary scale.

Table 3A.5: Secondary Education Salaries

Category	% in Gov't.-Funded Schools (EMIS 2007)	Annual Average Salary			
		2007 (Payroll)		2008 (New Scale Mid-Point)	
		MK (000)	as Units of GDP per Capita	MK (000)	as Units of GDP per Capita
F	0.8%	802	22.5	990	27.7
G	4.6%	620	17.4	777	21.8
H	3.0%	533	14.9	684	19.1
I	39.5%	452	12.7	552	15.4
J	8.2%	348	9.8	384	10.7
K	21.1%	264	7.4	274	7.7
L	22.9%	159	4.4	196	5.5
Total	100.0%	350	9.8	416	11.6

Source: EMIS 2007, salary scale.

Appendix 4.1: Internal Efficiency and Resources Management

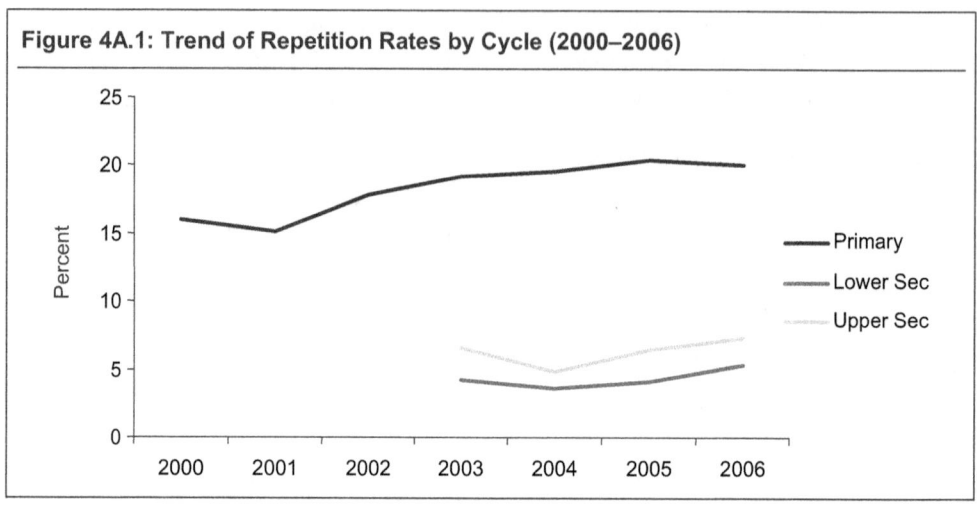

Figure 4A.1: Trend of Repetition Rates by Cycle (2000–2006)

Sources: EMIS 2000–2007.

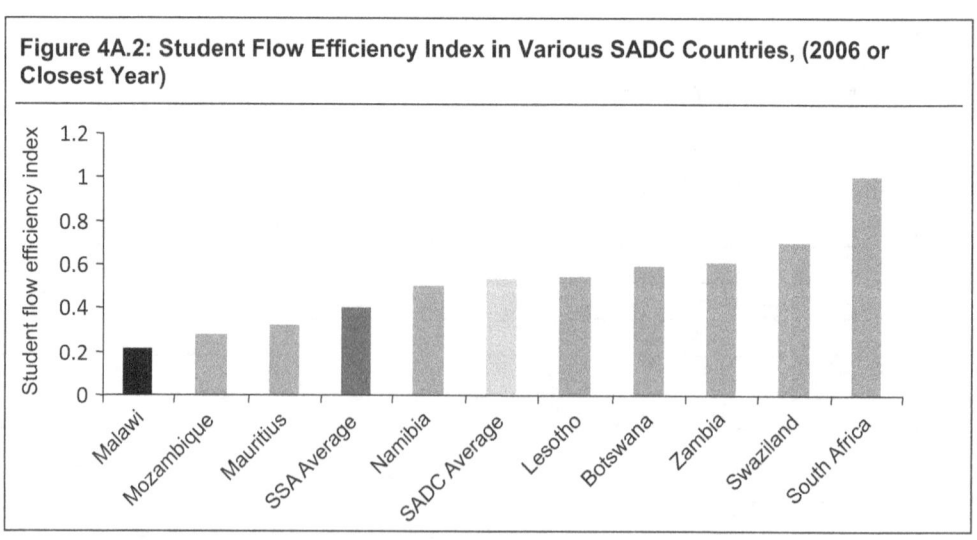

Figure 4A.2: Student Flow Efficiency Index in Various SADC Countries, (2006 or Closest Year)

Source: World Bank data 2009.

Figure 4A.3: Internal Efficiency Coefficient (IEC) in SADC Countries (2006 or Closest Year)

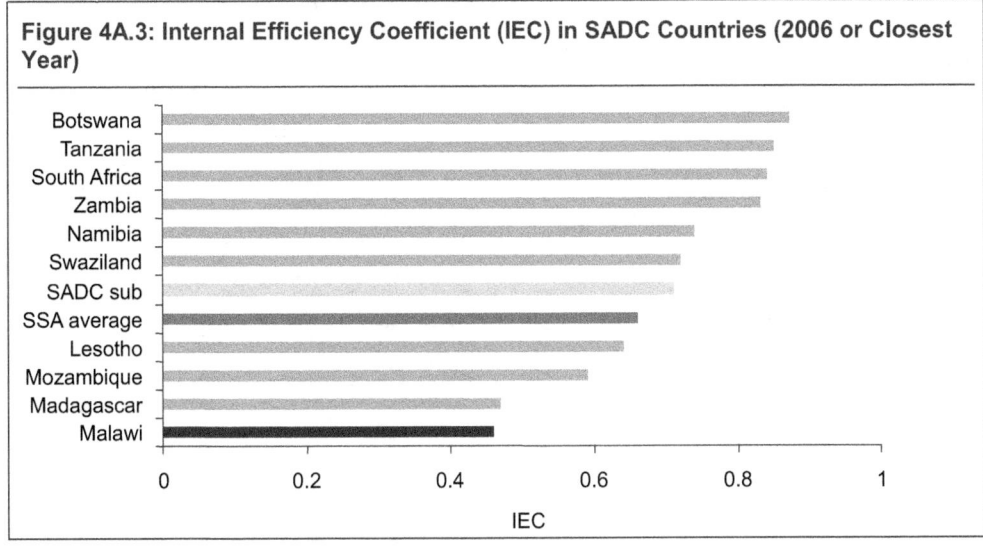

Source: World Bank data 2009.
Note: Based on a primary cycle of six years to allow for comparison.

Table 4A.1: Degree of Randomness ($1 - R^2$) in Public Teacher Allocations in Various African Countries (2002–2007)

Country	Gov't.-Funded Teachers (in %)	Gov't.-Funded and Volunteer/ Community Teachers	Country	Gov't.- Funded Teachers (in %)	Gov't.-Funded and Volunteer/ Community Teachers (in %)
Guinea (2004)	7	n.a.	Congo (2005)	38	35
Lesotho (2003)	18	—	**Malawi (2007)**	**42**	**42**
Niger (2003)	19	n.a.	CAR (2005)	46	24
Guinea-Bissau (2006)	20		Burundi (2004)	50	—
Burkina Faso (2007)	22	—	Benin (2006)	54	39
Mauritania (2004)	22		Cameroon (2002)	n.a.	45
Ethiopia (2002)	28	—	Mali (2004)	n.a.	27
Chad (2004)	33	34	**Average**	**31**	**35**

Sources: various CSR; Malawi: EMIS, 2007.
n.a. = not available.

Figure 4A.4: Consistency of Allocation of ORT at the Primary Level According to Enrollment at the District Level (2007/08)

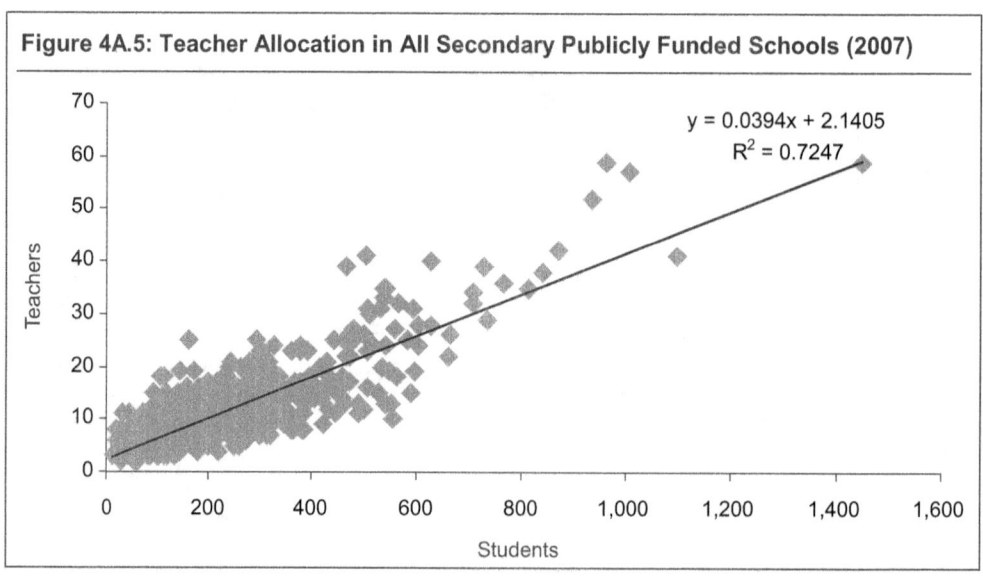

$y = 96.92x + 3E+06$
$R^2 = 0.8707$

Sources: ORT: 2007 budget data, enrollment; EMIS 2007.

Figure 4A.5: Teacher Allocation in All Secondary Publicly Funded Schools (2007)

$y = 0.0394x + 2.1405$
$R^2 = 0.7247$

Source: EMIS 2007.

The Education System in Malawi   245

Figure 4A.6: Coherence on Allocation of ORT Funds at the Secondary School Level (For Cost Center Schools and Grant-Aided Secondary Schools)

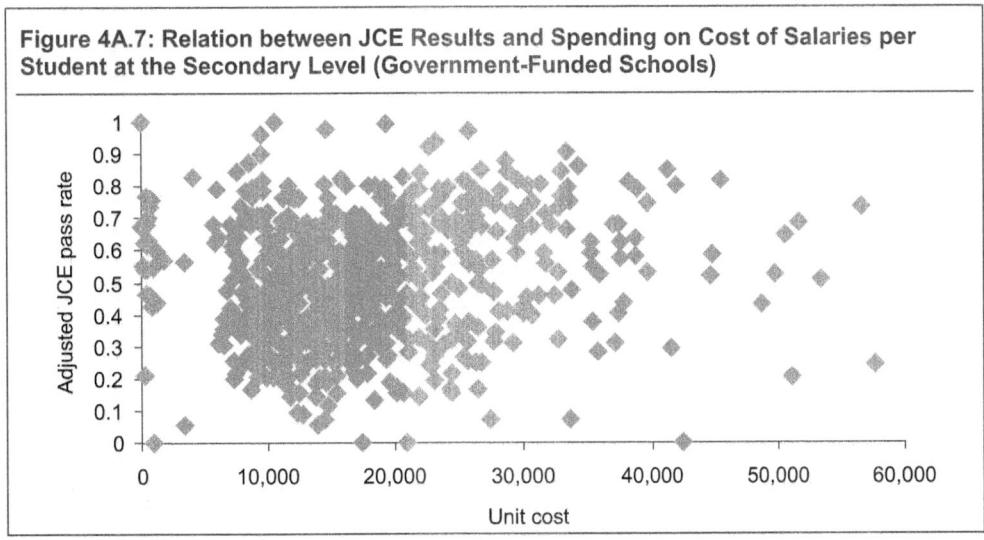

Sources: ORT 2007 budget data, enrollment; EMIS 2007.
Note: Based on 211 schools for which information is available (Cost center CSSs and CDSSs and grant-aided schools).

Figure 4A.7: Relation between JCE Results and Spending on Cost of Salaries per Student at the Secondary Level (Government-Funded Schools)

Sources: EMIS 2007, budget law 2008.
Note: Unit costs include school teachers and support-staff related expenses.

Figure 4A.8: Relation between MSCE Results and Spending on Cost of Salaries per Student at the Secondary Level (Government-Funded Schools)

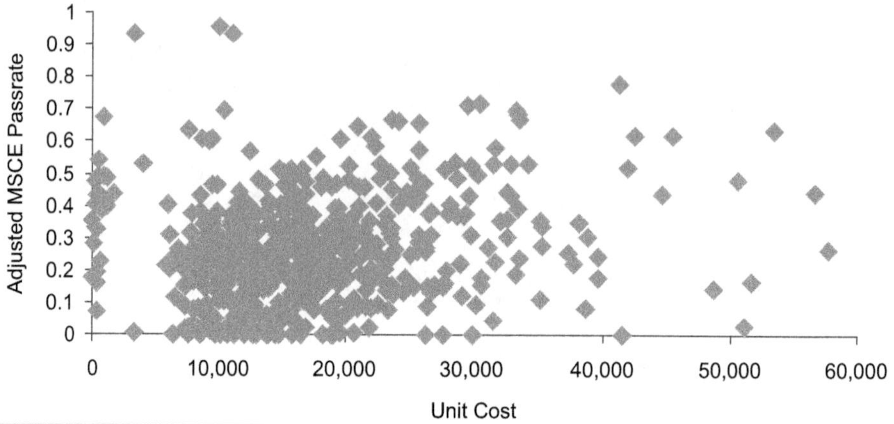

Sources: EMIS 2007, budget law 2008.
Note: Unit costs include school teachers and support staff-related expenses.

Appendix 4.2: SACMEQ Levels Definitions

Table 4A.2: Reading and Mathematics Skill Levels

Level	Reading	Mathematics
Level 1	**Pre-reading**: Locates familiar words in a short (one line) text. Matches words to pictures. Uses letters to help identify unknown words. Follows short, familiar instructions.	**Pre-numeracy:** Counts illustrated objects. Recognizes basic numbers and shapes. Carries out simple single operations of addition and subtraction
Level 2	**Emergent reading**: Reads familiar words. Identifies some new words. Uses simple, familiar prepositions and verbs to interpret new words. Matches words and phrases. Uses pictures for clues. Reads short simple texts with simple repetitive patterns	**Emergent numeracy:** Links simple verbal, Figureic, and number forms with single arithmetic operations on whole numbers up to two digits. Recognizes common shapes or figures in two-dimensions. Estimates accurately lengths of simple shapes
Level 3	**Basic reading**: Uses context and simple sentence structures to match words and short phrases. Uses phrases within sentences as units of meaning.	**Basic numeracy:** Recognizes three-dimensional shapes and number units. Uses a single arithmetic operation in two or more steps. Deals with place value and effects of a single operation.
Level 4	**Reading for meaning**: Interprets new words by referring to word parts. Interpret sentences and parafigure level texts. Matches phrases across sentences. Uses information outside the text to confirm opinion. Able to locate information in longer text passages.	**Beginning numeracy:** Interprets a visual or verbal prompt in order to count, recognize shape, number and time. Uses a single familiar basic (add, subtract, multiply, or divide) in simple arithmetic, measurement, and data tasks
Level 5	**Inferential reading**: Interprets and makes inferences from different types of more complex texts. Extracts information from unusually formatted text. Interprets maps, tables, and figures. Makes judgment about the author's intended purpose	**Competent numeracy:** Carries out multiple and different arithmetic operations using visual or verbal prompts where the order of operations is important. Converts basic measurement units. Understands the order of magnitude of simple fractions
Level 6	**Analytical reading**: Combines several pieces of information from a range of locations in complex and lexically dense text or documents. Analyzes detailed text or extended documents for underlying message. Identifies meaning from different styles of writing.	**Mathematically skilled:** Conducts multiple steps with a range of basic operations in a strict sequence using an analysis of a short verbal or visual prompt. Deals with three-dimensional perspective. Applies operations to units of time. Uses basic operations (additional and subtraction) on mixed numbers, multiplies larger numbers.
Level 7	**Critical reading**: Uses the structures of text to identify author's assumptions/aims/views and evaluates them. Offers a critical analysis of text.	**Concrete problem solving:** Can perform complex and detailed mathematical skills that require detailed knowledge of mathematics not supplied in the task. These tasks involve abstraction of verbal, visual, and tabular information into symbolic forms and algebraic solutions. Understands use of extended verbal or Figureic prompt (involving an analysis of steps) to identify correct sequence of calculations. Uses range of arithmetic operations on mixed number systems. Applies external knowledge or rules for problem solving. Converts and operates on units of measurement including time, distance and weight.
Level 8	**Insightful reading**: Identifies the author's motives, biases, beliefs, and suggestions in order to understand the main theme of the text. Interprets analogy and allegory and deeper significance and cohesiveness of ideas in the text.	**Abstract problem solving**: Identifies nature of problem, translates the information given into a mathematical approach and then identifies strategy for solving problems. Can readily apply the strategy and solve the problem. This is higher-order numeracy involving mathematical insight.

Source: SACMEQ 2005 report.

Appendix 4.3: Examination Pass Rates Analysis

Table 4A.3: Correlates of PSLE Results at National Level (2006)—Basic Statistics

Regression Variable	Sample Average	Min Max	Year
Pass rate	70.3%	0-100	2006
Contextual factors			2006
Division			
Northern	27.0%		
Central Eastern	19.0%		
Central Western	19.6%		
Southern Eastern	13.5%		
Southern Western	10.4%		
Shire Highlands	10.5%		
Location			
Urban	4.2%		
Rural	95.8%		
Type of school			
Government	30.6%		
Religious agency	67.3%		
Private	2.1%		
Classroom/pedagogical organization			2005–2006
STR>60	73.6%		
% of repeaters	19.7%	0-61.8	
Week teaching time (hour)	19.8h	0.2-48.1	
At least 1 book for 2 students (Chichewa) (Ref :less than one book per two students)	28.5%	0-100	
School conditions			2006
Single shift	84.1%		
Overlapping shift	15.9%		
Permanent classrooms	72.5%	0-100	
Temporary classrooms	15.0%	0-100	
Open-air classrooms	12.5%	0-100	
Has a library	7.4%		
Has latrines	92.4%		
Has electricity	5.4%		
Has water	89.2%		
PTA/SMC is active	89.1%		
Teacher characteristics			2005-2006
Proportion of female teachers	25.7%	0-99	
Proportion of teachers who are			
Civil servant	79.1%	0-100	
Temporary	10.9%	0-100	
Month-to-Month	3.6%	0-67.5	
volunteers	6.5%	0-100	
Proportion of teachers with			
PSLCE	0.6%	0-33.3	
JCE	49.5%	0-100	
MSCE	49.7%	0-100	
Higher education diploma/degree	0.2%	0-60	
Nb of Observations	3494		

Source: EMIS 2005, 2006, 2007.

Table 4A.4: Correlates of MSCE Results at National Level (2006)—Basic Statistics

Regression variable	Sample Average	Min. Max.
Pass rate	38.0	0-100
Contextual factors		
Division		
Northern	22.2%	
Central Eastern	16.4%	
Central Western	22.1%	
Southern Eastern	11.8%	
Southern Western	15.6%	
Shire Highlands	11.9%	
Location		
Urban	15.6%	
Rural	84.4%	
Type of school		
CSS	13.1%	
CDSS	60.4%	
Open school	2.5%	
Private	24.0%	
Classroom/pedagogical organization		
STR	21.7	3.6–122.2
% of repeaters	4.8%	0–53.1
Books per student	3.7	0–100.5
School conditions		
Type of classroom		
Permanent	94.6%	0–100
Temporary	5.4%	0–100
School facilities		
Has a library	44.0%	
Has a lab	23.0%	
Has latrines	84.9%	
Has electricity	38.4%	
Has water	83.3%	
PTA/SMC is active	75.8%	
Teacher characteristics		
Proportion of female teacher	14.6%	0–84.2
Proportion of teachers who are		
Not known	23.6%	0–100
I level	18.8%	0–100
H/G level	4.4%	0–70
F level	0.8	0–45
K/L/M/I level/primary (PT4-PT1)	52.3%	0–100
Proportion of teachers with		
PSLCE/JCE	1%	0–100
MSCE	68.0%	0–100
Higher education diploma/degree in education	23.5%	0–100
Higher education diploma/degree – non-education	7.5%	0–92.8
Nb of Observations	714	714

Source: EMIS 2006, 2007.

Table 4A.5: Some Characteristics of CSSs and CDSSs

	CSSs	CDSSs
Number and % of schools	141 (13.5%)	575 (55%)
% in rural areas	81%	92%
Number and % of students	55 464 (26.5%)	99 172 (47.4%)
School size	394	172
Number of teachers	2 662	4 813
% qualified teachers	72.9%	19.3%
% of female teachers	25.8%	20%
PTR	21:1	21:1
PqTR	29:1	107:1
Books/student	2.2	1.1
Has water	91.5%	92%
Has electricity	76.6%	21.3%
Has a library	82.2%	33.9%
Has a lab	74.5%	10.4%
House/teachers	0.47	0.25
Government grants per student	MK 5827 (52.5% of schools)	MK 1525 (14.4% of schools)
Share of government grants	86%	13%

Source: EMIS 2007.

Appendix 4.4: Consistency in Resource Allocations

Table 4A.6: Consistency of Teacher Allocation across Government-Funded Primary Schools at District Level (2007)

		Without Volunteers			With Volunteers		
	District	R^2 (in %)	STR	SqTR	R^2 (in %)	STR	SqTR
Central Eastern	Kasungu	55.0	83	89	56.0	80	85
	Nkhotakota	75.0	84	90	74.2	81	86
	Dowa	49.0	89	96	49.0	86	93
	Ntchisi	40.3	72	83	40.3	68	79
	Salima	56.5	87	97	56.4	80	92
Central Western	Mchinji	73.7	86	92	74.2	84	87
	Lilongwe City	61.5	44	46	61.5	44	46
	Lilongwe Rural East	66.2	101	108	66.8	98	102
	Lilongwe Rural West	43.8	79	83	44.2	78	81
	Dedza	28.2	110	120	38.1	96	113
	Ntcheu	43.9	102	111	47.4	89	104
Northern	Chitipa	56.4	68	73	47.5	61	70
	Karonga	77.3	78	82	72.9	70	79
	Rumphi	82.6	63	69	83.6	53	64
	Mzimba North	54.2	86	91	55.9	74	87
	Mzimba South	53.6	80	85	53.3	74	81
	Mzuzu City	91.4	44	45	91.4	44	45
	Nkhata Bay	52.7	95	102	50.7	78	96
	Likoma	93.6	51	54	93.8	49	51
Shire Highlands	Chiradzulu	33.8	86	90	33.8	86	87
	Thyolo	52.9	100	104	53.7	99	101
	Mulanje	55.9	110	114	55.9	109	110
	Phalombe	55.7	135	138	55.7	135	136
Southern Eastern	Mangochi	67.9	129	135	70.2	110	132
	Balaka	54.7	94	102	57.2	85	97
	Machinga	41.5	117	122	44.3	109	118
	Zomba Urban	85.8	37	38	85.8	37	38
	Zomba Rural	41.5	107	117	48.4	91	111
Southern Western	Blantyre City	57.7	50	51	57.7	50	51
	Blantyre Rural	71.1	71	77	71.9	68	73
	Mwanza	48.2	82	86	55.7	72	83
	Chikwawa	53.0	130	136	52.9	114	131
	Nsanje	65.4	116	126	66.7	98	120
	Neno	69.4	89	98	67.6	83	93

Source: EMIS 2007.

Table 4A.7: Consistency in Book Allocation across Government-Funded Primary Schools, by Divisions: R^2 Analysis

	Std1	Std2	Std3	Std4	Std5	Std6	Std7	Std8
English								
Northern	2.6	24.9	27.2	30.9	36.6	25.8	41.7	24.7
Central Eastern	0.9	13.6	12.9	14.4	14.1	15.3	22.9	18.0
Central Western	0.4	22.9	29.7	31.9	35.4	34.0	35.3	21.7
South Eastern	0.4	19.7	19.5	24.1	21.8	20.4	12.8	12.6
South Western	3.4	27.2	37.8	56.1	56.3	36.3	38.2	34.4
Shire Highlands	0.3	16.5	11.8	13.0	14.6	23.2	18.7	23.7
Chichewa								
Northern	2.4	24.3	16.7	32.4	43.6	44.6	48.1	41.6
Central Eastern	1.7	13.4	13.4	17.6	22.6	14.2	20.6	21.1
Central Western	0.5	19.8	28.9	25.9	34.3	32.3	28.4	22.5
South Eastern	0.6	16.7	22.9	21.2	30.9	34.2	37.0	18.2
South Western	5.2	28.2	41.3	54.7	49.9	42.6	42.4	35.7
Shire Highlands	0.4	13.0	15.3	11.4	14.4	23.0	20.0	15.2
Mathematics								
Northern	2.5	18.2	22.7	36.5	34.0	35.1	21.1	27.0
Central Eastern	0.8	9.8	12.6	13.7	15.4	20.9	24.3	22.9
Central Western	0.4	14.3	29.9	29.3	26.6	30.5	26.6	21.9
South Eastern	0.5	13.8	17.5	18.6	19.1	28.5	14.9	18.0
South Western	5.0	30.1	36.7	58.9	60.1	50.1	46.1	40.3
Shire Highlands	0.4	13.1	10.5	10.8	16.0	23.1	18.8	21.5

Source: EMIS 2007.

Appendix 4.5: Teacher Training

At the Primary Level

Malawi has experienced a few modes of training teachers over the years. Historically, up to 1994, teacher training for primary schools was a two-year pre-service program at a Teacher Training College (TTC) and all prospective teachers had to undergo this training before being engaged to teach. However there was the **MASTEP (Malawi Special Teacher Education Programme)** which used to train teachers, using the distance mode, at that same time. The MASTEP trained a teacher for three years so that by the end of the training period a MASTEP-trained teacher had covered the same syllabus as the ones who were training for two years in a residential mode. The MASTEP teacher was being trained while on the job.

The one-year teacher training program came into being in 1993 to replace both the two-year training and the MASTEP, and was run up until 1997. The objective was to increase qualified teacher numbers since teachers would be produced annually. However, this did not pay off because of the sudden introduction of free primary education (FPE) in 1994, which increased enrollment to about 3.2 million. A new program was designed to accelerate teacher training to meet the enrollment boom of the FPE. This was called **MIITEP, the Malawi Integrated In-service Teacher Education Program**.

Twenty-two thousand temporary teachers were recruited to be trained on the job before they could be engaged as full-time teachers. This training was partly residential but more time was devoted to distance learning while on the job. Initially, three cohorts of students went through the residential training in a year, which was later reduced to two in the year 2000 due to concerns with quality.

In 2006, the Ministry of Education introduced an improved mode of training teachers. This was called the 1+1 model or the Initial Primary Teachers Education Programme (IPTE). This meant that trainees would be one year in a TTC followed by another one year hands-on in a school under supervision by all the stakeholders (eg., the head teachers, mentor teachers, PEAs, college lecturers and ministry officials). Mentorship is another component of the IPTE program. Student teachers are assisted by trained mentor teachers in the second year of their training. This is the current training mode of teachers. The new distance mode of training primary school teachers, to start in 2009, will be a two-and-a-half-year program.

The recruitment of trainee primary school teachers is done by the Department of Teacher Education and Development (DTED) in liaison with the department of Human Resource Management and Development in the Ministry of Education. The appointment and disciplinary committee in the ministry selects student teachers using an aptitude test. The requirements for selection are that candidates should posses an MSCE with a credit pass in English and a pass in Mathematics and any one Science subject; be not more than 35 years of age; be ready to work in the rural areas ; and pass an aptitude test in numerical, communication, and reasoning skills.

The IPTE is mostly carried out in the five public and four private primary teacher training institutions. During the training, student teachers get an upkeep allowance of MK1,500.00 per month during the college-based phases and MK5,000.00 per month during the school-based phases. These allowances are paid by colleges from their ORT. The student teachers are also assisted professionally by trained mentor teachers during the field phase. The allowance for the field phase is not adequate considering the rise in the prices of commodities. (There is aneed to review it.)

From next year, October 2009, the total number of student teachers to be recruited will be 4,290. This will be after the completion of Liwonde TTC first phase and the expansion of St. Josephs TTC. The conventional mode of IPTE training has a non-residential progam component where 500 student teachers find their own accommodations outside of the campus. However, they enjoy the same privileges the residential student teachers do (e.g., meals at the college, teaching and learning materials). After qualifying from the TTCs, these teachers sign a bond before being deployed to teach in the rural areas for a period of not less than five years.

In 2009, the ministry will introduce the effective training of primary school teachers through distance mode. The decision to start this mode of training teachers was arrived at after realizing that the rate of teacher production cannot match the loss. The current TTCs do not have sufficient capacity to produce the required number of teachers to meet the projected target of 1:60 by 2017. The intake for the program will be 4,000 student teachers. Each student teacher will be attached to a study center / TDC and a college. Two hundred study center supervisors will be recruited for the program. Recruitment of open and distance learning (ODL) student teachers will be done locally, targeting those schools that have acute shortage of teachers. By 2012, the ministry will have recruited 12,000 student teachers through the program in addition to the yearly output of 4,000 teachers through the conventional mode from 2011.

All trained teachers are expected to perform and are all subjected to CPD. How the teacher is trained only depends on when that teacher-to-be was recruited and under what conditions.

At the Secondary Level

Secondary school teachers are trained at diploma and degree level. At diploma level, they are trained at Domasi College of Education which also started offering Bachelor of Education degree in primary education. The diploma program is offered as a preservice through conventional and distance mode of training. The distance mode targets under qualified teachers teaching in CDSSs. The University of Malawi and Mzuzu University are the main providers of degree programs.

The ministry of Education on the other hand piloted a program called Strengthening Mathematics and Science in Secondary Education (SMASSE). This program was introduced to remedy the low achievements of students in mathematics and science. It was piloted from 2004 to 2007 in the South Eastern Education division. On the basis of the achievements of the program, SMASSE is now being rolled out to the remaining divisions. The second phase will run from 2008 to 2012 and each division will have three INSET. Although the main focus of this intervention is the teacher, the main target is the learner in the classroom.

Other upgrading courses for teachers in Malawi:

- Domasi College of Education is running three programs aimed at improving the number of qualified teachers at secondary school level:

- 220 under-qualified teachers are admitted to upgrade to diploma level every year in subjects of their choice through distance mode and residential sessions at Domasi College of Education.
- 220 students are admitted to the normal entry program every year to study for a diploma in education in subjects of their choice. Out of these, 60 percent are recruited from serving primary school teachers.
- Up to 400 under-qualified teachers will be trained to diploma level in science subjects over the next three years with funding from the Africa Development Fund.
- Bachelor of Education degree in primary introduced at Domasi College of Education to reduce teacher shortage in TTCs. This targets qualified T2 teachers and secondary school graduates.
- An upgrading course at Chancellor College for TTC lecturers with diplomas to bachelors degree. This is supported by the Scottish government.
- Masters degree program for 19 TTC lecturers, including two DTED staff through Open and Distance Learning, sponsored by UNESCO through Indira Ghandi National Open University.

At the secondary school level, CPD is organized at cluster level.

Appendix 5.1: Internal Efficiency Tables by Gender

Table 5A.1: Repetition Rate Trends by Standard in Primary, 1999 and 2006 (All Types of Schools)

	Std 1	Std2	Std3	Std4	Std5	Std6	Std7	Std8
2006								
Male	24.8	21.9	23.4	17.9	16.4	13.2	11.0	16.4
Female	24.3	21.0	22.2	16.6	15.7	12.5	11.2	14.5
Total	24.5	21.4	22.8	17.2	16.1	12.8	11.1	15.6
1999 Total*	18.8	16.6	16.6	13.9	11.7	11.3	10.1	13.9

Sources: * CSR 2004; EMIS 2006, 2007.
Note: Repetition is calculated here as the number of repeaters in Standard X in year t divided by the total enrollment in Standard X in year t – 1. Thus, repetition refers to the year t – 1.

Table 5A.2: Repetition Rates by Form in Secondary, 2007 (All Types of Schools)

	Form 1	Form 2	Form 3	Form 4
Female	0.8	7.7	1.8	11.1
Male	1.1	12.1	2.9	13.6
Total	1.0	9.8	2.2	12.1

Source: EMIS 2007.
Note: Repetition is calculated here as the number of repeaters in Standard X in year 2007 divided by the total enrollment in Standard X in year 2006. Thus, repetition refers to the year 2006.

Table 5A.3 Dropout Rates in Primary By Gender, 1999 and 2006 (All Types of Schools)

	Std1	Std2	Std3	Std4	Std5	Std6	Std7	Std8
2006								
Male	6.3	5.4	4.7	4.6	4.3	4.1	3.8	3.9
Female	6.0	5.0	4.5	4.8	4.8	5.7	6.5	7.5
Total	6.1	5.2	4.6	4.7	4.5	4.9	5.1	5.5
1999 Total	13.9	11.1	9.3	8.9	7.7	8.3	8.3	8.2

Sources: * CSR 2004; EMIS 2006, 2007.

Table 5A.4 Dropout Rates in Secondary by Gender, 2006 (All Types of Schools)

	Form I	Form II	Form III	Form IV
Male	8.4	6.8	6.7	6.3
Female	11.7	8.6	10.1	8.2
Total	9.9	7.6	8.0	7.1

Sources: EMIS 2006, 2007.

Appendix 5.2: Disparities

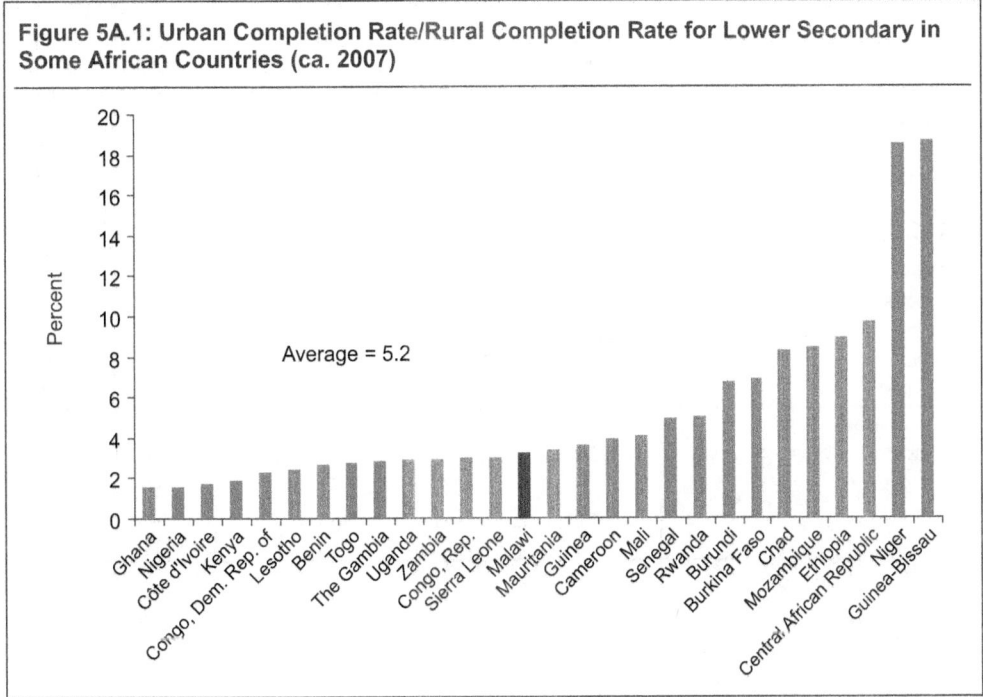

Figure 5A.1: Urban Completion Rate/Rural Completion Rate for Lower Secondary in Some African Countries (ca. 2007)

Sources: Calculation from MICS 2006 for Malawi, World Bank data base for other countries.

Table 5A.5: GER and PCR for the 28 Administrative Districts (2007)

	Boys		Girls		Total	
	GER	PCR	GER	PCR	GER	PCR
North						
Chitipa	159	88	134	66	146	76
Karonga	134	62	126	47	130	54
Rumphi	157	81	165	80	161	81
Mzimba	136	67	131	55	134	61
Mzuzu	98	53	102	56	100	55
Nkhatabay	136	75	135	63	136	69
Likoma	112	50	120	62	116	57
Central East						
Ntchisi	100	36	113	38	107	37
Nkhotakota	111	42	106	32	109	37
Salima	85	29	85	23	85	26
Dowa	110	35	117	33	114	34
Kasungu	119	45	129	40	124	42
Central West						
Mchinji	102	35	103	28	102	31
Lilongwe	88	31	92	26	90	29
Dedza	83	21	86	18	85	20
Ntcheu	111	40	115	36	113	39
South East						
Mangochi	79	22	81	17	80	20
Balaka	116	41	113	31	115	37
Machinga	90	26	91	19	90	22
Zomba	93	34	94	28	94	31
South West						
Nsanje	119	51	114	27	116	39
Chikwawa	96	38	93	21	95	30
Blantyre	77	38	78	34	77	39
Mwanza	117	39	121	28	119	33
Shire Highlands						
Phalombe	102	32	106	25	104	29
Mulanje	94	33	98	27	96	30
Thyolo	101	35	103	26	102	31
Chiradzulu	110	43	112	36	111	39

Sources: Calculation from EMIS 2007 and UN population estimates.

Table 5A.6: Leaving School Examination Results at the Primary Level by School Types, Location, Division and Gender (2006)

	Sat (%)			Passed (%)		
	Male	Female	Total	Male	Female	Total
School status						
Government	94.3	93.4	93.9	78.0	70.8	74.9
Religious	93.5	92.3	93.0	77.0	67.1	72.7
Public	93.8	92.7	93.3	77.3	68.4	73.5
Private	95.1	95.1	95.1	82.9	81.0	82.0
Location						
Urban	97.8	97.5	97.7	90.0	86.9	88.5
Rural	93.3	92.1	92.8	75.9	65.8	71.6
Division						
Northern	92.4	91.4	91.9	67.9	59.0	64.1
Central Eastern	93.6	86.9	90.5	71.0	59.7	66.0
Central Western	94.1	93.9	94.0	85.0	78.2	82.0
South Eastern	92.4	94.9	93.5	79.2	70.9	75.6
South Western	96.0	95.3	95.7	82.7	76.3	80.0
Shire Highlands	95.8	97.2	96.4	84.7	72.3	79.4
Total	93.8	92.8	93.4	77.4	68.8	73.7

Source: EMIS 2007.

Table 5A.7: JCE and MSCE Examination Pass Rates by School Types, Location, Division, and Gender (2006)

	JCE pass rates			MSCE pass rates		
	Male	Female	Total	Male	Female	Total
School status						
CSS	86.4	74.1	79.6	58.8	45.8	53.5
CDSS	63.4	41.1	54.2	39.1	20.7	33.0
Open day school	53.4	40.4	47.4	46.2	40.1	43.2
Public	69.3	50.0	61.2	46.6	33.0	41.5
Private	69.5	59.0	64.8	56.0	43.8	50.4
Location						
Urban	76.0	70.0	73.2	54.3	44.4	49.8
Rural	68.0	47.0	59.2	47.2	33.1	41.9
Division						
NED	72.3	52.8	63.7	51.0	35.9	44.9
CEED	60.0	39.0	51.3	45.4	29.4	39.4
CWED	68.4	52.5	61.4	52.2	36.7	45.8
SEED	70.1	58.2	65.0	52.0	43.4	48.5
SWED	70.3	56.0	64.2	45.0	39.7	42.9
SHED	77.6	53.7	67.6	45.6	30.2	40.0
Total	69.4	51.8	61.8	48.7	36.2	43.8

Source: EMIS 2007.

Table 5A.8: Access Rates to Standard 8 and GER, According to Education Division and Gender

	Access to Standard 8	GER
Central East		
Boys	38%	108%
Girls	34%	113%
Total	36%	110%
Central West		
Boys	31%	92%
Girls	26%	95%
Total	28%	94%
North		
Boys	69%	136%
Girls	58%	132%
Total	64%	134%
Shire Highlands		
Boys	36%	101%
Girls	28%	104%
Total	32%	102%
South East		
Boys	29%	91%
Girls	23%	92%
Total	26%	91%
South West		
Boys	39%	90%
Girls	30%	90%
Total	34%	90%
Malawi		
Boys	38%	100%
Girls	31%	102%
Total	35%	101%

Source: EMIS 2007.

Table 5A.9: Access Rates to Different Forms and GER on Secondary Education, According to Region, Education Division, and Gender

	Form1	Form2	Form3	Form4	GER
Region					
Central					
Boys	16.7%	17.8%	12.9%	14.6%	16.6%
Girls	14.2%	14.5%	8.6%	9.5%	12.9%
Total	15.5%	16.1%	10.8%	12.0%	14.8%
Northern					
Boys	33.2%	33.6%	25.8%	28.7%	32.2%
Girls	26.7%	27.1%	15.9%	18.8%	24.3%
Total	30.0%	30.3%	20.8%	23.7%	28.2%
Southern					
Boys	16.2%	17.2%	13.8%	15.7%	16.5%
Girls	13.7%	13.9%	9.2%	10.2%	12.7%
Total	15.0%	15.6%	11.5%	13.0%	14.6%
Education division					
Central East					
Boys	19.7%	20.7%	13.7%	15.3%	18.9%
Girls	16.9%	16.7%	8.9%	9.4%	14.8%
Total	18.3%	18.8%	11.3%	12.4%	16.9%
Central West					
Boys	15.0%	16.1%	12.4%	14.2%	15.3%
Girls	12.7%	13.2%	8.5%	9.5%	11.9%
Total	13.9%	14.7%	10.5%	11.8%	13.6%
North					
Boys	33.2%	33.6%	25.8%	28.7%	32.2%
Girls	26.7%	27.1%	15.9%	18.8%	24.3%
Total	30.0%	30.3%	20.8%	23.7%	28.2%
Shire Highlands					
Boys	16.6%	18.0%	14.9%	16.3%	17.2%
Girls	14.0%	13.4%	8.7%	9.1%	12.2%
Total	15.3%	15.7%	11.8%	12.7%	14.7%
South East					
Boys	12.3%	12.3%	10.1%	10.7%	11.8%
Girls	10.3%	10.5%	7.3%	7.1%	9.4%
Total	11.3%	11.4%	8.7%	8.9%	10.6%
South West					
Boys	20.5%	22.6%	17.2%	21.1%	21.6%
Girls	17.6%	18.3%	12.0%	14.9%	17.0%
Total	19.1%	20.4%	14.6%	18.0%	19.3%
Total Malawi					
Boys	18.4%	19.4%	14.8%	16.7%	18.4%
Girls	15.5%	15.7%	9.8%	10.9%	14.2%
Total	17.0%	17.6%	12.3%	13.9%	16,3%

Source: EMIS 2007.

Table 5A.10: Probability of Enrollment in Standards 1–8 of Primary School, by District

	Standard1	Standard8
North		
Chitipa	99%	49%
Karonga	98%	48%
Nkhatabay	98%	52%
Rumphi	99%	56%
Mzimba	99%	59%
Central		
Kasungu	98%	38%
Nkhotakota	94%	34%
Ntchisi	96%	26%
Dowa	98%	35%
Salima	98%	32%
Lilongwe	97%	42%
Mchinji	95%	33%
Dedza	88%	18%
Ntcheu	95%	29%
South		
Mangochi	92%	25%
Machinga	92%	24%
Zomba	97%	38%
Chiradzulu	98%	42%
Blantyre	97%	57%
Mwanza	96%	32%
Thyolo	95%	27%
Mulanje	97%	34%
Phalombe	94%	22%
Chikwawa	93%	30%
Nsanje	91%	33%
Balaka	97%	35%

Source: Calculation from MICS 2006 database

Table 5A.11: Probability of Enrollment in Forms 1–4 of Secondary School, by District

	Form1	Form2	Form3	Form4
North				
Chitipa	33%	26%	9%	4%
Karonga	35%	31%	21%	14%
Nkhatabay	34%	23%	11%	6%
Rumphi	43%	25%	16%	9%
Mzimba	45%	36%	24%	15%
Central				
Kasungu	23%	22%	15%	10%
Nkhotakota	22%	16%	12%	7%
Ntchisi	17%	14%	8%	5%
Dowa	19%	15%	10%	8%
Salima	14%	14%	11%	8%
Lilongwe	33%	29%	25%	17%
Mchinji	19%	14%	9%	5%
Dedza	11%	10%	7%	7%
Ntcheu	24%	18%	11%	6%
South				
Mangochi	15%	17%	13%	12%
Machinga	11%	6%	3%	2%
Zomba	28%	26%	15%	7%
Chiradzulu	34%	24%	13%	6%
Blantyre	47%	46%	33%	30%
Mwanza	26%	18%	11%	7%
Thyolo	19%	18%	13%	10%
Mulanje	23%	16%	11%	7%
Phalombe	14%	12%	8%	5%
Chikwawa	18%	19%	16%	9%
Nsanje	26%	19%	12%	8%
Balaka	29%	14%	7%	4%

Sources: Calculation from MICS 2006 database.

Appendix 6.1: TEVET Recurrent Unit Cost and Financial Management Issues

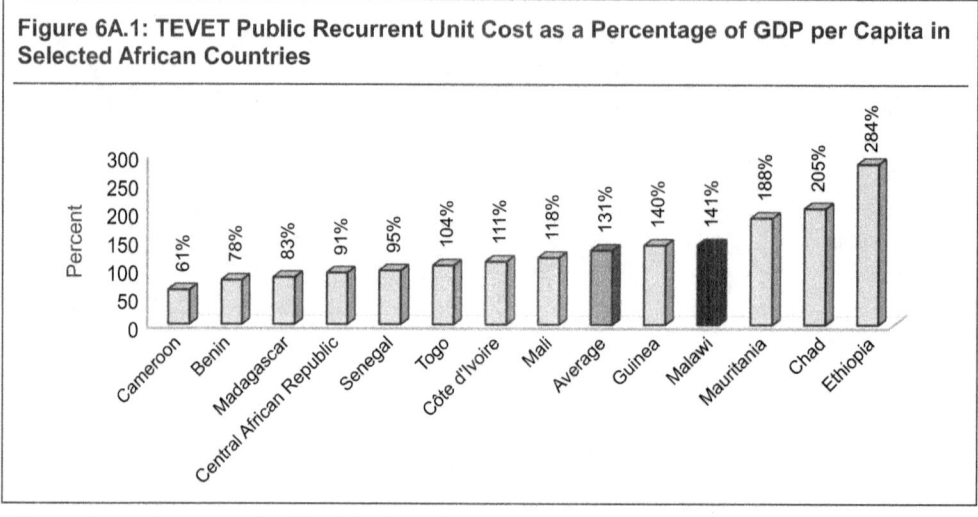

Figure 6A.1: TEVET Public Recurrent Unit Cost as a Percentage of GDP per Capita in Selected African Countries

Source: Calculations using the World Bank database.

Box 6A.1: Financial Management Issues in Technical Colleges

TCs are confronted with financial management procedures, which many of them consider cumbersome and bureaucratic. Generally, TCs operate with three different accounts:

1. Government Account No. 1 (ORT Account, PE account, and Development Account): All government allocations are administered through this account, which represents a treasury account rather than a physical account. Out of this account, payment is made for boarding, teaching materials for training TEVETA students, utilities, and full-time teachers on the government payroll. The money does not actually reach the institution, but is administered by treasury through vouchers.
2. Production Unit (PU) Account: PU is a physical account through which all income from the institution (i.e., fees, income generating activities, income from consultancies, exam fees) is channelled to the examination boards by the TCs on behalf of students and other income. This account is used to pay for all expenditure related to parallel programs and other activities apart from TEVETA training, such as salaries of directly hired teachers, part-time teachers, training materials for parallel courses, investment material, support staff, the cross-subsidization of utilities and other costs. This PU account actually provides the institutions with a flexibility necessary to survive. However, the legality and status of the PU is unclear. In the past, government auditors have queried the appropriateness of some expenses in audited colleges (especially expenses for part-time teachers' salaries) on the grounds that no legal basis is available.
3. TEVETA account, through which all allocations of TEVETA are channeled. EVETA is the principal signatory.

Appendix 6.2: Other TEVET Indicators

Table 6A.1: Number of Regular and Parallel Students in Technical Colleges (2007)

College	Regular Students			Parallel Students			Total
	Male	Female	Total	Male	Female	Total	
Soche	94	61	155	192	88	280	435
Namitete	35	38	73	50	94	144	217
Lilongwe	425	149	574	1,253	461	1,714	2,288
Livingstonia	113	63	176	160	12	172	348
Mzuzu	168	68	236	195	55	250	486
Nasawa	72	32	104	190	59	249	353
Salima	381	111	492	139	49	188	680
Total	1,288	522	1,810	2,179	818	2,997	4,807
in%			37.65			62.35	100.00

Source: Malawi Education Statistics 2007.

Table 6A.2: Records of the TEVET Provider Directory 1999

Type of Institution	Number of Recorded Institutions	Total Enrollment
Not classified	1	—
Church/religious organization	19	900
Community development program	3	152
Government institution	16	3,870
Grant-aided institution	4	31
In-company	2	204
In-company training center	1	72
Independent NGO	6	448
NGO affiliate	4	670
Parastatal	11	8,258
Parastatal/ government trust	1	500
Private commercial institution	101	7,835
Total	169	22,940

Source: TEVET Provider Directory Database 1999.

Table 6A.3: Enrollment in Regular Apprenticeship Programs (2003–2007)

Year	Total Enrollment
2003	1,036
2004	790
2005	817
2006	1,076
2007	1,330

Source: TEVETA.
Note: Figures represent total enrollment in regular apprenticeship system without students enrolled in Phwezi Technical College and in Press Trust Printing College.

Table 6A.4: Female Participation in TEVETA-Sponsored Courses by Applications, Short Listing, and Enrollment from 2001 to 2008

Year	Female Applicants	% of Total Applicants	Females Short-Listed	% of Total Shortlisted	Females Enrolled	% of Total Enrolled
2001					65	28.9
2002	1,472	15.0	472	17.8	50	22.3
2003	1,265	17.0	162	16.5	46	20.9
2004	1,771	18.7	537	15.6	82	31.4
2005	2,178	20.8	688	22.4	88	28.2
2006	3,063	22.8	1,909	31.0	243	31.6
2007	1,593	18.5	955	18.4	209	28.6
2008	1,583	17.6	1,222	24.9	205	29.4

Source: TEVETA.

Table 6A.5: Girls' Participation in Malawi Craft and Malawi Advanced Craft Examinations (in %)

Year	Malawi Craft	Malawi Advanced Craft	Combined
2003	10.4	11.0	11
2004	12.9	10.6	12
2005	16.8	10.8	15
2006	22.9	15.6	20
2007	24.9	18.7	23

Source: Malawi National Examinations Board.

Table 6A.6: Expenditure in Public Technical Colleges 2007/08 (Revised Budgeted) by Subprograms (in %)

Subprograms	Llgwe	Soche	Mzuzu	Namitete	Livngst	Salima	Nasawa	Average
02: Mgmt & support services (incl. PE)	68.0	50.2	67.9	54.6	27.3	82.6	57.8	56.6
06: Staff development	3.3	8.0	0.1	0.0	3.2	0.0	3.3	2.8
15: HIV/AIDS intervention	0.4	1.3	0.0	0.0	4.5	15.8	0.0	3.3
19: Special needs		1.3						0.2
26: Sports & culture		0.8	1.8					0.3
30: Boarding & feeding	15.6	25.3	24.9	35.4	18.6	0.0	25.1	19.6
31: Teaching services	12.7	13.0	5.3	10.0	46.4	1.6	13.8	17.3
Total	100	100	100	100	100	100	100	100
of which PE	*48.8*	*40.2*	*39.6*	*30.6*	*16.3*	*34.9*	*44.6*	*34.9*

Source: Government of Malawi, National Budget (Revised) 2007/08.
Note: Substantial differences can be observed by college, mainly because:
- Colleges attribute costs to subprograms in different ways. In the Salima TC budget, for example, costs related to boarding and feeding were included in the subprogram 15 (HIV/AIDS).
- Colleges use their income from other sources (see below) for different purposes. Notably, the PE budget depends on the posts that are actually filled. If this rate is low (typically in more rural locations), additional staff are recruited directly by the college and paid out of the PU (own income) account, which is not reflected in the government budget.
- First budget prepared under education, which follows other classification - confusion

Table 6A.7: Budget Execution Rates for Technical Colleges (2005/06)

	Execution Rate PE	Execution Rate ORT	Combined Execution Rate
Nasawa	44.5	53.3	50.0
Lilongwe	67.2	56.3	60.1
Livingstonia	127.2	69.9	89.9
Mzuzu	68.1	47.0	55.0
Salima	71.8	73.9	73.1
Average	73.0	59.7	64.5

Source: Government of Malawi, Budget (Revised) 2007/08.

Table 6A.8: TEVETA Expenditure 2002/03–2006/7, in '000 MK

	2002/03	2003/04	2004/05	2005/06	2006/07
Private sector training	3,295	10,216	11,391	17,444	42,355
Apprenticeship & other training	24,617	24,642	41,598	54,997	71,151
Informal sector outreach program	4,401	9,945	12,888	17,082	8,456
Quality assurance services	7,510	17,735	18,944	31,178	36,004
IEC activities	3,866	8,676	13,785	5,124	11,735
Planning, monitoring & evaluation	1,259	4,754	11,456	17,198	15,599
TEVETA Secretariat	45,753	68,910	79,049	88,831	96,434
Regional service centers	26,090	27,123	24,906	29,465	30,429
Fund management	4,035	9,284	17,855	18,954	25,069
Total expenditure	120,826	181,285	231,871	280,272	337,232

Source: TEVETA Secretariat.

Note: TEVETA expenditure is divided into (1) funding and subsidies for training activities, (2) funding of TEVETA's regulatory function of the TEVET system, and (3) funding of governance and administration.

Expenses for training activities:
- Cost of *Apprenticeship training*: Divided into (1) training material subsidies to Technical Colleges providing apprenticeship training, tuition for each apprentice payable to the TCs, bursaries for needy students, and occasionally support to the capital cost of TCs. Note that this budget line only covers TEVETA-administered apprentices (annual intake 760 at the moment), and not trainees in the parallel programs.
- *Private sector training program*: The program entitles levy-paying private companies to a reimbursement of 33 percent of their total training cost, while the upper ceiling is total training cost up to the total amount paid as levy. This means, employers can recover up to 33 percent of their levy payment through this scheme. The short-term training costs of employers to upgrade their own workforce are eligible. In 2006/07, a total of MK11.5 million was reimbursed to companies, representing around 30 claims. The program is structured into three windows: a company-specific private sector training program, common tailor-made private sector programs, and a private-sector training program through associations.
- *Informal sector training*: In this program, TEVETA funds tailor-made training to informal sector operators and workers.

Expenses for TEVET system regulation:
- *Quality Assurance*: costs related to assessment, certification, registration of training providers (in future also accreditation), standard setting, curriculum development, and verification.
- *Planning, monitoring, evaluation, research, information and communication*

Expenses for TEVET governance and administration
- *Governance*: Including salaries of TEVETA staff, both at central (TEVETA Secretariat) level and in the regional service centers, administrative costs, and cost related to the TEVETA Board.
- *Finance*: Mainly the administration cost of the levy and finance department (without salaries) of TEVETA finance division. This includes levy collection since 2004/05 directly done by the TEVETA Secretariat.

Table 6A.9: Examination Fees for Malawian Qualification

	MK
Trade Test 1	750
Trade Test 2	1,500
Trade Test 1	2,500
Malawi Craft	1,500
Malawi Advanced Craft	2,500
TEVETA CBET	none

Source: Based on MOEST records.

Table 6A.10: Calculation of Private Cost (Tuition Fees, Boarding, Testing Fees) for Formal TEVET in Technical Colleges (Prices as of 2008)

	MK	Unit
Fees TEVETA students not boarding	2,500	term
Fees TEVETA students boarding	5,500	term
Fees parallel students not boarding		
Min.	8,000	term
Max.	25,000	term
Malawi (Advanced) Craft Courses	15,000	term
Fees parallel student boarding		
Min.	18,500	term
Max.	35,500	term
craft courses	25,500	term
Exam fees (one time)		
TT3	750	one time
TT2	1,500	one time
TT1	2,500	one time
Malawi Craft	1,500	one time
Malawi Advanced Craft	2,500	one time
Total for parallel students	8,750	one time
Total TEVETA students boarding	33,000	program
Total TEVETA students not boarding	15,000	program
Total parallel students boarding		
Min.	119,750	program
Max.	221,750	program
Craft courses	161,750	program
Total parallel students not boarding		
Min.	56,750	program
Max/	158,750	program
craft courses	98,750	program

Source: Based on MOEST records.

Notes: Students have to pay tuition and boarding fees only when in college, which is normally a total of six terms. During the rest of the training time, trainees undergo industrial attachment. Only occasionally, fees are covered by the company of the apprentices.

Table 6A.11: Synopsis of Programs Offered and Qualifications Achieved in the Malawian TEVET Environment

Qualifications	TEVETA (Regular) Training in TCs and Aome Private Colleges	Parallel Apprenticeship and non-Apprenticeship Programs in TCs	Other Programs in NGOs and Private Commercial Training Institutions	Programs by Sector-Specialized Public and Private Institutions (e.g., MIT)	Informal Training (e.g., On-the-Job, Self-Learning)	Non-Formal Training
TEVETA CBET	Core			Core		Core
Malawi (Adv.) Craft		Core	Core			
NTT	X	X	Core plus X		(Core) if any	core
City & Guilds	X	X	X			
Other external qualifications		Core	Core	Core		
Institutional certificates			Core	Core		core

Source: Based on MOEST records.
Note: Core = Target qualification of the programs; X = Students also sit for exams parallel to their core target qualification.

Table 6A.12: STR in Technical Colleges (2007)

Enrollment	Number
Regular students only	**4,807**
Total enrollment incl. parallel	1,810
Teachers	**106**
Teachers incl. PU	150
T/S ratio teachers/regular students	1:17
T/S ratio all teachers/all students	1:32

Source: Based on MOEST records.

Figure 6A.2: Trade-Testing Candidates by Training Background and Year

	2003	2004	2005	2006	2007
external	789	282	438	527	1214
Other institution	656	715	520	682	1403
Public TCs	1814	1359	1564	1231	1948

Sources: Records of Trade Testing Services, MOL.

Table 6A.13: Trade Test Participation by Grade

	Number of Candidates	in %
Grade 3	9,805	57.2
Grade 2	5,473	31.9
Grade 1	1,854	10.8
Total specified	17,132	100.0
Unspecified	21	

Sources: Records of Trade Testing Services, MOL.

Figure 6A.3: Trade Test Candidates by Gender and Year (2003–2008)

Sources: Records of Trade Testing Services, MOL.

Table 6A.14: Trade Testing Candidates by Trade and Gender (2003–2008)

	Number of Candidates			In Percent	
	Female	Male	Total	Female	Male
Auto electrical	327	1,649	1,976	16.5	83.5
Bricklaying	149	1,124	1,273	11.7	88.3
Cabinet making		13	13	0.0	100.0
Carpentry & joinery	193	1,680	1,873	10.3	89.7
Diesel fitting		3	3	0.0	100.0
Electrical	282	2,278	2,560	11.0	89.0
General fitting	150	1,353	1,503	10.0	90.0
MVM	426	5,700	6,126	7.0	93.0
Painting & decorating	32	131	163	19.6	80.4
Panel beating	16	101	117	13.7	86.3
Plumbing	88	579	667	13.2	86.8
Printing	1	7	8	12.5	87.5
Refrigeration mechanics	19	162	181	10.5	89.5
Sheet metal work	11	63	74	14.9	85.1
Spray painting	17	104	121	14.0	86.0
Turning		6	6	0.0	100.0
Welding	9	193	202	4.5	95.5
Welding and fabrication	19	221	240	7.9	92.1
Wood work machining	9	34	43	20.9	79.1
Unspecified		2	2	0.0	100.0
Total	**1,738**	**15,403**	**17,151**	**10.1**	**89.8**

Sources: Records of Trade Testing Services, MOL.

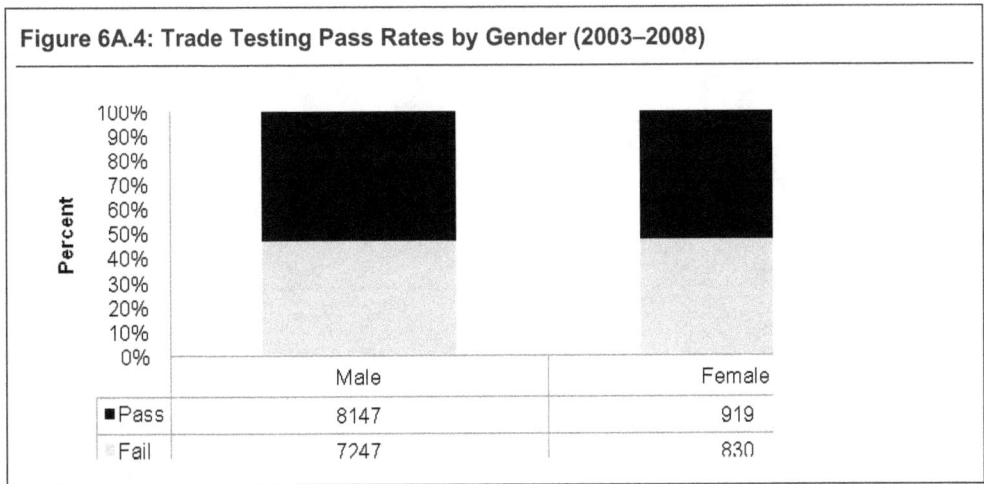

Figure 6A.4: Trade Testing Pass Rates by Gender (2003–2008)

	Male	Female
Pass	8147	919
Fail	7247	830

Sources: Records of Trade Testing Services, MOL.

Table 6A.15: Trade Testing Pass Rate by Type of Institution

Type of institution	Pass	Gesamt	Pass Rate in %
External	1,459	3,660	39.9
Other institution	2,532	4,477	56.6
Public TCs	5,074	9,013	56.3

Sources: Records of Trade Testing Services, MOL.

Appendix 7: Higher Education

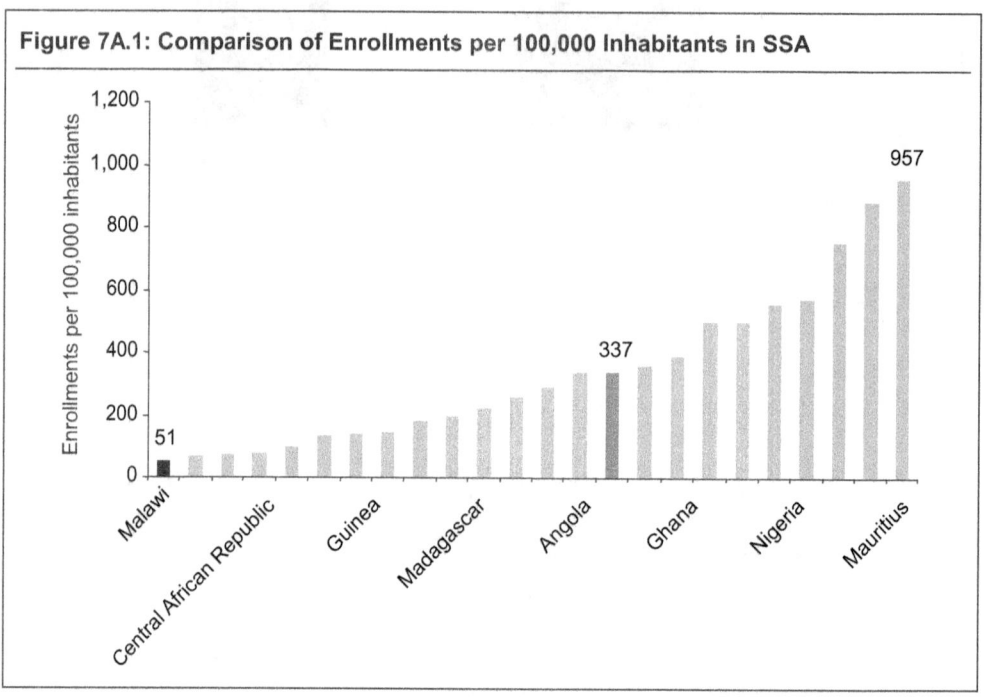

Figure 7A.1: Comparison of Enrollments per 100,000 Inhabitants in SSA

Source: Table 7.1 and UNESCO Institute for Statistics data.

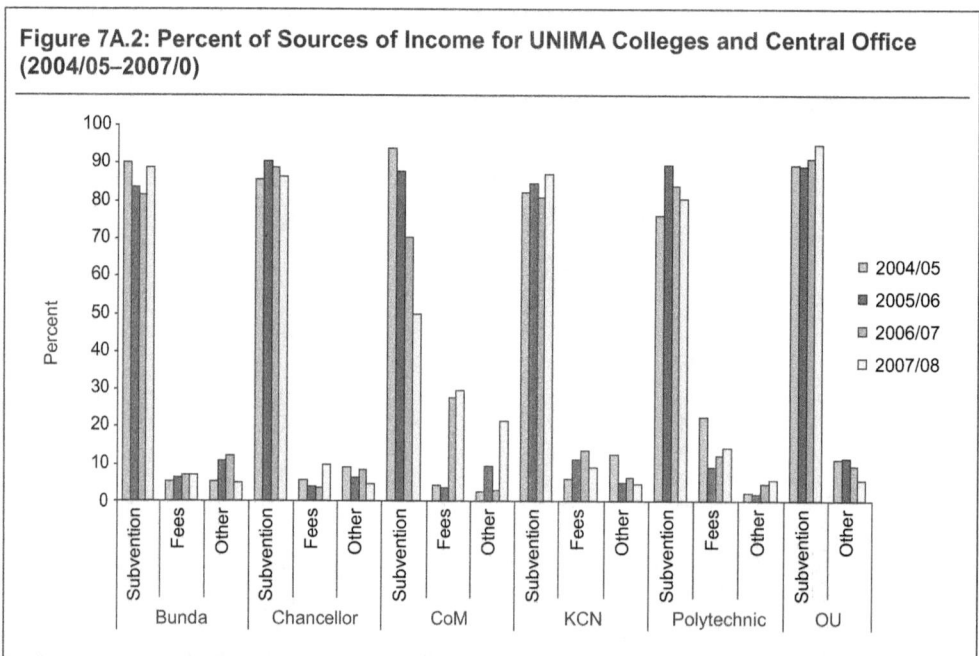

Figure 7A.2: Percent of Sources of Income for UNIMA Colleges and Central Office (2004/05–2007/0)

Source: Audited Financial Statements: 2004/05–2007/08 from the University Office.

The Education System in Malawi 273

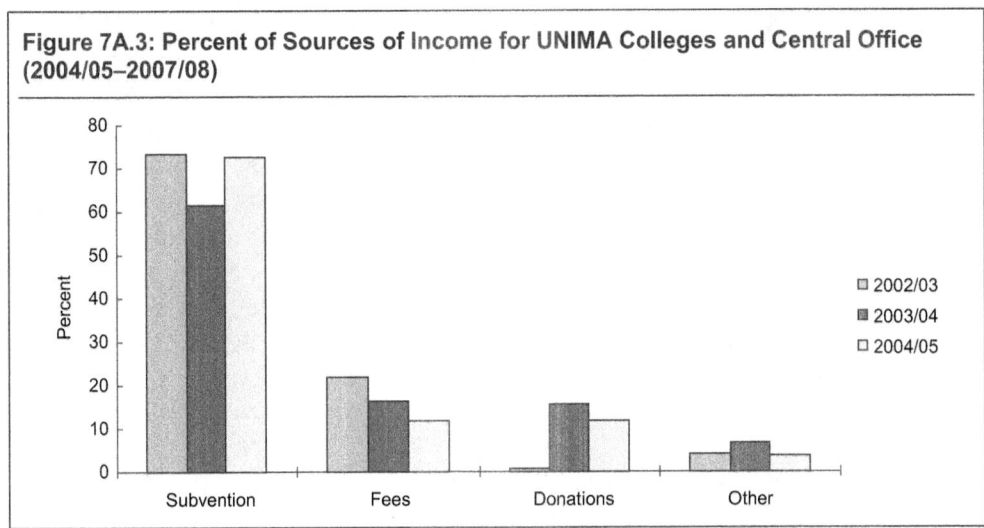

Figure 7A.3: Percent of Sources of Income for UNIMA Colleges and Central Office (2004/05–2007/08)

Source: MZUNI audited financial statements: 2002/03–2004/05

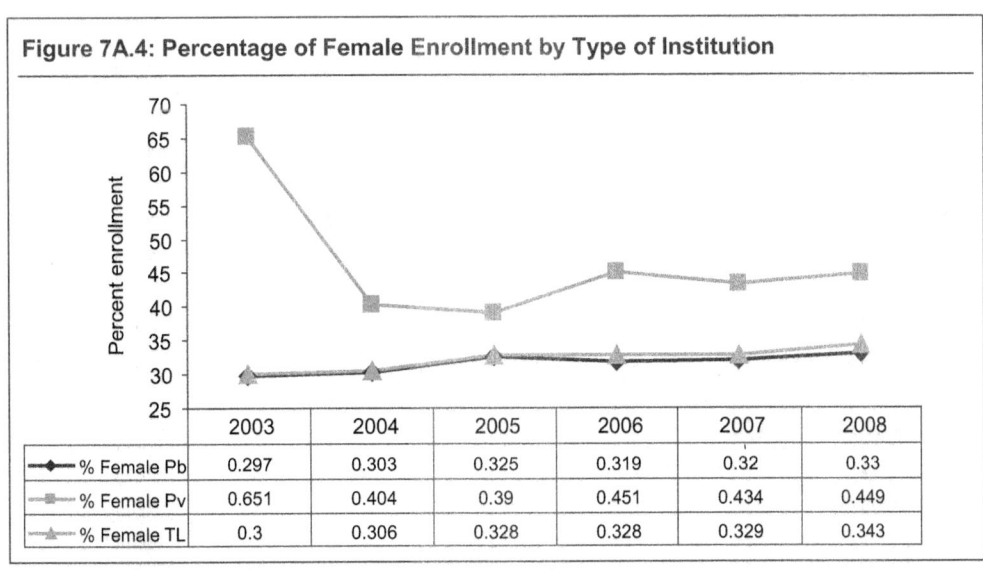

Figure 7A.4: Percentage of Female Enrollment by Type of Institution

	2003	2004	2005	2006	2007	2008
% Female Pb	0.297	0.303	0.325	0.319	0.32	0.33
% Female Pv	0.651	0.404	0.39	0.451	0.434	0.449
% Female TL	0.3	0.306	0.328	0.328	0.329	0.343

Source: Data from higher education institutions.
Note: Pb = Public, Pv = private, and TL= total.

Table 7A.1: Categories of Expenditure as Percentage of Total Expenditure: UNIMA

Percentage of Total Expenditure: UNIMA	2003/04	2004/05	2005/06	2006/07
Emoluments and benefits	59.9%	54.4%	53.6%	60%
Utilities	4.9%	5.8%	5.4%	4.7%
Student provision/allowances	6.3%	8.6%	7.2%	7.1%
Teaching materials/equipment	0.5%	0.7%	0.4%	1%
Books and periodicals	0.0%	0.9%	0.2%	0.2%
Travel subsistence	1.2%	1.6%	1.6%	1%
Vehicle maintenance/fuels and oils	3.7%	3.8%	3.6%	2.5%
Repair houses, buildings, equipment	3.6%	2.4%	2.7%	2.1%
Lease financing and assets purchase	1.1%	5.2%	6.1%	2.0%
Cleaning materials/rates and sanitation/kitchen equipment	0.4%	1.0%	1.2%	0.4%
Training and staff development	1.4%	1.5%	1.8%	1.3%
Research and publications/conferences and workshops	0.2%	0.3%	0.4%	0.4%
Common services (represents general administration)	13.3%	10.2%	13.8%	14.4%
Other	3.4%	3.5%	2.1%	3.1%
Total	100.0%	100.0%	100.0%	100.0%

Source: Data from Unima Colleges.

Table 7A.2: Categories of Expenditure as Percentage of Total Expenditure: MZUNI

Percentage of Total Expenditure: MZUNI	2003/04	2004/05	2005/06	2006/07
Emoluments and benefits	39.8%	46.2%	43.6%	50.6%
Utilities	8.1%	6.9%	3.2%	4.8%
Student provision/allowances	17.4%	13.6%	10.3%	9%
Teaching material/equipment	1.7%	3.7%	8.5%	8.8%
Books and periodicals	3.6%	1.8%	1.4%	1.4%
Travel subsistence	4.0%	8.2%	6.8%	9.2%
Vehicle maintenance/fuels and oils	4.1%	4.4%	0%	0%
Repair houses, buildings, equipment	2.7%	2.9%	0%	0%
Lease financing and assets purchase	9.8%	0.4%	15.7%	9.7%
Cleaning materials/rates and sanitation/kitchen equipment	0.2%	0%	1.1%	1.3%
Training and staff development	0.8%	1.7%	3.4%	2%
Research and publications/conferences and workshops	0.6%	0.8%	0.7%	0.8%
General Administration	6%	7.3%	1.5%	2%
Other	3%	2.1%	3.7%	0.4%
Total	100.0%	100.0%	100.0%	100.0%

Source: Data from MZUNI.

Table 7A.3: Categories of Expenditure as Percentage of Total Expenditure: Livingstonia

Percentage of Total Expenditure: Livingstonia	2003/04	2004/05	2005/06	2006/07
Emoluments and benefits	12.9%	36.9%	35.3%	34.7%
Utilities	1.4%	3.6%	2.4%	2.6%
Student provision/allowances	34.2%	29.4%	24.2%	23.2%
Teaching materials/equipment	3.4%	4.3%	3.7%	8.6%
Books and periodicals	3.1%	0%	0.1%	0%
Travel subsistence	3.2%	0.8%	2.9%	1.6%
Vehicle maintenance/fuels and oils	8.5%	10.9%	7.9%	15.1%
Repair houses, buildings, equipment	16.6%	0.2%	1.9%	3.6%
Lease financing and assets purchase	0%	0%	0%	0.0%
Cleaning materials/rates and sanitation/kitchen equipment	7.6%	2.8%	3.2%	2.7%
Training and staff development	0%	0%	2.5%	0%
Research and publications/conferences and workshops	0%	3.3%	1%	0.7%
Common services (represents general administration)	9.3%	7.8%	12.5%	5.5%
Other	0%	0%	2.2%	1.9%
Total	100.0%	100.0%	100.0%	100.0%

Source: Data from Livingstonia University.

Table 7A.4: Categories of Expenditure as Percentage of Total Expenditure: Catholic

Percentage of Total Expenditure: Catholic	Actual 2006–2007	Actual 2007–2008	Budget 2008–2009
Staff salaries and benefits	45.7%	58.8%	74.4%
Utilities (water and electricity)	7%	7.7%	5.6%
Student provisions/allowances	17.2%	11.5%	0.9%
Teaching materials/equipment	0.7%	1.1%	1.5%
Books and periodicals	0.7%	0.9%	0.8%
Travel/trips and allowances	0.2%	0%	2.3%
Vehicle maintenance/fuels and oils	2%	1.9%	3.1%
Repairs to houses and buildings	4.4%	0%	2.1%
Lease financing and assets purchase	5%	0%	2.1%
Cleaning materials, sanitation, kitchen equipment	0.4%	0.5%	0.3%
Training and staff development	0%	0.0%	0.2%
Research and publications/conferences and workshops	0.2%	0.1%	0.1%
Common services (general administration costs)	14.9%	11.0%	3.1%
Other stationery and duplicating services	1.5%	6.5%	3.5%
Total	100%	100%	100%

Source: Data from Catholic University.

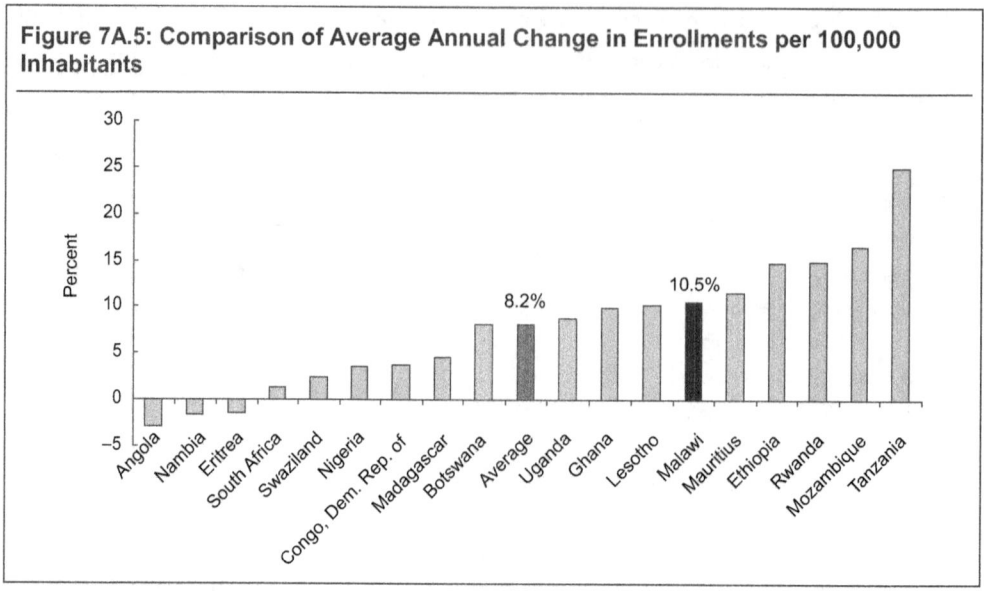

Figure 7A.5: Comparison of Average Annual Change in Enrollments per 100,000 Inhabitants

Source: UNESCO Institute for Statistics data.

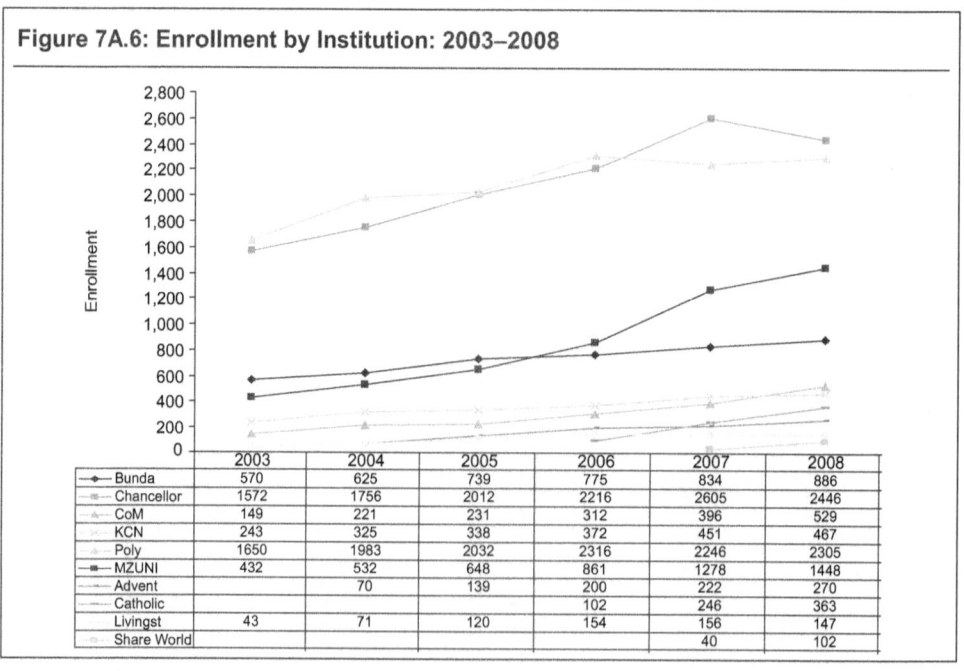

Figure 7A.6: Enrollment by Institution: 2003–2008

	2003	2004	2005	2006	2007	2008
Bunda	570	625	739	775	834	886
Chancellor	1572	1756	2012	2216	2605	2446
CoM	149	221	231	312	396	529
KCN	243	325	338	372	451	467
Poly	1650	1983	2032	2316	2246	2305
MZUNI	432	532	648	861	1278	1448
Advent		70	139	200	222	270
Catholic				102	246	363
Livingst	43	71	120	154	156	147
Share World					40	102

Source: Higher Education Institutions.

Table 7A.5: Enrollments in Higher Education by Gender

Year	Public				Private				Total for Both				
	Male	Female	Total Pb	% Female Pb	Male	Female	Total Pv	% Female Pv	Male	Female	Total	% Female TL	% Female Pv TL
2003	3,247	1,369	4,616	29.7	15	28	43	65.1	3,262	1,397	4,659	30.0	0.9
2004	3,793	1,649	5,442	30.3	84	57	141	40.4	3,877	1,706	5,583	30.6	2.6
2005	4,050	1,950	6,000	32.5	158	101	259	39.0	4,208	2,051	6,259	32.8	4.3
2006	4,701	2,200	6,901	31.9	246	210	456	46.1	4,947	2,410	7,357	32.8	6.6
2007	5,310	2,500	7,810	32.0	376	288	664	43.4	5,686	2,788	8,474	32.9	8.5
2008	5,412	2,669	8,081	33.0	552	449	1,001	44.9	5,964	3,118	9,082	34.3	12.4

Source: Data from Higher Education Institutions.

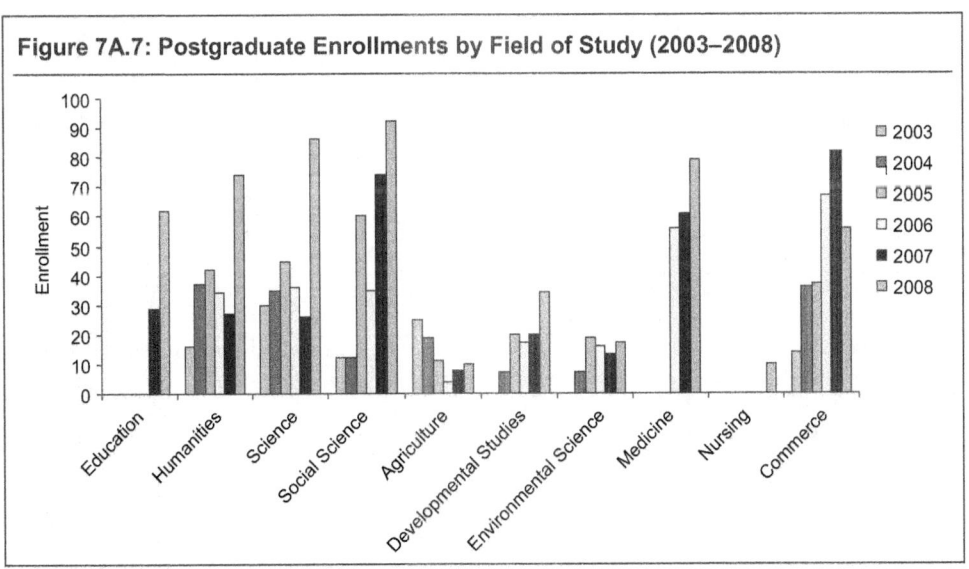

Figure 7A.7: Postgraduate Enrollments by Field of Study (2003–2008)

Source: Data from Higher Education Institutions.

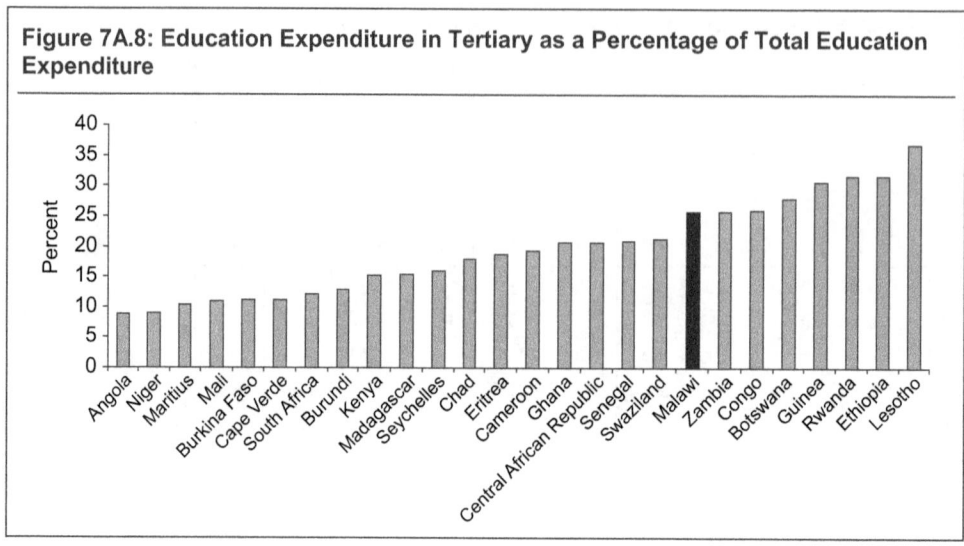

Figure 7A.8: Education Expenditure in Tertiary as a Percentage of Total Education Expenditure

Source: World Bank data.

Table 7A.6: Sources of Income for UNIMA

Year	Bunda			Chancellor			CoM		
	Subvention	Fees	Other	Subvention	Fees	Other	Subvention	Fees	Other
2004/05	459,475,000	26,538,000	25,757,000	566,192,000	37,058,000	59,979,000	371,634,000	15,935,000	9,888,000
2005/06	468,404,000	33,625,000	60,020,000	786,548,000	32,125,000	54,977,000	460,584,000	18,014,000	47,716,000
2006/07	486,320,000	40,779,000	70,741,000	850,955,000	32,478,000	77,493,000	467,328,000	183,558,000	18,017,000
2007/08	735,935,401	56,730,141	40,423,920	1,256,730,000	140,033,000	63,635,544	570,878,835	335,867,560	244,174,145

Year	KCN			Polytechnic			UO	
	Subvention	Fees	Other	Subvention	Fees	Other	Subvention	Other
2004/05	196,818,000	13,815,000	29,390,000	430,058,000	124,783,000	11,673,000	89,255,000	10,918,000
2005/06	303,486,000	38,957,000	17,631,000	695,436,000	70,339,000	14,544,000	133,668,000	16,760,000
2006/07	323,464,000	53,380,000	24,231,000	759,875,000	107,817,000	41,670,000	159,188,000	15,834,000
2007/08	519,099,000	52,925,000	25,857,000	1,070,288,110	187,959,520	73,395,041	259,182,000	15,290,000

Source: Data from UNIMA.

Table 7A.7: Percentages of Sources of Income for UNIMA

Year	Bunda			Chancellor			CoM		
	Subvention	Fees	Other	Subvention	Fees	Other	Subvention	Fees	Other
2004/05	89.8%	5.2%	5.0%	85.4%	5.6%	9.0%	93.5%	4.0%	2.5%
2005/06	83.3%	6.0%	10.7%	90.0%	3.7%	6.3%	87.5%	3.4%	9.1%
2006/07	81.3%	6.8%	11.8%	88.6%	3.4%	8.1%	69.9%	27.4%	2.7%
2007/08	88.3%	6.8%	4.9%	86.1%	9.6%	4.4%	49.6%	29.2%	21.2%

Year	KCN			Polytechnic			OU	
	Subvention	Fees	Other	Subvention	Fees	Other	Subvention	Other
2004/05	82.0%	5.8%	12.2%	75.9%	22.0%	2.1%	89.1%	10.9%
2005/06	84.3%	10.8%	4.9%	89.1%	9.0%	1.9%	88.9%	11.1%
2006/07	80.6%	13.3%	6.0%	83.6%	11.9%	4.6%	91.0%	9.0%
2007/08	86.8%	8.9%	4.3%	80.4%	14.1%	5.5%	94.4%	5.6%

Source: Data from UNIMA.

Table 7A.8: Sources of Income for MZUNI

Year	Subvention	Fees	Donations	Other	Total
2002/03	117,470,175	34,819,010	1,212,090	6,307,047	159,808,322
2003/04	129,275,846	34,410,398	32,429,330	14,302,655	210,418,229
2004/05	267,114,290	43,018,058	43,332,283	13,564,441	367,029,072

Source: Data from MZUNI.

Table 7A.9: Percentages of Sources of Income for MZUNI

Year	Subvention	Fees	Donations	Other
2002/03	73.5%	21.8%	0.8%	3.9%
2003/04	61.4%	16.4%	15.4%	6.8%
2004/05	72.8%	11.7%	11.8%	3.7%

Source: Data from MZUNI.

Table 7A.10: UNIMA Actual Expenditure: 2003/04 to 2006/07

Category	2003/04	2004/05	2005/06	2006/07
Emoluments	951,703,800	1,001,497,977	1,578,937,109	2,216,433,631
Benefits	114,472,606	174,634,124	186,637,115	209,712,597
Emoluments + Benefits	1,066,176,406	1,176,132,101	1,765,574,223	2,426,146,227
Utilities	87,234,871	124,375,851	177,846,221	188,649,621
Student provision/allowances	112,778,736	185,537,839	238,649,729	285,137,759
Teaching materials/equipment	9,445,555	15,770,575	12,994,817	39,055,036
Books and periodicals	875,613	20,149,505	6,476,935	8,229,474
Travel subsistence	21,265,548	35,529,454	52,019,297	40,310,104
Vehicle maintenance/fuels & oils	65,810,787	82,923,629	117,916,216	102,549,085
Repair houses, buildings, equipment	63,679,315	51,440,004	89,316,650	84,756,770
Lease financing &assets purchase	19,902,391	112,035,014	201,970,767	80,405,451
Cleaning materials/rates & sanitation/kitchen equipment	7,683,135	22,392,528	38,817,175	15,178,250
Training and staff development	25,570,425	32,162,261	57,798,683	52,849,620
Research & publications/conferences & workshops	2,971,503	6,054,851	11,607,916	16,700,247
Common services (represents general administration)	236,977,031	221,329,556	456,065,693	580,522,976
Other	60,582,570	75,688,000	69,922,000	123,391,966
Total	1,780,953,888	2,161,521,168	3,296,976,322	4,043,882,587

Source: Data from higher education institutions.

Table 7A.11: MZUNI Actual Expenditure: 2003/04 to 2006/07

	2003/04	2004/05	2005/06	2006/07
Emoluments			251,780,619	432,449,290
Benefits			4,775,607	5,263,787
Emoluments + Benefits	96,118,143	162,915,886	256,556,226	437,713,077
Utilities	19,447,567	24,216,217	18,944,322	41,525,064
Student provision/allowances	41,899,538	48,063,963	60,696,864	78,306,448
Teaching materials/equipment	4,086,825	13,123,493	49,956,123	75,895,730
Books and periodicals	8,737,707	6,404,670	8,253,304	12,318,578
Travel subsistence	9,586,289	28,798,405	40,260,325	79,348,412
Vehicle maintenance/fuels & oils	9,971,354	15,415,058		
Repair houses, buildings, equipment	6,540,767	10,132,796		
Lease financing &assets purchase	23,653,119	1,292,010	92,079,189	83,572,294
Cleaning materials/rates & sanitation/kitchen equipment	500,000		6,253,305	11,318,575
Training and staff development	1,840,681	5,902,264	19,942,013	17,566,730
Research & publications/conferences & workshops	1,467,821	2,978,408	4,253,304	7,318,576
Common services (represents general administration)	14,590,345	25,605,988	9,080,379	16,906,598
Other	2,882,648	7,447,108	21,591,504	3,820,735
Total	241,322,804	352,296,266	587,866,858	865,610,817

Source: Data from MZUNI.

Table 7A.12: Unit Cost by Institution

	2003		2004		2005		2006	
Institution	MWK	GDP	MWK	GDP	MWK	GDP	MWK	GDP
Bunda	546,945	15.05	765,489	21.06	868,900	23.90	1,047,979	28.83
Chancellor College	373,033	10.26	376,265	10.35	458,228	12.61	522,187	14.36
College of Medicine	1,753,554	48.24	1,521,271	41.85	2,043,182	56.21	1,900,964	52.29
Kamuzu College	685,948	18.87	515,687	14.19	719,346	19.79	1,145,240	31.50
Polytechnic	353,802	9.73	316,537	8.71	614,236	16.90	591,986	16.28
Mzuzu	558,618	15.37	662,211	18.22	907,202	24.96	1,005,355	27.66
Livingstonia	77,908	2.14	48,917	1.42	164,219	4.52	182,299	5.01
Catholic							494,532	13.60
Adventist							241,000	6.63
Shareworld							182,299	7.90

Source: Data from Higher Education Institutions.

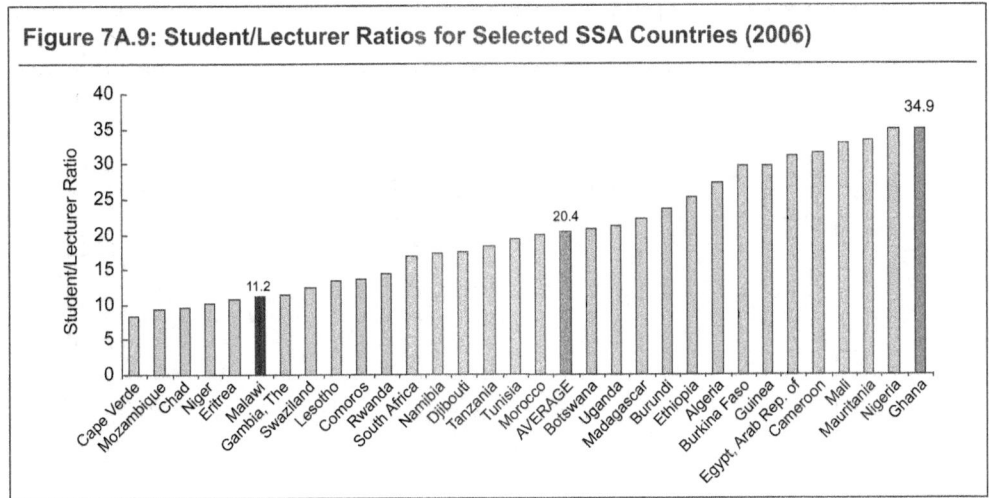

Figure 7A.9: Student/Lecturer Ratios for Selected SSA Countries (2006)

Source: UNESCO Institute of Statistics.

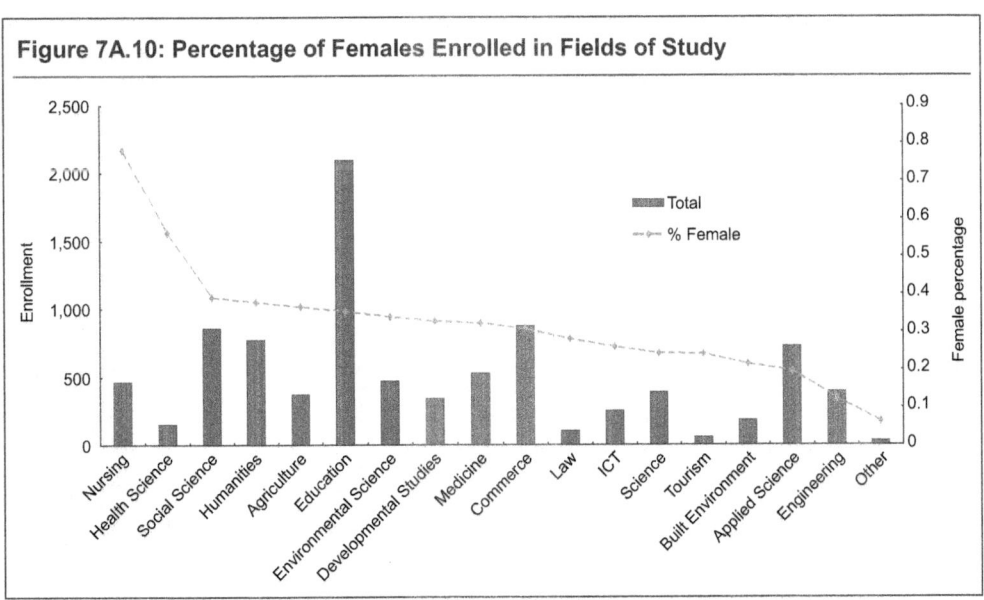

Figure 7A.10: Percentage of Females Enrolled in Fields of Study

Source: Data from Higher Education Institutions.

Table 7A.13: Percentage of Females in Postgraduate Studies

Year	Chancellor			Bunda			Com			KCN			Poly			MZUNI			Total			
	Male	Female	Total	Male	Female	Total	Male	Female	Total	Male	Female	Total	Male	Female	Total	Male	Female	Total	Male	Female	Total	%Female
2003	48	10	58	0	0	0							11	4	15	0	0	0	59	14	73	19
2004	61	23	84	0	0	0							28	8	36	0	0	0	89	31	120	26
2005	113	34	147	38	12	50							24	13	37	8	0	8	183	59	242	24
2006	82	23	105	24	13	37	32	24	56				45	22	67	31	2	33	214	84	298	28
2007	106	44	150	33	8	41	34	27	61				65	17	82	28	3	31	266	99	365	27
2008	201	74	275	48	13	61	42	37	79	0	10	10	51	5	56	34	6	40	376	145	521	28

Source: Data from Higher Education Institutions.

Appendix 8.1: Duration of Job Search

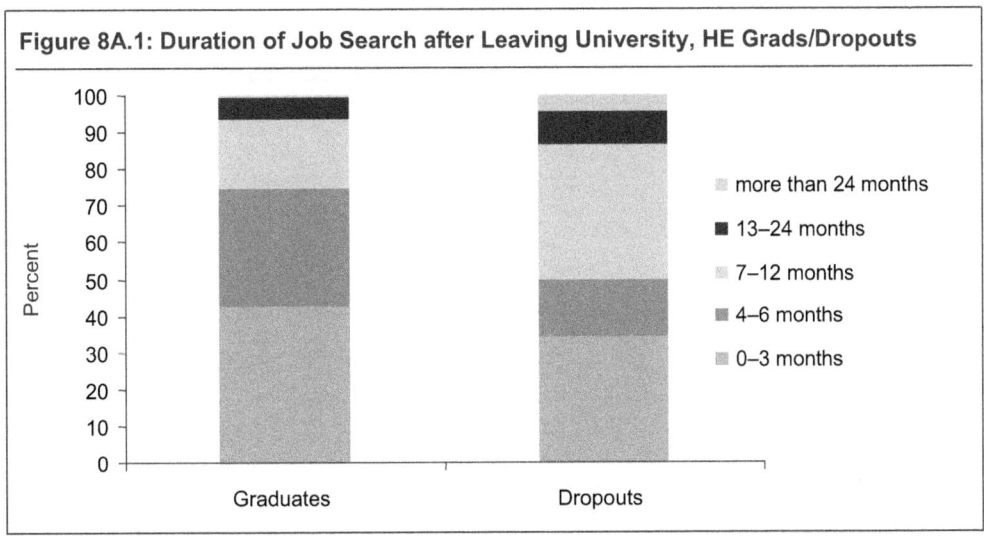

Source: GTZ/WB Tracer Survey (Appendix 9).

Appendix 8.2: Results of the Impact of Education on Social Behavior Calculations

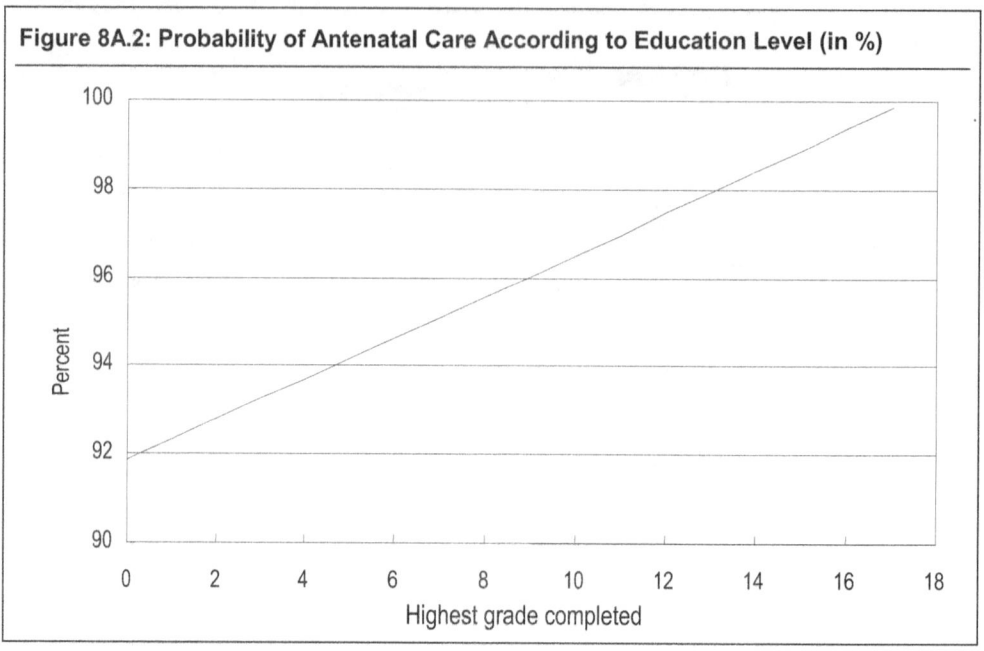

Figure 8A.2: Probability of Antenatal Care According to Education Level (in %)

Source: Calculation from MICS-2006 data.

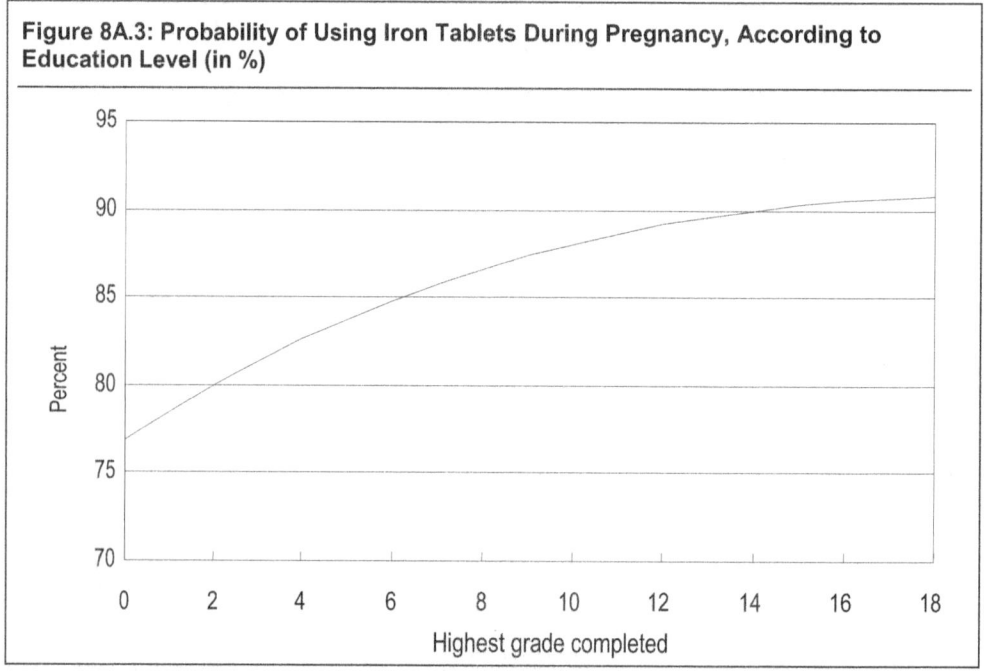

Figure 8A.3: Probability of Using Iron Tablets During Pregnancy, According to Education Level (in %)

Source: Calculation from MICS-2006 data.

Figure 8A.4: Probability for Women to Be Assisted at Delivery, According to Education Level (in %)

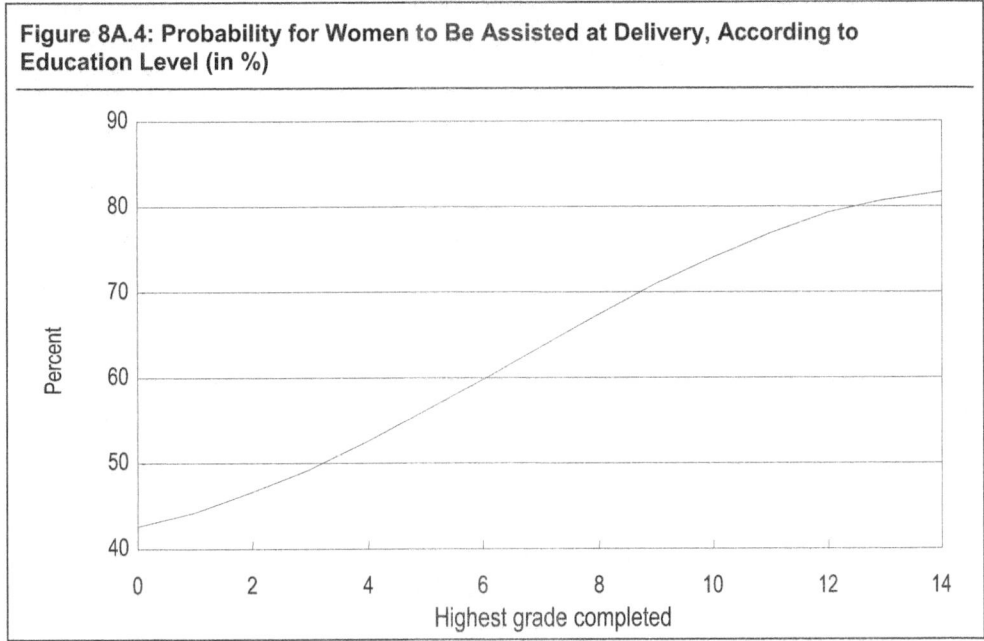

Source: Calculation from MICS-2006 data.

Figure 8A.5: Probability of Using Anti-Malaria Treatments for Children Under the Age of Five (in %)

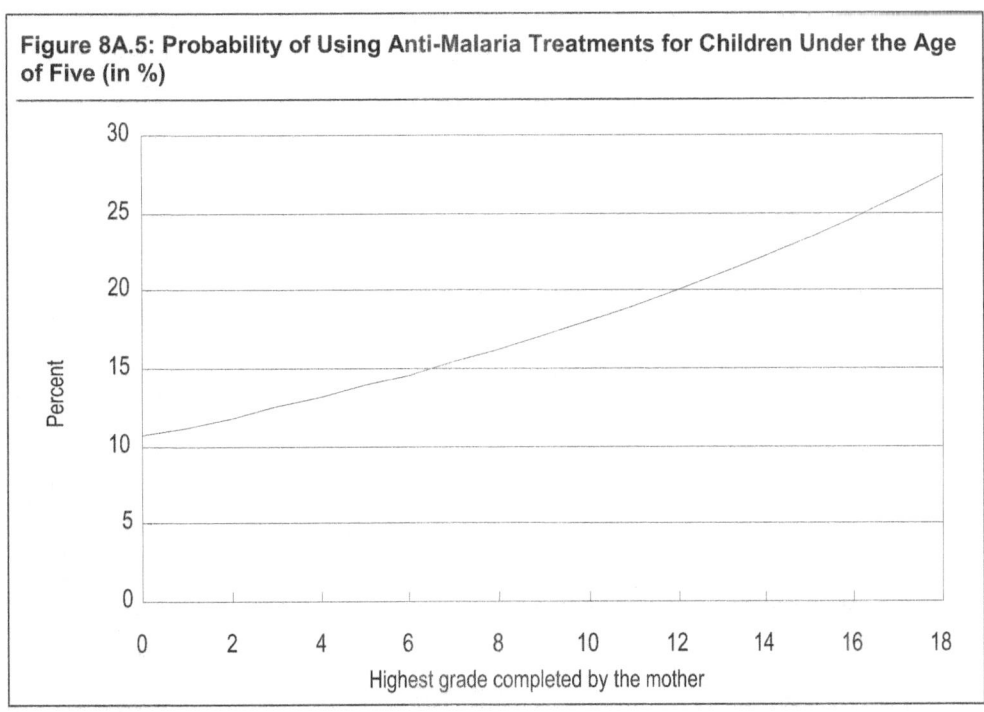

Source: Calculation from MICS-2006 data.

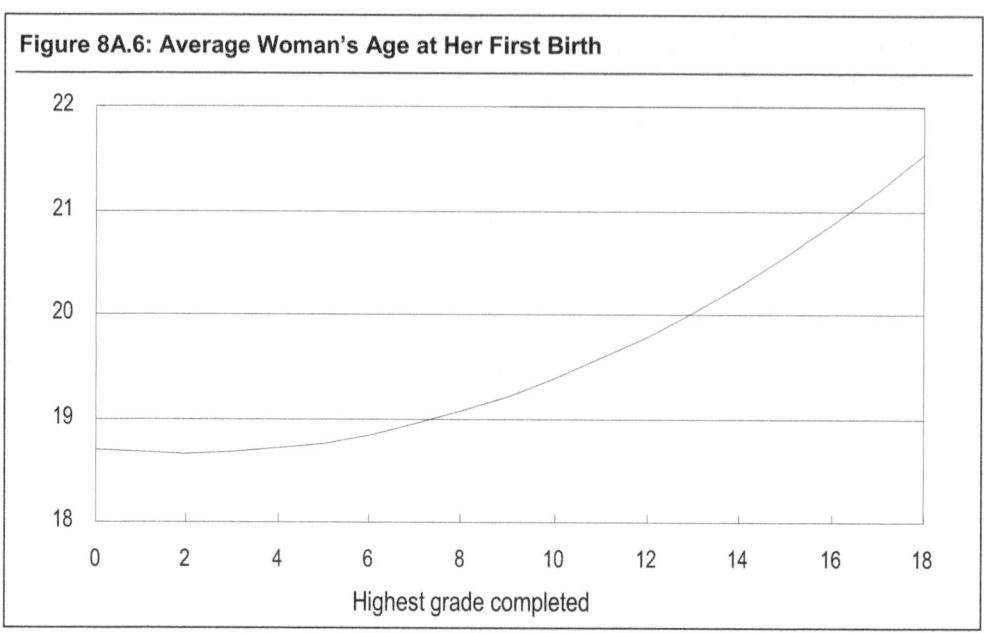

Figure 8A.6: Average Woman's Age at Her First Birth

Source: Calculation from MICS-2006 data.

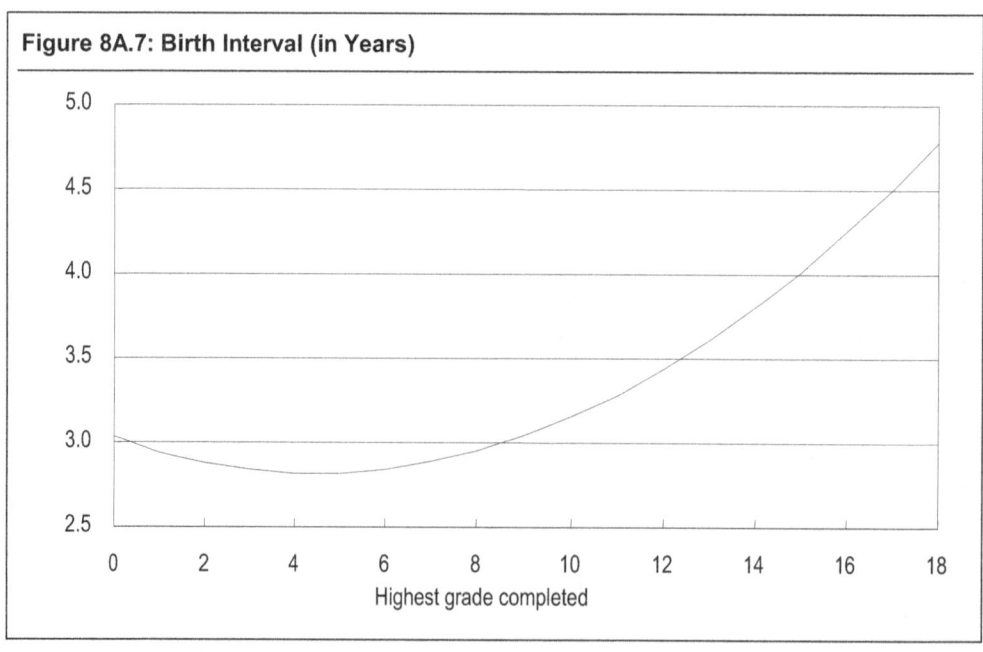

Figure 8A.7: Birth Interval (in Years)

Source: Calculation from MICS-2006 data.

The Education System in Malawi   287

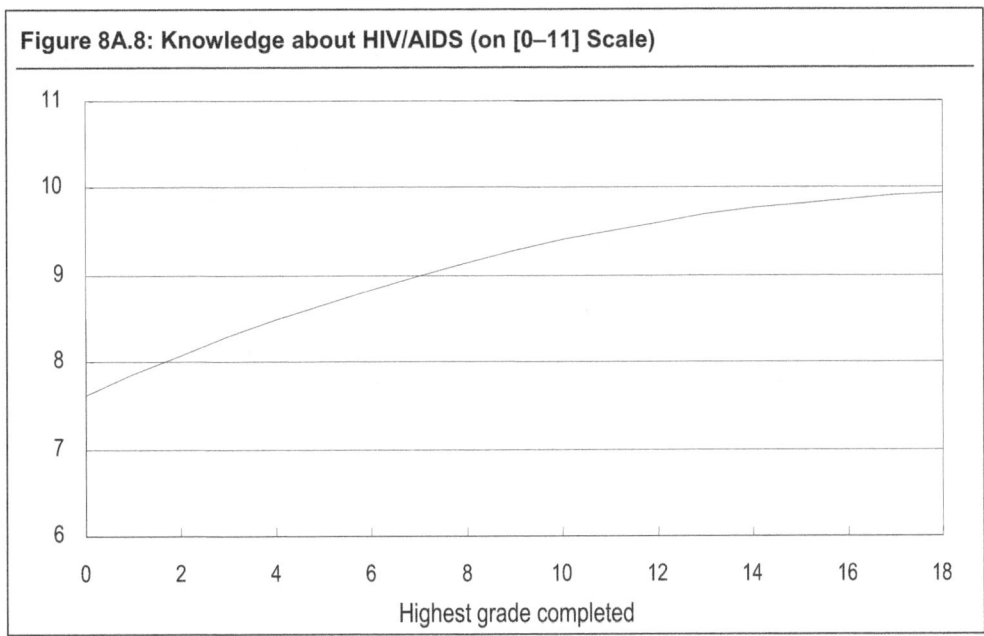

Figure 8A.8: Knowledge about HIV/AIDS (on [0–11] Scale)

Source: Calculation from MICS-2006 data.

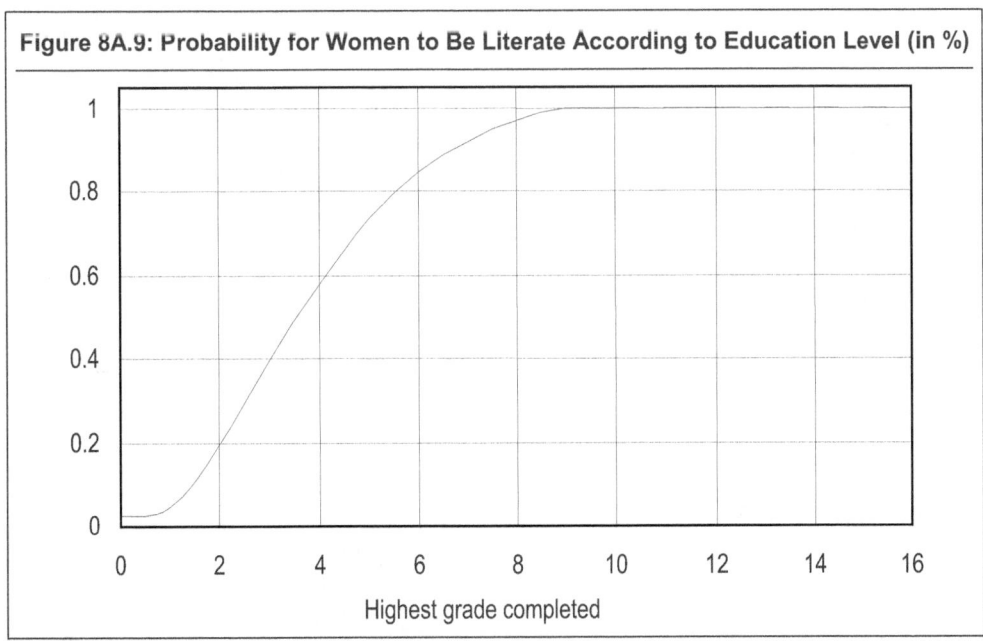

Figure 8A.9: Probability for Women to Be Literate According to Education Level (in %)

Source: Calculation from MICS-2006 data.

Appendix 8.3: Rates of Return of Education Investments: Calculation Method

Mincerian Earnings Functions

In order to calculate the rate of return of education, a common procedure consists in using the Mincer model, which estimates an equation based on the following:

$$Ln(Y_i^*) = \eta_0 + \eta_1 E_i + \eta_2 E_i^2 + \sum_{k=1}^{K} \eta_{3k} D_{ki} + \sum_{j=1}^{J} \eta_{4j} X_{ji} + u_i \quad (1)$$

Where:

$Ln()$ is the natural logarithm function; Y_i^* is the annual individual income (or annual wages); E_i is the professional experience (in years); $D_{ki} = 1$ if the individual has certification D_k (or attended the education level k) and $D_{ki} = 0$ if not; X_{ji} is the job sector of the principal occupation; u_i is a random term and is supposed to be Gaussian; η are parameters that are generated by the model itself.

In case of Malawi, using IHS 2004 data, results of such a model are shown in the table below. All parameters are statistically significant at usual levels (1 percent or 5 percent), and the R-squared is around 53 percent.

Table 8A.1: Mincerian Earning Function of Malawi (2004)

	Parameters	Standard Deviation
Constant	7.469***	0.00
Education level		
No school (reference)	—	—
Lower primary (stds. 1–4, LP)	0.078***	0.00
Upper primary (stds. 5–8, UP)	0.385***	0.00
Lower secondary (forms 1 and 2, LS)	0.810***	0.00
Upper secondary (forms 3 and 4, US)	1.548***	0.00
TEVET (technical colleges only)	2.427***	0.01
University (HE)	4.057***	0.01
Area of activity		
Informal sector agricultural (reference)	—	—
Informal sector non agricultural (ISNA)	0.810***	0.00
Public sector (PuS)	1.156***	0.00
Private sector (PrS)	1.294***	0.00
Professional experience (number of years)	0.051***	0.00
Squared professional experience	−0.0008***	0.00
R-squared (%)	52.6%	
Standard deviation of residuals	0.996	
The dependant variable is the natural logarithm of the annual income.		

Source: Calculations using IHS 2004 data.

***: significant at 1%

Simulation of the average income logarithm (and deduction of the average income) according to the education level

Using estimates from the Mincer model and the average of the experience variable, it is possible to simulate the logarithm of workers' average income according to their education level.

The estimated model is then the following:

$$Ln(Y) = 7.469 + 0.078\, LP + 0.385\, UP + 0.810\, LS + 1.548\, US + 2.427\, TVET + 4.057\, HE + 0.810\, ISNA + 1.156\, PuS + 1.294\, PrS + 0.051\, Exp - 0.0008\, ExpSqu \quad (2)$$

The estimated rates of return are net of the impact of control variables in the model, including professional experience (in terms of years). Once the earning function is estimated, the average annual income is simulated according to i) the different education levels and ii) the probability to work in each job sector according to the education level attended (using the average of job sector occupation according to education level as shown in table 8A.2).

Table 8A.2: Job Sector of Employed People According to Their Education Level, 15+ Years Old

	Non-formal Agricultural (Including Ganyu)	Non-formal Non-Agricultural (ISNA)	Formal Public Sector (PuS)	Formal Private Sector (PrS)
No school	69.3%	0.7%	6.9%	23.2%
Lower primary (LP)	65.0%	0.5%	6.8%	27.7%
Upper primary (UP)	52.2%	0.4%	9.1%	38.4%
Lower secondary (LS)	33.5%	0.2%	19.4%	46.9%
Upper secondary (US)	16.6%	0.8%	32.9%	49.7%
TEVET (technical colleges only)	2.2%	0.4%	65.7%	31.7%
University (HE)	0.5%	0.6%	41.9%	57.1%

Source: Calculations using IHS 2004 data.

Figures in Table 8A.3 below are the means of the other control variables (experience and squared experience) of the model. They are used to estimate the earning function.

Table 8A.3: Means of Variables Other Than the Highest Grade Completed

Experience	Experience-Squared
18.65287	535.0024

The simulated logarithm of income is the sum of two factors: a constant term and the factor that varies by the schooling duration, as shown in the following equation:

$$Ln(Y) = 7.469 + 0.051 \times 18.65 - 0.0008 \times 535 + 0.5\% \times 0.810 + 6.9\% \times 1.156 + 23.2\% \times 1.294$$
$$+ (0.078 + 0.5\% \times 0.810 + 6.8\% \times 1.156 + 27.7\% \times 1.294) \times LP + (0.385 + 0.604) \times UP \quad (3)$$
$$+ (0.810 + 0.833) \times LS + (1.548 + 1.030) \times US + (2.427 + 1.173) \times TVET + (4.057 + 1.227) \times HE$$

Table 8A.4: Logarithm of Annual Income According to Education Level

No school (reference)	= 8.371
Lower primary (LP)	= 8.505
Upper primary (UP)	= 8.975
Lower secondary (LS)	= 9.629
Upper secondary (US)	= 10.564
TEVET	= 11.586
University (HE)	= 13.271

The simulated income should take into account the variance of the error factor in equation (1) above.

$$Y_{simulated} = Exp\left[\left(Ln(Y)\right)_{simulated}\right] \times Exp\left(\frac{s^2}{2}\right) = Exp\left[\left(Ln(Y)\right)_{simulated} + \left(\frac{s^2}{2}\right)\right] \quad (4)$$

In that equation (4), s represents the Standard deviation of the residuals, and is shown in the last row of Table 8A.1 above.

$$s^2/2 = 0{,}996 * 0{,}996/2 = 0{,}496.$$

Table 8A.5: Expected Income According to Education Level, 15+ Years Old

	Expected Income Without Taking into Account Risks of Unemployment (a)		Unemployment Rate (b)	Expected Income Taking into Account Risks of Unemployment (a)*(1-b/100)
No school (reference)	= Exp(8.371 + 0.496)	= 7,095	1.1%	7,015
Lower primary (LP)	= Exp(8.505 + 0.496)	= 8,112	1.3%	8,005
Upper primary (UP)	= Exp(8.975 + 0.496)	= 12,983	2.1%	12,715
Lower secondary (LS)	= Exp(9.629 + 0.496)	= 24,969	3.7%	24,038
Upper secondary (US)	= Exp(10.564 + 0.496)	= 63,566	10.1%	57,121
TEVET	= Exp(11.586 + 0.496)	= 176,582	4.2%	169,221
University (HE)	= Exp(13.271 + 0.496)	= 952,027	2.4%	929,233

Source: IHS 2004 data and our own calculation.

Rates of Return

On the basis of the simulated incomes above, the rate of return of the level (k) relatively to the level (k-1) is estimated by dividing the difference of wages (between the expected income with a level k and the expected income with a level (k-1)) by the additional cost supported when pursuing schooling in level k.

On the income side, it is necessary to take into account the unemployment rate (which may vary with the education level) with the assumption unemployed people have no income (see table 8A.5).

The cost includes direct training costs as well as the foregone earning (or opportunity cost), which is the income one would forego while pursuing study to the level k. The foregone earning cost for the level k is estimated by using the expected income at level (k-1).

More precisely, the formula below is used to estimate the rate of return of education level (k) relatively to education level (k-1):

$$R_{k/k-1} = \frac{\pi_k \overline{Y_k} - \pi_{k-1} \overline{Y_{k-1}}}{N_{k-1/k} \pi_{k-1} \overline{Y_{k-1}} + N_k C_k} \tag{5}$$

with π_k the employment rate (therefore $(1-\pi_k)$ is the unemployment rate) of individuals with education level k; $\overline{Y_k}$ the simulated income of the level k, N_k is the average duration (number of years of schooling) within the level k, $N_{k-1/k}$ is the difference between level k and (k-1) in number of years of schooling attended and C_k the direct training cost.

The values of N_k and $N_{k-1/k}$ are shown in table 8A.6, as well as the annual unit direct cost (public and private) as calculated in Chapter 3.

With equation (5) it is possible to calculate both the **social** rate of return and the **private** rate of return. The two kinds of rate of return differ only by the components of the direct training costs. In the case of private rate, the only component of C_k is the training cost supported by the individual himself (or his family); in the case of social rate, the public cost is added.

Table 8A.6: Schooling Duration, Unit Cost, and Rates of the Different Education Levels

	Average Number of years of Schooling	Difference in Average Number of Years of Schooling $N_{k-1/k}$	Average Number of Years of Schooling within the Level k N_k	Unit Annual Cost (MK)		Rate of Return	
				Private	Public	Private	Social
Lower primary (LP)	2.78	2.78	2.78	252	3,019	5%	3%
Upper primary (UP)	6.65	3.87	2.65	252	3,019	15%	12%
Lower secondary (LS)	9.75	3.10	1.75	7,547	30,292	22%	11%
Upper secondary (US)	11.86	2.11	1.86	13,313	30,292	44%	25%
TEVET	14.18	2.32	2.18	34,444	51,408	54%	35%
University (HE)	16.14	4.29	4.14	63,725	780,479	171%	23%

Source: IHS 2004 and our own calculation.

For example the rate of return of upper primary compared to lower primary is calculated as follows:

The additional expected income is equal to (see table 8A.5): 12 715 − 8 005 = 4 710

Social cost of upper primary = $N_{k-1/k}$ Foregone earning + N_k (Annual Priv. cost + Annual Pub. cost)
= 3.87 x 8 005 + 2.65 x (252 + 3 019)
= 39 648

Private cost of upper primary = 3.87 x 8 005 + 2.65 x 252
= 31 647

Therefore, the social rate of return for upper primary is: 4 710/39 648 = 11.9 % and
The private rate of return for upper primary is: 4 710/31 647 = 14.9 %

Appendix 8.4: Employment and Income Data

Table 8A.7: Mean Income by Education Level as Units of GDP per Capita in Selected African Countries

	Mean Income (as units of GDP per Capita)					
	No School	Primary	Lower Sec.	Upper Sec	TEVET	Tertiary
Mali (2004, 25–35 years old)	1.38	1.78	2.45	2.77	3.37	3.59
Mauritania (2004, 25–35 years old)	1.43	1.68	1.85	2.10	2.78	5.05
Benin (2006, 30 years old)	0.81	0.98	1.16	1.86	1.85	3.46
Burkina (2003, 15–59 years old)	1.20	1.88	3.44	4.95	6.68	10.52
Congo, Rep (2005, 30 years old)	0.32	0.38	0.46	0.60	0.65	0.92
Malawi (2004, 30 years old)	**0.33**	**0.51**	**1.17**	**2.97**	**8.25**	**44.47**

Source: CSRs of the countries.

Table 8A.8: Expected Annual Income by Job Sector Taking into Account Unemployment Risk (MK)

	Public Formal Sector	Private formal sector	Non-Formal Agriculture	Non-Formal Non-Agriculture
No school	15,172	17,402	4,773	10,732
Lower primary	16,371	18,777	5,150	11,580
Upper primary	22,086	25,332	6,948	15,622
Lower secondary	33,219	38,101	10,451	23,497
Upper secondary	64,820	74,345	20,392	45,848
Technical college	166,464	190,924	52,369	117,742
Higher	865,518	992,700	272,291	612,193
Total	76,868	53,272	6,405	20,681

Source: IHS 2004.

APPENDIX 9

Tracer Study of TEVET and Higher Education Completers

Dietmar Pfeiffer
University of Münster-Germany

Gerald Chiunda
Malawi National Examinations Board

Part I: General Background

1. Introduction

The main concern of educational policy is the evaluation of the **internal and external efficiency** of programs, specifically in the sub-sectors of technical-vocational training on one hand and Higher Education on the other. Programs in these sub-sectors of the educational system usually generate higher unit costs than General Education (Primary and Secondary), which should result in appropriate returns. Therefore, maximum utilization of resources, demand orientation, and relevance for individuals and society are to be expected. Completer who does not find access to an employment or are overqualified or inappropriately qualified for the professional activities which they perform, mean a waste of economic resources and dissatisfaction and disappointment of qualified individuals.

Tracer Studies of beneficiaries of those programs (apprentices, trainees, graduates) can be considered as *one* powerful methodological tool in order to evaluate the impact of programs (outcomes, results, relevance) as well as identify problems and deficits experienced by the beneficiaries, which can provide important information for future policy options, quality monitoring and long term strategies. Tracer Studies are surveys that endeavor to follow up graduates of a program of study. The reason for the follow up is to evaluate the result of programs of studies in pursuant of quality assurance and the need to find out how graduates and leavers of the various programs are faring in the job market and workplace. The feedback provided by Tracer Studies can contribute to a better coordination between supply and demand in the labor market. Other possible objectives can be the evaluation of the learning environment, motivation processes, and general satisfaction with studies.

Education related tracer studies have been in the past directed mainly on individuals who have undergone **higher education** courses. Nonetheless they can track also participants in all other type of educational programs such as literacy courses, short-term **vocational courses** or formal **technical education** programs.

Traditionally, higher education related tracer studies cover graduates, who finished the course but not **dropouts**. The reason for this lack of interest for this field is that dropping out is considered mainly as a problem of internal efficiency of the institution and/or of a result of individual deficits.[1] Another reason is that the concept of drop-out is sometime difficult to define. On the other hand high dropout rates are causes of, for every year, high social and individual costs and therefore efforts to reduce the dropout rate are required. If the group of dropouts is clearly delimited to individuals who left university and did not re-enter neither in the same course nor in another one[2], they can be considered as a type of **control group** in a quasi-experimental design, which can contribute to estimate the impact of a university degree on employment chances and income of individuals. This may be important, because "one of the criticisms of tracer studies is that it is difficult to construct a control group of individuals who have not undergone the educational training".[3] In the case of TEVET, the control group does not comprise dropouts, but a small sample of worker who did not participate in any type of course or training program.

In the context of graduate surveys, sometimes **employer surveys** are conducted additionally. They can provide additional and complementary information which are not or only partially available for graduates (recruitment criteria and procedures, the reputation of universities etc). They can also give experiences and perceptions from a different point of view, so that a higher level of validity of data can be established.

2. Objectives of the Study

Existing data, generated by Tracer Studies conducted in Malawi in the past, are outdated and/or limited in scope.[4] The present Tracer Study aims to generate updated and valid information needed on relevance and external efficiency of Technical, Entrepreneurial, and Vocational Education and training (TEVET) and Higher Education (HE). This information is to be used as relevant input into the Malawi Education Country Status Report (CSR), which is currently being conducted by the government of Malawi.

> The general objective of the study is to assess the external efficiency of TEVET and higher education programs in Malawi, and identify needed improvement of existing educational structures and processes.

The specific objectives are related to generate information on the following topics considering disparities and differences by types of training and study, certificates, institutions, gender, origin, and levels:

- employment destinations of completers of the TEVET/HE programs
- professional success of completers of the TEVET/HE programs
- relevance of knowledge and skills acquired by TEVET/HE program
- match between field of study and field of occupation
- preparation for self-employment (if needed)
- job satisfaction of completers of the TEVET/HE programs
- assessment of training/study conditions, relevance, and effectiveness
- satisfaction of employers with the level of competencies of HE graduates
- satisfaction of employers with the level of competencies of TEVET completers
- reasons for leaving and present occupational situation of HE dropouts
- identification of practices that can contribute to improved efficiency of programs.

A complementary objective is to generate methodological experience and develop capacity in conducting Tracer Studies in Malawi.

3. Methodology

3.1. General Approach

According to the general rules of Survey Studies and taking into consideration the specific conditions in Malawi, the approach involved six steps with different activities outlined below.

Phase 1	Project Inception
Phase 2	Development of Questionnaires
Phase 3	Preparation of Field Phase
Phase 4	Data Collection and Data Entry
Phase 5	Data Analysis
Phase 6	Preparation and submission of Draft/Final Report

In the inception phase meetings with a Reference Group composed of representatives of different institutions and offices (GTZ, World Bank, MOE, MOLSD, and TEVETA) took place. The meetings intended to enable members to reach a consensual interpretation of the TOR, the target groups to be covered and the methodology of the study, including sampling frame, and questionnaires. Subsequent meetings were held with various officials of TEVETA and the JIMAT consulting group.

3.2. Target population

The following **four target groups** have been covered by the study:

- completers of formal, parallel and other (including informal) TEVET programs
- graduates of higher education courses excluding the health and education sector (medicine, nursery, teacher education) which is predominantly public organized
- employers that employ graduates and TEVET leavers
- higher education dropouts.

The survey accessed HE graduates/TEVET completers and HE dropouts, who finished their course in the four year interval 2004–07, a period that fit to the usual standards in Tracer Studies.

In addition to these three groups, employers of different size and sectors, which have actually employed TEVET people and HE graduate, have been targeted.[5]

3.3. Data collection

Generally, data collection was done in two phases. The first phase involved personal visits to the training institutions in order to get the initial database/personal contact details for the completers and graduates. The visit was complemented by phone calls, e-mails and fax. However, due to non completeness of database in most of the training institutions, an advertisement for the database was also made through the print media. This was an appeal to the targeted completers to forward their current contact details for a possible inclusion into the study.

Within this phase, phone calls were made directly to those who had left phone numbers in the training institutions. Where the phone numbers were for guardians/parents, attempts were made to get the contact details of their wards. This approach helped in updating and consolidating the database for the targeted completers and graduates. In addition, the phone calls helped to book for the interviews.

Nonetheless, not all the targeted 1,000 TEVET completers, 500 graduates, 200 employers and 100 university dropouts were contacted within the phase one.

In phase two, multiple methods were deployed in order to reach out and interview the targeted respondents. A total of 30 enumerators were trained to interview the respondents using structured questionnaires including some open questions. These enumerators were deployed initially in all the 28 districts, later on more enumerators went into the cities to complement those who were already there.

Another approach used was the area point sampling in which the geographical locations were demarcated then enumerators interviewed representatives of those locations. This approach was particularly helpful in the informal sector, which did not leave documentation of their localities at the training institution and indeed had changed locations several times after training. Snowball method in which enumerators asked for information for others from the one who had just been interviewed proved worthwhile especially in getting contact details and booking for university dropouts and graduates.

As for employers, a combination of approaches was used. Where graduates and completers indicated to be on employment, their employers were interviewed as well. The Business Information Register was also used to select targeted employers across the country and across sectors of the economy. However, where those employers did not or had never occupied either a TEVET completer or a graduate, such employers were replaced with others within the same locality and preferably the same sector.

3.4. Data entry and analysis

Before data entry, the returned questionnaires were checked for completeness and consistency. The data was analyzed statistically using the SPSS-PC, V.16 software. The analysis mainly included descriptive statistics, cross-tabulations, correlation, factor analysis, and cluster analysis. The graphs have been plotted by EXCEL.

Notes

[1] Tinto, V., 1975, "Dropout from Higher Education," *Review of Educational Research* 45, pp.89–125; Heublein, U., H. Spangenberg, and D. Sommer, 2002, *Ursachen des Studienabbruchs*, HIS: Hannover.
[2] Students who left the university and reenter after a certain time are defined as "interrupters."
[3] Hughes, Sarah, and Julia Lane. "Literature Review of Education-Related Tracer Studies in Developing Countries." University of Chicago.
[4] PJ Development Consultancy Company, 2005, "'Skills development Initiative' and 'On the job training' beneficiaries," Tracer study for TEVETA, Lilongwe; S.N. Zembere, and M.P.M. Chinyama, 1996, The University of Malawi Tracer Study, University of Malawi.
[5] The results of the employer survey will not be reported separately but will be included in the TEVET and the HE study in order to complete and cross validate the data collected by the interviews.

Part II: Higher Education Tracer Study

Introduction: The Context of the University System in Malawi

Soon after political independence, the government of Malawi established a public university called the University of Malawi. The principal aim seems to link to the provision of human resource base trained to be managers in both public and private sectors. Hence over the years, University of Malawi grew into five constituent colleges with one central control centre known as the University Office. With the coming of political and economic liberalization, a need for and indeed another public university of Mzuzu was established. Simultaneously, the church and other private entities established their own universities offering various curricula. At the time of the tracer study, there were four government-accredited universities, namely; University of Malawi, Mzuzu University, Shareworld Open University, and University of Livingstonia. Entry into the public universities is controlled by government policies, availability of space and resource consideration whereas the private universities are still in their infant phase of development. All this implies that student intake into the university system is largely limited.

Therefore the total enrolment is only about 7,000 students in all programs and about 1,000 students are awarded yearly, giving an `elitist` character to the system. "This capacity restriction is one of the principal causes for the disproportionately high cost of higher education per student, relative to regional levels, reported to be US$2,884 for the 2003/04 financial year. By 2006 the cost per student had grown to about $4,270 at UNIMA and US$5,169" at Mzuzu.[1]

The principal limit given in the public universities is the provision of free and guaranteed boarding and lodging to all students. The access to university is basically government financed. Nonetheless government introduced an annual student financial contribution of US$170 for UNIMA and US$390 for Mzuzu. Meanwhile some private institutions already started to operate and probably others will be created in the future. This diversification of the system can be a contribution to enhance delivery of Higher Education on the premises that a policy of regulation and quality assurance guarantee the necessary academic standards.

The systemic, managerial, and academic challenges of the system of higher education in Malawi are reflected in the National Education Sector Plan, which proposed goals and strategies with respect to higher education in order to expand access and improve his quality and relevance.

1. Methodology

The general methodological procedures of tracing, sampling, and data collection have been described above in Part I. The following section describes the construction of the specific questionnaires and the basic characteristics of the samples for each target group covered by the Higher Education study.

1.1. Questionnaires

The development of the questionnaires for the graduates as well as for the employees was based on standard instruments developed by the "Centre of Higher Education Research" (CHER) at the University of Kassel-Germany.[2]

Considering the focus of the study on aspects of external efficiency and the scope of the target groups (graduates of all field of studies; employees of the formal and the informal sector occupying graduates and/or TEVET leavers), the instruments were subjected to an adaptation and reduction of the issues to be covered. The questionnaires were developed and revised in consultation with all stakeholders involved in the study.

The questionnaire for the dropouts was compiled by the consultants using elements of instruments of different studies and self-developed items.

1.2. Size of Samples

In keeping with the TOR, a sample size of 500 HE graduates was envisaged. As some of the completers were out of the time range 2004-2007 or had earned a qualification less than Diploma the sample comprised **n=492 HE completers.**

As the decision of the CSR team to include also dropouts was taken after the inception phase, only a small sample of initially n=101 could be envisaged. Also in this case some units were out of the time range 2004-2007, so that final size was **n=91 dropouts.**

The limited employers survey suggested in the TOR included a total of n=220 employers (companies or organizations). Out of this number **n=134 employers** occupied university graduates and post-graduates. For purpose of the HE survey, only this subgroup is relevant and included in the analysis.

1.3. Characteristics of the Samples

According to the TOR, the sample of the **HE graduates**[3] included all field of studies less the health sector, teacher education and other areas providing mainly human resources for the public sector. The study targeted all government accredited University Institutions, namely University of Malawi, Mzuzu University, University of Livingstonia and Shareworld Open University. At the time of data collection, however, University of Livingstonia had graduated teachers only according to the initial database collection exercise. Consequently, all those graduates were working in government Institutions. This left the study with three Universities, University of Malawi, Mzuzu University, and Shareworld. Shareworld did not provide the initial database hence the data collection depended much on snowball approach. Resultantly, a few graduates from this University were reached out.

University of Malawi had five constituent colleges. These are: Chancellor College, Bunda College of Agriculture, Malawi Polytechnic, Kamuzu College of Nursing, and

College of Medicine. By their nature, Kamuzu College of Nursing, and College of Medicine train in health, therefore graduates from these did not qualify for the study as the graduates work in the public health sector. The study therefore targeted those graduates from Chancellor College, Malawi Polytechnic and Bunda College of Agriculture.

The demographic background characteristics of the samples are given in the sampling frame below, based on the number of valid cases.

Sampling Frame

	Graduates	Drop outs	Employers
Year of finishing course or leaving university			
2004	N=117	N=15	
2005	N=115	N=26	
2006	N=132	N=27	
2007	N=128	N=23	
Age			
Mean	28	27	
SD	4.8	3.5	
Gender %			
male	71	74,7	
female	29	25.3	
Region %			
North	13.9	17.6	40
Central	32.7	24.2	73
South	53.4	58.2	107
Location %			
Urban	77.7	70.3	
Rural	22.3	29.7	
No of employees in the branch of company %			
1-10			36.1
11-50			42.0
51-100			7.1
>100			16.8
No of employees in the whole company %			
1-10			22.2
11-50			29.8
51-100			11.7
>100			36.3

The sample meets largely criterions of representativeness. All relevant institutions had their completers covered in the study. All administrative districts were fully covered and special coverage emphasis was done for the four cities. This is why questionnaire retention rate was 100 percent.

The **drop out** sample as well included students from the universities mentioned above and all field of studies less the health sector, teacher education and other areas providing mainly human resources for the public sector. As there are no files or records available for this target group, the enumerators asked the graduates whether they knew drop outs (snowball system). Even not being representative in a strictly sense, all study areas, gender groups, regions, and locations were represented.

The sample of **employers** was comprised of companies of different sizes (small, middle, large companies) across all sectors of the economy, which occupied university and/or TEVET completers.

2. Results of Graduate Study

2.1. Assessment of Studies

The evaluation of the internal study conditions, the satisfaction with the studies and their usefulness done by the graduates are important subjective indicators, which have to be taken into account by the universities. They can be related to objective measures like occupational status, job success, and salary. However, such a relation cannot be interpreted directly as a causal one, because many intervening variables are of effect (table A9.1).

Table A9.1: Rating of Study Condition and Provision

	N	Mean	SD
Academic advice offered in general	487	2.21	1.00
Course content of major	486	1.88	0.88
Structure of study	485	2.24	0.95
Testing/grading	487	2.59	1.06
Practical emphasis of teaching and learning	488	2.51	1.08
Teaching quality of lecturers/professors	487	2.19	0.91
Chances to participate in research projects	489	3.16	1.34
Equipment, computer services, resources	490	3.20	1.28

Note: Scale from 1 (very good) to 5 (very bad)

The values achieved in the items referring to curriculum, didactic and structure and quality of the staff are highly positive. Lower mean scores are to be observed only in two aspects: material equipment and possibilities of research activities. However, a certain variance in all items, indicate the existence of different situations experienced by the graduates, which need further analysis. Most of the students completed their courses in time, diploma in three years and Bachelor degree in four years.

Additionally to the valuation of different aspects of the studies, a general **studies satisfaction index** has been included. According to the results exposed above, the table points out a high degree of general satisfaction with studies (M=2.14; SD=0.96) (table A9.2).

Table A9.2: General Satisfaction with Studies

Score	FREQ	PCT
1	125	25.6
2	225	46.0
3	99	20.2
4	25	5.1
5	15	3.1
Total	489	100

Note: Scale from 1 (very satisfied) to 5 (not at all satisfied)

Also with regard to the **usefulness of studies** for different areas, the results point out a very positive evaluation with means between 1.83 and 2.08 (table A9.3).

Table A9.3: Rating Usefulness of Studies

	N	Mean	SD
For finding adequate job after finishing studies	488	2.05	1.13
For fulfilling present professional tasks	488	2.08	1.06
For future professional development/career	488	1.97	1.12
For the economic development of the country	486	1.83	1.07

Note: Scale from 1 (very useful) to 5 (not at all useful).

The four items of usefulness have been submitted to a factor analysis, which resulted in a one-dimensional structure. Therefore a not weighted global usefulness index has been constructed with M=1.98 and SD=0.86. This result can be considered as very satisfactory. As it has been so expected, there is a high correlation (r=0.54) between study satisfaction and study usefulness.

Breaking down the usefulness index by field of studies it can be realized that there are significant differences between the fields, which can be interpreted as result of career chances, working environment and other factors. The highest mean scores are found in the areas of law, ICT, and agriculture. Gender imbalances referring to satisfaction or usefulness do not exist.

2.2. Transition to employment

One of the main concerns of the HE sector policy is the market labor orientation of the human capital formed at the universities. A mismatch between educational system and labor market, between demand and supply is, of course, a general concern of all sectors of education, but in case of higher education it reaches utmost importance due to the high unit costs of higher education compared with other educational sectors.[4] Therefore the transition from university to employment, the occupational situation (Section 2.4 below), and the match between profession and qualification (Section 2.3 below) are critical issues which must be considered.

The present data reveal the situation for the basic indicators of labor market integration in general. A break-analysis with gender and study area has been conducted.

- A need for searching employment was given in 76.7 percent of the cases; the remaining graduates continued in a job they had before graduation (8.4 percent), got a job without seeking (8.4 percent), set up their own business (1.9 percent)[5], continued to study (2.2 percent) or developed other activities (2.4 percent).
- For those who were seeking employment it took an average of 5.5 months to secure a job. It must be considered, however, that the distribution is extremely skewed pushing up therefore the average value. In fact, after six months 75 percent of all employment seekers had a job. The overall effect of gender and field of study on the duration of job seeking is insignificant, but once more the privileged labor market situation of graduates in law compared with other groups must be highlighted (mean=2.75 month).
- In general, after being awarded a university qualification 72.2 percent were full-time employed or had set up their own business (2.1 percent). A part-time employment had 11 percent of the graduates and still seeking employment were 10 percent. Once again no statistical significant gender or study field disparities occurred.

The typology[6] following up presents an overall impression of the predominant situation by year since graduation to now, showing that the labor market is not flooded by academically qualified manpower. There are good job opportunities for graduates of all cohorts even if not all of them can secure a job immediately after being awarded (figure A9.1).

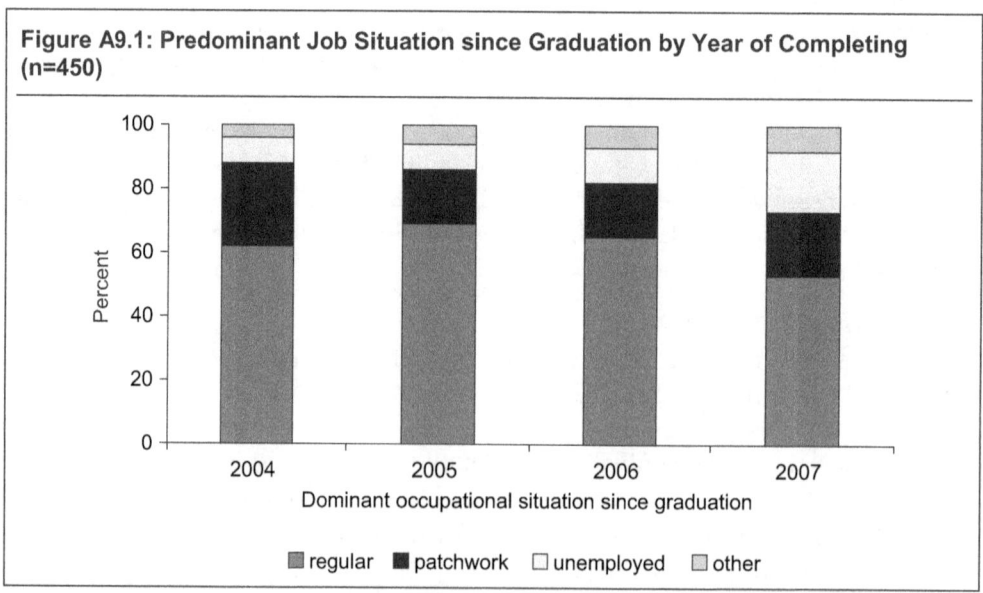

Figure A9.1: Predominant Job Situation since Graduation by Year of Completing (n=450)

An analysis of the situation by year, gender, and field of studies did not reveal significant differences. Only the cohort which finished one year ago (2007) has, of course, still a higher rate of unemployed.

2.3. Current employment and work situation

The integration into the labor market represents a first step in the chronological career of graduates and a basic indicator for the external efficiency of the system. However, it does not inform either about the professional progress or about the quality of jobs and their adequacy. Therefore further indicators are needed.

The indicators of **professional success** can be separated in subjective (depending on the individual perception) and objective (independent on the individual perception) indicators.

2.3.1 Subjective indicator

The most important subjective indicator is the satisfaction of the person with different aspects of the professional situation and their overall satisfaction (figure A9.2).

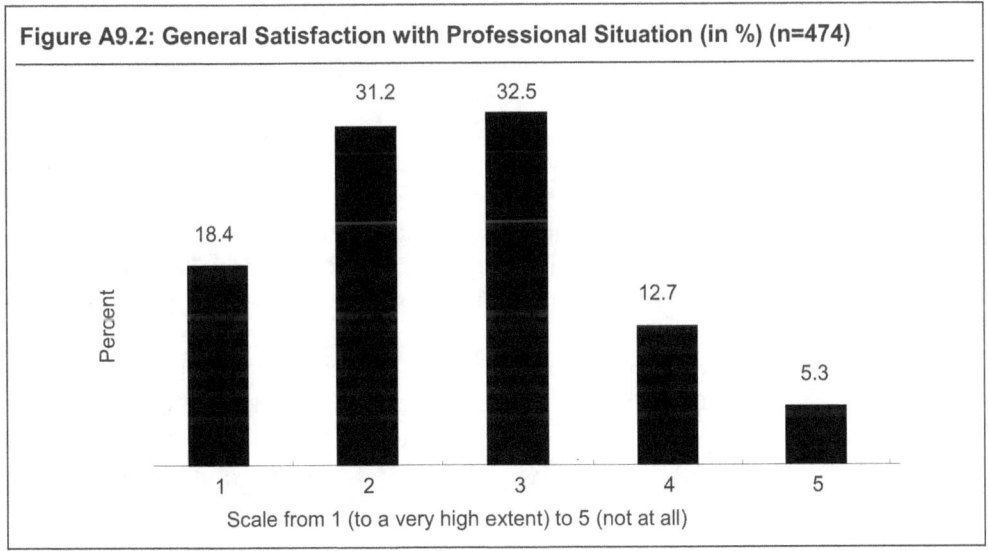

Figure A9.2: General Satisfaction with Professional Situation (in %) (n=474)

Generally, graduates were satisfied in their professional situation (M=2.55; SD=1.09) irrespective of year of graduation, gender or occupational status. Only 18 percent consider their situation as unsatisfying. An outstanding score of M=1.66 was presented only by the graduates of law. The importance of this result is founded in the empirically proven fact, that professional satisfaction is a decisive factor for the performance level, productivity, and motivation of the employees and finally the success of the company.

2.3.2. Objective indicator

These indicators include 'hard data' such as occupational situation, income, and duration of unemployment. In order to reveal the changes between the situation immediately after being awarded (Section 2.2) and the actual situation, the percentages for both data are presented next (table A9.4).

Table A9.4: Occupational Situation after Graduation and Present (in %)

Situation	After being awarded	At present
Full-time employed	72.2	83.4
Own business	2.1	2.7
Part-time employed	10.9	3.2
Unemployed but seeking	10.0	4.8
Advanced studies	1.0	2.5
Other	4.8	3.4
Total	478	476

It is apparent, that with pass of time the integration in the job market advances. At the time of interview, only 4.8 percent of the respondents reported to be unemployed and 86.1 percent to be fully employed.

This positive result in terms of external efficiency must be complemented by the observation, that professional success often requires a **high degree of mobility**, including phases of unemployment. 41 percent changed, at least once, the employer, mainly by reasons of career progress. In most of the cases such a change implies temporary unemployment.

Traditionally, the most important "hard" indicator of professional success is the **gross income**. In order to avoid a bias, only persons, who are actually employed will be considered (n=425). As income is a highly sensitive issue, the non-respondent number was 46 persons.

As it was to be expected, the distribution is characterized by a very large range (min=K 9,000; max=K 640,000) and an extreme right side skewness (v=3.48). The arithmetic mean per month is K 83,681 and the median K 65,000. The range within 80 percent of all subjects are located is from K 30,000 to K 150,000. Figure A9.3 shows the frequencies for intervals.

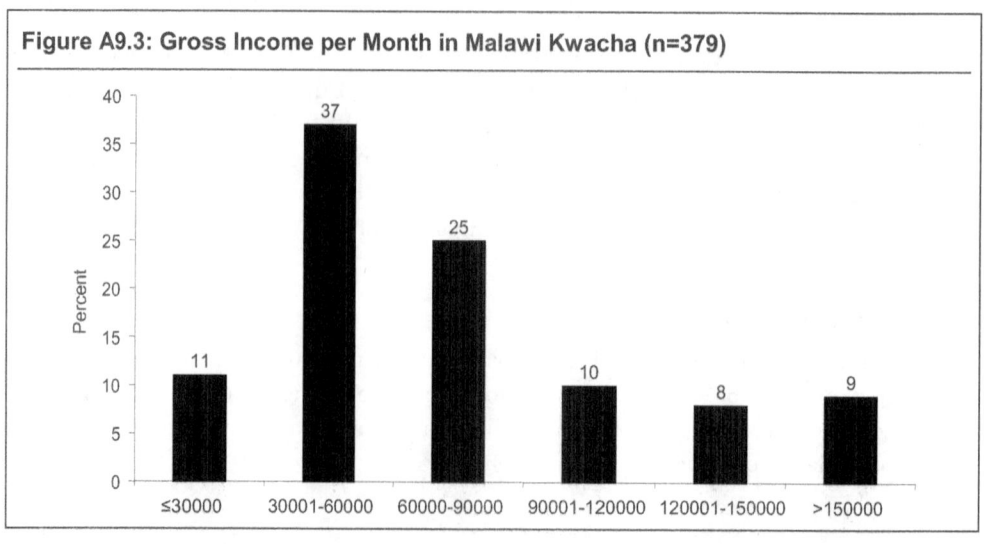

Figure A9.3: Gross Income per Month in Malawi Kwacha (n=379)

In order to get a realistic view about the income situation of graduates and their private rate of return, the values have to be compared with the average income per capita in Malawi, which is about US$230 (K 32,637) in a year.

While the indicators presented above did not reveal significant differences between groups, income, as a factor, registered some remarkable differences. Only significant differences will be reported in the following[7]:

- The average **income of male is 37 percent higher than that of female** (K 90,872 vs. K 66,047). This significant difference can be explained partly but not completely by the fact that male person are overrepresented in better paid work fields.
- The higher the academic degree the higher the income. This correlation correspond the basic theorem of human capital theory.
- The income in the southern region is significantly higher than in the central and northern regions.
- The average income of persons who at least changed once the employer is 41 percent higher than those of who did not (K 100,609 vs. K 71,490). This significant difference can be interpreted in the sense that mobility pays, but it must be considered that the chances to change the employer are not equally distributed for all.

In order to assess the career progress (promotion) a comparison between income in the first occupation and actual income is a strong indicator. This comparison has to be done by year, to control the effect of time (figure A9.4).[8]

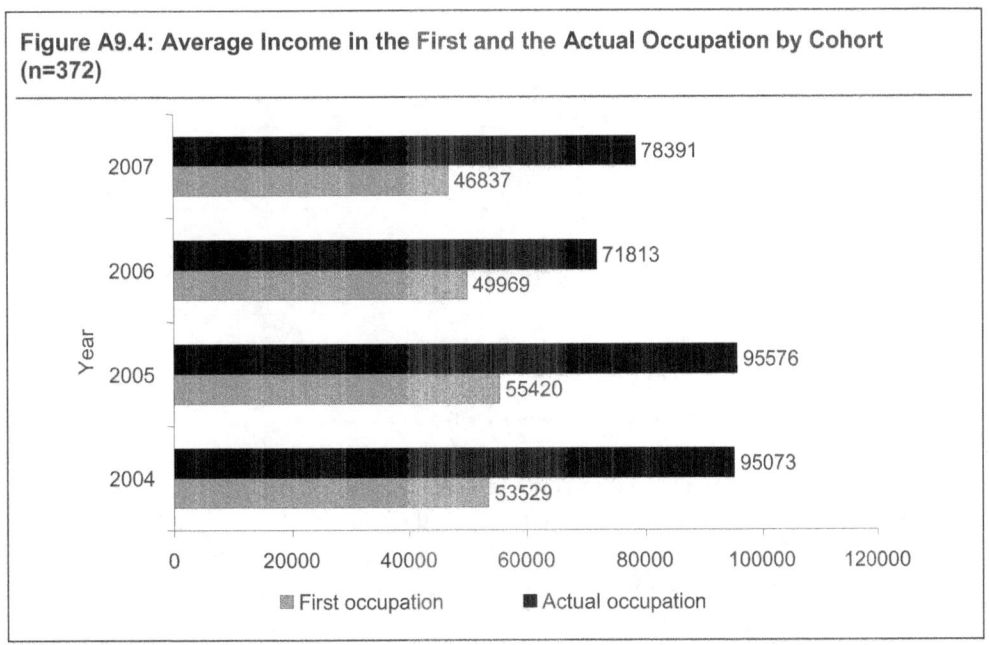

Figure A9.4: Average Income in the First and the Actual Occupation by Cohort (n=372)

For all cohorts an increase of income took place with 15-20 percent in average per year, except for the 2007 cohort which experienced in only one year a growth of 67 percent. In order to decompose these growth rates in a general component of economic growth and a component of individual promotion further econometrical analysis is needed. But it cannot be doubted that by and large the promotion progress for all employed graduates is fast.

2.4. Relation between studies and profession

Tertiary education is by nature a long-term project meanwhile the modern labor markets are short-term oriented. Therefore, **a synchronism between both subsystems is not easy to realize.** Lack or excess of academic qualified manpower, over-, under-, or miss-qualification are the consequence, and the external efficiency remains low.

As demonstrated above, the absorption of academic qualified manpower by the labor market in Malawi as well as the indicators of professional success can be considered as somewhat satisfying but with room for improvement. For a complete assessment of the external efficiency, however, the adequacy of the knowledge acquired at university is of utmost importance. This includes on one hand the possibility for the graduates to make use of their qualification and for the employers on the other hand to have at disposal the qualifications needed.

2.4.1. The view of the graduates

As pointed out in Section 2.1, the assessment of the utility of studies for fulfilling their professional tasks by the graduates was rather positive. Another aspect of the same issue is to what extent they could make use of qualifications acquired during their study. This measure can also be taken as an output indicator for the efficiency of study (table A9.5).

Table A9.5: Extent of Use of Qualification

Score	FREQ	PCT
1	153	33.9
2	147	32.6
3	107	23.7
4	31	6.9
5	13	2.9
Total	451	100.0
Missing	46	

Note: Scale from 1 (to a very high extent) to 5 (not at all).

It is quite encouraging, that the data reveal a high or even a very high extent of use (66.6 percent) with mean=2.12 and SD=1.05 on the five point scale. As to be expected there is a strong correlation (r=0.45) with the rating of usefulness of studies. Using the results of both indicators to carry out a cluster analysis, there is evidence that 78 percent of the respondents consider their studies as very useful for fulfilling their professional and effectively make use of the knowledge acquired. Only 17 percent assess their studies as not very useful and in consequence only make little use of their qualifications for fulfilling their professional tasks. The highest average score in this indicator is reached by law and ICT, because these are directly oriented to professional practice, whereas, i.e. pure sciences are more theoretical and different from the demands of everyday working tasks in a company. The gender-related mean difference (male=2.07; female=2.23) is not significant.

2.4.2. The view of the employers

To assess the utility and the use of qualification, the opinion of the graduates must be complemented by the **view of employers** in order to increase the degree of validity and triangulation of data, because the perception of both parts may differ.

A first strong indicator whether the contents of study and the demand of work fit, is the period of time the newly employed graduates need to carry out their professional tasks properly. Most of the employers (74.4 percent) consider a lapse of time until six months as sufficient for professional adaption, which is, in the international comparison, a good result.

A second indicator is the direct evaluation of knowledge and abilities of graduates by the employers (table A9.6).

Table A9.6: Degree of Abilities and Knowledge of the Graduates

	N	Mean	SD
Basic professional abilities and knowledge	129	2.09	.996
Special professional knowledge	129	2.45	.952
Knowledge in related professional fields	129	2.24	.974
Auxiliary characteristics	129	2.42	1.013

Note: Scale from 1 (very much) to 5 (not at all).

The evaluation given by the employers presents a satisfaction in all dimensions especially relative to basic professional knowledge. **A poor rating in all aspects of the graduate's abilities was expressed only by more or less 10 percent of the respondents.** All four aspects are strongly correlated, that means a general abilities and knowledge factor can be assumed. The evaluation given by the employers is not significantly correlated with the size of the company. Referring to the branch where the company is operating the evaluations differ somewhat, but the number of cases has not been sufficient to draw large conclusions.

Importantly it seems that many employers perceive certain differences in all aspects between the employees with academic degree coming from different institutions (figure A9.5).

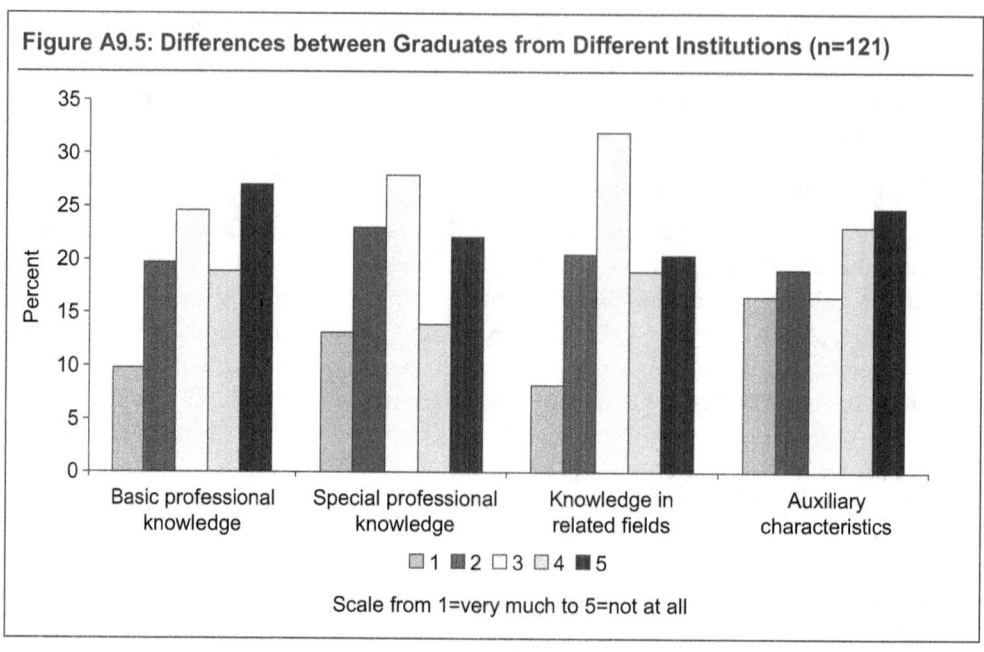

Figure A9.5: Differences between Graduates from Different Institutions (n=121)

Scale from 1=very much to 5=not at all

Little is known about the causes of this inter-institutional variance, whose analysis is beyond the scope of this study.

2.5. Appropriateness of professional situation and level of education

The question that how far the actual professional situation (status, income, tasks) corresponds to the educational level catches different areas. It summarizes the relation between studies and profession (Section 2.4), the professional success (Section 2.3) and finally the core issue in how far the educational and occupational system fit. The well-known phenomenon of over-qualification can be covered by this indicator—even if the viewpoint is a subjective one.[9]

Table A9.7: Extent of Appropriateness of Professional Situation

Score	FREQ	PCT
1	91	20.4
2	146	32.7
3	121	27.1
4	61	13.6
5	28	6.3
Total	447	100.0
Missing	45	

Note: Scale from 1 (very high extent) to 5 (not at all)

The average M=2.51 indicates a rather positive tendency and more than the half (52.9 percent) of all graduates, indeed, feel that their education qualifications are highly appropriate to their positions and status. Gender related differences do not exist at all in this indicator but there is a certain variance between groups in the field of studies.

There remains 19.5 percent, who felt that their positions and status did not match their qualifications. This is true especially for the group of only part-time employed graduates. Once more it must be emphasized that a 100 percent fit of the Higher Education system and the labor market system is a utopian benchmark, so that results as the above are not completely satisfying but quite reasonable.

As to be expected, the feeling of appropriateness has a strong influence on the satisfaction with the professional situation (r=0.55). Use of qualifications acquired, work satisfaction and correspondence between education level and occupational situation form a complex construct for measuring professional success. Submitting these core indicators to a non-hierarchical cluster analysis it becomes once more evident that there exists **a group of somewhat 19 percent of graduates with occupational problems** in a larger sense. This Group (Cluster 3) comprises persons not fully integrated in the labor market or in inadequate positions and therefore unsatisfied. Its composition is characterized by a strong over- representation of humanities (RR=1.63) and women (R=1.38).[10] In order to understand the patterns and causes of this problem further analysis is needed.

3. Results of Dropout Study

As pointed out above, studies which track university drop outs are rather rare. As far as it is known in Malawi, no reliable data about the reason and the destiny of drop outs are available. Even the quantitative dimension, the overall dropout rate, can only be estimated. The results presented below can give first empirical evidence about the reasons dropping out and the situation of the dropouts compared with graduates and completers of TEVET courses and programs.

3.1. Duration of studies and reason for leaving

The longer the student courses at university without success the higher the waste of resources. The average of 3.68 semesters in the present study does not seem very high in international comparison and especially students with financial problems leave university rather soon. Nevertheless it continues to be a matter of concern.

For possible policy options aiming at improving effectiveness, there is need for more information about the reasons for dropping out (figure A9.6).

Figure A9.6: Reasons for Dropping Out (in %) (n=90)

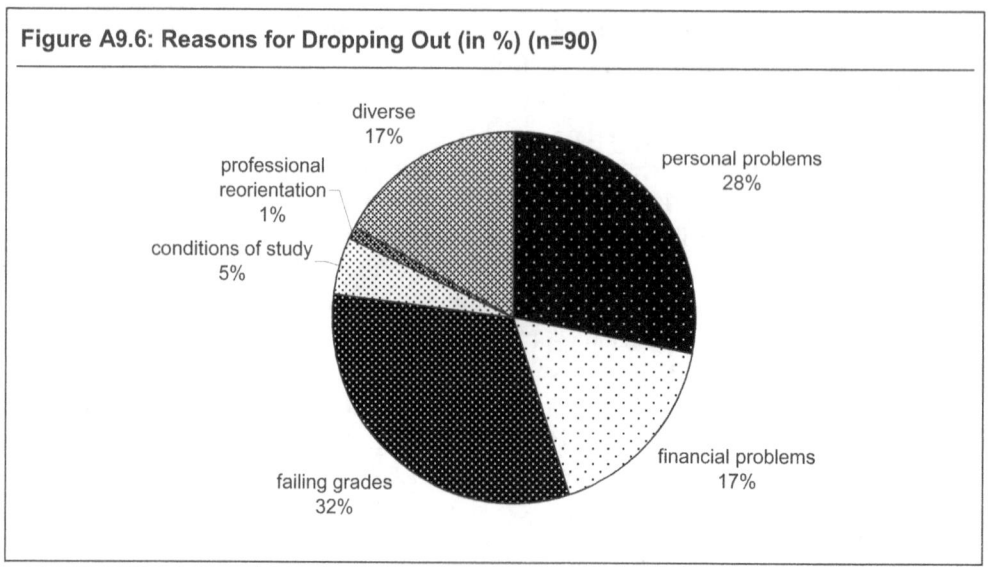

It is worth mentioning, that in case of female students personal problems are the main reason for dropping out (39.1 percent), in the case of male student it is failing grades (34.4 percent). Financial problems occur in both groups equally.

Basically there are two different constellations in the context of dropping-out: (1) lack of individual prerequisites and (2) systemic failures, which impede that gifted students continue their studies. Leaving university due to lack of academic performance, demotivation, or equivocal expectations makes part of a normal selection process and the earlier this reorientation takes place the better. But if the individual prerequisites are given and students cannot continue due to financial or personal problems institutional support is needed.

3.2. Actual Situation

A main concern is the situation of the persons after dropping out. Are there chances to insert in the labor market or is unemployment the consequence? The data reflect a split result: 55 percent are employed or put their own business; 35 percent are unemployed and 10 percent are coursing some kind of TEVET program. The gender differences referring to this issue are highly significant (p<0.01) with a female unemployment rate (21.7 percent) much lower than the average). The chances to secure a job vary also with the field of study.

It can be concluded, that dropping out does not lead automatically to social decline and poverty, but certainly the situation of those who did not finish their studies are in a less favorable position compared with the graduates: The unemployment rate is higher than in the case of the graduates, they need longer to find a job or put a business and when they finally are economically active they count with an average salary of only K 33,267 approximately 38 percent of the average that graduates receive. As is the case with graduates some between-group variances appear even not so expressive as in case of those. Furthermore only in a third of all cases the professional activities are related to the former studies, so that the knowledge acquired at university cannot be used effectively.

3.3. Future Plans

The plans of the dropouts for the nearer or longer future are an indicator for the degree of satisfaction with their actual situation. It is remarkable that about 62 percent of the dropouts plan to return to university, what this means is that by majority the dropouts are not definitive dropouts but so called potential interrupters. Only 26 percent are planning to try to secure a job or doing business and only 2.5 percent want to course a TEVET program. Even more than half of those who are integrated in the labor market are planning to return to the university. It is a matter of concern that also 60 percent of former students, who left the university due to performance problems did not give up the idea to return one day to academic studies. Obviously a vocational education does not represent an attractive option for those people. This is completely understandable in view of the income level of TEVET completers (cf. Part III, Section 2.4).

In spite of frustrating experiences and actual problems, the dropouts demonstrate an optimistic view of their future professional opportunities (figure A9.7).

Figure A9.7: Rating of Professional Opportunities in the Next Years (in %)

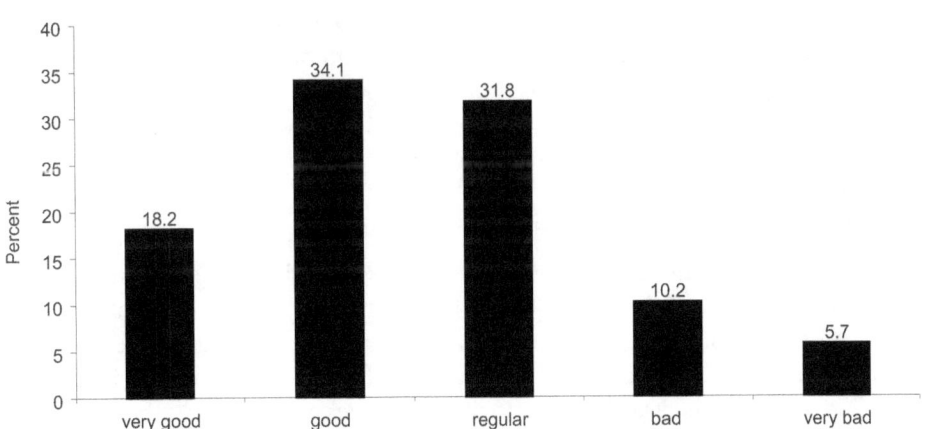

More than half of dropouts are rating their professional chances positively, especially those who had studied law (100 percent), pure sciences (66 percent), or business/economics (66 percent). In how far these expectations will be fulfilled in the future can be tested only by a longitudinal (panel design) study.

4. Summary and Conclusions

Summary

- The Higher Education Sector in Malawi fulfils widely its function to prepare highly qualified human resources, who are in general employable and succeed to integrate in the labor market.
- The graduates are mostly satisfied with their studies and evaluate them as useful for their professional activities.

- The scale of monthly gross income exhibits a wide range with a mean of K 87,000. Significant gender imbalance and differences between fields of studies are to be observed.
- The match between qualifications acquired (supply) and labor market needs (demand) is mostly given. The majority of the graduates perform activities and tasks appropriate to their qualification making use of their knowledge acquired at university.
- However, there is a segment of graduates (20 percent) not fully integrated in the labor market or situated in inadequate occupational conditions with salaries not corresponding to their level.
- The employers are somewhat satisfied with the level of knowledge and skills of the graduates. But there is also a stratum of 10-12 percent of graduates which does not exhibit the expected level of knowledge and abilities.
- Also little is known about the quantitative dimension of university dropout in Malawi, there is some empirical evidence that dropping out is not a singular phenomenon. Even being a small sample, first tendencies and trends appears. The main reasons for leaving university without being awarded are failing grades (32 percent) and personal problems (28 percent).
- The unemployment rate of the dropouts is rather high (35 percent) and the average salary of the active is about K 33,000.
- The majority of the dropouts plan to return to the university even when the reason for their dropping out was insufficient academic performance.

5. Conclusions and Recommendations

- The Higher Education system in Malawi is by and large aligned to its present economical and labor market environment. But knowledge weaknesses and problems of labor market integration for a certain segment of graduates should not be ignored. In the course of future development the enrolment rates must increase according to the manpower needed.
- The high income level reached by graduates justifies covering an adequate part of the real costs of services and introducing fees which must be used to enhance the material and academic infrastructure of the universities.
- The destination and situation of university dropouts must turn into a main concern of educational policy in order to avoid the waste of competent human resources by dropping out. Options of training and certification must be offered to those who cannot fulfill academic performance standards.

Notes

[1] Ministry of Education, Malawi. National Education Sector Plan. Higher Education. November 2006.

[2] Schomburg, H. (2003), *Handbook for Graduate Tracer Studies*. Centre for Research on Higher Education and Work. University of Kassel. The authors acknowledge gratefully the important support given by Harald Schomburg from the Center of Higher Education Research, University of Kassel.

[3] The sample includes also n=10 (2 percent) of post-graduates (Master's degree). It was decided not to exclude these cases because they may serve for comparative objectives.

[4] As known, in Malawi the costs are even higher than in other comparable countries due to some specific characteristics of the system. By 2006 the per student cost had grown to about US$4,270 at UNIMA and at Mzuzu US$5,169. Ministry of Education, Malawi. National Education Sector plan. Higher Education. November 2007

[5] It was surprising to note, that very few graduates are willing or able to set their own business. In case of graduates in economics, business administration and related areas the percentage was even lower (1.5 percent) than in general (1.9 percent).

[6] "Patchwork" means a situation of frequent change of jobs, mainly temporary jobs, more than one job at the same time, altogether an unstable situation.

[7] Due to the extreme skewness of the distribution, parametrical (t-Test, ANOVA) as well as non parametrical tests (U-Test, K-W-Test) have been performed. The results are identical; only in case of year of graduation the K-W-Test results significant and the ANOVA doesn't.

[8] In order to avoid a bias, only persons, who indicated both their first and present salaries made part of the comparison.

[9] Respondents, who are not seeking employment, whatever the reason may be or who are dedicated to advanced studies are not considered (n=448).

[10] The Relative Risk (RR) is a statistical measure which relates the conditional probability with the total probability for a determined group.

Part III: TEVET Tracer Study

Introduction: The Context of the TEVET System in Malawi

The evolution of TEVET system aligns very much to the political development of the country. At independence, the government of Malawi intended to develop a human resource base that would support the social-economic development of the country. This human resource base was soon to replace the huge expatriate level present in public and private sectors. However, it became clear that there was need to develop an equally important skilled craftsmanship that would meet the needs of the development agenda. So, an **apprenticeship program** was put in place.

The program was aimed at training artisans through public and private training institutions. Over the years, Technician Programmes were introduced into the apprenticeship scheme. External assessment for students in this program was initially done by City and Guilds of London Institute, an international examining and certifying body based in the UK. However, the need to localize the curriculum and its corresponding assessment procedures gave birth to the Trade Testing Examinations and, much later, the Malawi Craft Examinations. Recently (2006) the "Competency-Based Modular Education and Training" system (CBET) was implemented.

While it is clear from the foregoing that there were now three independent sources of external examinations, the advent of political multiparty brought liberalization of Tevet provision. The government, NGOs, churches, private formal and private informal operators established their own training bases, providing short and long-term non-formal programs. All these Tevet providers have choice on which examining body to subject their students to. In some cases, a student sits examinations from more than one of the three examining bodies for the same level of tuition. At the same time, the government established TEVETA with the mandate aimed at regulating Tevet system and facilitating formal and informal programs. Until now the coordination between the different public and private providers and authorities is poor and their roles are not clearly demarcated.

There should be a huge potential demand for TEVET among school-leavers in Malawi and the access to training facilities is limited. School attainments and educational level are further limiting factors in acquiring higher levels of skills, which are necessary for economic and social development. Those who do not gain access to formal institutional training undergo often some type of informal learning under craftsmen or members of the family, training on the job in a company or some informal program.

1. Methodology

The general methodological procedures of tracing, sampling and data collection have been described above (Part I). The following section describes the construction of the specific questionnaires and the basic characteristics of the sample for each target group covered by the TEVET completers study.

1.1. Questionnaires

The design of the questionnaires for the completers of TEVET Courses or programs has been performed by the consultants using elements of instrument developed for similar purposes.

1.2. Size of Samples

In keeping with the TOR a sample size of 1000 TEVET completers was envisaged. As the retention rate of the questionnaires was 100 percent, the final sample size was **n=1026 TEVET completers** and a small control group **n=73 without formal qualification.**

The limited employers survey suggested in the TOR included a total of n=220 employers (companies or organizations). Out of this number **n=206 employers** occupied skilled and unskilled manpower of different levels. For purpose of the TEVET survey, only this subgroup is relevant and included in the analysis.

1.3. Characteristics of the Samples

According to the TOR, the sample of the **TEVET completers** was drawn from all occupational fields in the formal and informal sector, wage employed, and self employed, with and without certificated qualification.

The sample meets largely criterions of representativeness. All relevant institutions from the formal TEVETA system (TC), parallel programs, and other programs in public and private institutions had their completers covered in the study. The questionnaire retention rate was 100 percent.

The demographic characteristics of the samples are given in the sampling frame on the following page, based on the number of valid cases.

Sampling Frame

TEVET PARTICIPANTS	
Age	
Mean	29
SD	6.1
Economic sector %	
Private formal	26.6
Private informal	20.4
Public	7.4
Other	0.5
Unknown	45.0
Gender %	
Male	71.7
Female	28.3
Region of living %	
North	20.3
Central	37.0
South	42.8
Location of work place %	
Urban	51
Rural	49
Education level %	
Standard 1-5	2.7
Standard 6-8	10.4
Junior Certificate of Education	29.2
Malawi School Certificate of Education or equivalent	47.7
Diploma or above	8.8
None	1.3

2. Results of TEVET Study

2.1. Type and level of qualification

Of all n=1099 respondents 93.4 percent obtained a form of qualification by one or more than one training course and/or program. Only those n=1026 cases are considered as TEVET completers in the context of this study. But also more traditional and informal ways of learning such as with members of the family, on the job or with a skilful craftsman still remain important (16 percent) specifically for the informal sector. Often young people start learning in a more informal way and later on insert in a formal training to acquire more skills by this way (14 percent). Table A9.8 informs about the qualifications obtained by those who completed a training course and were certificated.

Table A9.8: Type and Grade of Qualification

Type and Level	FREQ	PCT
City and Guilds 1	48	4.7
City and Guilds 2	33	3.2
City and Guilds 3	26	2.5
National Trade Test 1	174	17.0
National Trade Test 2	170	16.6
National Trade Test 3	112	10.9
Malawi Craft Certificate	34	3.3
Advanced Malawi Craft Certificate	18	1.7
Other Certificates	411	40.1
Total	1026	100.0

Note: Persons without certificates are not included in this table.

The traditional formal qualification and apprenticeship program continue to play a dominant role in the TEVET sector (60 percent). But the high percentage of "other certificates" demonstrates that the system as a whole has become very complex and heterogeneous. Beside the Technical Colleges with their long lasting apprenticeship programs there are multiple governmental, parastatal, nongovernmental, religious, and private profit-oriented institutions providing mostly short time or mid-term courses, which deliver to the participant basic knowledge and skills demanded by the market in the most different fields (table A9.9). The quality level of this "other certificates" is rather heterogeneous, since the category comprises simple certificates of attendance as well as diplomas of reputable institutes.

Table A9.9: Duration of Training Courses

Time	FREQ	PCT	Valid PCT	PCT cum
Until 6 months	189	17.3	24.7	24.7
Until 1 year	137	12.4	17.8	42.6
Until 2 years	171	15.5	22.3	64.8
Until 3 years	128	11.6	16.7	81.5
Until 4 years	126	11.5	16.5	98.0
More than 4 years	15	1.4	2.0	100.0
Total	766	69.8	100.0	
Missing	333	30.2		
Grand total	1099	100.0		

More than 40 percent of the courses do not exceed one year of duration. An analysis of the correlations between duration of the course and relevant key indicators of efficiency will follow later on.

2.2. Assessment of training

Although TEVET completers cannot be considered as experts in matters of qualification, their opinion about the usefulness of their course is a valid efficiency indicator because they experience finally the outcomes and effects in terms of labor market chances. Therefore it is very encouraging that the assessment of the usefulness of the training is very positive. The high rate of non respondents, however, should be taken into consideration (figure A9.8).

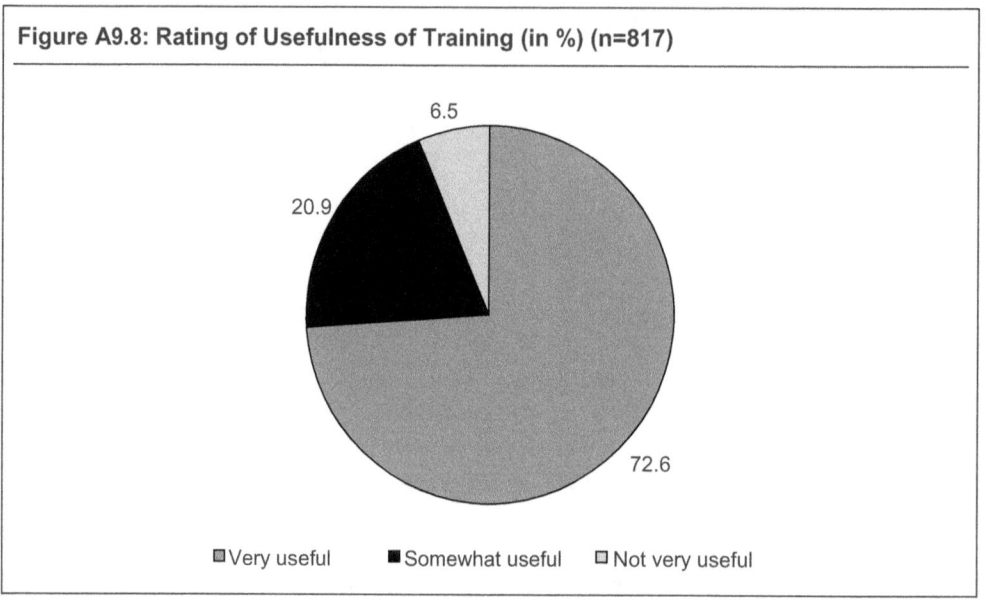

Figure A9.8: Rating of Usefulness of Training (in %) (n=817)

A detailed analysis of the factors which have influence on the rating of usefulness reveals interesting insights:

- Completers who rate the course as very useful have in average a 1.27 higher salary than the other two groups.
- In the group of unemployed persons only 53.1 percent rate the course as very useful.
- There is a zero correlation between duration and rating of the course.
- There are no gender differences in the rating.
- Self employed have a higher "very useful" rating (78.3 percent) than other groups

Variations referring to the type of course, institution and other intervening variables still need further analysis.

Another relevant indicator for the external efficiency is the matching of the type of course and actual employment field. A cross-tabulation between both variables reveals that around **80 percent of the completers are working in the professional field for that they have been trained.** A serious amount of misallocation of human resources is not to be stated.

This positive assessment can be cross-validated by real improvements of the work situation which the respondents attribute to the program/course they attended. In total out of n=1000 respondents only 145 (14.5 percent) experienced no change, half of them still without employment. The others report at least one positive change in their situation.[1] Table A9.10 reports the items which reached the highest approval.

Table A9.10: Changes as Result of Program/Course

Results of training	n	% of cases
I got a job	365	36.5%
I have been able to make better products	389	38.9%
I have been more frequently hired to provide my services	308	30.8%
I managed to open my own business	243	24.3%
n	1,000	

The positive evaluation of the programs in general does not mean, however, that there is no need for improvement. An overwhelming majority of respondents indicated in an open question a variety of weaknesses of the courses, which must be a matter of concern for all TEVET providers. Table A9.11 resumes the results:

Table A9.11: Weaknesses of Program/Course

Weaknesses	FREQ	PCT
Inadequate resources	335	34.7
Too long	167	16.3
Too short	237	23.2
Too theoretical	102	10.0
Others	90	8.8
No weaknesses	71	7.0
Gesamt	1,022	100.0

First of all it is notable, that nearly all respondents answered. This in case of open questions an exceptional result and a clear indicator that the completers attribute high relevance to this issue. There are obviously three main limiting factors: **Resources** (34.7 percent), **duration** (39.5 percent) and imbalance between **theoretical and practical elements** (10 percent). The factor "resources" comprise a wide spectrum of deficiencies: lack of material and tools for practical activities, outdated equipment, and syllabus, shortage of teachers and lack of books.

Furthermore, there is strong empirical evidence that exist a serious imbalance between duration of course, curriculum content and labor market chances. An in-deep analysis of the open answers show that on the one hand a lot of courses are too long, have too much superfluous subjects and require **too much effort compared with the salary they get later**. On the other hand, many courses are too short, that means for the students a work overload and not enough time for practical activities. A simple comparison of the duration of the courses shows the difference: The average duration in the group which considered the training period as too long was 29.3 months and in the group which considered too short was 14.9 months. There seems to be an urgent need to readjust the duration of the courses to the available resources and to real needs of the participants and the labor market.

Finally it must be mentioned that the misalignment between theory and practice is more serious as the 10 percent of responses indicates. In a lot of comments the critics about the long duration of the course and the lack of resources were combined with the complaint about too short practical periods, inadequate material to carry out practical works, theoretical overload, and insufficient industrial attachment.

2.3. Current employment and work situation

The successful integration in the labor market can be caught by different indicators. The most basic of them is the occupational status (table A9.12).

Table A9.12: Current Employment Status

Status	FREQ	PCT
Wage employed full-time	421	36.4
Wage employed part-time	88	7.9
Self employed (own business)	315	28.6
Self employed and wage employed	45	4.0
Unemployed but looking for employment	167	15.1
Unemployed and not looking for employment by personal reasons	15	1.5
Continue studying	48	4.5
Total	1,099	100.0

As to be expected the majority of completers are wage employed, but it is also a relevant percentage of self employed people. There is strong empirical evidence that self employment mainly takes place in the informal sector. As the number of non respondents was rather high in this issue an estimation had be done which results in a percentage **between 57 percent and 83 percent of the self-employed operate in the informal sector.** It is this group which in the question about problems in their actual professional situation indicates lack of capital or outdated tools as bottleneck for the growth of their business (85 percent).

Most of the subjects who were seeking employment after the course (n=456) secured rather rapidly a job: after six months 64 percent and after 12 months 85 percent were successful. The occupational stability is relatively high, because 70 percent did not change the employer (table A9.13).

Table A9.13: Duration of Employment Seeking

Time of seeking	FREQ	PCT
1-3 months	204	44.7
4-6 months	88	19.4
7-12 months	99	21.7
13-24 months	44	9.6
more than 24 months	21	4.6
Total	456	100.0

The positional level of the wage employed is another relevant indicator for the professional success. In general the completers operate on a rather low level considering the time, which they invested in learning processes (table A9.13).

Table A9.13: Level of Position

Level	FREQ	PCT
Ordinary hand (routine tasks)	349	58.7
Lower management (supervisor etc)	170	28.6
Middle management (foreman, group leader etc)	76	12.7
Total	595	100.0

Referring to the self employed and business men, most of them (77.5 percent) run their business with employees, the majority (41.6 percent) with 1-2 employees, creating a multiplicative effect for the labor market (table A9.14).

Table A9.14: Number of Employees

No of employees	FREQ	PCT
0	60	22.5
1-2	111	41.6
3-5	73	27.3
> 5	23	8.6
Total	267	100.0

In general, the data presented above reveal a somewhat positive panorama relative to the labor market chances of the completers.[2] But there exists also a stratum with serious problems of employability. Excluding those subjects who continue studying or who do not work by personal reasons results in an unemployment rate at present of 16.2 percent (cf. table A9.12).[3]

There is high empirical evidence, that certain social groups are more vulnerable than others in terms of unemployment and other factors of social relevance. This is shown also in this study where in some groups the percentage of employment seeker is significantly higher than the average. Table A9.15 presents the relative risk (RR) for those groups.

Table A9.15: Relative Risk of Unemployment for High Risk Groups

Groups	RR
Rural area	1.31
Women	1.39
Without education	1.87
Young (18-24 years)	2.46

Specifically young people and persons without education encounter serious problems to secure a job even having a qualification.

2.4. Income situation and its determinants

The core indicator for the quality and productivity of work—at least in the private sector—is the income of the persons (salary or net profit). Figure A9.9 shows the income distribution, which is concentrated in the range between K 5,000 and K 20,000 monthly (net). In case of self employment the income is the difference between sales and expenditures.

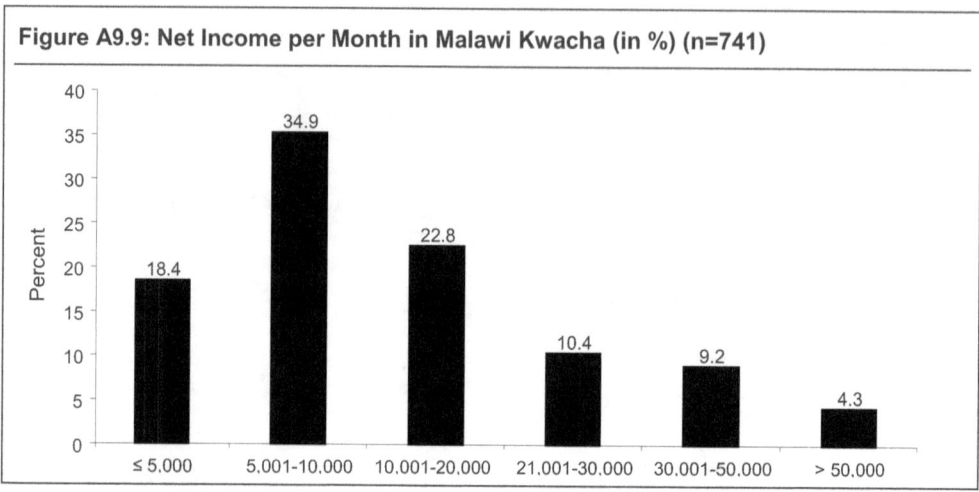

Figure A9.9: Net Income per Month in Malawi Kwacha (in %) (n=741)

The average is M=K 16,730. As in the case of higher education graduates the distribution is extremely skewed (v=3.0) and therefore the Median (K 10,000) is much lower than the mean.

In general terms the data reveal a rather **low level of income.** It should be a matter of concern for all stakeholders, when qualified people who coursed two years and more a training program and acquired recognized certificates are remunerated at such a level. Various completers complained about this serious disproportion in open questions.

On the other hand the high variance of income raises the question which variables have an impact on the income level of the completers. Some of them will be analyzed in the following.

Gender

Differently from the results in the HE sector no significant gender imbalances occur in the TEVET sector (Male: Mean=K 16,778; Female: Mean=K 16,591).

Location of living

There is a significant difference ($p<0.05$) in the income level between urban and rural areas (Urban: Mean=K 17,882; Rural: Mean=K 15,419).

Level of professional position

The higher the professional position the higher the income must be. This basic theorem of economics is verified by the data ($p<0.01$) (table A9.16).

Table A9.16: Mean Income by Positional Level

Level	Mean	N	SD
Ordinary hand	11332	319	10234
Lower management	18740	164	17064
Middle management	25822	72	24817
Total	15354	555	15813

The range between the lowest and the highest level is nearly one standard deviation. But not more than 13 percent of all completers reach a middle level.

Occupational status

The differences between the groups are significant ($p<0.01$). The highest mean income have those running their own business. This shows that it pays for the completers to start their own business venture (table A9.17).

Table A9.17: Mean Income by Occupational Status

Occupational status	Mean	N	SD
Wage employed full-time	16019	402	16402
Wage employed part-time	8979	70	7329
Self employed (own business)	20724	226	19411
Self employed and wage employed	15032	43	15878
Total	16731	741	17049

Educational level

The impact of the education level can be described like this: the upper and lower levels of education differ significantly in their income related to the average, but in the middle level (Standard 6-8, Junior Certificate of Education, Malawi School Certificate of Education) the differences are not significant.

Number of courses

The mean income of those who attended more than one training course is somewhat higher (M= K 19,582) than for the subjects with only one course (M=K 16,302).

Way of getting skills

As mentioned above, informal ways of learning and (friend, members of the family, on the job or with the help of a skilful craftsman) still remain important. For some it is the only way of skill acquirement, for others the first step which later on is completed by a formal training course (table A9.18).

Table A9.18: Mean Income by Way of Getting Skills

WAYS	Mean	N	SD
Informal way	13386	139	19408
Formal way	17235	484	16311
Both way	19192	110	16821
Total	16799	733	17085

The different income levels in the groups are a clear signal, that the market rewards work force which has practical abilities (acquired on the job or otherwise) **and** theoretical knowledge (acquired in a formal training). Only informal acquired skills usually mean a lack of theoretical basis and the formal courses by the TEVET provider are often too much theoretical without sufficient training of practical abilities (cf. table A9.11).

Duration of courses

As the accumulation of human capital depends basically on the time invested in education a strong correlation between duration of training and income should be expected. It appears, however, that the correlation in the case of TEVET completers in Malawi is rather weak. A correlation[4] rho=.05 was found including all occupied subjects; a rho=.18 including only the wage employed. This means that the market does not remunerate invested time but the shortage of certain competencies and qualifications.

Field of occupation

The shortage of competencies is reflected by the significant income differentials between the job fields of the completers. Table A9.19 presents the mean for all fields in descending order.

Table A9.19: Mean Income by Field of Occupation

Field of operating	Mean	N	SD
Steel fixing	33416	6	27850
Other[a]	27795	30	39485
Refrigeration & Air conditioning	25200	12	23603
Hawker	24122	18	15719
Computer Science	23222	9	17176
Secretarial, Administration and Accounting	21908	74	16668
Wood Machining/Fabrication and Welding	18733	46	15770
Carpentry and joinery	18498	92	16496
Beauty Therapy	17000	4	19493
General Fitting	15777	20	13025
Brick Laying	15755	36	13013
Painting and Decoration	15336	15	10716
Electrical Installation	14154	37	12249
Electronics	14095	19	19292
Car maintenance	14087	115	14139
Tailoring and designing	13044	57	16215
Plumbing	12957	23	13471
Food production	12676	14	16393
Hospitality Services[b]	10816	56	12082
Food processing	8833	6	1834
TOTAL	16899	685	17420

Notes: a. The category "other" comprises different fields of activities not registered in the list.
b. The low rank for "Hospitality Services" which comprises mainly the whole sector of tourism is somewhat surprising. But in this sector fringe benefits and tips don't make part of the official remuneration. Therefore the data probably underestimate the real income of the employed.

The between group differences are highly significant and reflect the demand-supply conditions of the actual labor market in Malawi. But also the in-group variances remain very high, because many other factors may have an effect on the income level.

Type of qualification

An important question is, in how far the labor market remunerates different type and level of certificates (table A9.20).

Table A9.20: Mean Income by Type and Level of Certificates

Type and Level	Mean	n	SD
City and Guilds 1	24250	28	22302
City and Guilds 2	18182	21	16972
City and Guilds 3	17569	19	18234
National Trade Test 1	15965	118	12986
National Trade Test 2	13585	119	11796
National Trade Test 3	14142	62	14572
Malawi Craft Certificate	22476	21	19300
Advanced Malawi Craft Certificate	14868	15	11745
Other Certificates	18750	283	20534
Without Certificates	11356	55	10301
Total	16731	741	170489

First of all it must be pointed out, that TEVET training does matter. Workers without certificated training course have an average income of only K 11,356, meanwhile the owner of a certificate reach K 17,162 in average. As the data reveal, the City & Guilds Certificate enjoy a definitely higher valuation in the labor market than the National Trade.[5]

A somewhat unexpected result appears in case of the Malawi Craft certificate. It should be expected, of course, that the owners of the Advanced Certificate have a higher income level than those of the Craft Certificate. A possible explication is the small sample size which means a high standard error and in fact the difference is not significant ($p>0.1$). But it should also be taken into consideration that a higher portion of Malawi Craft completers are self-employed implying a higher average income.

The owners of "other certificates" are characterized by an income a little above the general mean and the highest standard deviation in relation to the group mean. This demonstrates once more the very expressive heterogeneity of type and quality of courses and certificates offered by the market. Further analysis is needed in order to verify which type of certificates by which providers are rewarded by the employers.

2.4. Evaluation of the employers

Also in the case of non academic staff, the opinion of the employers is an important indicator in how far the system is able to provide market oriented qualifications.

First of all it must be pointed out that the employers confirm that a TEVET qualification makes a difference. For 76.8 percent there are notable differences in work performance between TEVET completers and the others. Only 10.6 percent don't perceive such difference and the rest do not know. Therefore it is not surprising that the companies put much emphasis on the qualification of their employees and organize by themselves the initial training if necessary or offer complementary training programs.

Another indicator for fit between demand and supply is the time the newly employed TEVET completers need to carry out their professional tasks. Most (82.4 percent) of the interviewed employers consider a lapse of time until six months as sufficient for professional adaptation.

Another core indicator for the market orientation of the TEVET system is the direct evaluation of knowledge and abilities of completers by the employers. The rather high non-respondent rate especially of City & Guild and TEVET Certificate shows that the employers employ few workers with this type of certificate (table A9.21).

Table A9.21: Degree of Abilities and Knowledge of TEVET Completers by Type and Level

Type and Level	N	Mean	SD
City & Guilds Part 1	72	2.13	1.020
City & Guilds Part 2	71	2.41	.935
City & Guilds Part 3	67	2.49	1.120
National Trade Test Grade 1	91	2.03	.983
National Trade Test Grade 2	91	2.63	1.007
National Trade Test Grade 3	89	2.70	.993
Malawi Craft Certificate	67	2.58	1.032
Advanced Malawi Craft	53	2.26	1.179
TEVETA Certificate Level 1	40	2.63	1.213
TEVETA Certificate Level 2	35	2.63	.877
TEVETA Certificate Level 3	58	2.29	1.377

Note: Scale from 1 (very much) to 5 (not at all).

The evaluations given by the employers vary in a relative small range from 2.03 (National Trade Test 1) to 2.70 (National Trade Test 3) in average. Neither outstanding nor poor rating is to be observed in general. But as the standard deviations indicate, the evaluation done by the employers is not completely homogeneous. **Especially in the lower grades of certificates there are around 15-20 percent of completers whose performance does not correspond to the expectations of the employers**.

Theoretically it is to be expected that the better the evaluation score the higher the grade achieved by the completers.[6] Indeed, the data verify very clearly this assumption. Especially in case of the National Trade Certificate, the difference between the lowest and highest level is more than half a standard deviation.

The between group variance in all type of certificates may be explained in part by the differences between institutions perceived by the employers (figure A9.10).

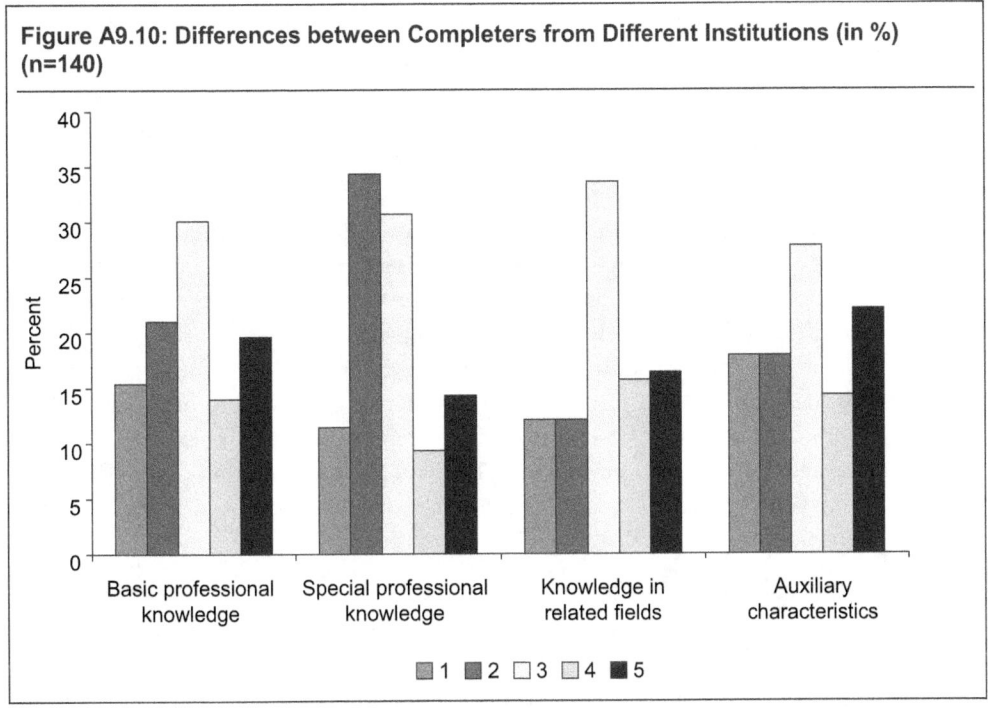

Figure A9.10: Differences between Completers from Different Institutions (in %) (n=140)

Note: Scale from 1=very much to 5=not at all.

There is an expressive inter-institutional variance, which is extremely high in case of special professional knowledge. This clearly indicates that not all TEVET providers adhere to the same set of quality standards and that quality assurance must become a main concern which goes beyond pure formal requirements in order to guarantee the acquisition of comparable skills for the Malawian workforce.

4. Summary and Conclusions

Summary

- The TEVET system is characterized by a high grade of complexity and heterogeneity in terms of duration, providers (public, parastatal, and private), quality of training courses and type and level of certificates on the other.
- Training programs are relevant for the formal and informal sector development, for self-employment and wage employment.
- The sector in Malawi fulfils widely its function to prepare a skilled workforce for various occupational fields, which is employable and ready to integrate into the labor market as wage employed or self employed. But there is still room for improvement.
- A risk group of around 20 percent of completers, specifically young people and women has problems to integrate successfully in the labor market.
- The completers rate the training program mostly as very useful (73 percent). But insufficient and outdated training materials, equipment, and infrastructure of institutions as well as limited places for industrial attachment

are serious constraints for a practical oriented training and skill development taking in account the prevailing demands of the labor market.
- The match between qualifications acquired (supply) and labor market needs (demand) is mostly given. 80 percent of the completers perform activities in the fields which they have been trained for.
- The scale of monthly gross income exhibits a wide range with a mean of K 16,730. There is no correlation between duration of training and income level, but a significant correlation between occupational field and income level. The remuneration for the owner of different types and levels of certificates differs somewhat but not so strong as to be expected.
- The employers are somewhat satisfied with the level of knowledge and skills of the graduates, but in the lower certificate grades there are around 15-20 percent of completers whose performance doesn't correspond to the expectations of the employers. They point out a rather large difference between completers coming from different institutions and sometimes poor practical abilities.

Conclusions and Recommendations
- Taking into account the high complexity of the Malawian TEVET system there is an urgent need to identify and demarcate the functions and responsibilities of different public, nongovernmental, and private providers, in order to optimize the efficiency of the system as a whole.
- All TEVET providers must keep track of those they trained and provide support and follow-up services to the completers in order to facilitate their integration in the Labor Market or to incentive the development of their business by giving loans.
- The mismatch between duration of training and income indicates an urgent need to make the curriculum flexible and to facilitate different entry and exit points to avoid waste of time and resources and enhance the efficiency of the system. The recently implemented modularized system may be a step in this direction.
- The insufficient and outdated training resources inclusive shortage of qualified teachers and insufficient industrial attachment is a serious constraint in preparing students for the actual and future needs of the economy. Strengthening synergy effects between the providers and the industry and commerce must be used.
- The high variance in the income distribution demonstrates that TEVET activities should be directed in emerging occupational areas beyond the traditional fields covered by the apprenticeship programs. For this purpose actual and future social and labor market requirements must be identified in close cooperation with stakeholders of the private and the public sector.
- As the employers perceive notable performance differences between the completers of different institutions, setting and assurance of quality standards are urgently needed in order to ensure that all TEVET providers adhere to certain standards. Not only registration but accreditation and permanent monitoring and evaluation of providers by TEVETA are needed. In this

context the multiple structures responsible for assessments and examinations should be reconsidered.

Notes

[1] As multiple responses have been possible the percentages sum up to more than 100 percent.

[2] The question what are the conditions for getting a work will be discussed later on.

[3] For data analysis concerned with issues of income, work place, professional tasks etc. both these groups (n=65) are excluded. In all questions related to professional qualification processes and their impact, however they will be included.

[4] Although the variables are metrical scaled, the Spearman correlation coefficient was calculated due to the strong skewness of both variables.

[5] This result is confirmed by the "Labor market Survey" conducted by JIMAT in 2008.

[6] The interpretation of the average scores must consider, that in case of City & Guilds and National Trade Certificates the levels are counting from 3 (lowest) to 1 (highest), but in case of the TEVETA Certificate it's inverse.

Part IV: Final Remarks

Education is a strategic sector for the promotion of economic and social development. The present study targeted two of the sub-sectors of the educational system: Higher Education and Technical and Vocational Education. Both of them are characterized by a *direct* relation with the labor market because their function consists in an economic point of view[1] in the formation of *specific* human capital needed by the private and public sector of a country's economy.

In general external and internal efficiency of educational processes has to be expected. *One* powerful tool[2] to assess efficiency and internal quality assurance in HE and TEVET programs are Tracer Studies which endeavor to follow up graduates of a program of study. The present study targeted graduates of Malawian Universities and completers of TEVET programs of the years 2004-2007. The results of the study indicate by and large a positive situation, and no evidence for a general trend of "over-production" of graduates was observed. However, there is still much room for improvement, in order to enhance the efficiency of the system as a whole according to the recommendations exposed above.

However, it must be emphasized that Tracer Studies are not a one-time data collection but should make part of institutionalized an integrated labor market oriented **Monitoring and Evaluation System (MES)**. Especially in dynamic environments which changing labor market demands, a regular monitoring must be realized at economically justifiable costs. The methodological experiences generated in the present study demonstrate the necessity to encourage universities and TEVET providers to develop databases which permit to track regularly their students providing a link between the supply side (universities and TEVET providers) and the quantitative and qualitative needs of the private and public sector of economy. The formation of alumni associations on both levels (HE and TEVET) could be a first and efficient instrument to put an effective MES and to collect needed data regularly. Incentives such us job and career information are helpful to attract members to join such alumni networks. Further steps such as regular reporting by part of the companies and self-employed can follow in the future in order to identify at time future occupational trends in the Malawian economy.

Notes

[1] Beyond the economic value of education there are a lot of non-economic social and individual effects to be considered.

[2] Another method to assess efficiency is the calculation of rates of return, which request, however, detailed information about the cost structures of programs.

References

Global

World Bank. 2004. *Cost, Financing and School Effectiveness of Education in Malawi: A Future of Limited Choices and Endless Opportunities.* Washington, DC: World Bank. August (first Education Malawi CSR).

Executive Summary

JIMAT Development Consultants. 2008. Malawi Labour Market Survey. Prepared for TEVETA, Draft Report. Lilongwe, August.

National Statistical Office. 2005. *Malawi Second Integrated Household Survey (IHS-2) 2004–2005.* October. Zomba, Malawi.

National Statistical Office and UNICEF. 2007. *Malawi Multiple Indicators Cluster Survey (MICS) 2006.* February. Zomba and Lilongwe, Malawi.

Chapter 1

OECD. 2008. OECD Stat Extracts (www.oecd.org). Paris.

UNAIDS. 2008. *Report on the Global AIDS Epidemic, 2008.* UN, New York

UNDP. 2008. *Human Development Report, 2007/2008.* UN, New York

United Nations. 2008. *World Population Prospects: The 2008 Revision.* Department of Economic and Social Affairs. UN, New York.

World Bank. 2008. *Live Database* (www.worldbank.org). Washington, DC: World Bank.

———. 2008. *Malawi Poverty Assessment Report, 2008.* Washington, DC: World Bank.

———. 2009 (forthcoming) *Education Performance Rating: How Do African countries Score? A Multi-Dimensional Tool for Benchmarking Education Outcomes and System Policies.* Washington, DC: World Bank.

World Health Organization. 2008. *Global Database on Child Growth and Malnutrition.* Geneva.

Chapter 2

Mingat, A., and S. Sosale. 2001. *Problèmes de politique éducative relatifs au redoublement à l'école primaire dans les pays d'Afrique Sub-saharienne.* PSAST/AFTHD. Washington, DC: World Bank.

Ministry of Education, Science and Technology (MOEST), Department of Education. 2008. *Education Statistics 2007.* Government of Malawi.

National Statistical Office. 2001. *Malawi Demographic and Health Survey (DHS)*. Zomba, Malawi and ORC Macro, Calverton, MD.

———. 2005. *Malawi Second Integrated Household Survey (IHS-2) 2004–2005*. Zomba, Malawi, October.

National Statistical Office and UNICEF. 2007. *Malawi Multiple Indicators Cluster Survey (MICS) 2006*. February. Zomba and Lilongwe, Malawi.

Reuge, N. 2008. *Schooling Profiles, Methodological Note n°2*. UNESCO-BREDA, Note du Pôle de Dakar (www.poledakar.org).

UNESCO BREDA. 2007. *Education for All in Africa: Top Priority for Integrated Sector-Wide Policies. Dakar+7*. Dakar.

World Bank. 2005. "Project Appraisal Document on a Proposed IDA Grant to the Republic of Malawi for an Education Support Project." AFTH3, Working Paper. Washington, DC: World Bank.

Chapter 3

Bellew, R. 2008. "Malawi NESP EFA-FTI Appraisal Report." Working Document. Cambridge Education, Mokoro, and Oxford Policy Management.

Foko, B., and M. Brossard. 2007. *Couverture scolaire des années 1970 et impacts sur la croissance entre 1970 et 2003*, UNESCO-BREDA: Document de travail du Pôle de Dakar (www.poledakar.org).

Government of Malawi. 2008. *Budget Statements* (revised), 2007/2008.

National Statistical Office. 2005. *Malawi Second Integrated Household Survey (IHS-2) 2004–2005*. October. Zomba, Malawi.

Ndem, F. 2008. *Education Household Expenditure*. Senegal: Pole de Dakar (www.poledakar.org).

World Bank. 2009 (forthcoming). *Education Performance Rating: How Do African countries Score? A Multi-Dimensional Tool for Benchmarking Education Outcomes and System Policies*. Washington, DC: World Bank.

Chapter 4

Bellew, R. 2008. "Malawi NESP EFA-FTI Appraisal Report." Working Document. Cambridge Education, Mokoro, and Oxford Policy Management.

Brossard, M. 2003. "Retention, redoublement et qualité dans les écoles publiques primaires béninoises: Quel diagnostic? Quelles pistes de politiques éducatives?" Pôle de Dakar Working Paper (www.poledakar.org).

Bruns, B., A. Mingat, and M. Rakotomalala. 2003. *Achieving Universal Primary Education by 2015: A Chance for Every Child*. Washington, DC: World Bank.

Mingat, A., and S. Sosale. , 2001. *Problèmes de politique éducative relatifs au redoublement à l'école primaire dans les pays d'Afrique Sub-saharienne*. PSAST/AFTHD. Washington, DC: World Bank.

PASEC, CONFEMEN. 1999. "Les facteurs de l'efficacité dans l'enseignement primaire: les résultats du programme PASEC sur neuf pays d'Afrique et de l'Océan indien." CONFEMEN (www.confemen.org).

———. 2004. "Le redoublement : pratiques et conséquences dans l'enseignement primaire au Sénégal." (www.confemen.org).

Pôle de Dakar. 2002. "Universal Primary Education: A Goal for All." Statistical Document for the Eighth Education Ministers' Conference for African Countries. MINEDAF VIII (December 6–12, Dar Es Salam). BREDA-UNESCO (www.poledakar.org).
SACMEQ II. 2005. *The SACMEQ II Project in Malawi: A Study of the Conditions of Schooling and the Quality of Education.* Working Report. Southern and Eastern Africa Consortium for Monitoring Educational Quality (SACMEQ) (http://www.sacmeq.org/).
UNESCO BREDA. 2007. *Education for All in Africa: Top Priority for Integrated Sector-Wide Policies. Dakar+7.* Dakar.
———. 2005. *EFA in Africa: Paving the Way for Action.* Dakar.
World Bank, in partnership with the Pôle de Dakar (UNESCO-France) and a national Cameroonian team. 2004. *Cameroun Country Status Report.* (www.poledakar.org).
World Bank, in partnership with the Pôle de Dakar (UNESCO-France) and a national Chadian team. 2005. *Chad Country Status Report.* (www.poledakar.org).

Chapter 5

Ministry of Education, Science and Technology (MOEST), Education Management Information System (EMIS). 2006, 2007. *Education Statistics.* Government of Malawi.
SACMEQ II. 2005. *The SACMEQ II Project in Malawi: A Study of the Conditions of Schooling and the Quality of Education.* Working Report. Southern and Eastern Africa Consortium for Monitoring Educational Quality (SACMEQ) (http://www.sacmeq.org/).

Chapter 6

Africa Private Sector Group. Investment Climate Assessment (ICA). Malawi: June 23, 2006.
Franz, Jutta, Marc Maleta, and Maston Mtambo. *A New Mechanism for Financing TEVET in Malawi.* A study commissioned by the TEVET Secretariat. Malawi: Ministry of Labour and Vocational Training, August 1998.
Gondwe, Clement. "TEVETA Informal Sector Outreach Programmes." Paper prepared as a response to UNESCO/International Centre for Technical and Vocational Education and Training call for papers. Lilongwe: March 2003.
Government of Malawi. *Budget Statements* (revised), 2007/2008.
Government of Malawi, Ministry of Labour and Vocational Training, Technical, Entrepreneurial and Vocational Education and Training (TEVET) Policy. October, 1998.
Government of Malawi. Technical, Entrepreneurial and Vocational Education and Training Act. No. 6 of 1999. February, 19, 1999.
Government of Malawi. Technical, Entrepreneurial and Vocational Education and Training (Registration of Education and Training Institutions). Regulation, 2006.
JIMAT Development Consultants. Malawi Labour Market Survey. Prepared for TEVETA, Draft Report. Lilongwe: August 2008.
Maganga, Dick. Apprenticeship Training Costs. Final Report. TEVETA, September 2008 (circulation restricted).

Ministry of Education, Science and Technology (MOEST), Education Management Information System (EMIS). 2006, 2007. *Education Statistics*. Government of Malawi.

MOEST. 2007. *National Education Sector Plan. Operation Supplement Containing Education Sector Analysis, Summary of Programme Profiles, Financial Details*. Draft, August.

Pfeiffer, Dietmar and Gerald Chiunda. Tracer Study of TEVET and Higher Education Completers in Malawi. Final Report. Lilongwe: GTZ/World Bank, 2008. (See Annex 9 of this report.)

PJ Development Consultancy Company. Tracer Study on "Skills Development Initiative" and "On-the Job Training" Beneficiaries. Prepared for TEVETA. Final Report. Lilongwe: August 2005.

Technical, Entrepreneurial, and Vocational Education and Training Authority (TEVETA), Government of Malawi. 1999. TEVET Provider Inventory. Lilongwe.

———. 2004. *A Guide to Better Understanding and Implementation of TEVET Qualifications*. TEVET Qualifications Framework Handbook. November. Lilongwe.

———. 2007. Strategic Plan for Technical Entrepreneurial Vocational Education and Training Authority (TEVETA) 2007–2012, March 2007. Lilongwe.

UNESCO. 2006. *Republic of Malawi: Report on Present Status and Future Directions of Technical and Vocational Education*. January. Paris.

Chapter 7

Barry, B., and A. Sawyerr. 2008. African *Higher Education and Industry: What Linkages*. Cape Town, South Africa: Association of African Universities.

Bloom, D., D. Canning, and K. Chan. 2006. *Higher Education and Economic Development*. Cambridge, MA: Harvard University.

Fielden, J., and K. Abercromby. 2001. *UNESCO Higher Education Indicators Study, Accountability and International Co-operation in the Renewal of Higher Education*. A study prepared by of the Commonwealth Higher Education Management Service (CHEMS), as part of the follow-up to the World Conference on Higher Education (UNESCO Paris 1998).

Helm, R. 2008. *University Admission Worldwide:* World Bank Education Working Series: Number 15. Washington, DC: World Bank.

Jackson, R. 2002. "The National Student Financial Aid Scheme of South Africa: How and Why it Works." *Welsh Journal of Education* 11(1), July.

Government of Malawi. 2006. Public Expenditure Review. Appendix V, *The Public Universities Students Loan Trust Loan Agreement Between The Public Universities Student Loan Trust in the Public of Malawi and the Student*. Lilongwe.

Hahao, N. L. 2003. "Towards Curriculum Relevance: The Reform Experience on the National University of Lesotho." Paper prepared for the Regional Training Conference on Improving Tertiary Education in Sub-Sahara Africa: Things that Work. Ghana.

JIMAT Development Consultants. 2008. "Malawi Labour Market Survey." Prepared for TEVETA, Draft Report. August. Lilongwe.

Kurasha, P. 2003. "Access to Tertiary Education as a National Strategy for Development: The Zimbabwe Open University Case." Paper prepared for the

Regional Training Conference on Improving Tertiary Education in Sub-Sahara Africa: Things that Work. Ghana.

Malawi Institute of Management. 2004. *University of Malawi Reform Study.* Lilongwe.

MOEST. 2008. *Trust Deed for the Public Universities Students Loans Trust, 2008.* Lilongwe.

Odebero et al. 2007. "Equity in the Distribution of HELB Loans in Kenya in Relation to Student Characteristics: An Empirical Analysis." *Educational Research and Reviews* 2(8): 209–219.

Otieno, W. 2004. "Student Loans in Kenya: Past Experiences, Current Hurdles, and Opportunities for the Future." *Journal of Higher Education in Africa* 2(2).

Pfeiffer, D., and G. Chiunda. 2008. "Tracer Study of TEVET and Higher Education Completers in Malawi. Final Report." Lilongwe: GTZ/World Bank. (See Annex 9 of this report.)

Shen, H., and A. Ziderman. 2008. "Student Loans Repayment and Recovery: International Comparisons." Discussion Paper No. 3588. Bonn: Institute for the Labour Study.

UNESCO. ISCED International Standard Classification of Education, 1997. Paris.

United Nations. *Recommendations Concerning the Status of Higher Education Teaching Personnel.* United Nations Education, Scientific and Cultural Organization, 1997. UN, New York.

University of Malawi. 2007. *University of Malawi Strategic Plan 2004/05–2009/10, Volume 1 Consolidated Version, 2007.* Zomba.

———. 2008. *Programmes and Entry Requirements for 2008–2009: University of Malawi.* University Office, Zomba.

Van Harte, M. 2002. "Can Student Loan Schemes Ensure Access to Higher Education: South Africa's Experience." International Comparative Higher Education Finance and Accessibility Project Discussion Paper, Graduate School of Education, University of Buffalo, Buffalo, NY.

Woodhall, M. 1992. *Student Loans in Developing Countries, Experiences and Prospects for Reform.* The Netherlands: Kluwer Academic Publishers.

World Bank. 1997. *Revitalizing Universities in Africa, Strategy and Guidelines.* Prepared by the Association of African Universities, 1997. Washington, DC: World Bank.

———. 2000. "Higher Education in Developing Countries: Peril and Promise (2000)." Paper commissioned by the Task Force on Higher Education and Society. Washington, DC: World Bank.

———. 2003. *Education in Rwanda: Accelerating the Agenda for Post-Conflict Development.* Human Development II, Africa Region, 2003. Washington, DC: World Bank.

Ziderman, A. 2004. *Policy Options for Student Loan Schemes: Lessons from Five Asian Case Studies:* UNESCO Bangkok.

Chapter 8

Africa Private Sector Group. 2006. Investment Climate Assessment (ICA). June 23. Malawi.

JIMAT Development Consultants. 2008. "Malawi Labour Market Survey." Prepared for TEVETA, Draft Report. August. Lilongwe.

Johanson, R., and A. Adams. 2004. *Skills Development in Sub-Saharan Africa.* Washington, DC: The World Bank.

Malawi Confederation of Chambers of Commerce and Industry (MCCCI). 2007. Report of the Results of the 2007 Malawi Business Climate Survey. November.

Malawi National Gemini MSE Baseline Survey 2000. 2001. Prepared by Ebony Consulting International and the National Statistical Office, with assistance of Kadale Consultants and Wadonda Consult, on behalf of DFID. February. Lilongwe.

Malawi Confederation of Chambers of Commerce and Industry (MCCCI). 2007. *Malawi Business Climate Survey*, p. 10. Blantyre, Malawi.

Ministry of Labour. 2007. *2006 Labour Yearbook,* March 2007. Malawi.

———. 2008. "Blantyre Sweeping Labour Inspections (The First Reports). Tables Generated from the Data and Some Highlights." February 15. Malawi.

National Statistical Office. 2006. Welfare Monitoring Survey (WMS). Malawi.

Pfeiffer, D., and G. Chiunda. 2008. "Tracer Study of TEVET and Higher Education Completers in Malawi. Final Report." Lilongwe: GTZ/World Bank. (See Annex 9 of this report.)

PJ Development Consultancy Company. 2005. Tracer Study on "Skills Development Initiative" and "On-the Job Training" Beneficiaries. Prepared for TEVETA. Final Report. August. Lilongwe.

Programa Integrado de Reforma da Educacao Profissional (PIREP)/C. 2007. "Lauchande, Analise Estatistica do Estudo de Base Sobre Educacao Técnica Profissional *(Mozambique)*." December. PIREP.

Republic of Malawi & The World Bank. 2006. *Malawi Poverty and Vulnerability Assessment. Investing in Our Future.* June.

Eco-Audit

Environmental Benefits Statement

The World Bank is committed to preserving Endangered Forests and natural resources. We print World Bank Working Papers and Country Studies on postconsumer recycled paper, processed chlorine free. The World Bank has formally agreed to follow the recommended standards for paper usage set by Green Press Initiative—a nonprofit program supporting publishers in using fiber that is not sourced from Endangered Forests. For more information, visit www.greenpressinitiative.org.

In 2008, the printing of these books on recycled paper saved the following:

Trees*	Solid Waste	Water	Net Greenhouse Gases	Total Energy
289	8,011	131,944	27,396	92 mil.
*40 feet in height and 6–8 inches in diameter	Pounds	Gallons	Pounds CO_2 Equivalent	BTUs

www.ingramcontent.com/pod-product-compliance
Lightning Source LLC
Chambersburg PA
CBHW060308240426
43661CB00059B/2697